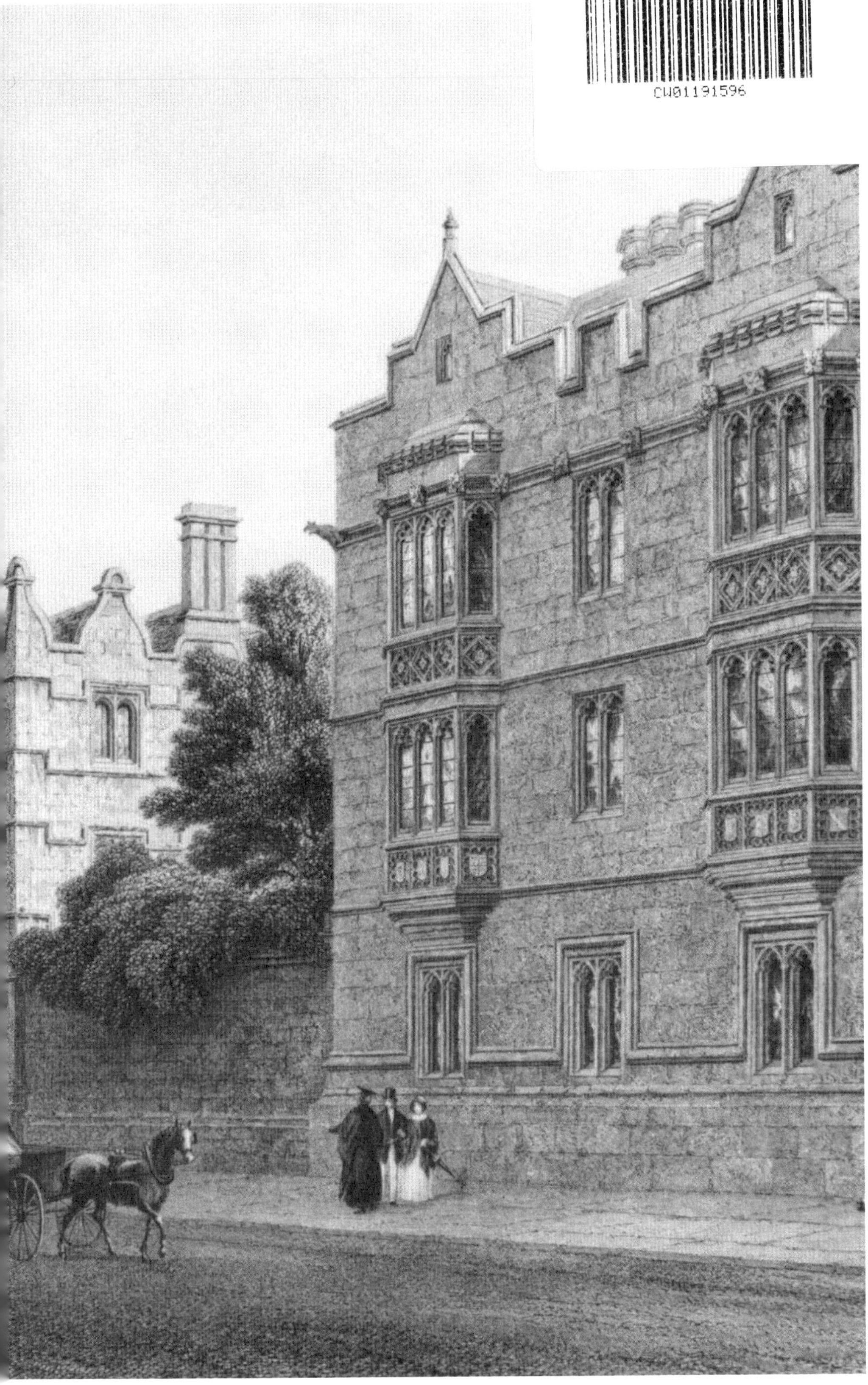

A HISTORY OF
UNIVERSITY COLLEGE, OXFORD

For Tania
with all best wishes
and many thanks for
your help in the
early stages

Robin D S
June 2008

An imagined portrait of an imaginary Founder: painting (*c.* 1661/2) of King Alfred, appropriated by University College as its Founder in the 1380s. No known likeness exists of the College's real Founder, William of Durham.

A HISTORY
OF
UNIVERSITY COLLEGE, OXFORD

ROBIN DARWALL-SMITH

OXFORD UNIVERSITY PRESS
2008

OXFORD
UNIVERSITY PRESS

Great Clarendon Street, Oxford OX2 6DP

Oxford University Press is a department of the University of Oxford.
It furthers the University's objective of excellence in research, scholarship,
and education by publishing worldwide in

Oxford New York

Auckland Cape Town Dar es Salaam Hong Kong Karachi
Kuala Lumpur Madrid Melbourne Mexico City Nairobi
New Delhi Shanghai Taipei Toronto

With offices in

Argentina Austria Brazil Chile Czech Republic France Greece
Guatemala Hungary Italy Japan Poland Portugal Singapore
South Korea Switzerland Thailand Turkey Ukraine Vietnam

Oxford is a registered trade mark of Oxford University Press
in the UK and in certain other countries

Published in the United States
by Oxford University Press Inc., New York

© The Master and Fellows of University College, Oxford 2008

Robin Darwall-Smith has asserted his moral rights
to be the author of this book.
Database right Oxford University Press (maker)

First published 2008

All rights reserved. No part of this publication may be reproduced,
stored in a retrieval system, or transmitted, in any form or by any means,
without the prior permission in writing of Oxford University Press,
or as expressly permitted by law, or under terms agreed with the appropriate
reprographics rights organization. Enquiries concerning reproduction
outside the scope of the above should be sent to the Rights Department,
Oxford University Press, at the address above

You must not circulate this book in any other binding or cover
and you must impose the same condition on any acquirer

British Library Cataloguing in Publication Data
Data available

Library of Congress Cataloging in Publication Data
Data available

Typeset by SPI Publisher Services, Pondicherry, India
Printed in Great Britain
on acid-free paper by
CPI Antony Rowe, Chippenham, Wiltshire

ISBN 978–0–19–928429–0

1 3 5 7 9 10 8 6 4 2

W. S.

C. J. F.

A. D. M. C.
inter mortuos

P. M. G.
inter vivos

Foreword

by Lord Butler of Brockwell, Master of University College

It is impossible to be a member of one of the ancient Oxford or Cambridge Colleges, or even to visit one, without being conscious of the past. It is there all around you—in the buildings, in the staircases, in the monuments, in the portraits. It would be an incurious person who did not want to know how these peculiar establishments—part monastery, part fortification, with their ancient traditions of self-governance, academic apprenticeship, and scholarly dialectic—come to be as they are.

People often say that new students find the antiquity intimidating. It is true that one cannot escape feeling the weight of Oxford's learning and it would be hard not to be daunted by one's consciousness of it. Yet I find the history comforting. As I sit in my office in the College—it is one of the seventeenth-century panelled student rooms in the Main Quad—I find it reassuring that more than ten generations, and ten times that number of student generations, have lived, worked, and agonized in this room, which is unchanged except for the electric light, the radiator, and the electronic gadgetry of a modern office. In that very room in 1850, Arthur Stanley and others planned a petition to Parliament for the reform of Oxford, which led to the establishment of a Royal Commission and the Oxford University Act of 1854. I think of generation after generation of students climbing the wooden staircase with candles in their hands, sharing much the same worries about forthcoming encounters with their tutors and ultimately with the examiners as students feel today. When I was an undergraduate in Univ. I found it comforting to be eating at the same table and seated on the same benches in the same hall as many thousands before me—and no doubt with much the same passions and preoccupations and jokes.

When, through reading this history, I can locate some of the events of the College's past, it gives me great pleasure. I cannot now go into the Winter Common Room without thinking of Samuel Johnson dining there with Master Wetherell, William Jones, Robert Chambers, and the Scott brothers (later Lords Eldon and Stowell). When I look at the portrait of the Earl of Leicester in that same room, I think of Queen Elizabeth I driving with him past the front of the College, on which the shrewd Fellows had hung a poem in her honour. When I look at the portrait of Edward Hales on the facing wall, I think of him reading a speech in honour of King James II on the latter's visit to the College. And I think of Shelley appearing before the

Fellows in that same room and refusing to answer their questions about the authorship of *The Necessity of Atheism*.

In other parts of the College, there is the room in which Obadiah Walker set up his private Chapel in his (by the standards of the times) illicit affair with Catholicism—in this part of the College we are said to have a real ghost. In the Antechapel, I think of the Fellows congregating in their efforts to resolve the eighteenth-century saga of the two rival Masters. I look at the window in the Main Quad from which a student opened fire on his colleagues and where John Wild, later Master, so bravely confronted him. In the Master's Lodgings I recall Master Bright being shot—fortunately not fatally—by the disappointed lover of one of the Fellows.

All this, and much more, is in the pages below. Of course, it is an article of faith with every Univ. man and woman that the College was founded by King Alfred. In 1872 the Fellows celebrated the thousandth anniversary of the College, and the Professor of Modern History is said to have sent us an offering of burnt cake. The reader will not find much about King Alfred in this history because there is nothing historical about the tradition—except the High Court's endorsement of it in 1727, which resulted in the sovereign becoming the College's Visitor.

What the reader will find is a fascinating account of the College's efforts to survive and grow from the vulnerable seed sowed by William of Durham in 1249; and the ups and downs which occurred along the way. It is clear that our predecessors were not always scrupulous about the methods by which they struggled for survival. There are legal tricks and illegal forged documents over the years. Yet one way or another the College did survive and grow, mainly through the beneficence of a long line of patrons who had their own reasons for supporting it, and ultimately helped along their way two British Prime Ministers, an Australian one, a President of the United States, as well as countless other statesmen, lawyers, scholars, artists, athletes, and people of distinction in every walk of life.

In 1999, the first full year of my Mastership, the College celebrated the 750th anniversary of its authenticated endowment in 1249. Since that is an earlier date than the foundation of any other College in Oxford or Cambridge, and since Oxford and Cambridge pre-date any other English-speaking University, University College can claim to be the oldest institution of higher education in the English-speaking world. That deserves a history.

A history needs a historian. The Fellows were fortunate in finding a historian in someone who is not only an Old Member of the College but its archivist. Dr Robin Darwall-Smith had already performed a valuable work for the College and for scholarship by completing the editing and publishing of the College's medieval accounts, begun by David Cox. Dr Darwall-Smith's love for the College, as well as his scholarship, shine out from the pages below.

The people and the episodes described come to life through Dr Darwall-Smith's sense of humour and wry regard for the humanity of those who played a part in bringing the College to where it is today.

The Fellows commissioned the history in the College's 750th anniversary year, which was the first full year of my Mastership. I rejoice that its publication, nearly ten years later, coincides with the last year of my Mastership. I want to thank Dr Darwall-Smith and all who have taken part in the production of this history and I commend it to all current and Old Members and all who are interested in the history of an institution which has had such a formative role in the lives of so many. Read and enjoy it.

Preface and Acknowledgements

This is the third attempt at a history of University College, Oxford. The first was William Smith's brilliant, if chaotic, *The Annals of University College* of 1728, and the second, William Carr's *University College* of 1902. Carr's book formed part of a complete series of histories of all the Oxford and Cambridge histories, and was somewhat hampered by the need for brevity. It is time for a fresh retelling of the story, and a new examination of the evidence.

Inevitably a book published in 2008 will eventually become as much a prisoner of its own period as one published in 1728 or 1902, and I should set down my own approach to writing this one. Covering the history of one institution over seven and a half centuries can lead to a loss of focus over the whole, and I have therefore attempted to keep two questions in mind throughout: what kind of institution has University College been throughout its history, and what has it meant to be a member of this College, be it as a Fellow, student, or member of staff? Perhaps as a result of this—or perhaps because of the essential nature of the genre—this book has become more of a social than an intellectual history. I do not, however, apologize for my interest in the inner workings of the College; whatever great things may have come out of University College would not have been possible without finances properly run, a staff to look after its members, and buildings to house them.

I have from time to time compared University College with other colleges. As archivist for two quite different Oxford colleges, I sometimes think that there is no such thing as a 'typical' Oxford (or Cambridge) college, and in that spirit, I hope that it will be of some interest to show what has made University College similar to or different from similar institutions.

The arrangement of many narrative chapters is guided by the terms of office of various Masters. The personality of Masters in a small college can have a considerable impact for good or ill, be they active or lazy, reformers or conservatives, conciliatory or divisive. A change in headship frequently marks a change in direction for the college as a whole, so that the dates of such events are often significant ones, and are worth marking with a break in the narrative.

College histories of previous generations sometimes concentrated enthusiastically on the college's 'great old members' to the exclusion of examining what was happening in the college itself. I have tried not to forget that this is first and foremost a history of an institution. Where people earn a mention here, it is either because their deeds and words have directly affected the workings of the College, or because they are especially representative of the College at a given period. Sometimes old members quite forgotten by posterity can provide information crucial to the understanding of their age, and the reader may more readily identify with such people than with grander—and remoter—personalities. I have, however, relented a little, by adopting the clever compromise of Clare Hopkins in her history of Trinity College in listing in an appendix the names of all the members of University College who appear in the *Oxford Dictionary of National Biography*.

I certainly do not regard it necessarily as my business to try to discuss the later careers of the College's 'great old members', because they are, in large measure, not very relevant to the theme of this book, and I am not sure that my attempts at a succession of rather dry rehashes of biography would make for very interesting reading. More apposite advice for the College historian was offered by Plutarch who, at the opening of his *Life of Alexander*, observed that 'a small matter and a phrase and jest made a greater revelation of a character than battles in which thousands die, the marshallings of very great armies, and the sieges of cities'. In that spirit, Clement Attlee appears in this book not as one of Britain's greatest twentieth-century Prime Ministers, but as an Old Member with a lifelong love of 'Univ.' (although there was one occasion when his Prime Ministerial power and his love of the College combined to significant effect); this is much more relevant to the matter in hand, and, I hope, may shed new light on Attlee himself. Likewise, others can discuss the later life and work of C. S. Lewis, but I do try to tell the story of his relationship with his first college. This is not mere parochialism: a college grants its members a degree of privacy from the outside world, and to focus on that private space and to explain it to that outside world is to present a more relevant, and revealing, picture of the nature of an institution like University College.

Finally, researching and writing this history has been an enjoyable journey, and if I have any hopes for the result, it is that some of that enjoyment may communicate itself to the reader.

I was commissioned to write the history in the autumn of 1998 on the initiative of the Master, Lord Butler of Brockwell, and I should start by thanking him and the Governing Body of University College for giving me the opportunity to write this book. Lord Butler deserves special thanks for his encouragement throughout, as well as for his helpful comments on the first draft of the history. The Estates Bursar, Frank Marshall, has also been on hand to oversee the project and discuss many details.

Within University College itself, I owe large debts of thanks to Peter Bayley, Catherine Holmes, Leslie Mitchell, Alexander Murray, Gwynne Ovenstone, Hartmut Pogge von Strandmann, and Tania Rawlinson, for commenting on the first draft of this history, and in some cases also for sharing their memories of the College with me. I have also benefited from the many articles on aspects of College lore written by both Peter and Leslie in past issues of the *University College Record*. I am very grateful to Christine Ritchie, the College Librarian, both for also looking at the first draft, and for helping me locate important books in our Library.

A glance through the footnotes of the last chapters will show the extent of my debt to many members of the College, past and present, who have talked to me, sometimes in formal interviews, sometimes informally at Gaudies and feasts. I am very grateful to them all, and my only regret is that some of them, such as Norman Dix, Sir Peter Strawson, and Lord Renton, are no longer alive to be thanked in person. I am also grateful to Richard Levitt (m. 1973), who made a generous donation towards the cost of the illustrations.

I have found help from many quarters outside University College. At my other home of Magdalen College, Christine Ferdinand, the Fellow Librarian, read and commented on several chapters. Magdalen is currently working on a history of its own, which should see publication in 2008, and in which I am collaborating, and I have had many beneficial discussions with its editors, Laurence Brockliss and Andrew Hegarty, on aspects of college history. Andrew in particular also deserves my hearty thanks both for letting me see his biographical register of members of St John's College from 1555 to 1660 in advance of publication, and for being the second sternest critic of early drafts of this book.

My colleagues in other college archives, including Judith Curthoys (Christ Church), Julian Reid (Merton and Corpus Christi), Anna Sander (Balliol), and Rob Petre (Oriel and Keble), have helped by discussing the workings of their colleges with me, or even just by offering encouragement over a drink, but I hope it is not invidious to single out for special thanks Clare Hopkins (Trinity), who shared many insights with me as she was working on her own excellent history of Trinity, and Michael Riordan (St John's and Queen's), who read and commented on the whole of the second draft. Within Oxford, Simon Bailey, Keeper of the University Archives, taught me how to mine the treasures of the papers of the Chancellor's Court, and the staff in the Bodleian Library were unfailingly helpful. Further afield, Ursula Mitchel, Archivist of Trinity College Dublin, helped me understand better the upheavals of the 1640s there, and the archivists at the Borthwick Institute, York, the British Library, Southampton University Library, the West Yorkshire Archive Service (Bradford), the Yorkshire Archaeological Society, Leeds, and the York Minster Archives, all generously assisted me when I visited their collections. I am also grateful to the many people who welcomed me when visiting places around the country with links to the College.

Some chapters have, I hope, benefited from the advice of some specialist readers. I am most grateful to Jeremy Catto and Alan Cobban for their comments on the medieval sections, to Mordechai Feingold on intellectual life in the early modern period, to Anne Gardiner and Jerry Murphy on the era of Abraham Woodhead and Obadiah Walker, to Jack Zoeller on the College's early American alumni and for disentangling the Bennet family, and to Mark Curthoys on the nineteenth century.

I also thank the following individuals and bodies for allowing me to reproduce these illustrations:

The Bodleian Library, University of Oxford (Figs. 5.1 and 5.2)
The Photographic Survey, Courtauld Institute of Art (Figs. 7.1–7.3, 8.1. 9.1, 10.3, 11.3, 13.1–13.4, 14.4, 15.3, 17.1–17.3, 18.2, 19.8, and 20.2)
The Governing Body of Christ Church, Oxford (Plate 3).
The President and Fellows of Magdalen College, Oxford (Fig. 16.5)
The Provost and Fellows of Worcester College, Oxford (Fig. 11.4)
David Hawkins (Fig. 19.7)
Graham Mason (Fig. 20.4)
Gwynne Ovenstone (Fig. 19.2)
Benjamin Sullivan (Plate 18)
Daphne Todd (Fig. 20.2)

I also wish to thank Jane Cunningham at the Courtauld Institute, Jacqueline Thalmann and Katherine Wodehouse at the Christ Church Picture Gallery, and Joanna Parker at Worcester College, for their assistance with their respective collections.

Of the remaining pictures Plates 2 and 7–9, and Figs.1.1, 6.1, 8.3, 14.2 were taken by myself or Peter Gilliver. Of the photographs taken for University College, Plates 1 and 6 and Fig. 6.2 were taken by the Bodleian Library Studios, and Plate 17 and Figs. 19.5–6 were taken by Thomas Photos. Almost all the other photos were taken by John Gibbons. The maps were drawn by Paul Simmons. The progress of this book through OUP was overseen first by Anne Ashby, and then by Sarah Holmes.

This leaves the dedicatees of this history. The first three are included because they cannot be thanked in person: William Smith and David Cox's names appear sufficiently often in the footnotes of the forthcoming pages to make one part of their contribution obvious; in addition, both they and Charles Faulkner in their respective centuries helped to preserve, sort, and add to the College's archives. Without all their work, there would be no history to write. The fourth dedicatee, Peter Gilliver, stands apart. For a decade he has lived with this project on the home front, he has joined me on many journeys to places with College links, yet throughout he has offered continual help and encouragement, some of which is reflected in the footnotes, and above all has been my sternest critic and greatest support.

Contents

Foreword	vii
Preface and Acknowledgements	x
Colour Plates	xviii
Figures	xix
Maps and Graphs	xxii
Abbreviations and Conventions	xxiii

1	William of Durham and the Idea of a College: 1249–1280	1
2	A College Takes Shape: 1280–1361	18
3	Crisis: 1361–1411	34
	The Gonwardby affair and the invention of King Alfred: 1361–1390	34
	A time for recovery: 1390–1411	44
	The Taint of Heresy: 1411	47
4	Medieval Equilibrium: 1411–1509	51
	Arrested growth: 1411–1441	52
	John Martyn: 1441–1473	57
	After Martyn: 1473–1509	63
5	Life in a Late Medieval College	68
	The College buildings	69
	The membership of University College	72
	The life of the College	78
	Estates and finances	81
	The late medieval College	87
6	Change from within and without: 1509–1572	89
	The failure of Ralph Hamsterley	89
	Leonard Hutchinson and the arrival of undergraduates	93
	Reformation and reaction	96
	Thomas Caius	104
7	In the Chancellor's Power: 1572–1632	109
	William James	111
	Anthony Gate and the puritans	114
	Elizabethan Fellows and Scholars: the case of John Browne	117

	George Abbot	120
	John Bancroft and the High Church Ascendancy	126
8	The Early Undergraduate College	132
	The membership of the College: The Yorkshire incursion	132
	Hierarchy triumphant: living within the College	139
	Study and recreation, behaviour and misbehaviour	142
	A new approach to estate management: entry fines and corn rents	152
	The growth of a college spirit?	153
9	Buildings, Civil War, and Commonwealth: 1632–1660	157
	Thomas Walker and New Beginnings: 1632–1640	157
	Civil war and chaos: 1640–1648	164
	Commonwealth and Protectorate: 1648–1660	171
10	The Rise and Fall of Obadiah Walker: 1660–1689	183
	The return of Thomas Walker: 1660–1665	183
	Finances restored, buildings completed: 1665–1676	187
	Scholars and scholarship, educators and educated	194
	'Old Obadiah, sing Ave Maria': 1676–1689	202
11	The Era of Arthur Charlett: 1689–1722	219
	Finding a New Master: 1689–1692	219
	Charlett Ascendant: 1692–1698	221
	'The evil Spirit that haunted the Master': 1698–1711	228
	John Radcliffe and Jacobite shadows: 1712–1722	237
12	Storm and Calm: 1722–1764	247
	Funeral Games: 1722–1729	247
	Thomas Cockman and the return to normality: 1729–1745	259
	John Browne and the Hutchinsonians: 1745–1764	266
13	Glory and Decline: 1764–1807	275
	The Great Awakening: 1764–1772	275
	Wetherell's web: architecture, literature, politics, and the Vice-Chancellorship	284
	Decline: 1780–1807	295
14	The Workings of a Georgian College	302
	Climbing the academic ladder	302
	Tutors, pupils, and libraries	309
	Social Life	315
	Servants	318
	The finances of the College and its Fellows	320
	Life after Oxford	325
	An Old Boy network?	328
	The problem of Georgian Oxford	333

15	From Shelley's Oxford to Stanley's Oxford: 1808–1850	336
	James Griffith and Percy Shelley: 1808–1821	336
	George Rowley and Travers Twiss: 1821–1836	342
	Frederick Charles Plumptre and Arthur Stanley: 1836–1850	351
16	The College Transformed: 1850–1881	367
	The Great Commission: 1850–1857	367
	The later years of Master Plumptre: 1857–1870	369
	The new broom: the arrival of George Bradley	386
	Bradley unravelled: Fellows versus undergraduates	401
17	The 'D.O.C.': 1881–1914	407
	James Franck Bright and the healing of wounds	407
	Reginald Macan	422
	The 'hearty' College: undergraduate life before 1914	425
	An era ends	439
18	Preserving Continuity: 1914–1945	440
	The First World War: 1914–1918	440
	Starting up again: 1919–1923	444
	The Mastership of Sir Michael Sadler: 1923–1934	447
	Arthur Poynton and Sir William Beveridge	452
	'The Pub on the High'	456
	The College and the Second World War: 1939–1945	469
19	The College Renewed: 1945–1979	475
	John Wild and Giles Alington	475
	The great benefactor: Arthur Goodhart	485
	The post-war College	491
	John Maud, Arnold Goodman, and the changes of the 1960s	500
20	Epilogue: 1979–2007	516
Appendix I.	Masters of University College to 2007	529
Appendix II.	Fellows of University College to 2007	530
Appendix III.	Members of University College in the *Oxford Dictionary of National Biography*	538
Appendix IV.	(1) Social backgrounds of members of University College, 1550–1807	
	(2) Ages of undergraduates on being admitted to University College, 1550–1807	547
Appendix V.	Properties outside Oxford acquired by University College before 1850	549

References	550
Index	575

Colour plates
(Between pages 278 and 279)

Frontispiece King Alfred, appropriated by University College as its Founder in the 1380s.

Plate 1. Page from the Missal (*c.* 1400) used in the Chapel of University College (University College MS 178 fo. 3^r).
Plate 2. St Oswald's Church, Arncliffe.
Plate 3. William James, Master 1572–84 (Christ Church Picture Gallery LP 45).
Plates 4 5. Two of the windows designed for the College Chapel by Abraham van Linge.
Plate 6. Illustration from Bede's *Life of St Cuthbert* (University College MS 165 fo. 12).
Plate 7. St Swithun's Church, Headbourne Worthy, Hampshire.
Plate 8. All Saints' Church, North Cerney, Gloucestershire.
Plate 9. The Radcliffe Quadrangle, built 1716–19.
Plate 10. Group portrait attributed to Benjamin Ferrers showing Thomas Cockman on the far left, and possibly his supporters in the Mastership dispute.
Plate 11. James Griffith's unbuilt design for a new Master's Lodgings (UC:FA11/1/P1/1).
Plate 12. James Griffith's executed design for altering the façade of the south range of the Front Quadrangle.
Plate 13. James Griffith, Fellow 1782–1808 and Master 1808–21.
Plate 14. University College's first rowing crew, 1827.
Plate 15. Conversation piece of Sir Michael Sadler and the Fellows of University College, 1934.
Plate 16. Design of the proposed interior of the Weir Common Room in the Mitchell Building.
Plate 17. A room in the Staverton Road Annexe.
Plate 18. Lord Butler of Brockwell, Master 1998–, and Lady Butler.

Figures

Front endpaper: The Oxford Almanack of 1853, showing the High Street frontage of the College, with the New Buildings in the foreground.

Fig. 1.1. The Minster Church of St Michael and All Angels, Sunderland.
Fig. 1.2. The first statutes of University College (UC:GB1/L1/1).
Fig. 2.1. Deed by which University College acquired Great University Hall (UC: E/A4/D/1).
Fig. 3.1. Extract from the 'French Petition' of 1384 (UC:E2/6/3L/9).
Fig. 4.1. Grant by Henry Percy, Earl of Northumberland, of Arncliffe Rectory (UC:E4/2D/1).
Fig. 5.1. Drawing of University College in 1566 (Bodl. MS Bodl. 13, fo. 10^v).
Fig. 5.2. Drawing of University College in 1668 (Bodl. MS Wood 376B, fo. 116^r).
Fig. 6.1. Memorial Brass of Ralph Hamsterley, Master 1509–18.
Fig. 6.2. Page from the College's Missal showing deletions of the word 'Papa' (Pope) (University College MS 178 fo. 7^r).
Fig. 7.1. Robert Dudley, Earl of Leicester, Chancellor of the university 1564–88 and benefactor.
Fig. 7.2. George Abbot, Master 1597–1610.
Fig. 7.3. John Bancroft, Master 1610–32.
Fig. 8.1. Edward Herbert, Lord Herbert of Cherbury, m. 1596.
Fig. 8.2. Extract from the accounts of John Elmhirst, F. 1621–51 (UC:BU3/F1/2 fo. 80^v).
Fig. 8.3. Monument to Sir George Savile, m. 1598, and family.
Fig. 9.1. Sir Simon Bennet, m. 1602.
Fig. 9.2. Ground-floor plan of a rejected design for a new quadrangle, *c.*1632 (UC:FA3/1/Y2/1).
Fig. 9.3. Model and plan of the approved design for a new quadrangle, *c.*1632 (UC:FA3/1/Y1/1 and 7).
Fig. 10.1. The newly completed College Library, 1674 (UC:BE1/MS1/3).
Fig. 10.2. University College, drawn in 1675 by David Loggan.
Fig. 10.3. Edward Hales, m. 1684.
Fig. 10.4. Title page of Catholic treatise published by Obadiah Walker.
Fig. 11.1. Image of King Alfred and William of Durham from the 1690s (UC:BE1/MS1/1)
Fig. 11.2. William Smith, m. 1668, F. 1675–1705, and Rector of Melsonby, 1704–35.
Fig. 11.3. John Radcliffe, m. 1666.
Fig. 11.4. Design for Master's Lodgings in Radcliffe Quadrangle (Worcester College drawings, no. 56).
Fig. 12.1. Thomas Cockman, m. 1691, F. 1700–1713, and Master 1722–45 (from T. Silvester (ed.), *Select Theological Discourses written by the late Rev. Thomas Cockman, D.D.*).

FIGURES

Fig. 12.2. Title page of *The Proceedings of the Visitors of University College*, 1723.
Fig. 12.3. The Oxford Almanack for 1735.
Fig. 12.4. The Oxford Almanack for 1753.
Fig. 13.1. William Jones, m. 1764 and F. 1766–83.
Fig. 13.2. Robert Chambers, F. 1761–75.
Fig. 13.3. William Scott, later Lord Stowell, F. 1764–82.
Fig. 13.4. John Scott, later Lord Eldon, m. 1766 and F. 1767–73.
Fig. 13.5. The Hall of University College showing the alterations made in 1766.
Fig. 13.6. Samuel Johnson.
Fig. 14.1. The title page of *A Tour from Oxford to Newcastle upon Tyne*.
Fig. 14.2. St Peter and St Paul's Church, Checkendon, Oxfordshire.
Fig. 14.3. Members of the University College Club (UC:O20/N1/1).
Fig. 14.4. Monument to Sir William Jones.
Fig. 15.1. The expulsion of Percy Bysshe Shelley and Thomas Jefferson Hogg (UC:GB3/A1/2 fo. 148^r).
Fig. 15.2. Travers Twiss, m. 1826 and F. 1830–63 (UC:O1/P1/1 fo. 2^r).
Fig. 15.3. Frederick Plumptre, m. 1813, F. 1817–36, and Master 1836–70.
Fig. 15.4. William Donkin, F. 1836–43 (UC:O1/P1/1 fo. 5^r).
Fig. 15.5. Arthur Stanley, F. 1838–51 (UC:O1/P1/1 fol. 6^r).
Fig. 15.6. Goldwin Smith, Stowell Law Fellow 1846–50 and F. 1850–68 (UC:O1/P1/1 fo. 15^r).
Fig. 16.1. Charles Faulkner, F. 1856–92 (UC:O1/P1/1 fo. 22^r).
Fig. 16.2. George Gilbert Scott's Library, in its original form (UC:P209/P1/6).
Fig. 16.3. The Chapel, after the alterations of George Gilbert Scott (UC:P209/P1/5).
Fig. 16.4. The University College Eight of 1862 (UC:O4/P1/1).
Fig. 16.5. University College undergraduate actors, 1860s (MCA MC:FA1/9/2P/1 fo. 61^r no 2).
Fig. 16.6. H. Neville, scout of John Hill (UC:P4/P/1).
Fig. 16.7. George Bradley, m. 1840, F. 1844–50, and Master 1870–81(UC:P167/P1/1 fo. 43^r).
Fig. 16.8. 'Tale of a Screw': cartoon about the sending down of the College (UC:P45/P/1).
Fig. 17.1. James Franck Bright, m. 1851, F. 1874–81, and Master 1881–1906.
Fig. 17.2. The Shelley Memorial.
Fig. 17.3. Reginald Macan, m. 1868, F. 1884–1906, and Master 1906–23.
Fig. 17.4. Interior of undergraduate room, 1901 (UC:P248/P1/1 fo. 15^r).
Fig. 17.5. The Martlets in 1904 (UC:P10/P/1).
Fig. 17.6. The last day of Eights Week 1902 (UC:P10/P/1).
Fig. 17.7. A coming-of-age dinner party, 1900 (UC:P248/P1/1 fo. 8^r).
Fig. 17.8. Prince Felix Yusupov in a College group photograph of 1911 (UC:O2/P1/1).
Fig. 18.1. Photograph of College members in 1917, including C. S. Lewis (UC:O2/P1/2).
Fig. 18.2. Arthur Poynton, F. 1894–1935 and Master 1935–7.
Fig. 18.3. Lord Beveridge, Master 1937–45, being presented with his portrait (from Gwynne Ovenstone's scrapbooks).

FIGURES

Fig. 18.4. The College Rugby XV of 1921/2 (UC:O2/P1/2).
Fig. 18.5. Edgar Carritt giving a tutorial in 1938 (from E. F. Carritt, *Fifty Years a Don*).
Fig. 18.6. The University College Servants Rowing Club in 1937 (photograph donated by Norman Dix).
Fig. 19.1. John Wild, F. 1933–45 and Master 1945–51, with several former College servants (from the 1948/9 *University College Record*).
Fig. 19.2. Giles Alington, F. 1944–56 (photograph lent by Gwynne Ovenstone).
Fig. 19.3. Gwynne Ovenstone, College Secretary 1947–87 (from the 1987 *University College Record*).
Fig. 19.4. Arthur Goodhart, F. 1931–51 and Master 1951–63, John Maud, F. 1929–39 and Master 1963–76, and their wives (from Gwynne Ovenstone's scrapbooks).
Fig. 19.5. The Alington Room shortly after completion.
Fig. 19.6. The Goodhart Building shortly after completion (UC:FA14/1/P2/1).
Fig. 19.7. Caricature of the Master and Fellows (from the 1962 *University College Record*).
Fig. 19.8. Lord Goodman, Master 1976–86.
Fig. 20.1. Kingman Brewster, Master 1986–8 (from the 1989 *University College Record*).
Fig. 20.2. John Albery, F. 1963–78 and Master 1989–97.
Fig. 20.3. Bill Clinton (m. 1968), President of the United States 1993–2001, with Douglas Millin, Head Porter of University College 1950–83 (UC:CA1/1/P1/4).
Fig. 20.4. Queen Elizabeth II in Radcliffe Quadrangle, May 1999.

Maps and Graphs

Map 2.1.   The first site of University College and its surrounding properties.
Map 2.2.   Great University Hall and the eventual site of University College.
Map App. V. Properties outside Oxford acquired by University College before 1850.

Graph 5.1. Income and Expenditure of University College 1381/2–1496/7
Graph 6.1. Income and Expenditure of University College 1504/5–1596/7
Graph 8.1. Matriculations at University College 1580–1674
Graph 9.1. Income and Expenditure of University College 1633/4–1689/90
Graph 10.1. Admissions to University College, 1675–1736
Graph 12.1. Admissions to University College, 1736–1807
Graph 14.1. Income and Expenditure of University College 1690/1–1807/8
Graph 15.1. Admissions to University College, 1808–1913
Graph 15.2. Income and Expenditure of University College, 1808/9–1881/2
Graph 18.1. Admissions to University College, 1914–2006

Abbreviations and Conventions

AO1	J. Foster, *Alumni Oxonienses. the members of the University of Oxford, 1500–1714; their parentage, birthplace, and year of birth, with a record of their degrees; being the matriculation register of the University* (4 vols., Oxford and London 1891–2)
AO2	J. Foster, *Alumni Oxonienses. the members of the University of Oxford, 1715–1886; their parentage, birthplace and year of birth, with a record of their degrees; being the Matriculation Register of the University* (4 vols., Oxford and London 1887–8)
ARUC	A. D. M. Cox and R. H. Darwall-Smith (eds.), *Account Rolls of University College, Oxford* (2 vols., OHS new ser. xxxix–xl 1999–2001)
BCL	Balliol College Library
BL	The British Library
Bodl.	The Bodleian Library, Oxford
BRUO	A. B. Emden, *A Biographical Register of the University of Oxford to A. D. 1500* (3 vols., Oxford 1957–9)
BRUO2	A. B. Emden, *A Biographical Register of the University of Oxford A. D. 1501 to 1540* (Oxford 1974)
Carr	W. Carr, *University College* (London 1902)
CCR	*Close Rolls of the reign of Henry III preserved in the Public Record Office* (15 vols, London 1902–75); *Calendar of the Close Rolls preserved in the Public Record Office 1272–1509* (61 vols., London 1900–63)
CSPD	*Calendar of State Papers, Domestic Series, preserved in the Public Record Office, 1547–1704* (92 vols., London 1856–1972)
F.	Fellow
Hearne, i–xi	*Remarks and Collections of Thomas Hearne Vol. I 1705–7*, ed. C. E. Doble (OHS ii 1885) *Remarks and Collections of Thomas Hearne Vol. II 1707–10*, ed. C. E. Doble (OHS vii 1886) *Remarks and Collections of Thomas Hearne Vol. III 1710–12*, ed. C. E. Doble (OHS xiii 1888) *Remarks and Collections of Thomas Hearne Vol. IV 1712–14*, ed. D. W. Rannie (OHS xxxiv 1897) *Remarks and Collections of Thomas Hearne Vol. V 1714–16*, ed. D. W. Rannie (OHS xlii 1901) *Remarks and Collections of Thomas Hearne Vol. VI 1717–19*, ed.

ABBREVIATIONS AND CONVENTIONS

Committee of the Oxford Historical Society (OHS xliii 1902)
Remarks and Collections of Thomas Hearne Vol. VII 1719–22, ed. Committee of the Oxford Historical Society (OHS xlviii 1906)
Remarks and Collections of Thomas Hearne Vol. VIII 1722–5, ed. Committee of the Oxford Historical Society (OHS l 1907)
Remarks and Collections of Thomas Hearne Vol. IX 1725–8, ed. H. E. Salter (OHS lxv 1914)
Remarks and Collections of Thomas Hearne Vol. X 1728–31, ed. H. E. Salter (OHS lxvii 1915)
Remarks and Collections of Thomas Hearne Vol. XI 1731–35, ed. H. E. Salter (OHS lxxii 1921)

HUO i	J. I. Catto (ed.), *The History of the University of Oxford, Vol. I. The Early Oxford Schools* (Oxford 1984)
HUO ii	J. I. Catto and R. Evans (eds.), *The History of the University of Oxford, Vol. II. Late Medieval Oxford* (Oxford 1992)
HUO iii	J. McConica (ed.), *The History of the University of Oxford, Vol. III. The Collegiate University* (Oxford 1986)
HUO iv	N. Tyacke (ed.), *The History of the University of Oxford, Vol. IV. Seventeenth-Century Oxford* (Oxford 1997)
HUO v	L. S. Sutherland and L. G. Mitchell (eds.), *The History of the University of Oxford, Vol. V. The Eighteenth Century* (Oxford 1986)
HUO vi	M. G. Brock and M. C. Curthoys (eds.), *The History of the University of Oxford, Vol. VI. Nineteenth-Century Oxford, Part 1* (Oxford 1997)
HUO vii	M. G. Brock and M. C. Curthoys (eds.), *The History of the University of Oxford, Vol. VII. Nineteenth-Century Oxford, Part 2* (Oxford 2000)
HUO viii	B. Harrison (ed.), *The History of the University of Oxford, Vol. VIII. The Twentieth Century* (Oxford 1994)
L & P Henry VIII	J. S. Brewer and J. Gairdner, *Letters and papers, foreign and domestic of the reign of Henry VIII, preserved in the Public record Office, the British museum, and elsewhere in England* (21 vols., in 33 1862–1910; new edn. of vol. i. in 3 pts. 1930; vol. of addenda in 2 pts. 1929–32)
m.	matriculated
MCA	Magdalen College Archives
ODNB	*Oxford Dictionary of National Biography* (online edition, with updates to summer of 2007)
OHS	Oxford Historical Society
Oswald	A. Oswald, 'University College', in *VCH Oxon.* iii. 61–81
OUA	Oxford University Archives

ABBREVIATIONS AND CONVENTIONS

Smith	W. Smith, *The Annals of University College* (Newcastle 1728)
SUL	Southampton University Library
Survey	H. E. Salter, *Survey of Oxford*, ed. W. A. Pantin and W. T. Mitchell (2 vols. OHS new ser. xvi 1964, xx 1969)
TCD	Trinity College, Dublin
TNA	The National Archives
UCR	University College Record
VCH Oxon. iii, iv	*A History of the County of Oxford* (VCH) iii, ed. H. E. Salter and M. D. Lobel (London 1954), iv, ed. A. Crossley (London 1979)
Wood, *Athenae*	*Athenæ Oxonienses. An exact history of all the writers and bishops who have had their education in the University of Oxford. To which are added the Fasti, or Annals of the said University*, ed. P. Bliss (4 vols., London 1813–20)
Wood, *City of Oxford*	A. Wood, *Survey of the Antiquities of the City of Oxford*, ed. A. Clark, *Oxford* vol. iii (OHS xxxvii 1899).
Wood, *Colleges*	A. Wood, *The History and Antiquities of the Colleges and Halls in the University of Oxford*, ed. J. Gutch (Oxford 1786)
Wood, *History*	A. Wood, *The History and Antiquities of the University of Oxford*, ed. J. Gutch (2 vols., Oxford 1792–6)
Wood, *Life* i–iii	*The Life and Times of Anthony Wood*, ed. A. Clark, vols. i–iii (OHS xix, xxi, and xxvi 1891, 1892, and 1894)
WRO	Warwickshire Record Office
WYAS (B)	West Yorkshire Archive Service (Bradford)
YAS	Yorkshire Archaeological Society, Leeds
YMA	York Minster Archives

CONVENTIONS

(1) Before 1752, dates are given in the new style, with the year starting on 1 January, rather than 25 March.

(2) William of Durham's bequest was reckoned in marks, and that term of currency will appear elsewhere in the earlier chapters. A mark is two-thirds of a pound (i.e. 13s. 4d. in pre-decimal currency). William's bequest of 310 marks, therefore, can also be written as £206 13s. 4d.

(3) Deciding what to call the College in this book posed something of a problem, because writing about an institution called University College in the University of Oxford can make for a certain confusion. The College is universally known by its abbreviation, 'Univ.', but this seems somewhat too informal for the present purpose, and in any event the nickname cannot be traced further back than the mid-nineteenth century. In the text, therefore, I tend to refer to 'University College'; all references to the University of Oxford in general allude to the

'university' in lower case. Likewise 'the College' always refers to University College; while 'a college' refers to colleges within Oxford in general.
(4) The names of the quadrangles of University College have been changed more than once. An Ordnance Survey map of the 1870s refers to the 'Quadrangle' and the 'Master's Quadrangle'; in 1902 Carr knew of the 'Large Quadrangle', and the 'Small', or 'Radcliffe Quadrangle', the latter being its present name. The former quadrangle has also more recently been known as the 'Front Quadrangle', but today is generally called the 'Main Quadrangle'. I have therefore used this name in the main body of the narrative.
(5) All documents referred to in the footnotes come from the archives of University College, Oxford, unless otherwise indicated.

I

William of Durham and the Idea of a College: 1249–1280

In the beginning the university of Oxford had no colleges. That this should have changed is due in no small part to a death at Rouen in 1249 and a misused legacy. Their tale is still told in a document in the archives of University College written when Henry of Staunton was Chancellor of Oxford in 1280–1.[1] The death was that of a theologian called William of Durham, the legacy a sum of money given by William to the university for an unusual purpose. The document is the report of a commission of enquiry set up three decades later to salvage the bequest. It also marks the start of a journey which takes that legacy, as embodied in University College, through seven and a half centuries, sharing in all the vicissitudes experienced by the university of Oxford since then.

One must begin with that early university without colleges. Oxford, like Bologna and Paris, effectively came into being before people had a clear idea of what a university was. A few masters had been teaching there in the 1090s, and a century later it had become home to a more organized group of masters and scholars, which one can best liken to a guild, the apprentices being the scholars, who would have arrived in their mid-teens, well grounded in Latin. In the curriculum, as it developed during the thirteenth century, all scholars began as members of the faculty of arts, being expected to study the Seven Liberal Arts, divided into the so-called *trivium* (grammar, rhetoric, and logic), and the *quadrivium* (arithmetic, geometry, astronomy, and music). They would also study the three philosophies (natural, moral, and metaphysical). Teaching was done by the masters, mainly through lectures and disputations (formal debates which trained one in logic and rigorous argument). There were no examinations in the modern sense; one was assessed on the basis of how many lectures one attended and how many disputations one participated in. After four years, if his masters thought he was ready, the scholar became a Bachelor of Arts. More study followed, during which, as

[1] UC:GB1/L1/1.

well as attending lectures, the scholar was expected to deliver some too. After at least three years, once again if one's masters were satisfied, one became a Master of Arts—although one could only actually call oneself an MA once one had stayed on to teach for a further year, a process known as 'necessary regency'. Those who wished could continue to teach at Oxford, and were known as 'regent Masters'.[2]

Not everyone took a degree: one had to pay for it, and some were content just to study for a short while. For the ambitious scholar, however, further degrees beckoned. These could be taken in the higher faculties of medicine, canon and civil law, and theology, which offered doctorates as their more senior degrees. Institutions which offered such higher degrees could claim the title of *studium generale*, or place of general study, the usual medieval term for a university. Until the mid-fourteenth century, however, theology degrees were only awarded at Paris, Oxford, and Cambridge.[3]

The early university and its members owned no property: all schools were rented out, and local churches, especially St Mary the Virgin, used for university ceremonies. Masters and scholars alike lodged in rooms in the town. This might appear insecure; but if the university took offence, it could easily migrate elsewhere, dealing a severe blow to the town's economy. This actually happened in 1209, when, after what the university regarded as the judicial murder of two students, its members did disperse, only reassembling in 1214 on the intervention of a papal legate (although some masters who had found their way to a town in the Fens remained there, and the university of Cambridge came into being).[4] As the century progressed Oxford's university put down more permanent roots. In particular, some enterprising masters began to purchase or lease halls, and rented out individual rooms to scholars. Many so-called academic halls grew up throughout Oxford during the next two centuries, providing scholars with decent accommodation, and masters with a good way of keeping their charges under control.

We are now ready to return to Rouen. For many years, little was known about William of Durham, and his College later found it expedient to forget him. His very identity was mislaid: some wondered whether he was an archdeacon of Durham; others found several Williams from the Durham area, and could not tell them apart. It was left to two Fellows of University College working over two centuries apart, William Smith and David Cox, to sweep away the detritus.[5]

---

[2] The early years of Oxford's university: Southern 1984; pre-university education: Orme 2006; education in early Oxford: Cobban 1988 and Fletcher 1984; early history of Paris: Tuilier 1994: i. 29–39. Leff 1992: 325–6 points out that the BA degree, as something more than a staging post to an MA, only became fully formalized by the middle of the thirteenth century.

[3] *Studium generale*: Cobban 1975: 23–7.

[4] Founding of Cambridge: Leader 1988: 16–19.

[5] Smith, 3–6, and Cox 1949 and 1981, as well as Cox's extensive notes on William (UC:S24/MS1/2). Murray 2000 re-examines the evidence in its European context.

William of Durham's name reveals him as a north-easterner; and a document of 1242, which called him 'William of Sedgefield', might reveal his birthplace, just a few miles from Durham, where he was probably educated. His earliest recorded appearance, however, is at Paris, where in the early 1220s he appears as a doctor of theology, working as one of eight so-called 'regent masters', or teachers, in that subject. Stephen de Bourbon, a student there at this time, reminisced that he once heard from 'Master William of Durham, Doctor of Theology' a tale of how St Bartholomew intervened in human form to save a master from the clutches of the Devil who was tempting him disguised as a beautiful woman.[6] The theology faculty at Paris in the thirteenth century was renowned throughout Christendom as a centre of excellence, and its regent masters, who later included such luminaries as St Thomas Aquinas and St Bonaventure, were its elite. His admission into such a company shows that William of Durham was a scholar of distinction.

Parisian doctors of theology could not take their degrees until they were at least 35 years old. If, therefore, William was teaching in the early 1220s, he was probably born in the late 1180s or earlier. This date makes a link with Oxford difficult, for William would have been of an age to be affected by the 1209 dispersal. In any event, Paris was popular with English scholars. It has been claimed that, until 1215, over a third of all MAs there were of English origin.[7]

William's teaching can be sampled by the survival of two manuscript volumes now preserved at Douai but once owned by the Benedictine Abbey of Marchiennes.[8] They form a collection of so-called *quaestiones* compiled at Paris in the early 1230s. The *quaestio* was an important part of the lecturer's armoury: having given a detailed exposition on a set text, he would then turn to some problems raised by it, and, having noted what previous authorities might have said on the subjects, then offer his own analysis.[9] Ten *quaestiones* in this collection are explicitly ascribed to William of Durham, and others have been attributed to him on contextual or stylistic grounds. The ones known to be William's cover such topics as the unity of the church, eternal life, sin, the body of Christ, and the giving of alms.

---

[6] William of Sedgefield: Bayley and others 1916: 33; William as teacher: Cox 1981: 116 (the passage in Latin is *a magistro Guillielmo de durennes [?] doctore theologie*).

[7] Age of theologians: Rashdall 1936: i. 473; Englishmen in Paris: de Ridder-Symoens 1992: 296. William's schooling would have left him proficient in French (Orme 2006: 73–8).

[8] Douai, Bibl. munic., MS 434, whose contents are summarized in Glorieux 1938*a* and 1938*b*. Glorieux 1938*b*: 256 lists the *quaestiones* explicitly attributed to William of Durham, and suggests others which might be by him. A fuller study of the manuscript, let alone an edition, is still needed. See too Cox 1981: 117 and (on where other *quastiones* of William might be preserved) Murray 2000: 65.

[9] The *quaestio*: Smalley 1952: 66–75.

Only William's *quaestio* on sin has been analysed in any detail. In it he notes a difference between 'sin' and 'evil': as he explains it, 'sin looks to the act, and evil to the state of mind, and by chance they are the same in thing and subject, but the reasoning is different' (*peccatum respicit actum, malum respicit habitum, et forte idem sint re et subjecto, sed ratio diversa est*). An analysis of this work claimed that William reflected the work of the early Franciscans, and that he was one of those masters whose work would later influence St Thomas Aquinas.[10]

William enjoyed his position until 1229. In that year, a brawl in a Paris tavern led to riots, which in turn led to a dispersal of the university. Some masters went to other French universities, others—at the eager invitation of Henry III—to Oxford and Cambridge. The contemporary historian Matthew Paris named five English masters among those who fled, including William of Durham. But where did William go? There is no evidence that he went to Oxford, and some think that he returned to Paris. All we know is that he next appears acting as the chief executor of Maurice, Archbishop of Rouen, who had died in January 1235.[11]

William was now archdeacon of Caux, in the diocese of Rouen, and prebendary of Laise, which brought him a canon's stall at Rouen Cathedral.[12] These posts, and above all his position as the executor of an archbishop well known for his incorruptible probity, mark him out as a man of consequence. In March 1235 William was elected archbishop by the Chapter of Rouen, though not without controversy. The Dean and one-third of the Chapter, protesting that William could not be both archdeacon and prebendary in the same diocese without a dispensation, boycotted the election, leaving the majority of the remainder to elect William. The Dean's objection was correct but not insuperable. The tensions almost certainly lay deeper: William's supporters and opponents will have hoped or feared that he was ready to continue Archbishop Maurice's reformist work.[13]

William did not wish to endure this discord: a contemporary chronicle says that William 'did not wish to agree to the election made about himself, but placed his consent in the will of the lord pope'.[14] Pope Gregory IX sent three delegates to Rouen to investigate the affair, sending them a letter in October 1235, in which he outlined the case and issued instructions: if William

---

[10] William's *quaestio*: Douai, Bibl. munic., MS 434 vol. i. fo. 84ʳ; analysis: Gillon 1937: 56–61.

[11] The dispersal and its aftermath: Tuilier 1994: i. 58–63 and Paris 1872–83: iii. 168; events at Rouen: Cox 1949: 14–19 and Auvray 1907: ii. nos. 2796, 2817, and 3281. Because of the date of the Douai manuscript, Glorieux 1938*b*: 260–1 thinks that William returned to Paris after the university reassembled in 1231.

[12] A prebendary was a canon in a cathedral who was supported by income from a particular estate, known as a 'prebend'.

[13] Archbishop Maurice: Murray 2000: 63–4.

[14] [William] *noluit consentire ad plenum electioni de se factae, sed consensum suum posuit in voluntate domini papae* (Chronicon Rhotomagense 1894: 336).

declined election, then a successor should be elected; but if he was willing to accept election, then the duties of his prebend should be investigated. Nothing further is known until Gregory wrote to the Chapter of Rouen on 12 August 1236 that William had refused to accept his election, and that a new archbishop had been elected.

David Cox wondered whether William refused the archbishopric because of concerns about the weakness of his position vis-à-vis his prebend.[15] However, a dispensation could have been obtained easily enough, and a man truly eager for preferment would have fought his corner more fiercely. William's conduct is more that of a man who had concluded that high preferment was not for him. Another of the English masters who fled Paris in 1229, Nicholas of Farnham, did become a bishop, but only reluctantly and after much persuasion.[16]

At the height of the Rouen affair, in August 1235, William had paid Richard Poore, the Bishop of Durham, an annual rent of 40 marks (£26 13s. 4d.), in return for receiving the income of the parish lands of Wearmouth, the manors of Wearmouth and Ryhop, and the town of Sunderland, for life. Although not explicitly stated, this document assumes that William was the rector of Wearmouth. Such a post did not necessitate residence: William could easily have employed a vicar to perform his parochial duties. Instead, William was content to go home, leaving Rouen, resigning his archdeaconry, but retaining his prebend. In November 1237 and April 1238 William was granted wood to build a house at Wearmouth, and other documents discovered by David Cox suggest that he remained consistently in residence until his death.[17]

William's final home, later known as Bishopwearmouth, whose church was renamed Sunderland Minster in 1998 (Fig. 1.1), is a wealthy parish, situated on the south bank of the Wear, just opposite the Venerable Bede's home at Jarrow. The parish's revenues, enhanced by his deal with Bishop Poore, and the income from his Rouen prebend, would have satisfied William's financial needs; as to his intellectual ones, barely a dozen miles away lay Durham Priory with its well-stocked library. There is evidence that William exploited this opportunity: among the manuscripts at Durham is one containing several books from the Old Testament and Apocrypha, with a thirteenth-century inscription that it was a gift to St Cuthbert from Master William of Durham.[18]

---

[15] Cox 1949: 19 and 1981: 119.
[16] Farnham: *ODNB* entry.
[17] Grant of lands: Durham Misc. Chart. 6430; grant of timber: *CCR 1237–1242*, 8 and 47; other material: Cox 1981: 120–1.
[18] Durham Priory: Dobson 1973: 358–9 and 369–71. The manuscript given by Master William of Durham has the reference MA A.II 7. William may have suggested purchases to the Priory: Murray 2000: 65 notes the presence there of a volume of Parisian theology acquired soon after its composition in 1235.

FIGURE 1.1 The Minster Church of St Michael and All Angels, Sunderland (formerly the church of Bishopwearmouth), where William of Durham was rector until his death in 1249. Only the tower dates from William's day.

William's end, however, came far from home. In his obituary notices for the year 1249 Matthew Paris in his *Chronica Majora* reports:

There died too in the same year Master William of Durham at Rouen, on his return from the Roman Curia, a most eminently learned man, and one abounding in many rents, but he gaped for more.[19]

In 1249, Pope Innocent IV and his court were resident at Lyon, and some documents shed light on why the elderly William, now in his sixties, made such a long journey. William's main objective was to protect his own rights: his erstwhile Parisian colleague, Nicholas of Farnham, now Bishop of Durham, was protesting against the agreement with Bishop Poore, and a mandate of 22 December 1248 settled the case in William's favour. However, William also appears on the endorsement of another mandate of 28 January 1249, now in the Durham muniments, concerning the Priory's attempts to recover some lands. The endorsement is barely legible, and William's exact involvement is

---

[19] *Obiit etiam eodem anno magister Willelmus de Dunelmo apud Rothomagum, rediens a Romana curia, literatus eminentissime et abundans multis redditibus, sed amplioribus inhiabat* (Paris 1872–83: v. 91).

unclear—even as to whether he was acting for or against the Priory—but he was evidently still at Lyon.[20]

William left Lyon some time after 28 January 1249, taking with him one last piece of recognition: the mandates of 1248 and 1249 both call William a papal chaplain. This honour lay in the Pope's personal gift, and lasted only during his reign. Innocent IV, a reformer, chose his chaplains with care (another chaplain, Jacques Pantaléon, later became Pope Urban IV), so that William's appointment was a tribute from someone properly appreciative of his stature.

Matthew Paris acknowledged William's stature, when he called him 'most eminently learned', and yet his obituary is more memorable for the sting in the tail, about William's alleged avarice. He was, however, being unfair. With his generous living and his other sources of revenue, William's wealth could have aroused envy. Furthermore, Matthew was unimpressed by papal honours. A modern assessment of William of Durham can be much more positive: a theologian of the first rank, who achieved the highest academic position, and was honoured by a Pope; a teacher whose pupils remembered his anecdotes fondly; a man who preferred a parish life to an archbishopric; and, as will be seen, a man aware of the latest trends in university education.

Yet William of Durham would have become just one more forgotten Paris theologian had it not been for the terms of his will. His will is lost, and our only evidence for its contents comes from the 1280/1 commission of enquiry mentioned at the start of this chapter, and a set of statutes for University College, dating from 1292.[21] The relevant passages are as follows:

From the 1280/1 commission:

(1) 'The said Master William bequeathed 310 marks to the University, under this condition, namely that they should purchase with this money annual rents for the use of ten or eleven or twelve or more masters who would be supported from the rents of this money.'[22]
(2) The decision of the 'masters deputed by the University and considering the will of the testator'[23] is to create a group of four masters studying theology.
(3) 'Furthermore it is to be forbidden to use the collected money for any other use except that which had been in the last will of the testator. Furthermore as soon as

---

[20] Mandate of 1248: Berger 1887: ii. no. 4274; mandate of 1249: Sayers 1999: no. 344 and Murray 2000: 65.

[21] On the 1280/1 document, see n. 1 above. The original of the 1292 set is lost, but medieval copies exist in the University Archives (OUA NEB/Supra/Register A, B, and C). Both documents are edited, not wholly satisfactorily, in Anstey 1868: ii. 780–3 and i. 56–61.

[22] *Dictus magister Willelmus trescentas marcas & decem universitati legavit sub hac forma scilicet quod ex illa pecunia emerentur redditus annui ad opus x vel xj vel xij vel plurium magistrorum qui essent de redditibus illius pecunie sustentati.*

[23] *Magistrorum ab universitate deputatorum et voluntatem testatoris considerantum.*

new rents have been purchased, the number and exhibition [i.e. income] of the masters is to be increased.'[24]

From the 1292 statutes, which are described as the production of 'the congregation of Regents and Non-Regents, on the request of the executors of the venerable Master William of Durham to the honour of his Scholars':[25]

Should all the Fellows of the College simultaneously die or resign, or otherwise cease to operate, the Congregation ordains 'according to the will of the founder, that in such a case Masters who have not been promoted, and live around Durham, should come to the Chancellor and Proctors or the senior theologian and the senior artists. These will admit some from the best of them to the aforesaid College, and, if there are not then such non-promoted Masters from that area, then Bachelors are to come forward, and, if necessary, Sophisters from the Durham area, and, as has been said concerning the Masters, some of them are to be received according to the said statutes.'[26]

These extracts leave clear clues about William's will: he left 310 marks (£206 13s. 4d.)—a sum equivalent to 100 times the annual wage of a builder[27]—to Oxford university, which it was to invest in land to support MAs studying theology, with preference given to candidates from the Durham area. It was also evidently expected that the masters would live together. Nothing quite like this had been given to Oxford before, and we must seek some kind of context for his bequest.

Although theology was the senior faculty at Paris, Oxford, and Cambridge, its study could deter even the most determined. In particular, there was the time factor. Theology could only be studied by a Master of Arts, who had already spent seven years in study. The theology course took longer still, especially if one sought a doctorate in it. Above all, it was not usually a lucrative subject: students in search of wealth or influence fared much better by studying law or medicine. Theology was thus very much the preserve of the intellectual, interested only in learning.[28]

---

[24] *Pecuniam vero collectam nulli liceat ad usus alios deputare nisi ad illum qui fuerat de ultimo voluntate testatoris; quamcito vero plures redditus empti fuerunt, augeantur numerus & exhibicio magistrorum.*
[25] *Congregacionis Regencium et Non-Regencium, ex procuracione executorum venerabilis M. Willelmi de Dunelm ad honestatem suorum Scholarium.*
[26] *Secundum testamentum fundatoris, quod in tali casu veniant Magistri non promoti propinquiores Donelm ad Cancellarium et Procuratores vel seniorem theologum et seniores artistas, qui eo ipso aliquos de melioribus illorum admittant ad praefatum collegium, et si non sint tunc tales Magistri non promoti illius patrie, veniant Bachilarii, vel, si necesse fuerit, Sophiste Donelmie propinquiores, et, ut de Magistris dictum est, recipiantur illorum aliqui secundum statuta dicta.* A Sophister was a student several years into his BA course.
[27] Murray 2000: 59.
[28] Theology losing out to more lucrative subjects: Murray 1985: 218–27; length of the theology course: Mitchell 1998: i. 305–6.

Where could one find money for such a long period of study? Most scholars depended on their family or a patron to help them achieve their MA, but few could have relied on receiving such aid thereafter. Some aspiring theologians might have private means, and others might be able to find a benefice, obtain the appropriate dispensation to study, and return to Oxford, paying a curate to do the parochial work. But few had such wealth or connections. There was also serious competition from the orders of Dominican and Franciscan friars. Only a few decades after their foundation in the early thirteenth century, both orders had houses in Oxford and Paris. Friars, and monks too, could study under the auspices of their orders, with little need for outside financial assistance. This started to give the regular clergy (clerics who belonged to religious orders) a numerical advantage over the secular clergy (clerics who did not belong to such orders). The problems grew deeper when the friars asked to be exempted from the arts course before reading theology, and bitter conflicts, first at Paris, and later at Oxford, would arise. Although these storms broke out after his death, it is significant that, after the dispersal of Paris in 1229, the friars stayed behind—unlike William—and, only two years later, three of the theology chairs at Paris, one of which William had once held, were now held by friars.[29]

The long years of labour, the financial problems, and the competition from the regular clergy made theology a daunting subject for the secular scholar, and William of Durham would have known this better than most. His bequest to the university of Oxford represents his own solution: an endowment to give budding secular theologians the time, the money, and the accommodation, to study in peace, under conditions comparable with those enjoyed by their regular colleagues. There may, however, have been another motive: the early thirteenth century was a time of anxiety about a lack of learned clergy in the parishes. The former regent master of Paris now settled in Bishopwearmouth was setting a good example, and it is reasonable to ask whether William may have hoped that other students of theology would follow his example.[30]

We need to look to Paris to understand William's actions.[31] By 1229 there were some three or four institutions there known as colleges, which had been created to support scholars in their study. The earliest was the Collège des Dix-Huit, founded in 1180 by an English crusader to provide a small income for eighteen scholars and clerks reading for their BA degrees, and first situated in a room in the Hospital of the Blessed Mary of Paris. Other early colleges were also intended for young scholars, or else for schoolboys preparatory to their entering the university. The organization of these first

---

[29] Sheehan 1984 and Leff 1968: 34–47.
[30] Concerns over a lack of learned clergy: Murray 1985: 292–306 and Murray 2000: 63–4.
[31] Rashdall 1936: i. 497–539 remains the key discussion of the Parisian colleges, but see too Reitzel 1971: 36–186, Cobban 1975: 126–32, and Tuilier 1994: i. 98–101 and 146–51.

colleges was loose: their statutes have little to say about their administration or course of study, and most of them, especially the Collège des Dix-Huit, were subject to outside jurisdiction, be it a local church, a hospital, or even the cathedral itself.

The appearance of this word 'college' opens up a new world. The word *Collegium* existed even in classical Latin to denote a group of people associated for a particular purpose. It then took root in the Christian world, and assumed more specific meanings. As a later observer, John Ayliffe, explained, a college is 'a *legal* Body, or Corporation, consisting in Three or more Persons, joined together in a Community'.[32] Colleges, therefore, could be set up in many contexts. There was, for example, the collegiate church, a church with a college attached, whose fellows would say services and celebrate masses for their founders and benefactors. If the college had a choir attached, then some of the fellows might teach the boys, but this was not the main purpose of the place.[33] Interestingly enough, the earliest university colleges at Oxford, as we shall see, took some time to acquire the exclusive name of 'college' rather than 'hall'.

The concept of a college at Paris university was becoming an attractive one, and assumed more complex forms. In the early 1250s, Robert de Sorbon, a royal chaplain who had evidently studied theology at Paris in the 1220s, began to purchase properties in Paris on whose site in 1257/8 he founded an institution open only to students of theology, which blossomed into the great college of La Sorbonne. Another significant foundation was the Collège du Trésorier, founded in the mid-1260s by Guillaume de Saône, Treasurer of Rouen Cathedral, William's former home, and open only to scholars from the city and diocese of Rouen studying theology.[34]

These dates and places are significant: Robert de Sorbon and Guillaume de Saône both moved in circles where they had the opportunity to know of William of Durham, and all three were wrestling with the concept of endowing institutions—colleges, if one will—for students of theology and learned priests who came from regions some distance away from the universities. More than that one cannot say, but the three men's activities do show that the idea of a college was evolving fast in mid-thirteenth century Paris, and that William's bequest makes sense when seen in that context.

That was, however, a Parisian context. England was different. Benefactions were being made to Oxford, but of a different kind. In 1240, on the suggestion of Robert Grosseteste, Bishop of Lincoln, and a former Chancellor of Oxford, the university created a loan chest, designed to hold the annual

---

[32] Ayliffe 1723: 2–3.
[33] Orme 2006: 214.
[34] Sorbonne: Tuilier 1994: i. 115–27; Trésorier: Reitzel 1971: 150–63; both colleges: Murray 2000: 61–4.

money given as penance by the city burgesses since 1214. Known as the St Frideswide's loan chest, this was kept in the priory of St Frideswide.[35] Others proposed to offer grants rather than loans. In 1243, the Prior of Bicester, evidently under the prompting of Robert Grosseteste, used a bequest from a certain Alan Basset to purchase lands whose rents were to support two chaplains, who were to be scholars at Oxford and were to pray daily for the souls of Basset and his wife, in return for an annual stipend of 8 marks (£5 6s. 8d.).[36] The Prior, however, left few details about how or where the two clerks were to live, or what they were to study, once they had carried out their daily duty. He even acknowledged the possible impermanence of Oxford by stipulating that its scholars are to study there 'or elsewhere where a *studium* will have been in England', and providing for the possibility of there being no university in England. This was a much less sophisticated arrangement than William of Durham's proposed group of theology students.

There is a headily experimental feel to English higher education in the 1250s and 1260s. It was still not impossible that Oxford or Cambridge might cease to have a university, while the example of Cambridge showed that new universities could be founded in England. Northampton was showing signs of developing a university until 1265, when Oxford and Cambridge successfully petitioned Henry III to close their rival down.[37]

Another approach was tried at Salisbury, where in *c*.1261/2 Bishop Giles de Bridport founded De Vaux College, the first college in England for secular clergy to study at university level actually to come into being. It was designed for two chaplains, and for twenty scholars to study arts and theology, under a Warden appointed by the cathedral. There was not yet a fully-grown *studium* at Salisbury, but one might have appeared, with this new college as catalyst. In fact, Salisbury never got its university, and members of De Vaux College had to go to Oxford to obtain a degree. England would have to make do with two universities jealous of all rivals: the last medieval challenge to their duopoly, a university created at Stamford in 1333, was closed down just two years later.[38]

William of Durham's idea of supporting a group of theologians in their studies therefore came at a time when there were many options for university education in England. In particular, his will of 1249 marks the moment when the concept of a college for educational purposes at university level crosses the Channel from Paris, and this is the reason why University College lays claim to the title of the oldest collegiate endowment in any British university.

---

[35] Loan chests, and other early benefactions to Oxford: Aston and Faith 1984.
[36] This document, known only from a seventeenth century copy, is printed in Salter 1924: 297–9. See too Rashdall 1936: iii. 175.
[37] Lawrence 1984: 128–30.
[38] De Vaux College: Edwards 1956 and Orme 2006: 79–81; the university at Stamford: Lawrence 1984: 131–2.

'Collegiate endowment' rather than 'college': William's Parisian concepts were too advanced for the Oxford of 1249. The next three decades saw his bequest mishandled, and almost lost for good. We may assume that his money was conveyed to Oxford and deposited, presumably in a chest, in the Priory of St Frideswide, where the university's other moneys were then stored. The legacy attracted the notice of Adam Marsh, a prominent Franciscan friar then at Oxford. In a letter written in the early 1250s, Adam asks a master of the university to help support a priest in need of financial assistance called Simon de Valence, and suggests that he could be lent £40 from 'the money deposited with the University of Oxford, from the charitable gift of Master William of Durham', in return for an appropriate deposit.[39]

Adam Marsh thought—quite wrongly, in the light of what we know of William's will—that William had created a loan chest. In any event, he was a master at pleading other people's cases, so that he may have been testing a previously untried source of assistance. Furthermore, one of Adam's best friends was Robert Grosseteste, who created Oxford's first loan chest. Aware of the arrival of William's bequest, Adam may have guessed that it was intended for a similar purpose. In any case, we do not know whether Simon de Valence received his money.

One suspects not; other documents suggest that, at least in the 1250s, the university was following William's instructions and investing his money in property. Four properties are known to have been bought: in June 1253, the Chancellor, Masters, and Scholars of Oxford gave the Hospital of St James at Brackley 36 marks (£24) for a house, later known as Little University Hall—now the site of the north-eastern corner of the front quadrangle of Brasenose College, facing onto Schools Street—which ran along the western end of what is now Radcliffe Square. A couple of years later they bought from Sherborne Priory, for an annual payment of 8 shillings, another house, later known as Drawda Hall (now the site of 33 High Street). In about 1262 the university bought the property directly to the south of Little University Hall for £55 6s. 8d., and which later became known as Brasenose Hall. Finally in about 1269/70, at a cost of ten and a half marks (£7), the university bought a rent of 15s. 8d. a year payable on a house which is now the site of 83 and 84 High Street, before receiving the whole property in about 1275.[40]

These purchases cost the University £86 7s. 8d.—just over two-fifths of William's bequest—and according to the commission should have yielded an

---

[39] Use of St Fridewide's Priory: Aston and Faith 1984: 279; Adam Marsh: *BRUO* ii. 1225–6; his letter: Brewer 1858: 256–7 (his own words are: *de pecunia universitatis Oxoniae deposita, ex munere caritativo magistri Willielmi de Dunelmia*).

[40] These transactions are recorded in UC:E/A1/D/4–5, UC:E/B1/D/1, UC:E/A2/D/3, and UC:E/B2/D1/1–3.

annual rent of about £12. So far, then, all appeared well, save that there is no record yet that the income was used to support theology students. Then trouble struck, as the commissioners of 1280/1 explained:

> The said Masters, enquiring further on the rest of the money, have found that the University of Oxford itself, being in need of money both for itself, and for certain magnates of the realm who were coming to the said University for aid, had taken some of the remaining money (viz. 100 pounds and 10 marks [£106 13s. 4d.]) as a loan for its own business, and gave the rest of it as a loan to others, from which nothing whatsoever has been returned.[41]

In short, the university had lost well over half William's bequest in ill-judged loans. It is easy to curse this folly, but Adam Marsh's mistaking William's money for just another loan chest shows that people were not sure what to do with it, even without outside pressure for funds. The 'magnates of the realm' are left unnamed, but Simon de Montfort had held a Parliament in Oxford in 1258, and his supporters revisited the city over the next few years. Discreet hints could well have dropped about how Simon's party would welcome assistance, and the contents of the chest in St Frideswide's, with the rather eccentric conditions attached to their use, seemed to be there for the taking.[42]

Yet, while the university was content to see part of William's money disappear, and to enjoy the income from the remainder, it made no attempt to put William's other plans into effect. In 1279, Edward I instituted a survey of property ownership, known as the Hundred Rolls. In the Oxfordshire section most of the properties bought with William's money are identifiable. Drawda Hall was now an academic hall, whilst the future Brasenose Hall and Little University Hall were being used as schools. All three are specifically called the property of the university, with no hint that they had been purchased for a special purpose. William's vision, it seems, had disappeared into the university's general funds.[43]

Something saved the day: between the creation of the Hundred Rolls, and the end of the Chancellorship of Henry de Staunton in 1281, the university suddenly appointed a group of masters to investigate how to put William of Durham's will into effect. It is not known what caused this change of heart: we shall see that some of William's executors were still alive in 1292—and, significantly, executors of wills who failed to carry out their duties could be excommunicated; perhaps some members of the university, aware of the

---

[41] *Dicti ... magistri ulterius inquirentes de residuo pecunie invenerunt quod universitas Oxon' ipsa indigens pro se & quibusdam magnatibus terre ad ipsam universitatem recurrentibus residuam pecuniam videlicet Centum libras & x marcas sterlingorum partem pro suis negociis mutuo acceperat & partem aliis mutuo concessit personis de quibus nichil est penitus restitutum.*
[42] Simon in Oxford: *VCH Oxon.* iv. 13–14. His party seem the likeliest beneficiaries precisely because of the vagueness in the text. Such circumlocutions might be prudent once Prince Edward, Simon's destroyer, became Edward I in 1272.
[43] The relevant entries from the Hundred Rolls are in Graham 1905: 29, 52, and 59.

FIGURE 1.2 The first statutes of University College, drawn up in 1280/1. The seal is that of the university of Oxford.

potential benefits of William's plan, might have considered it wise to do something more appropriate with his money.[44] Whatever the reasons, the masters appointed to investigate William's will submitted their report—the document with which this chapter opened (Fig. 1.2).

[44] Excommunication of negligent executors: Murray 2000: 59.

Having explained how over half of William's legacy had been lost, the masters then tried to enact his wishes as best they could, by outlining statutes for a new collegiate institution. Four Masters of Arts were to be selected by the Chancellor and Masters in Theology, with Masters from other faculties, if their presence was deemed appropriate. Later elections would also be held in this way, save that the new scholars would be allowed to participate. One of the four had to be a priest. The scholars would receive 50s. a year, and one of their number, who would receive an extra 5s. a year, would administer the College's finances, and be known as the Proctor (*Procurator*). The masters would live together, and read theology, although (perhaps to make the new Fellowships more attractive) they would be permitted to read texts on canon law if appropriate. The Chancellor and Masters of Theology, however, reserved the right to remove scholars, and a Master of Arts was to be appointed to help the Proctor in his financial activities. Any money in the institution's possession was to be kept in a chest, to which the Chancellor, the Proctor, and another master in the university would each have keys.

The last sections of the statutes show the commission's eagerness to prevent the repetition of past mistakes: the money raised from the rents was not to be used for any purpose contrary to William's will, and any spare money was to be invested in more property, and, if possible, more masters were to be appointed. No more dubious loans were to be taken from this source.

The little band of four Masters is a long way from William's hopes for up to a dozen of them. In any case, would William of Durham himself have considered that this new institution matched his own intentions? He certainly wanted to give financial aid to some scholars to study, but some have thought that he did not have the idea of placing them in a separate institution.[45] Yet this is to ignore William's Parisian experiences, and in particular his knowledge of the colleges there. We should not deny him the ability to conceive of a community of theologians, living together, especially when Robert de Sorbon's similar, if grander, foundation was founded barely a decade after William's death.

On the other hand, two institutions had appeared in Oxford since 1249 which modified and expanded the Parisian model, namely Balliol and Merton Colleges.[46] In about 1263, John de Balliol, a great north-eastern magnate, began to support a group of sixteen poor scholars in Oxford, allegedly as a penance imposed by the then Bishop of Durham. This foundation resembles closely the early Parisian colleges in offering charitable support to scholars in the early stages of their career. John died in 1268, which might have left his fledgling foundation open to the same dangers as that of William of Durham,

---

[45] Such as Mallet 1924–7: i. 84 (but Mallet was a Balliol man). Reitzel 1971: 191 wrongly claims that William merely envisaged a loan chest.

[46] See further Jones 2005: 1–12 and Martin and Highfield 1997: 1–24.

but he had an important advantage over William in his redoubtable widow Dervorguilla. Passionately devoted to her husband's memory, she took the little community at Oxford under her wing, setting aside money and lands for it, until she secured its future once and for all by giving it a set of statutes in 1282.

Soon after John de Balliol's scholars began to receive their bounty, Walter de Merton, a man eminent in both church and state as future Bishop and erstwhile Chancellor of England, created another foundation at Oxford in 1264. Merton College was the luckiest of the early colleges, both in the comparative longevity of its founder, who did not die until 1277, by which stage he had given his college property and a twice-revised set of statutes, and in his generosity—Merton remained the wealthiest college in Oxford, until New College was founded in 1379.

We do not know whether John de Balliol or Walter de Merton were aware of William of Durham's will. All three colleges, however, have links with Durham. William of Durham's links are already known; whether or not John de Balliol created his college at the instance of the Bishop of Durham, his power base certainly lay in the north-east; and Walter de Merton had spent much of the 1240s in the service of Nicholas of Farnham, Bishop of Durham, and William's former colleague. Furthermore it was Durham Priory that in 1289 created Durham College (the site of the future Trinity College), the first Oxford college for regular clergy, in this case Benedictine monks. Mere coincidence, some may say; yet it was useful for Durham to have outposts in Oxford for its brighter sons to receive the advanced education which could not be offered nearer home.

Of the three early colleges, Merton's fortunate birth undoubtedly helped it mature the most quickly, and Walter's concept of a college became the blueprint for Oxford and Cambridge foundations. As finally unveiled in 1274, his college was a community of fellows led by a warden, which offered its members the chance to study all subjects, not only arts but also the higher faculties of theology, law, and medicine.

Walter's model differed from most Parisian colleges in making its members responsible for administering its sources of revenue. The 1280/1 statutes of University College, quite possibly influenced by this example, as well as the activities of the university, make similar demands on the Fellows to take an active role in administering their own finances. This financial independence may have been an important factor in the development of the English colleges: however widespread the system of colleges became in European universities, nowhere else would colleges come to take over their universities quite in the way that the English ones did.[47]

---

[47] See Rashdall 1936: i. 531–3, Cobban 1975: 130–2, and Reitzel 1971: 5–14.

As one looks at the origins of Oxford's three oldest colleges, so it becomes ever harder to decide which one is the oldest, when one looks to its endowment, another to its property, and a third to its statutes.[48] This was a time when there was no settled concept of what a university college might be, and William of Durham, John de Balliol, and Walter of Merton—to say nothing of their Parisian counterparts—were each producing their own solution. Had William of Durham lived to see his scholars elected, or his executors been more vigilant, and University College begun in earnest much sooner, the history of Oxford's colleges might have had a very different start, one perhaps a little closer to the Parisian model. William's initiative, however, undoubtedly marked a significant moment in English university life, and, despite thirty years' apathy or downright incompetence, it had at last reached fruition by the 1280s. It was now time for the newly appointed scholars of Master William of Durham to administer this inheritance.

[48] Murray 2000: 66–7.

2

A College Takes Shape: 1280–1361

The commissioners of 1280/1 had done their work: presumably four Masters who wished to read theology were selected, and the university transferred to them the properties bought with William of Durham's money, with their title deeds and any remaining money.[1] But 'presumably' is all one can say. Although the next eighty years are crucial ones in the history of University College, they are also by far the worst documented. The names of its first Fellows are unknown; no accounts survive before 1381/2; our evidence consists largely of statutes, title deeds, and a few stray documents. Above all, we do not even know what the new institution was called, and the tale of how it came to be called 'University College' will play an important role in this chapter.

The first document after 1280/1 to mention the College is a second set of statutes, dating from 1292. Their swift appearance is unsurprising. The 1280/1 statutes were rather improvisatory, aiming merely to right the wrong done to William's will by appointing Fellows and preventing future misuse of his money: the fine details could wait. Thus they concentrated on such essentials as the election of Fellows, their stipends, and the choice of subject to read, but little else. By way of contrast, the statutes created by Walter de Merton and the Lady Dervorguilla for their colleges contained many more details regulating the life and conduct of their Fellows.[2]

It must have been considered appropriate that William of Durham's Scholars should receive similar regulations. Although the university remained in overall control of the new foundation's destiny, the 1292 regulations were drawn up at the request of the surviving executors of William of Durham, to the honour of his Scholars, which may suggest that pressure had been put on the university to produce them.[3]

---

[1] Although at least two deeds relating to College lands still remain in the Oxford University Archives (OUA F.17 and O.13).
[2] Statutes of Merton and Balliol: Martin and Highfield 1997: 13–24 and Jones 2005: 5–8 and 318–20.
[3] See p. 7 on extant sources for these statutes.

The 1292 statutes began with constitutional matters. Not only were the Bursar's duties restated, and his stipend increased to 10s., but a senior Fellow was appointed to regulate the conduct of the others, ensure observation of the statutes, check the College's finances, and oversee the holding of disputations. For these activities, he received half a mark (6s. 8d.) a year, with an additional half mark being given to him and the other Fellows for living expenses and servants.

The duties of the other Fellows were more clearly delineated: they had to keep their statutes secret, to place any sum greater than ten shillings in the common chest, and were forbidden to sell any College property or chattels without permission. They were to say a mass every year for their benefactors (the plural may imply that William of Durham's example had already been followed). Fellows who disparaged each other in public were to be fined (they should only correct each other 'decently and in secret'); they were to speak Latin 'often'; and they were encouraged in general 'to live decently as clerks, as befits holy men, not fighting, not uttering scurrilous or abusive words, not narrating, singing or eagerly listening to songs or tales about mistresses and loose-living people, or inclining them to lust; they are not to mock someone or rouse him to anger, and not to make a noise, so that those studying are hindered in their study or quiet.'[4] Another statute also referred, for the first time, to a College servant: a butler (*pincerna*) was asked to ensure that the College's weekly expenditure did not normally exceed twelve shillings without dispensation from the university.

Provision was made for a library—or at least a collection of books, in that 'one of any sort of book of the house' (*de quolibet genere librorum domus unus*) was to be put in a safe place for the benefit of present and future Fellows. This safe place was probably just a locked chest: the first reference to a library as an actual room is not until 1389/91. Arrangements were made for borrowing books, both by Fellows, and (in return for a pledge and the Fellows' permission) by others. An unexpected stipulation was that any scholar—not just Fellows of the College—about to participate in a theological disputation, or studying Peter Lombard's *Sentences*, had the right to borrow a book gratis.[5]

The university still exercised considerable influence: every year, before the Feast of Corpus Christi (the Thursday after Trinity Sunday), the College had to submit accounts to the Chancellor, and the statutes on the loan of books to

---

[4] *Vivant omnes honeste ut clerici, prout decet sanctos, non pugnantes, non scurrilia vel turpia loquentes, non cantilenas seu fabulas de amasiis vel luxuriosis, aut ad libidinem sonantibus narrantes, cantantes, aut libenter audientes, non irridentes vel aliquem ad iram moventes, non clamantes, ut studentes a studio vel quiete impediantur.*

[5] Statutes on books: Hunt 1950: 14–15; first reference to library: *ARUC* i. 81. Martin and Highfield 1997: 72–89 show that, although the library at Merton was only begun in the 1340s, it had already set aside space for a library.

outsiders suggest hopes that the new College might benefit other members of the university. However, the university did not intervene too much in the choice of Fellows: no rules on the method of electing Fellows were imposed beyond regulations for intervening, should all of them suddenly die, move away, be promoted, or be expelled *en masse*.

One other statute deserves quoting in full:

> Since the said Scholars do not yet have the means from which they can live usefully on their own, but sometimes it is useful for them to have others, good men, staying with them, it is ordained that every year, should anyone wish to stay with them, each Fellow is to make secret enquiries about his behaviour, and then, when unanimous agreement has been obtained, he is to be received, if they want him, on this condition that he himself promises in their presence that he will live honourably and peacefully according to the customs of the Fellows for the time of his stay there, will pay his debts, and do no harm to the affairs of the house, nor to himself, nor to his friends.[6]

This was unexpected: no such provisions appeared in the statutes of Walter of Merton or the Lady Dervorguilla. This society, however, was encouraged to welcome men who would not receive any of William's money, but would pay their own way, whilst obeying the same rules as the Fellows and involving themselves in the daily life of the College. The tone of the statute suggests that the Fellows were seeking, not young scholars reading for their BA, but rather maturer men seeking something better than a room in a private house, who preferred the company of Fellows to the atmosphere of an academic hall. Such men would become known as commoners.[7]

Finally, as mentioned in the previous chapter, the statutes declared that, in accordance with William's wishes, if the university had to choose Fellows for the College, then preference should be given to MAs from the diocese of Durham, and, failing them, BAs and, if necessary, Sophisters from there. William Smith suggested that this statute owed its existence to lobbying from William's executors, but it appears to provide evidence of William's own wishes.[8]

The 1292 statutes are above all pragmatic. Later colleges received statutes which were wildly optimistic in their founder's visions, such as Queen's, or excessively rigid in prohibiting any revision, such as New College, but these statutes provided William's Scholars with a simple set of rules, and even

---

[6] *Cum dicti Scholares nondum habent unde per se solos utiliter vivant, sed aliquando eis expedit secum alios honestos commorari, ordinatum est quod omni anno de quocumque commorari volente, queratur secrete ab omni socio de ejusdem moribus, et tunc, habito unanimi consensu, recipiatur, si velint, sub hac condicione, quod ipse idem coram eis promittat se honeste secundum consuetudines sociorum tempore sue more pacifice victurum, debita soluturum, rebus domus nec in se nec sibi adherentibus nociturum.*

[7] Other colleges, such as Oriel and Queen's, followed this example (Highfield 1984: 258–9 and Cobban 1992: 619–21). The modern, undergraduate, sense of 'commoner' is several centuries away.

[8] Smith, 43.

include an invitation to add further statutes if needed.[9] One omission, however, remained: although the 1292 statutes explicitly described the institution as a College with Fellows, they did not give it a name—all we learn is that William's executors were described as acting 'for the honour of his Scholars'.

After 1292, seven more years of silence fall until 19 September 1299. On that day, one Thomas de Clifford was ordained a priest at Lincoln Cathedral, and the Bishop's Register noted that he came from 'the house established for the soul of Master William of Durham at Oxford' (*de domo ordinata pro anima Magistri W. de Dunelmo Oxon.*). Thomas is the earliest known member of University College. He may have been a Fellow or a commoner, but the fact that he is described as belonging to this place faintly suggests the former as more likely—although, if Thomas belonged to the wealthy Clifford family, then he would have had less need of William's money. His career was certainly of the kind which William would have envisaged for his Scholars: by 1299 he was already an MA, and he was a Doctor of Theology by 1305. On leaving Oxford, he became, among other things, a Canon of Lincoln Cathedral and Dean of Auckland in Durham, and appears to have died before 1322.[10]

Thomas de Clifford came from a 'house'; even the 1280/1 statutes imply that the Scholars of Master William of Durham should live together. Yet the earliest home of the College is unknown (Maps 2.1 and 2.2). William Smith, who first examined this question properly, concluded that the Scholars would have used one of the properties transferred in 1280/1, namely Brasenose Hall, Little University Hall, and Drawda Hall. In the Hundred Rolls of 1279, Drawda Hall was an academic hall, but 'the house called Brasenose' was used for four schools, and the unnamed house next to it (Little University Hall) used for two. Smith suggested that the last-named was the likeliest home for the Scholars, because its name, versions of which, as we shall see, can be traced back to the early fourteenth century, is so suggestive. Furthermore, with such a small initial Fellowship, it made sense to live in a little house, leasing out a bigger one like Brasenose Hall for a larger rent. Although Smith diffidently observed that he was 'proceed[ing] upon Probabilities', Little University Hall remains the most plausible home for the first Fellows.[11]

One document in the College archives, damaged even in Smith's day, both enlightens and confuses. It records an arbitration of Simon de Faversham, Chancellor in 1304–6, concerning 'the hall called of the University of Oxford

---

[9] Statutes of Queen's (described as 'an Edwardian castle in the air'): Hodgkin 1949: 10–16; deadening effects of New College statutes: A. Ryan in Buxton and Williams 1979: 76–81.

[10] Clifford appears in Hill 1975: 121. Clifford's career: *BRUO* i. 442 and Cox 1972a.

[11] College properties in Hundred Rolls: Graham 1905: 29 and 52; Little University Hall: Smith, 56–7, followed by Carr, 31–2, Oswald, 61, and Darwall-Smith 2005a: 9–11 (although note the wise caution of Mallet 1924–7: i. 89).

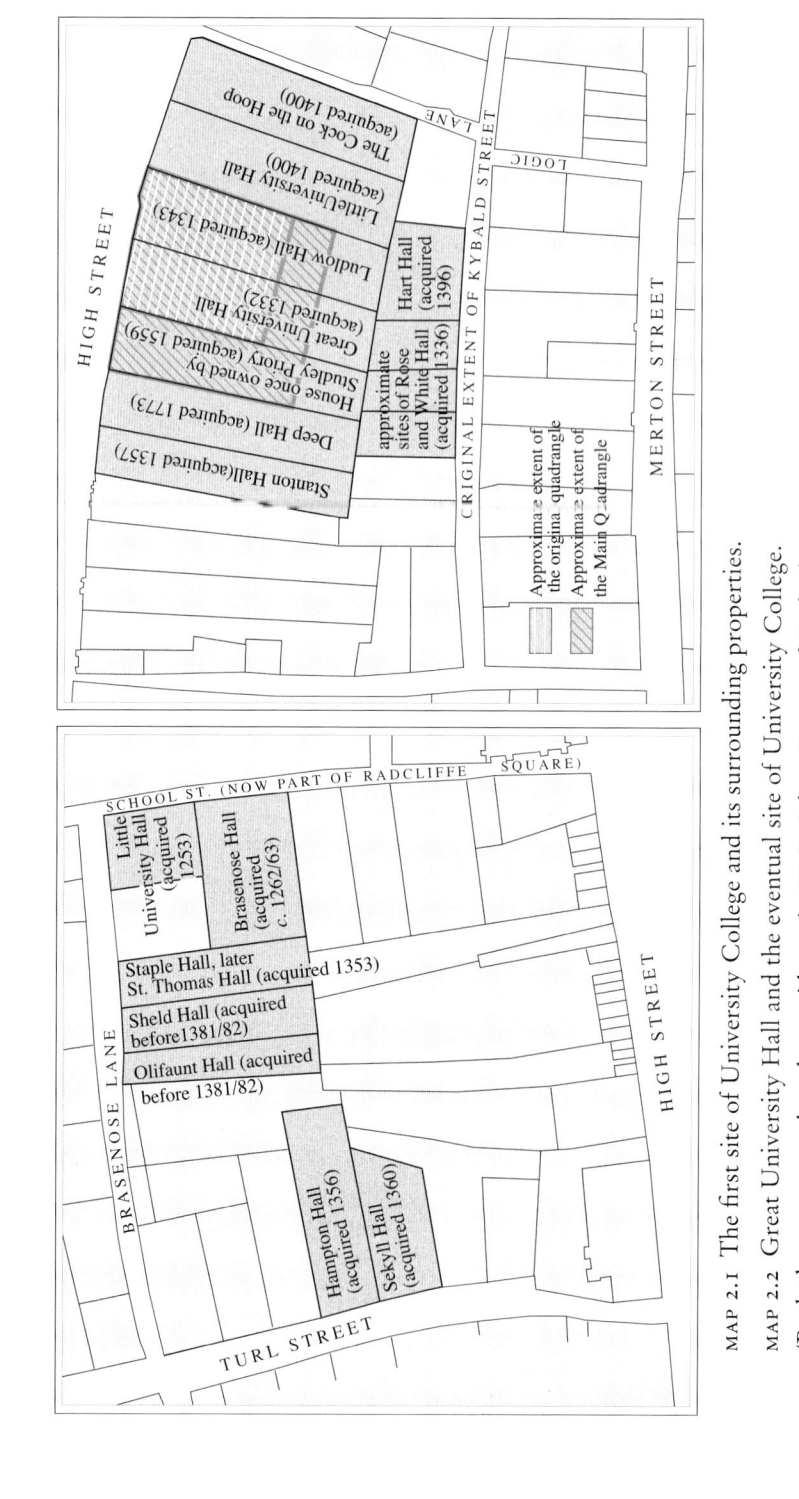

MAP 2.1 The first site of University College and its surrounding properties.
MAP 2.2 Great University Hall and the eventual site of University College. (Both these maps are based on evidence in H. E. Salter, *Survey of Oxford*).

situated in the Street of the Schools of Arts' (*aula dicta universitatis Oxon in vico scolarum artium situata*), and a dispute between an MA called John de Fridaythorpe and a group of other Masters. John, described as being 'actually in possession' of the hall, was accused of no longer using it for a school, in defiance of university statutes that buildings used for this purpose could not be used for any other, but he argued that an exemption had been made for the 'Scholars of Master William of Durham' (*Scholar[es] Magistri Willelmi de Dunelm*), under which houses owned by them could cease to become schools if a majority of the Scholars wished. The Scholars themselves intervened on John's behalf, and John won his case.[12]

This exemption is indeed mentioned in the 1280/1 statutes, but the reasons for John de Fridaythorpe's presence in 'University Hall' are unknown. One reading of the document could be that John was the Senior Fellow of the College, but because he was described separately from the Scholars, he could have been one of the College's first commoners, and his opponents were attacking him for being a lodger, rather than a teacher, with the Fellows brought in to support him. However, the matter remains difficult to resolve.[13] One detail, however, is clear. This document is the earliest yet known which names both the Fellows of the College and their home: they are 'the Scholars of Master William of Durham', living in a Hall 'called of the University of Oxford' in Schools Street.

Shortly after the Scholars of Master William of Durham assisted John de Fridaythorpe, they began to acquire more property: in July 1307, not only did they receive the final rights to 83–4 High Street, but they also acquired one tenement each in the parishes of St Mary the Virgin and St Peter in the East, later known respectively as Edward Hall and Maiden Hall. Soon after, in 1311, they acquired a house on the south side of New College Lane. No deeds record what price, if any, was paid for these properties.[14]

1311 also saw the appearance of a third set of statutes for the College, which took up the invitation made in 1292 for future rules to be drawn up if necessary. The new statutes were indeed intended as a supplement to the previous ones, and state that existing statutes not in disagreement with these new ones should remain in force.[15] Indeed many of the 1311 statutes merely refined earlier provisions: Fellows were still only to study theology, although during vacations they could read the basic texts of canon law, the Decretals and Decrees; the Bursar still received ten shillings a year, and the Fellows

---

[12] Document: UC:E/A1/D/6; Fridaythorpe himself: *BRUO* ii. 729; rules concerning buildings used for schools: Rashdall 1936: iii. 92.

[13] William Smith was sufficiently troubled that he dated it to after the College moved to its present site, notwithstanding the reference to Simon de Faversham (UC:AR2/MS1/1 pp. 27–8).

[14] See respectively UC:E/B2/D1/4, UC:E/A3/D/5, UC:E/B3/D/3, and UC:E/B4/D/5, and *Survey* i. 193, 214, 149, and 151–2.

[15] Text of 1311 statutes: OUA Wpβ/10 (original) and Salter 1920–1: i. 84–6.

their extra half a mark; two masses a year were to be said for the Founder; annual accounts were still to be presented to the Chancellor; and more Fellows could be elected if funds permitted.

There were some significant new regulations: the senior Fellow had to be a priest, and, if he was not, he should be ordained as soon as possible; any Fellow absent for more than a term without permission would lose his post, and any Fellow promoted to a living with an income worth five marks (£3 6s. 8d.) or more had to resign. A time limit was imposed on their study: every Fellow should formally oppose (see below) in the schools within seven years. It was also made explicit that the Scholars should live together; this had been taken for granted in 1280/1 and 1292, but not stated so baldly before. Finally, the statutes gave a name to the College: the Fellows were indeed to be called 'the Scholars of Master William of Durham'.

The 1311 statutes also attempt to clarify the relationship between College and university: the Chancellor and the Doctors of Theology had the right to ratify the election of new Scholars, to hear disputes about the conduct of Scholars and, if necessary, to expel them. This put the Chancellor and Doctors in the position of Visitors over the Scholars, to arbitrate on disputes, pronounce on statutes, and generally act as a court of last resort. Balliol and Merton had Visitors too, of a different sort: Balliol eventually ended up with the right to elect its Visitors, while Walter de Merton selected first the Bishop of Winchester and then the Archbishop of Canterbury to oversee his College.[16] What would become problematic in the case of University College was that, although the university clearly exercised a visitatorial function over the College, disputes would arise about which part of it could do so. Although the 1311 statutes ordain that only the Chancellor and Doctors in Theology had this right, later generations would start to ask whether the true Visitors of the College were actually the members of Congregation, the assembly of Regent Masters, or even Convocation, the assembly of both Regent and non-Regent Masters, and the ultimate decision-making body of the university.[17]

The nature of these new regulations suggests that the 1311 statutes were intended in part to prevent abuses for which no remedies had been stipulated in 1280/1 or 1292. The wealth limit sought to ensure that William of Durham's money went to the most deserving cases. The time limit would prevent Scholars from seeing a Fellowship as a mere milch cow, allowing them to stay as long in Oxford as they wished. Finally the explicit visitatorial functions given to the university could be a response to unknown tensions within the College.

---

[16] Balliol: Jones 2005: 13 and 17–18; Merton: Martin and Highfield 1997: 14–15 and 19–20.
[17] Convocation and Congregation: Mitchell 1998: 1–17. Mitchell (p. 5) observed that, 'roughly speaking, Convocation was the legislative body and Congregation the executive'.

A COLLEGE TAKES SHAPE: 1280–1361

If such a motive does lie behind the 1311 statutes, then they succeeded in their aim: no further statutes were drawn up until the 1470s. Instead, the Scholars of William of Durham began to grow in wealth and numbers. By 1381/2, over three-quarters of their property rental depended on estates acquired after 1311. This expansion, however, was relative: Merton's annual income from its estates at this time has been estimated at £340 a year, about eight times as much as that of the Scholars.[18]

The first new acquisition was the largest gift to the College since the bequest of William of Durham, and was also, perhaps surprisingly, its first property outside Oxford (Merton, Balliol, and Exeter had all from the first owned land elsewhere). In January 1318, a Doctor in Theology called Philip of Beverley (also known as Philip Ingelberd) who was the rector of Keyingham, a village in Holderness to the east of Hull, and, after his death, popularly venerated there as a local saint, obtained permission from the Crown through a licence of mortmain to grant to what he called 'The Masters and Scholars of the Hall of the University of Oxford' some lands in Keyingham and the neighbouring village of Paull. Philip asked that income from this land should support two Scholars, preferably selected among candidates from Beverley or Holderness.[19]

Philip might have been a Scholar of Master William of Durham, or availed himself of the opportunity to lodge at the College, but this remains uncertain. It is striking, however, that he resembles William in being another theologian who chose a parish life, and left money to support others seeking a similar career. He may have had links with Balliol, because he also asked that the Fellows regularly prayed both for himself and members of his family, and for the Lady Devorguilla de Balliol. It might simply be that Philip, as a north-easterner, desired to remember an institution with known links to his home country. Whatever the reasons, the gift was a major stroke of luck for the College: a rental dating from the early 1320s suggests that the land was worth almost £10 a year.[20]

Another benefaction proved harder to win, and once again a problematic will was the cause. Robert de Ripplingham, former Fellow of Merton, and latterly Chancellor of the Archdiocese of York, died in 1332, and in his will he left £40 to 'poor Arts scholars and Theologians at Oxford' (*pauperibus*

---

[18] 1381/2 rental: *ARUC* i. 1–2 (from that year's rental of £43 11s. 7d., £33 6s. 11d. comes from properties acquired in 1318–61); Merton's income: Martin and Highfield 1997: 68.

[19] Other colleges' properties: Aston and Faith 1984: 292–302; deeds relating to Philip's gift (which was finally completed in 1321): UC:E1/2D/1–10; Philip himself: *BRUO* i. 184 and Smith 2000: 43–8. Philip remains the only saint, even unofficial, with links to University College. Because corporations never 'died', so that the Crown received no feudal dues from them, from 1279 they were ordered to obtain a so-called licence of mortmain every time they acquired or were given new property.

[20] Devorguilla: UC:E1/2D/6 (although Philip appears to have given nothing to Balliol College); early rental: UC:E1/E1/1.

scolaribus Artistis et Theolog' Oxon'), and £300 'to sustain poor scholars, Masters of Arts, in Theology in the University of Oxford' (*ad sustentacionem scholarium pauperiorum magistrorum artium in Theologia in universitate Oxon*). The vague wording led to much dispute about Robert's intent, with several claiming that the money was intended for northern scholars in the university. One particular group of northern scholars, the Scholars of Master William of Durham, suggested that they should receive all the money. After a decade and a half of wrangling—and several visits by College Fellows to the Chapter at York—it was finally agreed that the College could get the bequest of £40. They eventually received £20 in 1346, but when in the autumn of 1348, two Fellows, Armand de Elstanwyke and John de Whixlay, turned up in York to collect the balance, the Chapter informed them they had not brought an acquittance bearing the seal of the Master and Scholars, and that they would have to return to Oxford and collect it. It is not known whether the College got its second instalment; in any event in 1349 the arrival of the Black Death in England would have distracted people's minds elsewhere.[21]

The College must have found money from somewhere before then, because in 1331, they had obtained a licence in mortmain to acquire lands and rents worth £10 a year, and in June 1332, they bought for an unknown sum a house called Selverine Hall or Spicer Hall, which lay on the south side of High Street (Fig. 2.1). Soon after, in 1336, they bought three properties adjoining Spicer Hall, Rose Hall, and White Hall to the south and Ludlow Hall to the east (Map 2.2).[22]

The purchase of these four properties was crucial to the history of University College, because some time after 1332 the Scholars of Master William of Durham took up residence in Spicer Hall, where their successors have remained ever since, for Spicer Hall and the three surrounding buildings now form the site of the eastern two-thirds of the Main Quadrangle, and part of the area behind. The exact date of the move is unknown, but it may have been before 1340, for a deed of that year (see below) shows that the College had no fewer than seven Fellows.[23] Initially the Fellows appear only to have used Spicer Hall, which by 1374 had become known as University Hall, and later Great University Hall. Ludlow Hall was leased out as an academic hall until the 1390s, and White Hall is still mentioned as a separate building as late as 1381/2.[24]

---

[21] Ripplingham's career: *BRUO* iii. 1577; his will: YMA L2(4) fos. 11–12ᵛ; disputes, and the College's attempts to obtain his money: YMA M2/4f fos. 9ʳ and 62ʳ, H1/1 fos. 1ʳ and 56ᵛ, and H1/2 fos. 2ʳ, 26ʳ, and 29ʳ (and UC:BE3/L1/1–2). See too Aston and Faith 1984: 291.

[22] Licence in mortmain: UC:GB2/L1/1; Spicer Hall: UC:E/A4/D/1–4; Rose Hall and White Hall UC:E/C1/D5–D6; Ludlow Hall: UC:E/B5/D/4–6.

[23] UC:E1/L1/1.

[24] Spicer Hall as University Hall: UC:E/B5/L/1; White Hall: *ARUC* i. 8.

FIGURE 2.1 Deed of 1332 by which University College acquired Great University Hall.

As the Fellows moved into their new home, so the names both for them and their College at last became more fixed. Indeed the very fact that they were members of a 'College' took time to settle. Although the 1292 statutes had referred to Fellows (*socii*) of a College (*collegium*), endowed institutions like University, Merton, Balliol, and Exeter were called halls (*aulae*) well into the fourteenth century.[25] The first change after 1311 was that the Scholars of Master William of Durham began to be named, not after their founder, but the place in which they lived. One of the deeds concerning Philip of Beverley's gift, from January 1318, refers to 'the Masters and Scholars living in the Hall of the University of Oxford and studying in the same University' (*magistris et scolaribus in aula Universitatis Oxon' commorantibus et in eadem Universitate studentibus*), and the seven Fellows of 1340 were called the 'Scholars of the Hall of the University of Oxford'. Later the two forms were combined: documents of the 1360s refer to 'The Hall of Master William of Durham, usually called the Great Hall of the University of Oxford', and a deed of 1374 refers to 'The College which William of Durham founded, now called the Hall of the University of Oxford', while the earliest extant

[25] Early colleges as halls: Highfield 1984: 228, and p. 29 below.

Bursar's roll, of 1381/2, refers to 'The College of Master William of Durham, commonly called Micheluniversitehall [i.e. Great University Hall]'. Accounts of the early 1420s, however, dropped William's name (reviving him briefly in the 1540s), and the College had become simply 'the College or Great Hall of the University of Oxford'.[26]

Little is known about the appearance of Great University Hall, but some conjectures can be made by examining other medieval halls in Oxford.[27] Its façade would have resembled an ordinary town house, and a passageway led from the street to the main courtyard behind. Rooms led off from this courtyard, including a central hall, the only common room in the building. The Bursar's accounts for 1381/2, compiled when the Fellows were occupying Great University Hall only, identify some of its rooms. Eight chambers are listed: a 'principal chamber', one next to it and another one underneath, two chambers above the garden, one of these next to the hall, a chamber with a hall, a chamber opposite the well, and a chamber next to it. There was also a latrine, a kitchen, and a courtyard.[28] Only rooms rented out to commoners are named; there will have been more for the Fellows' own use.

There was, however, no library, and neither was there a chapel. Fellows presumably worshipped at their local parish church, St Mary the Virgin. This left the College lagging behind its two contemporaries: as early as 1293, the Bishop of Lincoln had granted Balliol the right to a chapel, and Walter de Merton, in line with his grander visions for Merton College, bought up the neighbouring church of St John the Baptist, and transformed it into a college chapel.[29]

Why, however, should the Fellows have chosen to leave Schools Street?[30] The likeliest reason is that Spicer Hall, being significantly larger than Little University Hall, provided rooms for more Fellows and commoners. By the 1330s the Fellows must have realized that commoners could be very profitable: in the 1380s, they regularly received at least £5 a year from commoners, but, on average, only 33s. 4d. from Little University Hall. Great University Hall would certainly have yielded more income, purely as an academic hall, than Little University Hall, but when only two or three rooms at Great University Hall in the 1380s produced as much income as the whole of Little University Hall, it made sound economic sense to occupy the building with most rooms to let.

Meanwhile the Fellows were managing their properties successfully. While the house in New College Lane was sold to the founder of Queen's College on 19 May 1340, no fewer than six properties were acquired in the 1350s

---

[26] 1318 deed: UC:E1/2D/1; 1340 deed: UC:E1/L1/1; 1360s deeds: UC:E/B5/D/7 and UC:E2/6/1L/1; 1374 deed: UC:E/B5/L/1; accounts of 1381/2 and 1420s: *ARUC* i. 1, 301, and 308. The word 'mickle' in medieval times—especially in the north—tended to mean 'great' or 'large'.
[27] See further Pantin 1964.
[28] *ARUC* i. 2–3, 8, and 10.
[29] Jones 2005: 13–14 and Martin and Highfield 1997: 28 and 39–41.
[30] This is discussed further in Darwall-Smith 2005*a*: 12–14.

(Maps 2.1 and 2.2). Three, known as Staple (later St Thomas) Hall, Sheld Hall, and Olyfaunt Hall, formed a block directly adjoining the western end of Brasenose Hall; two more properties, Hampton Hall and an unnamed house later called Sekyll Hall, were on Turl Street; and the sixth, Stanton Hall, was on the south side of High Street, two houses to the west of Great University Hall. The costs involved in their purchases are not known: Stanton Hall at least appears to have been a gift. Their income was certainly welcome: by 1381/2, the six properties were yielding a rental of £10 7s.—almost one-fifth of the College's total rent roll.[31]

The College also received at least two bequests of books: in 1336 Stephen de Gravesend, Bishop of London, bequeathed an unknown book to the College, and in 1368 Simon de Bredon, a canon of Chichester bequeathed a 'book of the Master of histories' (*librum magistri ystoriarum*) to the Hall of the university of Oxford. Neither man appears to have had links with the College, and indeed it is not as if this College was singled out for special mention: both Stephen and Simon gave books to every college then extant in Oxford, and in Simon's case, Balliol, Merton, and Oriel received more books than University.[32]

This chapter has so far concentrated on statutes, property deals, and benefactions, but the Fellows of the Great Hall of the University of Oxford have remained an anonymous group, and it is time to rectify this. Unfortunately, sources for the names of Fellows remain scant, comprising merely stray references in title deeds, and other documents within and without the College archives. However, the loss is not as great as could be feared. Whereas the names of fifty-five Fellows are known from the better recorded fifteenth century, no fewer than forty-four Fellows have been identified from the fourteenth.

Most references to early Fellows tend to name them only singly or in pairs, but a few documents appear to name all those resident at a given moment. One of the best such examples dates from 8 July 1340, and concerns a dispute over the Paull property. In it, seven 'Scholars of the Hall of the University of Oxford' are named as Richard de Radford, Robert de Patrington, John de Poklington, William de Cundale, John de Suttone, William de Polmorva, and Robert de Scroton. Their origins and careers provide an excellent snapshot of a sample of early Fellows.[33]

---

[31] The house on New College Lane: UC:E/B4/D/6; Olyfaunt Hall: UC:E/D1/D/4 and *Survey* i. 60–2; Sheld Hall: UC:E/D2 *passim* and *Survey* i. 60–2; St Thomas Hall: UC:E/D3/D/3 and *Survey* i. 60–2; Hampton Hall: UC:E/D4/D/6–7 and *Survey* i. 51; Stanton Hall UC:E/A5/D/2 and *Survey* i. 88; Sekyll Hall: UC:E/D5/D/2–3 and *Survey* i. 50–1; rental for 1381/2: *ARUC* i. 1–2 (Sekyll Hall is the house rented out to Holwey).

[32] Summary of Stephen de Gravesend's will: HMC 1883: 46; college bequests from Simon de Bredon: Powicke 1931: 84 (Powicke suggested that Simon's book could be Univ. MS. 112, the *Historia Scholastica* of Peter Comestor). Simon called University, Balliol, Merton, and Exeter all halls.

[33] The deed is UC:E1/L1/1. Information on the Fellows is derived from the relevant entries in *BRUO*, but on Radford see too Magrath 1921: i. 87–90.

The presence of seven Fellows shows that the hopes of 1280/1 for the enlargement of the original group of four have been fulfilled, no doubt in part thanks to the Paull lands. The north-eastern links hoped for in 1292 and 1311 are also honoured, in that Richard de Radford came from the diocese of York, and the surnames of Robert de Patrington and John de Poklington suggest Yorkshire origins for them too.[34] William de Cundale was also a northerner, but from the diocese of Carlisle, to the west, but the Cornishman William de Polmorva was the College's only medieval Fellow from the south-west.

Some Fellows were recent arrivals—Suttone is known to have been at Balliol College until 1338, and Polmorva was still at Exeter in 1337—but Robert de Patrington and William de Cundale had appeared on College title deeds since 1332, and John de Poklington since 1336. Patrington, who would remain at the College until at least 1343, had an unusually long tenure: only two other fourteenth-century Fellows are known to have spent so long at the College.

Within Oxford the seven exemplify the fluidity of the world of early college fellowships: Radford and Suttone had both been at Balliol, whilst Polmorva had been at Exeter, serving as its Rector in 1336/7. When Queen's College was founded in 1341, Radford was its first Provost, and Cundale and Polmorva among its first Fellows. Radford's peripatetic career did not cease there: a document of July 1343 lists him as a Fellow of University College again, possibly persuaded to return to escape the difficulties faced by Queen's College in its early years.[35] As regards their academic achievements, Radford, Patrington, and Polmorva became Doctors in Theology, but Cundale, Poklington, Scroton, and Suttone remained MAs, so far as is known.

Outside Oxford, Radford, as a head of one college and possibly two, enjoyed a successful later career: as well as holding a succession of parishes in Essex, Kent, Nottinghamshire, Surrey, Suffolk, and Yorkshire, by the time of his death in 1369 he had become a canon and prebendary simultaneously at York and Hereford cathedrals. Although Patrington's career was shorter—he was dead by 1349—he had become Precentor of York by 1345. Scroton's later years were more modest: all that is known of him is that he became vicar of South Scarle, Notts., and was dead by July 1349. No evidence survives for the later careers of Poklington or Suttone, whilst all that is known of Cundale is that he returned to his homeland, dying in Westmorland in 1350, and leaving money only to Queen's College, which already had a special bond with that region.[36]

[34] Indeed the village of Patrington is close to Paull and Keyingham; Robert could have specifically benefited from Philip of Beverley's gift.
[35] Hodgkin 1949: 16–21 describes the college's early problems.
[36] Readers may wonder whether the deaths of c.1349 were linked to the Black Death. No Fellow is explicitly known to have died of the plague, but of all the twelve Fellows linked with the College between 1332 and 1348, at least two were already dead by 1348/9, and seven alive afterwards. This fits with the conclusions of Courtenay 1980, that the academic community escaped the Black Death relatively lightly, because it was better nourished and housed than average, and its mobility enabled it to escape trouble.

Perhaps the most successful Fellow was William de Polmorva. He served as Chancellor of Oxford in 1350–2—the first Chancellor with known links to University College—before taking up a succession of livings in Surrey, Exeter, and Sussex, and becoming canon and prebendary of St George's Chapel at Windsor, archdeacon of Middlesex, and canon of Lincoln. His career culminated in his appointment as King's Clerk and confessor to Queen Philippa in 1361, just before his death the following year. He left money to Exeter College, but nothing to University.

This snapshot from 1340 is representative of the world of the forty-four known Fellows of University College before 1400: of the twenty-one whose place of origin are known, over half are north-easterners; the average length of time which any of them are known to spend in the College is about six years. Indeed their time spent at University should be seen less as a culmination to a career than as a significant starting point: while the earlier careers of just nine Fellows are known, there are only seven Fellows whose later career remains unknown. Those careers match the 1340 sample well: half the Fellows spent the rest of their lives as parish priests, but eight became canons or prebendaries, and one, Peter de Curraff, Bishop of Limerick.[37]

Perhaps the most striking thing about the 1340 Fellows is that most of them never achieved a theology degree: just sixteen fourteenth-century Fellows are known to have obtained a theology degree, twelve as Doctors, and four as Bachelors. However, other surveys of medieval members of the university show similarly high drop-out rates; above all, degrees in medieval universities were not the necessary end point of a degree course, but rather the recognition of an achieved status, which would be of most use to those seeking high academic posts. This indeed was a world in which such an eminent scholar as William of Ockham never advanced beyond the degree of Bachelor of Theology, and one in which the vision of an Oxford harshly dominated by results is mercifully far away.[38]

The difficulties faced by students of theology, especially those from the secular clergy, were considered in the previous chapter; it is now time to survey briefly what the study of theology required of its practitioners.[39] We have seen that students could not start to study theology before they had first spent at least seven years in becoming Masters in Arts, during which time their minds would have been sharpened on lecture courses, with frequent opportunities for disputation.

---

[37] Dunbabin 1984 provides a general analysis of the careers of early Oxford men, which shows that the Fellows of University College were fairly typical.

[38] R. L. Storey in Buxton and Williams 1979: 17–20, provides evidence of an even greater wastage rate at New College between 1386 and 1540. On the medieval degree see too Catto 1984a: 189–90, Cobban 1988: 353–7, and Evans 1992: 500–2.

[39] Fuller accounts of the study of theology at Oxford, and indeed at Cambridge, may be found in Catto 1984b, Courtenay 1992, and Leader 1988: 170–91. See too Southern 1995.

For new Scholars of Master William of Durham studying theology, three main stages lay ahead.[40] First of all, one had to achieve the status of 'opponency', which meant that one had to participate actively in disputations, taking the role of formally opposing a proposition put up for discussion. Four or five years' study was considered appropriate to reach this stage, so that the time limit of seven years imposed on Fellows in the 1311 statutes was generous. During this time, one attended lectures and disputations, and studied the Bible and the *Sentences* of Peter the Lombard. Only after one had 'opposed' for a certain period of time was one ready to become a Bachelor of Divinity. To move on from this status chiefly required the actual giving of lectures on the *Sentences* or the Bible and even then one might need to lecture for a given time before one could achieve the summit of a Doctorate in Theology.

Because of their importance to theologians for so many centuries, Peter the Lombard and his *Sentences* require some introduction. Peter taught at Paris in the middle of the twelfth century, and compiled four books of so-called *Sententiae*. 'Sentences', the usual English translation for his work, does not do it justice; 'Opinions' would serve rather better. For Peter, in his lectures, had compiled a ready store of opinions on theological problems. His approach was consistent and simple: having identified a theological problem, he would assemble authorities to help him solve it, calling on the help of scripture and earlier theologians. Having analysed some relevant authorities, he then came to a conclusion. The four books containing his *Sentences* were carefully assembled, each one considering a different aspect of theology: book one, for instance, is devoted to the Trinity, providence, and the nature of evil. In addition, Peter, although no stylist, wrote good clear Latin. One could not wish for a better textbook, and the *Sentences* retained a central position in the study of theology for many centuries. As well as being clearly laid out, it offered the student a sensible methodology to adopt: one could take one of Peter's topics, add new sources to his, and perhaps modify a conclusion. Many scholars thus produced work which emerged as commentaries on Peter. Even William of Durham himself appears to have produced such a commentary, now lost.[41] Peter's *Sentences* offer the learned man an exhilarating opportunity to understand this world and the one beyond if he can but find the appropriate texts to aid him in his quest. A great medieval scholastic theologian, deeply erudite and possessed of tough argumentative skills, would have been a formidable figure in the lecture room or a disputation.[42]

---

[40] These stages are discussed more fully in Rashdall 1936: iii. 158–60.
[41] Cox 1981: 117.
[42] An example of the heights to which at least one Fellow of University College could climb may be found in Ashworth and Spade 1992: 50–4, a minute analysis of a treatise *De insolubilibus* (on insoluble things), a work on logic attributed to Henry Hopton, recorded as a Fellow of University College in 1356.

Such, then, was the condition of the Hall of the University of Oxford, its Fellows, and their studies in 1361. The previous eight decades had proved successful: the College was producing the theologians sought in William of Durham's will; it had acquired sufficient property for the number of Fellows to be increased slightly; it had even moved to larger premises. It remained one of the poorer colleges, far behind a wealthy institution like Merton, but nevertheless it had survived, and was performing its statutory functions. One former Fellow had served as Chancellor, and two, Adam de Pothow and Roger de Aswardeby, as proctors. Signs of a developing collegiate structure are detectable: Aswardeby is the first Fellow specifically called a Master of University College, an extension of the role of the senior Fellow adumbrated in 1292. In short, there was nothing to indicate that the next few decades would prove among the most calamitous in the College's history.

3

Crisis: 1361–1411

The later fourteenth century and early fifteenth should have been a period of consolidation for University College, a time to continue accumulating properties, and enlarging its Fellowship in the manner set out in the previous chapter. There were indeed successes: the College received its largest benefaction of land to date, and the process of turning a group of small halls into a unified quadrangle began. Yet these achievements were overshadowed by a serious crisis in the study of theology within the university and a property dispute which drained the College's finances and energies for thirty years amidst family intrigue, forgery, battles fought—sometimes simultaneously— through several different law courts, a change in the law, and an unexpected saviour who would assume a far greater significance for the College than anyone could have conceived at the time.

THE GONWARDBY AFFAIR AND THE INVENTION OF KING ALFRED: 1361–1390[1]

The Gonwardby affair began innocently enough. Between September 1359 and June 1361, the College acquired several properties in and around Oxford from a certain John Gonwardby, a citizen and pepperer of London, for the sum of £160, money which appears to have been given to the College. The properties comprised three large houses on the north side of the High Street (now part of the Covered Market) and another on the north-east corner of Carfax, gardens in the western parishes of St Peter-le-Bailey and St Thomas, fields in the Grandpont area, some islands in the Thames, and land on the north side of what is now Little Clarendon Street and to the north of St Giles's church, as well as many small portions of the common fields there. It appeared to be an excellent investment.[2]

---

[1] The accounts of this affair in Smith, 81–138 and Carr, 37–48 have been largely superseded by the work of David Cox. As well as his one published article on the case (Cox 1953), his papers in the College archives include an unpublished piece, 'University College, King Alfred and Edmund Francis' (UC:S24/MS2/2), and extensive notes and transcripts of primary sources (UC:S24/MS1/3).

[2] The deeds recording the transfer are UC:E2/5/2D/9–17, the last of which asks the College to celebrate masses for the soul of the otherwise unknown Robert Caldwell. Smith, 93–4 suggested that Caldwell had given the £160, which would certainly explain his presence here.

'Appeared' is the crucial word. Unfortunately, John Gonwardby had no right to sell the greater part of his estate. The land in the parishes of St Thomas's and St Giles's he had inherited from his father, and he could sell these as he wished. Not so the other properties, the inheritance of his mother Joan Goldsmith. Under the terms of two deeds of entail, drawn up back in 1307 and 1308 by her father John Goldsmith, this property could not be transferred outside the family whilst any descendants of John Goldsmith still lived—and in 1361 at least one did, namely Joan, niece of John Gonwardby and granddaughter of John Goldsmith.[3]

We shall never know how well informed the Master of University College, Roger de Aswardeby, and the Fellows were about the entails when they made their purchase. Whether they acted in good faith, or were party to John Gonwardby's disinheritance of his family, the consequences of their actions swiftly revealed themselves, as Joan and her husband Philip Jedwell (another pepperer of London) took the College to court in July 1362 to recover the properties which they considered their inheritance. Although the Jedwells had a strong case, and at least one jury found in their favour, they were, fortunately, willing to compromise, and in April 1363 allowed the College to retain the properties in return for two payments totalling £106 13s. 4d. And that, the College might have assumed, would be the end of the affair.[4]

The next few years saw a return to normality, apart from a dispute with the priory of St Frideswide over some unpaid rent (settled in April 1374). The most significant event from this time was the belated creation of a place of worship in Great University Hall. A document dated 10 January 1370 records that the Fellows will allow a representative of the Bishop of Lincoln to celebrate mass in 'the chapel or oratory' built inside the College, whose construction had recently been permitted by the Bishop. The description of the place suggests that this was not a separate building, rather an existing room specially converted for the purpose. Small as this would have been, nonetheless it enabled the Fellows of University College to carry out acts of worship in their own College for the first time.[5]

Unfortunately, as the dispute with St Frideswide's was ending, the descendants of John Goldsmith were stirring again, this time with greater menace. Joan and Philip Jedwell had a daughter, Idonea, married to a London merchant called Edmund Francis. The settlement of 1363 was not good enough for Idonea and her husband: they did not wish merely to be paid

---

[3] Deeds of entail: UC:E2/2/2D/1–2.
[4] Evidence for just one hearing in the 1362/3 case survives, transcribed by Brian Twyne in the seventeenth century from a document in the archives of Oxford City now lost (Bodl. MS Twyne IV (Θ), pp. 170–1); other documents concerning the settlement of the Jedwell case: UC:E2/6/1L/1–5.
[5] Dispute with St Frideswide's: UC:E/B5/L/1–3 (a damaged copy of the agreement between College and priory preserved in the Christ Church archives is in Wigram 1895–6: i. 343–4); 'chapel or oratory' (*capella seu oratorium*): UC:FA2/L1/1 and Oswald, 72.

off, but wanted their family estates returned. Furthermore legal opinion was divided on whether the type of document used in 1363, known as a final concord, could end an entail, and in Edmund Francis the Fellows were to encounter a tenacious opponent, wily and skilled in the ways of the law.[6]

Francis was evidently planning his attack as early as 1373, when he gave a box of deeds concerning the properties to one of the College's tenants in the disputed estates.[7] The storm finally broke in 1377, when the Francises opened proceedings in Oxford to recover their property. These proceedings were complex: because the disputed property was subject to the two entails of 1307/8, under common law the couple had to pursue the claims concerning each entail in two separate cases. In addition, much of the Grandpont property lay in another county, Berkshire, so that this had to be considered in a third suit.[8]

Another rule of common law played into Edmund and Idonea Francis's hands. In the 1370s, if a landlord leased property to its tenants for life (as University College had done), then any claim made against that property had to be made against the tenants, and not the real owner, who was deemed only to have a reversionary interest, which would come into effect only when the current tenants died. In 1377, therefore, Edmund and Idonea Francis sued, not the College, but its tenants. This was an obvious invitation to collusion: in return for, say, the promise of a more favourable lease, the tenants could simply not bother to appear in court, and thus lose the case by default. In any event, because there were almost a dozen tenants involved, it would have been hard enough to assemble them simultaneously, especially when some hearings took place in London.

The next two years went badly for the College: in a succession of hearings, some at the Hustings Court in Oxford, others at the King's Bench in Westminster, the tenants regularly defaulted, Edmund Francis could argue the injustice of his wife's loss of property, and the College was impotent to intervene. University College could not wholly rely on an impartial hearing, when some tenants, such as Richard Mercer, were city aldermen, likely to sit on the Hustings Court.[9]

The College's nadir came at the King's Bench in April 1379. Following a small procedural error at a hearing in Oxford in June 1378 when Idonea

---

[6] The problems of ending an entail: Simpson 1986: 126–37.

[7] These events are recorded in TNA CP 40/464, rott. 145, 230d, and 556, and TNA CP 40/474 rot. 305d.

[8] Surprisingly this does not seem to have been an issue in 1362/3, but perhaps the Jedwells and the College reached a settlement before it arose.

[9] The hearings of 1378–9 in Oxford and London (including Kexby's intervention below) are recorded in TNA KB 27/472 rott. 61–2. Richard Mercer (also known as Garston) also sat as an MP for Oxford regularly in the 1370s and 1380s.

Francis's attorney had not been admitted by due legal process, and so had no right to represent her, the Francises were now trying to sort this error out. The King's Bench agreed to set the error aside, but then suddenly decided to consider the question of landownership themselves—although neither the College nor its tenants were represented. On the third day of the hearing, the court received an unexpected visitor: William Kexby, the Master of University College, arrived asking to be admitted to plead the College's case. Not only was he late, but he had no supporting documentation with him—which suggests that Kexby had only just received news of the hearing, and had left Oxford in a hurry. The King's Bench threw his request out: in addition to his lateness, and lack of papers, it was argued, he had no right to represent the other Fellows, who should have come too. Having brushed the unfortunate Master aside, and noted the default of the tenants, the court found in favour of the Francises, and granted them seisin or possession of the property.

The verdict of 1379 was not totally unreasonable—Edmund and Idonea had a strong claim to the property, after all—but the methods employed in reaching it were not above reproach. It was not merely the muddle over Idonea Francis's attorney: the College had been deprived of a chance to put its case, and the King's Bench had reached its judgement simply because no one for the defence turned up in time. These small procedural injustices might yet offer the College future hope.

Few in the College would have hoped for much, however, in the summer of 1379. After his lamentable performance in Westminster, Kexby, perhaps fortunately, swiftly found preferment elsewhere: in November 1379 he became Archdeacon of Cleveland and later precentor of York, where he remained until his death some thirty years later.[10] He left a College facing financial disaster. In 1381/2, the College's gross income was just under £50 a year, but almost a third of this—£15 8d.—came from the properties now in Edmund Francis's hands. When debts from other properties were included, University College during the 1380s received less than half the rents it thought it was due (Graph 5.1).

In this crisis, the Fellows showed their mettle. Since the King's Bench had proved unhelpful, and the Hustings Court unreliable, the next place to look for aid was the Crown. Litigants worsted in the common law courts frequently petitioned the Crown to seek a hearing of their case in the King's Council, where special circumstances justified intervention on the grounds of equity, and so the Fellows of University College tried this method.

On 12 May 1381 a writ was sent to the Sheriff and Mayor of Oxford asking for aid to University College following a petition sent to the King.[11] As well

---

[10] Kexby's career: *BRUO* ii. 1044–5.
[11] Cox 1953: 19–20. The writ is calendared in *CCR 1377–1381*, 450; a copy of the petition: UC:E2/6/3L/10.

as reciting their claims in this petition, the Fellows had tried to attract royal attention, claiming that 'This College is the foundation of the University of Oxford founded by King Alfred former king of England, and which is held by you in chief.'[12] Links between the university of Oxford and King Alfred had only recently been 'discovered': Ralph Higden, in his *Polychronicon*, written in the 1350s, had suggested that Alfred, advised by St Neot, had established 'public schools for the various arts' (*scholas publicas variarum artium*) at Oxford. Higden's thinking is logical enough: Alfred was famous for his support of learning, and Oxford was undeniably the oldest university in England, so he must have had some dealings with it. Higden's work quickly became popular, and the Fellows of University College (whether or not they actually believed it) were evidently exploiting his account of the founding of Oxford in framing their petition to Alfred's heir.[13]

The 1381 petition seems to have achieved nothing. The accounts for 1381/2–1383/4 include expenses for Fellows' journeys to and from London, but nothing concrete occurs until the spring of 1384. The 1384/5 accounts show payments for journeys to Salisbury being made not only to Fellows but also to the Chancellor of the university, Robert Rygge. Parliament sat in Salisbury in April and May 1384, so the reason for these journeys is clear. So is the outcome: on 22 May 1384, Edmund Francis received a writ ordering him to cease prosecuting the College over the property in Grandpont, and to let the case be heard before the King's Council.[14] The Fellows, with heavyweight help from the Chancellor, had at last achieved a modest success.

Their new petition covered much the same ground as the earlier one, but it significantly enhanced the role of King Alfred (Fig. 3.1). In the preamble, it tells Richard II that the 'College called Mikeluniversite Halle in Oxenford' was 'first founded by your noble ancestor King Alfred, whom God protect, to maintain 24 theologians in perpetuity', and later on even claims that 'the noble saints John of Beverley, Bede, and Richard of Armagh and several other famous doctors and clerks were once scholars in your very college'. The petition bore an endorsement declaring that testimony was given in Parliament as to the foundation of the College; no doubt this was where the Chancellor fully justified his travel expenses.[15]

---

[12] *Quelle College est la foundacion del Universitie d'Oxenford founde par Roi Alfrid jadis Roi d'engleterre & la quelle est tenue de vous en chief.*

[13] Higden on Oxford: Higden 1865–86: vi. 354; see too Keynes 1999: 235–6.

[14] Chancellor's travel expenses: *ARUC* i. 41; writ of 1384: UC:E2/6/3L/7 (*ARUC* i. 41 records a payment of 20s. to Robert Gower, one of the Fellows, to collect such a writ from London in 1384/5).

[15] The petition is UC:E2/6/3L/9; the original quotations read: *Quel college estoit primement fondue par votre noble progenitour le Roi Alfrid qe deu assoille pour la sustenance de vint et quatre divines perpetuels* and *nobles seintz Johan de Beverley, Bede et Richard armachan et autres plusieurs famous doctours et clerks estoit iadys escolers en mesme votre college.* Cox 1953: 22–4 dates it to May 1384.

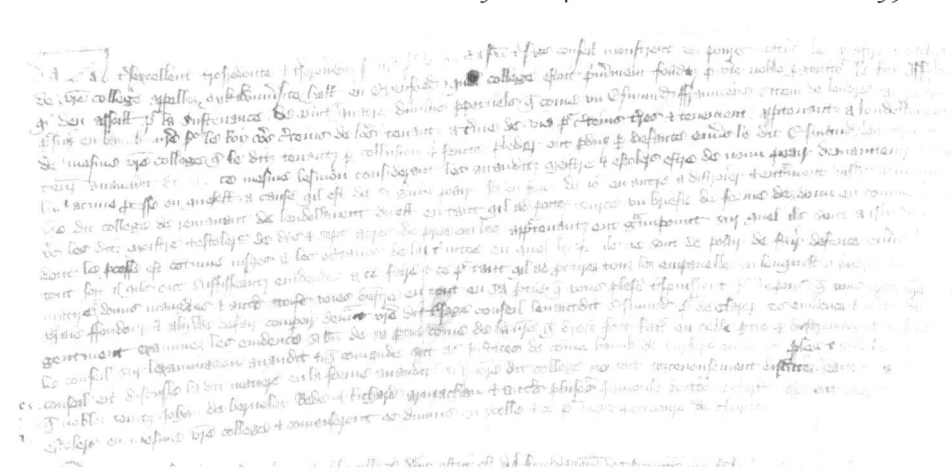

FIGURE 3.1 Extract from the 'French Petition' sent to Richard II by University College in 1384, in which King Alfred is first claimed as the College's Founder. The extracts quoted in note 15 start halfway through the second line from the top and at the start of the second line from the bottom.

Over 300 years later, William Smith called this petition the 'French Petition', and used it as the foundation for his brilliant deconstruction of the College's mythical origins. Of the presence of the early eighth-century saints John of Beverley and Bede, he sarcastically observed:

I need take no other pains to shew the Falshood and Absurdities of this Petition than to inform the Reader, that it is impossible to be true, as it is for any Person, King or Subject, to build COLLEGES, or endow them a hundred Years, and more, before he was born.[16]

How did the Fellows assemble this fascinating farrago, in which they leapt from claiming Alfred as the founder of the university to making him the founder of their College, and why did they think that it might help them? We should return to the writ of 1381, issued in reply to the College's first petition. The clerk drafting this had misread the original petition, and wrote that the College, and not the university, was 'of the foundation of our [i.e. the King's] ancestors' (*de fundacione progenitorum nostrum*). It would be hard to resist following where the Crown's functionary had led, and embellishing the tale with fancy corroboration. The involvement of the Chancellor shows that the university was nothing loath to add its support to the College of which it was Visitor.[17]

---

[16] Smith, 129–30.
[17] Cox 1953: 23–4 first noticed this beneficial error.

The Fellows may also have hoped that this subtly modified petition would better attract the attention of its recipient: by 1384 Richard II had taken greater control of government. The young King took considerable interest in his status and lineage, choosing Edward the Confessor as his patron saint. Amongst all the petitions coming to him, the claim of a college, however small and insignificant, to be a royal foundation might just have been enough to catch his eye.[18]

The College nevertheless would need an influential friend to help attract Richard's attention. They already had the Chancellor of Oxford on hand, but, significantly, the Keeper of the Privy Seal in 1384 was one Walter Skirlaw. Skirlaw, who had helped in the negotiations for Richard's marriage with Anne of Bohemia, was a Yorkshireman from the village of Skirlaugh near Beverley. He is known to have studied theology at Oxford in the early 1360s, and, although there is no evidence that he was ever attached to University College, yet it would be surprising if someone ideally placed to benefit from Philip of Beverley's benefaction had not exploited it. The fact that Skirlaw kept a kindly eye on the College for the rest of his life suggests a more than casual acquaintance.[19]

The success of this petition did not solve everything, for it only concerned the Grandpont properties. University College now had to repeat the whole process with the other two lawsuits, but each time the College secured a writ for one lawsuit, Edmund Francis promptly pursued another lawsuit back in the common law courts. With the 1379 King's Bench judgement in his pocket, Francis preferred to avoid the King's Council, where his chances of victory were less sure. A swift resolution was also made harder because in 1386–8 Richard II was engaged in a struggle with some of his opponents, which culminated in the so-called Merciless Parliament of February 1388, when several of Richard's advisers were executed.

The Fellows kept their nerve. In addition to submitting more petitions, they found the law changed in their favour: in October 1385, Parliament passed an act which allowed landlords to take action against plaintiffs who had successfully sued their tenants, and even explicitly declared that it was retrospective with regard to University College.[20] Finally, in July 1388 the Fellows achieved a breakthrough when the Sheriff of Oxford was ordered to return to University College all the properties awarded to the Francises in 1379, and to find out what rent arrears were due it. Then, on 2 August 1388 a final writ ordered Edmund and Idonea Francis to cease all actions on any of the cases. No litigant—not even one as spirited as Edmund Francis—could

---

[18] Richard and his ancestors: Saul 1997: 311–12; presenting petitions to him: Tuck 1971: 4–7.
[19] Skirlaw's role: Clarke 2006, who argues cogently for Skirlaw's links with University College; Skirlaw's life and career: Jarratt 2004.
[20] Three of these later petitions are edited in Toulmin Smith: 1896: 143–6 (although Cox thought that her dates were a few years too early); the Act of Parliament of 1385 is transcribed in Anon. 1816: 38–9.

fight that. It may not be coincidental that at the end of July and the beginning of August of 1388 Richard II himself was staying in Oxford.[21]

Although these events did not mark victory for the College, they did return the case to the status quo before April 1379, and provided an opportunity for that fair hearing which had been sought since 1377. In November 1388, therefore, the unnamed Master of University College was summoned to appear in person at Chancery on 20 January 1389, where the case would be arbitrated by Thomas Arundel, the Archbishop of York, and two others, one appointed by each party.[22]

Nothing is known about the subsequent hearings, save that the accounts for 1388–91 show especially large expenses relating to the case: there were again journeys to London and elsewhere; a payment of 6s. 8d. 'in wine to the Chancellor of England' (*in vino Cancellario Anglie*) in 1388/9 hints at meetings at the highest level, and similar payments for wine to Edmund Francis himself suggest that agreements were being reached.[23]

The College may have tried other methods than wine. Among the documents concerning the Gonwardby lands are some deeds with an interesting tale: in 1191, they say, one Henry le Ferrour had sold them all to one Geoffrey Goldsmith, and then that in 1233, Geoffrey mortgaged his lands to Gilbert de Gonwardby for £1,000, which he could not repay. Geoffrey generously allowed Gilbert to live in his properties for life, after which the lands would revert to him. This duly happened, and the final deed in this sequence records their sale by John de Gonwardby to University College in 1361.[24]

The outrageous sum of £1,000 should sound an alarm. There are other egregious errors: the 1191 deed is dated to 'The Feast of St Lawrence in the second year of King Richard the First'—as William Smith said, 'the calling of any King the *first* before there is a *second* is absurd'[25]—and the handwriting of these deeds is closer to the fourteenth than the twelfth or thirteenth centuries. In short, these deeds are all forgeries, created to provide a history of the estates which ignores the 1307/8 entails. Worse still, evidence for the authorship and the date of manufacture of these deeds points strongly towards the Fellows of University College in the late 1380s. They stood to gain most from their creation, especially during the hearings of 1389, when they had a chance to present their case. For all the misplaced ingenuity bestowed on them, it is unlikely that the forged deeds provided much assistance. It would have been clear enough to the arbitrators that, after almost three decades, a compromise was the only equitable solution,

---

[21] Writs of July and August 1388: *CCR 1385–1389*, 516–17; Richard's movements in 1388: Saul 1997: 471.
[22] *CCR 1385–1389*, 546.
[23] Payments recorded at *ARUC* i. 75–6 and 80–1.
[24] These deeds are UC:E2/6/MS/4–12. See too Darwall-Smith 1996.
[25] Smith, 116.

whereby the College did not suffer for its purchase of 1361, and Idonea Francis received compensation for the deceptions of John Gonwardby. The decision reached in January 1390 satisfied both aims: the College retained the property, but had to pay Edmund and Idonea Francis £113 6s. 8d.[26]

The case had already cost the College dearly. Even before the expenses of the arbitration, much of its already reduced income had been swallowed up in legal expenses. In 1384/5, for example, one-third of the College's actual income was spent this way. It is little wonder that the College was running at a deficit almost every year in this decade. It is little wonder either that the numbers of Fellows fell from the seven of 1340: weekly payments of commons to Fellows, which appear in the accounts until the 1410s, show that in the 1380s there were never more than three or four Fellows resident in the College at any one time, and that it was not until 1391 that even five Fellows are first recorded.

At least the final settlement proved less crippling than could have been feared: Francis agreed to receive his money in an annual payment of 4 marks, or 53s. 4d., which he finally renounced in 1399, having received barely a quarter of the money owed him. However, back in 1388 it had been calculated that the College had the right to claim over a hundred pounds in rent arrears from him. Evidently, then, the College and Francis agreed to cancel out each other's debts, and Francis and his descendants never bothered the College again.[27]

The dispute with Edmund and Idonea Francis has dominated discussion of the 1380s, but of course it was not the only event taking place in the College. Sometimes Fellows may have considered their lives almost too eventful: on 19 February 1386 the body of Edmund Strete, a Canon of Chichester and commoner at the College, was found in his room hidden in the straw of his bedding. An inquest held that day concluded that Strete had been murdered over a month before by his servant John West, who had promptly fled. Two years later, on 22 May 1388, two Fellows of the College, John Alkebarow and John Taylor, were among a group of graduates summoned before the King and his council on account of conflict between northern and southern members of the University. Alkebarow had already shown a propensity to be obstreperous when in 1377, before he joined the College, he had been forbidden to carry arms and engage in threatening meetings at a time when the university was in dispute with the Dominicans.[28]

Grisly as the tale of Edmund Strete is, it does show that the College's troubles did not deter scholars from seeking lodgings there; indeed, in the 1380s, the College was renting rooms to seven or eight commoners every

---

[26] Deeds settling the case: UC:E2/6/4L/1–5.
[27] Payment of arrears: dorse of UC:E/6/3L/9; Francis's quit-claim: UC:E2/6/4L/7.
[28] Strete's career: *BRUO* iii. 1802; his inquest: Salter 1912: 47 (one hopes that the winter of 1386 was cold enough to render a month-old corpse not too malodorous for others living in University College); Alkebarow and Taylor: *BRUO* i. 24–5 and iii. 1850.

year. Likewise, Alkebarow and Taylor remind us that scholars also still wished to become Fellows of University College. Any Master of Arts planning to study theology in Oxford in the 1380s would have known of the College's difficulties, and realized that all its Fellows would have to help solve them, and not just ensconce themselves in their studies; yet the attractions of a guaranteed income and accommodation remained great enough to attract new Fellows.

The names of most of the Fellows of University College from the 1380s, as well as the disputatious John Alkebarow and John Taylor, are known, but several are now little more than mere names. Even the identity of the Master at this period remains uncertain. One Fellow of undoubted stature was John Middelton, who may have been Master for much of the decade. A Durham man, Middelton's later career was outstandingly successful. In addition to collecting canonries and prebends (see p. 4) from as far afield as Dublin, St David's, York, and London, he became King's Clerk and Physician to both Richard II and Henry IV.[29]

The other Fellow especially worthy of note was Robert Gower. Nothing is known of his origins or his later career (save that in 1391 he became a Bachelor in Theology), but the Bursars' Rolls show him as a doughty defender of the College's rights. Bursar in 1381/2 and 1387/8, he is the only Fellow whose name appears in every itemized list of travel expenses, often several times in one year. Although all the Fellows of the 1380s, in particular John Middelton and John Taylor, deserve remembrance for not giving up the fight, Gower's contribution seems especially worthy.[30]

Even if the Fellows were in a mood to claim victory in 1390, it had been earned at great cost. In 1361–90 the development of the College had stalled and almost regressed to the point where they were sometimes unable even to afford the four Fellows recommended in 1280/1. University College was not unique among Oxford or Cambridge colleges in having to defend its property, but few other colleges were faced with the potential loss of almost one-third of their annual rental.[31]

On the other hand, the College had retrospectively acquired another benefactor. The effect of King Alfred on the outcome of the Gonwardby affair remains debatable: William Smith thought it was crucial, but it may have done little more than attract royal attention sufficiently to give the College a fair hearing in a more sympathetic court. That, for now, was enough; the full usefulness of Alfred to his unilaterally adopted College lay in the future.

---

[29] Middelton may have been Master because in several lists of Fellows (e.g. UC:EB5/F2/2) he is regularly named first. His later career: *BRUO* ii. 1276–7.
[30] Gower: *BRUO* ii. 707–8 (where he is erroneously called Richard).
[31] Disputes over college land in general: Evans and Faith 1992: 639–41; particular instances: Jones 2005: 11–12 (Balliol) and Martin and Highfield 1997: 64–8 (Merton).

A TIME FOR RECOVERY: 1390–1411

University College recovered its momentum surprisingly quickly. The accounts for the two decades after 1390 show a net income at last returning to between £40 and £50 a year, and the number of Fellows rising again to between five and six, with no fewer than seven recorded in 1396/7. As the Fellowship grew, so it began to express itself as a community: the accounts for 1400/1 record a 'gaudy of St Cuthbert' (*gaudia sancti Cuthberti*)—the earliest known reference to the St Cuthbert's Day Feast.[32]

The College also acquired more property: in 1399 it was given a building in Schools Street opposite Brasenose Hall (now the site of part of Radcliffe Square) containing a set of schools and in 1400 a pair of buildings directly adjoining the main site of the College, of which the western one was called Little University Hall (usually described as 'Little University Hall in the High Street' to avoid confusion with the other University Hall), and the eastern one called, picturesquely enough, 'The Cock on the Hoop'. Finally the College purchased a house on the site of 9 High Street in 1401 for £5 6s. 8d.[33]

These new properties did not greatly enrich the College, but they were useful: the schools were let to young MAs having to do their stint of necessary regency (p. 2)—before long some Fellows of University College itself were renting them—whilst the properties adjoining the College could either be let out, or else be subsumed into its main site.

The greatest sign of the College's confidence was the decision to enlarge itself in the 1390s. First of all, there was the transformation of Ludlow Hall, next door to Great University Hall (Map 2.2). Rents were paid on Ludlow Hall for the last time in 1389/91, but in that same period just over £8 were spent on repairs to it, and in 1391/2 the wall between it and Great University Hall was removed. The accounts for the next few years are missing, but when they resume in 1396/7, something extraordinary has happened: in 1391 the College was letting seven rooms, with a rental of £4 6s., but in 1396/7 it was letting eighteen, with a rental of £9 8s. 4d. This increase was clearly caused by the decision to incorporate Ludlow Hall into the main site of the College.[34]

The incorporation of Ludlow Hall did not only offer opportunities for extra income from more commoners; there were also possibilities for development. In the later 1390s the College erected a Chapel on the site of the southern ends of Great University Hall and Ludlow Hall to replace the space for worship created in 1370. The accounts for 1396/7 and 1397/8 show £5 and £14 respectively being spent on the Chapel and other College expenses, and in the latter year the Fellows apparently forewent some of their allowances in

---

[32] Seven Fellows: *ARUC* i. 109; St Cuthbert's Feast: *ARUC* i. 132.
[33] Schools: UC:E/A6/D/1; Little University Hall on High Street: UC:E/B6/D1/6–8; 9 High Street: UC:E/E1/D/4–5 and *ARUC* i. 144. See also *Survey* i. 73, 190–1, and 107–9 respectively.
[34] Repairs on Ludlow Hall: *ARUC* i. 81 and 102; room rentals: *ARUC* i. 86 and 108–9.

order to pay workmen building the Chapel. Finally, in November 1398 the Bishop of Lincoln permitted the College to consecrate the altar in the choir of the new Chapel to St Cuthbert. The new building was not intended for the exclusive use of the Fellows: we would expect commoners to participate in the religious life of the College, and indeed they and the Fellows jointly gave 8*d*. in 1430/1 for cleaning the altar cloth in the Chapel.[35]

The 1390s also mark the beginning of an almost complete list of Masters of University College, and shed some light on the method of their appointment, thanks to a document, dated 16 March 1393, which records the appointment by the Chancellor of Thomas Foston as Master of University College.[36] This document shows both College and university acting within the boundaries set by the statutes of 1292 and 1311: Foston was elected Master by the Fellows of the College, and their choice was then ratified by the Chancellor acting with the Regent Masters in theology and the proctors of the university. As, however, the concept of a Master of University College took root, and the rule of 1292 became interpreted to mean that in a vacancy the senior Fellow automatically became Master, so the election of Foston, the senior Fellow, was hardly unexpected.[37]

The end of the document contains a surprise: the Chancellor records that Foston's appointment will last only two years. There is no other evidence that the Mastership of University College was thus restricted (as was the Rectorship at Exeter at this time), yet there are several Masters of the College during the 1390s: Foston's successor, Thomas Duffeld was in office by September 1396, and his successor, Edmund Lacy, appears to have taken over by 1398/9. Nor had all these Masters obtained preferment to entice them away: both Foston and Lacy stayed on as commoners after they had ceased to be Master. This swift turnover, however, is not reflected in the new century: the next known Masters, John Appleton and John Castell, each served for the better part of a decade. Whether, therefore, the time limit had been a long-standing rule, or something created in special circumstances is not known.[38]

John Appleton, Master by *c*.1401, had a fortunate Mastership, as his tenure saw a most impressive benefaction to the College through the agency of an old friend. At the end of 1403, evidently acting at the request of Walter Skirlaw, Henry IV gave University College his manor of Marks Hall, near Margaret Roding, in Essex. Since the mid-1380s, Walter Skirlaw had pros-

---

[35] Building expenses: *ARUC* i. 110 and 113–14; Fellows allowances: this is a possible interpretation of an obscure note by William Smith (*ARUC* i. 112), but his reference to work carried out 'in the time of the building of the chapel' (*tempore edificacionis capelle*) is clear enough; consecration of the altar: UC:FA2/L1/2; cleaning the altar cloth: *ARUC* i. 379.

[36] Salter 1924: 9.

[37] The statutes of 1475 (see next chapter) explicitly say that the old statutes ordained that the Master succeeded according to seniority.

[38] Duffeld as Master: UC:E/C2/D/1; Lacy as Master: UC:E2/9/1D/1; Exeter College: Southern 1954: 108; possible special circumstances affecting Foston's time limit: Oswald, 62.

pered, becoming Bishop of Durham in 1388, and even survived the deposition of Richard II with his influence intact. Now Skirlaw was in a position to help University College more than before. He was asked by Henry to arrange the conditions of the gift, and duly obliged: income from the manor would support three new Fellows, who had to be priests, and were expected to pray for Skirlaw and the King. Preference was to be given to Masters or Bachelors from Oxford or Cambridge who originated from the dioceses of York or Durham, and they would be expected to study theology. In all other respects, the new Fellows should obey all the existing statutes of the College. Skirlaw ensured that existing Fellows should not feel left out, by asking that they all perform an obit for him—that is to say, they should perform an annual mass for him on the anniversary of his death—and each receive 6s. 8d. both then, and on St Cuthbert's Day. It is rather surprising that Henry IV was prepared to let Skirlaw assume so much prominence in this benefaction, to the point that it became all too easy to assume that Skirlaw, and not his King, was the actual donor of the manor. Skirlaw, however, did make further benefactions of his own, bequeathing University College books and money on his death in 1406.[39]

The manner in which Skirlaw chose to administer the King's gift, namely by supplementing the College's existing statutes with a set of new ones applicable only to the new group of Fellows, set a precedent for future benefactions. Although it would ensure that a body of Fellows in the College would always be associated with particular benefactors, to keep their memory green, in the long run it would lead to the College's statutes becoming a tangle of potentially contradictory jurisdictions, which would lead eventually to explosive results in the 1720s.

That lay far in the future: the Fellows of the early fifteenth century could rejoice in the good fortune, or careful lobbying, of their Master and their great patron. Marks Hall yielded an income of over £20 a year—half the College's existing rental—and the first payment is recorded in 1406/7. The Fellows certainly felt themselves personally indebted to John Appleton, as shown by a touching gesture made much later. In 1438, when Appleton was old and ill, the Fellows obtained a dispensation from the Chancellor to allow him to live in the College, receiving the income from a Fellowship funded from Marks Hall. This use of a Fellowship as a kind of pension is unique in the history of the College, and shows how much the Fellows thought they owed to Appleton.[40]

---

[39] The gift of Marks Hall: UC:E3/D1/1–9 and UC:GB1/L1/2 (see too Clarke 2006); Skirlaw's will: Jarratt 2004: 163; his gift of books: UC:E3/D1/10; bequests of money worth £7 6s. 8d.: ARUC i. 164 and 173. The error about the donor of the manor has been made by, among others, Carr, 58, BRUO iii. 1708, and indeed myself at ARUC i. xxix, yet the documents concerning the gift show beyond doubt that the manor was in Henry's possession and that it was Henry's alone to give.

[40] First payment from Essex: ARUC i. 162; Appleton's special Fellowship (which lasted five years): UC:MA6/L1/1.

THE TAINT OF HERESY: 1411

Whilst the Gonwardby affair and the benefaction of Marks Hall had dominated events in University College, the university as a whole had been affected by a serious crisis which in the early fifteenth century would break over University College. That crisis was the legacy of John Wyclif.[41]

John Wyclif was undoubtedly the most famous Oxonian of the later fourteenth century: a daring and original thinker and a great and influential teacher, as well as something of a self-publicist. Any theologian studying at Oxford in the 1360s or 1370s—which would have included all the Fellows of University College and several of its commoners—would have at the very least known of Wyclif in the small world of the theology faculty, almost certainly attended his lectures and disputations, and possibly known him personally. For all, therefore, that Wyclif's career, which took him to Balliol, Merton, and Queen's, never took him to University College, he would not have gone unnoticed there.

Had Wyclif merely been a brilliant teacher, that would have been all. Wyclif, however, began to be heard well beyond the lecture rooms of the university, both through his own efforts and those of his disciples. When he began to express doubts about the nature of clerical privilege, he found friends in high places such as John of Gaunt, Richard II's eldest uncle, who found such opinions convenient for their own political ends. However, when Wyclif went further, proposing that every Christian should have the right to read the Bible, even in English, and began to doubt the doctrine of transubstantiation, he was dropped by his alarmed former allies. By the time of his death in 1384, he had been forced to withdraw to his parish of Lutterworth, and his teaching had been officially condemned.

Matters were not so simple within Oxford. Robert Rygge, the Chancellor who had helped University College with its petition in 1384, was reluctant to allow the Archbishop of Canterbury to interfere with the university's autonomy, even to investigate heresy; and such evidence as exists for what was actually discussed within the schools for the 1380s and 1390s suggests that Wycliffite ideas remained at the core of academic theological discussion.[42] It remained only a matter of time before church and state might jointly decide to examine Oxford more closely.

In the 1390s University College began to be drawn more closely into the web, thanks to an Irish Cistercian monk called Henry Crumpe. In the early 1380s Crumpe had first been notable as a violent opponent of Wyclif, supposedly coining the term 'Lollards' for his followers, but when he returned to Oxford in the early 1390s he began to teach views, especially on the eucharist, which were dangerously close to Wyclif's. In May 1392,

---

[41] See further Catto 1992a, and also Martin and Highfield 1997: 100–5.
[42] Catto 1992a: 219–20.

Crumpe was summoned before a council of bishops at Stamford, which included both archbishops, and was forbidden to engage in any scholastic act without permission from the Archbishop of Canterbury. At just this time Henry Crumpe was also a commoner of University College, and indeed rented a room there for much of the next decade. Evidently the Fellows of the 1390s considered that Crumpe was not contravening the statutes of 1292 which required that commoners live 'honourably and peacefully' and 'do no harm to the affairs of the house'.[43]

Another commoner of University College got into trouble in the following decade. Richard Fleming, a Yorkshireman, lived there from at least 1404/5 to 1408/9, becoming proctor in 1407. Handsome, intelligent, well connected, and perhaps a little full of himself, Fleming seems to have involved himself in speculation in the theology faculty which was sufficiently daring to offend the orthodox. Forty years earlier, Fleming might have passed unnoticed, but he was not so lucky now. The Archbishop of Canterbury, Thomas Arundel, a determined foe of Lollardy, was taking a keen interest in the theologians of Oxford, and had in 1407 issued constitutions, or rules, controlling what could and could not be discussed in the theological schools through a board of censors.[44]

In 1409 six Masters accused Fleming of promulgating erroneous doctrine, and the matter reached the notice of these censors, who seem to have condemned him. Arundel rebuffed an appeal from Fleming, but thanks to some careful string-pulling, Fleming eventually escaped punishment, and reinvented himself as a paragon of orthodoxy, reappearing two years later as a member of a university board sending Arundel in March 1411 a list of 267 errors which they had found in the works of Wyclif.[45]

At the same time as Fleming was extricating himself from trouble, two other members of University College were diving into it. In December 1409 Arundel wrote to the university protesting at the conduct of four scholars, who had spoken out against his constitutions, and asking that they be punished. Of the four, one, John Kexby (a nephew of William Kexby), was a commoner of University College, and another, Robert Burton, was a Fellow.[46] Kexby and Burton need not have been protesting simply on account of Lollardy; equally at stake was the autonomy of Oxford, which had never endured such interference before. Burton was clearly of a combative disposition: he was to be named in letters patent of 13 May 1411 as one of several scholars to be arrested for causing riots in the city.[47]

---

[43] Crumpe's career and activities: *BRUO* i. 524–5 and Catto 1992a: 216–17 and 230–2; Crumpe at University College: *ARUC* i. 102.
[44] The main sources for the story of Fleming and the visitation of 1411 are documents in BL Faustina C. vii, edited in Salter 1924: 115–93. See too Catto 1992a: 243–54.
[45] Salter 1924: 128–30.
[46] Ibid. 123. It is not known how far this matter proceeded.
[47] Ibid. 103.

Greater intervention was yet to come. In the summer of 1411, Arundel let it be known that he intended to include the university in his general visitation of the diocese of Lincoln—something never done before by an Archbishop of Canterbury.[48] Despite the best attempts of the university to stop him, which included barring his entrance to the university church of St Mary the Virgin, he did succeed in beginning a visitation in August that year.

The Fellows of University College were as heavily implicated in these events as any member of the university. In the College's archives is a copy of an appeal to the Pope made after 17 October 1411, by John Ryvell, Fellow and Bursar of University College, against a sentence of excommunication published by Archbishop Arundel against him, the Master, John Castell, the other Fellows, Robert Burton, Adam Redyford, and John Hamerton, and against the College as a whole, and posted in three Oxford churches.[49] On 21 September, Ryvell formally protested on behalf of the College against the sentence. It went, he said, far beyond the Archbishop's authority, and was carried out without warning and when he and his colleagues had done or said nothing wrong. No other evidence for this excommunication of the whole College exists, but the date suggests strongly that it was closely linked to the Archbishop's visitation, and it seems likely that the excommunication was lifted as part of a compromise achieved between Arundel and the university later in the year.

Accusations of unorthodoxy made against individual members; defiance of an Archbishop; and excommunication: University College in the early fifteenth century has the appearance of an institution in which Lollardy has run riot. Yet this is to oversimplify matters. Alongside such figures as Henry Crumpe or Richard Fleming, University College also accommodated as a commoner from 1399–1407 John Orum, who later wrote addresses on the Apocalypse which show his orthodox credentials. Richard Fleming himself ended his days as Bishop of Lincoln, founding Lincoln College in 1427 specifically to nurture theologians who would fight heresy. Edmund Lacy, successively Fellow, Master, and then commoner from 1391 to 1406/7, became Dean of the Chapel Royal at Windsor, accompanied Henry V to Agincourt, and became Bishop successively of Hereford and Exeter. As for the excommunicated Master and Fellows, John Castell was appointed a King's Clerk in 1420, and served as Chancellor of the university in the 1420s, whilst Robert Burton succeeded him as Master in 1420, and later became precentor of Lincoln and archdeacon of Northumberland, also

---

[48] Only as recently as 1370 Oxford had been exempted from the jurisdiction of the Bishop of Lincoln, and in 1395 it had tried unsuccessfully to free itself from the jurisdiction of the Archbishop of Canterbury too (Cobban 1988: 283–4).
[49] UC:GB2/L4/1, supplemented by UC:AR2/MS1/10 pp. 9–13.

being appointed a member of the English delegation to the council of Basel in 1432.[50]

Such men were not out-and-out Lollards. They were young men, at the start of their careers. It is not surprising that they were attracted by new and daring ideas in their youth, which they put away as they grew older, but which at the time would have aroused the suspicions of Archbishop Arundel. Furthermore, if Fellows and commoners in University College had listened to Wyclif's views more sympathetically than might have been wise, they were not alone in Oxford. Perhaps the chief sin of the Fellows of University College in the crisis of 1411 was not so much any possible lack of orthodoxy as a certain stubbornness in defending what they considered to be the university's privilege to study and teach without outside interference—a danger greater, in the long run, than anything threatened by Edmund and Idonea Francis.

[50] Catto 1992a: 258–9 (Orum), and *BRUO* i. 319–20 (Burton) and i. 368 (Castell).

4
Medieval Equilibrium: 1411–1509

After the tumultuous events of 1411, the remainder of John Castell's Mastership seems to have passed quietly. Much the same could almost be said of the history of University College in the whole fifteenth century: although it did not completely escape lawsuits, internal embarrassments, and outside influences, there were no lawsuits as damaging as that with Edmund and Idonea Francis, nor did any other bellicose prelates disturb the Fellows' studies. Furthermore, the College witnessed significant changes to its statutes, its membership, and its very fabric, as the College's first quadrangle at last came into being.

By 1411 the idea that members of Oxford university, at whatever level, should live together had become increasingly the norm. Other colleges had been founded by now: most, like Exeter or Queen's, quite modest, and one, New College with its seventy Fellows, far grander than anything yet seen in Oxford. All catered for fellows, and New College was the first to offer awards to scholars reading for their first degrees. The great majority of undergraduate scholars instead looked for their accommodation and, increasingly, some of their teaching to the academic halls.[1] In *c.*1410 the university even passed a statute ordering all scholars to live in halls or colleges. Oxford was not alone in this: Cambridge and Paris both had, as well as colleges, equivalents to halls known respectively as hostels and 'pédagogies', and both were trying to tighten up the rules of residence throughout the fifteenth century.[2]

University College's endowment, however, continued to support only Fellows reading Theology, and apart from a few exceptions to be encountered

---

[1] The word 'undergraduate' has yet to be recorded before the early seventeenth century (and the same seems to be true of its Latin equivalent, *subgraduatus*). Before then, the word 'scholar' tends to be used instead. For this period, therefore, I tend to use the term 'undergraduate scholar' to describe specifically a scholar who had yet to become a BA.

[2] Statute of *c.*1410: Gibson 1931: 208 (the presence of later statutes enforcing the same rule suggests that it was difficult to enforce); growth of halls: Catto 2004; Cambridge: Leader 1988: 45–8; Paris: Tuilier 1994: i. 249–52 and 441. Oxford, Cambridge, and Paris were not the only medieval universities with colleges, but colleges were less pervasive in southern Europe (see further Denley 1991, Gieysztor 1992: 116–19, and Schwinges 1992: 213–22).

later, its commoners were of BA status or higher. Just one document hints at some provision for undergraduate scholars, namely a set of regulations compiled at an unknown date after 1380, known only from a transcript made by Thomas Walker, Master from 1632.[3] It differs from the earlier statutes in containing a series of 'customs' (*consuetudines*) rather than rules. Many of the customs build on what was there already: junior Fellows will give way to their seniors; a cap is placed on a Fellow's 'commons' or weekly allowance; and Fellows will take part in weekly disputations or lectures. But one custom is very new:

> The whole company must have two portionists, each of whom in alternate weeks must read the bible and guard the gate: and for whom provision is to be made once a day from common alms.[4]

'Portionist' (later apparently corrupted to 'Postmaster') was the term used at Merton for its scholars, and it is interesting to find the term used here. The idea of a poor scholar nourished by alms in return for duties like reading the bible at meals or acting as a porter has parallels elsewhere, where the term *bibliotista* or bible clerk is also used. Unfortunately, the portionists or poor scholars of University College are distinguished by their complete absence from College records, save for a payment of 4*d.* to the *bibliotista* in the accounts of 1496/7. The fact that they were supported by Fellows rather than the College may in part explain this absence, but in the end this early glimpse of undergraduate scholars at University College remains a mystery.[5]

ARRESTED GROWTH: 1411–1441

Castell's successor as Master in 1420 was his fellow troublemaker of 1411, Robert Burton. Burton's succession is marked by a striking entry in the Register of Henry Chichele, then Archbishop of Canterbury, in which he grants a request made in May 1420 by the Chancellor and Congregation of the university that Burton receive a dispensation to remain Master of the College, whilst obtaining promotion to benefices worth more than 5 marks a year. The reason for this, the petitioners say, is the poverty of the College, its many debts, its goods held in pawn, and its tenements in ruins or else completely destroyed. In painting such a bleak picture, the university may have been talking up the College's plight. Furthermore, by trying to arrange regular dispensations for Masters of University College, the authorities might hope that an experienced academic would be encouraged not to move on too soon.[6]

---

[3] UC:GB1/MS1/1 pp. 3–4.

[4] *Tota comitiva duos habeat porcionistas, quorum uterque alternis ebdomadis, bibliam legat, et alternis portam custodiat: quibus saltem semel in die de communi eleemosyna ministretur.*

[5] Poor scholars: Leader 1988: 62–3 and Cobban 1992: 592–3; 1496/7 accounts: *ARUC* ii. 170.

[6] Burton: Jacob 1947: 223–5 (also Carr, 60 and Oswald, 64).

Financially, however, all was not well. In 1419/20, the College's real income was £55 5s. 5¾d., whereas in 1418/19 it had been £72 6s. 8¾d. This in itself was not a great problem: such fluctuations occurred throughout the fifteenth century (Graph 5.1). However, the College usually succeeded in making its real expenditure match its real income, or creating a small surplus. In 1419/20 the College ran a deficit of just over £4, its worst performance for a generation, and even in the 'good' year of 1418/19, half its income was spent on repairs to College properties.

At the same time, the College's population was alarmingly low. Over the previous two decades, it had usually comprised four or five Fellows living with an average of ten commoners, but in 1419/20 and 1420/1, there were only three Fellows and three—and then two—commoners. University College was having recruitment difficulties. Until 1419/20, it seems to have obeyed William of Durham's wish only to elect Masters, and although the 1292 statutes—and Walter Skirlaw's statutes too—had permitted Bachelors to be elected Fellows in the absence of a suitable Master or Arts, this option seems rarely to have been invoked. The College accounts scrupulously indicated whether someone was a 'Master' or not, and almost every known Fellow to date had been an MA. Another dispensation of 1420, this time granted by the university itself, suggests that this standard was now proving unsustainable.[7] Robert Burton was permitted to appoint as Fellows up to seven scholars who could be Bachelors or even Sophisters (p. 8), even before they had become Masters and were ready to read theology—although they were still expected to do this in due course.

What had gone wrong? One plausible theory is that, even without the attractions of other, wealthier, foundations to attract would-be theologians elsewhere, the convulsions of the previous decades may have made the study of theology less popular at Oxford, and there may not have been enough eligible MAs to come to University College. Entry requirements, therefore, had to be lowered. The two dispensations of 1420 evidently put something to rights: the accounts for 1421/2 show six Fellows (of whom only two, including Burton himself, were MAs) and six commoners. This unusually high proportion of Bachelors may indeed have reflected an immediate crisis; but later fifteenth-century accounts usually include one or two Bachelor Fellows. Even if it is not directly attributable to these dispensations, a change has certainly taken place in the College's personnel.

Robert Burton's term as Master was short; by 1423/4 he had embarked on his solidly successful later career, and been replaced by Richard Witton. Unfortunately for the College, whereas Burton's only known act as Master was to bolster the College's delicate finances, Witton's only known act

---

[7] UC:GB6/3/A1/1.

produced the opposite effect. The College's house on the site of 9 High Street was, in theory, liable to an annual quit-rent of 15s. 8d. payable to Osney Abbey, the greatest corporate landowner in Oxford. This quit-rent had already been the subject of dispute between the Abbey and the property's then owner in the 1370s. Now in the late 1420s, the arguments flared up again. It is not clear who started the dispute, but it was unwise for the College to take on the Abbey. At the very least it was expensive: from the first mention of a payment made 'for the Osney business' (*circa materiam Osney*) in 1426/7 until 1431/2 the College was regularly spending money on the case, sometimes as much as £12 or £13 a year—a significant sum for a College whose rental was still not much more than £60.[8]

In a further parallel with the 1380s, Witton and the Fellows invoked King Alfred again, embellishing the tale further. The Fellows of 1384 had concocted an Aluredian foundation of twenty-four Fellows; now Witton claimed that Alfred had endowed the College with no less than seventy-eight Fellows, comprising three equal groups of grammarians, philosophers, and theologians. The history of 9 High Street was also rewritten: a set of deeds supposedly dating from the late twelfth and early thirteenth centuries suggests that this house was once owned by the Goldsmith family no less, and was not subject to any quit-rent. These documents are forgeries. Better forgeries than those of the 1380s, with no anachronistic howlers, and written in an apparently 'old' hand, but not quite good enough: the handwriting is not quite right for the period, and several people mentioned in them were actually extracted from genuine deeds dating from up to a century later.[9]

This brew of forgery and King Alfred had worked in the 1380s. It did not work now: in May 1432, the Chancellor of the university and the Mayor of Oxford were brought in to arbitrate, and they agreed that the Abbot of Osney had the right to claim his quit-rent from University College. This defeat was borne by a new Master: Witton had moved on in 1428, and it was left to his successor, Thomas Benwell, to see the case out to its sorry conclusion—and suffer recriminations. In July 1432, Chancellor and Mayor united again, this time to declare that there was no truth in a rumour that Thomas Benwell had secretly sold the disputed rents to Osney Abbey.[10]

---

[8] The background to the quit-rent: Salter 1929: 396–400; documents concerning the 1420s case: UC:E/E1/L/1-8; 'Osney business': *ARUC* i. 349.

[9] The only evidence for Witton's statement is Smith, 144–6, where he provides an English translation, without indicating his source (New College, then the wealthiest college in Oxford or Cambridge, supported just seventy fellows)—Smith's typically robust comments (Smith, 146–50) make good reading; forged deeds: UC:E/E1/MS/1-5 and Darwall-Smith 1996.

[10] Arbitration: UC:E/E1/L/5-6 (Clarke 2006: 112–14 suggests that the lack of a patron comparable with Walter Skirlaw also played a part in this fiasco); Benwell: UC:E/E1/L/7.

That Thomas Benwell should first appear under a cloud is typical. It is almost impossible meaningfully to assess the character of any medieval member of University College, yet something seems to hover over Benwell, as if the archives of Oxford have determined to blacken his name. This is not simply due to his bad luck in inheriting the Mastership during the hopeless struggle with Osney Abbey: other records raise doubts about his financial competence. When he was Bursar in 1428/9, the accounts for that year note that John Humfray, the College's tenant in Marks Hall, claimed he had paid the College 28s., but that no one, including the Bursar, could remember having received it, and in February 1436 a former tenant of the manor, Geoffrey Athelham, had to swear that he had paid two years worth of rents to Benwell, because some Fellows had disputed this.[11]

Sometimes Benwell was plain unlucky. In May 1426, the Bursar of University College arrived in the village of Good Easter, near Marks Hall, with a sick horse, telling those who would listen that it had not fallen ill due to any excessive work or sudden illness, but because it had been unwell for a long time—in other words, before the Bursar had bought the horse. That Bursar was Thomas Benwell. The people of Good Easter agreed to witness an affidavit to this effect which Benwell took back to Oxford, although readers may be forgiven for suspecting that the agreement owed less to the villagers' veterinary skill, and more to the pleading of a Bursar desperate not to be left out of pocket.[12]

Money and horses were not Benwell's only problems: on 28 January 1436, he was summoned to appear before the Chancellor's Commissary to answer a charge of 'incontinence' with one Agnes Babelak and other unnamed women. At the hearing, however, Agnes suddenly withdrew all her charges, saying that she had made them all up, and Benwell was therefore declared innocent. Neither does Benwell's career outside University College appear very successful. He spent two decades there, as Fellow and Master; and yet nothing is known of his later career, and unlike Castell or Burton he apparently did not combine his Mastership with any benefice.[13] In short, history has painted him as either a rogue or a fool: the Bursar who is lumbered with a sick horse; the Master who inherits a hopeless legal dispute; and who is, or is not, caught with his trousers down.

Yet such a portrait overlooks Benwell's twenty years of service to the College; the nine occasions when he acted as Bursar, more than any Fellow for over two centuries; and a warm letter of recommendation written on his behalf by the university to an unnamed bishop in 1427.[14] He represents a

---

[11] *ARUC* i. 366 (1428/9) and UC:E3/L3/1 (1436).
[12] Affidavit: UC:MA10/L2/1.
[13] Agnes Babelak: Salter 1932: i. 17–18 (readers can decide whether Benwell was unjustly accused, or merely capable of buying silence: prostitution existed in medieval Oxford (Cobban 1999: 138–40)); Benwell's career: *BRUO* i. 171.
[14] Anstey 1898: i. 31–2.

type of Fellow or Master who chose to spend more of his career attached to the College than his predecessors. Thomas Benwell may also have been a man with connections: during his Mastership, three well-born youths—the nephew of a Bishop and two future peers—rented rooms at University College, when they were barely into their teens. As the next chapter will show, although such people regularly studied at Oxford in the fifteenth century, they are apparently only recorded at University College under Benwell.[15]

Before leaving Benwell, we need to return to a theme mentioned earlier, namely the reinvention of the history of University College. Whether or not the Osney trial was a catalyst for reviving the story of King Alfred, the fact remains that during the early fifteenth century the College was very interested in trying to square the claim that it had been founded by King Alfred with the clear allusion in the 1280/1 and 1292 statutes to the endowment of William of Durham, whose identity was now forgotten.

Two documents, now only known in seventeenth-century transcripts, show how the Fellows tried to reconcile these accounts. The first is a document titled 'Some Annals of the College from the year 800 to the year 1400', which William Smith called the *Memorandum*.[16] It is a very brief account of some important benefactions to the College, up to the gift of Marks Hall. The first entry shows its level of accuracy:

Memorandum that around the year 800 King Alfred founded this College whose expenses were paid for by the Royal Exchequer right up until the Conquest. Then William the Conqueror, aiming forcibly to destroy the English language, withdrew the said grant, unwilling to nurture further any clerks who would preach the faith on our own tongue, and then the Scholars of the College lived for a long time only from the devotion of those who loved our language.[17]

It then notes the bequest of William, Archdeacon of Durham (*sic*), who, it is said, first gave the College an endowment, and then the benefaction in 1292 of the otherwise unknown 'Gilbert in Gilbera'.

Although the *Memorandum* is worthless as history, it is crucial for the historiography of University College in its ingenious solution to its double foundation. King Alfred did indeed found the College, they say, but his

---

[15] The three youths are Robert Fleming (Richard Fleming's nephew), Robert Hungerford (later Lord Hungerford and Moleyns), and John Tiptoft (later Earl of Worcester).

[16] The best source for the *Memorandum* is UC:BE1/MS2/2 pp. 7–8 (a volume compiled in the 1670s). See Smith, 204–5.

[17] *Memorandum quod circa annum Domini Octingentissiam* [sic] *Rex Alredus alias Alfredus fundavit Collegium istud cujus Exhibitio sumebatur e Scaccario Regis continuo usque at Conquestum saltem exclusive. Tunc Willelmus Conquestor pre viribus nitens destruere linguam Anglicanam dictam Exhibitionem retraxit nolens ulterius nutrire Clericos ad predicandum fidem in nostro vulgari idiomate, et tunc vixerunt Scholares Collegij diu ex solâ (devotione) diligentium Linguam nostram.*

foundation was destroyed in 1066, and William of Durham merely re-founded it. The question of what endowments the 'old' University College possessed was sidestepped neatly by turning it into an Anglo-Saxon precursor of the King's Hall, Cambridge, a college funded by Exchequer grants.[18]

The second document is a charter supposedly created in 1219 for the then Chancellor of the university, Louis de Chapernay (henceforth the Chapernay charter). In this document, dated to 'the fourth year of King Henry the Third after the Conquest', Chapernay, noting that William, Archdeacon of Durham, has left 400 marks to invest in rents to support six masters, now with the agreement of the Doctors of Theology and proctors makes over to Roger Caldwell, 'Warden or Senior Fellow' of University College, various properties purchased with his money. The forgery is transparent: neither Louis Chapernay nor Roger Caldwell ever existed; Henry III was actually styled 'King Henry the son of King John'; and the properties, although genuinely owned by University College, were actually acquired during the later thirteenth and fourteenth centuries. Antony Wood, who observed that the handwriting was consistent with a date after Richard II, was no more fooled than William Smith. Smith also noted that, remarkably, the deed bore the seal of the university, making it a most ambitious forgery. Access to the seal need not have been impossible: John Castell was Chancellor of Oxford in 1421–5, and Gilbert Kymer, Chancellor in 1431–4, rented a school from University College in 1432/3–1433/4.[19]

The purpose of the Chapernay charter is uncertain, not least because it contradicts the *Memorandum* by apparently leaving no room for King Alfred. It certainly offers a clearer exposition of the College's foundation than the real statutes of 1280/1, by naming exactly which properties were handed over to the College, and omitting the embarrassing details about the loss of half William's bequest, but, unlike the legends of King Alfred, or the forged deeds of the 1380s and 1430s, there is no obvious benefit in its creation. However, the existence of this and the *Memorandum* do show that the College was trying hard to explain the legends of its foundation, and to include King Alfred in them.

JOHN MARTYN: 1441–1473

The custom whereby the senior Fellow of University College automatically became Master did not always work to the College's advantage, providing Masters as different as John Appleton and Thomas Benwell. In 1441 the

---

[18] On King's Hall (incorporated into Trinity College in 1546) see Cobban 1969.
[19] The original document has been missing at least since 1887 (UC:AR3/MS1/1), and so one must rely on Smith's transcript (UC:AR2/MS1/7 pp. 1–3); handwriting: Wood, *Colleges* 44; Castell: *BRUO* i. 367–8; Kymer: *BRUO* ii. 1068, and *ARUC* i. 397 and 407. Such use of the university's seal for dubious documents was not unique: Emden 1968: 138–43.

College was fortunate: the senior Fellow was John Martyn, a Durham man who had been a Fellow since 1427/8. Martyn spent at least forty-five years at University College as Fellow and Master, a term not to be surpassed there until the seventeenth century, and his term of thirty-two years as Master has been exceeded only twice in the College; indeed no Oxford college head before 1500 seems to have surpassed him. He also exploited the dispensation granted to Robert Burton: Martyn has been linked with five parishes, in Warwickshire, Northamptonshire, and Oxfordshire, frequently holding at least two of them in plurality. For Martyn, then, the Mastership was not a stepping-stone on his way to higher things, as it had been for his predecessors. Instead it became the foundation for the rest of his life.[20]

Martyn became a significant figure in Oxford: from c.1447/8 until 1457, he served on the committee overseeing the building of the new Divinity Schools, and a letter from the Mayor of Oxford to the Mayor of Bristol from the 1460s called him 'a man off grete worship and of noble fame within the Universite of Oxford and eke withoute'. In contemplating the career of John Martyn, therefore, we see the first glimmerings of what a college headship could signify, in particular how he could shape policy and could use his position to win respect and patronage both inside and outside the university. Three themes run through Martyn's Mastership: a transformation in the physical appearance of the College; success in fund-raising activities; and changes in the composition of the College community.[21]

The College's appearance in 1441 had apparently changed little since the erection of the Chapel in the late 1390s. The accounts for the intervening years regularly refer to general repairs, but not to fresh building work. This suggests that most of Great University Hall and Ludlow Hall were still standing, especially their street frontages. Although the College had a Chapel, there seems to have been no attempt made to replace the hall which presumably stood at the centre of Great University Hall, and which everyone, Fellows and commoners alike, would have had to use. University College therefore still lacked any recognizable quadrangle: significantly, the Bursars' accounts make no mention of a quadrangle after the incorporation of Ludlow Hall until 1487/8. Medieval colleges did not necessarily have to have a quadrangle—Exeter lacked one until well into the seventeenth century—but all new foundations since at least New College had been equipped with them, and older ones, such as Balliol and Merton, now featured them too.

[20] Martyn's career: *BRUO* ii. 1235.
[21] Martyn and the Divinity Schools: Salter 1932: i. 183–4, and ii. 252 and 256 (some building accounts of 1452/3 for the Schools may owe their presence in College (UC:P61/F1/1) to his involvement); Martyn's character: Salter 1920: 224.

It is impossible to construct an exact chronology of the building of the first quadrangle of University College, but much of the work was almost certainly done under John Martyn. Already the accounts for 1434/5–1435/6 had mentioned the construction and repair of a 'new chamber' in the College, costing just over £16. Then, in 1441/2 and 1442/3, just after Martyn became Master, there were references to building a new house and a new storehouse in the College. The interpretation of 'house' (*domus*) is problematic: it may denote a separate building, or part of a residential range. However, there is little doubt about the next known development: work on a new Hall started in 1448/9 and continued at least into 1450/1. The new Hall ran north–south, situated to the east of Great University Hall, and almost exactly covering most of Ludlow Hall.[22]

The resources of a small College would not have run to such a building, and although University College did spend some of its own money on it (including £9 17½ d. in 1450/1), it seems that much money came from elsewhere. Antony Wood, who examined this Hall before its demolition in the 1660s, certainly thought that it had been built 'partly at the College's Charge and partly by the benevolence of well-disposed people', basing this assumption on various inscriptions and coats of arms he saw there. There was, for example, a window commemorating John Chedworth, commoner in 1435/6–1440/1 and later Bishop of Lincoln, as a benefactor to the College. Wood also noted the coats of arms of Robert, Lord Hungerford and Molyns, who had shared a room with Chedworth, no doubt as his personal pupil.[23]

How many of these people contributed to the Hall is not known; but the College certainly did receive benefactions for buildings. In a covenant of June 1458 Martyn and the Fellows of University College record receiving a bequest from one Joan Danvers, to be used on building a tower and main entrance to the College. Joan Danvers was the widow of William Danvers, a former MP for Berkshire, but it is not known why she should have taken an interest in University College (she also gave estates to the newly founded Magdalen College). A tower was certainly in place by 1465/6, when repairs were carried out on it, and may have become Martyn's residence: it certainly functioned as the Master's Lodgings in 1531, and it was an ideal place from which to watch the comings and goings of the College. By the time of Martyn's death in 1473, then, the College had changed completely since 1441. At least three sides of a quadrangle—those with the Chapel to the south, the Hall to the east, and the tower and main entrance to the north—were in place, and two of them were partly or wholly erected under Martyn.[24]

---

[22] *ARUC* i. 421, 428 (new chamber); 496, 505 (new house); 559, 572 (new Hall). See too Darwall-Smith 2005a: 15–17.

[23] Wood, *Colleges* 59. His description of the Hall is at *Colleges* 59–61. Hungerford is discussed in the next chapter.

[24] Covenant: UC:BE5/L1/1; repairs of 1465/6: *ARUC* i. 703; the tower as Master's Lodgings in 1531:UC:GB3/A1/1, p. 7; the use of towers by heads of other houses: Harvey 1992: 754.

John Martyn exerted his fund-raising skills elsewhere. In the 1440s, the most eminent living former member of University College was Edmund Lacy, Bishop of Exeter, but he seems to have given nothing to the College. John Martyn changed that: the accounts in 1443/4 record a gift of £10 from 'our special Lord the Bishop of Exeter' (*Domino nostro speciali episcopo Exon*'), and other gifts followed until Lacy's death in 1455. Occasional visits were also made to Lacy to maintain the link so profitably renewed. Others were willing to give Martyn's College cash donations. In January 1448, for example, the College received a bequest of 50 marks (£33 6s. 8d.) from Henry, Cardinal Beaufort, who had died the previous year.[25]

The greatest benefaction from these years, however, took place in 1443 when Henry Percy, Earl of Northumberland, presented University College with the rectory of Arncliffe, a large parish in the Yorkshire dales (Fig. 4.1 and Plate 2). Percy had no known link with the College and his benefaction is unexpected. Antony Wood thought that the gift resulted from the university lobbying the Earl to assist an old College with strong links to the north-east. There is no evidence for this, but the university certainly wrote an effusive letter of thanks to Percy, and urged the Archbishop, Dean, and Chapter of York to consent to the gift.[26]

The rectory of a large parish was a great prize: not only did the College receive the right to appoint to the living—its first piece of patronage—but it could make money through the practice of 'appropriation'. The owner of an appropriated living was permitted to receive all its tithes (a right usually farmed out for a fixed annual rent) so long as he paid the stipend of a vicar to manage the parish. Appropriating the living was expensive—the College had to spend £25 in 1443–4 to arrange this—but worthwhile. After the death of the sitting rector in 1451, the College received over £20 a year by renting out the tithes of Arncliffe, and increased its rental to about £80.[27]

Percy presumably knew that the College would appropriate the living, for he asked that, in return for his gift, it would elect three Bachelors or Masters from the dioceses of Durham, Carlisle, or York, with special preference given to candidates from Northumberland, to read theology. The new Fellows would receive the same allowances as other Fellows. In return the College agreed to say two masses a year for Percy and his family, for which they would receive payment.[28]

---

[25] Gifts from Lacy: *ARUC* i. 513, 567, 602; visits to him: *ARUC* i. 533–4, 545, 573; Beaufort's bequest (the reason for which is unknown): UC:BE4/L1/1.

[26] The gift: Darwall-Smith 2006: 83–7; related documents: UC:E4/2D/1–8; the university's role: Anstey 1898: i. 219–22, and Wood, *Colleges* 46, and Carr, 62. Evans and Faith 1992: 637–8 note that such lay benefactions were commoner in fifteenth-century Cambridge than in Oxford.

[27] Expenses concerning the appropriation: *ARUC* i. 506 and 516.

[28] Percy's statutes (very reminiscent of Walter Skirlaw's): UC:E4/2D/1.

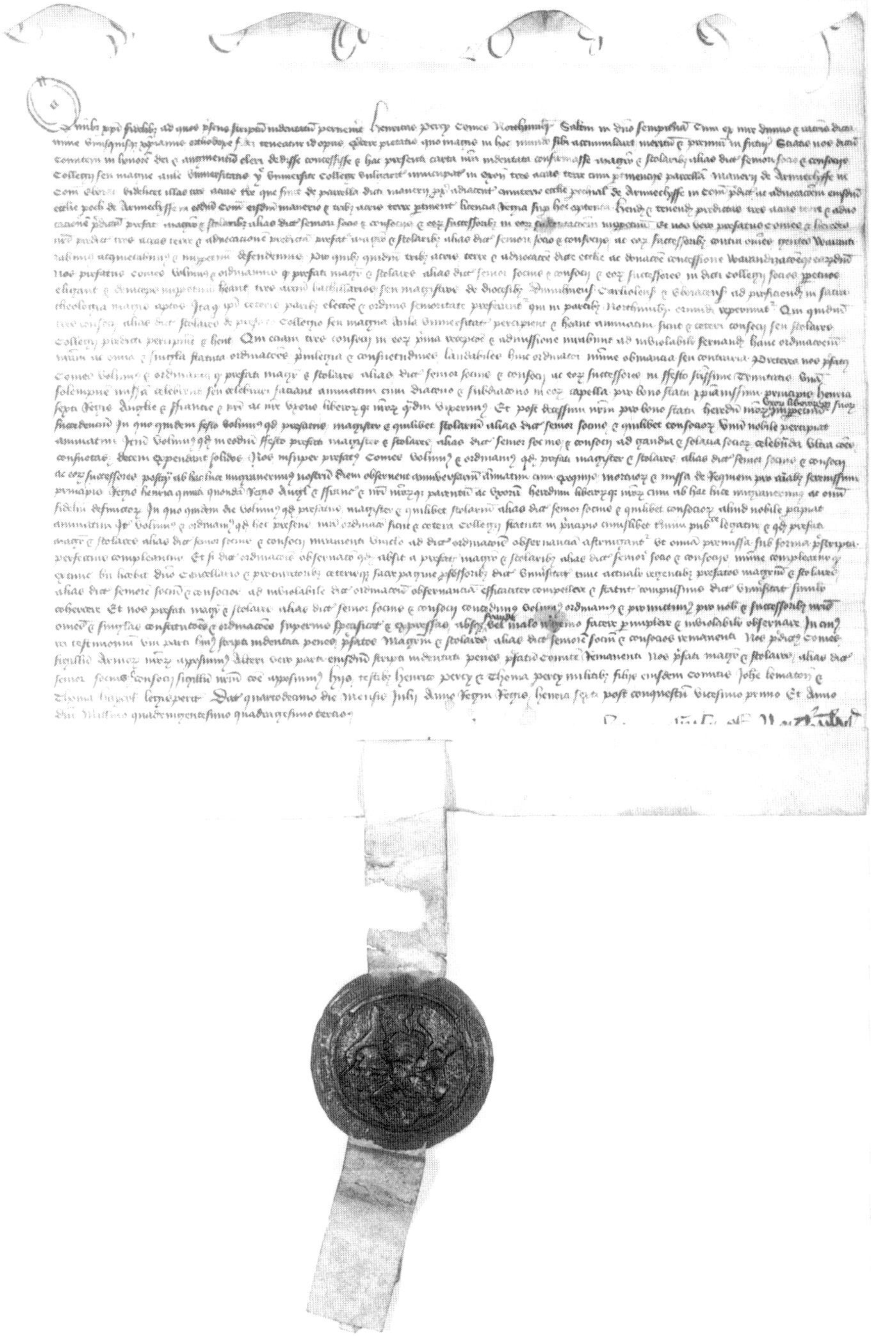

FIGURE 4.1 Deed of 1443 by which Henry Percy, Earl of Northumberland, granted Arncliffe Rectory to University College. Percy's signature is just visible at the bottom of the deed.

As Martyn and the Fellows were settling Arncliffe rectory, they engaged in another property transaction. In 1447, they received a collection of houses and rents in Newcastle-upon-Tyne from one Alice Bellasis which promised to yield £6 14s. 2d. a year—not as impressive as Arncliffe or Marks Hall, but welcome nonetheless. However, the Newcastle property did not prove as profitable as expected, and Alice proved a tough negotiator: in February 1451, the College agreed to pay her an annuity of 8 marks and 10 shillings (£5 16s. 8d.—almost equivalent in value to the Newcastle rental itself) for life, to be charged on the revenue from Marks Hall: no small strain on the College's resources, and one which continued to be paid until 1473/4.[29]

In addition to soliciting money from others, Martyn apparently gave, or at least lent, money of his own to the College. In November 1455, when he was owed no less than £34 18s. 10d., he agreed to remit all but £20, which would be paid him in instalments over the next five years.[30] Martyn also appears to have overseen a stabilization in the College's finances. References to money paid into or from a College chest can be traced back to the 1380s, but from the mid-1450s the College's accounts regularly record the sums of money in the College chest at the start and end of each year. The sums are not large (only once getting above £10 during the 1460s), yet they suggest a College capable of creating a reserve fund, rather than living from hand to mouth.

One curious episode relating to the College's properties from this period might have radically changed its future course. In 1448, William Waynflete, Bishop of Winchester, founded Magdalen Hall in what is now Bostar Hall. Waynflete was interested in expanding his site, and in 1450/1 was negotiating with John Martyn about the possibility of the Hall purchasing a perpetual lease on Little University Hall in High Street, the Cock on the Hoop, and 83–4 High Street, to the point of drafting some deeds for the transaction. The plan fell through—Waynflete dissolved Magdalen Hall in 1458 and instead created Magdalen College on a new site further to the east—but it leaves an interesting vision of how University College might have grown without the site of the Radcliffe Quadrangle.[31]

The new College buildings and the increase in its endowment were accompanied by a change in the College's population. Between the incorporation of Ludlow Hall in the 1390s and 1441, the College's contingent of commoners usually averaged between eight and twelve, at a time when the average number of Fellows was never more than four or five. Then, in the early 1450s, as the number of Fellows stabilized at six or seven, so the number of commoners collapsed to barely two or three. Commoner numbers grew a

---

[29] The gift of the property and Alice's annuity: UC:E5/2/1D/2 and 5 (the former is calendared in Oliver 1924: 159–62); also on Alice's annuity: *ARUC* i. xxix.

[30] Salter 1932: i. 354–5.

[31] Salter 1914: 260–3. The Magdalen Hall created in the early sixteenth century was a different institution.

little in the late 1460s and early 1470s, but soon fell away again, and by the late 1480s sometimes no commoners were recorded at all. This decline occurs just as the income from Arncliffe starts to arrive. The College was able to elect more Fellows, it needed more rooms to accommodate them, and it was less dependent on income from commoners. From a financial point of view, commoners had proved a mixed investment. Some commoners were irregular payers, whereas the money from Arncliffe came from one reliable source only.[32]

Just once did the money from Arncliffe fail, but this was due to special circumstances. Readers may have wondered to what extent College life was affected by such major events as the Hundred Years War or the Wars of the Roses. On the whole, the answer appears to be not at all, except in 1460/1 when the College collected barely a quarter of the money due from its properties outside Oxford (Graph 5.1). This year, however, saw the bloodiest phase of the Wars of the Roses, with some of the worst fighting, such as the battle of Towton, in Yorkshire. The Fellows evidently concluded that any journeys north would be unwise in the circumstances, and chose to sit that year out safe in Oxford.

When John Martyn died, not long before July 1473, he had altered University College more profoundly than almost any of his predecessors. In the absence of official registers or minutes, it is not always possible to assign a set of policies to the head of a medieval College. Yet something happened to University College under Martyn—its buildings were changed; its finances reached a new sense of stability; and the dominant presence of the commoners ceased—and it is surely right to give him some of the credit for this transformation.

AFTER MARTYN: 1473-1509

The Senior Fellow of University College in 1473 was William Gregford, a Fellow since 1453/4 and vicar of the west Oxfordshire parish of Shipton-under-Wychwood since 1465.[33] Anyone succeeding John Martyn had a hard act to follow, and it seems that Gregford did not have an easy time. Almost at once he encountered difficulties over Arncliffe. Just before John Martyn's death, the current Earl of Northumberland had been taking an interest in the property given away by his grandfather. He wished to reward his chaplain, Thomas Holton, and had hoped to give him the living of Arncliffe, which

---

[32] In 1436/7, for example, the College hoped to receive £3 16s. 8d. from its rooms, and received £4 18s. 10d., but in 1437/8, these figures were £6 6d. and £2 4s. 4d. respectively. These difficulties were not unusual: in 1454/5, King's Hall, Cambridge, was owed £63 3s. 10¼d. by eleven commoners (Cobban 1988: 332). The building of the new Hall will also have meant the demolition of several rooms in Ludlow Hall.
[33] Gregford's career: *BRUO* ii. 817.

was now in the gift of University College. The outcome of a dispute between a small College and the greatest magnate of north-east England was unsurprising: in December 1473, the College had to agree that, in return for Holton's not claiming the parish, it would give him an annuity until he received promotion. In return the Earl graciously released the College from the need to maintain the number of its Fellows for six years. The College also agreed to say a mass once a year for the Earl and his wife. This clause no doubt stuck in the Fellows' throats, especially because Holton received an annuity of £3 6s. 8d. for over twenty years.[34]

Two relevant pieces of evidence suggest tensions in the College at this time, although their testimony is ambiguous. They are two new sets of statutes, compiled in July 1475 and April 1478, and the first ones given to the College since 1311.[35] Both drawn up by the Chancellor of Oxford, its doctors of theology, and its proctors, they imply that some tightening up was needed. The rule forbidding Fellowships to be held in conjunction with benefices appears to have caused considerable trouble: Fellows were reminded in 1475 that they must resign if they accepted a benefice worth more than 10 marks a year, and in 1478 that they could not seek a dispensation from the Visitors without first gaining the Master's permission. Other statutes also reinforced existing rules on the sale of College chattels without permission of the Master. The changing nature of education within the university and the growing presence of Bachelors among the Fellows were also reflected: Fellows were enjoined in 1475 to hold regular disputations in the Chapel, in theology for Masters, and in philosophy for Bachelors, and the 1478 statutes updated the rules of 1292 on the length of time for which Fellows could study theology, clarifying that this period started after a Master had completed his period of necessary regency. The College was also reminded in 1475 that servants must not be punished without the permission of the Master, and that commoners must not be forced to leave without reasonable cause, and the will of the Master and the majority of Fellows.

The new statutes also cover new ground: the 1475 set included the first detailed regulations for the holding of services in the College's Chapel (p. 80), but also reminded the Fellows that at least one of them who is an ordained priest must remain in residence at any time, to prevent divine service being neglected when most of the Fellows are absent. In 1478, Fellows were given procedures for commemorating the founder and benefactors in Chapel services. The state of the College's finances was also

---

[34] Documents concerning this case: UC:E4/2L/1–5; the power of the Percies: for example, Lander 1969: 185–7.

[35] UC:GB1/L1/3–4. These documents are now damaged, but their texts can be reconstructed from Thomas Walker's seventeenth-century transcriptions (UC:GB1/MS1/1).

touched on: the 1475 statutes said that each Bursar would be personally liable for any deficit in the accounts and would have to enter into a bond with the College to this effect.

The greatest innovation from either set, however, came from 1475, and concerned the appointment of a Master. Whereas the senior Fellow at a vacancy had automatically become Master, just like Gregford, the new rules declared that the Mastership would now be decided by canonical election, and that the candidate should be a Fellow and 'from the bosom and company of the College' (*de gremio ac comitiva eiusdem Collegij*).[36] More rules on College elections were added in 1478, in particular that Fellows should keep details of elections secret, and not spread them about the university, but the 1475 rule was the important one: any Fellow of the College could now stand for Master.

The statutes of 1475 and 1478 are significant documents, not just for their contents. They raise questions about the state of the College under William Gregford: why should the first major revision of the College's regulations for over a century and a half take place now? It is tempting to think that some Fellows were unhappy at the imposition of Gregford as Master solely on the grounds of his seniority,[37] and a look at the College in 1473 is suggestive. Gregford was not the only Fellow of long standing: Richard Marshall was also first recorded as a Fellow in 1453/4, but had always been listed in the accounts as Gregford's junior. It would be understandable if years of being deemed junior to Gregford, irrespective of ability, generated some resentment. Marshall ceased to appear in the lists of Fellows after 1474/5, only reappearing briefly in 1479/80–1480/1, and of the other four Fellows present in 1473/4, one, Alan Hyndmersh, last appeared in 1474/5, and another, Simon Baxter, in 1475/6.[38] One could therefore construe the intervention of 1475 as an attempt to strengthen the authority of a Master in trouble, and to prevent a recurrence of these circumstances.

Yet it may be too simple an analysis merely to make Gregford a scapegoat. Some statutes, especially those concerning worship in the Chapel, or pluralism among Fellows, could equally well be seen as a response to a College grown soft under the last years of the ageing John Martyn, when corners were cut, debts allowed to pile up, and not enough questions asked. Gregford was not the only Fellow who had held a living in conjunction with his Fellowship: both Richard Marshall and Alan Hyndmersh appear to have

---

[36] The actual words are: *per canonicam electionem proviso semper quod ille qui electus est in officium magistri olim fuerat socius et de gremio ac comitiva eiusdem Collegij.*

[37] As Carr drily expressed it, 'the advantages of seniority were discovered to be not always the best qualification for headship' (Carr, 69).

[38] *BRUO* ii. 1229 (Marshall), ii. 995 (Hyndmersh; although contrary to *BRUO* he seems to have remained a Fellow until 1474/5), and i. 133 (Baxter).

done likewise. It is typical of our evidence for this period that, although the 1475 and 1478 statutes testify to some tension within University College, the reasons for it remain unknown.

Other mementoes of Gregford's reign are more positive: on 30 April 1476, the College Chapel was dedicated (until now, only its altar had been consecrated), and accounts for the later 1470s suggest that considerable rebuilding was taking place in the College. People continued making gifts to the College: in February 1474, William Asplyon, a former Fellow who was now a priest at Syon Monastery in Middlesex, gave University College a collection of books, and in March 1482, John Crosby, a former commoner, bequeathed £40, partly to be used in saying prayers for his memory.[39]

William Gregford died in 1487 or 1488, and his death theoretically gave the Fellows their first opportunity to elect the Master of their choice. In fact they chose the Senior Fellow, John Roxborough, anyway. Another Durham man, Roxborough was a pluralist like his predecessors, holding parishes in Hampshire, Wiltshire, and Surrey.[40] Little is known of the College during the twenty years of his Mastership: there was a dispute over a house in Newcastle; land was acquired in Merton, just outside Oxford, in c.1505/6; some small benefactions came to the College; and that is all.[41]

One detail, however, suggests that all was not wholly well in Roxborough's College. Two seventeenth-century copies exist of a lost document, titled simply 'Concerning Bachelors' (*de Bachilariis*), which regulates the behaviour of Fellows of University College who are Bachelors, and have not yet incepted as Masters.[42] The preface portrays a College in disarray. Bachelor Fellows have been acting disgracefully by spending five or six years doing nothing about becoming Masters—this, when the 1292 statutes had bound Masters to oppose within seven years—and in the meantime are disobeying their seniors, not participating in their academic exercises, not wearing the gowns appropriate to their rank outside the College, and attending Chapel services either late or not at all. The Visitors were stern towards the Bachelors: they must treat the senior Fellows with respect; they must incept as Masters within three or four years; they must wear the clothing appropriate to their status, and cause no trouble within the College;[43] they must improve their attendance rate at lectures and chapel services, and speak Latin more

---

[39] Dedication of the Chapel: University College MS 178 fo. 3ᵛ and *ARUC* ii. 41; other College expenses: *ARUC* ii. 60 and 68; Asplyon's gift: UC:BE6/L1/1 and p. 79; Crosby's gift: UC:BE8/L1/1 (Crosby left similar sums to Lincoln and Queen's).

[40] *BRUO* iii. 1602.

[41] Newcastle: Oliver 1924: 165–7; Merton: *ARUC* i. xxix; small benefactions: UC:BE9/L1/1.

[42] UC:GB1/MS1/1–2.

[43] As if to leave no room for doubt, the rules say that they must not cause trouble 'inside the College, its rooms, the quadrangle, the garden, the Hall, or any other places' (*infra Coll^m, cameras, quadratum, ortum, Aulam, vel loca alia quæcumque*).

often; and a table of penalties, culminating in expulsion, was set up for infringements of these rules.

The lack of a date for this remarkable document is tantalizing. Both extant sources place it between the statutes of 1475 and 1478 and documents concerning the 1509 Mastership election, which narrows it down somewhat. Fortunately the College accounts' scrupulous care in indicating which Fellows are Bachelors or Masters makes it possible to date it more exactly. The Fellows of the 1470s and early 1480s included very few Bachelors, all of whom became Masters after a couple of years, but matters changed in 1484/5, with two new Fellows, Edward Underwode and Richard Hyndmersh. Underwode and Hyndmersh were both Bachelors when appointed, and Bachelors they remained throughout their time in the College, although Underwode stayed until 1491/2, and Hyndmersh at least until 1493/4 (the accounts for 1494/5 are lost). Then, in 1493/4, no fewer than four new Fellows appeared, all Bachelors. In 1495/6 a change took place: Hyndmersh, although at least now given the title of Master, was no longer a Fellow, but was renting a school, and, of the four young Fellows, one was called a Master and the other three, described as 'inceptors', were on the way to becoming Masters soon.

Underwode and Hyndmersh, hanging around so long without taking their MAs, are perfect candidates for these Bachelor troublemakers, and after the sudden influx of four more Bachelor Fellows in one year, all young men, it is not hard to imagine University College turning into the place described in the preamble, and the consequent need for action. The regulations on Bachelors, therefore, almost certainly date from the mid-1490s, in response to this highly unusual situation, when the Fellowship had more Bachelors than Masters, and one or two Bachelors, at least, were not prepared to play by the rules.[44]

Roxborough does not emerge well from this business—one wonders whether John Martyn would have let matters reach such a pass—but it is a salutary lesson in the extent of our knowledge of University College in the late fifteenth century. Mere chance enables us to date this document to Roxborough's time, and one cannot tell whether the events of the mid-1490s were typical of College life, or merely an isolated incident in a quiet Mastership. This episode does reveal, however, that even a College as small as University was capable of internal trouble. Just how capable was to become appallingly clear when Roxborough died in 1509.

---

[44] Underwode did at least end his days as a canon of St Pauls (*BRUO* iii. 1931), but nothing definite is known of Hyndmersh's later life (*BRUO* ii. 995 confuses him with another Hyndmersh).

5
Life in a Late Medieval College

The last chapters have been primarily narrative in their intent, and certain topics which are best tackled thematically have been put to one side. Before we embark on the story of a century which will change University College completely, we should consider some of these themes, in particular the College's appearance, its finances, and its members, their backgrounds and later activities.

First of all, however, we should ask how typical University College was at this time. It was not unusual in being small. There were two divisions of Oxbridge colleges, large foundations like Merton, New College, All Souls, and Magdalen at Oxford, and the King's Hall at Cambridge, possessed of generous endowments, dozens of Fellows and (sometimes) scholars, which permitted their Fellows to study in all the higher faculties; and smaller institutions like University College and Lincoln, whose Fellowship rarely attained double figures, and which were still largely intended for theologians. There were some idiosyncratic foundations, such as Trinity Hall, Cambridge, intended almost exclusively for lawyers, and Balliol College, whose Fellows had to resign once they had taken their MA, but most colleges fitted into one of these categories. Some new Cambridge colleges even appear to have taken a reactionary stand in renewing a bias in favour of theologians: some 97 per cent of the Fellows of Queens' College before 1500 were theologians, and St Catharine's College, founded in 1473 for a Fellowship of four, was likewise only open to theologians. On the other hand, University College was not alone in having to relax its admission requirements by electing bachelors to posts once open only to masters; Oriel was doing this after 1441.[1]

A fifteenth-century scholar of Oxford might have been rather surprised that University College—or, indeed, any of the smaller colleges—might merit a history of its own. It is well-nigh impossible to calculate how large the university was at this time, but it is clear that the campaign to get

---

[1] Henry Chichele, founder of All Souls College, asked that no less than two-fifths of its Fellows should study law (McConica in McConica 1996: 36–43). Other colleges: Jones 2005: 6 (Balliol); Leader 1988: 85–6 (Trinity Hall); Twigg 1987: 104 (Queens'); Cobban 1973 (St Catharine's); Pantin 1954: 119 (Oriel).

undergraduate scholars into academic halls had proved successful. Such people, however, did not as a whole attend colleges, unless they received scholarships there. Most commoners in colleges, especially those in University College, were mature men who already had degrees of their own. It would, indeed, have been quite possible for someone to study up to the rank of MA without needing to set foot in a college, and possibly remaining unaware of a foundation as small as University College.

THE COLLEGE BUILDINGS

By 1500 University College's first quadrangle was complete. Unfortunately, above ground nothing survives of it, and only two pictures of it are known: John Bereblock's bird's-eye view, drawn in 1566, and Anthony Wood's sketch of the south and part of the west range, drawn just before their demolition in the 1660s (Figs. 5.1–5.2). When combined, however, with Wood's detailed notes on the old quadrangle and other pieces of evidence, a partial reconstruction is possible.[2]

This quadrangle was small—barely two-thirds the size of its successor—and, as Wood observed, it 'was not uniform in its windows, which shews that the quadrangle was not built all at one time, but at several', an assessment borne out by his drawing. The High Street frontage was dominated by the Tower which housed the Master. Inside the College, to the east, was John Martyn's Hall and probably the kitchen too; straight ahead lay the south range, with the Chapel, built in the late 1390s, and the Library above the Antechapel. The west range, to the right, appears to have been entirely residential. Wood thought that the front and most of the west ranges were the oldest parts of the College, to judge from their poor condition when demolished.

As mentioned in the last chapter, the windows of the Hall contained images, coats of arms, and inscriptions commemorating former members and benefactors of the College. Such decoration was used elsewhere: Wood noted many chamber windows which bore similar images and inscriptions, such as one in the west range which depicted King Alfred kneeling before St Cuthbert, and another in a chamber near the Chapel which showed St John of Beverley, appropriated as an Old Member in the 1380s. Another room, on the front range, showed Alfred holding a model of the College. Some of this decoration probably dates from the sixteenth century, if not the early seventeenth, but other parts must come from the fifteenth, on account of the choice of names or coats of arms.

---

[2] Bereblock: Bodl. MS Bodley 13 fo. 10ᵛ; Wood: Bodl. MS Wood 276B, fo. 116ʳ, and Wood, *Colleges* 56–69. Durning 2006 provides a facsimile of Bereblock's whole manuscript, showing the drawing of University College in context, and explains his artistic conventions. On the quadrangle of University College see also Darwall-Smith 2005a: 17–23.

FIGURE 5.1 Drawing of University College by John Bereblock in 1566.

FIGURE 5.2 Drawing of the north and west ranges of the old quadrangle of University College made by Antony Wood in 1668.

Wood thought that the Chapel was built in the 1470s, presumably on the basis of its dedication in 1476, but the style of its windows, as drawn by Wood, suggests that little work had been done to it since its construction in the 1390s. He saw several memorial brasses and inscriptions inside, all dating from the sixteenth century, but there may have been earlier memorials. Although there was no great east window, Wood noted that the side windows were filled with stained glass, comprising a mixture of images of saints (St Jude, St Cuthbert, St John of Beverley), benefactors (William of Durham, Walter Skirlaw), and coats of arms of benefactors.

There is other evidence for the internal arrangements of the Chapel: the 1478 statutes refer to its having a choir, at whose entrance Fellows could stand and recite the names of their founder and benefactors, and Wood mentioned the presence of a side altar, and there may have been others, for occasions, especially in the commemoration of benefactors, when more than one mass needed to be said at once.[3] The Chapel was also a place of burial. Antony Wood was unable to name anyone buried here before 1633, but he thought that there were older bodies there.

The College's Library was situated directly above the Antechapel, which would have made for rather a poky entrance to the Chapel proper. This Library must have been a tiny room—a world away from the spacious libraries of Merton and Magdalen—which suggests that the College's collection of books was also small. It has been said that the history of University's manuscript collection 'is harder to make out than that of any other Oxford College';[4] this history becomes easier to understand if the College did not own many manuscripts in the first place.

The rest of the quadrangle appears to have been entirely residential. Surviving medieval buildings elsewhere in Oxford and Cambridge have provided some evidence for accommodation elsewhere, notably that much of it was shared. Frequently there would have been a communal bedroom, with individual studies leading off it—exactly the opposite practice to modern sets of shared rooms, where it is the bedrooms which are private. The situation in University College at this time is harder to work out: if one adds up the number of Fellows and commoners, even at their peak, and considers the possible number of rooms within the quadrangle, it is not immediately obvious that they would have needed to share rooms. That is not to say that they enjoyed complete privacy: the case of Edmund Strete, murdered by his servant in 1386, shows that commoners certainly were allowed to have their servants stay with them, and some lists of room rents sometimes give two names as occupying one room. On at least one occasion, when John

---

[3] Larger Chapels, like those at Merton or Magdalen, had several altars in their Antechapel.
[4] Hunt 1950: 13.

Chedworth and Robert Hungerford rented a room in 1437/8, the two occupants appear to have been a young commoner and his tutor, but this seems to have been very unusual, if not unique in the medieval College.[5]

Although the medieval quadrangle of University College might have had a certain quaint charm, it would have been, architecturally speaking, something of a mess: any attempt to look for the unity of quadrangles like those at All Souls is fruitless. University College could not afford William Wynford or William Orchard, the architects of New College and Magdalen, but built when it could. The best parallels for University College, the medieval quadrangles of Balliol, Oriel, and Queen's, have disappeared either totally or in great part, so that next to no trace of an interesting development in Oxford's architectural history has survived.[6]

THE MEMBERSHIP OF UNIVERSITY COLLEGE

The strong northern presence in the fourteenth-century College becomes overpowering in the fifteenth. Out of fifty-five known fifteenth-century Fellows, the geographical origins of some twenty-eight are known, and, of these, twenty came from the diocese of Durham, and six from Yorkshire. Indeed seven Fellows had previously been secular scholars at Durham College, a college intended for monks from Durham Priory which also supported eight non-monastic scholars.[7] Only one Fellow is known to have been a southerner, Gilbert Haydok from Hampshire. Almost nothing is known about these men's social status, but since Fellowships of University College were still intended for scholars who had no other funding for their theology studies, and since it was the wealthier classes—those notionally ineligible for Fellowships—whose pedigrees are best known, this is only to be expected.

As in the fourteenth century, a Fellowship at University College was an important first stage in a career, rather than a career in itself. This is borne out by the general absence of information about Fellows' careers before their election. Most fifteenth-century Fellows, therefore, were young men in their twenties or early thirties, who spent an average of only ten years in the College.[8] A few Fellows stayed for longer periods, nine of them for sixteen years or more. Some, such as John Martyn, owed the length of their stay to being elected Master, but others, such as John Elwyk, Fellow in 1420/1–1438/9, and Richard Marshall, Fellow in 1453/4–1473/4 and again in 1479/

---

[5] Chedworth and Hungerford: *ARUC* i. 449. A century later, more evidence survives for how the rooms in the quadrangle were occupied (p. 140).
[6] Darwall-Smith 2005a: 22–3.
[7] Durham College: Dobson 1992: 550–2.
[8] The average age of Fellows will have fallen once Bachelors began to be elected Fellows in the 1420s.

80–1480/1, seem to have regarded their position as a chance to remain in Oxford studying and (one presumes) teaching.[9]

Neither the regional bias nor the average length of tenure is unique to University College. At Queen's College, Oxford, for example, what had been merely recommended as a preference for candidates from Cumberland and Westmorland became an essential condition for membership, and at Queens' College, Cambridge, the average tenure of pre-1500 Fellows was six and three-quarter years, with only three Fellows remaining for more than twenty, while at All Souls the average tenure had risen to ten years by 1500.[10]

The fact that Martyn and his two successors all died in office after fairly substantial terms shows that the role of Master was changing. For such Masters as Edmund Lacy, John Castell, or Richard Burton, the Mastership was but a staging-post on the way to a higher career, but for John Martyn and John Roxborough, it was a foundation on which to construct the rest of their lives.

The College offered other possibilities for its Fellows: four Fellows became principals of halls owned by the College, and no less than fourteen rented rooms in the College's own set of schools teaching there during their stint of necessary regency. A Fellow did not have to retain his Fellowship to remain within the College: one-third of all known Fellows from 1381/2 to 1450/1 became commoners there after resigning their Fellowships. It was clearly a common enough career to be a Fellow for a few years, and then to be appointed to a benefice but obtain the appropriate licence to remain in Oxford studying, paying a curate to administer it if required. One former Fellow, Thomas Nafferton, remained in College for eighteen years after his resignation, but most stayed for a shorter time, like Thomas Pray, who became rector of a parish in Wiltshire in 1453, and resigned his Fellowship, but remained a commoner for another ten years.[11] Some Fellows returned as commoners in their old age. Robert Burton returned to his old College as a commoner in the late 1440s, as did Gilbert Haydok in the late 1470s—in each case some twenty or thirty years after their resignations. There was also the unique instance of John Appleton receiving a special Fellowship in 1438.

One aspect of the Fellowship remained unchanged from the fourteenth century, namely the wastage rate: of the 22 Fellows known to have been elected in the first half of the century, 10 took a theology degree (3 Doctors

---

[9] Only one Fellow from the first half of the century is known to have died in College, but no fewer than seven from the second half did so.

[10] Queen's: Hodgkin 1949: 49; Queens': Twigg 1987: 78; All Souls: J. McConica in McConica 1996: 39.

[11] *BRUO* ii. 1336 (Nafferton) and iii. 1514–15 (Pray). Nafferton was at various times rector of three Oxford city parishes, and so had every incentive to remain at University College.

and 7 Bachelors)—a decent proportion—but the 33 Fellows known from the second half of the century yield up only 5 (4 Doctors and one Bachelor). Even John Martyn remained a mere Bachelor of Theology to the end of his days. University College was not unusual: only eight out of the 162 MA Fellows of fifteenth-century All Souls became a BD or DD. Moreover the university charged high fees for bestowing a Doctorate of Theology, so that people only chose to go through the ceremony if it might benefit them. By the late sixteenth century, indeed, it had become rather unusual to become a DD if one was not head of a college or a Canon of Christ Church.[12]

The careers of University College's later medieval Fellows were hardly stellar: no other Fellow achieved the distinction of Edmund Lacy, Bishop of Exeter, and companion of Henry V at Agincourt. Many of them, nevertheless, enjoyed successful 'middle-ranking' ones. We have already encountered Robert Burton as one such example; John Castell, his predecessor as Master, became precentor of York Minster, where he was buried in 1457.

Over half the Fellows of fifteenth-century University College, however, ended their days as parish clergy. Some do seem to have led quiet lives in their parish, such as John Fayt, Bursar in 1399–1401, who moved to Simonburn, Northumberland, in 1406, and then Aycliffe, County Durham, in 1425, where in 1435 he petitioned his Bishop for a licence of non-residence because he was old and ill. Seen in context, Fayt was perhaps something of a failure: other Fellows were unashamed pluralists. Henry Strother, Fellow in the 1450s, held three livings simultaneously in the 1470s, in Cambridgeshire and Suffolk, and Robert Middelham, Fellow a decade later, was for over thirty years, until his death in 1511, simultaneously rector of Loughton, Essex, Canon and Prebendary of the chapel of St Mary and Holy Angels in York, and vicar of All Saints, Northampton, where he asked to be buried.[13]

These careers parallel that of the founder of the College. The Fellows of the fifteenth century presumed that William had been Archdeacon of Durham, but the real William of Durham had ended up in a country parish, albeit a wealthy one. In short, although the late medieval College produced no Fellows of national importance, by helping to create a learned parish clergy it was following its founder's example. This was not so unusual among Colleges with a strong theological bias: many Fellows of New College and Lincoln, for example, also became parish priests. That being said, such Colleges were very different from the rest of the university: one survey of late medieval Oxonians' careers concluded that 'only a small proportion of the parish clergy was trained in a university and most university men did not obtain a parish cure'.[14]

[12] McConica in McConica 1996: 38–41.
[13] *BRUO* ii. 673 (Fayt); iii. 1808 (Strother); ii. 1273 (Middelham). Admittedly some positions, like prebends (p. 4), did not require the cure of souls.
[14] Careers of New College and Lincoln men: R. L. Storey in Buxton and Williams 1979: 21–2, and Green 1979: 45–9; careers of other Oxonians: Evans 1992: 538.

University College, however, was very unusual among Oxbridge colleges in the number of its commoners. The College accounts for 1381/2–1496/7 identify almost 220 commoners as staying at University College during this time. The only other college in either university with comparable figures is King's Hall, Cambridge, which during a similar period had about 120 commoners and 100 semi-commoners; and yet King's Hall was one of the largest colleges in either university, with a Fellowship of over thirty. The character of University College, especially in the early fifteenth century, must therefore have been rather different from other small colleges, with such a large population of mature non-Fellows.[15]

The 1292 statutes had created a mechanism for accepting commoners, ordering the Fellows to hold elections once a year, before Pentecost, and enquire about applicants' behaviour, and requiring them to obey the rules of the house, not to fall into debt, and not to harm the College. No evidence survives to show whether these rules were carried out, but it seems likely. In February 1510, the Fellows voted that, in order to avoid disturbance and to prevent disputes, one commoner (and former Fellow), John Barnaby, should no longer have a room in the College. This suggests that they had previously voted to accept him as a commoner.[16]

Commoners did not tend to stay very long, remaining for three years on average throughout this period: indeed seventy-four commoners spent only one year there. Apart from former Fellows of the College, many of them were mature men, vicars or rectors, taking time away from their parishes to study—almost a kind of sabbatical leave. Some Fellows from other colleges also stayed here, and there were a few monks, such as Henry Crumpe, and some cathedral clergy, including poor Edward Strete. Commoners did not have to come from the north-east: the geographical origins of about a quarter of them are known, and a significant proportion of them come from the midlands and the south. There were also two Irishmen and one Norman. They did not have to study theology, either: barely a tenth of them are known to have obtained higher degrees, but over half of these were in civil or common law, and one commoner, Thomas Southwell, became a Bachelor in Medicine.[17]

A few commoners were not of postgraduate age. Three stand out in particular, Robert Hungerford, later Lord Hungerford and Molyns, John Tiptoft, later Earl of Worcester, and Robert Fleming, nephew of Bishop

---

[15] Analysis of commoners: Cobban 1969: 44–5 and 259–62, Cobban 1992: 620–1, and Cobban 1999: 97–106. Interestingly, King's Hall, like University College, apparently curtailed its intake of commoners in the second half of the century.

[16] UC:GB3/A1/1 p. 2. Barnaby's case is discussed in the next chapter.

[17] The Norman was Peter Provost from Coutances, a commoner in the late 1430s (*BRUO* iii. 1523). The lack of commoners taking degrees may owe something to the fact that many of them came to Oxford for a year or two's study, before returning to their parishes.

Richard Fleming, all admitted by Thomas Benwell.[18] All three arrived at University College as mere boys, barely 13 years old, Hungerford and Tiptoft sharing their rooms with tutors. Hungerford stayed for only three terms in 1437/8, but Tiptoft remained three years from 1440, and Robert Fleming stayed longer, from 1430/1 to 1443/4. Fleming, as the nephew of a Bishop, might be expected to follow his uncle in a university career. Hungerford and Tiptoft, however, were heirs to peerages, noblemen who later led active political careers (so active indeed that both were executed during the Wars of the Roses), and in theory had no need of the fairly vocational education offered by late medieval Oxford. By the end of the sixteenth century, a period at Oxford had become a far more regular part of a young nobleman's education, but even in the fifteenth century well-born young commoners were not so unusual—some members of the Paston family attended Cambridge, for example, and other colleges, such as Balliol and Queen's, also occasionally accepted them.[19]

One had to have means to rent a room in a college. In the fifteenth century rooms at University College cost between 6s. 8d. and over £1 a year, which was fairly typical for a college (Robert Fleming, Hungerford, and Tiptoft all rented rooms at the upper end of the scale). On the other hand, the only known accounts for a hall, dating from 1424, show scholars being charged only about 6d. a year for accommodation. However, a commoner in University College would have a room for himself and his tutor or servant, whereas a room in a hall was divided between four scholars. In addition to the better accommodation on offer, a college's primarily adult environment would in theory afford fewer opportunities to associate with unsuitable company.[20] Hungerford, Tiptoft, and Fleming, however, remain unusual figures at University College. Indeed, apart from these three and the mysterious 'portionists', the College remained as it had been for over a century, a place for the mature scholar. It was, however, starting to appear rather unusual in this. As will become clear in the next chapter, other colleges by the end of the fifteenth century were increasingly assuming some of the characteristics of academic halls in offering cheaper accommodation to undergraduate commoners.

The medieval commoners of University College were often rather more interesting figures than its Fellows. Some are interesting for sensational reasons, such as Thomas Southwell, a commoner in 1418/19 and 1421/2–1422/3, who later helped found the College of Physicians, but was condemned to death in

---

[18] *BRUO* ii. 985 (Hungerford); i. 699–700 (Fleming); iii. 1877–9 (Tiptoft), and on the latter also Mitchell 1938: 13–27. *BRUO*'s claim that Fleming returned to University College in the 1460s is not supported by the relevant sections of *ARUC*.

[19] Noble commoners in general: Cobban 1988: 313–18 and 329–30 and Cobban 1999: 108–12; at other colleges: Jones 2005: 34–5 and Hodgkin 1949: 42–7; Pastons at Cambridge: Cobban 1999: 20–1.

[20] Cobban 1999: 102–3 (rents in colleges) and 38–9 (rents in a hall). University College's accounts talk only of rooms being rented, so food and fuel would have been extra.

1441 for committing necromancy with the Duchess of Suffolk, and found mysteriously dead in his cell on the morning of his execution. Hungerford and Tiptoft, on the other hand, bring the glamour of nobility, high politics, and tragic ends, with Tiptoft adding a certain voyeuristic horror by the atrocities committed by him during the Wars of the Roses, which included impaling his enemies.[21]

Three commoners (John Chedworth, Robert Fitzhugh, and Richard Fleming) became bishops in the fifteenth century, and Chedworth and Fitzhugh also had successful careers in Cambridge: Chedworth was Provost of King's College in 1446–52, while Fitzhugh was Warden of King's Hall in 1424–31 and Chancellor of Cambridge in 1423–8. Another commoner and Warden of King's Hall, this time in the 1480s, was Christopher Urswick, who undertook diplomatic missions for Henry VII and became one of his executors.[22]

It is tempting to claim such eminent men as great Old Members; but this begs the question whether someone who was not a Fellow should be regarded as a member of a college at all. Commoners were evidently not bound by the same rules concerning residence—no questions were asked about the month-long disappearance of Edmund Strete in 1386, when his body was still in his room. Some commoners, especially in the first half of the century, stayed in more than one college, such as Richard Fleming at Queen's and Robert Fitzhugh at Exeter. On the other hand, under the 1292 statutes, commoners were to live 'according to the customs of the Fellows' during their stay, so would have been expected to attend Chapel and dine in Hall with them.

The pattern of benefactions is similarly mixed: Robert Fleming's magnificent collection of books was bequeathed to his uncle's foundation of Lincoln College—not one came to the College where he had lived for so long—whereas other commoners, John Chedworth and John Crosby, proved greater friends.[23] It seems that the strength of a commoner's feelings towards the College was a personal matter: the later concept of a general 'college spirit' is not readily applicable to University College in the Middle Ages.

Last among the inhabitants of University College we should consider its servants. There were usually no more than four of these in the Middle Ages, a butler, a barber, a cook, and a laundress. Very few of them were named, so that we do not know how long they tended to work for the College. About half a dozen servants certainly seem to have rented College properties, such as Matilda Hawsten, employed as laundress in the later 1430s, who occupied 83 High Street for a term in 1439/40.[24]

[21] *BRUO* iii. 1734–5 (Southwell); Mitchell 1938: 126–35 (Tiptoft).
[22] Chedworth: *ODNB* entry; *BRUO* ii. 689–90 (Fitzhugh); *BRUO* iii. 1935–6 (Urswick).
[23] Robert Fleming's books: Green 1979: 34–6 (Fleming's only gift to University College appears to have been a debt of 4*s*. for room rent, recorded as unpaid until 1472).
[24] *ARUC* ii. 568.

The position of laundresses is interesting. Other colleges, who seem to have been rather frightened of employing women, restricted their access, and some, such as New College and Magdalen, had strict rules that they should only employ laundresses of such an age and appearance that no suspicion might fall on them. At Magdalen, indeed, laundresses were not even listed among the College's servants.[25] University College, with its less detailed statutes, had no such rules, but one may suppose that a similar approach was employed.

The fullest information about University College's medieval servants concerns their salaries. These show once again how poor it was: for example, while the laundress at King's Hall, Cambridge, was receiving 26s. 8d. a year in 1475/6, and her counterpart at New College no less than 40s., the laundress of University College earned just 8s. a year in the 1490s. Even the butler, who always earned the largest salary in the College (26s. 8d. in the later fifteenth century), must have looked with some envy at the 40s. a year received by his colleagues at New College and Merton.[26]

THE LIFE OF THE COLLEGE

Analysing the origins and careers of the Fellows and commoners of University College leaves them in a vacuum: it reveals nothing of their daily lives. It also runs the risk of compartmentalizing the College's members too greatly. For example, Fellows would have spent time attending lectures, participating in disputations, and reading books, all connected with the study of theology; but then so would an ex-Fellow of the College, staying on as a commoner, and it is reasonable to assume that the parish priest, on his 'study leave', would have done the same—that was, after all, the theoretical reason for their stay. Such men would have had much in common in their daily lives, and had frequent opportunities to exploit this within the College. And yet no evidence for this survives.

For all that theology remained the only course of study open to a Fellow, and its prestige in theory remained high, even sympathetic observers agree that it did not prosper in the fifteenth century.[27] There are signs that the traditional scholastic method was starting to lose favour. The heroic visions of the twelfth and thirteenth centuries which set such store by erudition and the careful evaluation of one source against another, to say nothing of the excitement of minute logical argument, were in danger of evaporating in the arid sands of pedantry—or at least, that was how some might caricature them. It is tempting to wonder to what extent this was a reaction to the trouble caused by the theologians' dangerous flirtation less with outright

---

[25] Cobban 1999: 137–8; on Magdalen, Darwall-Smith 2000*b*: 86.
[26] Other colleges: Cobban 1969: 235–6. University College's servants probably earned extra from its commoners, and the laundress could have worked for more than one institution.
[27] See further Catto 1992*b*.

heresy *per se* than with 'fashionable Wycliffist radical chic',[28] which in itself was sufficiently disturbing to the authorities. Whatever the reason, fifteenth-century theology has an atmosphere of cautious consolidation, and Oxford produced no major thinkers in the field.

Nevertheless this was not a period of complete ossification: theologians were expected to preach extensively (as would former Fellows now living in parishes), and there was an increasing interest in personal devotion and contemplation. Certain religious houses, such as the London Charterhouse, and the convent of Brigittine nuns at Syon, were particularly respected as centres of such spiritual activity, and one Fellow of University College, William Asplyon, became a priest at Syon in the decade before his death in 1485. Asplyon was a benefactor to the College Library, and among his gifts pride of place is given to 'one beautiful Bible' (*unam pulchram Bibliam*). The donation included certain important authors of medieval philosophy and theology, such as commentaries by Nicholas de Lyra and St Augustine, as well as Boethius' *Consolation of Philosophy* and books by Duns Scotus. Asplyon clearly felt that such books would be relevant to his old College.[29]

Another aspect of late medieval theology was an increasing interest in patristics—the study of the earliest Christian writers. In this respect one remarkable document is the commonplace book of John Castell, which found its way to the manuscript collection of University College.[30] Among notes on such miscellaneous topics as monks and friars (fo. 18^v), angels (fo. 20^v), and indulgences (fo. 44^v), Castell also made excerpts from authors who interested him, both scholastic authorities like Peter Lombard and St Thomas Aquinas, and older figures, like St Augustine, Bede, and Cassiodorus.

On the other hand, the few works whose authorship can be definitely assigned to any Fellows of the fifteenth century are not very theological. Thomas Pray, Fellow in 1444/5–1453, and commoner for a decade after, collaborated with Thomas Killingworth of Merton, one of the best astronomers then working in Oxford, while Thomas Thurlby, Fellow and then commoner from 1463/4 to 1473/4, wrote a treatise on arithmetic.[31]

A greater departure from traditional study can be seen in Robert Fleming and John Tiptoft, two of those three young commoners from the 1430s and 1440s. Both men became luminaries of the early humanist movement, travelling extensively, and assembling large libraries of classical texts and of works reflecting the latest scholarship, Fleming even learning Greek. Yet no contemporary Fellow of University College seems to have matched Fleming or Tiptoft in the modernity, so to speak, of their scholarship. For

---

[28] Catto, in McConica 1996: 7. The fact that All Souls, founded by an Archbishop of Canterbury, was intended to support both lawyers and theologians, is significant.
[29] Asplyon's career: *BRUO* ii. 61–2; his books: Hunt 1950: 30–1.
[30] This manuscript (University College MS 76) is discussed in Catto 1992c: 771–2.
[31] North 1992: 124–7 and 138–9.

all that University College was clearly not completely devoid of intellectual vitality, it is unfortunately not the kind of vitality which later ages would find to their liking.[32]

If the content of study was not changing greatly, the method of its transmission certainly was. The traditional system of centralized university teaching was breaking down, especially once people were allowed to evade their term of necessary regency in return for a fee. Academic halls filled the void by themselves providing lectures to their students, and Magdalen College went further still in the 1480s by endowing three 'praelectorships' or lectureships whose lectures were open to all members of the university. The faculty of arts was most affected by this revolution, but the Fellows of University College were starting to look to their own resources for their education. The 1475 statutes specified that Bachelors and Masters of Arts alike should hold disputations once a fortnight in the Chapel, and once a week if four or more Fellows were in residence.[33]

The holding of disputations of course formed only part of the life of the College Chapel. Fortunately there survives a fragment of a missal which was used there before the Reformation (Plate 1).[34] Originally this missal would have contained prayers for all services and all seasons of the year, but only the calendar listing saints' days and feasts is preserved. Richly decorated, the feasts are written in different coloured inks according to their status, and some extra occasions have been added, namely the date of the dedication of the Chapel (30 April 1476) and the dates of the deaths of Walter Skirlaw and Henry Percy, Earl of Northumberland. The missal was therefore probably bought in the early fifteenth century almost as an 'off-the-peg' job, and updated to take account of special College feasts.

More evidence for the liturgical life of the Chapel is to be found in the 1475 statutes. In particular, they remind us how central a part the daily round of divine worship played in the College as a whole. Apart from daily prayers and the daily celebration of mass, every resident Fellow had to attend services for first and second vespers, compline, matins, and high mass on all feast days. For major festivals, provided that enough Fellows were present, they were expected to hold sung services, which, in the absence of any choir, would have probably just meant the use of plainchant only—there is no evidence that the medieval Chapel had an organ. It is reasonable to suppose that regular attendance was also expected of the commoners.

Fellows and commoners alike played their full part in the life of the university as a whole. Both groups provided proctors and custodians of the university's loan chests, and one commoner, William Dowson, was Chancellor's

---

[32] Weiss 1957: 97–105 (on Fleming) and 112–22 (on Tiptoft). Green 1979: 34–6 suspects that the humanist texts given by Fleming to Lincoln were little used by its Fellows.

[33] Teaching at non-university level: Cobban 1988: 198–204 and Cobban 1999: 55–6 and 179–80.

[34] Bodl. MS Univ. 178 (discussed in Wordsworth 1904: 38–40). My thanks to Dr Beth Lee-de Amici for discussing this fragment with me.

Commissary in 1444–9, and heard some cases in the College itself.³⁵ The university itself also played a role as Visitor of University College, although it generally guided the College with a fairly light hand: the College was allowed to elect its own Fellows and (after 1475) its Master, and appoint its own commoners. This is quite a difference even from Merton College, where in electing a Warden the Fellows had to send a short list of candidates in order of preference to their Visitor, the Archbishop of Canterbury, for him to make the final choice.³⁶ The sixteenth century would see University College's autonomy disappear, as Chancellors discovered how to exploit their powers.

Fellows did not spend all their time in Oxford. The College's accounts from 1381/2 to 1413/14 record in detail the payment of commons, or allowances, to Fellows, noting how many were in residence every week. These show that all Fellows were usually present from February to April, and from October to December. Most were there in January, May, and June; but almost none were in the summer, between July and September. In 1407, for example, there were an average of six Fellows resident in November and December, but just one for the whole of August and most of September. Although later accounts do not record this information, the order in the 1475 statutes that at least one ordained priest should remain in College at all times suggests a similar summer exodus. Some absences were clearly due to the demands of College business, such as visiting its estates, and others would be due to Masters (and sometimes Fellows) visiting the parishes where they were incumbent, but the fact that so many Fellows were away at once suggests that some took the opportunity to visit families and others.

Any account of the life of the medieval members of University College would be incomplete without looking at its disagreeable aspects. The College's history to 1500 encompassed litigation, forgery, riot, accusations of indecency, and even murder. There were times when members of the College were actively at variance with each other, as with the troublesome Bachelors of the 1490s. It was a place of chance violence, in which John Crosby, commoner and future benefactor, had to be absolved from excommunication for wounding a glover who had failed to make him a pair of gloves in the required time, and Thomas Eslake, commoner in 1448/9–1450/1, was found guilty of stabbing offences in 1458 and 1459. The only extenuating factor is that all such events were typical of medieval Oxford.³⁷

ESTATES AND FINANCES

Almost every medieval college depended largely on income collected from its estates, and University College was no exception. By 1500 it owned property

---

³⁵ Proctors: Cobban 1992: 623–4; Fellows as custodians of chests: Pantin and Mitchell 1972: index; Dowson: *BRUO* i. 590–1; his hearing cases in College: Salter 1932: i. 116.
³⁶ Merton and its Wardens: Martin and Highfield 1997: 19.
³⁷ Green 1979: 40 (Crosby); *BRUO* ii. 647 (Eslake).

in Oxford and Oxfordshire itself, and also in Yorkshire, Essex, and Northumberland (Appendix V). The management of these properties and the income which they yielded were crucial to its survival, and so an examination of the College's finances should begin with a survey of its properties.[38]

University College had a problem with its properties: even after the gift of Marks Hall in 1403, almost two-thirds of its rental came from estates in Oxford. Only in the 1450s, with the arrival of money from Arncliffe, did the proportions become roughly half-and-half.[39] This would not have been a problem had Oxford been a prosperous city, but it was not: the late fourteenth and fifteenth centuries saw a steep decline in its wealth, as many houses fell vacant or were demolished, and rents became harder to collect. This was advantageous for a college looking to purchase land cheaply on which to build, like New College or All Souls, but one aiming to be a landlord within Oxford faced problems.[40]

University College suffered worst in the 1420s and 1430s; most accounts from these decades include a section for Oxford properties 'in the hand of the College' (*in manu Collegij*)—in other words properties standing empty because there was no tenant there. In some years, the value of empty properties amounted to almost one-fifth of the College's total rent roll. The westernmost of the three houses in the parish of All Saints shows how dangerous a combination of defaulting tenants and a slack property market could be. This was one of the College's most expensive properties, regularly rented out at over £3 a year, equivalent to an entire year's income from Paull in Holderness. From 1430/1 to 1435/6 the tenant of this property was a certain Isabel Colet. Unfortunately Isabel fell behind with her rent payments, and by 1435/6 she owed the College over £4. She was taken to court, and judgement was awarded in the College's favour. Unfortunately the verdict achieved little: Isabel and her executors continued to owe the College money well into the 1450s, while the house itself appears to have remained 'in the hand of the College' from 1436/7 until 1443/4, and the College had to spend £23 18s. 7½d. over two years making the house ready for its new tenant, John Weskew to move in.[41]

The College also owned several halls within Oxford. Other colleges owned halls too, but used them rather as Queen's College used St Edmund Hall, whose Principal was a Fellow of Queen's and ran the hall almost as a private speculation. Although some of its Fellows were occasionally Principals of its halls, University College seems mostly to have regarded its halls

---

[38] Evans and Faith 1992 provide an overview of medieval colleges' finances.
[39] *HUO* ii. Map 4, a guide to college properties outside Oxford in 1500, shows that only Exeter owned fewer properties outside Oxford than University College.
[40] The decline of medieval Oxford, see Cooper and Crossley 1979: 15–19, 28–35, and 40–3; clearing a site for All Souls College: Colvin and Simmons 1989: 2–9.
[41] *ARUC* i. 435 (court case), and 505 and 515 (repair bills).

solely as investments, and was buying them until the early fifteenth century.[42] In one instance it even appears to have created a hall. In 1360 the College bought an unnamed property on the east side of Turl Street, next door to Hampton Hall (which it already owned), and rented it out as a private house. In 1444/5 the house, still unnamed, was listed among the College's halls, rather than its houses, and by 1455/6 it had received a name, Sekyll Hall.

By the middle of the century, however, University's interest in halls was on the wane. While half its rental in 1381/2 derived from its halls, that proportion was just over one-fifth by the late 1440s. This was not merely because properties had been acquired: the College's halls were gradually disappearing. Some were incorporated into the College's central site (Ludlow Hall), others re-let as private houses (Stanton Hall and Drawda Hall); and others sold to other colleges. This was the fate of Maiden Hall (sold to New College in 1389), Edward Hall (sold to Oriel College in 1486), and three halls (Hampton Hall, Sekyll Hall, and Olifaunt Hall, now a garden) sold to Lincoln in 1463.[43]

University sold these last properties for an annual quit-rent. In the case of the Lincoln properties, the rental from Hampton Hall and Sekyll Hall alone amounted to 70s. in 1461/2, but the quit-rent agreed with Lincoln was only 46s. 8d. This might seem a very poor deal, until a closer look at the accounts for 1461/2 shows that the College was owed about 5s. in unpaid rent from these properties. Lincoln College would prove much more punctual in paying, and the Fellows of the 1460s evidently preferred a regular, if smaller, payment to wild fluctuations.

The disappearance of these halls marked not so much a decline in the academic hall, as a change in its nature, as exemplified by Brasenose Hall, Little University Hall in Schools Street, St Thomas Hall and Sheld Hall, which were the only halls owned by University College by the 1480s. Sheld Hall (now a garden) and St Thomas Hall had been leased to the same tenant as Brasenose Hall since 1434/5, as had Little University Hall since 1452/3 (except for 1466/7). After 1481/2 only Brasenose Hall was named in the accounts, so that all four properties had effectively become one large hall. When these properties were leased as a single entity to the newly founded Brasenose College for 92 years in 1508, it was as if what had been *de facto* for several decades was at last *de jure* as well.[44]

---

[42] Queen's College and St Edmund Hall: Hodgkin 1949: 56; University College and its halls: Cobban 1988: 156–7 (where he coins the term 'aularian imperialism' to describe University College's appetite for acquiring halls).

[43] See further *ARUC* i. xx–xxiv and ii. 559–68. In addition to New College, Oriel, and Lincoln, the central sites of Queen's, Brasenose, Somerville, and St Hugh's also incorporate land bought from University College—a record possibly unique in Oxford or Cambridge.

[44] Lease of 1508: UC:E/A2/D/6; the growth of Brasenose Hall: Catto 2004: 216–18. All these old halls were swiftly replaced by the front quadrangle of Brasenose College after 1509 (Madan 1909 and Allfrey 1909). Significantly the first Principal of Brasenose College, Matthew Smyth, had also been the last Principal of Brasenose Hall.

University College enjoyed mixed fortunes with its estates outside Oxford. Some yielded incomes far beyond anything in the city, but their remoteness made for administrative troubles. The estate at Paull unfortunately proved a disappointment. A property thought to be worth £10 a year in the 1320s, and which had enabled the Fellowship to expand to seven in 1340, was yielding just over £4 in the 1380s and just over £3 for much of the fifteenth century. The low-lying Humber coast proved all too vulnerable to the sea, and much land was permanently lost in the fourteenth century, some of which, one fears, belonged to University College. The College assisted in the melancholy task of keeping the sea back—the accounts for 1448/9 mention a payment of £3 for making sea dikes (*pro factura de ly see dykes*).[45]

Marks Hall, however, proved a happier acquisition. Some initial expenditure proved necessary, as when £6 13s. 4d. was spent on sheep in 1410/11, but the College came to receive a more regular income from Essex than from its properties in Oxford. Rather than manage this manor directly, the College chose to farm it out to tenants, in return for a fixed rent. The comparative closeness of Essex meant that leases often required tenants to deliver their rent money directly to London, where a Fellow would collect it and bring it to Oxford.[46]

Arncliffe (Plate 2) lies in Littondale in North Yorkshire, some 30 miles west of Ripon. The setting is idyllic but remote, and the parish was large, comprising several villages in two dales separated by a steep hill. One village in the second dale, Hubberholme, had its own chapel, and incumbents always faced the dilemma of either paying for a curate there, or attempting to serve both places themselves. As with Marks Hall, the College farmed out the tithes, usually to a syndicate which normally included the vicar of Arncliffe. At this stage the College were more interested in Arncliffe's cash potential than its usefulness as a piece of patronage. As part of the deal to appropriate the rectory, it had agreed to pay a vicar a stipend of just 20 marks (£13 6s. 8d.), which was evidently not a particularly attractive income: no Fellow of University College became vicar of Arncliffe until 1506.[47]

The last of the College's non-Oxfordshire properties, at Newcastle-upon-Tyne, proved an unhappy investment, and not just on account of the annuity to Alice Bellasis mentioned above: even after her death the estate rarely yielded its expected income of £6 14s. 2d., as the College had trouble collecting its rents—frequently receiving less than the full amount, and

---

[45] Sea damage: Smith 2000: 37–8 (William Smith (Smith, 169) himself suspected that much of the Paull land was lost in this way); sea dikes: *ARUC* i. 561.

[46] Sheep: *ARUC* i. 205: fifteenth-century leases for Marks Hall: UC:E3/D2/1–10; Fellows' expenses for collecting rents from the tenant in London: (e.g.) *ARUC* i. 205 and 238; the wider context: Evans and Faith 1992: 670–6.

[47] Arncliffe in general: Darwall-Smith 2006; extant fifteenth-century leases: UC:E4/3D/1–10. The inclusion of the vicar among the tenants of the rectory seems to have been common (thus Evans and Faith 1992: 675–6).

sometimes nothing at all—and by the 1480s, the rental from these properties was never more than about £3 13s. It was not just a problem of difficult tenants: late medieval Newcastle, like Oxford, was evidently not as prosperous as it had once been, and its population was in decline.[48]

Efficient collection of these rents would seem crucial to the stability of University College's finances, but, to judge from its accounts, it seems to have failed in this regularly.[49] Until 1485/6, the College's accounts recorded not just the expected rent from its properties, but also the respective sums owed by its tenants at the start and finish of the year (called 'arrears' and 'allowances' respectively). Examination of the pre-1485/6 accounts quickly shows how large the arrears and allowances were allowed to grow. In 1415/6, for example, at a time when the College's rental was £59 19s. 4d., its allowances had climbed to £143 6s. 10¼d., and in 1468/9 the equivalent figures were £84 19s. 6d. and £148 4s. 3d. Fortunately, it is possible to reconstruct what the College actually received in any given year by subtracting the allowances from the sum of arrears and the rental, and the results are given in Graph 5.1.[50]

This shows the violent oscillations in the College's income during this period, sometimes receiving considerably less than its rental, sometimes considerably more. Very occasionally, as at the height of the Wars of the Roses in 1460/1, this was due to outside circumstances; often these fluctuations owe more to the difficulty of travelling to distant estates. There was little point in visiting Paull every year, for example, and indeed the Bursars did not do so: in 1424/5–1440/1, a period when journeys on College business are documented very thoroughly, someone seems to have travelled to Marks Hall in Essex almost every year, whereas only nine visits to Paull are recorded. Nevertheless, unpaid rents were a problem. Every so often, a Bursar prepared a list of arrears which he seems to have despaired of recovering, and omitted them from the actual accounts. There were, furthermore, problems with collecting rents even within Oxford itself, as seen with Isabel Colet.[51]

It is therefore to the credit of the College's Bursars that they generally kept its accounts under control for most of the fifteenth century. Sometimes there were lucky breaks, as when Edmund Lacy was persuaded to make a donation in 1443/4.[52] There were certainly difficult times, such as in the early 1420s,

---

[48] Oliver 1924: 134–68 calendars many of the College's deeds on these properties. Butcher 1978 provides a detailed analysis of the College's management of them, and considers the economic decline of Newcastle.

[49] *ARUC* i. xxxvi–xli provides an analysis of the College's early accounting methods.

[50] The main reason for such a complex system was that Bursars were personally liable for deficits in the accounts, and had to explain every defaulter to protect themselves.

[51] Two arrears lists are preserved for 1416/17 and 1470/1 (see *ARUC* i. xxxix–xl). An instance of a defaulting College tenant, who actually ran away to avoid paying his rent, is in Salter 1920: 224–5.

[52] Evans and Faith 1992: 701 note that other colleges called on their friends to make cash gifts in difficult times.

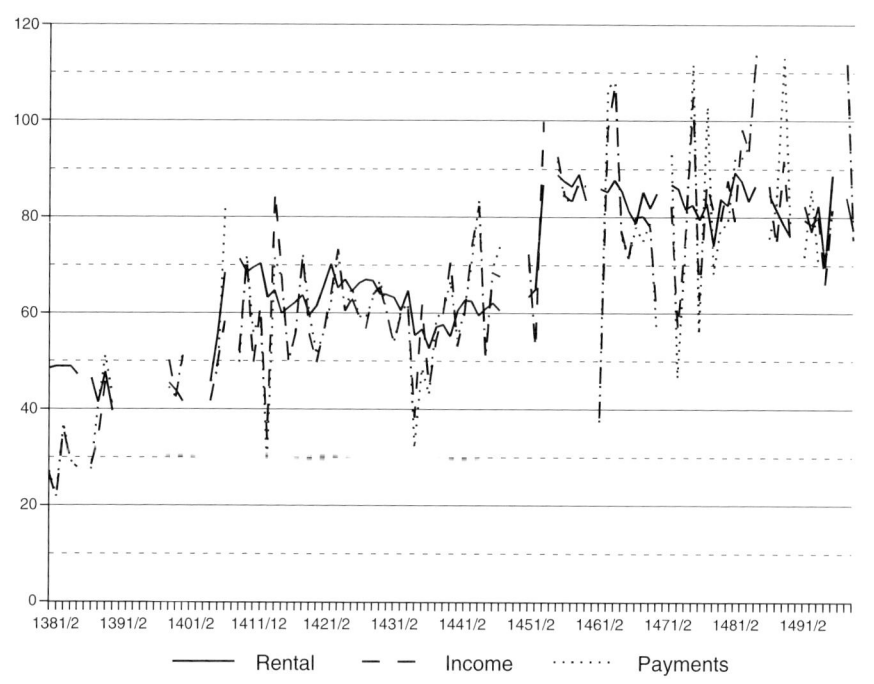

GRAPH 5.1 Income and Expenditure of University College 1381/2–1496/7. 'Rental' is the rental in any one given year (i.e. the income which University College expected to receive); 'Income' is University's real income (calculated as by subtracting allowances from the sum of arrears and rentals); 'Payments' is self-explanatory. Gaps are caused by missing rolls.

and one can never overestimate the extent to which individual Bursars might rearrange expenditure to go into a different accounting year if necessary, but for most of this period, University College managed to keep its expenditure at least within reasonable distance of its income. Furthermore, the fifteenth century was generally good to the College, for its rental effectively doubled to about £80 at a time when prices and wages were generally stable. This rental was typical for a small college: Lincoln, for example, had a slightly smaller rental in 1455, and almost all the Cambridge colleges had rentals under £100. On the other hand, Magdalen College in 1490/1 had an income almost ten times that of University College—although of course Magdalen had to support forty Fellows, thirty Scholars, a men and boys' choir, four chaplains, and ten servants, whereas University College only had seven Fellows. University College was not alone in its problems with arrears and fluctuations in net income. All Souls' income also varied greatly from year to year, and in 1425 Merton was having trouble maintaining a full complement of forty-four Fellows because of reductions in its income.[53]

THE LATE MEDIEVAL COLLEGE

Small as it was, by 1509 University College had become a well-established institution in the university of Oxford, and not atypical of the kind of college which had become part of the world of the medieval English university. Before leaving that world behind, however, we ought once again to look beyond England. Although, as R. C. Schwinges has observed, by now 'the situation over much of Europe was dominated by the colleges, above all in England and France', yet the English college was becoming rather an unusual institution. In Paris, for example, although there were by now many more colleges there than at either Oxford or Cambridge, and although there were some similarities (such as that several Parisian colleges were open only to members from particular regions or countries), yet, apart from the Sorbonne, magnificent and anomalous in its size and influence, the Parisian colleges had never acquired the autonomy of those in England, many of them being supervised by outside authorities, and being institutions intended mainly for students reading for their first degrees. Many were poorer even than University College: some, accepting that they were too poor to fund in-house teaching, arranged to send their students to other wealthier foundations. Newer universities had colleges too, such as St Andrews in Scotland, but they again were slightly different: for example, St Salvator's College, founded there in 1451, was intended not just to support students in the Faculty of Arts, but also Masters and Bachelors who seem to have been teaching within the university as a whole, with no hint of their having to move on once they had completed any degree, to the extent that by the end of the century they were close to becoming a permanent professorate. These glimpses from beyond serve to remind us that the path followed by University College and Oxford since 1249 was not absolutely pre-ordained.[54]

Some compromises had been made at University College, such as allowing Bachelors of Arts to become Fellows, or admitting so many commoners, but in general the Fellows had stayed remarkably true to William's vision of an institution intended to support theology students, even to the extent of staying aloof from other degree courses and admitting only a handful of undergraduate scholars. And, for all that University remained one of the

---

[53] Green 1979: 29 (Lincoln); Evans in McConica 1996: 50 and 59–61 (All Souls); Martin and Highfield 1997: 121 (Merton); incomes in 1490/1: MCA *Liber Computi* for 1490/1, and *ARUC* ii. 140–4; prices and wages: Phelps Brown and Hopkins 1956.

[54] The European scene: Schwinges 1992: 214, Rashdall 1936: i. 511–39, Verger 1992: 61, and Tuilier 1994: i. 146–51 (Paris) and Cant 1970: 23–41 and Rashdall 1936: ii. 308–10 (St Andrews). Parisian colleges had also—unlike Oxbridge ones—suffered badly during the Hundred Years War (Tuilier 1994: i. 249–52).

poorest colleges in England, it was successful: it retained a special link with the north-east; its former Fellows were serving parishes up and down England; its current Fellows were playing a full part in university life; it remained able to attract new benefactions; above all, it had survived and even prospered, with the original Fellowship now almost doubled. It would be during the next century that University College would change into something very different.

6

Change from within and without: 1509–1572

When John Roxborough died in 1509, he left a College little changed since the thirteenth century, still comprising a community of students of theology and mature commoners. By the death of Master Thomas Caius in 1572, the Fellows of University College still studied theology, and a few mature commoners still resided there, but much else had changed. It was not merely that all members of the College now had to profess allegiance to a new form of Christianity; there was a community of fee-paying undergraduates, whose presence would oblige the Fellows to change themselves from students of theology into teachers, and whose ubiquity meant that, by the end of the century, 'commoner' had come more generally to mean 'undergraduate commoner'; and, last but not least, the College now looked to outsiders for its Masters.

THE FAILURE OF RALPH HAMSTERLEY

This last change occurred first: a majority of Fellows, unable or unwilling to elect a new Master from among themselves, chose Ralph Hamsterley, a former Fellow of Merton College. At first glance, it appears equally surprising that the Fellows sought an outsider and that a member of one of the wealthiest Oxford colleges wished to lead one of the poorest. Nevertheless, there were some mutual attractions. For the College, Hamsterley's prosperous career, during which he had acquired livings and canonries in Durham, Northamptonshire, and Essex, made him a man of known means and possible expectations. Hamsterley himself had failed to be short-listed for the Wardenship at Merton both in 1507 and 1508: he would not satisfy any ambitions to become head of a college there. Whatever the reason, the Fellows and Hamsterley were taking an interest in each other. In May 1509, even before John Roxborough's death, the Fellows agreed that they would hold an obit for Hamsterley on the day after Trinity Sunday, in return for an unspecified benefaction.[1]

---

[1] Hamsterley's career: *BRUO* ii 864–5; the Merton elections of 1507–8: Salter 1923: 334 and 370. Hamsterley's benefaction is known only from a seventeenth-century transcript (UC:GB1/MS1/1 pp. 18–19).

When on 23 September 1509 five Fellows met to elect a Master, four of them voted for Hamsterley. All sides then moved carefully: the Fellows agreed to seek a dispensation from the 1475 statutes, while Hamsterley (staying nearby at Oddington, in Otmoor, where he had been rector) said that he would only accept the Mastership if his election was unanimous. Unfortunately the fifth Fellow, Peter Person, had voted for John Barnaby, a former Fellow currently renting a room in the College. When informed of Hamsterley's request, Person replied that if Hamsterley could either prove he had been a Fellow of University College, or else obtain a dispensation, then everybody (including himself) would support his election. The former was impossible; the latter (perhaps as Person had hoped) proved difficult.[2]

When the Visitors of University College, in the persons of the Vice-Chancellor, Proctors, and Doctors of Divinity, met on 11 November to discuss Hamsterley's dispensation, one of the Doctors and both Proctors opposed it. The matter was therefore referred to the Chancellor, William Warham, Archbishop of Canterbury. Warham's reply revealed his sympathies: praising Hamsterley as a learned and good man, he sternly declared that he should be elected Master, and that any Fellow who disagreed should be threatened with imprisonment, if necessary, to help him change his mind.[3]

Warham's tough language was ill-advised. Although the Visitors, on receiving his letter, announced to a meeting of Congregation that Hamsterley was to be elected Master, several members present, including both Proctors, attempted to overrule the College's traditional Visitors by holding a second meeting of Congregation at which they tried to elect Barnaby. This action probably owed less to Barnaby's innate qualities than to irritation at an interfering Chancellor.[4]

The Chancellor's authority nevertheless prevailed. On 13 January 1510, Warham summoned Hamsterley and Barnaby to Lambeth Palace, where a group of clerics, summoned to give advice, formally upheld Hamsterley's election on condition that his successor be a Fellow of the College. That was that: there was no more opposition in Congregation and on 4 February 1510 the College Register reported that, 'on account of the disturbance to [the Fellows'] studies, and to avoid disputes and divisions', John Barnaby was forbidden to stay in the College. Even Peter Person apparently made his peace, being elected Bursar in May 1510 (although he died the following year). Of the other Fellows who had elected Hamsterley, only one was still in

---

[2] Hamsterley's election: UC:GB3/A1/1 pp. 1–2; Person: *BRUO* iii. 1482–3.

[3] Warham's letter: Mitchell 1980: 13–15. The Archbishop of Canterbury is *ex officio* the Visitor of Merton, so Warham may have known Hamsterley.

[4] Warham was quite an interventionist Chancellor anyway (Cross 1986: 119). See p. 24 above on Congregation.

place by the end of 1511. After such a complete change in personnel, Hamsterley might have enjoyed a peaceful reign.[5]

Unfortunately he threw away this opportunity. In April 1512, the Register of Merton College recorded that Hamsterley was granted a room and commons there for the rest of his life, in return for a gift of £20 to be distributed as an obit. For one college to offer a bolthole to the head of another is bizarre, and indicated that something was amiss again in University College. Just how amiss became clear in November 1512, when Warham appointed a deputy, Richard FitzJames, Bishop of London (and former Warden of Merton), to investigate the College. Every Fellow, even the last survivor of 1509, Thomas Thomson, was accused of rebellion and disobedience towards his Master, and ordered to mend his ways.[6]

The Fellows might have disputed the impartiality of a Mertonian commissioner; they could not dispute that matters had once again reached such a pass that intervention was necessary. The legitimacy of Hamsterley's election was no longer a problem: one is rather left wondering at the essential competence of a Master who united all the Fellows against him.

The remainder of Hamsterley's Mastership (he died in August 1518) apparently passed peacefully. Noting the lack of entries in the College Register (begun by Hamsterley in 1509 in conscious imitation of Merton's) from April 1511 until his death, some have suggested that Hamsterley moved out of College, perhaps to Merton. He did, however, appear in some official documents, such as Thomas Thomson's will of December 1514, which named him and the Fellows of University College as his executors, so that he was at least nominally involved in College business to the end of his life. It therefore remains an open question whether he did escape to Merton, or some other congenial retreat such as Oddington.[7]

Hamsterley did not completely forget University College: he had a memorial brass of himself placed in the middle of its Chapel, as if to show that he could not be easily expunged from College memory. However, he also gave brasses to Durham, Merton, and Queen's Colleges, and the church at Oddington. The Durham brass is lost, as is that of University College, which, according to Anthony Wood, simply depicted 'the effigy of a man in a gown'; just the silhouette of the Merton brass (which apparently depicted him and a

---

[5] Barnaby's ejection and Person as Bursar: UC:GB3/A1/1 p. 2; Person's inventory (OUA Register F (reversed) fo. 130ʳ) is dated to 1511; tenures of Fellowships deduced from accounts for 1509/10–1511/12.

[6] Merton's offer to Hamsterley: Salter 1923: 424; FitzJames's report: OUA, Senior Proctor's Book, Lib. B p. 86.

[7] Thomson's will: OUA Register F (reversed) fo. 247ᵛ. *BRUO* ii 864 and Martin and Highfield 1997: 143 think that Hamsterley moved to Merton, but its archives do not substantiate this (information from Dr Michael Stansfield, then Archivist of Merton). Furthermore, the early portion of University College's Register survives only as a later copy—some pages for the years 1511–18 could have been lost.

FIGURE 6.1 Memorial Brass of Ralph Hamsterley, Master 1509–18, in Oddington Church, Oxfordshire.

former Warden) survives; and the inscription for his brass at Queen's, but not the figure, remains. Only the Oddington brass survives complete: this spectacular and grisly monument depicts Hamsterley as a skeleton in a shroud being eaten by worms (Fig. 6.1). Such is the earliest known depiction, albeit schematic, of a Master of University College.[8]

John Barnaby had the final word. On leaving Oxford, Barnaby took a living in London, where he died in 1517 or 1518. Hamsterley left the College nothing, but Barnaby bequeathed £20 for an obit, payments for which appear in the accounts from 1524/5. It was perhaps fortunate that there was no Fellow from 1509 to wonder whether the wrong Master had been elected.[9]

---

[8] Hamsterley's monuments: *BRUO* ii. 865; University College's brass: Wood, *Colleges* 62–4 (Wood claims that it was moved to the new Chapel, but it was missing in the 1780s); Merton's brass: Bott 1964: 21–2; Martin and Highfield 1997: 142 call Hamsterley 'something of a connoisseur of funeral monuments'.

[9] Barnaby's will: Darlington 1967: 44–5. No trace of any obit for Hamsterley appears in the College accounts, which makes one wonder whether the money for this was ever paid.

LEONARD HUTCHINSON AND THE ARRIVAL OF UNDERGRADUATES

The College's next choice of Master appears to have been a happier one. Leonard Hutchinson, formerly of Balliol and first recorded as a Fellow of University College in 1514/15, was elected Master without controversy on 16 September 1518 and remained in office for twenty-eight years. Although this period is not well documented (perhaps indicating that there were no disputes to settle), enough evidence survives to show Hutchinson played an important role in the College's history.[10]

Outside the College, Hutchinson acted as the Chancellor's Vice-Commissary in June 1531, and in February 1544, after the catastrophic burglary of the contents of the university's loan chests from the Convocation House in St Mary the Virgin, it was Hutchinson with whom the university entrusted the little that was left. Within College, Hutchinson had ideas about the status of the Master: in 1518, the Master's Lodgings were still in the tower above the entrance to the College, but in 1531 the Fellows permitted Hutchinson to occupy Little University Hall in High Street, situated next door to the College (and offering significantly more room), leaving the tower for the College's use. He also seems to have kept order. Fellows absent without permission were expelled, and action was taken against former Fellows who had not paid their debts. He may also have used his position to help members of his family: it may be more than coincidental that the Fellows elected during his Mastership include John Hutchinson (F. 1518–42), George Hutchinson (F. 1526–after 1530), and Hugh Hutchinson (F. 1537–after 1547). A Fellowship at University College, however, was not a particularly enticing post. One young Cambridge scholar, elected a Skirlaw Fellow in 1524, promptly declared himself unwilling to accept it, and found a place back in Cambridge. Thus University College lost Nicholas Ridley, future Bishop and Protestant martyr.[11]

Hutchinson also seems to have taken an interest in the management of the College's estates. The land at Paull, remote and consistently underperforming financially, was sold in 1529. At much the same time, in 1528, the College acquired half the manor of Eastwick in Grandpont, then in Berkshire. Eastwick (also Eastwyke) Farm, as the property became known, proved a more profitable investment than Paull, yielding more rent more consistently, not

---

[10] Hutchinson's career: *BRUO2* 302–3.
[11] Hutchinson acting for Chancellor: OUA Register EEE fo. 185ʳ; loan chests: Pantin and Mitchell 1972: 429–30; leaving the tower: UC:GB3/A1/1 p. 7 (Little University Hall had been a private house since the 1470s (*ARUC* ii. 565–6), and an allusion in the 1532/3 accounts to 'the tower and other rooms within the College' (*ARUC* ii. 279) shows that Hutchinson had moved out); absent Fellows sacked: UC:GB3/A1/1 pp. 6–7; Fellows in debt: OUA Register EEE fo. 7ʳ; Nicholas Ridley: UC:GB3/A1/1 p. 6 and *BRUO2* 496. Ridley's election is undated, but probably happened c.1524, since he returned to Cambridge then. He may have applied in case he failed to win a more desirable post at Cambridge.

least because it became a stock ground for dealers bringing animals to Oxford market. In 1541 land at Hailey, near Witney, was acquired, while the house at 9 High Street was sold in 1542. Unfortunately Hutchinson's desire to make College estates profitable (essential in a period experiencing high inflation) sometimes smacked of sharp practice, as when the College was accused in the 1530s of selling the next lease of its tithes at Arncliffe to two different parties, and pocketing payments from both of them.[12]

However, the most important development in Hutchinson's College concerns its membership. As has been regularly observed, University College's membership to date comprised almost exclusively Fellows and mature commoners who rented rooms within the College, a few undergraduate scholars under Thomas Benwell, and the 'portionists' being simply the exceptions to prove the rule.[13] Something unexpected then occurred in 1519/20. That year's accounts record twelve men renting rooms in the College. Two are Doctors of Theology; four are Masters of Arts; but six men, named as Johnson, Waneman, Savege, Bringnell, Knylt (or Knytt), and Bemmerton, have no title, and are renting three rooms between them at very modest rates. The absence of titles suggests that they have yet even to achieve their BAs. It has therefore been suggested that these six men are the first real forerunners of University College's fee-paying undergraduate commoners.[14]

Much remains uncertain. No record survives of any College decision to admit undergraduate scholars as commoners; and the summary nature of the College's accounts for the next four decades makes it impossible to track precisely the growth of their presence. On the other hand, the commoners of the previous two decades have been almost exclusively mature men, and there have never been more than five in any given year. It is also suggestive that nothing is known of the later careers of Johnson and his colleagues: young men coming up to study for a short while, with no interest in a degree or an ecclesiastical career, would be less likely to leave any traces behind.

The appearance of these undergraduate scholars comes at a significant time, as many Oxford colleges were following the academic halls in accepting such men in larger numbers, and the remaining academic halls began to grow ever larger or else (like Brasenose) to be re-founded as colleges. New foundations, led by Magdalen College, whose statutes were promulgated in 1480, specifically permitted commoners below the rank of BA to live and receive teaching in the college. Meanwhile several older colleges were changing their

---

[12] Sale of Paull estate: archives of St John's College, Cambridge (which bought it in 1530) D62.104; purchase of Eastwick Farm UC:E/H1/1D/3–7; sale of 9 High Street: UC:E/E1/D/14; purchase at Hailey; UC:E6/1D/10–11; the Arncliffe imbroglio: UC:E4/3L/3 and UC:E4/3D/12; inflation in the sixteenth century: Phelps Brown and Hopkins 1956.

[13] An obscure entry of 1514 in the university's registers (OUA Register F (reversed) fo. 215ᵛ) may suggest that some Fellows were then accepting pupils on a private basis.

[14] ARUC ii. 250–1 (this account survives only in William Smith's transcripts, but he is a reliable witness); interpretation of these names: Carr, 71.

ways: undergraduate scholars are attested at Balliol and Queen's, and Lincoln may have been accepting them in the previous century. The poorer colleges, glad of possible extra income, followed the fashion most eagerly: wealthier foundations like New College and All Souls stayed aloof for the time being.[15]

Various explanations can be offered for this development, two of which were mentioned in the previous chapter. Undergraduate scholars could be monitored more easily in a hall or college than in private lodgings—indeed the authorities had been trying to forbid students to use the latter for over a century. Another factor was the breakdown of the system of 'necessary regency' (p. 2), so that it fell upon the halls and the colleges to supply the deficiency. The schools owned by University College and once leased to young Masters reflect this breakdown. They ceased to pay any rents after 1545/6, and by 1560/1 the College had cut its losses: the building had been demolished, and the property was merely 'a garden on Schools Street'.[16]

The financial attractions of undergraduate scholars are clear enough: they needed to spend money on accommodation, on food and drink (with potential benefits to college servants)—and above all on tuition. There were not enough college lectureships yet to carry the full teaching burden of the university, and so, during the sixteenth century, Oxford's fellows began informally to take on tutorial work. They were paid directly by their pupils, and a fellow with a taste for teaching and sufficient entrepreneurial spirit could significantly supplement his stipend. If other colleges and fellows were benefiting from these new circumstances, then it would be foolish for a poor foundation like University College to be left behind.

There can be no doubt of the significance of the step which University College took in accepting undergraduate scholars as commoners on a regular basis. The College's earliest statutes had provided for a body of Fellows studying theology, joined by commoners who wished to carry out study of their own at Oxford: they did not provide that the Fellows would teach. Now the whole function of the College was starting to change: the Fellows would have to dilute their studies with teaching, and eventually create a system for the management of the welfare and discipline of their young charges. In modern terms, University College would change from an institution of postgraduate study into one of undergraduate teaching.

These changes would occur gradually, and when we return to the six young commoners of 1519/20, a sense of perspective is needed. They do not yet differ significantly from earlier young occupants of College rooms like John Tiptoft in the 1440s. In particular, nothing is known of how they were taught

[15] See variously McConica 1986a, Jones 2005: 34–5, Hodgkin 1949: 57, Green 1979: 55, Williams in Buxton and Williams 1979: 44–5, and above all, on this 'triumph' of the academic hall, Catto 2004.
[16] Decay of necessary regency: Fletcher 1986: 185–7; University College's schools: *ARUC* i. xxvi and *ARUC* ii. 587–91; college lectureships: McConica 1986a: 5 and 21–2.

within the College—if indeed they received any teaching there at all. It is also unclear whether University College accepted undergraduate scholars as commoners continuously. In 1519/20 it received £3 17s. from its rooms, the highest total for several years. During the next few decades, this amount fluctuated between 10s. in 1529/30 and over £4 in 1532/3 and 1533/4. The lack of names in the accounts also means that we cannot tell what proportions of commoners were undergraduate or mature until the 1560s. We know of at least one mature commoner, William Hall, a former Fellow of Merton, who was accepting pupils of his own when lodging in University College in 1562.[17] More seriously, the College had no educational provision to speak of, lacking both lectureships and scholarships—a far cry from the three lecturers and thirty demies or scholars at Magdalen. Nevertheless, the students of 1519/20 mark the start of a development which would transform the College's population more profoundly than any other before or since, and that gives Leonard Hutchinson's Mastership an especial significance.

REFORMATION AND REACTION

Leonard Hutchinson's Mastership was affected by events far beyond his or the College's control, namely the consequences of Henry VIII's desire to divorce his queen in his search for a male heir. The universities were dragged into the affair and obliged to support the King at each stage of his journey, until there was a complete break with Rome, and the creation of a separate Church of England. The College then witnessed the upheavals created by the Reformist regime of Edward VI, the reunion with Rome under Mary I, and the final break with Catholicism under Elizabeth I. In observing these events from within one small Oxford college, we must forget that we know the end of the story. The Fellows of University College would not know that Henry would die unreconciled to Rome, that Edward and Mary would both die childless, or that Elizabeth would live to a great age. Therefore a Fellow of the mid-1550s might have been hopeful that England's reunion with Rome would be permanent, and a Fellow of the 1560s or 1570s fearful that Elizabeth's regime could be overturned at any moment.

Under Henry VIII Hutchinson and the Fellows were outwardly conformist. The one former member of the College known to have resisted was Richard Fetherstonehaugh (F. 1513–15), who became a chaplain to Catherine of Aragon and then tutor to Princess Mary. His determined opposition to Catherine's divorce led to his imprisonment and finally execution for treason in 1540. Hutchinson, however, was one of the Oxford divines who agreed that Henry was entitled to divorce Catherine. He also seems to have profited personally from the dissolution of the monasteries: in 1543 he was granted a share in land in Northamptonshire which had belonged to Dingley priory,

---

[17] Clark 1887–9: ii. 6.

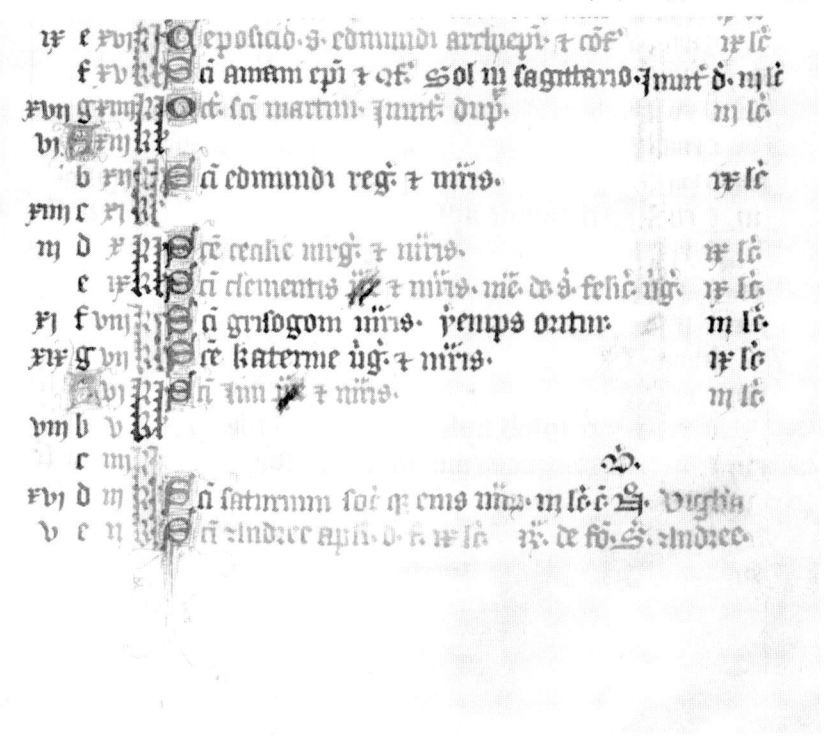

FIGURE 6.2 The Reformation comes to University College: page from the College's Missal showing the word 'Papa' (Pope) deleted from the feasts of St Clement and St Linus (23 and 26 November).

and which he was then permitted to sell—one suspects at a decent profit—barely a year later.[18]

Under Henry VIII at least, England was not really a Protestant country. Henry himself remained a traditionalist at heart, and kept religious reformers and conservatives in careful equilibrium, rarely allowing one side complete dominance. Evidence for how the Fellows of University College dealt with change is provided by the calendar in the College's missal (Fig. 6.2). Every reference in it to the Pope has been scratched out, as have the feasts of St Thomas à Becket on 5 January, 7 July, and 29 December. The Fellows had clearly deduced that, having made the appropriate gestures, their liturgical life could carry on much as before.[19]

---

[18] Richard Fetherstonhaugh: *BRUO2* 204; Hutchinson and the divorce: *L & P Henry VIII* Vol. 5, 6; his property dealings: *L & P Henry VIII* Vol. 18 Part 1, 541, and Vol. 19 Part 1, 45.
[19] College Missal calendar: Bodl. MS Univ. 178; a wider picture: McCulloch 2003: 198–204 and Duffy 1992: 379–447 (and 412 on Thomas à Becket).

Such dangers as Oxbridge colleges faced under Henry VIII were less religious than financial. Some problems were minor: University College lost some small quit-rents from colleges funded by religious orders. A greater danger came in 1545, when, after the passing of an act for the suppression of chantries, plans were mooted for a second act, to affect all remaining colleges, including those at the universities. Early in 1546, all the colleges were compelled to send the King valuations of their lands. This had happened to the monasteries before they were dissolved, and the colleges would have been all too aware of the unhappy parallel. But they were lucky: a speedy deputation from both Oxford and Cambridge, and an expression of surprise on Henry's part that so many scholars could survive on such little income, saved the day. Arguably the very existence of the Oxbridge colleges was never in greater danger than at this time.[20]

The claim of poverty which had so surprised Henry was certainly justified in the case of University College. The Commissioners overseeing the valuation noted that its expenditure usually exceeded its revenue, due to the cost of victuals, and that the gap was usually made up by legacies and donations. The accounts support this picture of a financial crisis (see Graph 6.1). In spite of all Leonard Hutchinson's best efforts, the College's net income barely increased at all during the first half of the sixteenth century, at a time when prices doubled. The accounts after 1518 cease to mention reserve funds in a College chest, and, although for much of the 1520s and 1530s, income usually exceeded expenditure, this changed during the 1540s, until by 1548/9–1556/7 the College ran at a loss every year. Eastwick Farm provides a good example of the short-term measures to which the Fellows were reduced. In 1541 the farm was leased to Thomas Monday, an Oxford brewer, for twenty years at a rent of £6 13s. 4d. Then in 1547, the College granted another Oxford brewer, Roger Hewett, a reversionary lease (one, in other words, which would not come into effect until 1561, when the preceding lease had expired) of twenty-one years. Ten years later, in 1557, the College granted a second reversionary lease to Thomas Hutchinson, a former servant of Master George Ellison, to take effect in 1582 (Hutchinson then sold his lease—presumably for a profit—to Hewett in 1562). Hewett himself then obtained a third reversionary lease in 1567, due to start in 1603. Money will have changed hands to secure these leases, bringing short-term relief and a long-term burden to the College. By 1567 Eastwick Farm was tied up with reversionary leases for over half a century, all of which set the rent at £6 13s. 4d., and it was not until 1621 that the College could at last lease it more profitably.[21]

---

[20] Quit-rents: *ARUC* ii. 314. The crisis of 1545/6 is discussed variously in Howard 1935: 22–4, Green 1979: 85, Cross 1986: 132–3, and Loach 1986: 366.

[21] The Commissioners on the College: *L & P Henry VIII* Vol. 21 part 1 p. 141; leases of Eastwick Farm: UC:E/H1/2D/1–10; inflation: Phelps Brown and Hopkins 1956.

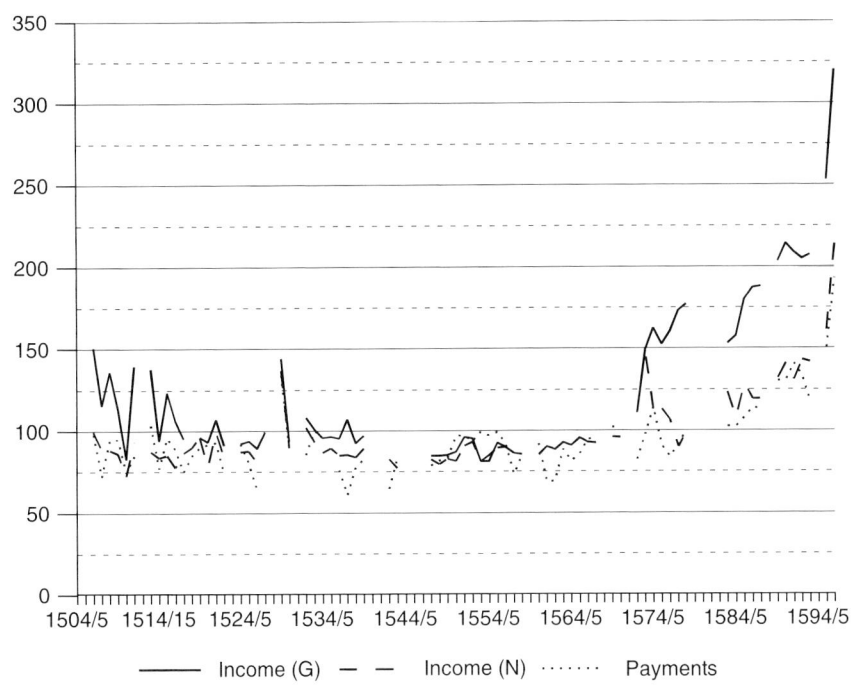

GRAPH 6.1 Income and Expenditure of University College 1504/5–1596/7. 'Income (G)' is the gross income in any year, including allowances and money in the College chest, where they are mentioned; 'Income (N)' is the College's net income, with allowances and money in the chest deducted; 'Payments' are self-explanatory. Gaps are caused by missing rolls.

Meanwhile Leonard Hutchinson had resigned the Mastership in September 1546. His departure is the most surprising event in his career. He is not known to have moved on to any higher post, and he did not die until 1554. He had, however, acquired several livings during his Mastership, and he seems to have moved to one of these (possibly Croughton in Northamptonshire, where he asked to be buried), thus making him the first Master of University College to enjoy what was effectively retirement.[22]

His successor was John Crayford. Crayford had been a Fellow of University College in the early 1520s, but had then become Master of Clare College, Cambridge, in 1530–9 (the only Master of University College also to have headed a Cambridge college). At Cambridge, he acquired a reputation as something of a bruiser—he was more of a gladiator than a Vice-Chancellor,

[22] BRUO2 302–3.

thought one contemporary—and stories were told of how his rage once led him to throw someone bodily out of the Regent House, and, on another occasion, to cut off a man's hand. However, his strength of character had served Cambridge well, when, as Vice-Chancellor in 1533–5, he had helped ensure the university's support for the King's divorce. He remained carefully aware of Henry's religious policy: in 1540 he had been one of the commissioners for enforcing the Act of Six Articles (Henry's main attempt to bring religious reformers to heel) in London; and was made a Chaplain to the King in 1545. In the uncertain atmosphere of the 1540s, the College presumably hoped that such a well-connected Master would be a sturdy defender of their interests.[23]

It was therefore unfortunate that Crayford died in August 1547, barely a year after his election. For his successor, the Fellows turned to Richard Salveyn, Fellow since 1526. By now, the government of the young Edward VI had revealed its Reformist sympathies: the following years saw England's first major iconoclasm, and the compulsory introduction of a prayer book in the English language. In the summer of 1549, Royal Visitors were sent to Oxford to ensure compliance. Within University College, the Chapel would have been stripped of its ornaments, and elaborate vestments no longer worn; the medieval missal was now obsolete; prayers for the dead were forbidden, bringing the relationship between the College and its past benefactors under close scrutiny; and, above all, the Fellows would have had to explore new and approved areas of theology. Life, in theory, would be harder for those attached to the old ways.

Yet the College, like the university in general, proved surprisingly resistant to reform. It is true that in May 1549 Henry Brachinburye was elected Fellow on the orders of the Visitors, but an examination of the Fellows of University College from 1545 to 1560 shows the remarkable tenacity with which many of them retained their posts. There were regularly six Fellows at any one time, in addition to the Master. Three Fellowships were held by men who straddled every religious change in this period, namely Edmund Thomson (elected in May 1543 and replaced in 1556), and Christopher Greenwell and Ralph Cockey (both elected in June 1545, and in place at least until December 1557). A fourth, George Ellison, elected Fellow in 1543, became Master in 1551, and died in post in June 1557. As for the other Fellows, their dates of resignation show few obvious signs of purges or mass resignations, a pattern repeated over much of the university.[24]

The College showed its ability to preserve some independence after October 1551, when Richard Salveyn resigned the Mastership, because, as he

---

[23] Crayford's career: *BRUO2* 148–9 and Forbes 1928: i. 129–30; Crayford as 'gladiator': Caius 1568: 160 (although, as will be seen, he is not an impartial witness); other tales: Caius 1574: 121 and Fuller 1840: 215.

[24] Brachinburye's election: UC:GB3/A1/1 p. 9; the Oxford context: Duncan 1980.

explained, 'I colde in noe wise, for my infyrmyte of bodye, do suche thynges as the office requirethe' (since Salveyn was later deprived of his livings under Elizabeth I, one wonders whether his ill-health arose less from bodily infirmity than an allergy to Protestantism). A month later George Ellison was elected his successor, and was approved by the traditionally minded Vice-Chancellor, Owen Oglethorpe. Then, in March 1552, the university Registrar, Thomas Caius, unexpectedly produced a document at a meeting of Congregation which, he claimed, showed that he was the representative of Richard Salveyn, that Salveyn's resignation had been forced, and that Ellison's election was illegal.[25]

Thomas Caius, Registrar since 1534, who preferred to be known under this Latinized version of his surname Key or Kay, had been elected a Fellow of All Souls in 1525. He was a man apparently in sympathy with Protestantism: he had translated into English some works of the Swiss reformer Heinrich Bullinger. One therefore wonders whether Caius' intervention was quite what it appeared. The compiler of the College Register suspected—probably rightly—that certain people, in particular the Royal Visitors, who included the Chancellor Richard Cox, were hoping that Caius might become Master. Nevertheless, the Fellows succeeded in having their way. Congregation referred the matter to a committee, which concluded that Ellison's election had been legal, and that Caius' intervention should be set aside. Soon afterwards Caius was sacked as Registrar, allegedly for incompetence.[26]

In August 1552, not long after Ellison was confirmed in his Mastership, the deputy Vice-Chancellor attempted to list the members of every college and hall. This so-called 'Academic Census' therefore gives the first full list of residents of University College in a generation. Twenty-five names are given, comprising a Master, seven Fellows (four MAs and three BAs) and seventeen men who are with no title—what we would call undergraduate commoners, in other words. At last the tentative undergraduate presence of 1519/20 has become something more permanent and more closely akin to the standard modern model of a college. On the other hand, University is the smallest college on the list, and of the eight halls named, only three had fewer members.[27]

A year later, the College and the country witnessed yet more religious change: Mary I, on succeeding her brother in July 1553, tried to reverse the revolution of the preceding two decades and reunite England with the

---

[25] Salveyn's resignation and Ellison's election: OUA Hyp/A/5 fo. 55ᵛ and UC:GB3/A1/1 p. 9 (although the dating there is a little wrong); his later career: *BRUO2* 503; Thomas Caius' protest: OUA Register FF fo. 130ᵛ. See too Duncan 1980: 228–9.

[26] Caius: *BRUO2* 325–6; Wood, *Athenae* 397–401; and *ODNB* entry; his work on Bullinger: Dent 1983: 10. Significantly Owen Oglethorpe was obliged to resign his post as President of Magdalen in 1552.

[27] Boase 1885: xxiv.

Catholic faith. George Ellison appears to have been at the very least content to accept the change, for he remained Master until his death in 1557. Indeed there is evidence that he and most Fellows welcomed it: the entries concerning St Thomas à Becket in the missal were restored, and large sums were spent on the Chapel. During the previous decade or so Chapel expenses had ranged from 7s. 7d. (1552/3) to 26s. 8d. (1548/9); in 1553/4, however, the Fellows spent 39s., on it and over £3 in 1554/5. Similar sums were spent every year until 1558/9. These sums are especially significant when one remembers the College's meagre finances. A less enthusiastic Fellowship would have desisted until it had little choice but to obey.[28]

Some Fellows, however, could not accept the changes. Henry Brachinburye is not heard from again after 1552, and Edmund Thomson revealed himself as a Protestant and fled to Frankfurt. Other Fellows, past and present, found the new sensibilities more to their taste, such as Thomas Pentland (F. 1537–c.1540), appointed a chaplain in 1557 to the new Archbishop of Canterbury and Chancellor of Oxford, Reginald, Cardinal Pole.[29]

A chance for the Master and Fellows to show their loyalty came when the former Archbishop Thomas Cranmer, and Bishops Latimer and Ridley were brought to Oxford for a series of disputations with a group of theologians picked from both universities. On 16 April 1554, following a day of disputations in the Divinity Schools, Cranmer was led off to the town prison of Bocardo, while his interlocutors were dined at University College.[30]

The day was marred by the unexpected intervention of the College's earliest known undergraduate to have been more than a name, William Holcot. Holcot, a Berkshire gentleman, MP for Old Sarum in 1545, had, according to Anthony Wood, studied at University College as a young man, but returned there regularly to study theology, which, despite his lay status, remained his chief passion. Under Edward VI, Holcot obtained a licence to preach, and appeared in churches, clad, according to Wood, in 'a velvet Bonnet, a damask Gown, and sometimes a Chain of gold or silver about his neck'. Under Mary, his preaching ceased, and he resided in University College again (which suggests that Ellison's College showed some religious toleration). Having attended the disputation, Holcot noted that Cranmer was charged with misquoting some of his sources. Since he owned one of the relevant books, he decided to visit Bocardo that evening and lend it to the Archbishop. Needless to say, he was promptly arrested, and himself locked up in Bocardo. It became clear that Holcot was working on his own, and, after several days of pressure to bring him round, Holcot signed allegiance to the new regime. Only the Vice-Chancellor's intervention prevented the

---

[28] Exact figures for Chapel expenditure are in the relevant pages of *ARUC* ii.
[29] Thomson and Pentland: *BRUO2* 571 and 441; Marian Oxford in general: Russell 1985.
[30] Foxe 1583: 1430 and 1441.

undoubtedly furious Master and Fellows from expelling him outright. Holcot seems to have lain low, until, under Elizabeth, he resumed his preaching career. John Foxe wrote that Holcot 'though then an apostate is yet now a penitent preacher', and Anthony Wood claimed that he distributed copies of the Catechism to children in the streets of London.[31]

George Ellison died in June 1557, and was succeeded by Anthony Salveyn, probably the brother of Richard, and a former Fellow of the College, who had become a canon at Durham Cathedral. Salveyn's tenure was short: he resigned in December 1558. Perhaps he was aware of changing times. The previous month, Elizabeth I had succeeded her sister as Queen, and although it took some months for a new ecclesiastical settlement to mature, many will have guessed its nature. As it was, Salveyn appears in 1561, described as 'meanly learned, but of estimation in his county', on a list of recusants ordered to keep within fixed bounds—in Salveyn's case, within five miles of Kirkbymoorside, in Yorkshire.[32]

If Salveyn had hoped to draw some fire away from the College, he failed. Faced with a university supportive of Mary's religious policies, the new regime ruthlessly eliminated dissent. This can be seen in the rapid replacement of nearly all the Fellows of University College. We do not know whether they jumped or were pushed; we do know that, in May 1559, four new Fellows were elected, and that by January 1563 only one of the Fellows present in November 1558 was still there. Of the Marian Fellows, one at least remained loyal to Catholicism to the end: Henry Stapper, elected in June 1558, was working as a recusant priest in Yorkshire as late as 1609.[33]

The new Master, James Dugdale, had been a Fellow since 1547 and, like Ellison, had weathered the previous religious changes, yet retained a conservative sensibility. When William Hall, a Fellow of Merton, was expelled from there in 1561 for opposing a new Protestant Warden, he found shelter in Dugdale's College, where he died a year later. Dugdale's most important act as Master, in April 1559, was to exchange the College's property in the village of Merton for a house adjoining the west side of the quadrangle, which offered useful scope for expansion. Otherwise Dugdale, evidently aware of the dark clouds around him, stayed away from Oxford. He was certainly away in May 1561, when the Vice-Chancellor, Thomas Coveney, drew up new statutes declaring that, to stop the College falling into ruin in the Master's absence, the number of Fellows was not to be increased, and any Fellow elected Bursar who refused to take it on would be deprived of his stipend until he agreed to do so. Finally, in November 1561, the authorities

---

[31] Holcot's career: Wood, *History* ii. 128–9, and Wood, *Athenae* i. 420 (Holcot is one of the undergraduates in the 1552 census); Holcot and Cranmer: Foxe 1583: 2135.
[32] Salveyn: *BRUO2* 503 and *CSPD Addenda 1547–65* 522.
[33] Stapper's later career: Russell 1985: 225 and Wainewright 1911–12. Cambridge was also purged at this time (Morgan 2004: 65).

lost patience with Dugdale. Having been summoned before the Royal Visitors and failed to appear, he was formally stripped of the Mastership.[34]

THOMAS CAIUS

The College had to elect its sixth Master in fifteen years. Its choice—surprisingly—was Thomas Caius, the rejected candidate of 1552. In the intervening decade, Caius had managed to appear sufficiently conformist to escape attention under Mary, and his career was prospering under Elizabeth. In 1560 he had been appointed a prebendary at Salisbury Cathedral, and in 1563 he became rector of Tredington, a rich Worcestershire parish. All the Fellows who had opposed Caius in 1551 were gone, and Elizabeth's Visitors were more ruthless at imposing their will than Edward's. The ground seems to have been laid carefully, as the Vice-Chancellor's register reports that Caius was elected 'not without a previous dispensation' from the Chancellor, because he had no prior links with the College. There are also hints that some Fellows were actually interested in electing Thomas Caius. Some Fellows, but not all: the recusant Henry Stapper refused to vote for Caius.[35]

Fortunately for Caius there was a surprising lack of religious strife in University College. While places like Gloucester Hall, Balliol, Exeter, or New College, to say nothing of the new foundations of Trinity and St John's, contained many crypto-catholics, accepted with varying degrees of tolerance, there is no evidence for such activity at University College, apart from Henry Stapper, soon to leave, and William Hall, soon to die. However, the College would have been fairly easy to monitor: the Chancellor, as Visitor, could keep a careful eye on it; the Fellowship was small enough that it would take little time to remove those deemed unsound; and the usual rapid turnover of undergraduates would assist matters. Families with recusant sympathies would have considered it wiser to send their sons elsewhere.[36]

Caius has acquired a reputation for incompetent administration—Anthony Wood quotes a letter of 1573, which alludes to 'the late wasted, spoiled and indebted University college in Oxon'—but this is not wholly fair. The accounts for the late 1560s and early 1570s show regular deficits, but the College's problems dated back to the mid-1540s. Little new building took place—Caius' only known architectural contribution was to rebuild the Master's Lodgings—and the College's rental showed a slight increase. Some

---

[34] William Hall: Martin and Highfield 1997: 155–6; acquisition of property: UC:E/A7/D1/1; Coveney's statutes: UC:GB1/L1/5; Dugdale's dismissal: UC:GB3/A1/1 p. 11, OUA Hyp/A/7 fo. 18ʳ, and *CSPD 1547–80* 188.

[35] Caius at Salisbury: Le Neve 1986: 75; his election: Dent 1983: 27; prebendaries: p. 4.

[36] Williams 1986: 405–15 shows that the conversion of University College went especially smoothly.

emergency asset-stripping occurred: in additional to the creation of such reversionary leases as those for Eastwick Farm mentioned above, properties at Hanborough and Headington were sold, and in February 1562, the College sold the rights to the next two presentations at Arncliffe for an unspecified sum. However, Caius struck three deals which proved profitable for his successors. The first was with Brasenose College, which since 1508 had paid an annual quit-rent of £3 for its site. In 1571, in lieu of this rent, Brasenose leased University College a field adjoining Eastwick Farm called Irish Mead, for it to sublet. The field was first sublet in 1574, and it immediately brought in more income. The second deal was with one Thomas Gold of Oxford, who left some houses (now 49–51 St Giles) to his son on the curious condition that he could only sell them to University College. A little later, the College was given the reversion on the Crown Inn in Cornmarket Street. This third benefaction acquired greater significance under a supplementary agreement of 1571 that, when the property came to the College, its income would support two lecturers in Logic, or one lecturer each in Logic and Philosophy. Although the College did not receive the Inn for over a decade, this document of 1571 is the earliest evidence for the College trying to create its own undergraduate teaching system.[37]

University College also attracted some men of letters. William Adlington, whose version of the Roman novel, Apuleius' *Metamorphoses*, is a classic of Elizabethan translation, wrote at least part of his work at University College in 1566. Among actual undergraduates of the College, the rising star was the Irishman Richard Stanyhurst, said by Anthony Wood to have come up in 1563, and certainly renting a College room in 1565/6 and 1567/8. While still an undergraduate, he wrote a commentary on Porphyry, which was published in 1570 with commendatory verses from such diverse sources as Thomas Caius himself, Laurence Humphrey, the Reformist President of Magdalen, and Edmund Campion, future Catholic martyr. Perhaps fortunately Caius never saw his protégé become University College's most eminent Catholic convert, almost certainly thanks to Stanyhurst's friend Edmund Campion, who spent time with him in Ireland on their leaving Oxford. Stanyhurst, however, did not follow Campion to martyrdom. Instead he moved to Flanders, from where he travelled widely, writing extensively on historical and theological matters. His advice as an English specialist was sought from Philip II of Spain, and he died in Flanders in 1618 as chaplain to Philip's daughter. He also produced a verse translation of

---

[37] Poor state of the College: Wood, *Athenae* ii. 204; Master's Lodgings: Wood, *Colleges* 58; sold properties: ARUC i. xxxi; Arncliffe sale: UC:GB3/A1/1 p. 12; the quit-rent from Brasenose: UC:E/A2/D/6; the transfer of Irish Mead: UC:E/H2/1D/4–6 (eventually Brasenose gave outright possession of Irish Mead in exchange for University College ceding its rights to the site of Brasenose); 49–51 St Giles: UC:E/G1/1D/1; the Crown Inn: UC:BE1/MS2/2 pp. 315–22.

the first third of Virgil's *Aeneid* which has deservedly been hailed as among the worst in English.[38]

Caius' own literary activities, meanwhile, centred on the history of Oxford. When Elizabeth I visited Cambridge in 1564, she heard speeches about that university's superior antiquity, and Caius decided that an Oxonian riposte was required. His short treatise, 'An Assertion of the Antiquity of Oxford University' was mainly concerned with strengthening the claim that King Alfred had founded University College in particular, and Oxford in general, but he also waxed lyrical on the medieval fantasy that Oxford's university had been founded at Cricklade—claimed as a corruption of 'Greeklade'—in Wiltshire, which allowed him to bring in pre-Christian legends. Nevertheless, Caius did do some research among the College's archives—possibly the first scholar to do so—and his little work includes a list of eminent alumni of University College, including John Castell, Thomas Benwell, and John Martyn, and, more recently, Leonard Hutchinson and John Crayford. He also noted the claim in the medieval *Memorandum* (p. 56) that William the Conqueror had almost destroyed the Saxon university. Meanwhile William of Durham had faded from memory: Caius knew him only as 'a certain Archdeacon of Durham called William' who had revived the university and college.[39]

Caius had a chance to publicize his work (which still existed only in manuscript) when the Queen visited Oxford in September 1566. One account recorded that 'Mr Keis, Provost [*sic*] of University College wrote a little book on the antiquity of the University of Oxford, which he wished to be presented through the Chancellor of Oxford, Robert Dudley, Earl of Leicester, to the Queen's Majesty.' Whereas others had presented their books in person to the Queen, Caius had to hope that Leicester would act for him, and it is unclear whether Dudley obliged, let alone what the Queen thought of it. The only certain moment when University College received royal attention was on her last day in Oxford, when, progressing through High Street, she saw the façades of the church of St Mary and of All Souls and University College festooned with verses lamenting her departure.[40]

Caius' brief work may have attracted little attention in the bustle of a Royal visit; it was not unnoticed elsewhere. A copy came into the hands of a Cambridge man, Matthew Parker, Archbishop of Canterbury, who passed it to his friend John Caius, Master and refounder of Gonville and Caius College, Cambridge (and no relation of Thomas). Caius of Cambridge

---

[38] Adlington: the introduction to his translation is signed from University College, although he appears in no College or university records; Stanyhurst: Lennon 1981, Wood, *Athenae* ii. 251–8, and *ARUC* ii. 379 and 388.

[39] Caius' reasons for writing the *Assertio antiquitatis Oxoniensis Academiae*: Caius 1730: ii. 316.

[40] Presentation of Caius' book: Plummer 1887: 183; verses: Wood, *History* ii. 163.

decided that Caius of Oxford needed rebutting, and so in 1568 published a 300-page counterblast, 'On the Antiquity of the University of Cambridge' (*De antiquitate Cantabrigiensis academiæ*). Thomas's little treatise was printed at the end of the book, with a note that it was by an 'unknown author'. John Caius adopts all the ploys of the polemicist—feigned impartiality, sarcasm, bluster—to destroy his opponent. If Thomas could summon up Cricklade and Alfred for Oxford, John found for Cambridge Cantaber (a Spanish king from the time of 'Gurguntius', a British king 'discovered' by Geoffrey of Monmouth), and Sigibert, a seventh-century king of the East Saxons. University College is brushed aside as 'a single Hall, so very tiny' (*una tantilla Aula*). John must have hoped that, when readers finally reached Thomas's little work, it would be mocked as presumptuous nonsense.[41]

Thomas Caius' reaction to John Caius' publication is easy to imagine—and indeed a copy of John's book bearing Thomas's angry annotations came into the hands of the eighteenth-century antiquarian Thomas Hearne. Thomas Caius also wrote a long counterblast, in which he repaid John's polemic with interest. Again he returned to the College archives, proclaiming of the *Memorandum* on King Alfred's gifts, 'see, here is irrefutable proof of this matter, not from glass windows, as you like to mock, but copied from a most ancient document in the College.' Unfortunately for Caius, although the document was genuine, its contents were false. It is typical of Caius' bad luck that, although later antiquarians like Bryan Twyne knew of his work, it was not until 1730 that Thomas Hearne published an edition of it.[42]

Modern readers may well think that the battle between Caius of Oxford and Caius of Cambridge has all the significance of that between Tweedledum and Tweedledee: John's book has been called 'the largest and most calamitous of its author's works' and it is hard not to think the same of Thomas's. The scholarship of both men was equally at fault, in their uncritical acceptance of legends passed down at second or third hand, and in their unhistorical reading of texts. Yet this is to misjudge Thomas and John. Both their works show great erudition, and in their time the legends which they cited were generally accepted as true. They were not alone, either, in searching for the oldest possible origins for their institutions.[43] For good or ill, Thomas's works mark a significant, if misguided, advance in the historiography of Oxford.

Thomas Caius died in Oxford in May 1572. He remains one of the unluckier Masters of University College. Memories of the unwise attempts

---

[41] John Caius on University College: Caius 1568: 252 and also Brooke 1996: 74–5. An enlarged edition of John Caius' book was published posthumously (Caius 1574).

[42] Thomas Caius' annotations on John's book, with his own counterblast, are in Caius 1730. His comment on the *Memorandum* is at ii. 429. Other dubious documents, such as the 'Chapernay Charter', are read with an equally uncritical eye (ii. 430–2).

[43] John's history: Brooke 1996: 75; other examples of 'invented' history: Fox 2000: 227–35.

to foist him on the College in 1551/2, the lack of success in his literary battles with Cambridge, and the greater achievements of his successors, have not served him well. Yet Caius' record is a happier one than that of the previous outsider, Ralph Hamsterley. University College was apparently spared the religious disputes suffered elsewhere; attempts were made to rationalize its finances; and Caius was the most eminent man of letters to have led the College for many years. If later Masters enjoyed greater success, then Thomas Caius had undoubtedly sown some of the harvest they would reap.

7

In the Chancellor's Power: 1572–1632

In the decades following the death of Thomas Caius, the inner life of University College becomes increasingly visible, as more letters, memoirs, and other personal documents survive. It was also a time when the College enjoyed an increased measure of prosperity and stability. That stability, however, came at a cost. Between the resignation of James Dugdale in 1561 and the death of Thomas Walker in 1665, almost every Master of University College was an appointee of the Chancellor (as effective Visitor of the College). The Mastership election of 1610 provides a good example. George Abbot resigned as Master on 23 February, and ten days later the date of election was fixed as 7 March; but on 24 February, the Chancellor, Richard Bancroft, had written to the College. Noting his right of dispensation, and anxious that the College should retain its high standards, he offered as a suitable candidate his nephew John Bancroft—and even granted the Fellows a licence to elect him Master, because he was not a member of the College. On 7 March the Fellows duly did their Chancellor's bidding.[1]

Although the Fellows retained more autonomy in electing to their own body, even this process was monitored. After 1587, every Fellowship election in the College Register listed all the Doctors and Proctors who formally approved it. This process had precedent—the statutes of 1311 had ordered the College to present new Fellows for approval to the Chancellor, doctors of Theology, and proctors—and at least one election, that of John Hartburne in June 1511, was thus approved, but this scrutiny had now become more regulated.[2]

Other colleges suffered similar pressures. Robert Dudley, Earl of Leicester, Chancellor of Oxford from 1564 (Fig. 7.1), and his immediate successors were lay courtiers, powerful at court, and keen to exploit their powers of patronage in Oxford. In one respect at least, University College was luckier than most: some other colleges were 'persuaded' by Leicester and others to

[1] Election of 1610: UC:GB3/A1/1 pp. 29–31.
[2] Hartburn's election: OUA Register F (reversed) fo. 140ᵛ.

FIGURE 7.1 Robert Dudley, Earl of Leicester, Chancellor of Oxford 1564–88 and benefactor. Portrait attributed to William Segar or Federigo Zuccaro.

lease property to a patron's friend on generous terms, sometimes with disastrous long-term consequences.[3]

University College was also fortunate in having some distinguished Masters and Fellows. It was also a successful period for benefactions; a system of undergraduate tuition took root; a grand building project was mooted; and, of the Masters themselves, two became bishops and one an archbishop. Furthermore the power and status of the Master within the university increased. The Vice-Chancellor was now chosen only from among the heads of colleges and Canons of Christ Church, and Congregation, formerly the main forum for transacting university business, suffered a process of emasculation during the later sixteenth century, as its agenda was increasingly decided in advance by a committee comprising the Vice-Chancellor, Proctors, heads of colleges, and Doctors in Divinity. This received legal sanction in the Laudian

---

[3] Powerful Chancellors: Williams 1986: 423–39 (and at Cambridge, where William Cecil was Chancellor, Morgan 2004: 388–436); interference in elections: Brooke 1996: 106 and Twigg 1987: 79; interference in leases: D. Hoyle, in Cunich and others 1994: 77–83 and Stevenson and Salter 1939: 223.

statutes of 1636, and was called the Hebdomadal Council, because it met every week in term time. These developments benefited the head of a small college, as he could meet his wealthier colleagues on comparatively equal terms, and a head with sufficient energy and connections could win influence throughout the university. The power granted to their heads meant that colleges of Oxford and Cambridge came to exercise a power over their universities not shared by colleges elsewhere in Europe. Although colleges in European universities continued to be numerous, not least in Paris, and well filled, yet it was the faculties, not the colleges, which dominated these institutions.[4]

There was one other aspect to what became the Hebdomadal Council which was specially relevant to University College: its composition happened to overlap closely with the body ordered to act as the College's Visitor in the 1311 statutes (p. 24), and during the period covered by this chapter the Council came increasingly to act as *de facto* Visitor of the College.

WILLIAM JAMES

The Master selected by the Earl of Leicester in 1572 was a young man, barely thirty years old. William James, an alumnus of Christ Church, had become Theology lecturer at Magdalen in 1571. Leicester thought well of him—he appointed him one of his chaplains and would make him Vice-Chancellor in 1581—and the Fellows responded: the 1572/3 accounts record two of them making a 'Jorney to London att the masters Comminge first to the Colledge'. James was also the first Master to marry. Although it is not known whether Katherine James lived in the College or in his Oxfordshire living of Kingham, his eldest son, William (m. Christ Church in 1593 aged 16), was born during his Mastership. He is also the first Master of whom a reasonably authentic likeness survives (Plate 3).[5]

The first significant event of James's Mastership was the defining of University College's legal status. This had been of concern to Oxford in general. In 1571 both Oxford and Cambridge universities were incorporated under an act of Parliament, and older colleges, which lacked foundation charters (having been founded before such things were necessary), were seeking to rectify this. Merton had already received a charter by letters patent under Mary, and Balliol would receive one in 1588. In February 1573, James procured University College a charter of incorporation. Apart from giving the College legal status, the charter also settled its name. The preamble noted seven variants of its name—was it the Hall, or the College, of the Great Hall of the University of Oxford? Was it led by a Master and Scholars, or a Master and Fellows?—and formally decreed that William James and the Fellows

---

[4] Congregation and its undermining: Cross 1986: 117–18 and Fletcher 1986: 164 (similar developments occurred at Cambridge (Morgan 2004: 84–8 and 303–12)); European colleges: de Ridder-Symoens 1996: 158–64, 167–75, and 190–5, and Müller 1996: 333–9.

[5] James's election is described in UC:GB3/A1/1 p. 13. Journey to London: *ARUC* ii. 415; James and Leicester: Harington 1804: ii. 268; James's wives: Wood, *Athenae* ii. 203–4.

should be incorporated as 'The Master and Fellows of the College of the Great Hall of the University of Oxford' (*Magister et Socij Collegij Magnae Aulae Universitatis Oxon.*), a title which remains to this day.[6]

By the 1570s University College had also assumed its current coat of arms. Although arms attributed to William of Durham were known, as King Alfred came to be accepted as the Founder of the College, it began to adopt arms attributed to him. 'Attributed' is the important word here: there was no heraldry in Alfred's day, and the shield with a blue cross and four or five martlets was assigned only retrospectively to him and other Anglo-Saxon monarchs. It is not known when University College assumed the bogus arms of its bogus founder, but a heraldic visitation of Oxford in 1574 showed that the College was certainly using it by then, and it has been using it ever since.[7]

William James also turned to the College's finances. One modest piece of good fortune came in 1572/3 when the College acquired 49–51 St Giles (p. 105). Then the section of 'unexpected receipts' (*recepta preter spem*) in the accounts of 1573/4 recorded a sum of £54 22*d*. We do not know whether James had attracted a benefactor, or arranged the College's accounts so that its reserve fund reappeared, but the accounts after 1573/4 regularly record a College reserve fund (now usually called the 'Bursar's Bill' (*billa bursarii*)) of between £50 and £90, thus giving University College greater stability than it had enjoyed for many years.[8]

Another innovation in the 1583/4 accounts is a payment of £4 'for greeke and logicke Lecture'. The Crown Inn (p. 105) was now in the College's possession, and its funds for lectureships at last released. An undated entry in the College Register from this period shows the College exploiting this development. The Fellows created five new College officials: a Dean, who ensured that the undergraduates attended prayers in Chapel, and readings and disputations in the Hall; three Praelectors, or Lecturers, one each in Greek, philosophy, and logic, who would lecture once a week; and a Catechist, who, under university regulations of 1579, would provide religious instruction. These offices mark a decisive change in the culture of University College: it had been one thing to accept undergraduate commoners, and offer them internal tuition on an informal basis; but the College's acceptance of its duty to appoint and pay official lecturers for its undergraduates marked the final passing of the medieval College as a community of students of theology.[9]

[6] 1571 act: Williams 1986: 402; colleges: Martin and Highfield 1997: 154 and Jones 2005: 80–1. University College's charter: UC:GB2/L3/1.

[7] Forrester 1969 and Turner 1871: 98–100. Either four or five martlets can be used. William of Durham's arms (a fleur de lys) were still visible in College in 1574, but someone had written 'Skerloo' above them. It is unclear how genuine William of Durham's arms are.

[8] 49–51 St Giles: *ARUC* ii. 411 (the deed by which the College purchased the property from Thomas Gold's son is lost, but it was issuing its leases from 1573/4 (UC:E/G1/2D/2)); receipts of 1573/4: *ARUC* ii. 421.

[9] Payment to praelectors: *ARUC* ii. 488; new College offices: UC:GB3/A1/1 p. 17. Praelectors did not have to be Fellows: John Waldridge, the first known Logic praelector (*ARUC* ii.

New benefactions came to the College. There was the bequest of William Hearne, or Heron, of Clerkenwell, who left money in 1580 to the Clothworkers' Guild in London to give £5 a year each to University College and to Peterhouse, Cambridge, to educate poor scholars. Hearne apparently had no link with either institution, but the reference in his will to helping 'twoe poore Colledges' suggests that he just wished to support the oldest colleges in each university. There was also the gift of Simon Perrot, a former Fellow of Magdalen College. In July 1584 he gave University College a house in Woodstock and lands in Waterstock, to pay for a sermon to be preached on St Simon and St Jude's day in St Peter in the East, the first choice of preacher being a Fellow of the College. Twenty shillings should also be distributed among the poor of the parish that day.[10]

The third significant benefaction of James's Mastership came from William Holcot. In spite of his tangle with the College authorities in the 1550s, Holcot, on his death in 1575, bequeathed books to University and Queen's Colleges in a disarmingly affectionate manner:

I herewith will that certayne of my said hawks and howndes my Books ... be in tyme conveniently conveyede to the mewes and Kennells I meane the Librarye of the Queens Colledge and of the University Colledge in Oxford where I ones was to learn soo to hawke and hunt. They those books mentyonede therefore to be fastenede and cheyned to the use of the students there, not doubtinge but those my Colleagues and Companyons will in studye soo hawke and hunt with theyme that they will remember their Colleagian the gever.[11]

Less disarming were the conditions attached to a bequest of £20 to each college, to be spent on poor scholars and the Master and Fellows for as long as funds held. The scholars benefiting from Holcot's bequest would say the following grace every day at Hall:

[Scholar] Lyft upp your hartes.
[Response] We lifte them upp unto the Lord.
[Scholar] Lett us geve thankes to the Lord our god for William Holcotte.
[Response] Yt is meete and right soo to dooe.

Evidence from College accounts suggests that its members endured this daily display of egotism until the funds ran out after a decade.[12]

---

492), only became one in 1586. Elsewhere, Queen's created lecturers in 1535, with Merton following in 1560, Balliol in 1571, and Lincoln in 1573. Only Oriel introduced them later (McConica 1986a: 57–62). University College was also slow to appoint catechists, although Oriel and Merton only created them in 1585 and 1589 (Greenslade 1986: 326–7).

[10] Hearne's bequest: UC:GB3/A1/1 p. 16, UC:BE1/MS1/1 p. 7; transcription of his will: UC:BE1/MS2/2 p. 506; Perrot's gift: UC:BE1/MS2/2 pp. 445–53 (on Perrot himself, see *BRUO2* 442–3); the Woodstock house: Crossley 1990: 347–8.

[11] Date of Holcot's death: Wood, *History* ii. 129; his will: UC:BE11/W1/2. UC:BE1/MS1/3 fo. 2 lists the books he gave, which included works by Foxe and Calvin.

[12] The responses: UC:BE11/W1/2; payments from Holcot's fund: *ARUC* i. xxxiii.

James's reputation spread. In 1573 the chaplain and fellows of the Savoy, a London hospital, unsuccessfully asked Lord Burghley to make James their Master, recording his 'wisdom and policy in restoring and bringing to happy quietness the late wasted, spoiled, and indebted University College'.[13] In 1577 James was appointed Archdeacon of Coventry, after which he had less time for College affairs.

Evidence for this comes from the letters of Robert Batt, a young Brasenose BA. Batt came from a landed Yorkshire family, but, as the third son, had to shift for himself for a living. In 1583 he applied for a Fellowship at University College, first writing to the senior Fellow, John Browne, and then to James himself. He presented his credentials: he came from Yorkshire; he could not remain in Oxford without a Fellowship; and his tutor could supply a reference. He would also have hoped that his elegant Latin would tell in his favour. Unfortunately, after he had written three times to James tactfully finding new ways of asking about his application, it became clear where James's real interests lay. In a letter to a friend at University College, Stephen Waterhouse, Batt grumbled that he was getting nowhere because 'your Master is hanging around court, gaping for the Deanery' (of Christ Church, then vacant).[14]

James did become Dean of Christ Church in 1584, and resigned as Master of University College that September. Having presided over the second visit of Elizabeth to Oxford in 1592, he became Dean of Durham in 1596, and then Bishop there from 1606 until his death in 1617. If, as Batt feared, William James was most interested in his own advancement, he did at least achieve this by proving his competence. The College, its finances enjoying a much-needed stability, its legal status established, and its undergraduate teaching provided for, had much to thank him for.

ANTHONY GATE AND THE PURITANS

Once again the Fellows of University College (now including Robert Batt, whose persistence was rewarded in July 1584) received a new Master from their Chancellor. Leicester's candidate, Anthony Gate, showed how far one could overrule a College's statutes, for not only was Gate's highest degree in medicine, but he was also a layman—indeed he was the College's only lay Master until 1906. Gate's links with the College, however, were strong: he had taken both his MA in 1572 and his B.Med. in 1580 there, and a 'Master Gate' was renting a College room in 1573/4–1583/4. He could also have been an undergraduate there—the first Master for whom such a claim could be made.[15]

---

[13] Wood, *Athenae* ii. 204.

[14] Batt's letters: Bodl. MS Rawl. D 985 fos. 30[r]–53[v]; his comment on James (*Magister vester curiam frequentat, decanatum inhians*) is at fo. 47[r].

[15] Robert Batt's election: UC:GB3/A1/1 p. 20; Gate's election: UC:GB3/A1/1 p. 21 (supplemented by UC:AR2/MS1/11 pp. 36–7). The wording of his dispensation is curious: noting the 1475 statutes' demand for a Master 'from the bosom and company of the College' (*de gremio ac*

Gate was another married Master, and his wife Judith lived with him in the Lodgings. He also seems to have sent his children to the College. Four young Gates, all described as 'gentlemen' of Oxford, matriculated from University College during this time, namely Peter and Nathaniel (m. October 1590 aged 11 and 10 years, Nathaniel being the youngest known member of the College), Timothy (m. February 1592 aged 12), and Thomas (m. April 1602 aged 12). These activities suggest that Gate had treated his College rooms much like William Holcot, as an occasional residence. Gate's origins are unknown, although he may have come from East Anglia—his brother, Geoffrey, lived in Norfolk. Furthermore, although still quite young when elected (probably in his mid to late thirties), Gate seems not to have sought advancement. He may have had private means—he had been renting expensive rooms in College, usually at 20s. a year, and in 1588 he bought the College's lease on Irish Mead.[16]

An explanation for Leicester's unorthodox choice of Master may be found in the religious background to this period. Although University College was free from any taint of crypto-catholicism, it was not quite free from other kinds of religious controversy. The religious consensus of Elizabethan Oxford was strongly Calvinist: excessive ritual in services aroused disapproval; the minister was seen less as an intermediary between God and the congregation, than a preacher and teacher, leading a congregation in its worship; it was thought that man would be justified before God by faith rather than good works; and, above all, there was a strong belief in the doctrine of predestination, which taught that God, being omniscient, knew in advance who would be saved or damned. Some took this a stage further, claiming that the saved would have shown themselves worthy by leading appropriately godly lives. Thus far, at least, the majority of Oxford Protestants were in general agreement, but some felt that the Elizabethan church was not sufficiently reformed. For them, the Book of Common Prayer still contained too many remnants of the old ritual, not least its regulations concerning the wearing of vestments, and they opposed the concept of an ecclesiastical hierarchy, which they argued was contrary to scripture. It was such people who first attracted the nickname of 'puritans'. Leicester gave patronage to puritans, although not exclusively so, and in the mid-1580s, a time when the Catholic threat was considered particularly dangerous, he would have taken pains to seek a Master of impeccably Protestant credentials.[17]

---

comitiva ... Collegii), the Fellows said that, although Gate was not *de gremio Collegii*, he was *de comitiva*. The best explanation for this distinction is that the Fellows were trying to differentiate commoners from Fellows.

[16] Ages of undergraduates: p. 547; Gate's brother: UC:MA23/1D/1; Gate's room rents are in the relevant pages of *ARUC*; lease of Irish Mead: UC:E/H2/2D/2.

[17] A wider exploration of these matters as seen in Oxford: Loach 1986, Williams 1986, and Tyacke 1997, and (elsewhere) MacCulloch 2003: 109–12 and 374–5; Leicester's religion: Williams 1986: 430–1.

It is therefore unsurprising that the few known facts about Anthony Gate suggest that he, and much of the Fellowship, held distinctly 'puritan' views on religion. In April 1586, Gate and the Fellows of University College were summoned before the Vice-Chancellor and rebuked for not wearing surplices. A letter from an unnamed Fellow, preserved only in copies, claims that they defied the Vice-Chancellor, declaring that this was not enjoined by their statutes, and that they were answerable only to their Visitor, the Chancellor himself (who, they hoped, would not have enforced the rule too firmly).[18]

Gate appears again when Richard Bancroft, a prominent opponent of Elizabethan puritans, observed in 1593 that one 'Gate of Oxford' supported the *classis* movement.[19] This must be Anthony—no other possible Gates were then around—and this accusation was more serious, for the *classis* movement was the most significant manifestation of dissent among Elizabethan puritans. *Classes* were informal groups of ministers and laymen, who met to discuss religious topics of mutual interest, and regulated themselves without reference to the ecclesiastical hierarchy. The church authorities devoted much energy in the 1580s and 1590s to destroying the movement. It is therefore suggestive that Gate was a known sympathizer. Further evidence for strong Protestant feeling comes when the 1586/7 accounts record payment for 'fagottes for the fire at the death of the Scottish Quenne'. Gate and his colleagues clearly agreed that the execution of the Catholic Mary Stuart was well worth celebrating. Gate was also known to Sir Francis Walsingham, Elizabeth's spymaster, and a patron of the reformers, who endowed a theology lectureship in Oxford.[20]

Leicester died in 1588, attended at the last by William James. Perhaps thanks to the latter's lobbying, he did not forget University College, bequeathing it property in Wales 'to the maintenance of two Schollars in the University College in Oxford'. The Scholars were to be nominated by his wife during her lifetime, and then by his heirs, and would receive £20 a year. Unfortunately Leicester continued:

This fee farm I know not the name of it, but the present rent is about Five Pounds a year, and worth fifty or threescore pounds when the years be out, which are about Twenty as I guesse.[21]

The property was eventually identified as a collection of farms in Montgomeryshire, but Leicester had conveyed these lands to two trustees upon a secret

---

[18] Surplices: OUA HYP/A/16 fo. 132ʳ; the letter: BL Add MS 38492 fo. 80ʳ and BL Add MS 48064 fo. 92ʳ⁻ᵛ (the presence of several copies shows that the affair aroused some interest): puritans and surplices: Dent 1983: 67.
[19] Dent 1983: 132–3.
[20] Mary's bonfire: *ARUC* ii. 511; Walsingham: Williams 1986: 436–7.
[21] The relevant portion of Leicester's will is transcribed at UC:BE1/MS2/2 pp. 469–70.

trust in 1580, and had died before the estate was returned. Unsurprisingly, therefore, the College had trouble proving its claim to this estate. Indeed the Fellows had to go to law to prove it, taking on the powerful Herbert family in the 1610s, and only in 1617 could the Countess of Leicester recommend the College's first Leicester Scholars.[22]

ELIZABETHAN FELLOWS AND SCHOLARS: THE CASE OF JOHN BROWNE

During the Mastership of Anthony Gate some of the other members of the Elizabethan College emerge from comparative anonymity. In particular, Gate was not alone in his advanced Protestant views. Richard Parker, who rented a College room in the early 1570s after taking his BA there, became a leading member of the *classis* near his living of Dedham in Essex, which he had to resign in 1590, and Alexander Cooke (F. 1587–97) became vicar of Louth in Lincolnshire, of which he was briefly deprived in 1604, for refusing to wear a surplice. In later years, he wrote several treatises, ferociously attacking both Catholics and Anglicans who he felt had grown too close to Rome.[23]

Robert Batt at least had a quieter life. His younger brother Thomas matriculated from University College in 1591, presumably so as to benefit from Robert's supervision. Robert resigned his Fellowship in 1597 to marry, and in 1598 became rector of Newton Tony, Wiltshire, where he died in 1617, leaving a collection of over sixty books behind him. After his two elder brothers died young, he also inherited his family estate in 1607.[24]

Undoubtedly, however, the dominant presence in the College at this time was John Browne (F. 1575–1612), the first person whom Batt had contacted in applying for a Fellowship. The survival of several of his papers, including an account book recording his pupils' finances, also makes Browne the best-documented Fellow of his generation. His early academic career is unclear— he may have been at St Alban Hall—but he devoted his life to University College. Batt's letter of 1583 hints at Browne's prominence: undoubtedly, as William James was seeking preferment, a vacuum was growing in University College, and Browne was evidently interested in filling it.[25]

Under Anthony Gate, Browne threw himself into procuring benefactions for the College from his relatives. First, there was his uncle Thomas Browne, vicar of Basingstoke and former Fellow of Balliol. Before his

---

[22] Lawsuit with Herbert family: UC:BE1/MS2/2 pp. 479–87; first Leicester Scholars: UC:GB3/A1/1 p. 34.
[23] Parker: Greenslade 1986: 339, and Collinson 1990: 222–39 and 438–9: Cooke: *ODNB* entry and Babbage 1962: 174–7.
[24] My thanks to Mrs Joan Edwards for providing more information on Batt's later life.
[25] His entry in *AO1* confuses him with a different John Browne of Christ Church. Browne's papers are catalogued as UC:S13.

death in 1587, he had given £10 to purchase books for the College Library, and he also paid for the repair of five ground-floor rooms. Finally, he bequeathed money to endow two scholarships at University College and one at Balliol.[26]

More impressive still was the benefaction of Browne's cousin John Freeston, who in 1592 gave the College various lands in and around Pontefract, including the site of a hospital called Knowles Almhouses, or the Trinities, to support one Fellow and two Scholars, and to increase the stipends of the Catechist and the Master. The College, however, had to use the income from these properties also to support an almshouse at Kirkthorpe near Pontefract, pay the stipends of a master and usher at Normanton School, also near Pontefract, and supplement the stipend of the master of Wakefield School. Freeston's Fellow and Scholars should be chosen from the grammar schools at Normanton, Wakefield, or Pontefract, or, failing these, the grammar schools of the West Riding of Yorkshire, or, failing that, anywhere in Yorkshire. Freeston's generosity was not exhausted: in his will of 1594, he gave the College £60 to purchase the lease on the house west of the College, asking that a new building be erected there, its best rooms assigned to his Fellows and Scholars, and free lodgings given to John Browne. He also gave 200 marks (£133 6s. 8d.) to be used to purchase land at Normanton, and build a grammar school there. The master would be selected by the Master of University College, the Master of Emmanuel College, Cambridge, and the Rector of Lincoln College, as well as several local vicars.[27]

Such a generous gift was unlikely to reach the College without obstacles, and so it proved. Freeston left a widow, who needed provision, and it took almost twenty years to see the property safely in the College's possession. When James Harrison became the first Freeston Fellow in August 1598, it emerged that, during Mrs Freeston's lifetime, he could only receive one-third of his allowance, with free lodgings, and in 1609 it was agreed further that the Freeston Fellow should not receive a share of the fines and dividends received by other Fellows. Freeston's gift never quite realized its full value, for eventually it subsidized merely one senior and two junior Freeston Scholars.[28]

Not every benefaction to the College from this period owed its origin to Browne—in addition to the Earl of Leicester's bequest, Otho Hunt, Fellow and commoner between 1559 and 1565/6, in 1590 left property in Methley, Yorkshire, where he was rector, to support one or two Scholars from the

---

[26] Thomas Browne's benefactions: UC:GB3/A1/1 p. 22, UC:BE1/MS1/1 p. 8, and UC:E9/W1/1–4. John Browne invested his uncle's bequest in land at Rotherwick in Hampshire, arranging for its tenant to pay quit-rents to both Colleges to support their respective scholars. The Balliol donation is discussed in Jones 2005: 82–3.
[27] Copies of Freeston's deeds of gift are at UC:BE1/MS1/2 pp. 323–50.
[28] UC:GB3/A1/1 p. 25 and UC:GB3/A1/1 p. 27. See p. 152 below on dividends.

Yorkshire area—but Browne's contribution is especially notable. All these Elizabethan bequests, however, are notable for another reason. Whereas the College's benefactions before 1500 were intended to increase the number of Fellowships, almost all its sixteenth-century ones were to benefit men below the rank of Fellow. This was prudent: now that almost every college was open to undergraduate commoners, it was important for University College to attract the best men it could, and the obvious means was by Scholarships, of which it had had none, but other colleges several.[29]

Nevertheless, not every early Scholarship was bestowed on undergraduates. The first Browne Scholar, James Harrison, and Freeston Scholars, Timothy Gate (a son of the Master) and Lancelot Gryme, were created in July 1597, the latter two at John Freeston's insistence that his first scholarships go to Gryme and to 'Mr Gate his sonnes'. All three had matriculated in 1592, and were all of BA status. In August 1598, by contrast, Thomas Gate became a Freeston Scholar, and William Mason a Browne one, both at John Browne's nomination. The only known Thomas Gate (another of Anthony's sons?) from this period matriculated from University College in April 1602 aged 12, and the only known William Mason from Magdalen Hall in June 1606 aged 16, before moving to Magdalen College. If these identifications are correct, then they would have been very young indeed. Both Harrison and Gryme were former pupils of John Browne, and Browne appears to have been using these Scholarships to help non-Fellows whom he thought needed them, irrespective of status. Only in the 1610s, after Browne's death, did the Browne and Freeston Scholarships become scholarships in the modern sense, of awards given to undergraduates.[30]

In the 1580s and 1590s, John Browne's prospects looked good: he was known to Sir Francis Walsingham; he had been a preacher in the university; he became a Bachelor of Theology in 1594; and in 1593 he was awarded the reversion of a prebend at Ely Cathedral the next time the Crown had the right to make a presentation there. Walsingham had died in 1590 and it might be some time before a vacancy at Ely occurred, but Browne still had reasons for optimism.[31]

He was certainly at his most optimistic in the late summer of 1597 when Anthony Gate died in the Master's Lodgings, since he campaigned to be elected Gate's successor. He, or one of his supporters, wrote memoranda explaining why he should be appointed. Apart from suggesting that the College should revert to the old tradition of electing the senior Fellow (i.e.

---

[29] Hunt's bequest: UC:BE1/MS1/1 p. 9 and UC:BE1/MS2/2 p. 354. University College was not alone in creating undergraduate scholarships (Stone 1975: i. 20, claims that Oxbridge colleges created some 500 of them between 1560 and 1640).

[30] Scholarship appointments: UC:GB3/A1/1 p. 24 & UC:GB3/A1/1 p. 25; Harrison and Gryme as John Browne's pupils: UC:S13/F1/1 pp. 1–6.

[31] Walsingham: UC:S13/MS1/4; prebend at Ely: UC:S13/L1/1–7.

Browne), the documents recalled the benefactions which Browne had procured, and the efforts which he had made in securing the Earl of Leicester's bequest. Browne also won the support of Gate's widow, Judith. In a draft letter to the widow of Sir Francis Walsingham—the earliest known document written by the wife of a Master—she laments the loss of her husband, 'who hathe left behind him fiue younge children very slenderly provided for', and hopes that Lady Walsingham will put in a good word for John Browne, since Sir Francis had been well disposed both to Browne and to Gate. She also clearly hoped that Browne might help her eldest son win a Fellowship in the College, and help her remain in the Master's Lodgings, which, following her husband's death, she would otherwise have to leave with no obvious place to go—a fate which would hang for several centuries over the wives of improvident Masters.[32]

Unfortunately, Browne's lack of a patron proved fatal. The current Chancellor, Thomas Sackville, Lord Buckhurst, already had a candidate of his own in his chaplain, George Abbot, a Fellow of Balliol since 1583. Buckhurst made the College's decision easier by issuing a dispensation for Abbot before election day. The Fellows, faced with the Chancellor's man and the Chancellor's dispensation, did what was expected, and Browne had to accept the inevitable.[33]

GEORGE ABBOT

In George Abbot (Fig. 7.2), University College had a Master similar to William James: a young man, in his mid-thirties, possessing the same potent combination of ambition and a powerful patron. Buckhurst seems to have been a pragmatist in religious matters, and Abbot was just that. Although a staunch Calvinist in his theology, Abbot was moderate in other respects, such as in his willingness to work within the existing Church of England. Buckhurst showed his estimation of Abbot by appointing him Vice-Chancellor in 1600/1, 1603/4, and 1605/6. He had difficult times, which he handled skilfully. In 1601, he had to suppress shows of support for the Earl of Essex and his abortive revolt; and in 1603 he had to soothe feelings severely ruffled within Oxford by some controversially anti-Calvinist statements made by his predecessor. A more comic attack on his authority came in 1605, when, just before a visit from James I, he committed 140 undergraduates to prison for daring to keep their hats on in his presence in the university church.[34]

---

[32] Browne's lobbying activities: UC:S13/MS1/2–4 (whose claims are treated with justified scepticism by William Smith at UC:AR2/MS1/4 pp. 283–4); Mrs Gate's letter: UC:S13/MS1/1 (transcribed in Darwall-Smith 2002b).

[33] Abbot's election: UC:GB3/A1/1 p. 25.

[34] Abbot's religion: Dent 1983: 218; his Vice-Chancellorships: Welsby 1962: 19–21 and Fincham 1997: 182–6; the hats: Nichols 1828: i. 559.

FIGURE 7.2 George Abbot, Master 1597–1610, by an unknown artist.

Abbot's career proved even more successful than James's. In 1600, barely three years into his post, he was made Dean of Winchester. He then attracted the notice of the new monarch, James I, when they met at Woodstock in 1603 during Abbot's second Vice-Chancellorship. James showed his regard for Abbot by sending him to Scotland in 1608 to a meeting of the Scottish Church to discuss episcopacy, and to defend the King in a lawsuit. Abbot's scholarship was also recognized when in 1604 he was appointed a member of the team which translated the Gospels, Acts of the Apostles, and the Book of Revelation for the Authorized Version of the Bible.[35]

One may reasonably ask what time Abbot had left for the interests of University College. Other, larger, colleges had known heads who were more courtiers than academics, but University College had never experienced anyone quite like George Abbot. Evidence, however, suggests that Abbot

[35] Welsby 1962: 17, 26, and 29–31.

did not forget his College completely, especially in his dealings with undergraduates, some of whom came to be very fond of him. Of one such, Dudley Digges (m. 1600), Abbot said, touchingly, in 1627 that 'he calleth me Father and I term his Wife my Daughter, his eldest Son is my God-Son and their Children are, in love, accounted my Grandchildren.' Another former undergraduate, Sir George Savile (m. 1598), appointed Abbot, 'my antient loving tutor in Oxford', one of his executors in his will of 1614.[36]

Abbot wrote at least one student textbook, *A Briefe Description of the Whole Worlde wherein is particularly described all the Monarchies, Empires and Kingdomes of the same*. The first edition was published in 1600; the second, much enlarged, in 1605. It is clearly arranged, taking the reader first through the oceans, then continental lands, ending with islands. Within each country Abbot discusses its boundaries, its previous and current systems of government, its religion, and anything else of interest. Abbot's biographer calls it 'not wildly exciting', but it is accurate and well-informed for someone of Abbot's date and situation, becoming more hazy the harder a country was to reach for a Western European. It is also very level-headed: there are no travellers' tales in this book. His only vices are those of a Protestant Englishman, assured of his superiority over all other nations and religions. For him, Islam is 'a new religion, consisting partly of Jewish ceremonies and partly of Christian doctrine, and some other things of [Mohammed's] owne invention'. Abbot says of the Spaniards that their 'insolence...is very great, even over Christians, tyranizing and playing all outrages, wheresoever they set men in subjection'. Nearer home, the Irish 'are naturally rude and superstitious', and Scots 'do barbarously speake' English. One of Abbot's early charges (and later no mean scholar himself), Edward Herbert, Lord Herbert of Cherbury (m. 1596), considered geography essential for the young scholar, noting that 'it will bee requisite to learne something concerning the Gouernements, manners and Religions, either anncient and new, as also the Interests of state, and Relations in Amity, or strength in which they stand to theire neighbours'—all subjects precisely covered in Abbot's little book. The *Description* was certainly a great success, being regularly reprinted, even after Abbot's death.[37]

Another example of Abbot's teaching activities is a set of thirty sermons preached on the Book of Jonah between 1594 and 1599 in the university church, mainly to a student audience. Abbot's biographer rightly describes them as 'vigorous and swiftly moving, such as to retain the interest of the hearers'. Abbot avoids talking over his audience's heads, and tailors his words to their needs: he expresses disapproval of long hair in men, and on another

---

[36] Digges: Rushworth 1659: 451; Savile: Clay 1920: 23.
[37] Welsby 1962: 8; quotations from Abbot 1605 (which lacks page numbers); Herbert's comments: Herbert 1976: 20.

occasion, aware of the future careers of many of his listeners, discusses the challenges faced by a parish minister. His theological position remains carefully balanced, combining Calvinist beliefs on predestination and the importance of preaching, with a willingness to accept the ecclesiastical structure of his day.[38]

Nevertheless, such were the other demands on Abbot's time, that University College would regularly have had to take second place. He had, however, John Browne on hand. Browne may have been disappointed of the Mastership, but his influence within the College remained undiminished. It was later said of him that he was 'a reverend, learned and carefull man, in everye way for the good and government of the Colledge' and that 'there hath not to our remembraunce any matter of strife broken out for visitation in the said College since his first election'. Relations between Abbot and Browne even appear cordial: in his will, Browne described Abbot as 'my ever worshipful and equall kynde friend' and left him 40s. with which to purchase a gold ring. Browne continued to strive for promotion, both academic and ecclesiastic. In 1608 he became a Doctor of Divinity, an honour by now rarely sought by those who were neither heads of colleges nor Canons of Christ Church, and, perhaps aware that the Ely prebend might be some time coming, secured a promise in 1603 of the Essex living of Stanford Rivers, when it fell vacant.[39]

Abbot was fortunate in having a Fellow like John Browne willing to help; but there were other Fellows on whom he could rely, especially two Yorkshire cousins, Charles Greenwood (m. 1592; F. 1597–1614) and Jonas Radcliffe (m. 1592; F. 1600–26). Jonas Radcliffe was an unusual figure in Jacobean Oxford in that he was very badly lame. University records noted his exemption from attending Congregation in 1608, because he 'could not attend without great pain to himself', and when in 1614 he was studying to become a Bachelor of Theology, he was exempted from professorial lectures on account of his lameness. His disability deprived him of any hope of ecclesiastical or academic promotion, but did not prevent his becoming an important College figure. He sometimes acted as deputy for the Master when absent, and above all he was a much-loved and respected tutor. One pupil wrote an affectionate elegy upon his death, praising him for his even-handedness towards his pupils, writing:

---

[38] Abbot 1613: 570 (long hair) and 343–4 (parish life); opinions on the sermons: Welsby 1962: 9–14, and Tyacke 1997: 570–1 (who compares Abbot with the puritan Provost of Queen's, Henry Airay, showing that, although both men shared similar theological views, Airay expressed greater opposition to the ecclesiastical settlement).

[39] Praise of Browne: UC:S13/MS1/5; his will: UC:S13/W1/1; the titles of his doctoral disputations, which include 'Papacy is heresy', or 'Faith alone justifies, but does not save without good works': Clark 1887–9: i. 205; offer of Stanford Rivers: UC:S13/L1/8.

> Thou wast alike to all; or if there were
> any that felt thy temper lesse severe
> Itt was their industrie their favour wanne
> not to the gentler, but the better mann
> Thus all encourag'd were...

Another pupil erected a memorial to him in the Chapel where he was buried, and significantly, when it was demolished, it was one of just three memorials transferred to the present building.[40]

Charles Greenwood's equally considerable abilities as a tutor are similarly revealed by his former pupils. One such was George Radcliffe (m. 1609), himself another cousin of Greenwood and Jonas Radcliffe, whose letters home to his mother provide the earliest known significant correspondence from an undergraduate of University College. George's letters show Greenwood as more than a mere teacher. he was given an allowance to spend on George, as was typical at the time; he looked to his pupil's health, buying a pomander for George at a time of plague. He also provided careers advice: many years later, George wrote that 'This Mr Greenewood was the cause of my takinge upon me the profession of the law, his intent beinge to make me serviceable to Sir George Savile my godfather.'[41]

Greenwood's abilities were recognized elsewhere: he was one of the proctors of 1609, undoubtedly thanks to Abbot's support, and early in 1610, George wrote about a sermon preached by his cousin in St Mary the Virgin 'which he performed with great approbation, I might say admiration, of all', and in June 1610, he joined a team appointed to produce a revised edition of theological works by early Christian writers. Others wanted the benefit of his teaching: between 1611 and 1613 he was asked to travel to France with a young Yorkshireman called Thomas Wentworth, a graduate of St John's College, Cambridge, and future minister of Charles I. A deep friendship grew up between the two men, with significant results. Although Wentworth's father had left instructions that his youngest sons, Matthew, Philip, and George, should go to Cambridge, all three went instead to University College, where Matthew became a Fellow. Greenwood, and George Radcliffe too, later became Wentworth's chief advisers on estate matters, and, when Wentworth was sent to Ireland, Radcliffe joined him. Eventually, Greenwood achieved some well-deserved preferment, becoming rector of Thornhill, to which he was appointed in 1614 by the father of his former pupil—and Wentworth's brother-in-law—Sir George Savile (m. 1598), and

---

[40] University records on Radcliffe: Clark 1887–9: i. 92 and 133; Radcliffe as Master's deputy in 1620: OUA CC Papers 1620 1620/154:1; the elegy: Kay 1976. His memorial now stands on the north side of the Antechapel, immediately to the east of the door.

[41] Radcliffe's letters: Whitaker 1810 (see too Darwall-Smith 2002a); George's pomander: Whitaker 1810: 41; Greenwood's careers advice: Cooper 1973: 322.

resigned his Fellowship that year. However, he did not forget his College, and will re-enter the story later.[42]

Greenwood's last years at University College were spent under a new Master. Like William James, George Abbot was destined for greater things. In May 1609, he was appointed Bishop of Lichfield and Coventry, and was enthroned there in December. Almost at once, however, he was appointed Bishop of London, where he was enthroned on 12 February 1610. Eleven days later, Abbot resigned as Master of University College. To become Bishop of London so quickly was remarkable in itself, but Abbot's ascent was not complete: on 20 November 1610 Richard Bancroft, the Archbishop of Canterbury, died, and in February 1611 Abbot was appointed his successor—barely two years after his first episcopal appointment. No one previously attached to University College had ever achieved such ecclesiastical success.

Unfortunately Abbot remains a controversial Archbishop: Edward Hyde, Earl of Clarendon, said dismissively that Abbot 'had been head or master of one of the poorest Colleges in Oxford, and had learning sufficient for that province', but others take a more nuanced view, noting that his early years were fairly successful, but he lived too long, enduring a new king who had little sympathy with his brand of pragmatic Calvinism, and had become all but ignored by the time he died in 1633. A shadow was also cast over his later years by an incident in 1621, when, whilst out hunting, the Archbishop accidentally shot a gamekeeper dead.[43]

University College might have hoped to receive a few crumbs of archiepiscopal generosity: heads of other colleges, when promoted, were usually generous to their colleges and kindly patrons to their Fellows. If such hopes were entertained in 1611, they were disappointed. No Fellow of University College appears to have enjoyed significant promotion in the 1610s and 1620s, and the College itself received nothing from Abbot except for a silver communion dish, until, just before his death, he gave it £100 to spend on books. More seriously, in the 1610s, Abbot was made the senior member of a group of trustees who had been given £5,000 by a certain Thomas Tisdale to support scholars and fellows at an Oxford college. Balliol was to have first refusal on the offer, and University College had second. Balliol overplayed its hand, and did not receive a penny from the fund. However, rather than then turning to University College, the trustees instead used Tisdale's money to refound Broadgates Hall in St Aldates as Pembroke College in 1624. One

---

[42] Greenwood's sermon and his work on the Church Fathers: Whitaker 1810: 37 and 62; his travelling to France: Wedgwood 1961: 24; Wentworth's brothers' education: Cooper 1973: 55; Greenwood's estate advice: Wedgwood 1961: 29 and Cooper 1973: 269. The Savile, Wentworth, and Radcliffe families are discussed more fully at the end of the next chapter.

[43] Clarendon 1888: i. 118–19; more positive analyses: Holland 1987 and Fincham 1990: 301–3.

wonders whether an Archbishop with a little more interest in his second former college might have fought harder to help.[44]

This raises a question mark over George Abbot. He was undoubtedly an effective Master and an important figure in the university, yet there remains something slightly elusive about him. His Mastership was not a time of great benefactions, nor a time of reforms. Indeed, when something important took place, it owed rather more to John Browne than George Abbot. There is nothing to indicate that Abbot disliked University College, but little either to show that he saw it as much more than a useful staging post on his glittering path to success.

JOHN BANCROFT AND THE HIGH CHURCH ASCENDANCY

Another Magisterial vacancy led to another Cancellarial intervention: as we saw at the start of this chapter, Richard Bancroft persuaded University College to elect his nephew John as Master in March 1610. Few Masters arrived under worse omens than John Bancroft (Fig. 7.3). It was one thing to be the Chancellor's nominee, but quite another that he was also his nephew—and above all there remained John Browne. As it became clear that George Abbot would resign, Browne campaigned a second time to be elected Master. Memoranda were again written, presumably for the Chancellor's eyes, extolling Browne's achievements in the College, but again Browne was passed over, this time for a young man born only a year before he had been elected a Fellow.[45]

This blow struck when Browne was formulating one last scheme for University College, namely a new quadrangle. Little architectural activity had occurred in Oxford during the second half of the sixteenth century, but after 1600 several colleges began to expand or remodel themselves, especially Lincoln, Merton, and Oriel, and in 1610–13 the splendid buildings of the newly founded Wadham College took shape—whilst University College still inhabited its mishmash of medieval architecture. Browne's campaign had taken gradual shape. First of all, there was the house to the west of the College. Browne's cousin John Freeston had already left money to buy up the lease on it, and in 1605 a certain Thomas Frognell, with no known links to University College, gave 40s. for the same purpose, so that in November

---

[44] Kindness to former colleges: Henry Robinson, Provost of Queen's, appointed Bishop of Carlisle in 1598, promoted several Queen's graduates (Fincham 1990: 195), and William Laud, former President of St John's College and Abbot's successor at Canterbury, apart from similarly helping St John's men, also gave St John's a magnificent new quadrangle; Abbot's silver dish: UC:BE1/MS1/2 p. 1; his gift of £100: UC:BE1/MS1/3 fos. 5^{r-v}; the Tisdale affair: Jones 2005: 86–8 and Welsby 1962: 117–18. It is also possible that Abbot disapproved of the theological direction in which the College travelled under his successor.

[45] Browne's memoranda: UC:S13/MS1/5–6.

FIGURE 7.3 John Bancroft, Master 1610–32, by an unknown artist.

1606, the College at last bought the surrender of the lease, and demolished the house. Browne then began to raise funds and material for a new building. He bought timber in Wytham Wood, and in November 1610 entered into a contract with the masons currently working on the north side of a new quadrangle at Merton.[46]

No more, however, was heard of Browne's scheme, and almost a quarter of a century passed before the rebuilding of the College was reconsidered. Several reasons may be offered for this failure: insufficient funds; a lack of appetite for the huge fund-raising effort required; and perhaps a feeling that the College's efforts might better be concentrated elsewhere. Above all, the one man who might have had the energy to see the project begun soon left the

---

[46] The wider context: Newman 1997: 135–7; Frognell's gift: UC:GB3/A1/1 p. 26; the surrender of the lease: UC:E/A7/D1/9; Browne's purchase of timber: UC:S13/MS1/6; his contract: UC:FA3/1/L1/1–2.

College: in 1611 the living of Stanford Rivers at last became vacant, and Browne won the preferment which had eluded him so long. Browne moved to Essex, and resigned his Fellowship in July 1612, having, true to form, nominated his replacement. Unfortunately, he did not enjoy his new life long: on 11 May 1613, George Radcliffe, now in London, wrote to his mother that 'Dr. Browne died upon Saturday last [8 May], miserablie and fearefullye on a dead palsey; he is found to be worth 15s 2d and 600 pounds indebted to University College.' Little else is known of this astonishing debt—gossip may have enlarged the figures—but other documents imply that all was not well; and the College received no bequests from him. Browne's death arouses pity after all that he had done for his College, but it makes a sadly appropriate end to a career which had never quite fulfilled its promise.[47]

John Bancroft might well have been relieved at the departure of such a massive figure; as it was, Bancroft proved himself a better Master than had been feared. Like Abbot, he took pains to get to know the undergraduates, encouraging them to share in his sports: in May 1610, George Radcliffe wrote to his mother, asking for some money to buy a bow and arrows, 'for our Master loves shooting well, and we must follow'. Bancroft also acquired a reputation for financial efficiency. Anthony Wood claims that 'he was at great pains and expence to recover and settle the antient lands belonging to that foundation'. University College's Newcastle estate shows there was need for this. An anonymous report on these properties in the 1590s says of one house that 'This tenement is in lease, and the rent payd dewly', but of another that 'These tenements cannot be found out, nor the streates or the places', and yet the Newcastle lease of 1596 listed all these properties, as if nothing was wrong. At least in this instance the College accepted reality—its next Newcastle lease, of 1605, named just one house, in Westgate Street—but, even then, a letter of 1635 alludes to an enquiry made in Newcastle 'for howses and rents belonging by right vnto Vniuersitie Colledge whereof some wer conceited [sic] and the Colledge hath had no rents thus long tym.'[48]

Any assessment of Bancroft's approach to the problem is made difficult because only two draft accounts from his time survive, for the years 1616/17 and 1629/30, but these provide some support for Wood's assertion. The appearance of income from the Freeston properties in 1616/17 suggests that the College's ownership was now settled, and the appearance in the 1629/30 accounts of income from the Montgomery properties bequeathed by the Earl of Leicester suggests a similarly happy outcome. Perhaps the

---

[47] Browne's promotion: UC:S13/L1/11–12; nomination of a replacement: UC:S13/C1/6; his death: Whitaker 1810: 93–4; his will and related papers: UC:S13/W1/1–9.
[48] Archery: Whitaker 1810: 61; finances: Wood, *Athenae* ii. 893–5; the 1590s report: UC:E5/2/MS1/7; 1596 lease: UC:E5/2/D6/1; 1605 lease: UC:EB1/A1/1 fo. 312ᵛ; 1635 letter: UC:E5/2/C1/7.

greatest testimony to Bancroft's competence is that, when the official sequence of accounts resumed in the early 1630s (just after Bancroft had ceased to be Master), the College's rental was almost treble that of the 1590s—an increase well above the rate of inflation over that time.[49]

Bancroft's College also received some fresh benefactions. The most important one came from Robert Gunsley, rector of Titsey, Surrey, and supposedly a former member of University College—although no record of his Oxford career survives. In 1618, Gunsley bequeathed to the College the rectory of Flamstead, near Harpenden in Hertfordshire, stipulating that its income should support four Scholars, two each from the Grammar Schools at Rochester and Maidstone. As with Arncliffe, this living would be appropriated, so that the College would pay for a perpetual curate out of its income from the parish's tithes. The creation of fresh undergraduate Scholarships was, by now, nothing new, but, significantly, Gunsley had endowed the first awards in the College which gave preference to candidates in any other part of England than the north-east.[50]

Unfortunately not all the Fellows shared Bancroft's financial competence. One Fellow, in particular, showed a magnificent financial incompetence: the story of John Elmhirst (F. 1621–51), Bursar in 1623/4, 1629/30, 1633/4, and 1635/6, illustrates both the enduring fragility of University College's finances, as well as the patchiness of its accounting records. Elmhirst's extant official accounts are apparently all in good order; the problem lay in tradesmens's bills for food and drink. Bursars were then responsible both for paying tradesmen, and for being reimbursed in turn by members of the College. Unfortunately, Elmhirst was not very efficient at the latter duty, and therefore fell seriously behind in paying his creditors. As a result, during the four terms of his Bursarship he succeeded in running up a debt with a local brewer which came to over £500—when the College's rental for 1635/6 was not quite £440.[51]

Elmhirst was inefficient rather than fraudulent: when pressed about one debtor, he wrote pathetically in August 1641 that 'I am one of the most unhappy men liveing, thus to tyre and weary out your goodnes...that my ill husbandry, carelessness, oversight, kindheartedness or whatsoever you shall please to calle it, should be (as it is) a vexation to you.' Gradually Elmhirst found himself having to pay back his losses. After he left the College in 1651, the pressures grew greater, and he had to sell the contents of his rooms, including his library. Even in the 1660s he was still repaying his debts.

---

[49] Draft accounts for 1616 and 1629 (preserved in two Bursars' journals): UC:BU3/F1/1–2; accounts for the 1630s (which show Bancroft as tenant for some of the Montgomeryshire estates): UC:BU2/F1/1; inflation: Phelps Brown and Hopkins 1956.
[50] Gunsley: UC:BE1/MS2/2 pp. 355–62 (the first Gunsley Scholar was appointed in 1627 (UC:GB3/A1/1 p. 37)) and Edwards 1999: 270–1. See p. 60 on appropriating livings.
[51] The story is told in Cox 1977; papers concerning Elmhirst's plight are in UC:S7.

Meanwhile, the Fellows themselves, shutting an open stable door, decreed in March 1638 that all future Bursars should appoint two sponsors to underwrite their debts.[52]

For a contemporary observer, however, the most striking feature of Bancroft's Mastership would have been a change in the College's religious life. Bancroft arrived at a time when the Calvinist consensus of Oxford was starting to be attacked. Several theologians had found the doctrine of predestination too extreme, and, influenced by the teaching of the Dutch theologian Jacobus Arminius, began to ask whether God's grace might sometimes intervene to bring salvation. Some of these so-called 'Arminians', however, went further: believing that the sacred nature of the ministry had been eroded, and that insufficient attention had been paid to the priest's (not minister's) role as a divine intermediary, they thought that more should be done to enhance the beauty of holiness, be it through liturgical practice, priestly dress, or the decoration of churches and chapels. A leading exponent of these new ideas in Oxford in the 1610s was the President of St John's College, William Laud, who had already attracted the dislike of George Abbot.[53]

The College of Anthony Gate and George Abbot had been strongly Calvinist, but Bancroft would show himself more supportive of the new, 'Arminian', beliefs. We do not know where he stood in 1610, but his uncle Richard had fought vigorously against radical Protestantism—he had had his suspicions about Anthony Gate, after all—and by the 1630s, John Bancroft had revealed himself as a prominent anti-Calvinist, admired by one Italian observer in 1636 for his experience in ecclesiastical politics, and called 'molto nostro amico'—a far cry from the passionate anti-Catholicism of George Abbot.[54]

The Master was no lone Arminian: a list of John Elmhirst's books, made in October 1651, showed that, although he owned works by Calvin, he also owned Richard Montagu's tract *A New Gagg for an old Goose*, which had been attacked by George Abbot in the 1620s, and some works of William Laud and John Cosin, one of Laud's most enthusiastic supporters.[55]

Bancroft had accumulated several ecclesiastical posts, including a canonry of St Pauls in 1609 (just before coming to University College), and parishes in Kent, Middlesex, Berkshire, and Oxfordshire; but in 1632 he became Bishop of Oxford, and resigned the Mastership of University College that August.

---

[52] Elmhirst's letter: UC:S7/C1/1; valuation of the contents of his room, and lists of his books: UC:S7/MS1/1–3; creation of Bursars' sponsors: UC:GB3/A1/1 p. 48.

[53] Laud and the English 'Arminians': Tyacke 1987, Tyacke 1997: 572–90, and Parry 2006 (Costin 1958: 29 claims that George Abbot lobbied to prevent Laud's election as President in 1611). In calling Laud and his sympathizers 'Arminians', we should note that they were influenced by Arminius only on the subject of predestination, and certainly not on the question of ritual. Furthermore, Arminians did not have a monopoly on the beauty of holiness: in the 1620s, even Abbot commissioned painted glass for a chapel he had built (Parry 2006: 104).

[54] Fincham in Fincham 1993: 85, and Milton 1995: 365.

[55] Elmhirst's books: UC:S7/MS1/3; Robert Montagu: Fincham 1990: 61.

He had taken time to achieve promotion, but he had been at least as good a Master of University College as James or Abbot, and had also shown yet again the effects of the Chancellor's control of the College. Successive Chancellors had appointed Masters who variously cleared the College of Catholicism, steered it dangerously close to extreme radicalism, brought it back to a more pragmatic Calvinism, and then shifted it towards Arminianism. These changes could be witnessed in many other Oxbridge colleges, but University College reflected them more keenly than most. The next few years would see the College's close links to the Chancellor continue to prove beneficial, only in time to receive an abrupt, and catastrophic, reverse.

8

The Early Undergraduate College

On 3 September 1566, during Elizabeth I's visit to Oxford, Robert Dudley, Earl of Leicester and Chancellor of the university, gave the Spanish Ambassador a tour of some colleges, including University College, where, as a contemporary account wrote, 'they saw its little Hall and little Chapel' (*Aululam et Sacellulum*), before going on to Magdalen.[1] Little Hall and little Chapel: these words, not meant maliciously, cruelly remind one that, however much University College exulted in its antiquity, it remained comparatively insignificant. On the other hand, its population in the sixteenth century was the largest it had ever been, thanks to its undergraduate presence. Like other colleges in Oxford and Cambridge, University College was affected by the determined efforts of university authorities to force all students out of private accommodation so that their behaviour—and religion—could be better monitored, a process culminating in the matriculation statutes of 1581 when the university ordered undergraduates and their tutors to subscribe to the 39 Articles, and to be attached to a college or hall—a moment which effectively marks the transformation of Oxford into a collegiate university.[2] It is time to examine the effects of this change in population on University College.

THE MEMBERSHIP OF THE COLLEGE: THE YORKSHIRE INCURSION

We begin at the top of the College hierarchy, with the Fellows, and find that the Durham presence, previously so strong, fades away. In the first half of the sixteenth century, when the origins of 19 out of 52 Fellows are known, 11 came from Durham and 5 from Yorkshire; but, in 1551–1600, when the figures are 24 out of 50, only 2 came from Durham and 15 from Yorkshire. Finally, 17 of the 28 Fellows elected in 1601–42 came from Yorkshire and 3 from Durham. Nevertheless, the northern tone of the Fellowship remained: throughout this period, only six Fellows are known to have come from south of Yorkshire and Lancashire. More information can be found about Fellows'

---

[1] Plummer 1887: 180.   [2] 1581 statute: Gibson 1931: 421–2.

social status, where another surprise is in store: no fewer than six Fellows from the early seventeenth century were sons of esquires, and one, Matthew Wentworth, the son of a baronet. Few medieval Fellows, if any, appear to have been so well born. Another change was that, after University College acquired an undergraduate community, the Fellows, in common with those at other colleges, looked kindly upon former pupils when vacancies arose. Of the Fellows of 1551–1600, twenty-one were former undergraduates of the College, and the Fellows of 1601–42 were more inbred still: all but eight of these were College alumni.

The early Tudor Fellows stayed an average of six and a half years—as opposed to ten in 1451–1500—but later Fellows remained longer (ten years on average in 1551–1600, and just over thirteen in 1601–42). The shorter tenures in the early sixteenth century cannot be attributed simply to religious changes, since the greatest purges within the College took place after 1558; the fragility of University College's finances may rather have encouraged Fellows to look elsewhere. After 1558, however, as more Fellows assumed tutorial duties, there were greater inducements, both financial and personal, for good tutors like Charles Greenwood or Jonas Radcliffe to remain. Indeed some Fellows were particularly durable: whereas five out of the 102 Fellows of the sixteenth century remained in the College for more than twenty-one years, no fewer than eight of the twenty-eight early Stuart Fellows stayed this long. Since the total Fellowship rarely exceeded eight or nine during this period, the significance of these long-serving Fellows is clear.[3]

Fellows, however, were increasingly allowed to combine their Fellowships with activities outside Oxford. Leave of absence for a term was regularly given, and even longer periods were allowed. A quarter of the Masters and Fellows elected between 1551 and 1642 held benefices in conjunction with their College posts; but other reasons enticed them away. Charles Greenwood was granted three years' leave in August 1604, and in November 1611 was allowed to escort the young Thomas Wentworth around France, while Thomas Radcliffe (F. 1613–48 and 1660) received three years' leave in April 1636, and then three years more in March 1639. Radcliffe was Secretary to the Lord Treasurer, Bishop Juxon, which would explain the College's acquiescence.[4]

Part of the reason for this flexibility was financial. The only detailed summary of a Fellow's income from this period, for John Elmhirst in 1640, gives his official College stipend as just £10. Elmhirst, however, also received £15 10s. as his share of that year's entry fines, and £7 from a student renting

---

[3] Fellows at Queens' College Cambridge at this time stayed on average six or seven years (Twigg 1987: 78–9), and few fellows at Lincoln College or Magdalene College Cambridge stayed more than five (Green 1979: 142 and D. Hoyle in Cunich and others 1994: 69–70).
[4] Greenwood: UC:GB3/A1/1 pp. 26 and 32; Radcliffe: UC:GB3/A1/1 pp. 47–8, and Whitaker 1810: 10 (compare Green 1979: 191).

his room. Elmhirst was also allowed to hold the living of Aston Ingham, Herefordshire. Fellows therefore had to execute ingenious balancing acts to keep their personal finances healthy.[5]

The commoners of University College during 1500–1642 are rather harder to analyse than the Fellows of the period. Not only did the College itself not keep admission registers of its undergraduate commoners, until the 1670s, but the university did not keep full matriculation records until the 1580s, and even afterwards people still escaped administrative notice. Any analysis of the College's commoners, mature and undergraduate alike, therefore has to accept that the picture is incomplete.[6]

Graph 8.1, which shows matriculations at University College as recorded in university registers up to 1674, suggests an astonishing explosion of entrants in the early 1580s, followed by a slump in the succeeding decades, before another rise in the 1630s—a trend paralleled throughout Oxford. However, the matriculation statute of 1581 would have obliged unattached undergraduates quickly to join any college willing to receive them—hence the 'blip'—and the 'decline' represents a return to normality. The graph deceives in another particular: over one-tenth of the thousand or so commoners known to have been at University College between 1550 and 1642 appear in no matriculation registers, and are known only from College records, especially Buttery Books and Bursar's Books, which record the weekly expenditure of everyone resident in the College. As only a few of these books survive, there will have been many more commoners whose names are lost. Two other significant sources are a pair of account books compiled by John Browne between 1584 and 1611 and John Elmhirst in the 1630s: tutors at this time regularly received money from their undergraduate charges when they came up, and spent it on their behalf. In these account books Browne and Elmhirst record their pupils' income and expenditure, and thus supply useful information about student life from this period.[7]

Many 'extra' members appear as only surnames in lists, but sometimes enough survives to show that, at least within College, they were treated like everyone else. One such is John Wolveridge, a Hampshireman who appeared in John Elmhirst's accounts as a pupil in 1630/1, and who was living in College in 1634. Wolveridge never took a degree, and does not even appear in any matriculation register, yet Elmhirst treated him identically to his other students, even down to the books purchased for him. Years later, in the 1670s,

---

[5] UC:S7/F1/3. See p. 152 below on entry fines.
[6] The following analysis is based on a list of members of University College extracted from *AO1* by Peter Gilliver, supplemented, mainly from College sources, by myself.
[7] Effects of 1581 statutes: Russell 1977 (the conclusions about student population in Stone 1975 do not take sufficient account of these factors); Browne and Elmhirst's account books: UC:S13/F1/1 and UC:BU3/F1/2. We should also take account of lazy or incompetent university registrars (hence the apparent lack of matriculations in 1608 and 1627).

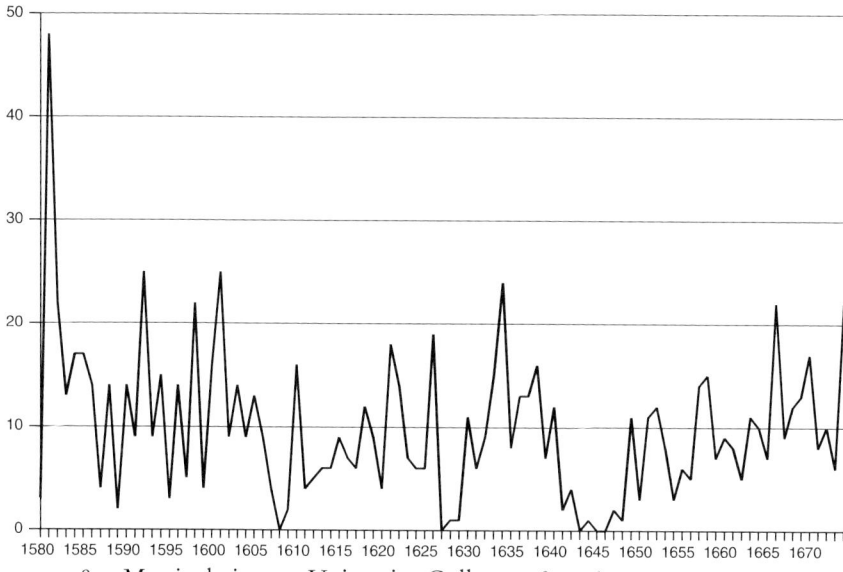

GRAPH 8.1 Matriculations at University College 1580–1674.

another Elmhirst pupil, Obadiah Walker, was corresponding with Wolveridge as one Old Member to another, and even soliciting contributions towards the new quadrangle (Wolveridge gave £20). In theory, Wolveridge had never been a member of University College; yet he and his contemporaries clearly saw himself as such.[8]

It is also hard to draw firm conclusions about the careers of undergraduate commoners, when nothing is known of the later lives of well over half of them. Over a third of those whose later careers are known, however, took orders, and, in one of his lectures on Jonah, George Abbot called Oxford 'this Seminarie and store-house of the Ministerie'.[9] At the higher end of society, at least forty Old Members of University College in 1551–1642 became Members of Parliament, two dozen were knighted, nine became baronets, and two were raised to the peerage.

More is known about the geographical origins, social status, and age of undergraduates in 1551–1642, especially from the 1580s, when such information appears in the university's matriculation registers. The origins of some two-thirds of commoners from 1551 to 1600 are known (356 out of 532), and they show a wide variety. The commonest county of origin is

[8] Wolveridge as Elmhirst's pupil: UC:BU3/F1/2 fos. 74^v, 75^v, and 78^{r-v}; resident in 1634: UC:AR2/MS1/9 p. 152; correspondence with Walker: UC:MA30/2/C5/1–3; his benefaction: UC:BE1/MS1/1 p. 41, where he is called a commoner of the College.
[9] Abbot 1613: 343.

Yorkshire, with 48 commoners, followed by Cheshire (27) and Oxfordshire (23). The south-west is well represented, with 58 men, but just 3 men each came from Durham and Northumberland. Nine came from Ireland and 26 from Wales.[10]

In 1601–42, when the origins of over four-fifths of commoners are known, some areas have fallen from favour: Ireland and Wales have only one member each, and Cheshire just two. Durham and Northumberland, with 8 and 5 men respectively, remained marginal, but Kent, which sent just 13 undergraduates in the previous half-century, now provided 40. However, Yorkshire now assumed a dominant presence, with 111 commoners—almost a quarter of all the College's undergraduates. Yorkshiremen within Oxford as a whole apparently made up barely 5 per cent of the known undergraduate population, so that University College's Yorkshire bias is all the more striking.[11]

Less is known about the social status of a significant number of commoners (see Appendix IV), especially before 1600, although it is clear that about a third of all commoners were the sons of so-called 'plebeians', and after 1601 a similar proportion the sons of esquires, knights, baronets, and peers. Only a handful of members were the sons of clergy. Indeed University College seems to have accepted a higher than average proportion of undergraduates from the upper classes—quite striking for one of the poorest colleges in Oxford. Meanwhile, the status of 'plebeian' covered anything from the son of a yeoman farmer or city merchant down to the so-called 'servitor', students of poor birth who took on menial tasks to help pay for their education. Furthermore, while some plebeians might have discreetly overstated their status, for others with an eye to their finances, a sliding scale of matriculation fees had been introduced in 1565, by which, for example, the son of a prince, duke, or marquis paid 13s. 4d., but the son of a 'plebeian' 4d. One example of such financial mobility is Edward Fradisham, who matriculated from University College in November 1591 as a plebeian, and then paid extra to sit with other well-born undergraduates on the Bachelors' table.[12]

The average age of University College's first undergraduates on matriculating was between 16 and 17 years, especially after 1601 (see again Appendix IV). The oldest undergraduates were aged 40, and the youngest only 10. The few youngsters were rather special cases: several of the very youngest were the sons of Anthony Gate, so presumably lived in the Master's Lodgings; others came up with their older brothers. It is possible, however, that the average age of undergraduates may have been a little lower: these figures are based on ages at matriculation, but College records show undergraduates regularly taking up

---

[10] Curiously, Wood, *Athenae* ii. 146–7 claims that in the sixteenth century University College was, along with Hart Hall and Gloucester Hall, popular with Irishmen.

[11] See the tables given for selected years in Stone 1975: i. 102 and Porter 1997: 59.

[12] Upper-class undergraduates: Stone 1975: i. 83 and Porter 1997: 55; matriculation fees: McConica 1986a: 49–51; Edward Fradisham: UC:S13/F1/1 p. 12.

residence weeks, months, and sometimes years before actually matriculating. For example, Obadiah Walker, who officially matriculated on 5 April 1633 aged 16, was being taught by John Elmhirst as early as July 1631.[13]

Finally, it was easy for Tudor and Stuart undergraduates to change college. In 1551–1642, some three dozen men migrated to University College to take their BA or MA, and some sixty undergraduates of University College took degrees elsewhere. A few moved several times: Thomas Wentworth's brother Philip, for example, matriculated at University College in December 1626, took his BA from Magdalen College in 1629, and returned to University College in 1631 to take his MA next year. These migrations are recorded because degrees were taken. Sometimes otherwise unknown migrations come to light by chance: John and William Burdet, for example, matriculated from University College in November 1591, but their tutor John Browne paid 6*d*. for transferring their bed there from St John's College.[14]

Nothing has so far been said about the mature commoners who loomed so large in the medieval College. University College was still admitting them during the first two decades of the sixteenth century, but when, after four decades' silence, the accounts of the 1560s once again name commoners, a change has occurred. There are one or two former Fellows and some mature scholars, but most rooms are rented out to younger men, some BAs and others still undergraduates. Furthermore, only a handful of mature commoners (46 out of 532 known commoners from 1551–1600, and just 5 commoners from 1601–42) had no previous links with the College. Instead, most commoners of BA status or higher were former undergraduates of the College. Many were potential Fellows: almost half the Fellows elected between 1580 and 1600 rented College rooms before their election. A career structure was now developing, whereby a young undergraduate came up to University College, took his BA, and then stayed on, renting a room and awaiting a vacant Fellowship. This structure had, of course, existed in other Oxbridge colleges; it was only possible in University College now that it had an undergraduate population of its own.

Not every undergraduate who remained became a Fellow; some appeared content with, or at least resigned to, staying on under any pretext. Lists extracted by William Smith from lost Buttery Books regularly include about half a dozen men like Thomas Hopkinson, who took his BA from University College in 1606, but was resident in 1614/15, or Philip Francklin, who had matriculated there in 1612, and was still resident in 1624/5. Some returned to the College after a break. Leonard Digges (m. 1603) travelled abroad, after taking his BA in 1606, producing important translations from Latin and Spanish, and writing poems of his own, some showing an early

---

[13] UC:BU3/F1/2 fo. 74^v.
[14] Wentworth in 1631: UC:AR2/MS1/9 p. 151; the Burdets' bed: UC:S13/F1/1 p. 35.

appreciation of Shakespeare. In 1626 he returned to University College to take his MA, and rented a room there until his death in 1635, when he was buried in the Chapel.[15]

University College's mature commoners are at least reasonably visible. This cannot be said for our penultimate group of members, who were largely unknown but for one document, a list of numbers of members of college and halls, taken, for reasons unknown, in 1612. University College, yet again the smallest college, is said to comprise a Master, 9 Fellows, 36 commoners, 7 servants, and 19 'poor scholars and servitors' (*pauperes scholares et servientes*). Who are these poor scholars? Contemporary lists of College residents, from a lost Buttery Book of 1614/15, and the Bursar's Book of 1616, show a College containing a Master, Fellows, and about three dozen others, and comparison between these lists and the matriculation registers shows an almost complete overlap—there is no room for these 'poor scholars'. Wherever one looks, these 'poor scholars' are completely invisible.[16]

External evidence provides some aid: Magdalen College's Visitor, the Bishop of Winchester, wrote to its Fellows in 1636, complaining that 'you have a multitude of poore schollers or Servitors, which hang upon the Colledge in an idle and unschollerly way, by reason that every man takes unto himselfe a liberty to take in whom he will to wayt upon him, without any order of admittance'.[17] In other words, some Fellows supplemented their income by taking in scholars of modest means who might not matriculate, but, in return for performing menial duties, received informal tuition. Living in Fellows' rooms, they would not rent rooms themselves, and, if the Fellows paid for their upkeep, they would not appear on buttery lists. Thus University College's 'poor scholars' of 1612 evade every record, and reveal again the informal structure of the early undergraduate college.[18]

Finally there are the College's servants. Fortunately, more information survives concerning Tudor servants than for their predecessors. The old categories of servant continue to be listed in the accounts—butler or manciple, cook, sub-cook, barber, and laundress—but evidence now emerges of others. In January 1532, two so-called common servants of University College, William Nixon and William Gylis, protested to the Chancellor's Court that they were owed money by a commoner, claiming that everyone living in

---

[15] Hopkinson and Francklin: UC:AR2/MS1/8 pp. 148 and 149; Digges: *ODNB* entry, and UC:GB3/A1/1 p. 47 and UC:BE1/MS1/2 p. 8 (which charmingly says Digges chose University College as his 'retreat' and 'grave' (*recessum* and *sepulchrum*)); mature commoners elsewhere: Green 1979: 220 and Costin 1958: 38.

[16] The 1612 census: Bodl. MS Tanner 338 fo. 38 rev., and printed in Walker *c.*1809: 247–56 (in comparison, Christ Church and Magdalen each had over 240 members); names from the 1614/15 Buttery Book: UC:AR2/MS1/9 p. 148; the 1616 Bursar's Book: UC:BU3/F1/1.

[17] Macray 1901: 51–2.

[18] The 'poor scholars' slightly resemble the medieval 'portionists' (p. 52), whose presence remains undetectable during this period.

College had to pay them an agreed rate. These 'common servants', who performed personal tasks for College members, being paid directly by them, and receiving nothing from College funds, were therefore not mentioned in the accounts. More explicit evidence comes from John Browne's account book, which records pupils paying not only to laundresses and barbers, but also 'one to make his bedd'—the first clear reference to scouts. Some wealthier pupils even brought their own servants to the College.[19]

The references to barbers and laundresses show that 'official' servants received extra money from College members. Some servants certainly prospered: in November 1620 when an inventory was made of the possessions of Gabriel Cracknell, former cook of University College, he was found to have in ready money £350 (the College's rental in 1616 was about £270), and his possessions were valued at £1,210 11s.—wealth far beyond the aspirations of most Fellows. Cracknell enjoyed other benefits, as when he was admitted a 'privileged person' (*privilegiatus*) of the university in June 1604, which meant he could be sued only in the Vice-Chancellor's court, and was exempted from certain local taxes.[20]

Gabriel Cracknell seems to have been exclusively a College servant, although a most successful one. Other servants, however, combined their work with study, such as Richard Lewis, a native of Carnarvon who was appointed manciple of University College in April 1581, but died before September 1584, when his successor was appointed. Like Cracknell, Lewis became a privileged person when in December 1581 he was listed as one of six servants—not, curiously, as manciple—of William James (then Vice-Chancellor) who were thus honoured. An inventory compiled after his death shows that Lewis owned a sizeable library, comprising an extensive range of Roman literature, including Cicero, Ovid, Virgil, and Terence, and some works of Plato and Aristotle, a collection of which any undergraduate would have been proud. Lewis lived and died the manciple of University College, and might never have taken a degree, let alone matriculated, yet, if he is not an undergraduate, he is certainly more than a servant.[21]

HIERARCHY TRIUMPHANT:
LIVING WITHIN THE COLLEGE

This examination of the Fellows and undergraduates has had, unavoidably, a rather theoretical air. It is time to examine the College's buildings, and to see

---

[19] Nixon and Gylis: OUA Register EEE fo. 196ᵛ; John Browne's pupils' servants: UC:S13/F1/1 pp. 32–3 and 35.

[20] Cracknell's inventory and will: OUA HYP/B/20; becoming a privileged person: Clark 1887–9: i. 399; the College's rental in 1616: UC:BU3/F1/1. Clifford 1996 shows that although college cooks could become wealthy, Cracknell was exceptional.

[21] Lewis appointed manciple: UC:GB3/A1/1 p. 19; his successor appointed: UC:GB3/A1/1 p. 20; made a privileged person: Clark 1887: i. 392; his inventory (OUA HYP/B/15) is undated, but the apparent date of his death supports a date of 1584. We might see Lewis and William James's other servants as analogous to, if not examples of, the 'poor scholars' discussed above.

how its members lived together as a community. These were essentially the same as of the medieval college (Figs. 5.1–5.2), but until now little evidence has survived to show how they functioned, except for the Chapel, Library, Hall, and kitchen. Some room inventories, however, from the late sixteenth and early seventeenth centuries provide a much fuller picture.[22]

The inventories suggest that there were nine residential staircases in the quadrangle. Each originally led to one room on the ground floor, and one above, but University College, like other Colleges, installed 'cocklofts'—attic chambers with dormer windows—on most staircases to produce a third storey, so that the quadrangle contained just over two dozen rooms, or sets of rooms. The first-floor rooms were the most spacious and were deemed the most desirable. The inventories always name these rooms—for example, the 'Garden chamber', the 'Chapel chamber', or the 'north street chamber'—while the ground-floor rooms were just called 'chamber under the garden chamber' or suchlike. Ground-floor rooms elsewhere tended to have only earth floors and no hearths. We may assume that the better, first-floor, rooms went to the Fellows. They appear to have been suites rather than individual rooms—College accounts carefully differentiated between repairs to Fellows' studies and those to their chambers.[23]

This leaves the cocklofts and ground floors. The most detailed accounts for this period, from the 1570s and early 1580s, usually list only about a dozen commoners renting rooms, and between six and eight Fellows. This total almost matches the number of first-floor and ground-floor rooms in the inventories. If the Fellows lived on the first floor, then these commoners presumably lived on the ground floor. Meanwhile the inventories treat cocklofts as appendages of first-floor chambers, while the 'underchambers' are listed separately. This suggests that most undergraduates lived in cocklofts above their tutors, paying them and not the College for their accommodation, but ground-floor rooms went to those willing to pay for comparative privacy. For the wealthy lodger, however, better accommodation was on offer. There tended to be more first-floor rooms than there were Fellows, and, each year, one or two Lodgers paid up to £1 a year, twice the rent for cheaper rooms. One can guess where these men were accommodated.[24]

---

[22] UC:EB1/A/1 fos. 372–7 (whole College and Master's Lodging, 1580–6); UC:FA1/3/MS1/2 (ditto, 1587); UC:FA1/3/MS1/4 (ground-floor rooms only, 1620); UC:FA1/3/MS1/5 (first- and second-floor rooms only, early seventeenth century); and UC:FA1/3/MS1/6 (Master's Lodgings only, 1632). See too Darwall-Smith 2005*a*.

[23] Ground-floor rooms and cocklofts: Newman 1986: 627–31; repairs to Fellows' rooms: *ARUC* ii. 404, 474–5, and 499–501. In comparison, rooms in the three storeys of Wadham's new quadrangle were called 'ground chambers', 'middle chambers', and 'upper chambers'. Fellows tended to live on the second floor, renting out the cocklofts above, and the ground-floor rooms were occupied for a time by servants (Mallet 1924–7: ii. 251–2).

[24] One such wealthy commoner was Anthony Gate, future Master.

The Master's Lodgings, now physically separate from the College, changed in atmosphere, now that Masters could marry. Although Masters' wives took no part in College life, their very existence marked an innovation. The Lodgings also sometimes accommodated commoners. The 1575/6 accounts refer to repairing the lock on 'Hughes chamber doare' in the Master's Lodgings, and the inventory compiled after the death of Thomas Caius suggests that he lived with at least three commoners.[25]

The College would have been well filled: the 1612 census, including the 'poor scholars', suggested that there were over sixty people living there. The wealthy commoner might have been able to rent a room more or less to himself, but everyone else, Fellows included, enjoyed little or no privacy. Where a suite of rooms was shared, people occupied a communal bedroom, but each had a separate study (a reversal of modern practice). This was a very hierarchical world, in which the quality of one's accommodation depended on one's ability to pay. One is not so aware of such distinctions in the medieval College, but by the later sixteenth century they were deeply embedded in university life.

The Hall particularly emphasized these distinctions. The weekly summaries of batells bills in the Bursar's Book for 1615/16 listed the names of College residents in four groups, arranged in strict order of seniority. The Master and Fellows occupy the first group, while the second comprises mainly senior BAs and some undergraduates. Every undergraduate here whose origin is known is the son of either a gentleman, an esquire, a knight, or a baronet. The third group comprised other BAs and some undergraduates who are all plebeians' sons, and the fourth comprises undergraduate sons of plebeians, except for one gentleman's son. Some of John Browne's pupils paid 3s. 4d. to sit on the 'Bachelors' table', which suggests that the second group is that Bachelors' table, containing BAs and wealthy undergraduates, and that therefore each group represents a table at which one sat according to one's social status. The most exalted sat with the Fellows: a lost Buttery Book of 1631 showed William Savile (m. 1626 aged 14), who had inherited his family's baronetcy, sitting there. Unsurprisingly those sitting on the higher tables spent more freely. Of those on the Bachelors' table in 1616, Edward and Richard Tildesley, sons of a knight, were charged an average of £5 a term for their batells, and Edward Monyns, son of a baronet, was charged slightly more. People on the third table paid an average of £3 a term, but some of those on the fourth table paid barely £1.[26]

Although we have concentrated on a snapshot of the College in 1616, the structure it uncovers held true for well over 200 years (indeed College rooms

---

[25] 1575/6 accounts: *ARUC* ii. 436; Caius' inventory, printed at *HUO* iii. 635–41, mentions 'Merickes Chamber', 'Mr Sherborns chamber', and 'Mr Hopkins chamber'.

[26] Bursar's Book of 1615/16: UC:BU3/F1/1: John Browne's pupils on the Bachelors' table: UC:S13/F1/1 pp. 9, 12, and 35; William Savile: UC:AR2/MS1/9 p. 151; examples of this division by tables elsewhere: Stevenson and Salter 1939: 283.

were rented out at different prices until 1939).[27] Most changes only enhanced the differences: for example, later in the seventeenth century commoners of higher status acquired the names of 'gentleman commoner' and even 'fellow commoner', and wore special gowns to indicate their different status.

The preceding discussion assumes that undergraduates lived in College. This was not necessarily so, as the memoirs of Edward Herbert, later Lord Herbert of Cherbury (Fig. 8.1), show. Matriculating from University College in June 1596, he then had to leave to attend his father's deathbed. Soon after returning to Oxford, his mother found him a wife. On marrying in February 1599, he then returned, taking a house outside College in which he lived with his wife and mother and continued his studies—all the while, presumably, remaining attached to University College.[28]

STUDY AND RECREATION, BEHAVIOUR AND MISBEHAVIOUR

We have seen who were the members of University College in 1500–1642, and where they lived within it. It is time now to turn to what they did, what they studied, and how they occupied their spare time, and what happened when problems arose.

Among the Fellows, the study of theology remained central—law and medicine could not be studied. The methods of learning theology, through lectures and disputations, were not so different, but the theology studied had, of course, changed greatly. Some light can be shed on this from the books which Fellows owned themselves or which were in the College Library, which, while not explicitly for the exclusive use of Fellows, as at some colleges, nevertheless consisted primarily of books acquired for the benefit of Fellows rather than undergraduates. We do know, however, that it was largely, if not wholly, a reference library: chains were purchased for library books to prevent their removal.[29]

The College's Library was still squeezed into a small room above the Antechapel. Knowledge of its contents depends largely on a donations book compiled retrospectively in 1674, and apparently based on books still on the shelves. Few donations before 1570 are recorded, presumably more on account of the inevitable turnover of library stock than because of miserly donors. Between 1570 and 1640, University College depended for the expansion of its Library largely on donations—the College accounts almost never mention books being purchased—but most smaller colleges did likewise. Choice as to acquisitions was thus very much at the donor's whim: thus

---

[27] Room rents in 1939: UC:BU3/F3/108.
[28] Herbert 1976: 15–17.
[29] The theological context: Greenslade 1986 and Tyacke 1997; chaining library books: *ARUC* i. 713 and ii. 434 and 478.

FIGURE 8.1 Edward Herbert, Lord Herbert of Cherbury, m. 1596 (copy of a contemporary portrait).

the literary Leonard Digges offered a geographical treatise by Mercator, an English translation of Plutarch, and an edition of Froissart. Fortunately, gifts may not always have been so random. Since almost half the donors were Fellows, and a few were undergraduates (and, in one case, an undergraduate's mother), they may have been given some idea of what was wanted.[30]

Some donors gave money for the Fellows to buy books of their choice for the Library: John Browne's uncle Thomas gave £10 for this purpose in 1586 and George Abbot £100 in 1633. Such gifts enabled the purchase of large multi-volume works: Thomas Browne's money bought for the College some important early Christian writings, including the works of St Augustine, and Abbot's gift bought eight volumes of St John Chrysostom, eleven volumes of St Thomas Aquinas, and much else.

---

[30] The Library benefactors' book: UC:BE1/MS1/3; the wider context: Ker 1959 and 1986; hints to donors: Fuggles 1981 suggests that this was common practice at St John's College.

The books given to the Library in 1570–1640 have a strongly theological tone: they include such medieval writers as Bede, St Bonaventure, Thomas à Kempis, and Peter Lombard and his commentators, including Duns Scotus, but also editions of books of the Bible in Hebrew, Latin, and Syriac, and the works of such Church Fathers as Eusebius, St Basil, and St Jerome. There were Protestant thinkers, including Beza, Calvin, John Foxe, Luther, Peter Martyr, and Zwingli. Some Greek and Roman authors were represented, albeit mostly philosophers or scientists (such as Aristotle, Galen, Pliny the Elder, and Ptolemy), or authors relevant to Judaeo-Christian history (e.g. Josephus). These books would be useful largely to Fellows only: it seems that undergraduates had to purchase their own textbooks.

Inventories of Fellows who died in the early sixteenth century show them owning mainly theological texts, including Albertus Magnus and Duns Scotus, but also works of Aristotle, although William Thomson, who died in 1507 also owned Juvenal's *Satires*. Later Fellows owned their share of theological works, including, of course, their own copies of Protestant thinkers; they also purchased more recent works of scholarship, such as commentaries of Aristotle by the sixteenth century cardinal Gasparo Contarini.[31]

The survival of Peter Lombard and Duns Scotus into the seventeenth century might at first glance appear surprising, but such writers remained essential resources for the biblical commentator, be he Calvinist or Arminian: in the ninth of his sermons on Jonah, George Abbot said of one argument 'I haue borrowed this reason from the maister of the Sentences', assuming that his audience would understand him exactly, and John Bancroft presented works by both authors to the Library.[32]

Abbot's sermons on Jonah have one other paradox to a modern reader: apart from showing his erudition in religious texts, he peppers his sermons with classical allusions. His deep knowledge of Greek and Latin literature, however, was employed only for theological ends. This was typical of English scholarship of the day: new approaches to the study of classical texts were known, and, as we shall see, were taught to undergraduates, but for the scholar embracing an academic career, they remained but a prelude to the study of theology. It is not until later in the century that men of University College begin to explore other approaches.[33]

---

[31] Inventories: OUA Register No. 3, fo. 28ᵛ (William Thomson); OUA Register F (reversed) fos. 130ʳ, 179ᵛ, and 247ᵛ (Peter Person, d. 1511, Willam Bydnell, d. 1512, and Thomas Thomson, d. 1514); OUA HYP/B/18 (Richard Slatter, d. 1576, who owned Contarini on Aristotle). These men's libraries are analysed in Fehrenbach and Leedham-Green 1993: 13–18 (W. Thomson), 58–9 (Bydnell), and 99–102 (T. Thomson), and 1995: 253–5 (Slatter).

[32] Abbot 1613: 187. Fletcher 1981 contrasts Oxford and Cambridge's preference for tried and tested studies with the greater openness to change shown in German and Scottish universities.

[33] See further Feingold 1997a: 261–9.

In turning to undergraduate study, we enter a world new to University College.[34] The Arts course as outlined in Chapter 1 and as remodelled in the Laudian statutes of 1636, with its aim of taking the student through a wide range of subjects, remained the basic degree for undergraduate study, but few people had studied—let alone taught—it in the College before. By now Greek and Roman literature lay at the heart of a student's reading, but it was there less for its own sake, than for its usefulness and relevance. Students of rhetoric looked to Cicero and Quintilian; logicians and philosophers to Aristotle; and mathematicians to Euclid. That is not to say that more recent authors were not read and taught, but the classics were there as a point of reference.

We even know what books some undergraduates of University College read—or at least owned. Now that, thanks to printing, books were more affordable, undergraduates could create private libraries to a degree previously impossible. From the 1570s come two inventories, for John Dunnet, who died in 1570, and Thomas Bolt, who died in 1578. Both owned several dozen books, mainly Greek and Roman texts: works, for example, by Plato, Cicero, Ovid (his *Metamorphoses*), Virgil, and Terence. Both men also owned books on logic, and a few theological texts. Dunnet also had, for light reading, *The Palace of Pleasure*, an anthology of 'Pleasant Histories and excellent Novelles', assembled and translated by one William Painter, and first published in 1566.[35]

The accounts kept by John Browne and John Elmhirst for their pupils show what books they were expected to acquire. Browne's pupils purchased classical authors, especially Cicero, Ovid (his *Tristia*), and Xenophon (his *Cyropaedia*, or *Education of Cyrus*), chosen, it seems, for their excellent style and fitting sentiments. At least one pupil bought Homer. They also purchased Latin and Greek grammars, bibles, and catechisms. More modern books included the *Logicæ artis compendium* of Robert Sanderson, a basic textbook of the day, at least one 'law booke', contemporary works on rhetoric, and the *Dialectic* of Peter Ramus, which promulgated a different kind of logic from Aristotle's. Elmhirst's pupils bought both Cicero and the philosopher and tragedian Seneca. They also bought texts on logic, but Elmhirst, to a greater degree than Browne, had them buy religious works, like Calvin's *Institutions*, or the *Heidelberg Catechism* of Zacharias Ursinus, a work of religious instruction recommended by the university; and some

---

[34] On this large and still not thoroughly explored subject, see further Fletcher 1986 and Feingold 1997*a* and 1997*b*. They show that the studies of University College's undergraduates can readily be paralleled in other colleges.

[35] Dunnet: OUA HYP/B/12 (and Fehrenbach and Leedham-Green 1994: 222–7); Bolt: OUA HYP/B/10 (and Fehrenbach and Leedham-Green 1998: 204–17). Tales from the *Palace of Pleasure* were among versions used by Shakespeare (such as *All's Well that Ends Well* and *Romeo and Juliet*) and his contemporaries (such as John Webster's *The Duchess of Malfi*).

undergraduates bought such popular books of modern history as Johannes Sleidan's *De quatuor summis imperiis*.[36]

Of the two undergraduates who provided first-hand testimony of their time at University College, George Radcliffe said nothing about his studies, but Edward Herbert remembered that, soon after coming up, he participated in logic exercises, and received a thorough coaching in Greek. But Herbert, by his own account at least a studious lad, claimed that he also taught himself French, Italian, and Spanish. He also had suggestions for the syllabus: he disapproved of elder sons being taught 'the subtilyties of Logicke,... whiche art, though it may bee tolerable in a mercenary Lawyer, I can by noe meanes commend it in a sober and well-gouerned Gentleman'. Herbert thought that logic should take its place equally among philosophy, medicine, geography, arithmetic, geometry, and rhetoric.[37]

Once University College had appointed logic, philosophy, and Greek praelectors, and a catechist, much basic teaching would have been handled by them. For the complementary contribution of tutors, we turn to John Browne's accounts. These show that Browne was not so much his pupils' teacher, as their director of studies. Several students' accounts record payments 'to his tutor', which suggests that Browne had found someone else to teach his charges, not least as sometimes he writes 'Item my dueties his tutor', when, presumably, he did his own teaching. Browne distinguishes between a 'tutor' and a 'reader', which suggests that some teaching might have had rather a mechanical feel, with the undergraduate obliged to do little more than passively take in a text. George Radcliffe, in his letters home, never speaks of being 'taught' by his tutor, but once wrote 'Mr [Jonas] Radcliffe doth read to me.' As with tutoring, Browne sometimes performed this task himself, and sometimes hired others: in 1601, for example, he paid an old pupil, James Harrison, now a Fellow, to read to one of his charges. Nevertheless Browne saw the undergraduates in his account book very much as his own pupils.[38]

Good tutors would modify the basic syllabus if a pupil showed ability in a particular direction. One such was Thomas Henshaw (m. 1634), later one of the first Fellows of the Royal Society. Henshaw was a pupil of John Elmhirst, and the latter's accounts show him purchasing books on varied subjects, including history and logic, and even spending 6s. on shelves for his room. Unfortunately, Henshaw found Elmhirst an indifferent tutor, and later admitted to benefiting more from his informal links with two younger Fellows, Abraham Woodhead (F. 1633–48 and 1660–78) and Obadiah Walker

---

[36] Ramus: Fletcher 1986: 177–8 and Feingold 1997a: 289–95; Sanderson: Feingold 1997a: 294–7; Ursinus: Loach 1986: 388; Sleidan: Feingold 1997a: 344–5.

[37] Herbert 1976: 15 and 17–20.

[38] Browne doing his own teaching: UC:S13/F1/1 pp. 15, 25, 31, and 49; James Harrison's help: UC:S13/F1/1 pp. 47–8; George Radcliffe: Whitaker 1810: 72.

(F. 1635–48 and 1660–76). Woodhead and Walker, observing Henshaw's interest in the sciences, encouraged him to stay with William Oughtred, a Surrey rector and the foremost mathematics teacher in the land. Thanks to their advice, Henshaw spent nine months with Oughtred before returning to College.[39]

Such flexibility extended to the taking of degrees, for the acquisition of a degree remained as optional as before. Of the 532 commoners known for 1551–1600, just over 200 took their BA degree (of whom over half proceeded at least to MA status), and between 1601–42 again just over 200 out of 469 commoners are known to have received a BA degree (of whom about three-fifths proceeded at least to MA status). Some undergraduates regarded degrees as more optional than others. In the late sixteenth and early seventeenth centuries, it became fashionable for young men of gentle birth to learn something of the law at the Inns of Court in London, for all that the Inns were not, like universities, set up specifically for educational purposes. Sixty-seven undergraduates from University College from 1551–1600 are known to have attended the Inns of Court, and eighty from 1601–42. They were particularly uninterested in degrees: barely one-third of the later group achieved a BA, and only one-quarter of the earlier group are known to have done so.[40]

George Radcliffe's attitude towards degrees is typical of his class. In 1611 he was admitted to Grays Inn, and, that winter, as his time at Oxford was drawing to an end, he was uncertain about whether to take his BA. Charles Greenwood his tutor wanted him to do so, but his mother seemed undecided. By the new year he was writing 'the Degree of Bacchelour is a thing not necessary, and therefore (according to the counsel of my friends) I am resolved to let that passe.' Radcliffe eventually took his BA in May 1612, but it was clearly not thought essential for his prospects.[41]

It was mainly sons likely to inherit their estates or enter the law who came up to Oxford knowing that they would not spend long there, while younger sons like Robert Batt needed degrees to set themselves up in later life. An example of this contrast is provided by two brothers from Kent, Herbert and Edmund Randolph, who both matriculated from University College in November 1616 aged 16 and 15 respectively. Herbert, the eldest son, never took a degree, and presumably returned to the family home. Edmund, however, took his MA, then remained in Oxford to become a Bachelor of Medicine in 1626, before continuing his studies at Padua, where he received a

---

[39] Henshaw's accounts: UC:BU3/F1/2 fo. 83^{r-v}; his teaching: Wood, *Athenae* iv. 444–7 and Pasmore 1982: 177–8.

[40] Inns of Court: Prest 1972. Of the undergraduates of 1616, the only ones who went to the Inns of Court were those wealthy enough to sit on the Bachelors' Table.

[41] Letters of 9 and 18 December 1611, 11 January 1612, and 13 February 1612 (Whitaker 1810: 55–6, 65, 67, and 77).

doctorate in 1628. It could be a little too easy for a well-born dilettante to pass through the College, staying long enough to acquire some polish whilst receiving the privileges due his rank. Some contemporaries certainly feared the risk: the elegy on Jonas Radcliffe, by praising him for giving preference 'not to the gentler, but the better mann', suggested that others might not.[42]

The sources which shed light on College members' studies also reveal something of their other activities.[43] We start with the contents of their rooms in the early sixteenth century. Most people's rooms tended towards the utilitarian, if not humble. Apart from his books, William Thomson (died 1507) owned just a gown, a 'lityll pot of pewtyr', a chair, and three chests, while several of John Hartburne's possessions (died 1513) are described as 'old' or 'broken'. Occasionally people tried to bring some colour into their rooms with coverlets or painted cloths—the latter hung on walls as a cheap substitute for tapestry. Thus William Thomson owned several 'peynted clothys', and 'a coverlyt of wyt with flowrys', but John Roxborough, as Master, owned a little piece of tapestry, some pieces of say (a fine cloth resembling silk), and two candlesticks. As the century progresses, further home comforts appear. John Kytley, a mature commoner who died in 1531, owned several carpets and five 'censys or drynkyng potts', and the lengthy inventory of the Master's Lodgings on the death of Thomas Caius shows that the move to Little University Hall had enabled the Master to live in a grander manner.[44]

Other information on room furnishings comes from John Browne and John Elmhirst's accounts: their pupils bought wood, candles, paper, gowns (with fur lining), shoes, slippers, stockings, and hats—although the last three categories were only acquired by wealthier undergraduates. However, Elmhirst's pupils seem to have had more spending money than Browne's, for they also purchased chairs, curtain rods, desks, fire shovels and tongs, waistcoats, laced cuffs, and clothes made of fine materials.

Students' spending varied according to their background. In autumn 1592, the lowly born Lancelot Gryme paid Browne just 9s. for his general expenses; in the previous autumn, Francis Palmer, a gentleman's son from Hampshire, paid 22s. 10d. One rather foppish undergraduate, Christopher Martyn, a Dorset gentleman's son (m. 1584), purchased several pairs of shoes and slippers, knives, 'spice and figges', several pairs of gloves, one pair of knitted yellow stockings and one of green. During one year his expenses totalled over

---

[42] See Stone 1975: i. 9–10.
[43] McConica 1986b and Newman 1986 provide details on the wider Oxford context.
[44] Thomson: OUA Register No. 3, fo. 28ᵛ; Roxborough and Hartburn: OUA Register F (reversed) fos. 98ʳ and 191ʳ; Kytley: OUA Register No. 4 fo. 305ʳ (other painted cloths appear in the inventories of Peter Person and the will of Thomas Thomson (OUA Register F (reversed) fos. 130ʳ and 247ᵛ)): Thomas Caius' inventory: *HUO* iii. 635–41; fuller accounts of the possessions of Fellows and undergraduates: Newman 1986: 626–33.

£20 (Gryme spent just over £6 over a similar period), and Browne ruefully noted that he had so far received barely half this sum from Martyn's parents. An Elmhirst pupil, Thomas Rockley (m. 1633) from Yorkshire, a godson of Thomas Wentworth, had still more extravagant ways, spending money on dancing and fencing lessons, 'a paire of laced cuffes', books—including more than one copy of the same work—5s. 'at the reuells', and three maps (Fig. 8.2). At one point, Elmhirst recorded that his pupil had run up expenses of over £100.[45]

Fencing was not the only sport enjoyed at this time. George Radcliffe practised archery with John Bancroft (p. 128), and one Fellow, Richard Slatter, owned a bow and arrows at the time of his death in 1576. Undergraduates also played tennis, and the College seems to have had its own courts: the draft College accounts of 1615/16 record 6d. spent on 'removing the bordes of the Tenniscort'. College members also enjoyed music. John Dunnet owned a lute at the time of his death, and Browne's pupil Robert Hartwell (m. 1587) bought fresh strings for his lute. Even George Radcliffe cultivated a taste for music, confessing to his mother in May 1610 that he had just spent 30s. on a bass viol, and hoping that part of his grandmother's legacy could be put towards this. Thomas Caius' inventory of 1572 records that he owned a pair of virginals, currently lent out. In addition, College members with a taste for singing would leave few obvious records. It is rather unexpected to find the early modern College echoing to such music-making: Edward Herbert notes that he learned to play the lute and to 'singe my part at first sight in Musicke', commenting that such activities kept him out of trouble; he also engaged in fencing and riding. Although he claimed, somewhat primly, that he never had time for dancing, 'as imploying my minde always in Acquiring of some Art or Science more vseful', he conceded that it improved one's deportment.[46]

Herbert was anxious to avoid trouble, observing that students could get into bad company, and needed 'the Company of graue, learned men' as a counter-weight. Unfortunately, little is known about the bad behaviour of University College's undergraduates. For example, some colleges had 'initiation ceremonies' of sorts for young students, but no evidence for their existence survives from here. Edward Herbert and George Radcliffe had few opportunities for misbehaving—Herbert lived with his mother and wife, and Radcliffe lived under his cousins' watchful eyes—but Radcliffe once revealed what could go on when he wrote in December 1610 'The University I find very much

---

[45] UC:S13/F1/1 pp. 4–6 (Gryme), 8–9 (Palmer), and 25–6 (Martyn); UC:BU3/F1/2 fos. 76ᵛ, 79ʳ, 80ᵛ–81ʳ, 84ᵛ, and 86ʳ (Rockley). Browne and Elmhirst's troubles with Martyn and Rockley compare interestingly with their financial competence elsewhere (pp. 128 and 129).

[46] Slatter: OUA HYP/B/18; Tennis players: UC:S13/F1/1 pp. 33 and 45; tennis court: UC:BU3/F1/1; Dunnet: OUA HYP/B/12; Hartwell's lute: UC:S13/F1/1 p. 33; Radcliffe's viol: Whitaker 1810: 52–3; Caius's virginals: *HUO* iii. 641; Herbert 1976: 17 and 31.

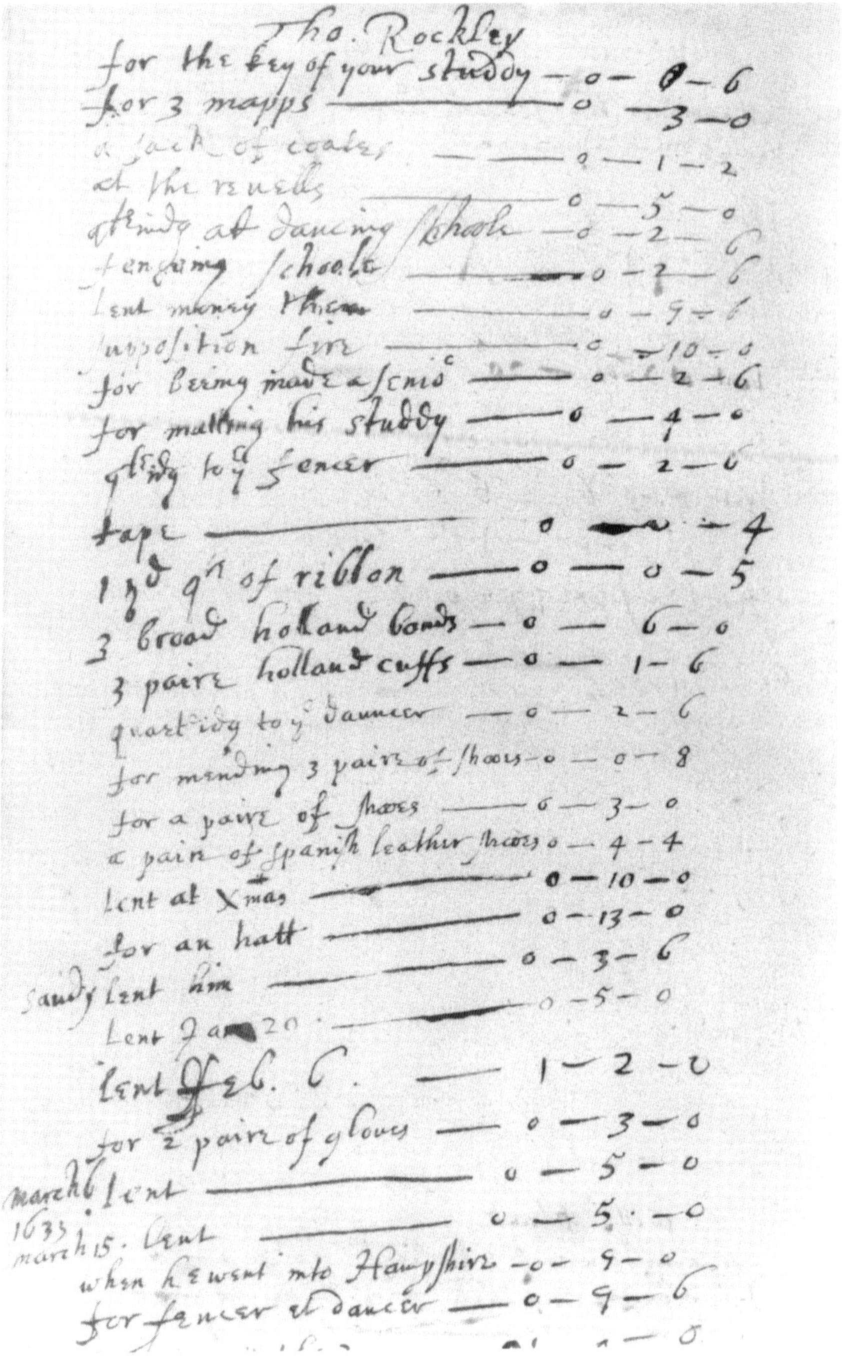

Tho. Rockley

	£	s	d
for the key of your studdy	0	0	6
for 3 mapps	0	3	0
a Jack of coales	0	1	2
at the reuells	0	5	0
q[uarter]rudg at dancing schoole	0	2	6
fencing schoole	0	2	6
lent money him	0	9	1
apposition fire	0	10	0
for being made a sen[io]r	0	2	6
for matting his studdy	0	4	0
q[uarter]rudg to y[e] fencer	0	2	6
tape	0	0	4
1 y[ar]d q[uarte]r of ribbon	0	0	5
3 broad holland bands	0	6	0
3 paire holland cuffs	0	1	6
quart[er]idg to y[e] dauncer	0	2	6
for mending 3 paire of shoes	0	0	8
for a paire of shoes	0	3	0
a paire of spanish leather shoes	0	4	4
lent at Xmas	0	10	0
for an hatt	0	13	0
sandy lent him	0	3	6
Lent Jan 20	0	5	0
lent Feb. 6.	1	2	0
for 2 paire of gloues	0	3	0
march 6 lent	0	5	0
1633 march 15. lent	0	5	0
when he went into Hampshire	0	9	0
for fencer & dancer	0	9	6

FIGURE 8.2 Extract from the accounts of John Elmhirst, Fellow 1621–51, showing the large sums spent by Thomas Rockley, m. 1633, on his clothing and his dancing and fencing lessons—but not on his books.

reformed, about drinking, long hair, and other vices, especially our house, out of which 2 have lately gone, to avoid expulsion for drunkenness.'[47]

Debt was a particular problem. Some undergraduates, then as now, were poor payers: in March 1612 the Fellows drew up sanctions against defaulting commoners, which culminated in possible expulsion. More extreme sanctions were sometimes required: in 1617, one Fellow, Thomas Radcliffe, prosecuted Richard Browne (John Browne's nephew) in the Chancellor's court over a debt of £5. One feels slightly less charitable towards Radcliffe on learning that when Michael Thomson (F. 1614–after 1623/4), who had regularly been summoned before the Chancellor's court for debt during 1615–18, was once arrested in Catte Street by John Addams, a bookseller, Radcliffe apparently came to the rescue by beating Addams up, so that Thomson could make his escape.[48]

While few records of the misdemeanours of University College's undergraduates survive, those of the Fellows are revealed both in the College Register and the records of the Chancellor's Court. Their problems lay in the allurements of the town. In October 1608, for example, James Harrison, one of John Browne's protégés, was rebuked by the Master in Chapel, for spending the night outside the College, and for going to the King's Head tavern and other places of ill-resort, while in April 1619, a Leicester Scholar, Samuel Wilson, was ordered not to spend nights away from College, nor to enter town houses to drink or to smoke, and certainly not to do these things in the College.[49]

Few Fellows, however, ended up in a worse predicament than Matthew Wentworth, one of Thomas Wentworth's brothers, who had matriculated in 1622, and was elected a Fellow in 1626. In March 1635, he was summoned before the Chancellor's Court to answer for a debt of £25, supposedly borrowed from Gregory Ballard, a Fellow of St John's. Wentworth denied the claim strenuously, but his defence was a humiliating one: he and Ballard had been gambling in an inn, and Ballard had won £50 from Wentworth, so that Wentworth's 'loan' was actually a gambling debt. Worse still, Wentworth had to confess that 'how much money the sayd Ballard did lend the sayd Wentworth then at gaming by reason it is a good while since and by reason of their watching all that night at gaming this respondent doth not certainly know'. Ballard was evidently an accomplished gambler and the hapless Wentworth an easy victim: one witness reported that Ballard had won £140 that evening from several people, including Wentworth. Wentworth was

---

[47] Herbert 1976: 19; initiation ceremonies: Wood, *Life* i. 133–4 and 138–40, and Morgan 2004: 144–5; Radcliffe: Whitaker 1810: 65 (also note Abbot 1613: 570 on hair).
[48] Sanctions against defaulters: UC:GB3/A1/1 p. 32; Radcliffe *v* Browne: OUA HYP/A/32 fos. 30ʳ and 32ᵛ; Thomson and the bookseller: OUA Hyp/A/32 1617 fo. 87ᵛ.
[49] Harrison: UC:GB3/A1/1 p. 27; Wilson: UC:GB3/A1/1 p. 34.

spared further embarrassment when he died, not yet 30, in June 1635, and was buried in the College Chapel.[50]

Such an early end was not unique: death was a regular visitor to the College, and John Browne and John Elmhirst's pupils had to pay for visits from the surgeon or physician. Oxford was always vulnerable to outbreaks of plague, and in 1525/6 and 1577 University College temporarily abandoned the city. While wealthier colleges had official plague refuges, University College simply rented accommodation, as in 1577. More usually, however, the College tended to sit it out within its walls: George Radcliffe's arrival in Oxford in June 1609 coincided with an outbreak, and his letters show that the College was staying put. He claimed that 'not only the University in general, but every colledge in particular, hath been so looked to, that there hath been little or no danger'.[51]

A NEW APPROACH TO ESTATE MANAGEMENT: ENTRY FINES AND CORN RENTS

The previous two chapters have discussed University College's troubled finances after 1500 (see too Graph 6.1). Two important factors in their improvement were the development of entry fines and the creation of corn rents. Because they influence the College's finances until well into the nineteenth century, it is necessary briefly to explain their workings.[52]

Entry fines arose alongside so-called 'beneficial' leases, which became the norm among colleges during the sixteenth century. The annual rent remained unchanged from one lease to the next, but, each time one was renewed, the tenant also paid a lump sum, calculated on the land's value, known as an 'entry fine'. The administration of fines at University College is documented from the 1630s, when its earliest 'Fine Book' begins. This shows, for example, that in 1639 the tenant of Stanton Hall, whose annual rent was 18s., paid a fine of £5. Fines could be reduced or waived, on account of rebuilding costs, previous good services, or hard-luck stories (in 1701, a Welsh tenant, Thomas Whittington, had his fine reduced 'for having been Robbed...since the last renewall'). A misbehaving tenant, however, might be charged a larger fine. Proceeds from fines went directly to the Master and Fellows, and came to be omitted from the general accounts. By the 1670s, money from fines was divided into equal shares, one to each Fellow, one to the Treasury, and two to the Master. Thus in 1673/4, each Fellow received a dividend of £21 5s. 3d., and the Master one of £42 10s. 5d. These terms were indeed generous to

---

[50] Wentworth's debt: OUA CC Papers 1635/46:1–3; his burial: UC:GB3/A1/1 p. 47. Ballard later became Registrar to the Bishop of Oxford, and in 1660–2 Registrar and Secretary to the Royal Visitors to Oxford (information from Andrew Hegarty).
[51] *ARUC* ii. 267, 446 and 458, and Whitaker 1810: 40–1.
[52] General discussions of entry fines and corn rents: Aylmer 1986: 521–58 and Howard 1935: 29–33 and 38–47.

tenants, but it was the tenants, not the college, who were responsible for the upkeep of their properties.[53]

The system of corn rents was created by an act of Parliament in 1576, which specified that in all future leases on agricultural property granted by Oxbridge colleges and by Eton and Winchester Colleges one-third of the rent should be paid, either as an agreed quantity of wheat and malt barley, or else as the cash equivalent of their current market price—which was how colleges preferred to receive it. The quantity of wheat and malt was calculated on their respective prices in 1576 (or, presumably, the price when the first new-style lease was drawn up for a property), and remained unchanged, offering a kind of index linking against inflation. One of University College's first leases with corn rents was issued in 1588 for Arncliffe, whose annual rent of £27 was now recalculated as £18 in cash, plus 6 quarters of wheat and 28 of malt, or the cash equivalent. This remained unchanged in every Arncliffe lease until 1797, but the annual sum sent to Oxford fluctuated, depending on the price of wheat. In 1591/2, for example, the College received £39 5s. 4d. from Arncliffe, but in 1596/7, a time of dearth and high grain prices, it received £97 9s. 4d. Corn rents undoubtedly helped increase the College's endowment income. They did, however, produce considerable fluctuations. For example, the College's rental veered between £423 17s. 5d. in 1634/5 and £523 15s. 5d. in 1637/8.[54]

THE GROWTH OF A COLLEGE SPIRIT?

The most intangible aspect of University College in the time of its first undergraduates is the extent to which the College saw itself as a community. This question has a significance beyond its obvious sentimental appeal to old college members and others. In later centuries University College, like other Oxbridge colleges, did see itself as a community, living, working, and playing together, and did develop a special relationship with former undergraduate members. It is therefore a reasonable question to ask how far back such attitudes can be traced.

Arguably, the early undergraduate commoners of University College were little more than paying guests, especially before the introduction of a tutorial system. They could stay for as long or as briefly as they wished, and easily switch colleges. There were, however, undergraduates who were prepared to remember the College fondly. In bequeathing books to Queen's and University Colleges, William Holcot had asked that his 'Colleagues and Companyons...in studye' at both places 'will remember their Colleagian the gever'. Although Holcot was only a commoner at both colleges, he nevertheless saw

---

[53] Administration of entry fines: UC:EB2/F1/1 pp. 3–4 (other colleges were similarly flexible over fines: Howard 1935: 68–9); misbehaving tenants: UC:EB2/F/1 pp. 46–7; Whittington's fine: UC:EB2/F/1 p. 33; division of fines: UC:BU3/F2/2.

[54] Arncliffe lease: UC:E4/3D/21; rents in 1591/2 and 1596/7: *ARUC* ii. 529 and 549.

himself as an Old Member, and felt a bond with future students. Similarly George Radcliffe gave £100 towards the new quadrangle in 1635 'out of a deep love for the College', as the Benefactors' Book put it, and the College once lent him documents concerning its Pontefract estate, so that he could provide legal advice. John Browne remained in contact with his pupils John and William Burdet, advising on their finances, and became one of John Burdet's executors.[55]

An atmosphere of gift-giving was growing throughout the university. Well-born undergraduates were expected to show their appreciation of their college by giving a piece of plate when they left. Some fifty gifts of plate are known to have been made to University College in the half-century before the Civil War, most from undergraduates, but some from Fellows and tenants, and even one gift from Gabriel Cracknell, the College's wealthy cook. Beauty apart, plate has other uses: it can be recycled or sold in time of need. In the early 1630s, for example, some plate was melted down and turned into spoons.[56]

The strong north-eastern presence in University College, comparable with the ties between Queen's and north-west England, Exeter and south-west England, and Jesus and Wales, will have enhanced a sense of community. There remained a need for sympathetic environments for undergraduates from distant parts of the country where they could find others who shared their backgrounds, who might know their families—and, indeed, who could understand their accents.[57]

With such regional ties, it is not surprising that we find several family networks at University College in 1551–1642. Perhaps the most remarkable one surrounds Sir George Radcliffe of Thornhill and his cousins Jonas Radcliffe and Charles Greenwood. Jonas's brother Joshua was the father of Savile Radcliffe (m. 1600) and Thomas Radcliffe (m. 1606; F. 1613–48 and 1660), and Savile's own son, another Joshua, matriculated in 1621, while George's son Thomas briefly attended the College in 1641–2. Furthermore George's godfather and distant cousin (and neighbour at Thornhill) Sir George Savile matriculated at University College in 1598. In turn, Savile's two sons George and William both matriculated from the College in 1626. Finally, Savile's wife was the sister of Thomas Wentworth, who sent his younger brothers to University College, and befriended George Radcliffe

---

[55] Holcot: p. 113; Radcliffe's gift: UC:BE1/MS1/1 pp. 12–13; Pontefract documents: UC:AR1/MS1/3; John Browne and the Burdets: UC:S13/C2/1–13.

[56] Gifts of plate: UC:BE1/MS1/2; recycling plate: UC:EB1/A/1 fos. 460^v–461^v.

[57] Fox 2000: 53–79 discusses contemporary awareness (and incomprehension) of regional dialects, and observes (p. 63), 'The enduring regional affiliations of many colleges in Oxford and Cambridge were probably due, in large measure, to the need to find a tutor familiar with a boy's manner of speech.'

FIGURE 8.3 Monument in Thornhill Church to Sir George Savile, m. 1598, and his wife Anne (née Wentworth). Lying in front of them is their son George, m. 1626.

(Fig. 8.3). This Thornhill network shows how local links could be mirrored in the membership of a College.[58]

Loyal families did not just require Yorkshire connections or a kinsman in the Fellowship, as shown by the Digges family of Kent. As well as Dudley (m. 1600) and Leonard (m. 1603) Digges, Dudley's sons Thomas (m. 1626) and Dudley (m. 1630) also went to University College.[59]

Some perspective should be maintained: in describing his undergraduate life, Edward Herbert barely mentions University College, and about a hundred members of University College from this period had relatives in other colleges. Furthermore, University College still had its 'little Hall' and 'little Chapel'. When, in 1592, each college contributed towards the expenses of Elizabeth I's visit that year according to its means, Christ Church paid £2,000 and Magdalen £1,200, but University and Balliol, the two poorest colleges,

---

[58] Genealogical information from Whitaker 1810 and Nuttall 1986. George Radcliffe's son Thomas never matriculated, but appears in Buttery Books for 1641/2–1642/3 (UC:BU4/F/3–4).

[59] Some antiquarians claimed Dudley and Leonard's father Thomas (d. 1595) and grandfather Leonard (d. 1571) for University College, but this is unsubstantiated. Wood, *Athenae* i. 414–15 merely says that Leonard was 'educated for a time in this university (but in what house, unless in Univ. coll. I know not)'.

paid just £100 each. Nevertheless, it is possible to see in University College during the early modern period the first signs of a sense of community. It is becoming a place which one's relatives or neighbours might attend—and which sometimes engenders affection among what one might even start to call its Old Members.[60]

Finally, there is one curious aspect of early modern University College, namely the apparent lack of internal strife. Fellows are disciplined; some undergraduates are asked to leave; the university authorities sometimes have to enforce outside orders, as in the surplice incident of 1586; but, after the fiasco of Ralph Hamsterley, there are no known instances before 1642 of the university having to intervene to settle internal strife. John Browne had claimed that these peaceful times were thanks to his influence. Whether or not he is to be trusted, the peacefulness of this period is striking.[61]

During the sixteenth and early seventeenth centuries University College was transformed from an institution intended for study into one intended primarily for teaching; its rooms were fuller than ever; benefactions were now given as much to help undergraduates and young graduates as Fellows; and above all, it had achieved a basic structure which has survived to the present day. While the College's structure had changed, however, its appearance had not. It was now left to the next generation of the College to take up the challenge of John Browne's failed building project.

---

[60] College contributions: Fletcher 1976: 287; affection towards Cambridge colleges: Morgan 2004: 104–5.

[61] Lovatt 1995/6 considers factional strife as a 'given' in the early modern college, but notes too the forces for cohesion, such as the sharing of rooms and meals, and the surprising detail that some people forced out of a College later became its benefactors—like John Barnaby. Examples of problems elsewhere: Green 1979: 170–87 on the abrasive Paul Hood (Rector of Lincoln 1621–68), and Gray and Brittain 1979: 61–5 on the financial and personal irregularities of Roger Andrews (Master of Jesus, Cambridge, 1617–32).

9

Buildings, Civil War, and Commonwealth: 1632–1660

THOMAS WALKER AND NEW BEGINNINGS: 1632–40

When John Bancroft resigned the Mastership of University College on 23 August 1632, William Laud, Bishop of London and Chancellor of Oxford, swiftly followed precedent. On 28 August he recommended to the Fellows one Thomas Walker, whom they elected unanimously three days later. The new Master was Laud's protégé. Both were natives of Reading, and Walker had been a Scholar and Fellow of St John's College, where Laud had been President. Walker acquired preferment, becoming rector of two Oxfordshire parishes, Little Rollright and Mixbury, and, in 1630, a Prebendary of Bath and Wells. On resigning his Fellowship in 1631, he married Sarah, daughter of Laud's half-brother, Dr William Robinson.[1]

Walker arrived at an important moment. Just before John Bancroft's promotion, news had arrived of a remarkable bequest, which played a dominant role in College life for the next three decades. Sir Simon Bennet, a Buckinghamshire gentleman and former pupil of Charles Greenwood (m. 1602; Fig. 9.1), died childless in 1631, bequeathing a large estate in Northamptonshire called Handley Park to the College, subject to a life interest for his widow. Bennet had planned this benefaction for some time: he acquired Handley Park in the 1620s, so that in leaving property to University College, he would not deprive his heirs of any family estate.[2]

The 863 acres of Handley Park were arguably the most generous gift yet made to the College: rent from its other estates averaged about £450, but Handley Park alone was expected to yield at least £350 a year. Bennet wished to endow an equal number of Fellowships and Scholarships, respectively worth £20 and £10 a year, and requested that the College give a feast for his

---

[1] Walker's election: UC:GB3/A1/1 pp. 39–40; his background: information from Andrew Hegarty; Walker at Bath and Wells: Le Neve 1979: 73 and 110.
[2] See further Cox 1971a and 1972b. The house itself shows signs of having been substantially rebuilt at this time, as if made ready for a suitable tenant.

FIGURE 9.1 Sir Simon Bennet, m. 1602, donor of Handley Park, by an unknown artist.

Fellows and Scholars on St Simon and St Jude's day (28 October). Nothing was said about how many of them would be appointed, nor how they would be selected; presumably the College would appoint as many as the estate could support. Bennet also permitted the College, during his wife's lifetime, to sell as much timber on the estate as they wished to pay for rebuilding the College. The College had probably been forewarned of such a large benefaction, so that some discussions about its use—including rebuilding plans—may have occurred before Bennet's death. Others were ready to support a new building programme, including Bennet's old tutor, Charles Greenwood, who gave £1,000 towards the rebuilding at once, and £500 more in 1636. Another Greenwood pupil, George Radcliffe, now an adviser in Ireland to the Lord Lieutenant Thomas Wentworth, offered £100 in 1635.[3]

The College therefore began to discuss the appearance of its new quadrangle. Designs for two quite different schemes are known. Only a ground-floor

[3] Greenwood and Radcl gifts: UC: E1/MS1/1 p.11.

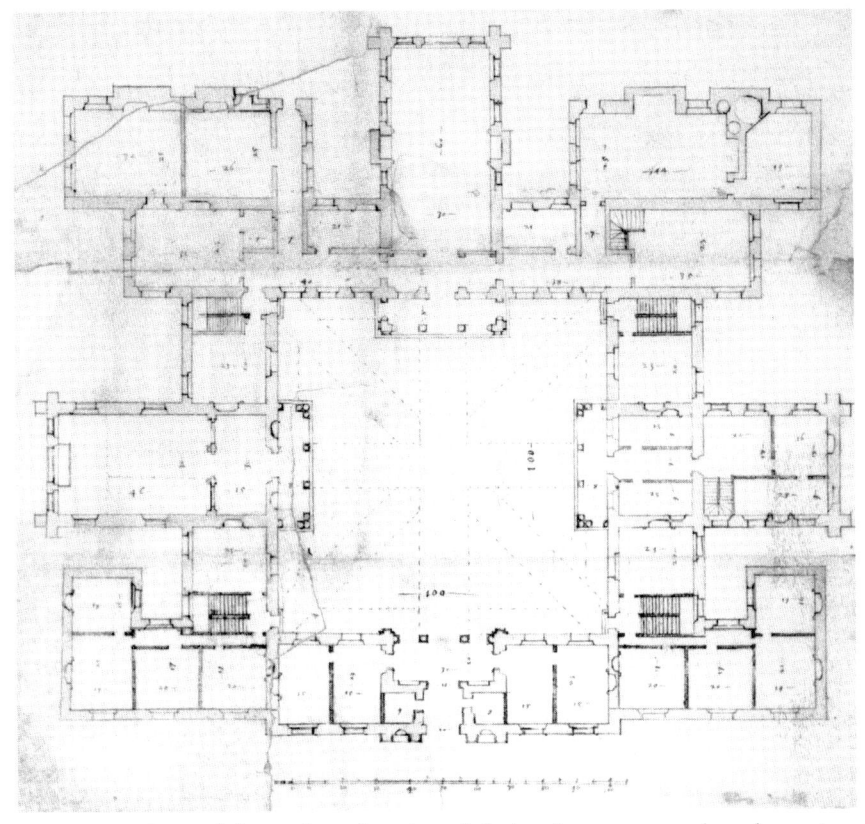

FIGURE 9.2 Ground-floor plan of a rejected design for a new quadrangle, c.1632. The High Street frontage runs along the bottom of the plan.

plan survives for the first, more daring, one (Fig. 9.2). Breaking with tradition, its unknown architect proposed a classicizing design, comprising a quadrangle with three porticos, two of which led to a Chapel and a Hall. The idea was revolutionary, and appears to be the earliest classical design for an Oxford or Cambridge college. The alternative was inspired by the new quadrangles at Wadham and Oriel. Its traditional plan was straightforward and almost square, with the Hall and Chapel placed on the south range. In the manner of Wadham, a wing jutted out to the south to contain the kitchen on the ground floor and a library above. Its style followed the modified Gothic of both colleges, borrowing from Oriel a fan-vault for the main entrance and rows of little gables at roof level. There survive for this design both plans and fragments of a pasteboard model—the oldest model of its kind in Britain (Fig. 9.3).[4]

[4] The classicizing design (ref. UC:FA3/1/Y2/1): Colvin 1983: 10–12; the Gothic design (ref. UC:FA3/1/Y1/1–9): Colvin 1983: 9–10, Honeyball 1986, and Sturdy 1990 and 1991; the wider context: Newman 1997, especially 144–5, 146, 158–9, and 169.

FIGURE 9.3 Surviving portions of a model of the approved design for a new quadrangle, c.1632, standing on one of its accompanying plans, which shows an unbuilt proposal for a cloister.

No records survive of the ensuing discussions, but the conclusion is clear: Thomas Walker wrote on the back of the classicizing design 'This modell was refused as inconvenient.' Daring as the rejected plan was, it could only be achieved by fussy, potentially expensive, and thus 'inconvenient' uses of space in the College. The Gothic design was also easier to build in stages. Even with Bennet's bequest, the College could not afford to build the quadrangle in one go. The mason for the project was Richard Maude, who is generally thought to have designed it as well. Maude would have been known to Walker, having worked on Canterbury Quadrangle at St John's College—although he was discharged from there in 1633.[5]

Maude's plans suggest that the west, north, and east ranges would contain about three dozen sets of rooms between them. Most sets had one large room, and two smaller ones, but it is not known how many people would occupy each set. Whereas medieval sets had comprised a communal bedroom with separate studies, one plan for the first floor of the new quadrangle labels all the larger rooms as 'chambers', and the smaller ones 'bedrooms' and 'studies', which implies just one occupant per set. Rooms in the second floor, which appear to have been divided up into smaller groups, would have gone to undergraduates, as had the cocklofts in the old quadrangle.

[5] Maude: Newman 1997: 159 and Sturdy 1990: 67; leaving St John's: Costin 1958: 40.

Ground-floor rooms could have gone to undergraduates, other lodgers, and perhaps servants. This would have been perfectly adequate: in March 1639, the College's Buttery Book listed as being in regular residence a Master, 8 Fellows, 8 MAs, 10 BAs, and 34 undergraduates—some 60 people who could have comfortably occupied the new building.[6] The Master might also have put people up in his Lodgings, and Fellows might have accommodated some so-called 'poor scholars' (p. 138) in their rooms.

On 17 April 1634, the first stone of the new quadrangle was laid by John Bancroft, and a promising young Fellow, Abraham Woodhead, gave an elaborate Latin speech. As befitted a son of Thomas Caius' College, Woodhead observed that University College had been the cradle of Oxford, 'while its little sister Cambridge was not yet the chimaera of a slumbering brain', and he charmingly compared Alfred and William of Durham with Charles I and 'William of Canterbury' (Laud). More practically, in May the College made an agreement with Sir Simon Bennet's widow regarding the sale of timber from Handley Park, tactfully agreeing that the new buildings should be called 'Sir Symon Bennetts Lodgeings and Hall'.[7]

Thomas Walker's detailed building accounts record the progress and cost of the work. Since the new quadrangle would be one-third larger than the old, work started on the west range, where no existing buildings required demolition. This range was completed in the spring of 1635, and the builders moved to the north, High Street, range, completing it by March 1637, and installing the great gate during the following year. The new buildings were quickly filled. The income from rented college rooms more than doubled to £20 in 1635/6, and rose to £36 in 1637/8, while the 1637/8 accounts allude to 'removing Chestes into the new treasury'—the new tower on the north range.[8]

The next stage was the south range, with the Hall and Chapel, which could be built around the remnants of the old quadrangle which were still in use, but here the project met a delay. Sir Simon Bennet's widow died in 1636, and ownership of Handley Park should have reverted to University College. Unfortunately, as we have seen, Bennet had left the number and selection of his Fellows and Scholars unresolved. Bennet's nephew and heir was a minor, but his guardians, exploiting this vagueness, refused to hand the property over. The College therefore had to take them to court, not winning their case and the property until November 1639.[9]

---

[6] The labelled plan: UC:FA3/1/Y1/9; for analysis of occupation, compare Sturdy 1990: 68–9; absent Fellows could also rent out their rooms (UC:S7/F1/3 shows John Elmhirst doing this); College in 1639: UC:BU4/F/1.

[7] Woodhead's speech: UC:GB3/A1/1 pp. 45–6; agreement with Lady Bennet: Pyx ι fasc. 2 no. 7.

[8] Completion of west range: UC:MA26/F1/1 p. 53; completion of the north range: UC:MA26/F1/4. Thomas Walker reckoned that the west range cost £1,405 3s. 3d. and the north range £1,711 10s. 4d (UC:MA26/F1/4), and that by May 1637 the College had raised £1,802 9s. 8d. from selling timber at Handley Park (UC:MA26/F1/2). Room rents from UC:BU2/F1/1.

[9] This lawsuit is documented in Pyx ι fascs. 3–5 (Pyx ι fasc. 5 no. 1 is the Court's decision).

As work began on the south range, Maude and his team evidently had difficulties fitting a chapel, hall, buttery, a passageway to the yard by the kitchen, and a staircase to the Library into this space, and plans for several different configurations survive. Even the Chapel interior took time to evolve—early designs proposed three windows on the south side, and one on the north (which later became five and three), and an Antechapel which occupied one-third the total length of the Chapel, as opposed to one-sixth as it does now. It was also proposed to place a little cloister to the south-east, bounded by the walls of the Chapel and the kitchen wing (visible on Fig. 9.3). Such a cloister would have offered opportunities for exercise in bad weather and, as with the cloisters of New College and All Souls, possibly burial for members of the College. The existence of several designs for this cloister shows that the proposal was treated seriously.[10]

Walker and the Fellows also considered the furnishing of the Chapel. English Arminians were especially eager to worship God in appropriately magnificent surroundings, and they led the way in reintroducing painted glass windows into churches and chapels. The finest glass painters in contemporary Oxford were two brothers from Emden in East Friesland, Bernard and Abraham van Linge, who worked with enamelled, rather than painted, glass—that is to say, they applied enamel paints to clear glass which they then fused by firing it in an oven. Bernard had designed windows for Wadham, while Abraham had worked at Lincoln, Queen's, Christ Church, and Balliol. Abraham may not have been an easy man—a letter at Magdalen College says of him 'This duch is a slye fellowe and stronge headed and must have a ruffe muzell or els there is no doinge with him'—but University College commissioned from him eight side windows and an east window, paying £190 between August 1641 and May 1642, with an extra £100 to follow when the east window was complete.[11]

Abraham van Linge's windows for University College were his last in Oxford and, in many people's opinions, also his best (Plates 4–5). The enamelling process allowed him to paint windows with the freedom granted to an oil painter, and his windows teem with exuberant detail, be it a mountain range, a seascape, or a simple domestic scene. Their subjects were carefully chosen. In the Antechapel (as originally conceived) would be two New Testament scenes of Christ respectively in the house of Mary and Martha, and in the Temple casting out the money-changers, and one from

---

[10] UC:MA26/F1/2 shows that work on the south range began in 1639; evolution of the south range: UC:FA3/1/Y1/2–9 (some of these are redrawn in Honeyball 1986); Chapel layout: UC:MA26/F/10 p. 15; All Souls cloister (now demolished): Colvin and Simmons 1989: 16–17.

[11] College chapels in the 1630s: Parry 2006: 59–86 (the van Linges are discussed on 60–2 and 103); Abraham van Linge's early work: Archer 1975; van Linge at Magdalen (where he received no commissions): MCA MC·FA5/1/2F/18; University College's commission: UC:MA26/F1/2 fo 42ᵛ and UC:MA26/F1/10 p. 14.

the Old, showing Jacob's dream. These scenes of purification and of listening to God's word would have created an appropriate mood in which to enter the Chapel itself, which showed scenes from the Old Testament on the theme of obedience and disobedience—be it Adam and Eve in the Garden of Eden, or Abraham agreeing to sacrifice his son—or ones which prefigured the New Testament, such as Jonah and the whale (Jonah's three days in the whale prefiguring Christ's three days in the tomb).[12]

By February 1642, Thomas Walker calculated that the new quadrangle had so far cost £5,429 11s. 11½d., of which all but £1,800 came from Handley timber. The south range was still incomplete: the walls were standing, but they lacked roofs or internal fittings. Nevertheless, within a decade, over half the quadrangle had been built.[13]

The 1630s were a confident decade for the College. As well as the Bennet bequest and the great building programme, Walker's College enjoyed intellectual vitality—and improvements in its living standards. The College accounts for the 1630s note the first known regular purchases of napkins in the Hall, and, in 1634/5, 4s. spent on a cushion for the Master's use there. The College's finances, in spite of John Elmhirst (p. 129), were also in good shape, as its profits from corn rents were divided among the Fellows every year from 1633/4 to 1640/1. Sometimes, as in 1635, the sum was a mere £5 13s. ¼d., but in 1638, the Fellows shared a dividend of £100.[14]

The College eagerly displayed its loyalty to the King and his Church. Bonfires were lit on the 'King's Holy Day' until 1645/6, and, when Charles I visited Oxford in August 1636, the Hall and buttery were whitewashed and the quadrangle levelled 'against the K. comeing to Oxf.' (although, so far as is known, the King did not visit University College). Meanwhile, although the old Chapel was due for demolition, the Fellows maintained standards there: £8 was spent on a new pulpit in 1633/4, and in 1636/7 large sums were spent on 27 yards of blue serge and green broadcloth for an unspecified purpose, and almost £1 on just one cushion.

The College's loyalty did not go unnoticed. Thomas Walker was appointed to two more Oxfordshire parishes, Somerton in 1633, and Hanborough in 1638. Some Fellows prospered. William Laud was also Chancellor of Trinity College Dublin, and in August 1640, when the Provostship there fell vacant, the post was filled by Richard Washington (F. 1626–40 and 1644–51), Dublin's first Oxonian Provost.[15]

---

[12] The fullest analysis of the windows remains Black 1977, but see too Sherwood and Pevsner 1974: 210 and Parry 2006: 67–9, who agree on their excellence.

[13] Cost of the quadrangle: UC:MA26/F1/6 p.11.

[14] Information in this and the next paragraph is derived from UC:BU2/F1/1.

[15] Walker's parishes: information from Andrew Hegarty; Washington was admitted Provost on 1 August 1640, according to the Board Register of the College (TCD MUN/V/5/1; my thanks to Ursula Mitchel, Archivist of Trinity College, for this reference). See too McDowell and Webb 1982: 13–15 and 17.

CIVIL WAR AND CHAOS: 1640–1648[16]

After the confident 1630s, the 1640s began badly. The political and religious beliefs of Charles I and William Laud, although generally welcomed in Oxford, were less well regarded elsewhere, not least on account of the heavy-handed methods sometimes employed to promulgate them. Oxford, indeed, had almost been cocooned from the worst of this opposition. There was also a local problem: although University College now owned Handley Park, it had yet to settle with Bennet's trustees on the implementation of his endowment. The size of Sir Simon Bennet's gift posed a problem. Doubling the rental could double the number of Fellows and Scholars in the College, but could such an increase be readily accommodated? Would the new Fellows share in existing Fellows' privileges and duties? Could the new College buildings accommodate them all?

Bennet's trustees wanted the estate to support as many Fellows and Scholars as possible, and to receive compensation for what they considered the loss of family property. They proposed that the lands be rented out at £500 a year, to endow eight Fellows and eight Scholars, half of whom should be relatives of Sir Simon Bennet. For the College, the first demand was financially imprudent, and the second had not been stipulated by Bennet. They turned to William Laud, who in October 1640 wrote a memorandum on the bequest. His advice was sensible: recommending a smaller but surer income, Laud proposed that the property be rented out for £350, to endow four Fellows and four Scholars. The new and existing Fellows should comprise one united body, sharing revenues from old and new properties, and to prevent, as he said, 'faction and other Inconveniences which might otherwise growe within the said howse to the utter ruyne of the said Colledge'.[17]

Laud's advice was wise, but his power was fading: the Long Parliament imprisoned him in December 1640. Rumours spread that the trustees were attempting to have a bill passed in Parliament, which was unlikely to be sympathetic towards a College so close to the hated Laud. Early in 1641 Walker and the Fellows wrote to the Earl of Pembroke, the new Chancellor of the university, protesting that they 'could not yeeld to the propositions of the kindred, without great losse to themselves'. War stopped future discussions, and the Bennet benefaction remained in limbo until the end of the decade.[18]

The political crises of the early 1640s touched College members directly. Hearing that a creditor threatened to complain about him to Parliament, John Elmhirst asked Walker in November 1641 to sell the contents of his room, in order 'to stoppe [his creditor's] mouth from farther complaint, especially there where he threatens (for I had loth there be sifted, where

---

[16] See further on these years Roy and Reinhart 1997.
[17] Laud's memorandum: Pyx κ fasc. 5 no. 5a; the views of Bennet's trustees: Pyx κ fasc. 5 nos. 8a–8b and Pyx μ fasc. 11 nos. 3a–3b.
[18] Fellows' petition: Pyx κ fasc. 5 no. 8b.

they winnow with a whirlwind)'. Richard Washington fled Ireland for Oxford when rebellion broke out there in autumn 1641, and Abraham Woodhead, elected Proctor in March 1641, led a successful campaign preventing Oxford's enemies from imposing new statutes on the university, even defending himself before Parliament. Thomas Walker himself suffered personal troubles as well as political ones, when between May 1640 and October 1641 he lost his wife Sarah and all three of his children.[19]

Deep as the political crisis was, there remained hope of resolution while both sides still spoke to each other, and the College tried to function as normal. In particular, the building programme continued: Abraham van Linge delivered his eight side windows with an east window promised to follow, while preparations were made for completing the Chapel and Hall. Above all, the College still received fresh Fellows and undergraduates.

The appearance of normality slowly wore thin, as shown by the College's Buttery Books for 1639/40–1642/3.[20] In March 1639 University College comprised a Master, 8 Fellows, 8 MA and 10 BA commoners, and 34 undergraduates. During the year, about a dozen new undergraduates arrived, and the College remained fairly well filled. Figures were similar for 1640/1, but only three new undergraduates arrived in 1641/2, and the College emptied almost completely of its wealthier undergraduates in August 1641 (the poorer ones remained, presumably because they could not afford to leave). The servant keeping the Buttery Book found wry humour in this, for in the week of 27 August 1641 he wrote against one person's name 'hy ho noe body at home'. Numbers only returned to normal in November.

In March 1642, twenty-seven undergraduates were in residence, and attendance remained steady even during early summer, as all hope of agreement between King and Parliament vanished. Members of the College drifted away only in August, when active preparations for war began in Oxford. Magdalen Bridge was blocked, and members of the university took part in army training. From 28 August until 10 September some Royalist troops were resident in Oxford, and the university appointed a delegacy to find maintenance for the troops, and to provide arms for the safety of the university. The delegacy included Thomas Walker and Obadiah Walker.[21]

The arrival of soldiers was the last straw. Most College members left in the week beginning 2 September, and two weeks later only two MAs, two BAs,

---

[19] Elmhirst: UC:S7/C1/3; Washington: the Board Register of Trinity College (TCD MUN/V/5/1) records that he left Dublin on 29 October 1641 (see too McDowell and Webb 1982: 17), and the 1641/2 Buttery Book (UC:BU4/F/3) shows him in Oxford by December 1641; Woodhead: YAS MS 46 (a memoir by Francis Nicholson) and Roy and Reinhart 1997: 690; Thomas Walker's family: Wood 1899: 180.

[20] UC:BU4/F/1–4. In comparison, Lincoln College in Michaelmas 1641 comprised 12 Fellows, 12 fellow commoners, 36 undergraduates, and 10 servitors (Green 1979: 244).

[21] Wood, *History* ii. 442–9 provides a fuller account of these events. Antony Wood the antiquarian first appears here as a chronicler of his own time. He will appear regularly in the next few chapters, not least because he knew several members of University College.

four poor undergraduates, and four Fellows remained. Thomas Radcliffe and John Elmhirst had long been absent anyway, and Abraham Woodhead left for Europe in the autumn of 1642, travelling with Sir George Radcliffe's son Thomas and two other pupils. Some undergraduates returned for brief periods between October and March, but otherwise University College closed down as a teaching institution. The building programme also ceased: the south range remained incomplete, and Abraham van Linge never produced his east window, his aisle windows stored away for installation in better times. The College was left an architectural mess, with remnants of the old quadrangle surrounded by the new.[22]

Worse followed. Within days of the Royalists' departure, some Parliamentarian soldiers arrived in Oxford, followed by one of their leaders, Lord Saye and Sele (also High Steward of Oxford), seeking hidden munitions, arms, and plate. Several houses were searched, including that of one Thomas Smith, where some of University College's plate was hidden. Presumably to discourage others, Saye confiscated what he found. The College also endured the presence of soldiers: in the weeks of 9 and 16 September 1642 the Buttery Book recorded sums 'drank by the soulders'—presumably Royalists—and in the week for 7 October 1642 someone wrote 'billet our ten men or else'. Whether or not this recorded a verbatim (Parliamentarian?) threat, it evokes the tense atmosphere.[23]

The Parliamentarians left Oxford early in October, and shortly afterwards Charles I took up residence in Christ Church. With the King came his court, and the empty Colleges filled up. From the middle of November 1642, people appear in University College's Buttery Book who are clearly not students, but probably attached to the court (the Bursar's Book for 1643/4 identifies almost thirty such non-academic lodgers). Some were Old Members: that loyal alumnus, Sir George Radcliffe, arrived in summer 1643, and a Sir Francis Carew resident from November 1642 may be the Francis Carew who matriculated in 1619. Other residents, however, had no prior links, such as Sir Thomas Aylesbury, Master of the Mint, who stayed for parts of 1642 and 1643, and Sir Orlando Bridgeman, Keeper of the Rolls in the Common Pleas and solicitor-general to the Prince of Wales, who stayed briefly in early 1644. The College may also have seen its first resident women: the Bursar's Book for 1643/4 noted a debt for £13. 6s. from a Lady Boswell in a context which suggests that she was renting a College room.[24]

[22] Empty College: UC:BU4/F/4; Woodhead: Wood, *Athenae* iii. 1157 and YAS MS 46; Thomas Radcliffe signed a Buttery Book in the week of 17 September 1641 (UC:BU4/F/3) but never matriculated; van Linge's career after 1642 remains a mystery.

[23] Saye and Sele: Wood, *History* ii. 450–2: Thomas Smith had lent the College money (UC:BU8/1/F2/1–6; perhaps he retained the plate as security?), and his son Oliver rented Eastwick Farm and the Grandpont fields (*ARUC* ii. 580 and 592); soldiers in College: UC:BU4/F/4.

[24] Charles in Oxford: Wood, *History* ii. 454; Buttery Book: UC:BU4/F/4; Bursar's Book: UC:BU3/F1/6; Lodgers in other colleges: Roy and Reinhart 1997: 700–5 and de Groot 2002; Aylesbury and Bridgeman: *ODNB* entries; Lady Boswell: UC:BU3/F1/6 fo. 8५.

The remnants of the College tried to maintain some continuity. Two Scholars were elected in 1643–4, and in 1644 Richard Washington was re-elected Fellow. Messengers were sent to Handley Park and Wales in 1643–5, and some standards were kept up: 1s. 6d. was spent in 1646/7 on 'rubbing the bookes and making cleane the library'. There were occasional glimpses of royal approval, as when Obadiah Walker preached twice before the King, the second time at Charles's request.[25]

Nevertheless the effects of the war were unavoidable. In June 1643, a list of all scholars aged between 16 and 60 was drawn up, who could spend one day a week building fortifications. This work could be dangerous: one undergraduate, Richard Tennant (m. 1641), was buried at St Clements on 2 June 1643, having drowned, perhaps while working by the Cherwell.[26]

In addition to demands on their labour, College members endured demands on their purse. In 1642–5, the College made several payments 'towards the bulwarcks in Oxon', and during the siege of Oxford in 1646, Thomas Walker calculated that the College spent £15 11s. 7d. 'in provision against the seige in reparacions, in Contributions towards the soldiers maintenance, and other occasions'. The King's presence also proved expensive. In July 1642, the College lent Charles £150, and in July 1643 he wrote to the Fellows asking them to support as many infantrymen as they could for a month. When Charles commended this proposal, 'not doubting but you will soe farr expresse your selves this way that Wee shall not be disappointed of Our expectation', the Fellows knew what this delicately expressed hint meant. In addition, in 1642/3, the College gave £2 12s. 6d. to the trumpeters, footmen, and coachmen of the Prince of Wales and of the King, and the trumpeters of Prince Rupert. The greatest loss of all, however, was the College's plate. In January 1643, when most colleges loyally gave their plate to the King, inevitably to be melted down for coin, University College's contribution was assessed at just over 60 lb., the third smallest quantity (this suggests that not all its plate had been confiscated by Lord Saye and Sele).[27]

The College also had trouble collecting its annual rent (Graph 9.1). This is not always easy to detect: the accounts then recorded merely expected, rather than actual, rent, and only once, in 1643/4, is the gulf between appearance

---

[25] Elections: UC:GB3/A1/1 p. 51; messages to properties: UC:MA26/F1/12 pp. 7–9; books: UC:BU2/F1/1 p. 204; Walker's sermons: Smith, 256–7.
[26] The university at war: Wood, *History* ii. 462–4 and 470. Tennant: Wood, *City of Oxford* 214.
[27] Payments for fortifications: UC:MA26/F1/12 pp. 7–9; loan to King: UC:MA30/3/F/1 (and payment of soldiers: UC:MA30/3/F/2); payments to servants: UC:BU2/F1/1 p. 155 (de Groot 2002: 1210, notes similar payments made in 1643 by Corpus Christi College); weight of College plate: Bodl. Tanner MS 338 fo. 65 (Carr, 108, claimed that the plate was worth £190 4s. 2d., but supplies no source); Saye and Sele's confiscation: an entry in the College accounts of 1654/5 'in making enquiry for the Coll' plate wch my Lord Say tooke away' (UC:BU2/F1/1 p. 292), suggests that the College never got this returned.

GRAPH 9.1 Income and Expenditure of University College 1633/4–1689/90. 'Income (N)' signifies net income, as calculated in Graph 6.1. Income from the Bennet foundation is not recorded on these accounts until 1665/6, hence the great increase in income that year.

and reality revealed. The official accounts of the Bursar, William Richardson, give the College's income as almost £470, but in his Bursar's Book, Richardson recorded that some £220 was still unpaid, and £70 more was owed in batells bills. Some arrears were due to defaulting tenants—in February 1648, parishioners at Arncliffe refused to pay tithes, claiming that they did not belong to the College—but some College properties faced actual danger. When Oxford was besieged in May and June 1645, Eastwick Farm was occupied by Royalist soldiers as an outpost. Eastwick survived reasonably unscathed, but the College's house in Woodstock was recorded in March 1646 to be 'much decayed by reason of these unruly times', and the College had difficulty finding a tenant for it. Meanwhile room rents declined from about £30 a year in the early 1640s to nothing in 1645/6–1646/7. The College normally received payments from commoners on their admission, but no such payments were recorded in 1646/7 and 1648/9 (see Graph 8.1). Something had to give: most Fellows and Scholars did not receive their full stipend, and the College's overall expenditure declined from an average of £450 a year in the 1630s to £275 in 1646/7.[28]

Meanwhile University College's old members found themselves having to choose sides or else leave the country altogether. The College took most interest, unsurprisingly, in its Royalists: one Fellow drew up a list of thirty-three former undergraduates and one Fellow who fought for the King. Three of them had been at the College before 1620, but the remainder came up between 1630 and 1640. They were well-born, too, for ten were the sons of esquires, and nine the sons of knights or baronets. Some were born soldiers, such as Philip Monckton (m. 1638), knighted at the age of 24, who became a Major-General and participated in the Second Civil War of 1647/8, but even the mathematician Thomas Henshaw joined a cavalry regiment. Five men died or were killed, including the youngest, George Boteler, who had only come up in October 1640, and Thomas Rockley, the godson of Thomas Wentworth, Earl of Strafford, and erstwhile dandy of the 1630s.[29]

On the Parliamentarian side was Henry Bulstrode (m. 1592), Parliament's governor of Aylesbury. There was also Henry Nevill, who lived at University College in the late 1630s; he spent the earlier part of the war abroad, but returned in 1645 joining the Parliamentarians, and attracting the favour of Oliver Cromwell, until he refused to tolerate the latter's control of power. Another old member, William Say (m. 1619), signed Charles I's death warrant. Undoubtedly, however, the most prominent Parliamentarian from University College was Henry Marten (m. 1617). Marten was unusual in being a political, rather than religious, reformer, and he led a distinctly 'unpuritanical' way of life. As early as 1640, Marten was heard to comment 'I do not think one Man wise enough to govern us all', and, like Say, he signed Charles I's death warrant; but he grew to mistrust Cromwell's power, and spent the later 1650s out of favour.[30]

After Cromwell's victory at Naseby in 1645, the defeat of the Royalists became inevitable. In April 1646 Charles left Oxford, and Thomas Fairfax besieged the city. When Oxford surrendered on 24 June 1646 Fairfax was generous: the university and its colleges kept their buildings, privileges, and possessions intact. Nevertheless, in 1644/5 Cambridge had received

---

[28] Richardson's accounts: UC:BU2/F1/1 pp. 163–75; his debts: UC:BU3/F1/6 fos. 87–92; Arncliffe: UC:E4/1C/6; Eastwick Farm: Wood, *History* ii. 475–6 mentions 'Mr. Oliver Smyth's house, (held by him of University Coll.)', and Smith leased Eastwick Farm (*ARUC* ii. 592); Woodstock: UC:EB2/F/1 p. 5; room rents: UC:BU2/F1/1; other colleges' financial troubles: Twigg 1997.
[29] College members abroad: Wood, *Athenae* iv. 447 and 271; Royalist soldiers: UC:MA30/3/F/3; Monckton: *ODNB* entry. Some other Royalists were omitted from this list, such as Sir William Savile (m. 1626), Governor of York (Nuttall 1986: 41–58).
[30] Bulstrode: Wood, *Athenae* iii. 472; Nevill: Wood, *Athenae* iv. 409–10 (probably to be identified with a 'Nevill' who appears in the Bursar's Book of 1637/8 (UC:BU3/F1/4) and the Buttery Books of 1639/40–1642/3 (UC:BU4/F/1–4)); Marten: Clarendon 1759: 41 (republicanism), Wood, *Athenae* iii. 1237–44 (very hostile), and Waters 1973 (more balanced).

a Parliamentary visitation, during which its colleges were purged of Royalist sympathizers. Thomas Walker, kinsman of William Laud, and recipient of a sapphire ring in his will, would have had few illusions about the future.[31]

In May 1647 Parliament created a board to make a visitation of Oxford university. Oxford was ready: on 1 June 1647, its members elected a group of delegates who 'should in the name of the University have power given them to answer and act in all things pertaining to the public good of the University'. Their intention was to create trouble for the Visitors, by refusing to cooperate. One Delegate was Obadiah Walker, and University College's archives hold papers relating to the delegates, including advice on polite non-cooperation, which suggest that University College was a centre of anti-Parliamentarian activity.[32]

At first Visitors and university warily circled each other. Requests for interviews were met with excuses—Thomas Walker fell conveniently ill when summoned to see the Visitors—and the authorities were distracted by a Royalist uprising, the so-called Second Civil War. By the spring of 1648, however, Oxford could no longer escape, and during April Magdalen, All Souls, Wadham, Trinity, St John's, and Brasenose witnessed ejections of their Fellows.[33]

On 18 May 1648, the first members of University College were summoned before the Visitors, and asked to submit.[34] Obadiah Walker stonewalled, saying 'I am not yet satisfied that I may submit to this Visitation', and another Fellow, Henry Watkins, and a Leicester Scholar, Thomas Silvester, gave similar replies. Others yielded, including two young BAs, William Woodward and Ezreel Tonge. Richard Washington, however, gave a more complex reply.

I doe freely and conscientiousely submitte my selfe to this Visitation, authorised by Parliament, as I thinke I ought to doe, and as I have donne formerly in another kingedome to a like Visitation sent from the Parliament there, to the Colledge where I then lived.

Some have interpreted this statement as a sign of Washington's Parliamentary leanings, but William Laud would not have tolerated an unsympathetic Provost in Dublin, and a Parliamentarian would hardly spend the Civil War in Royalist Oxford. It is better to characterize Washington as a pragmatist who thought he could do more good by submitting to the inevitable than

---

[31] Oxford: Wood, *History* ii. 479–85; Cambridge: Leedham-Green 1996: 81; Thomas Walker: information from Andrew Hegarty.
[32] Creation of the board of visitors: Roy and Reinhart 1997: 723; the delegates: Wood, *History* ii. 507, 512, and 520; documents about delegates' activities: UC:MA30/3/MS/1–75.
[33] Thomas Walker: Wood, *History* ii. 533; visitations of other colleges: Wood, *History* ii. 568–73; the early stages of the Visitation: Roy and Reinhart 1997: 723–7.
[34] Burrows 1881: 102–3 and 121.

BUILDINGS, CIVIL WAR, AND COMMONWEALTH: 1632–1660

by making a foolhardy stand. He had already been ejected from one academic position, and was no doubt unwilling to endure this again. The fact that he served as Bursar continuously in 1646/7–1649/50 suggests that he was trying to preserve some continuity.[35]

Others paid the price for their courage. On 7 July 1648, Obadiah Walker, Henry Watkins, and Thomas Silvester were expelled (although Silvester later submitted, and was readmitted), with Thomas Walker suffering the same fate three days later. Thomas Radcliffe and Abraham Woodhead, lying low outside Oxford, were deprived in October 1648. Of the two other non-resident Fellows, John Elmhirst and William Richardson were eventually deprived of their Fellowships in 1651. Only four other colleges lost a larger proportion of their Fellows.[36]

COMMONWEALTH AND PROTECTORATE: 1648–1660[37]

The Visitors' choice of Master, Joshua Hoyle, was installed on 11 July 1648. Hoyle, an elderly Yorkshireman, had studied at Magdalen Hall, and then moved to Trinity College Dublin, taking his BA there in 1610 before becoming a Fellow and then, in 1623, Professor of Divinity. Hoyle and Richard Washington will therefore have known each other, and Hoyle, like Washington, had fled Ireland in 1641. Hoyle was academically distinguished—soon after becoming Master, he was appointed Regius Professor of Divinity at Oxford—and his religion was to the Visitors' liking. Of two publications attributed to him, one, *A Reioynder to Master Malone's Reply concerning Reall Presence* (Dublin, 1641), is a learned, ferocious, and exhausting diatribe against the doctrine of transubstantiation. In the other, a sermon preached after William Laud's execution in January 1645, Hoyle exults at the death of this modern priest of Baal. One should, he writes, 'cloth not proud offenders with the robe of Martyrs... When transgressors are cut off, let God have the glory.' Antony Wood was unimpressed by Hoyle, finding his inaugural address as Regius Professor 'a very miserable trite speech', and he characterized him as 'a person of great reading and memory, but of less judgement, and so devoted to his book that he was in a manner a stranger to the world and things thereof, a careless person, and no better than a mere scholar'.[38]

---

[35] Burrows 1881: cxxvii writes: 'The Register shows how implicitly [Washington] was trusted by the Visitors.' Carr, 113 even claims that Washington 'was the leader of the Parliamentarian party in the College'. No other record of the Dublin visitation is known (information from Ursula Mitchel).

[36] Walker, Watkins, and Silvester: Burrows 1881: 145; Silvester's recantation: Burrows 1881: 228; Walker: UC:MA26/F4/1 p. 1; Radcliffe and Woodhead: Burrows 1881: 199; other colleges: Roy and Reinhart 1997: 730.

[37] For the wider context, see Worden 1997.

[38] Hoyle's installation: Wood, *History* ii. 600; his academic career: Wood, *Athenae* iii. 382, McDowell and Webb 1982: 12–13, and Burtchaell and Sadleir 1935: 413; Hoyle on Laud: Hoyle 1645: 16; Wood on Hoyle: Wood, *History* ii. 607 and 609, and Wood, *Athenae* iii. 383.

After Hoyle's installation, the Visitors selected fresh Fellows and Scholars. The compliant BAs Ezreel Tonge and William Woodward were rewarded with Fellowships on 14 and 17 July 1648; three more Fellows and eight Scholars were appointed in October and November, and others followed in 1649 and 1650.[39]

Meanwhile the expelled Master and Fellows had to shift for themselves. Thomas Walker at least seems not to have been ejected from any of his livings. Obadiah Walker chose to travel widely in Europe, where, according to Antony Wood, he 'advantaged himself much as to the knowledge of the world, men and languages'. Abraham Woodhead drew on Royalist patronage, such as from the Duke of Buckingham, and devoted himself to private tuition.[40]

The expelled and intruded Fellows, however, found themselves conducting business with each other. In autumn 1648, Thomas Walker helped settle debts from William Richardson's Bursarship of 1643/4, and in 1653/4 a messenger was sent to 'Dr. Walker' on unspecified business, while John Elmhirst corresponded with Joshua Hoyle about his debts. It even seems that Abraham Woodhead kept a room in College. On 29 December 1648 the Visitors ordered that 'Mr. Woodhead shall have a chamber in University Colledge, with consent of the Fellowes', and in October 1649 they ordered Richard Washington and the same Mr Woodhead to report on the Bennet benefaction. No other 'Mr. Woodhead' had such knowledge of University College, and so he has plausibly been identified with Abraham.[41]

The arrival of so many new Fellows threatened a loss of continuity in College life, and much depended on Richard Washington to preserve it. Unfortunately a situation in which the former Provost of Trinity College was subordinate to his erstwhile Professor of Divinity required a tact which perhaps Hoyle did not possess. Washington continued as Bursar until March 1650, and regularly represented University College before the Visitors, but he then withdrew from College life, moving to London, where he died in August 1651.[42]

Instead, Hoyle turned to Ezreel Tonge. Tonge, who had matriculated from University College in 1638, remained in Oxford at the start of the Civil War, but according to Antony Wood he had Parliamentary sympathies, and after March 1644 left to become a schoolmaster at Churchill, near Chipping Norton. Having returned and submitted to the Visitors, Tonge now appeared alongside Hoyle, attempting to settle College debts.[43]

---

[39] These appointments are recorded in UC:GB3/A1/1 pp. 54–8.
[40] Thomas Walker: information from Andrew Hegarty; Obadiah Walker: Wood, *Athenae* iv. 437–8 (also Firth 1962: 97–8); Woodhead: Wood, *Athenae* iii. 1157 and YAS MS 46.
[41] Walker: UC:BU3/F1/6 fos. 87–93 and UC:BU2/F1/1 p. 282; Elmhirst: UC:S7/C1/4–5; 'Mr. Woodhead': Burrows 1881: 214, 271, and 556, and Carr, 116.
[42] Washington and the Visitors: Burrows 1881: 271, 289, and 329; his death: UC:GB3/A1/1 p. 61.
[43] Tonge's career: Wood, *Athenae* iii. 1260–1, and the Bursar's Book of 1643/4 (UC:BU3/F1/6); Tonge acting alongside Hoyle: OUA UC Papers 1651/18:31–2.

Unfortunately, the inexperienced Master and Fellow faced tremendous problems. Hoyle himself quickly realized the poor state of the College's finances: in autumn 1648, he petitioned the Parliamentary Visitors concerning his stipend, which at £30 was the second smallest for any college head. The Visitors tried to help—in October 1649 they ordered three Fellowships to be frozen, and their income used to settle debts—while the College was getting back in touch with its more distant properties, and soon issuing leases on the scale of the 1630s. Carr even argued that the College may have come close to temporary dissolution, on the basis of an order issued by the Visitors in March 1650 'that the Master and Fellowes of Universitie Colledge be required to repare to the said Colledge with all convenient speede, to the end that the affaires of the Colledge may be thoroughly settled'. In fact this may mean nothing more than that not all the Fellowship was in residence.[44]

Next there was the Bennet benefaction, left in suspended animation since 1641. The Bennet trustees now had the ear of the current Chancellor, the Earl of Pembroke, who in May 1648 wrote an abusive letter to the College, castigating them for not carrying out any building work, or electing any Bennet Fellows over the last few years, 'the which', he raged, 'occasions a greate Scandall not onely upon your particular Society but the University alsoe, and a generall Discouragement to all Persons charitably affected, to see soe bountifull and eminent a Gift soe much abused.'[45] Pembroke conveniently overlooked the fact that a civil war had caused this inactivity.

With such a Chancellor, the College could expect little help. Some gestures were made—the Visitors appointed the first Bennet Fellow in November 1648, and five more in 1649—but when the Court of Chancery decided on the benefaction in December 1649, the Bennet trustees were victorious: the estate would be leased at £400 a year; there would be eight Fellows and eight Scholars, half of whom would be relations of Sir Simon Bennet, but with no restrictions on the selection of the rest (these were thus the College's first open Fellowships); the new Fellows and Scholars would be funded separately from the old foundation, so that a second Bursar would administer the Bennet money. There would therefore be an old foundation and a new foundation, living side by side. Ezreel Tonge, who had led the College's defence, admitted that matters had not gone well, writing in May 1650 to an unnamed expelled Fellow with an almost embarrassed deference: 'Perhaps our follies may be some pleasure unto you to read at leasure ... and it would be a great delight unto mee to heare the impartiall iudgement of what is approvable and what not in those articles.'[46]

---

[44] Hoyle's petition: Burrows 1881: 207–8, 210, and 251; vacant Fellowships: Burrows 1881: 269; contacting properties: UC:BU2/F1/1, pp. 225–6; possibly empty College: Burrows 1881: 289 and Carr, 119.

[45] UC:MA26/C1/3.

[46] The 1649 judgement is reported in Pyx κ fasc. 5 nos. 12a–13b; Tonge's letter: Pyx μ fasc. 11 no. 4 (William Smith wrote on it that he thought it was addressed to Obadiah Walker).

A decade earlier, Thomas Walker had warned that the trustees' proposal would 'occasion murmurings, and hart-burnings, if not factious Division'.[47] He was right: it was one thing to give each Fellow a stipend and profits from corn rents or entry fines, from his own foundation, and to assign College offices to all Fellows; but how would one-off payments to the College, such as admission fees, be divided? How would the two Bursars agree on the payment of repairs to College buildings, expenses for journeys on College business, or the settling of tradesmen's bills? No answers were forthcoming to these questions. The only extant set of accounts from the new—Bennet—foundation, for October 1651–January 1653, shows that it had run up a deficit of over £200, but was also making regular payments to the old foundation to settle debts between them. It also shows a physical division between the foundations: by November 1651, the Bennet Fellows were holding a separate feast on St Simon and St Jude's day.[48]

The old foundation was in no happier state, in large part thanks to Ezreel Tonge, who was Bursar in 1650/1. Tonge ended his term of office with unpaid debts of £280, and with the old and new foundation each claiming that the other owed them money. Tonge resigned his Fellowship soon after his Bursarship expired, but left few happy memories behind: Tonge claimed that the College still owed him money, but the new Bursar, Thomas Jennings, claimed that Tonge owed them money, and had sold College furniture to pay his debts. In 1652 or 1653 Tonge angrily rounded on his accusers, writing 'am I not well rewarded by Washington and his partie Genings who endeavour for my good will to hange me as a theafe before the whole world and to robb me of my mony laid out for the College and of my good name too'. Ultimately the Parliamentary Visitors had to attempt to adjudicate on who owed what.[49]

Even after Tonge's departure, the Fellows' financial problems remained: between 1651/2 and 1656/7, the expenditure of the old foundation regularly exceeded its income, and in 1653 the old foundation had to sue the new before the Chancellor's Court for debts payable on the goods of Richard Washington. By February 1654, so great were the disputes between the foundations that the Parliamentary Visitors made a drastic intervention: the new foundation should pay the old almost £200, and the old would write off its debts. However, because the new foundation was found to owe £700 elsewhere, the Visitors also ordered that, in order to discharge these debts,

---

[47] UC:MA26/MS2/4. Several Cambridge colleges had so-called 'bye-fellowships', whose holders were excluded from receiving dividends, from administering the college and its estates, and from holding college offices—and who were in frequent disputes with ordinary fellows (Morgan 2004: 219–21).

[48] The account book is UC:S11/F1/1. The feast is mentioned on p. 5.

[49] Tonge's debts: UC:S8/F1/1; muddled finances: UC:S8/F1/4; Tonge's self-defence: UC:S8/C1/3; the Visitors' intervention: Burrows 1881: 366 and 368.

the Fellows of the new foundation should not be paid for three and a half years (although they could remain in College if they wished): a woeful outcome of Sir Simon Bennet's great benefaction, thanks to his overambitious trustees.[50]

Financial troubles apart, University College still lacked any autonomy, with all Fellowships and Scholarships being appointed by the Parliamentary Visitors. Sometimes greater names were involved, as when in 1652 Oliver Cromwell himself recommended one John White to a Fellowship. When in June 1651 the College tried to elect a Fellow, the Visitors declared that the College was still 'not in a statutable way to make their own elections', and made the election void—but appointed the College's candidate anyway. Only in 1653 could the College elect its own Scholars and Exhibitioners; and it does not seem to have elected Fellows until 1657.[51]

The elderly Joshua Hoyle had proved unequal to these challenges, and his health was declining: in October 1651, he was unable to carry out his duties as Regius Professor due to illness. He fell ill again late in 1654, and died on 6 December, being buried in the old Chapel (the new one being still incomplete).[52]

As Hoyle lay dying, Ezreel Tonge, unbowed by his past dealings with the College, planned a triumphant return. In autumn 1654 he began lobbying to succeed Hoyle as Master, and attracted support from several eminent men. It was also rumoured that he directly approached some Fellows. Tonge must have thought the moment opportune. Of the College's fifteen Fellows—seven and eight from the old and new foundations respectively—all but one of the Bennet Fellows, their stipends still suspended, were living out of College. Of the seven Fellows of the old foundation, three, including George Gale, the senior Fellow, were not in residence, which left Sampson Eyton, Edward Terry, Thomas Thornton, and William Offley. The five resident Fellows were determined that Tonge would not be their Master. One of them later called him 'a man so active in his owne concernients, so desirous of the place, and so very well knowing the litle respect the Fellowes of the Colledge did beare to him'. The five Fellows tried to summon their colleagues as Hoyle's death drew near, but some did not reply, and others said they were too unwell to travel. The five therefore had to act on their own initiative. On the day after Hoyle's death, even before his burial, Sampson

---

[50] The old foundation's debts: UC:BU2/F1/1; Washington's goods: OUA CC Papers 1653/71; the Visitors' intervention: Burrows 1881: 386–9 (Bennet Scholars continued to be paid, so long as they remained in College).

[51] White's election: UC:GB3/A1/1 p. 64 (unfortunately, he obtained this support through a fraudulent petition, so that the Visitors had to declare the election void); attempts at autonomy: UC:GB3/A1/1 p. 60; first known free elections of Scholars and Exhibitioners and of Fellows: UC:GB3/A1/1 pp. 65 and 68.

[52] Hoyle's illness: Burrows 1881: 339; his death and burial UC:GB3/A1/1 p. 66.

Eyton, the senior Fellow present, held a Mastership election, at which Thomas Thornton was unanimously chosen.[53]

The instincts of Eyton and his colleagues to save the College from Ezreel Tonge were surely sound, but the legality of an election held so quickly with only a third of the Fellows was questionable. Tonge himself quickly protested before the traditional Visitors of the College (the Vice-Chancellor, Doctors of Divinity, and Proctors). After some uncertainty over whether the traditional or the Parliamentary Visitors had greater authority, the traditional ones confirmed Thornton's election, and Tonge disappeared from the College's affairs, to re-emerge two decades later.[54]

Unfortunately, Thornton now faced internal opposition. George Gale claimed that he should have been consulted, and he and another Fellow of the old foundation, Edward Farrar, appealed against the election in March 1655, claiming that greater efforts should have been made to contact non-resident Fellows. Gale neglected to mention that he had been incommunicado in a remote part of Devonshire, and that Farrar had not replied to several letters from Oxford. Although the other non-resident Fellows declared their support for Thornton, nevertheless, the procedural points proved decisive, and the Chancellor's Court overruled the Visitors, declaring the election void.[55]

The College held fresh elections in May. Thornton won again, but never took office. The exact course of events is unclear; it seems that the Chancellor, Oliver Cromwell, intervened and, following such predecessors as William Laud, installed his own candidate, Francis Johnson, one of his chaplains (although he did appoint Thornton rector of Wheathampstead as compensation). Unfortunately, Johnson, a former Fellow of All Souls in his forties, was an uninspiring character: even Edmund Calamy, the historian of dissenting ministers, admitted that he 'had no very good elocution', and, rather ungallantly, that 'he was encompassed with Job's Afflictions, and among the rest, with the Dins of a foolish Woman, but he patiently bore all.'[56]

Before contemplating the Mastership of Francis Johnson, let us look more generally at the College in the 1650s, its members and their activities. There is a great change among the Fellows, which was perhaps inevitable while they continued to be appointed by the Parliamentary Visitors rather than elected in the customary way. Before 1648, they had largely been drawn from among

---

[53] Tonge's campaign for the Mastership: UC:AR2/MS1/11 pp. 90 and 92; his approaches to Fellows, and their opinion of him: OUA CC Papers 1655/42:7; Thornton's election: OUA CC Papers 1655/42:4, 7, 10, 16, 21, and 28.
[54] UC:AR2/MS1/11 p. 93 and OUA CC Papers 1655/42:43 and 45.
[55] OUA CC Papers 1655/42:4, 7, and 10.
[56] Thornton's second election: UC:AR2/MS1/11 p. 92 (no contemporary evidence for Cromwell's intervention is recorded, but Johnson's comments in 1660 (p. 181), and *CSPD 1660/1* 235, on Thornton's preferment, make clear the course of events); Calamy on Johnson: Matthews 1934: 299.

the College's junior members, but of the thirty-four Fellows appointed or elected in 1648–60, only thirteen were former members of the College. Many of them were not even Oxford graduates. Three had been to Cambridge, three more, including Joshua Hoyle, to Trinity College Dublin, and one, Edward Farrar (F. 1651–89), to St Andrews. Furthest travelled of all were Ambrose Bennet (F. 1649–c.1658), a nephew of Sir Simon, and Sampson Eyton (F. 1650–60), who had helped repel Ezreel Tonge. Bennet had lived in Virginia in 1635–48, while Eyton had spent eight years studying at Harvard College in New England, and they are thus the first members of University College to have come from America.[57]

The College's regional links weakened in the 1650s: only five Fellows came from Yorkshire, and the remainder came from as far afield as Devon or Shropshire. The turnover was quicker: only three Fellows remained longer than ten years. Furthermore the Parliamentary Visitors were less observant of the regulations which restricted Fellows to the study of Theology: three Fellows of the 1650s obtained medical degrees, and one a Doctorate in Civil Law. There was one other difference: only eight Fellows were appointed with MA degrees, and eleven were appointed possessing no degree at all—reflecting, undoubtedly, the upheavals which had prevented many young men from attending university in the previous decade.

Undergraduate numbers gradually revived: 163 commoners attended University College during the 1650s, either as MAs, BAs, or undergraduates. The university's matriculation registers for this period, which record only family background or status (and not age), reveal a change (see Appendix IV). Whereas in 1601–42, 12 per cent of undergraduates were the sons of knights or baronets, only one knight's son attended University College between 1642 and 1660. There were some sons of esquires, but again the proportions are smaller than in 1601–42 (7% rather than 18%). Instead, a much larger proportion of undergraduates are the sons of gentlemen, clergy, or 'plebeians'. These figures support Antony Wood's claim that, although the university's numbers remained high, few nobles or esquires sent their sons there, 'unless to Colleges where an old Head and some Fellowes remained', but instead sent them abroad—as with George Radcliffe's kinsmen, the Savile family of Thornhill. The Royalist Sir William Savile had died in 1644, his family home was destroyed in 1648, and his son George was indeed educated abroad.[58]

---

[57] Eyton: Zoeller 2005 (which proves that he studied at Harvard); Ambrose Bennet: Zoeller 2007. Zoeller 2005 also lists the earliest members of University College with American links, including Henry Colman (m. 1597), the first known member to emigrate there (in the 1620s). Perhaps unsurprisingly many of these emigrants were at Oxford under the 'puritans' Anthony Gate and George Abbot, rather than the 'Arminians' John Bancroft and Thomas Walker.

[58] Data on College members. AO1 and College Buttery Books UC:BU4/F/5–7; university membership: Wood, *Life* i. 301; the Saviles: Nuttall 1986.

The students of the 1650s were slightly more eager to obtain degrees than their predecessors: well over half are known to have left Oxford with a degree, ranging from a BA to a DD, while barely 40 per cent of the 1601–42 intake did so. They also moved around Oxford less. Only six undergraduates are known to have taken a degree elsewhere and only ten migrated to take a degree at the College. As in previous years, nothing is known of the later careers of well over half these undergraduates. Forty-three of the remainder took orders, but the College recorded only one knight, one baronet, and two MPs: a great decrease on pre-war years. One unexpected feature was the brief appearance—sometimes for no more than a week—of visitors whose names suggest that they came from the Protestant community in Transylvania. One such was Caspar Titzabetsi, who stayed in College for much of 1653/4, and was made an MA in March 1654; a note in the Buttery Book for the week of 4 February 1654 referring to 'Mr Tizebetsi Collection' suggests that the College was willing to assist him financially.[59]

The 1650s saw the supposed dominance of puritanism in Oxford, as elsewhere in the country. The Book of Common Prayer was proscribed, and new forms of worship recommended, yet the university's religious life enjoyed an unexpected diversity. The breaking of the Church of England's monopoly had encouraged many to give free expression to individual interpretations of Christianity, and observers detected two main factions in Oxford, the 'Presbyterians' and 'Independents'. Presbyterians sought an English church similar to the Scottish model, in which religious life centred on a parish church governed by a minister and elders, while Independents, of whom Cromwell was one, fearful that a tyranny of elders would replace that of the bishops, urged greater flexibility in men's individual relationship with God, and supported the principle of a voluntarily gathered congregation. Antony Wood satirically mocked each group, claiming that the Presbyterians 'seemed to be very severe in their course of life, manners or conversation, and habit or apparell; of a Scoth [sic] habit, but especially those that were preachers', whereas the Independents 'were more free, gay, and (with a reserve) frollicksome; of a gay habit, whether preachers or not', and that both parties were 'void of publick and generous spirits'.[60]

No Presbyterian members of University College are known for certain, but Wood identified as Independents Francis Johnson—unsurprisingly for a chaplain of Cromwell—and Edward Farrar. Several members gladly supported the new order: almost a quarter of the undergraduates who had taken orders were ejected from their posts after 1660. One such was John Flavel, who according to Wood studied at University College in the late

---

[59] Titzabetsi: Wood, *Fasti*, in Wood, *Athenae* ii. 181, and (on Transylvanian Protestantism) MacCulloch 2003: 457–64.
[60] Presbyterians and Independents: Wood, *Life* i. 148, and Worden 1997: 754–63.

1640s and then became a minister in Dartmouth. Some Oxonians, however, secretly observed the Anglican liturgy, among them University College's first known Scotsman, William Annand (m. 1651), born in Ayr in 1633. His father, a supporter of Laud, fled Scotland to find a living in Kent. The son followed the father's sympathies. Wood wrote of his time at Oxford that 'tho' then put under a presbyterian tutor and discipline, yet he took all occasions to frequent sermons preached by loyal [i.e. Anglican] persons in, and near, Oxon.'[61]

Whatever their denominational sympathies, College members were not necessarily more godly than before. In November 1651, fines were imposed on Fellows, Scholars, and commoners alike for non-attendance at Chapel, and the Fellows were ordered to 'pray in the Chappell every one a week by turne' (which suggests that their attendance had been poorer than this). There were other disciplinary problems: in June 1651, the Visitors ordered the Master and Fellows to say exactly how many Fellows were in residence, and to explain why the absent Fellows were not there; in October 1658, Anthony Fidoe (F. 1650–8) was found to have married, and was promptly expelled; and Thomas Harley (F. 1658–60) was declared in February 1660 to have been absent for a year without permission, and was expelled the following month. A somewhat less dangerous diversion for members of University College arrived in 1654, when one 'Jacob a Jew' opened Oxford's first coffee house at the Angel Inn, just to the east of 83 High Street.[62]

The clearest sign of the College's complex religious life is the fate of Abraham van Linge's windows for the Chapel. In 1648, the new Chapel remained incomplete, its windows placed in storage, and the old Chapel was still used. Painted or stained glass was a frequent target of puritan iconoclasm in the 1640s and 1650s, but University College seems to have escaped this. Even the glass in the old Chapel survived long enough for Antony Wood to describe it in detail, and he never alludes to its destruction. More surprising still is the purchase in 1651/2 of 'a new lock to lock up the new Chappell glasse in the storehouse', which implies that van Linge's windows were being afforded protection.[63]

Although the Chapel remained unfinished during Francis Johnson's Mastership, he did oversee one major building project: in December 1655 he and

---

[61] Johnson and Farrar: Wood, *Life* i. 148 and 370. Flavel: Wood, *Athenae* iv. 323–6 (although Flavel is mentioned in no College records, and did not matriculate); secret Anglicans: Wood, *History* ii. 613; Annand: Wood, *Athenae* iv. 257–9. Green 1979: 256 discusses the religious divisions of Lincoln College in the 1650s.

[62] Chapel attendance: UC:AR2/MS1/7 p. 97; Fellows in College: UC:GB3/A1/1 p. 60; Anthony Fidoe: UC:GB3/A1/1 p. 71; Thomas Harley: UC:GB3/A1/1 p. 73; Jacob's coffee house: Wood, *Life* i. 168–9 (the site of the Inn is now part of the Examination Schools).

[63] The old Chapel windows: Wood, *Colleges* 62–6; storing the windows UC:BU2/F1/1 p. 257. Spraggon 2003: 217–49 shows that, apart from such notorious instances as the destruction of many windows at Christ Church, Oxford colleges escaped puritan iconoclasm better than might have been feared.

the Fellows decided to complete the Hall. William Offley (F. 1651–9) was put in charge of soliciting benefactions. Offley's task proved difficult: whilst the College in the 1630s raised over £5,000, most of it from two benefactions, in 1655–6 it raised just £450 from almost sixty benefactors. Johnson himself gave £40, and the Fellows all dutifully chipped in with smaller contributions, but only four Old Members and one pre-war Fellow, Richard Clayton (F. 1629–39), gave anything. University College therefore turned to members of other colleges, London aldermen, and Oxford tradesmen. Some eminent men contributed, including the republican divine Hugh Peters, and the scientist Robert Boyle, then occupying Deep Hall, a house owned by Christ Church situated between University College and Stanton Hall. The Hall's fine hammer-beam roof was built between March 1656 and July 1657, at a cost of £533 2s. (the date of '1656' is still legible on its lantern). Nevertheless, the old Hall remained in use for some time after this, to judge from a payment made in 1659/60 'for takeing down the Eschucheons & removeing the tables in ye old Hall'.[64]

Johnson evidently had a taste for building: in 1656/7 almost £60 was spent on repairing the Master's Lodgings. Whether the Lodgings really needed repairs, or whether Johnson had ideas of how a Master should live, the College could ill afford this sum, and a dispute arose over who should pay it, the Master or the College. Matters were made only more complicated—and unpleasant—by the fact that the old foundation was considered responsible for repairs to College buildings, and that it was Fellows of the new foundation who helped pass a motion that the College should pay for the repairs. The Fellows of the old foundation protested to the Parliamentary Visitors, and refused to settle their accounts for 1656/7. Eventually in January 1658 the Visitors patched up an agreement that the College should pay for the repairs, but that the Master would contribute £10.[65]

Unfortunately the later 1650s saw a potential benefaction elude the College. Charles Greenwood had died in 1644, at the height of the Civil War; in his will he asked his trustees to purchase lands worth £100 to support two Fellows and two Scholars at University College. One trustee, Thomas Radcliffe, was one of the Fellows expelled in 1648, and the other, Anthony Foxcroft, for unknown reasons would not carry out Greenwood's wishes.

---

[64] Offley's appointment: UC:BE23/L1/1; benefactors: UC:BE1/MS1/1 pp. 13–26 and UC:BE23/MS1/1 (Boyle's residence at Deep Hall—not owned by University College until 1773—is marked by a plaque facing the High Street); building accounts for the roof: UC:BU3/F1/8; emptying the old Hall: UC:BU2/F1/1 p. 373

[65] Repairs to Lodgings: UC:BU2/F1/1 pp. 317–19 (in 1656/7 expenditure exceeded income by £24, so this work had a substantial impact); payment for repairs: Burrows 1881: 436.

Although the College spent considerable sums in 1656/7–1658/9 on suing Foxcroft, it never received Greenwood's bequest.[66]

By 1659, the College had worse things to worry about than Foxcroft's dishonesty. After Oliver Cromwell's death the previous year, no one person or group proved capable of replacing him, and fears of a return to anarchy spread even to Oxford: when preparing a lease for Eastwick Farm in November 1659, the College offered a generous entry fine 'in consideration of the present troublesomeness of the times'. It was only early in the following year that a solution was reached by inviting the exiled Charles II to return to Britain. Charles was proclaimed King on 5 May 1660, and returned to London at the end of that month. Amidst the rejoicings in Oxford, there were some who hoped for personal profit from the upheavals: on 8 May Ambrose Bennet, now the College's tenant at Handley Park, wrote an emollient letter to Thomas Walker, offering his 'best Assistance to procure your Return after your Tedious Banishment', and clearly hoping that a College under Walker would prove a more malleable landlord. In his reply, Walker replied politely but warily that 'it is not fitt that I should be too forward to presume of my returne'.[67]

Walker need not have been so cautious: a fresh visitation of Oxford occurred a few months later, and the events of 1648 were replayed in reverse. On 1 August 1660 the Visitors came to University College. Francis Johnson defended himself stoutly: when asked by what right he was Master, he declared that 'hee was putt in Master there by Oliver Lord Protector and the Lords and Commons, which was then the Supreame power'. They were brave words, but futile: Johnson was expelled and Thomas Walker restored. A few days later, the three surviving expellees of 1648, Thomas Radcliffe, Abraham Woodhead, and Obadiah Walker, were reinstated, and four Fellows, Edward Terry, Sampson Eyton, Marmaduke Lambert, and Thomas Cupper, were expelled. The other Fellows seem to have acquiesced in the change of government, including Edward Farrar, castigated by Antony Wood for preaching a sermon in 1660 ferociously attacking the Independents with whom he had once associated. Wood added the censorious observation that 'you may know [Farrar] by his red beard, a slabberer of Boyes'.[68]

---

[66] Greenwood's will: UC:BE22/W1/1; lawsuit with Foxcroft: UC:BU2/F1/1 pp. 319, 332, and 344. Greenwood left a similar benefaction to Lincoln College, who also failed to extract any money from Foxcroft (Green 1979: 260).

[67] Eastwick Farm: UC:EB2/F/1 p. 9: Thomas Walker: Pyx μ fasc. 11 nos. 12–13; Ambrose Bennet: Zoeller 2007.

[68] The visitation of University College: UC:GB3/A1/1 pp. 74–5: Edward Farrar: Wood, *Life* i. 370. Cox 1960 provides a fuller account of these events. Zoeller 2005: 96 shows that Sampson Eyton had just married in secret, so his departure was opportune.

Daunting problems now confronted Thomas Walker, now in his late sixties, and the restored Fellows. The great building programme remained far from complete, with the quadrangle a fragmentary jumble of old and new buildings; the Bennet benefaction had created a bloated, disputatious, and impoverished Fellowship; and the College's finances were in an appalling mess. The 1640s and 1650s had proved one of the unhappiest periods in the history of University College, and Thomas Walker now had to spend his last years attempting to restore it to its condition of twenty years earlier.

10

The Rise and Fall of Obadiah Walker: 1660–1689

No previous member of University College has dominated it to quite the same extent as Obadiah Walker. Having already been an important Fellow in the 1640s, he assumed an increasingly prominent role in College life after 1660. Both its reputation and his grew together, only to suffer in the late 1680s a calamitous reverse, which left the College in disarray, and made Walker, if not the greatest Master of University College, certainly its most fascinating and tragic.

THE RETURN OF THOMAS WALKER: 1660–1665

The early 1660s belong, however, not to Obadiah Walker but to his unrelated namesake Thomas, now restored as Master. Thomas Walker returned to an Oxford which joined the country in seeking to reverse the changes of the 1640s and 1650s. The Church of England was restored, its episcopate intact, the Book of Common Prayer reintroduced in a slightly revised form, and almost every surviving high-ranking churchman of the 1630s restored to a position of authority. Within Oxford the undoubted leader of this refreshed Anglicanism was John Fell, the formidable Dean of Christ Church who dominated the university until his death in 1686.[1]

Walker restored some Laudian practices to University College, although Anthony Wood had to smile at the dangers in which this placed the elderly Master:

Dr. Walker, Mr. of University Coll., when he was at prayers in his chappell as he came in bowed low to the east; when he came out he bowed soe low that he sounded [i.e. swooned], such it seems was his formality that brought that inconvenience upon his body.[2]

The College followed Walker's example. The coronation of Charles II was celebrated with a dinner and a bonfire; copies of the Book of Common

---
[1] The wider context: Beddard 1997a; Fell at Christ Church: Bill 1988: 28–30. Fell is (slightly unfairly) immortalized in the epigram 'I do not love thee, Dr Fell'.
[2] Wood, *Life* i. 445 (in June 1662).

Prayer were purchased; and Christmas, banned during the Commonwealth, was celebrated again as the Hall and Chapel were decorated with holly and ivy. The views of the remaining Commonwealth Fellows on these changes are unrecorded: presumably, like Thomas Thornton, so nearly Master in 1654/5, who sent his son Joshua to University College in 1671, they accepted the inevitable.[3]

Thomas Walker, however, faced greater challenges than restoring good religious practice, namely the College's finances and the disastrous state of the Bennet foundation (matters were not helped by the fact that Ambrose Bennet, the College's tenant in Handley Park, was embezzling income from its timber and crops, and evaded the College by fleeing to the Caribbean in 1671/2): in September 1661, the Visitors ordered that no new Bennet Fellows or Scholars be elected until their foundation's debts were settled. In that same year Thomas Walker returned to the Court of Chancery to dispute the 1649 settlement. Not only did he claim that he, not Joshua Hoyle, had been the true Master then, but he could also prove that the settlement had failed. Walker's appeal succeeded: the Bennet trustees accepted defeat, requesting unsuccessfully that, if the decree was reversed, then at least two or three Fellowships and Scholarships should still be reserved for Bennet's kin. In October 1662 the court ordered that the Bennet foundation should support four Fellows and four Scholars only; that Handley Park be rented out for no more than £350; and that all the College's finances be administered by one Bursar—almost exactly the same proposals made by William Laud twenty years earlier. From 1665/6 onwards the accounts of both foundations were recorded in one set of accounts, and this unhappy episode drew to a close.[4]

Unfortunately, lawsuits cost money, and Thomas Walker spent at least £150 over the Bennet benefaction. There also remained the campaign against Charles Greenwood's executor, Anthony Foxcroft. By 1665, Walker calculated that the College still had debts of about £350, and in March that year the Visitors allowed the income from any vacant Fellowships to be used to settle its debts, and agreed that up to four Fellowships could be frozen at any time.[5]

Nevertheless, for the remaining years of life and Mastership allotted him, Thomas Walker displayed an undimmed energy for turning the College around. He also, it would seem, had acquired a new enthusiasm, for in 1661/2, University College commissioned a portrait of Alfred the Great (see frontispiece) at a cost of £3 10s., which may have been met by Thomas Walker himself, and whose face, it has been suggested, may derive from

---

[3] Coronation: UC:BU2/F1/1 p. 376; Book of Common Prayer: UC:BU2/F1/1 p. 398; Christmas: e.g. UC:BU2/F1/1 pp. 408 and 419; Joshua Thornton: UC:AR2/MS1/11 p. 147.

[4] Elections suspended: UC:GB3/A1/1 p. 79; Ambrose Bennet: Zoeller 2007; the new settlement: Pyx λ fasc. 6 nos. 1–14b.

[5] Cost of Bennet lawsuit: UC:MA26/F3/1; dispute with Foxcroft; UC:BE22/L1/1–18; total debts: UC:BU8/1/F3/1–7; appeal to Visitors: UC:GB3/A1/1 p. 83.

images of Charles I.[6] Although University College's claims on Alfred had never been forgotten—as seen in Abraham Woodhead's speech on the laying of the foundation stone for the quadrangle (p. 161)—they had not been much emphasized since the days of Thomas Caius. Indeed William Smith suspected that Walker himself revived the cult of Alfred. Shortly after coming up in 1668, he remembered:

I heard King *Alfred* mentioned in our Prayers, which causing some Discourse upon that Subject; I was told by one of the Seniors that heard it, that Dr. *Clayton*, after he was chosen Master, when he first heard King *Alfred* named in the Collect before *William* of *Durham*; openly and aloud cried out in the Chapel, There is no King Alfred *There*.[7]

Observing that Clayton had been away from College for many years, Smith concluded that Thomas Walker in exile had read Brian Twyne's *Antiquitatis Academiæ Oxoniensis apologia* (itself influenced by Thomas Caius), and was enthused by the links with Alfred.[8] The commissioning of Alfred's new 'portrait' certainly supports Smith's analysis, and it was appropriate to proclaim University College's royalist links at a time when the monarchy was being restored.

While Walker settled in quickly, matters were not so easy for the three restored Fellows. The senior Fellow, Thomas Radcliffe, had little time to enjoy his restoration, dying in December 1660. Abraham Woodhead, however, lived until May 1678, resigning his Fellowship only a month before his death. Although he assisted in the College's lawsuit against Foxcroft, and corresponded with successive Masters—and money was even spent on his rooms in 1661/2—Woodhead never lived in College again, being instead granted leave of absence regularly from September 1660 until his resignation. Eventually he withdrew so completely from College affairs that in 1676 Obadiah Walker wrote that Woodhead was 'so enamoured of retirement, that he corresponds not at all or very litle with any of us'.[9]

Woodhead kept a low profile with good reason. When in Europe, he had come into direct contact with Roman Catholicism, and secretly converted. Had he come to Oxford, he would have had to refuse to attend Chapel, and thereby forfeited his Fellowship. Fortunately the Master and Fellows, mindful perhaps of Woodhead's past services, did not wish to bring matters to a

---

[6] The portrait: Keynes 1999: 261–3 and 271–2; payment: although the 1661/2 accounts record payment 'ffor King Alfreds picture' (UC:BU2/F1/1 fo. 389), one of Walker's notebooks (UC:MA26/F3/2) lists it in a section 'Laid out by ye Master', which suggests that he provided the money. The College used a portrait of Elizabeth of York, Henry VII's queen, for an image of Alfred's wife Ealhswith.
[7] Smith, 242.
[8] Ibid. 242–3.
[9] Woodhead's rooms: UC:BU2/F1/1 p. 388; Woodhead acting for the College: UC:MA26/F3/1 and 5 and UC:BE22/L1/10; his retired life: UC:MA30/2/C5/1.

head, and never called his bluff. In return, Woodhead lived a retired life in Hoxton near Shoreditch, and, although he devoted himself to writing works of Catholic theology, he published nothing under his own name and did nothing to draw attention to himself.

Through his writings Woodhead became arguably the most respected English Catholic apologist of his day. Even the Protestants William Smith and Antony Wood could respectively call Woodhead's books 'praised' (*laudatos*) and commend 'his calm, temperate and rational discussion of some of the most weighty and momentous controversies under debate between the Protestants and the Romanists'. Some also wondered whether Woodhead wrote *The Whole Duty of Man*, an immensely popular manual of piety anonymously published in 1658.[10]

It is usually thought that Woodhead owed his protection to the third restored Fellow, Obadiah Walker, who certainly kept in closest touch with him (although Thomas Walker's approval would also have been essential). Obadiah Walker himself took time to settle back into a College life. He was granted leave for most of the early 1660s, and apparently continued to travel. In 1676, he looked back on this time, writing to his undergraduate contemporary John Wolveridge:

> My selfe a greate part of the troublesome times & some years also since his Majesty's returne have been a stranger even in our own country; but being heaved out of my place, & wandred along time up & downe, I am at last, by the good providence of God, set down iust as I was.[11]

Meanwhile, Thomas Walker resumed building the new quadrangle. As matters currently stood, the Chapel remained unfinished with van Linge's great windows still in storage, while the Library and kitchen and the whole of the east range all remained unbuilt. Walker began with the Chapel. There were no grand gifts like those of Charles Greenwood or Simon Bennet, but the College did receive a large bequest of £180 from Catherine Read, the sister of a former commoner, and a further £135 from eleven other donors. Walker, of course, was well placed to renew pre-war contacts, and eight donors had current or previous links with the College. One of the most generous, the chief justice Sir Orlando Bridgeman, who gave £50, had lodged there in the 1640s. The Chapel was intended to live up to van Linge's windows: the roof alone cost over £100, part of which was spent on fourteen carved angels. There were two differences from the existing Chapel: the screen separating the Antechapel was placed slightly further east, so that both van Linge's New Testament scenes could be seen in there, as intended, and the east window

---

[10] Smith: UC:AR2/MS1/11 p. 141; Wood: Wood, *Athenae* iii. 1158; Woodhead and *The Whole Duty of Man* (usually attributed to John Fell's friend Richard Allestree): Hearne x. 319 and Hearne xi. 90; a modern assessment of Woodhead: Gardiner 2003.

[11] Walker's absences noted variously in UC:GB3/A1/1; his travels: UC:MA30/2/C5/1.

only had plain glass. Finally, on 20 March 1666, the Chapel was consecrated by the Bishop of Oxford, and permission was granted in the following month to demolish the old Chapel.[12]

Sadly, Thomas Walker was not present. He had died on 6 December 1665 and been buried in the church of St Peter in the East alongside his first wife and their children. Walker's last years had been a worthy conclusion to his Mastership, and he made the College one last gift, a large collection of medieval manuscripts and books for the Library.[13]

FINANCES RESTORED, BUILDINGS COMPLETED: 1665–1676

Upon Thomas Walker's death, the Fellows of University College found themselves rediscovering a privilege for the first time in a century: the free election of a new Master. The Chancellor had no candidate up his sleeve, and the College could choose whom it pleased. Antony Wood heard rumours that Obadiah Walker might have been chosen, but 'refused it, and chose rather to live an obscure and retired life, than take that trouble upon him'. Instead on 11 December the College elected a former Fellow, Richard Clayton.[14]

Wood was unimpressed by the new Master—'Good for nothing but eating and drinking' was his view—but this was unfair. Clayton was a sensible choice. Having matriculated from University College in 1618, he had been a Fellow in 1629–39, and then retained a room at least until 1643/4. Rather unusually for his generation, he maintained contact with his old College during the 1650s: he was mentioned as a possible Master in 1654/5; he gave £5 towards the Hall roof; and his son John matriculated from the College in 1657. A Prebendary and then a Canon of Salisbury Cathedral from 1661, Clayton spent more time in Salisbury than in Oxford, but could rely on the assistance of Obadiah Walker, now regularly resident in College.[15]

In December 1668 Clayton reflected on what had drawn him back to the College, and what he saw as the challenges ahead:

---

[12] Read's benefaction and the angels: UC:MA26/F3/1–3 (Parry 2006: 95 notes that angels regularly appeared in Laudian church furnishings, especially on roofs); other donors: UC:BE1/MS1/1 pp. 27–9; the ceremony: UC:MA30/1/L1/1; destruction of the old Chapel: UC:MA30/1/L1/2; glass installed in the east window in later 1660s: UC:BU2/F1/1 p. 447 and UC:BU2/F1/2 fo. 2ᵛ. The 1660s screen was removed thirty years later (see below).

[13] Walker's death and burial: Wood, *Life* ii. 52 and *City of Oxford* iii. 180; his books: UC:BE1/MS1/3 fos. 7–8. Walker's bequest included texts on theology and law, a copy of Twyne's history of Oxford, and—perhaps unsurprisingly—a defence of William Laud.

[14] Walker's refusal: Wood, *Athenae* iv. 438; Clayton's election: UC:GB3/A1/1 pp.87–8, and UC:MA29/L1/2.

[15] Wood and Clayton: Wood, *Life* ii. 53; the 1654/5 election: OUA CC Papers 1655/42: 4–5 and 16; gift for the roof: UC:BU3/F1/8; John Clayton: Wood, *Life* i. 406; Clayton at Salisbury: Le Neve 1986: 59, 63, and 99.

I have been above 50 years of this College; and in my old age I was sollicited to undertake the Government of it; I knew the Coll: was much in debt; the imperfect Building required a creditable person to further it & the Discipline was much altered from that good order, which had made the Coll: to flourish, when there was scarse a dry chamber for a Gentleman to lodge in; notwithstanding these great discouragements, I adventured on it... But all our Debts will be paid in a very short time... Our ruinous Old Building we have pulld down: & wee have brought up the Foundation, towards the completing of the new... To recover our Antient Discipline, hath been a hard taske I yet groane under it & am resolved through ill report, as well as good report, to prosecute it.[16]

A meeting between the Fellows and the College's Visitors in January 1667 sheds light on two of Clayton's problems, namely the state of the College's finances, and the fact that—contrary to statute and custom—Commonwealth Fellows had been allowed to read subjects other than theology. The meeting was initially called because Thomas Laurence, who had been elected a Fellow the previous July, protested to the Visitors that the College was refusing to pay him. It was revealed at the meeting that the two Fellows elected immediately before Laurence also had yet to be paid, because, the College explained, they were still bound by the rules of March 1665 about freezing Fellowships. The Visitors agreed that the three Fellows could now be paid. That ended the official agenda of the meeting, but John Fell, the Vice-Chancellor, now innocently asked whether the Master and Fellows wished to bring anything else to the Visitors' attention. No, they replied. Fell pounced: he had been reading the College's statutes, he said, and wanted to know whether all the Fellows were reading Theology, or were in holy orders. Clayton, caught off guard, had to admit that this was not so. Fell swiftly ordered that now every Fellow would have to take deacon's orders within four years of receiving his MA on pain of expulsion.[17]

Natural wastage would remove the non-theologians among the Fellows. Restoring the finances was harder work. Fellows agreed to forgo financial perquisites to ease the burden: in September 1673, the entry fine of £520 on Handley Park was spent, not on the Bennet Fellows, but on settling debts. Steps were taken to improve the College's financial administration, as when in 1681 John Hopkins, the College's steward, bequeathed £50 to be used as a 'stock', to help the College's cash-flow. Eventually, by the end of Clayton's Mastership, the College had achieved some kind of stability. Although we have already learned to look at them with a cautious eye, the College's accounts of the later 1670s start to appear unusually healthy, certainly when compared with the doldrums of the 1650s (see Graph 9.1), and no

---

[16] Letter from Clayton to Lord Halifax (OSB MSS file #3318, from James Marshall and Marie-Louise Osborn Collection, Beinecke Rare Book and Manuscript Library, Yale University).

[17] UC:GB3/A1/1 pp. 89–91. Smith, 283 records that one Fellow, John Armitage (elected 1660), a physician, took holy orders to retain his post, but eventually chose to resign in 1675.

more Fellowships are left vacant for financial reasons, while the number of Bennet Fellowships gradually declined to the new limit of four.[18]

The College now faced another challenge. Although the Fellows had chosen their own Master, their independence in electing Fellows came under serious threat. After 1660, Oxford and Cambridge colleges came closer than they had ever done before or since to becoming pawns in the patronage game, as Charles II and James II issued a long series of mandates ordering Colleges to admit people of their (or their ministers') choosing as a Fellow or Scholar—or even a head.[19]

An example of what could happen occurred at University College in October 1668, when the Master and Fellows received a mandate from the King asking that they elect John Savile (m. 1662) to the next vacant Fellowship. It was immediately clear whose hand was behind this document: John Savile was a distant relative of George Savile, Marquis of Halifax, and a minister of Charles II—that same George Savile whose father, uncle, and paternal grandfather, and three of whose Wentworth great-uncles, had all gone to University College, and who himself might have followed them had he not come of age during the Commonwealth (p. 177).[20]

Richard Clayton showed his mettle: accepting the mandate would set an unwelcome precedent, but it was unwise to alienate a potential friend. He therefore wrote to Halifax expressing delicate surprise: 'one Line from your Lordship' would have been enough. Clayton also sent Obadiah Walker to speak to Halifax. Fortunately Halifax was willing to play by the rules: in replying to Clayton, he noted his apprehension about setting a precedent, and reassured him that 'I am so tender of doing anything which may come within that possibility.' Agreeing to set aside the mandate and wait for a vacancy, he graciously concluded that 'though I had not the good fortune to bee a member of your colledge, I shall ever bee ready to pay the homage I owe it as a Yorkshire man.' Unfortunately Clayton then had to inform Halifax that John Savile had committed a misdeed (unfortunately unspecified) which had 'so fouledy forfeited his reputation, & hath cast such a Blott upon it' that it would be imprudent to elect him a Fellow at once; he proposed that Savile's election be delayed until the following year. So it transpired: Savile was elected to a Percy Fellowship in October 1669, but was soon presented by Halifax himself to Charles Greenwood's old living of Thornhill, and his Fellowship was declared vacant in February 1672.[21]

---

[18] Handley Park: UC:EB2/F/1 p. 17; Hopkins's gift: UC:GB3/A1/1 p. 104. University College's financial difficulties were not unique: Balliol College lost one-fifth of its rental in the Great Fire of London, and suspended two Fellowships in 1666 (Jones 2005: 114–15), and Merton and Lincoln also had problems (Martin and Highfield 1997: 214 and Green 1979: 273).
[19] Mandates: Twigg 1987: 150; individual examples: Costin 1958: 132, Twigg 1987: 145–8, Trevelyan 1990: 51, and Brockliss and others 1988: 26–8.
[20] John Savile's mandate: UC:MA29/C2/1; see further Cox 1973.
[21] Clayton's letters to Lord Halifax: OSB MSS file #3318, from James Marshall and Marie-Louise Osborn Collection, Beinecke Rare Book and Manuscript Library, Yale University; Halifax's reply: UC:MA29/C2/2.

In spite of such distractions, Clayton and the Fellows gradually completed the new quadrangle. In 1668/9 work began on demolishing the last parts of the old College, laying the foundations of the east range, and building the kitchen and Library wing, all of which was estimated as costing £394 1s. 10d. A sum of £252 was raised for this stage of the project from twenty-six people, of whom fifteen were past and present members of the College, including Abraham Woodhead, and a future College butler, John Pricket, who gave £10. By 1671/2 the new Library appears to have been in use, and in 1682/3 the College appears for the first time to have purchased books for the Library. When a register of benefactors to the Library was compiled in 1674, the fine new room—tragically dismantled in the 1860s—was proudly depicted on the frontispiece (Fig. 10.1). Parts of the old quadrangle nevertheless continued in use. Antony Wood noted on his drawing of the south and west sides (Fig. 5.2) that these were demolished in 1668, but the east side, which Wood never drew, lasted longer. The 1671/2 accounts mention work carried out on 'the roofes of the old and new building', and in 'the old Hall', and in 1674/5 2s. was paid 'for 2 dayes worke in the old Hall'.[22]

Nevertheless, the old quadrangle's time was past, as the Fellows geared themselves up for one last push to complete the project with a fund-raising campaign more intense than any other until the twentieth century. First of all, in April 1669, it was agreed that, 'whilst the College is in building', gentlemen commoners should give money at their admission, rather than plate, as had been the custom. The College also borrowed extensively—possibly over £800 between 1661 and 1682. Most loans came from individuals, but the university lent £50 in 1673 and £200 more in 1675.[23]

Finally it was time to start a letter-writing campaign. The accounts for 1675/6 have these entries:

Item for gilt paper for our Letters to Benefactors	00-00-04
Item for sending those Letters	00-00-06[24]

Examples of the College's begging letters survive, most of them in the hand of Obadiah Walker. Some, however, were written by other Fellows, which shows the collective nature of the venture. These extracts from a letter in the hand of Nathaniel Boyse (F. 1674–89) typify the arguments used:

---

[22] Estimates for kitchen and Library: UC:MA26/F4/2 pp. 8–9; gifts for the same: UC:BE1/MS1/1 pp. 29–36 (non-College donors included John Fell); the Library in use: UC:BU2/F1/2 fo. 16^v includes payments for its stairs; buying books: UC:BU5/F1/1; depiction of the Library: frontispiece of UC:BE1/MS1/3 (Cox 1956 describes traces of the Library found when the Alington Room was created); 1671/2 accounts: UC:BU2/F1/2 fo. 17^v; 1674/5 accounts: UC:BU2/F1/2 fo. 32^r.

[23] Money from gentleman commoners: Bodl. MS Ballard 49 fo. 24^r; possible loans for building work: UC:FA3/1/F1/11–20 and UC:EB2/F/1 pp. 20–2.

[24] UC:BU2/F1/2 fo. 37^v.

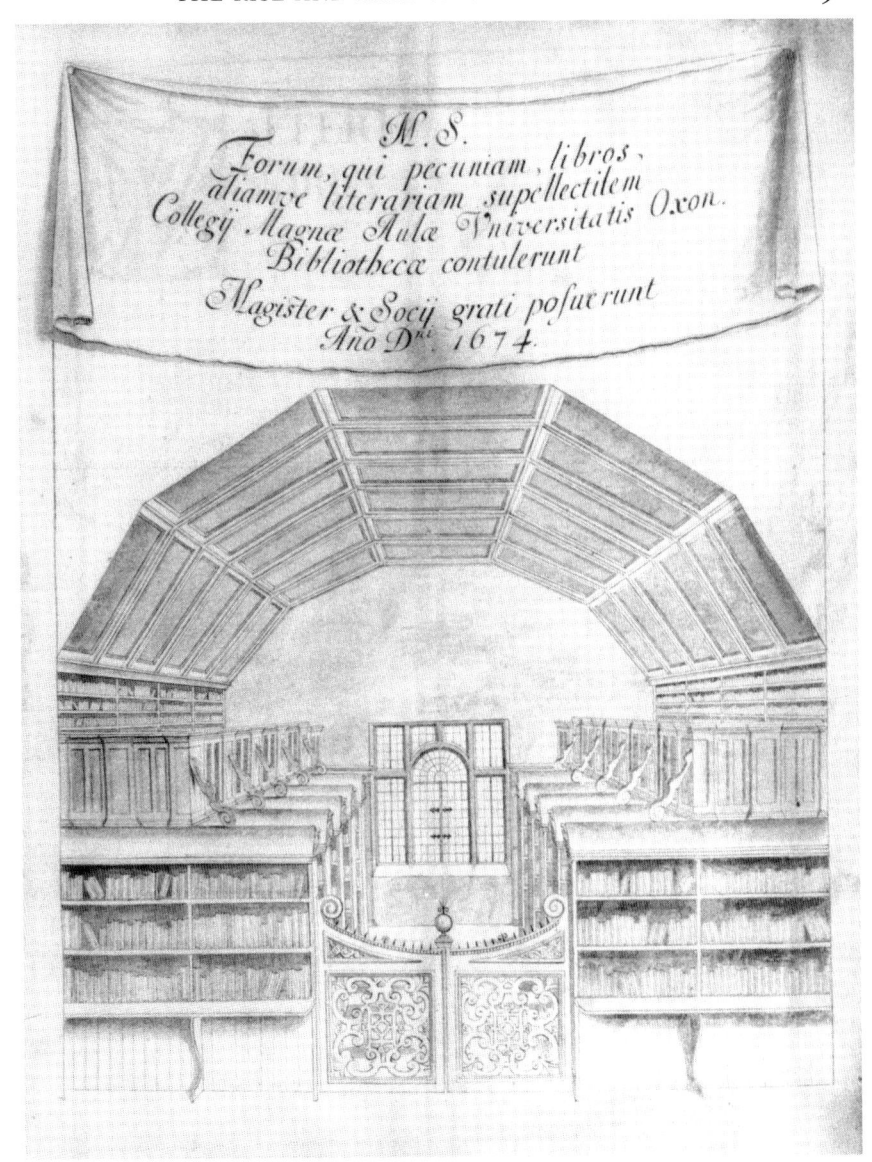

FIGURE 10.1 Frontispiece for a Library Benefactor's Book compiled in 1674, showing the newly completed College Library.

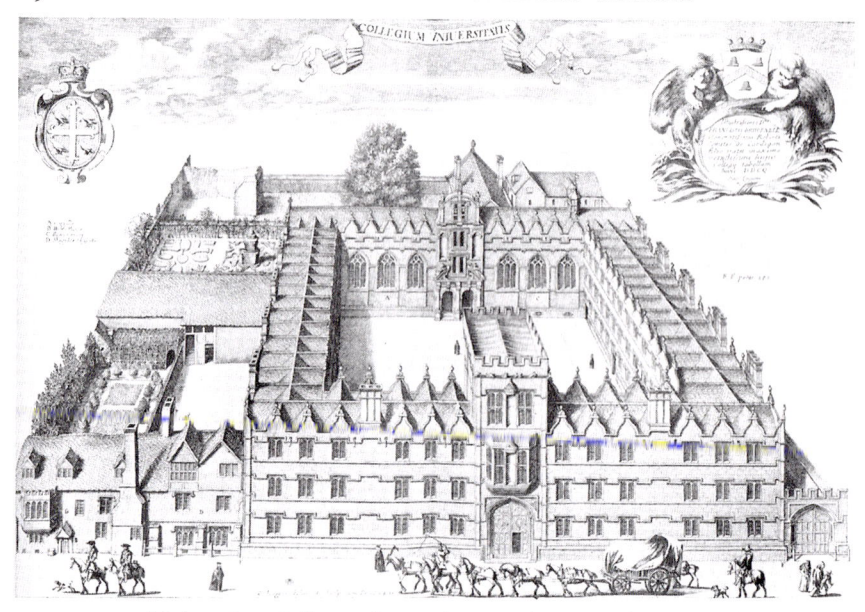

FIGURE 10.2 University College, drawn in 1675 by David Loggan for *Oxonia Illustrata*. To the left of the quadrangle is the Master's Lodgings.

Gentlemen,
Your aged Mother, and not yours alone, but of this whole University, if not of all other such nurserys of learning at least in this nation, craves your assistance in the time of her necessity...there remains a great part of the fourth side of the Quadrangle unfinished. The present Maister and Fellows have used their utmost endeavours with their freinds in these parts for the supplying of what they have already done, and now apply themselves unto you...And we have very great hopes that you will not be wanting to us in this our necessity; This being a Colledg cheifly design'd for, and most of the preferments in it limited to Northen Schollars...She may justly expect that as she hath fostered your youths, so you would cherish her age.[25]

At this time David Loggan was preparing his great series of engravings of Oxford, *Oxonia Illustrata* (published 1675). Loggan was evidently prevailed upon to show University College with its quadrangle complete (Fig. 10.2), and the engraving was dedicated to Francis Brudenell, son of Robert, Earl of Cardigan. Brudenell himself had no links with the College, although a relation, Thomas Brudenell, matriculated from it in 1675. In a draft letter

---

[25] Fund-raising correspondence: UC:MA30/1/C/1–20; Boyse's letter (UC:MA30/1/C/1) is transcribed in *UCR* Vol. XI no. 2 (1994), 79–80 (other letters are transcribed in Darwall-Smith 1998: 57–9); Bodl. MS Ballard 49 fo. 26[r] is another appeal in Boyse's hand.

Obadiah Walker thanked Francis for 'sending to us for education one of your own family', and pushed his luck by noting that 'you have been pleased to complete [the quadrangle] in picture; we humbly beseech you to assist the finishing of it in reality.'[26]

£424 is known to have been raised from forty donors, half of whom were College men (again including Woodhead). Other contributions came from John Fell, Gilbert Sheldon (Archbishop of Canterbury and Chancellor of the university), and Thomas Thinne, one of the MPs for the university. The donors of the 1660s and 1670s were a mirror image of those of the 1650s: several old members from the 1630s were willing to contribute towards the building of the Library and east range, as were members who had come up after 1660, but there were just two donors who had matriculated in the 1650s. Furthermore, generous as the gifts were, they failed to cover the expenses: it seems that, by July 1676, the east range had cost £696 17s.[27]

In spite of this shortfall, the new quadrangle was finally completed. On 13 April 1675 Humphrey Prideaux, a student of Christ Church, wrote that University College had just started work on the east range, 'which [he rightly observed] will make that colledge looke very handsom, and not inferior in beuty to any other in the University', and, on 6 August 1676, that 'University Coll: is now all built up.'[28]

After over four decades the great work was at last finished, at a cost of at least £7,500.[29] This was not unreasonable, in comparison with similar projects. Wadham College in 1610–13 appears to have cost almost £11,000, while the Canterbury Quadrangle at St John's College (which had three sides) cost over £5,500. However, University College remained a small player in architectural terms, when compared with Trinity College, Cambridge, which had raised £11,879 2s. 1d. by 1695 for the Wren Library alone.[30]

Richard Clayton survived to see the project almost complete: he died at Salisbury on 10 June 1676. Twelve days later Obadiah Walker was unanimously elected Master, for all that Antony Wood suspected that Walker only 'accepted of that office, rather than a stranger should come in (as 'twas designed)'.[31]

---

[26] Walker's letter: UC:MA30/2/C1/3. No donation from Brudenell is recorded.
[27] Donors for the east range: UC:BE1/MS1/1 pp. 36–46; costs: UC:MA26/F4/2 fo. 15ʳ.
[28] Thompson 1875: 40 and 50.
[29] The total cost is calculated thus: in February 1642, Thomas Walker calculated that the new quadrangle had cost £5,429 11s. 11½ d (UC:MA26/F1/6 p.11); the Hall roof in 1655/6 cost £533 2s. (UC:BU3/F1/8); £315 was raised for the Chapel; and £1,090 18s. 10d. spent on the Library and east range. This figure, however, differs from the estimate of £8,500 given in Newman 1997: 146. The Chapel did lack some furnishings until the 1690s, so the final cost lies somewhere between these two amounts.
[30] Wadham and St John's: Newman 1997: 145–6; Trinity: Trevelyan 1990: 49.
[31] Election: UC:GB3/A1/1 pp. 99–100 and Wood, *Athenae* iv. 438.

SCHOLARS AND SCHOLARSHIP, EDUCATORS AND EDUCATED

Obadiah Walker began his Mastership in a fortunate position. Thomas Walker and Richard Clayton had—admittedly with help from Obadiah himself—settled the College's finances, and completed the great building programme, and although still small and poor, the College was flourishing intellectually almost as never before, largely, thanks to Obadiah's example. It is time to look at the life of the College in the years following 1660.

In many respects, the Restoration College looked back to the 1630s. First of all, there was the selection of its Fellows. Twenty-five were elected in 1660–88, of whom all but five were former undergraduates, and one more had migrated there to take his BA. Eighteen of these Fellows had held College Scholarships before their election. Their geographical origins were, however, more widespread than before the war. Although Yorkshire still supplied more Fellows than elsewhere, there were only eleven of them. Two each came from Northumberland and Cumberland, and one from Durham. The remainder came from Kent to Worcestershire to Cambridgeshire: the lack of restrictions on the Bennet Fellowships was opening up the College a little. For many, a Fellowship was the height of their aspirations. They remained in post for an average of twelve and a quarter years; four Fellows stayed for twenty-one years or longer; and ten died in place. Some also benefited from contact with wealthy students, for example by accompanying them on tours of Europe. One such, John Ledgeard, was travelling with Sir John Bland, Bt. (m. 1679) when he died in November 1683 from injuries received in a coach accident in Picardy.[32]

Analysing the junior members of the College becomes much easier than in previous decades because in 1674 the College decreed that all new members, irrespective of status, should enter their names and other personal details in an Admissions Register, a practice still followed today. These registers are more reliable than the university's ones—not least because they record migrations from other Colleges—and therefore become the primary source for University College's membership. In 1660–88, some 318 commoners came to University College, 22 of them arriving at BA or MA level. On average, the College admitted between 10 and 15 new members a year (Graphs 8.1 and 10.1), roughly the same number as in the 1620s and 1630s, with occasional 'peaks', as in 1666 and 1674, when over 20 new members were admitted. This contrasts with other colleges, where numbers were starting to fall.[33]

---

[32] Ledgard: UC:BE1/MS1/1 p. 47 and Wood, *Life* iii. 82–3.

[33] Falling numbers elsewhere: Williams in Buxton and Williams 1979: 59, Bill 1988: 191, Attwater 1936: 81, and Davies in Davies and Garnett 1994: 36. I use the word 'commoner' advisedly: Scholarships at University College (except for the Leicester and Gunsley awards) were usually awarded to undergraduates several months—and sometimes several years—after matriculation.

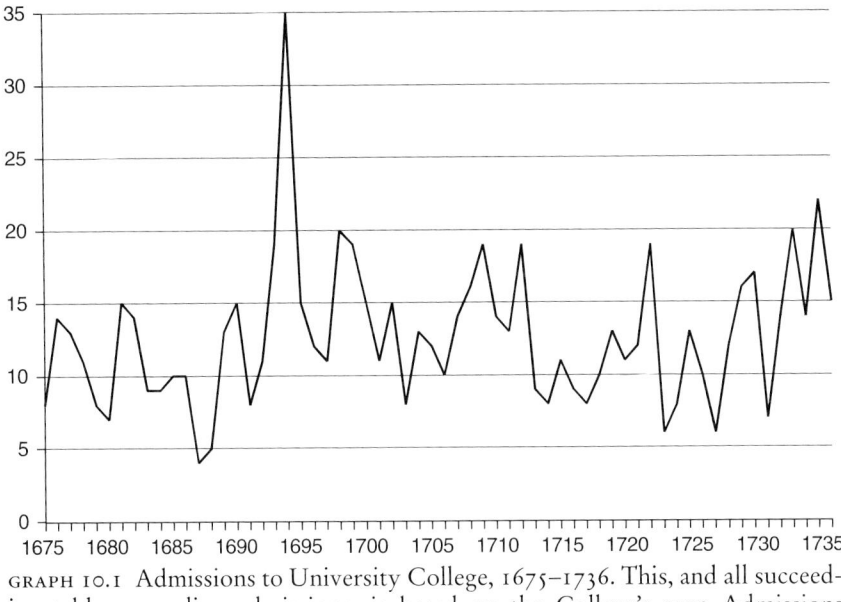

GRAPH 10.1 Admissions to University College, 1675–1736. This, and all succeeding tables recording admissions, is based on the College's own Admissions Register.

University College became a Yorkshire stronghold once again: in 1660–88, 100 of its 318 commoners came from there. The next most popular county was Kent, with twenty-four commoners: the Gunsley Scholarships were having an effect. Only ten men came from Durham and Northumberland. The remaining students came from most regions of England, fairly evenly spread out. Richard Clayton was therefore quite correct to appeal to Lord Halifax's 'love to Yorkshire-students, who are best provided for in this College by our Founders, more than they are in all our other Colleges within this University'.[34]

Although the Restoration commoners were of a slightly higher social status than those of the 1650s, especially as regards the sons of esquires and the sons of knights, baronets, or peers, there was not quite a return to pre-war levels (see Appendix IV). There were rather more undergraduates who described their fathers as belonging to such non-clerical professions as medicine or the law. As with the early years of the century, well over half of all undergraduates matriculated aged 16 or 17, but there were fewer very young members, and rather more who were aged 18 or above.

[34] Letter to Lord Halifax, OSB MSS file #3318, from James Marshall and Marie-Louise Osborn Collection, Beinecke Rare Book and Manuscript Library, Yale University.

More undergraduates were now choosing to take a degree: 170—more than half—are known to have done so, of whom 60 received a BA, 86 an MA, with the remaining 24 all proceeding to higher degrees. There remained some mobility: 11 undergraduates took their BA at other colleges, and 12 their MA, while 8 commoners came to University College to take their BA, and 2 their MA. As little is known about the careers of this generation as their predecessors: nothing is known about 148 of them. It is clear, however, that the College remained a source of recruits for the church: 91 of its members took orders.

These undergraduates came up to an increasingly stratified College, as the groupings seen in pre-war Bursar's Books and Buttery Books become more complicated. Buttery Books now include below the MA commoners a group of gentlemen commoners, who, on account of their status, are also called 'Mr.', whether they have a degree or not. Commoners of very high status (such as sons of peers) are listed among the Fellows, among whom, therefore, they ate their meals. There then follow the BAs of higher status, the ordinary commoners, and the BAs of lower status. Below them there are now two groups of poorer undergraduates, called 'batelers' and servitors. The servitors we have met already, as the poorest class of undergraduates, who performed menial duties for their keep. The batelers are harder to pin down, because their role differs from one college to another, but they seem to occupy an intermediate rank between commoners and servitors, paying for some of their food and drink, and supplementing their income by performing servants' duties. One or two undergraduates worked as College servants: a list of servants from 1673/4 shows that the porter was William Courtney (m. 1669). This hierarchy is clearly seen in a set of regulations compiled in April 1669, in which, for infringing rules of access to the buttery, commoners were to be fined 12*d*., batelers 6*d*., while servitors were to deliver a public declamation in the Hall.[35]

The College still sat at table according to status—in 1682/3 three table cloths were bought 'for Gent Commrs. Commr. & Batlers Table'—but the university's rules on academic dress were now tightened up. In August 1666, Fell issued regulations concerning the cut and shape of the gowns and caps to be worn by all members of the university, be they noblemen or servitors. No one could hide his status, either with the gown which he wore, or the table at which he sat for meals. Even the College's gardens appear to have been divided by class: draft accounts for 1688/9 refer to money spent in 'dressing the Comoners Garden', which suggests that there were separate gardens at least for the commoners, Fellows, and the Master.[36]

---

[35] Courtney: UC:BU3/F2/2; 1669 rules: Bodl. MS Ballard 49 fo. 24ʳ. Balliol also had servitors, batelers, commoners, and gentlemen or fellow commoners (Jones 2005: 137–8).

[36] Table-cloths: UC:BU2/F1/2 fo. 73ʳ: academic dress: Wood, *Life* ii. 84–5, and Beddard 1997*a*: 842; the commoners' garden: UC:BU3/F2/5 fo. 67ʳ. These divisions held true at Cambridge; see Cunich and others 1994: 143–7.

Although no undergraduate testimony comparable with that of George Radcliffe or Edward Herbert is preserved from this period, there survives for the first time something approaching an undergraduate timetable. On his return to University College, Thomas Walker made extensive notes about what he found, including the weekly round of classes and lectures for junior members of the College. The junior and senior 'Formes' had an identical timetable:

After morning prayer every day except Tuesday and so-called 'sleeping days [sic]', lectures.
After morning prayer on Saturdays: 'repetitions' (the repeating of texts supposedly learned from memory).
Mondays and Tuesdays, 10 a.m.: disputations.
Wednesdays and Fridays, 4 p.m.: disputations.
Thursdays, 10 a.m.: declamations.
Saturdays, 10 a.m.: speeches and disputations.
Saturdays, 2 p.m.: 'corrections and themes' (themes were an exercise; the former presumably refers to corrections of the themes).

The Bachelors of Arts had separate declamations on Wednesdays at 9 a.m., and disputations on Fridays at 6 p.m. These exercises took place in the Hall—in 1662/3 the College bought a 'frame for the quæstions in the Hall'—as was common practice elsewhere.[37]

One of the people who taught at the College published his own thoughts on teaching. This was, perhaps inevitably, Obadiah Walker, with his book *Of Education, Especially of Young Gentlemen*, published in 1673, and reprinted five times during his lifetime.[38] Although not intended for the teaching of undergraduates, Walker's book nevertheless reveals much about his views on education in general. He knows young people well— 'The great inclination of Youth is to *pleasures*; and that, either to *idlenes* and *sleep*' (p. 11)—and approves of good solid hard work: 'Never have I seen parts, how great soever, without industry and study to produce any good' (p. 8). He has advice for teachers too. They should be '*religious*, virtuous and grave', 'Prudent and discreet', 'Master of [their] *tongue*', and 'Not *covetous*'—in other words they should not hope to benefit from wealthier pupils (pp. 26–8).

Walker favoured a non-specialist curriculum. A student's basic syllabus should be 'the *History* of his own or other Countreys, search of *Antiquity*, and *Languages*, *Natural History*, and experiments; *Medicine*; forreign *Laws*, *Mathematicks*, *Astronomical* observations; *Mechanicks*, and the like; It being a noble study to observe, how God governs *natural*, as well as *free* Agents'

---

[37] Walker's timetable: UC:MA26/F4/1 p. 4; the frame: UC:BU2/F1/1 p. 398. Of course this timetable omits private sessions between tutors and pupils (see Bill 1988: 196–7).

[38] Page numbers are taken from the third edition (Walker 1677). For further discussion of it, see Woodcock 1998 and Bill 1988: 1–16.

(p. 35). He therefore disapproved of recreations which required specialized knowledge. He approves of dancing, 'so much whereof is to be learn'd as may give a good and *graceful* motion of the body', but protests at 'the use, which is frequently made of it, especially since it is become a *difficult study*, and many years, besides infinite practise, required to a reasonable perfection in it' (p. 71). Music, he says, is 'not worth a Gentlemans labor, requiring much industry and time to learn, and little to lose, it', although singing, which, as he says, 'needs no instrument to remove or tune', is acceptable (pp. 115–16). Walker was not alone in criticizing specialization so forcefully, but his approach had its own risks: the pedant would be replaced by the dilettante. By the end of the century, several theorists, John Locke in particular, were criticizing such a broad, but shallow, approach.[39]

Finally, Walker also suggests how an Oxford tutor might structure his teaching timetable, describing 'the manner now generally used' in universities as follows:

First an account of the former Lectures; *then* to read and write about half an hour; *then* to explicate that about an equal time. Experience since hath added an hour more for the Scholars *conferring* one with an other in circles, in presence of their Reader, and *disputing* upon questions given them the reading before. The hour that remains, the Master begins another Lecture, explains it to them, and gives them questions for the next disputation. (p. 127)

Walker implies that the rather passive relationship whereby George Radcliffe was 'read to' by his cousin has been replaced by something which involves the pupil more directly.

Readers may smile at Walker's maxims, and wonder how successful he was in practice. Fortunately, some evidence survives of this dealings with his pupils. Firstly, we should remember that Thomas Henshaw found Walker and Abraham Woodhead more congenial than his official tutor. Secondly, some of Walker's papers show how seriously he took his duties as a tutor. On one occasion, he was faced with the difficult task of writing to the father of an undergraduate, John Leigh, who had died in the College in January 1675, having matriculated only the previous October. Having opened with a warning that he is the bearer of bad news, Walker breaks it to Edward Leigh gently, by taking him through the stages of his son's illness before revealing what Leigh must by now have been prepared to expect; even then nowhere in the letter do the words 'death' or 'died' appear. He ends with one last anecdote showing the son's excellent character:

A few daies before his sickness he told his Tutor & mee what good resolutions he had made of wel-husbanding his time &c. And tho' Almighty God thought not fit to give him time to put them in execution, yet I doubt not of their sincerity & that our

---

[39] The wider context (including Locke's criticisms): Feingold 1997a: 218–42.

mercifull & good Lord will accept the will for the deed, when him-selfe takes away the possibility of performing it.[40]

Walker published works on other subjects: he wrote a book on logic, which was still read at Christ Church in the eighteenth century, and in 1675 and 1678 published a *Paraphrase of the Epistles of St. Paul*, which was apparently intended as a specimen for a large project to compile a set of commentaries on the Bible by several hands, and was even reprinted in 1684.[41]

As well as being a prolific author himself, Walker supported the work of other scholars. He was a friend of John Fell's, and assisted him in the running of the University Press, where he may have helped design the Oxford Almanack for 1677. Furthermore Antony Wood, who had first met and befriended Walker in June 1667, thought that Walker also played a leading role in encouraging the Press to publish his history of the university. Walker's interests ranged in other directions: he was involved in the donation of the Arundel Marbles to Oxford in the 1660s; he was interested, albeit rather amateurishly, in Anglo-Saxon coins; and he participated in the creation of the Ashmolean Museum, helping to draft a memorandum on its administration.[42]

Walker's presence encouraged scholars to move to University College, even those who did not have Fellowships, and the College briefly resembled once again the medieval college with its mingling of Fellows and mature commoners. In particular, three important early scientists were drawn there. First, in the early 1660s, Peter Stael, a German emigré and pioneer in Oxford science, rented a room in University College. Next was Robert Morison, the university's Professor in Botany, who rented a room in the College at least from 1671/2 until his death in 1683. Morison was an important figure in scientific studies of the day: apart from his lectures, he also managed the Botanic Garden, and his *magnum opus*, the *Plantarum historia universalis Oxoniensis*, was published posthumously in 1693. Antony Wood was sure that he became professor because Walker recommended him to John Fell and others. The third scientist was Robert Plot, the first Keeper of the Ashmolean Museum and Professor of Chemistry, sometime secretary to the Royal Society, and author of the *Natural History of Oxfordshire* (1677) and the *Natural History of Staffordshire* (1686). Plot apparently moved to University College in 1676—he was certainly renting

---

[40] UC:MA30/2/C1/4 (transcribed complete in Darwall-Smith 1998: 60).
[41] Walker's logic: Bill 1988: 264; the paraphrase of St Paul (parts of which may have been the work of Abraham Woodhead): Carter 1975: 86–7 and Tyacke 1997: 609–10.
[42] Walker and the Press: Keene 2003; the almanack: Petter 1974: 30; Wood's history: Wood, *Life* ii. 172–3 and Carter 1975: 48 and 73–4; Wood's friendship: Wood, *Life* ii. 109; marbles: Bodl. MS Ballard 9 fo. ±9ʳ and Wood, *Life* ii. 119–20; coins: Burnett 2005 (who is unimpressed by Walker's numismatic expertise); the Ashmolean: Ovenell 1986: 25–7 and 52.

rooms there in 1678–80—and gave the College a statue of King Alfred in 1682.[43]

Some Fellows also became respected scholars. One was the Yorkshireman William Smith (m. 1668; Fig. 11.2), elected in 1675. In his youth, Smith had various interests—in chemistry, for example—but eventually he was drawn to the history of University College itself. Previous chapters have drawn frequently on Smith's work; now we encounter him in person, as recorder of and participant in his own times. Another Fellow, Hugh Todd (m. Queen's 1672) was elected in 1678. A Cumberland man, he assembled notes, published posthumously, on the history of his county and he also contributed to translations of Plutarch. He refers in a letter of April 1682 to work carried out by him towards a catalogue of baronets.[44]

Walker himself felt confident in his colleagues' scholarship. Not only did he and Todd contribute to an atlas published in 1680, but in 1677, Walker planned an ambitious publishing venture for the College itself, an annotated Latin translation of an unpublished life of King Alfred written in the 1640s by Sir John Spelman. His choice was wise: Spelman's life has been called 'the first "modern" biography of the king', which effectively 'determined the parameters of Alfredian studies which have endured to the present day.'[45]

In a letter of April 1677, Walker explained his reasons for publishing the life:

The book is not made by any of us, but divers of the society have assisted with their paines and learning to fit it for the presse... For the society is willing that the world should know that their benefactions are not bestowed on mere drones. We intend also to print it at the charge of the College & hope to make some advantage by it towards finishing our chappel, & furnishing our library.[46]

Most of the translation was by Christopher Wase, Superior Bedel of Civil Law, and printer to the university, and Elias Ashmole helped supply illustrative material, especially contemporary coins. The authorship of the footnotes is unknown, although almost all the annotations in the proof copy of the work in the Library of University College are in Walker's hand, suggesting that his was a dominant role in the project.[47]

---

[43] Stael: Wood, *Life* i. 472 says he stayed in the College, but the archives do not corroborate this; Morison at University College: UC:GB3/A1/1 p. 105, UC:BU3/F1/10–12 and UC:BU4/F/10–12; Morison and Walker: *Fasti* 314–15 in Wood, *Athenae* (also Morison's *ODNB* entry); Plot in the College: UC:BU3/F1/13 and UC:BU4/F/12; Plot's work: Ovenell 1986: 31–63, and *ODNB* entry; statue of Alfred: UC:BE1/MS1/1 p. 47 and Wood, *Life* iii. 35. The statue was installed above the gate to the quadrangle but was moved in 1687 (see below). It was in the Master's Garden in the 1940s, in a ruinous condition, and has since disappeared.

[44] Smith's chemistry: Magrath 1913: 103–4 and Wood, *Life* iii. 75; Todd's work: Wood, *Life* iii. 75 and *ODNB* entry; letter of 1682: Magrath 1913: 49–51.

[45] Keynes 1999: 254–6.

[46] UC:MA30/1/C1/13 (transcribed in Keynes 1999: 263–4).

[47] Translation: Keynes 1999: 264; Ashmole and coins: UC:MA30/2/C7/1 (transcribed in Darwall-Smith 1998: 63). Several original copper plates of coins for the life survive (UC:MA30/2/AR/1–7).

The final product, published by the University Press, was as fine a piece of work as Walker and his colleagues could have hoped. In addition to its elegant engravings, it is also clear that someone in the College had a more than adequate command of Anglo-Saxon, using Anglo-Saxon types which had only been given to the University Press the previous year. The Master and Fellows of University College could hardly have produced a better tribute to their 'founder'.[48]

Spelman accepted that Alfred had founded, rather than re-founded, Oxford, but—as a good Cambridge man—fell back on the tale that Sigebert had founded Cambridge in the seventh century. However, he does not allude specifically to University College, so Walker's team duly filled the gap. Their argumentation could be shaky: in dismissing Wood's doubts about the Alfred legend, they said that he had a grudge against the College, and too great a love of his own College of Merton, and that there was no point in going over old ground again (p. 135). In discussing the comparative lack of evidence for Alfred's links with Oxford, they claimed that William of Malmesbury and Asser did not mention Oxford in regard to Alfred's schools, simply because there were no other universities in England beyond these (pp. 136–7).[49]

Walker and his team encountered more controversial material when Spelman discussed Alfred's dealings with the Papacy, mentioning his visit to Rome when a child, and suggesting that Alfred ruled supreme over the English Church even after his visit to Rome (pp. 70–1). Spelman's comments, with the equally non-condemnatory footnotes, were guaranteed to raise hackles: some might infer that the head of the Church of England could still be subject in some way to Rome.[50]

Although University College enjoyed a period of especial intellectual vitality, there was still time for recreation. For the first time, the Fellows had a common room set aside for socializing. The earliest allusion to such a Common Room appears in the accounts for 1682/3, in which money is spent both 'for mending & whiting the Old Common room', and for 'glass in the Com: room', which suggests that there was already a Common Room in operation. The new room (known now as the Winter Common Room) was apparently fully operational by 1684/5, and by 1688/9 Fellows were even paying common room dues.[51]

The College regularly paid for musicians, especially at the Feast of St Simon and St Jude. In November 1682 three musicians gave the Bursar, Thomas Bateman, 'an afternoon's musick on demand'. The 1660s also saw the earliest recorded performances of plays at the College, Henry

---

[48] Saxon types: Carter 1975: 124–5. Page numbers below are from Spelman 1678.
[49] Spelman and Oxford: Keynes 1999: 255.
[50] See further Beddard 1997*b*: 864 and Tyacke 1997: 610.
[51] 1682/3 and 1684/5 accounts: UC:BU2/F1/2 fos. 73^v and 84^r; payment of dues: UC:BU3/F2/55 fo. 76^v. Lincoln College, by comparison, had a common room by 1662 (Green 1979: 275).

Glapthorne's *Wit in a Constable*, performed in January 1664, and *The Wedding* (unattributed) in January 1665. The performers may have been members of the College: Oxford witnessed a short-lived attempt to revive student drama in the early 1660s. For the sports-minded, Loggan's 1675 engraving of University College includes a space which has been identified as a tennis court.[52]

University College was now regularly included on the itineraries of eminent visitors to Oxford. In December 1670, the College greeted Prince William of Orange (later William III); in May 1682 it was the turn of the ambassador of Morocco; and in May 1683, the College received a visit from the Duke and Duchess of York, and their daughter the Lady Anne.[53]

Even in its fine new quadrangle, the authorities at University College, as elsewhere, had to be vigilant against disciplinary problems. Antony Wood, ever fearful of a deterioration in student behaviour, claimed that William Shippen (F. 1659–68), when Proctor in 1664/5, 'flattered [undergraduates] which made them the ruder and debaucht'. Although there is no evidence at University College for anything resembling the pastime of senior undergraduates at Queen's College in the 1680s of turning junior ones over a coal fire, the Fellows did have to lay down the law. The regulations of April 1669 (p. 196) enjoined students to 'forbear pissing & other nastines against the Walls of the College, or in the Quadrangle; as also that they forbear to make any noise or disturbance in the Quadrangle, particularly to toll the bell except for meales & exercises; under the penalty of six-pence for every fault.'[54]

'OLD OBADIAH, SING AVE MARIA': 1676–1689

Obadiah Walker's election as Master of University College in 1676 might seem the happy culmination of his career. The College enjoyed its healthiest state for decades, and Walker was widely respected as a scholar, teacher, and patron of learning. Walker himself might have hoped for a peaceful time, writing in autumn 1676 that 'Old-age with its infirmities having already seized mee, render me uncapable of any other than a reposed, sedentary employment.'[55] This was not to be: his later years proved to be dramatic, successful, and eventually calamitous, and he ended up as the only Master of University College to appear in a nursery rhyme.[56]

[52] St Simon and St Jude: for example, UC:BU2/F1/1 p. 420, from 1664/5; Thomas Bateman's music: UC:BU3/F2/3; plays in the College: Wood, *Life* ii. 2 and 28 and Elliott 1997; tennis: Potter 1994: 52–3, which shows that most colleges had tennis courts at this time.
[53] Visits: Wood, *Life* ii. 208 (William), iii. 16–17 (ambassador), and iii. 49 (Duke of York and party).
[54] Shippen: Wood, *Life* ii. 34 (although we should remember Matthew Wentworth from the 1630s); Queen's: Hodgkin 1949: 121; 1669 rules: Bodl. MS Ballard 49 fo. 24.
[55] UC:MA30/2/C5/1.
[56] Firth 1964 provides another account of Walker's life after 1676.

The problem was religion. Abraham Woodhead was not the only member of University College having trouble deciding between Rome and Canterbury. There was William Rogers (m. 1663), a Gloucestershire gentleman's son of an antiquarian bent and an acquaintance of Antony Wood and Thomas Hearne. In 1670 Rogers gave the College a magnificent collection of books and manuscripts, including a twelfth-century manuscript of Bede's *Life of St Cuthbert* (Plate 6). However, soon after being admitted to Lincoln's Inn in 1666 Rogers had converted to Catholicism. Another Gloucestershire antiquarian, John Theyer, had also converted during the reign of Charles I. Surprisingly, Theyer's son Charles matriculated from University College in 1668, which he could only have done as a member of the Church of England.[57]

Another friend of John Theyer at University College was Timothy Nourse (m. 1655), Fellow from 1659, whom Antony Wood described as 'a vainglorious man, conceited of his worth'. In September 1672, while in Paris, Nourse wrote to Clayton denying rumours that he was inclining towards Catholicism. Yes, he had attended the Catholic Chapel at Somerset House, but only because he was asked to go and 'hear the Musick'. Nevertheless, Nourse's claim that 'I am at present as I was when I left Oxford of the same Judgement I was formerly' was not a very firm refutation. Nourse kept on finding excuses for avoiding taking communion either in the College Chapel or in St Mary the Virgin, until the College lost patience: Nourse was summoned in January 1674 to answer charges that he had stayed away without permission, that he disagreed with the Church of England, and that he had received an inheritance worth more than the statutes permitted. Nourse failed to appear: he was deprived of his Fellowship, and his Catholicism became public.[58]

By the late 1670s, questions were being asked about Obadiah Walker's beliefs, partly on account of his friendship with Abraham Woodhead. Some found it suspicious that, on being elected Master, Walker had not proceeded to a doctorate in theology, as was the norm for heads of colleges in holy orders, but remained an MA. Nevertheless, Walker remained within the Church of England, officiating at communion services in the Chapel. Besides, anyone of High Church beliefs was vulnerable to accusations of Popery from extreme Protestants; and among such High Church men as John Fell, himself no friend of Catholicism, Walker's religion was not doubted.

---

[57] Rogers's life and interests: Fendlay 1996/7; his gift: UC:BE1/MS1/3 fos. 8^{r-v}. Charles Theyer also had antiquarian interests, presenting a manuscript life of Catherine of Aragon—a subject with interesting religious connotations—to the College Library (Wood, *Life* ii. 485–6).

[58] John Theyer and Nourse: Wood, *Life* ii.143; Nourse's character: Wood, *Life* ii. 276; letters to Clayton: UC:MA29/C1/1–4 (quotations from the first letter); deprivation: UC:GB3/A1/1 p. 97.

Trouble arose for Walker from an unexpected and unwelcome quarter. After his failure to become Master in 1655, Ezreel Tonge's career had been chequered. Cromwell had appointed him Fellow of a university at Durham which was never created; the London church where he was minister was destroyed in the Great Fire; and he had even served as a chaplain in Tangier. By the late 1670s, Tonge had had time enough to nurse grievances, and acquire a paranoid hatred of Catholicism. When, in the summer of 1678, he met a renegade Catholic called Titus Oates who spun him fantastic tales about a Catholic plot, Oates's lies and Tonge's fanaticism succeeded in setting alight the national hysteria which has come down to us as the Popish Plot.[59]

In November 1678 Tonge turned his attentions to his former tutor Obadiah Walker. Even in October, questions had been asked in the House of Commons about both Woodhead's bequeathing his house at Hoxton to Walker, and incautious comments in the edition of Spelman's *Life of Alfred*, but matters had gone no further. Nevertheless, a Fellow of Queen's, Thomas Dixon, had heard rumours that Walker 'is much suspected of late to be a Papist', and that he had refused to take the oath of Allegiance and Supremacy. Then Tonge struck. Wood wrote that:

Israel Tonge fellow of University and Mr. [William] Shepen made freinds in the parliament house to have Mr. Walker turned out because a papist, that either of them might succeed. Base ingratitude! False Tonge was his freind, and formerly his servitor.[60]

Tonge's ingratitude was as obvious as his ambition: in the late 1660s he had written in friendly terms to Walker, and in 1670 he gave a book to the Library. William Shippen, however, had for some time been disputing a claim that he owed the College money, and in October 1678 had written to Walker protesting his innocence and peevishly commenting 'I must desire you to make a litle stricter enquiry into this busyenesse.'[61]

Walker was protected by John Fell, who in October 1679 prevented Titus Oates from receiving an honorary DD. Not even an attack made in April 1679 by the aged Master of the Rolls, Sir Harbottle Grimston, on 'the printing of Popish books at the Theater in Oxford', specifying the Spelman translation and Antony Wood's history of the university, damaged him. For Grimston, however, anyone prepared to discuss the pre-Reformation church in terms other than fiery denunciation was suspect. Furthermore, he was no friend of University College: in 1665 he had browbeaten Thomas Walker into electing his kinsman, Thomas Laurence, to a Fellowship. Tonge, at least, did

---

[59] Tonge's later career, and the origins of the Popish Plot: Kenyon 1972: 45–54; the Oxford context: Beddard 1997b: 863–905.

[60] Questions in Parliament: Wood, *Life* ii. 421; gossip in Queen's: Magrath 1903: 269; Tonge and Shippen: Wood, *Life*, ii. 422; see too Beddard 1997b: 863–8.

[61] Tonge to Walker: UC:S8/C2/1–2; gift of book: UC:BE1/MS1/3 fo. 8r; Shippen to Walker: UC:MA30/C6/4.

not plague the College much longer: he died in December 1680. Thomas Jones (F. 1649–58), another survivor from the Commonwealth College, preached at his funeral.[62]

There was further trouble in June 1680, when Francis Nicholson (m. 1666), a former pupil of Walker, preached a sermon at St Mary the Virgin which was thought to hint at the existence of purgatory. Complaints were made and Nicholson was obliged to submit a written apology to the Vice-Chancellor. After this incident, however, Walker was left in peace. Although the university generally remained anti-Catholic, it was willing to stay quiet out of loyalty to the Crown, and to the heir presumptive, James, the Catholic Duke of York.[63]

When James acceded to the throne following his brother's unexpected death in February 1685, Oxford, trusting in his assurances to protect the Church of England, loyally celebrated. University College paid 'For Torches and Faggots at the King's proclamation', and on the evening of his coronation, created a so-called 'illumination': two or three candles were lit in every window facing High Street. A few months later, one member, Hugh Brawne (m. 1674), joined an army mustered at Oxford to suppress the Duke of Monmouth's rebellion.[64]

After the crushing of the rebellion, a service of thanksgiving was held at St Mary at which Nathaniel Boyse, last seen helping raise money for the College, preached a sermon. Several listeners thought that it 'savour[ed] of popery', and Boyse, like Francis Nicholson, had to recant before the Vice-Chancellor. Soon afterwards, more controversy emanated from University College when Walker published at the University Press *An Historical Narration of the Life and Death of our Lord Jesus Christ*, a life of Christ compiled from the four Gospels, other books of the Bible, and some non-biblical sources such as Josephus. It was thought at the time to be Walker's work, but it is almost certainly the work of Abraham Woodhead. The book provides a good, if pedestrian, collation of the sources, and sold well at first, until people examined its contents more closely. In particular, Protestant readers would not have appreciated the author's observations that the Virgin Mary's 'graces and perfections in all vertues...surpassed those of the greatest Saints whatever' (p. 11), and that Peter 'was ordained by God his Father to be the chief and prime Pastor of them, under Christ' (p. 328). Rumours spread that John Fell had enjoined Walker to tone down his text, but that Walker had published it unchanged.[65]

---

[62] Fell and Oates: Wood, *Life* ii. 465; Grimston and Obadiah Walker: Wood, *Life* ii. 449; Grimston and Thomas Walker: UC:MA26/C1/7–9; Tonge's end: *ODNB* entry.

[63] Nicholson's sermon: Wood, *Life* ii. 488–9 and 490–1. In Charles II's last years the University Press published no books specifically attacking Catholicism (Beddard 1997*b*: 872).

[64] Torches: UC:BU2/F1/2 fo. 84ᵛ; the illumination: Wood, *Life* iii. 141: Brawne: Wood, *Life* iii. 147. Beddard 1997*c* supplies a general account of Oxford in 1685–8.

[65] Boyse's sermon: Wood, *Life* ii. 152 and 156 (see too Beddard 1997*c*: 918); the *Life of Christ* (page references from Walker 1685): Wood, *Athenae* iv. 443 said that Walker claimed authorship, but others, like Slusser 1979–81: 414, are certain that Woodhead wrote it; the book's success: Magrath 1913: 141–3; attempts at rewriting it: Keene 2003: 86 and Bodl. MS Ballard 49 fo. 27.

These events attracted royal interest. In October 1685, Boyse was granted an audience with the King where James called his sermon 'an ingenious discourse' and the *Life of Christ* 'a very good book', innocently wondering 'how any one shall find fault with it'. Something was brewing, but Walker's friends took no notice. In November 1685, Antony Wood noted a conversation with Walker about the vestments of John Leyburne, the papal nuncio, without considering why he knew so much about this, and when, in January 1686, Walker visited London for several weeks, Wood dismissed rumours that he was spending time with Catholics, as coming only from 'jealous men'.[66]

The rumours were correct. On returning from London, Walker ceased to attend services in the Chapel, and on the first Sunday in Lent, Nathaniel Boyse and another Fellow, Thomas Deane, pointedly turned up for Chapel, but remained in the Antechapel, taking no part in the service. Finally, the issue of the *French Gazette* published on 18 March (and dated 8 March, in the Gregorian calendar) reported Walker's conversion to Catholicism. Soon afterwards Boyse and Deane followed him.[67]

Few other events have given University College such public prominence as Walker's conversion. The shock can be imagined, as much among Walker's friends as his foes. Rumour claimed that John Fell, already gravely ill, died all the sooner from grief at his friend's action. Ever since, people have been asking how long Walker had been preparing for this move. Antony Wood, forgetting that he had previously noticed nothing untoward, wrote bitterly that Walker had 'continued a concealed papist 30 yeares or thereabout', and others have suggested that University College after 1660 was a nest of Catholics, secretly transmitting their faith within a closely-knit community.[68]

Caution is needed here: because we know what happened, it is tempting to detect popery in Walker's every deed or word. Had Walker died on the same day as Charles II, his troubles during the Popish Plot, and his friendship with Woodhead would have been noted, but nothing else would have suggested a potential convert or crypto-Catholic. William Smith's testimony is significant here. Many years later he wrote that in the 1650s, Walker was '(as some Zealots stile it,) rather poysoned than converted' to Catholicism, either by an unnamed priest or by Abraham Woodhead. The word 'poysoned' is significant: it implies that Walker was not actually converted in the 1650s, but that the seductive charms of Catholicism had begun, as Smith saw it, to corrupt his soul. Smith also observed that 'Mr. *Walker* received the Sacrament from

---

[66] Wood, *Life* iii. 165–6 (Boyse and the King), iii. 171 (Leyburn's vestments), and 176–7 (Walker in London).

[67] Wood, *Life* iii. 182. The *French Gazette*, properly titled the *Gazette de Londres*, was a French version of the *London Gazette*, the official government newspaper. Intended for a European audience (Walker 1974: 706–7), it often included different material from the English edition. Presumably the report of Walker's conversion was intended to inform Catholic readers abroad of this significant *coup* for James.

[68] Wood, *Life* iii. 182; a recent view: Beddard 1997c: 922.

the Hands of the Master of the College, 'till he became Master himself, and continued to distribute it to others' until his conversion. No Catholic could have received communion in the Church of England—it was his refusal to do this which had given away Timothy Nourse.[69]

Walker himself revealed nothing about his spiritual journey. Smith wrote:

> When it was enquired of [Walker], by several Persons, whether he was a Papist before or not, 'till his Majesty declared himself such? the Answer he gave was, usually, this, *That he Thought no Man's Salvation depended upon his answering this Question.*[70]

When summoned before the House of Commons in 1689, however, Walker claimed:

> I cannot say That ever I altered my Religion, or that my principles now do wholly agree with those of the Church of Rome...If they are Popish I have not changed my Religion: But they will not be found to be wholly agreeable with the Doctrine of the R.C. Church.[71]

These words of a frightened old man should be treated with caution. Nevertheless, they fit Smith's picture of someone who, while remaining in communion with the Church of England, gradually withdrew from it. One might recall, from a later age, John Henry Newman, another High Church Anglican drawn towards the more 'catholic' aspects of its doctrine—like Walker and John Fell—but one who eventually concluded that his beliefs could better be accommodated within the Church of Rome. Walker may have travelled a similar path, although the moment when he accepted Catholicism in his heart will always remain unknown.[72]

Nathaniel Boyse readily admitted that he and Thomas Deane 'were both drawn from their Religion by the Perswasions of Mr. Obadiah Walker', although he never said when the persuading began. Both men had matriculated from University College on the same day in 1669, but while Boyse was elected Fellow as early as 1674, Deane had to wait a decade longer to join him. When a Bennet Fellowship fell vacant in June 1684, Walker clearly wished the Fellows to elect Deane, but another man, Thomas Bennet (m. 1674), was chosen. Twenty years later, in an unpublished note, William Smith wove a dramatic tale of how one Fellow, John Naylor, arrived at midnight on the day before the election, so that Deane lost, and how Walker successfully promised preferment to tempt another Bennet Fellow to resign in October 1684, whereupon the Fellows elected Deane with rather a bad grace. Smith's second account, however, published in 1728, is rather different. Because, he

---

[69] Smith, 257.
[70] Ibid. 258.
[71] Bodl. MS Ballard 49 fo. 27ʳ.
[72] Tyacke 1997: 610 plausibly suggests that Walker may have been ill-at-ease with the English Church, but at the same time unsure about Roman Catholicism.

said, the Bennet settlement in 1662 stipulated that provision should still be made, if someone suitable arose, for relatives of Sir Simon Bennet, of whom Thomas Bennet was one, Smith threatened to make a formal complaint if Deane got elected, and his ploy succeeded. Smith, as we shall see, had a legalistic, if not pedantic, mind, so that it would be characteristic of him to oppose Deane's candidature solely on procedural grounds. Furthermore, even in his first account, Smith had caustically commented that Deane was more highly thought of outside the College than inside. The fact that Deane got his Fellowship so long after his matriculation suggests that the Fellows may have doubted Deane's academic competence as much as, or more than, his religious orthodoxy.[73]

If Walker had been attempting to create a crypto-Catholic cell in University College, then the events of 1686 were hardly encouraging. Boyse and Deane converted, as did Francis Nicholson and a Fellow of Brasenose called John Barnard; there were rumours too about John Massey, a former undergraduate of University College (m. 1666) and now a Fellow at Merton. However, no other member of University College followed the Master's example—with one significant exception. This was Edward Hales (m. 1684; Fig. 10.3), the eldest son of Sir Edward Hales, a Kentish baronet. As the latest representative of a wealthy family well disposed towards the College (two of his uncles had attended the College in the 1660s), Hales was already a significant figure—in 1685, he persuaded the College to make a friend of his a Gunsley Scholar—but he soon became more important. Sir Edward, who had converted to Catholicism the previous November and had therefore been deprived of an army commission, participated in an important test case, Godden *versus* Hales, in June 1686, which decreed that the Royal prerogative could overrule the laws preventing Catholics from becoming army officers. Hales now joined the privy council, and became Lieutenant both of Dover Castle and of the Tower of London.[74]

James II, well aware of Walker's significance, gave him his full protection: in March 1686, he dispensed him and his followers from attending Anglican services, and in May 1686 exempted them from the provisions of the Test Act so that they could retain their positions. Thus far James could claim that he was not seeking to impose Catholicism on the unwilling, merely to relieve Catholics from persecution, and that he would tolerate freedom of conscience in religious matters. Unfortunately, at University College, as elsewhere, the enthusiasm of the convert propelled James into tactless actions which smacked less of toleration than of Catholic aggression.[75]

---

[73] Boyes's conversion: Hearne viii. 264; Smith's accounts of Deane's election: UC:AR2/MS1/11 pp. 149–50 and Smith, 332–3. The dishonest Ambrose Bennet was Thomas Bennet's uncle (Zoeller 2007: 101).

[74] Walker's disciples: Wood, *Life* iii. 176–7; Nicholson: Wood, *Athenae* iv. 449–50; Hales and the Scholarship: UC:AR2/MS1/11 p. 151; Godden *versus* Hales: Miller 1978: 156–7.

[75] Dispensation of March 1686: *CSPD 1686/7* 80; exemption of May: UC:GB3/A1/1 pp. 111–12 (see too Wood, *Life* iii. 184).

FIGURE 10.3 Edward Hales, m. 1684, who welcomed James II on his visit to the College, by an unknown artist.

In May 1686, Walker was given a royal licence to print and sell thirty-six specified books of Roman Catholic theology, most of which were unpublished works by Abraham Woodhead. Next, after his conversion, Walker turned some rooms in the Master's Lodgings into a Catholic Chapel. As this grew too small, the non-Catholic Fellows later claimed that he procured by unknown means a key to a vacant room on the ground floor of the east range of the quadrangle, and made this a Chapel instead. Wood's diary suggests that this room was opened for public Mass in August 1686. This was still not large enough, and so in that same month, Walker received a royal warrant empowering him 'to make use of any chamber you shall think convenient in the College' as a Catholic Chapel. At a later date—the Fellows thought not long before Christmas 1686—Walker summoned a College meeting at which Boyse read the warrant out. As the Fellows digested this alarming news, Walker, displaying a courtesy which his king might have wisely used, said:

Gentlemen, you perceave I may take any Room. Your Common-Room is the Largest, but out of respect for the Society I will take only that which is on my side of the College next to my Lodgings.[76]

The non-Catholic Fellows, relieved that Walker had not selected the Chapel (as they had feared), were in no position to oppose royal and magisterial authority combined, and Walker took over the sets which today are numbered VII.1 and VIII.1, knocking them into one large room. He was gracious in victory: the accounts suggest that no College money was spent on this work (presumably Walker—or possibly James himself—paid for it).

Walker's powers were still growing. In November 1686, a Fellow, Edward Hinchliffe, died, and in January 1687 came a letter from the King ordering that the revenue from his Fellowship be sequestered to the Master 'to be applied to such uses as we shall appoint'. The use turned out to be maintaining a priest for the Catholic Chapel. Fellowships had been left vacant for financial reasons, but never before had income from a Fellowship been explicitly transferred to other purposes. Walker promptly appointed a Jesuit chaplain, Edward Humberston, who was later succeeded by another Jesuit, Joseph Wakeman. The College attracted sons of recusant families: Antony Wood noted four 'Gentlemen-commoners under Mr. Walker that are papists', three of whom, Charles Dormer, Robert Scarisbrick, and Cuffield (first name unknown), can be identified from College records. The fourth may have been John Dryden, the son of the poet laureate, and later Catholic Fellow at Magdalen.[77]

In July 1687 Walker was appointed a JP for Oxfordshire, and his protégés were making headway elsewhere. After John Fell's death in July 1686, James appointed a Dean of Christ Church with no previous links with the College who lacked the stature of his predecessor—but the King thought him suitable, not least when he soon converted to Catholicism. This new Dean was Walker's former pupil John Massey, and one suspects that James had sought Walker's advice. Walker was also drawn into the affairs of Magdalen College. When its President died early in 1687, James twice attempted to impose a successor on the Fellows. The ensuing battle of wits resulted in the expulsion of almost all the Fellows of Magdalen, thereby creating a group of Protestant martyrs. Walker was generally assumed to have recommended James's first candidate, Antony Farmer. Even after Farmer withdrew his candidacy, his

---

[76] Licence to print books: *CSPD 1686/7* 119–20 and Wood, *Life* iii. 198; Walker's search for a Catholic Chapel: Bodl. MS Ballard 16 fos. 15–16 (an account in William Smith's hand); the first Chapel: Wood, *Life* iii. 194; warrant: *CSPD 1686/7* 241; Walker to the Fellows: Bodl. MS Ballard 49 fos. 27^v and 72^r.

[77] The sequestered Fellowship: UC:GB3/A1/1 p. 110, and *CSPD 1686/7* 350; Walker's Chaplains: Wood, *Life* iii. 276, *Athenae* iv. 440, and Beddard 1997c: 928; recusant undergraduates: Wood, *Life* iii. 214. John Dryden appears in no College records, but the poet Thomas Shadwell—whose son John attended University College at this time—in his *The Address of John Dryden, Laureat, to His Highness the Prince of Orange* (1689) talks of his studying 'under the great Gamaliel Obadiah'.

character blackened by unsavoury rumours about his past life, Walker continued to involve himself in Magdalen's affairs. When its Fellows were expelled in November 1687, Walker was among those who dined in the College that same evening, and he gave advice on the Crown's powers of visitation—naturally giving them a broad interpretation. Meanwhile Cambridge also endured James's attentions: in 1687 he mandated the Fellows of Sidney Sussex College to elect a Catholic head.[78]

Unsurprisingly Walker swiftly encountered opposition. His first publication, an edition of Woodhead's *Two Discourses concerning the Adoration of our Blessed Saviour in the Holy Eucharist* which appeared in January 1687, was entrusted to a local printer, Leonard Litchfield—who let a young Fellow of Trinity College, Arthur Charlett, see the proofs, enabling Charlett to publish his rejoinder virtually simultaneously with Walker's book. Walker therefore set up a private press at the back of his Lodgings. By November 1688, he had published a dozen books, seven of which were certainly by Woodhead (Fig. 10.4), and almost all of which promptly received Protestant counterblasts, many of them—to the undoubted discomfiture of John Massey—written by Christ Church men.[79]

The Catholic Chapel, however, became the focus for the greatest hostility—and indeed for the display of the elderly Walker's courage. Services became something of a spectator sport, as people entered the College to peer into the Chapel, listen, and mock. William Smith recalled how Protestant spectators once embarrassed Walker's first Jesuit chaplain. When he was giving a sermon,

many Protestants were harkening at the Out-side of the Windows, in the Quadrangle, one of them discovering that it was one of Mr. *Henry Smith's* Sermons which he had at Home by him, went and fetched the Book, and read at the Out-side of the Windows, what the Jesuit was preaching within.[80]

In February 1687 Walker sought to prevent such barracking by restricting access to the Chapel, but this failed. That August, a gentleman commoner of Christ Church pointedly broke into laughter during a catechizing, and a year later, a boy brought a cat into the Chapel, making it squeal at inappropriate moments. Christ Church men took especial pleasure in causing trouble. Once they sent 'old Job', one of their kitchen servants, to sing outside the Master's Lodgings:

---

[78] Walker the JP: Wood, *Athenae* iv. 440; Dean Massey: Wood, *Life* iii. 197 and 200–1 and Wood, *Fasti*, in Wood, *Athenae* ii. 348; events at Magdalen in 1687–8: Brockliss and others 1988: 31–76; Walker and Farmer: Bloxam 1886: 71, 73, and 79; Farmer's defects: Brockliss and others 1988: 48–51; Walker at Magdalen: Bloxam 1886: 210 and Wood, *Life* iii. 250; advice on visitations: Bloxam 1886: 236–7; Sidney Sussex College: Goldie 1996.

[79] Litchfield and Charlett: Wood, *Life* iii. 209; Walker's books: Carter 1975: 117–19 and Wood, *Life* iii. 209; Protestant counterblasts: Beddard 1997c: 935–7.

[80] Smith, 259.

FIGURE 10.4 Title page of *A Compendious Discourse on the Eucharist*, one of the treatises by Abraham Woodhead which Obadiah Walker published on his private printing press.

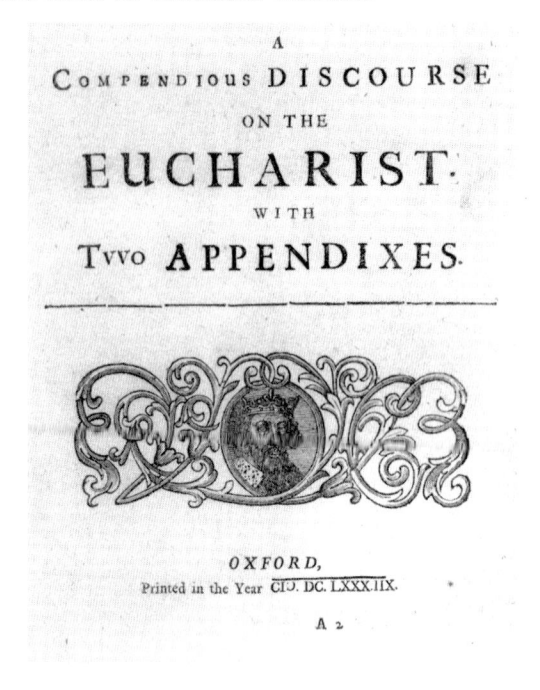

> O old Obadiah
> Sing Ave Maria,
> But so will not I a
>   for why a
> I had rather be a Fool than a Knave a.[81]

The excellent rhyme in 'Obadiah' survived long afterwards: even in the early twentieth century, 'Old Obadiah, sing Ave Maria' was used as a children's playground rhyme on 5 November.[82]

The world now grew suspicious of Oxford in general, and of University College in particular. In June 1686, when Hugh Todd, whose Protestantism never wavered, was visiting north-west England, one member of Queen's had heard 'of Mr. Todd's inclineing much towards Popery in several sermons which he has lately preached in the country, and that the Bishop has sometimes rebuked him for it'. Wood claimed that 'the University emptied and

---

[81] Walker barring entry: Wood, *Life* iii. 213; the laughing undergraduate: Wood, *Life* iii. 223; the cat: Wood, *Life* iii. 273–4; old Job's song: Magrath 1913: 158; similar troubles at Magdalen College: Brockliss and others 1988: 66–7.

[82] Michael Sadler wrote in 1931 that it was sung on 5 November 'within my memory' (UC:MA44/6/C/1 no. 36).

THE RISE AND FALL OF OBADIAH WALKER 213

many were afraid to send their son thereto', and University College certainly suffered. In the early 1680s, it admitted about ten men a year, but in 1687 and 1688 respectively only four and five signed the register; the recusants were not making up the balance (Graph 10.1). Numbers also fell at Christ Church and Magdalen.[83]

Meanwhile, Walker and the College somehow maintained a *modus vivendi*. Leases were drawn up and the accounts for 1686/7–1688/9 kept as usual. A significant factor may have been that, unlike the other, intruded, heads, Walker at least had been statutably elected Master. Although the College attracted few new members, its existing ones seem to have remained. Protestant undergraduates appear to have accepted Catholic tutors: in the Bursar's Book for March 1687, Thomas Deane underwrote the batells of several undergraduates, almost all of whom appear to have been Protestant. Meanwhile, Protestant Fellows and Scholars continued to be elected. Even John Hudson, elected Fellow in March 1686 following a mandate from James himself, proved not to be a Catholic. The Protestant Hudson and the Catholic Deane travelled to Maidstone in November 1686 to select a new Gunsley Scholar—although Hudson spent an uncomfortable two days defending Protestantism against Deane and other Catholics in the coach.[84]

Walker himself appears to have tolerated acts of defiance against Catholicism. When Edmund Heron (m. 1682) got drunk outside the College in December 1687, and tripped John Barnard, no less, into the gutter, his only penalty was to make a formal apology the following morning. When James ordered his Declaration of Indulgence, which offered freedom of worship to Catholics and dissenters alike, to be read in all churches and chapels, John Hudson alone of the Fellows agreed to read prayers that day, but pointedly omitted the Declaration. Yet, he remembered later, 'Mr. *Walker* did not seem at all to resent [his action], as People imagined that he would do.' Hudson was involved in another remarkable act on St John's Day (24 June) 1688. The university sermon that day is usually preached in Magdalen College, but Magdalen's chapel was then used for Catholic services. Therefore, although a sermon was preached at Magdalen that day, the 'official' university sermon was preached at St Mary the Virgin by John Hudson. Walker could presumably have prevented Hudson from doing this, had he wished.[85]

Most remarkably of all, Walker welcomed the gift of an east window for the Protestant Chapel in 1687 from an Old Member called John Radcliffe.

---

[83] Todd: Magrath 1913: 162; an empty university: Wood, *Life* iii. 202: Christ Church and Magdalen: Wood, *Life* iii. 257 and Bill 1988: 36.

[84] Deane's pupils (who include Thomas Shadwell's son John): UC:BU3/F1/15; Hudson's mandate: *CSPD 1686/7* 84; Fellows' fears: UC:AR2/MS1/1 pp. 152–3; journey to Maidstone: UC:GB3/A1/1 p. 110; Hudson's experiences: Hearne i. 104.

[85] Heron: Wood, *Life* iii. 245 (where he is wrongly called 'Edward'); Hudson's prayers: Hearne i. 104; his sermon: Wood, *Life* iii. 270.

A Wakefield lad, Radcliffe matriculated from University College in 1666, and became a Hunt, then a Freeston Scholar. In 1670, he was elected a Fellow at Lincoln College, but he resigned in 1675 amidst some bitterness over his refusal to take orders. Lincoln's loss was University College's gain, for Radcliffe, moving to London, became a successful society doctor. Radcliffe's window was designed by Henry Gyles of York, and depicted the Nativity. This was a daring choice of design, for it may have been the first painted glass window in England since the 1640s to depict a biblical scene. Although it was intended for a Chapel where Walker no longer worshipped, he nevertheless wrote Radcliffe an enthusiastic letter of thanks. Phrases, however, like 'nor can we salute the morning light without meditating on the shepherds and the Angells adoring the true sun' and a description of the window as 'an object moving our devotions' were too exuberant for the Fellows, who sent a second letter to Radcliffe explaining that this letter represented Walker's personal views, and not the College's.[86]

Radcliffe's own relations with Walker show how a difficult situation could be kept under some sort of control. In May 1688, Walker wrote to Radcliffe suggesting that he convert to Catholicism. Although Radcliffe rebuffed him firmly, yet he concluded his letter with a remarkable expression of affection:

Yet, tho' I shall never be brought over to confide in your Doctrines, no one breathing can have a greater Esteem for your Conversation, by Letter, or Word of Mouth, than
   Sir,
  Your most Affectionate and Faithful Servant,
  John Radcliffe.[87]

Others also had a personal regard for Walker which survived the latter's conversion, as his personal magnetism somehow kept such friendships alive. Antony Wood continued to discuss historical matters with him, and praised him both for 'the great stock of various erudition and science amassed together in himself', and for 'his great prudence and discretion, his philosophical and unpassionate temper, and lastly his great love of a private and sedate life, joyned with a great hatred of idleness both in himself and others'. Likewise, appalled though William Smith was at Walker's conversion, he wrote in 1728 that 'I have many good Things to say of him, as that he was neither Proud nor Covetous', and a few years later generously copied extensive extracts from his transcripts of College records

---

[86] The window: UC:BE1/MS1/1 p. 48; Radcliffe and Lincoln: Green 1979: 290–1; although Radcliffe's window was removed in 1862, some designs for it, as well as some fragments, still survive (see further Brighton 1970); Walker's letter (transcribed in Darwall-Smith 1998: 64–5): UC:MA30/1/C/3.
[87] The letter is transcribed in Pettis 1715: 19–21.

for Cuthbert Constable, a recusant eager to find out more about Woodhead and Walker.[88]

Walker could also rely on a visceral loyalty to the Crown. While many of James's subjects might deplore the King's religion, and some of his activities, they accepted that he was the anointed monarch of the realm. Even John Hudson, despite his anti-Catholic actions, was suspected of staying loyal to James after his deposition. Thomas Bennet, elected in preference to Deane in 1684, had to serve as Proctor from March 1687, which landed him in some difficult situations, such as when in October 1687, he helped entertain the Commissioners who had been sent to force Magdalen to accept the King's choice as President.[89]

There was therefore little protest when William Rogers added to his gift of books by paying for a statue (generally attributed to John Bushnell) of James II to be erected in the quadrangle, in place of the statue of Alfred given by Robert Plot, which was moved to a niche above the Hall. The King's statue was installed on 7 February 1687, amid great celebration. There was a dinner to which all comers were welcome, music was played in the Hall, and there was another 'illumination'. Just before the dinner, Edward Hales gave a speech which extolled James for his courage, loyalty, and religious toleration.[90]

In September 1687, the statue's subject himself visited Oxford, and University College was on his itinerary. Although several members of the royal family had visited the College, no reigning monarch seems to have visited University College before.[91] There could be no greater sign of royal approval for Walker. As James entered the College, Edward Hales was on hand again to deliver a speech, which was later printed. Although Hales carefully observed that the King left 'the Duty towards God, to every Conscience', his speech's triumphalist opening would have made a Protestant shudder:

We, your Majesties Humblest Subjects of this House, have the great reason to rejoyce in this your Majesties presence, in as much as this being the most Antient Colledge, and Mother of all the rest in your Dominions, hath been chosen out to begin the restitution of the Religion which was first Planted and Watred by so many Eminent, Devout and Learned Persons.[92]

After the speech, James attended the Catholic Chapel to hear vespers, but, to show his tolerance, was also shown round the Anglican one.[93]

---

[88] Wood and Walker: for example, Wood, *Life* iii. 204, and Wood, *Athenae* iv. 442; Smith on Walker: Smith, 258; Smith and Constable: YAS MS 45.
[89] Hudson's loyalty: *ODNB* entry; Thomas Bennet: Bloxam 1886: 142–3 and 164.
[90] Rogers's gift: UC:BE1/MS1/1 p. 49 (see further Esdaile and Toynbee 1952–3, who attribute it to Bushnell); statue of Alfred: Smith, 251; the ceremonies: Wood, *Life* iii. 209–12.
[91] And none would do so again until 1999.
[92] *A Speech, spoken by Mr. Hayles, a Student of University-Colledge of Oxford, and Son to the Honourable Sir Edward Hayles, With his Majesties Gracious Acceptance*. A copy is in the College archives as UC:P166/X1/1.
[93] Wood, *Life* iii. 233.

This occasion would cheer Catholic members of the College—William Rogers came up for the occasion—but non-Catholic members were also caught up in the excitement. Thomas Bennet planned a further 'illumination' (but set the lights up a day early), and on the following day delivered a speech to James in the Bodleian Library asking that he 'be good to' the Church of England. James graciously permitted Bennet to kiss his ungloved hand.[94]

Forty years later William Smith, ever the canny Yorkshireman, could still not conceal his bewilderment at Walker's unworldliness at this moment of his greatest glory:

Mr. *Walker* that had the King's Ear, and entertain'd him at *Vespers* in their Chapel, and shewed the King the painted Windows in our own; so that the King could not but see his own Statue in coming out of it, never had the Prudence nor Kindness to the COLLEGE, as to Request the least Favour to the Society from him; tho' the COLLEGE at that Time was worse provided of Benefices, than any ancient COLLEGE in the whole UNIVERSITY.[95]

Even the Protestant Smith hoped that the College might derive some benefit from James.

James visited University College after an uneasy meeting with the Fellows of Magdalen, at which he had rebuked them ferociously for their defiance. University College, with its Catholic head, two Chapels, and a mixed membership united in welcoming him, provided a happier model for the future Oxford. Indeed, as James departed, there was nothing to hint that his reforms might fail, especially after the birth of a Prince of Wales in June 1688. The College purchased a collection of celebratory verses for the Prince, and, during a day of Thanksgiving the following month, the College was illuminated again, and allegorical pictures hung facing the High Street.[96]

James's rule, however, was soon in trouble. By September 1688, rumours had reached Oxford of an invasion led by William of Orange. James panicked, and in October restored the expelled Fellows of Magdalen. Walker (like John Massey) remained in his College. Nevertheless, time was running out: on 7 November, two days after William had landed at Torbay, a crowd tried, unsuccessfully, to break down the High Street entrance of Walker's Lodgings. On 9 November Walker accepted that all was lost, and left University College for ever, leaving his printing press and its contents to be seized.[97]

Others fled in different directions. Edmund Heron joined a troop which mustered at Oxford towards the end of November in support of the Dutch,

---

[94] Rogers at the College: Fendlay 1996/7: 291–2; Bennet: Wood, *Life* iii. 231 and 233 (illuminations) and 235 (speech).
[95] Smith, 260.
[96] Book of verses: UC:BU3/F2/4 fo. 76ᵛ; College celebrations: Wood, *Life* iii. 271.
[97] William's invasion: Wood, *Life* iii. 278; Magdalen: Brockliss and others 1988: 70–2; trouble at the Lodgings, and Walker's departure: Wood, *Life* iii. 282; his printing press: Magrath 1913: 243.

and soon afterwards Thomas Deane and the Jesuit Joseph Wakeman fled to London with the contents of the Catholic Chapel—and with John Massey. Massey made good his escape; but Walker was captured in Kent and was sent to the Tower of London to join Sir Edward Hales. The Catholic experiment at University College was over.[98]

The fates of Walker's colleagues can be quickly told: Edward Hales was killed fighting for his king at the battle of the Boyne in 1690; his father, Sir Edward, ended his days at James's court in exile in 1695. Francis Nicholson and Nathaniel Boyse lived out their days in Portugal, taking several of Woodhead's manuscripts with them, but Deane remained in England. Sadly, Boyse and Deane fell out over Walker's will, Boyse claiming that Deane had cheated him.[99]

There remained Obadiah Walker, incarcerated in the Tower of London. He could not possibly continue as Master, and the Fellows sent a deputation to persuade him to resign. Unfortunately Walker refused to go, and the Fellows eventually petitioned the Visitors for help. On 4 February 1689 the Visitors duly came to the College, where the Fellows charged Walker with defecting to the Catholic church, sequestering money from a Fellowship 'for sinister uses', and printing books opposing Protestantism. The Visitors duly declared the Mastership vacant, and at the same meeting stripped Boyse and Deane of their Fellowships for leaving the Church of England.[100]

Walker was eventually released from the Tower in January 1690. He was by now in his mid-seventies, and his experiences would have crushed a lesser man. Yet Walker lived on until 1699, his spirits undaunted. Although he lived a quiet and retired life, his thirst for scholarship remained unquenched, as he published books on grammar and classical history. He maintained links with Oxford, asking William Smith to send him books, and advising on the use of an estate set aside for charitable purposes, and in 1694 advised the College on the history of John Freeston's benefaction. Most remarkably of all, despite Walker's unsuccessful attempt to convert John Radcliffe, the latter kept his word in retaining his affection for his old tutor to the end, and sending him every year a new suit of clothes, and a dozen bottles 'of the Richest Canary to support his Drooping Spirits'. When Walker died, Radcliffe had this inscription placed on his tomb in St Pancras' cemetery (which Walker had asked to be placed next to that of Abraham Woodhead):

---

[98] Heron: Wood, *Life* iii. 284; Deane, Wakeman, and Massey: Wood, *Life* iii. 285; Walker's capture: Wood, *Life* iii. 287–8.

[99] The Haleses: respective *ODNB* entries; Nicholson corresponded with Cuthbert Constable in the late 1720s (YAS MS 46) and even gave Constable his Woodhead manuscripts; Boyse and Deane: Hearne viii. 264, and *ODNB* entries.

[100] Persuading Walker to resign: UC:GB3/A1/1 p. 113 and Magrath 1913: 243–4; sacking Walker, Boyse, and Deane: UC:GB3/A1/1 pp. 114–15 and Wood, *Life* iii. 297–8.

> O.W.
> per bonam famam et infamiam [through good reputation and bad][101]

In fact Walker had summed himself up over a quarter of a century earlier, in this meditation on the benefits of scholarship, which describes perfectly the character he preserved throughout his remarkable life:

Learning and study makes a young man thinking, attentive, industrious, confident and wary; an old man cheerful, and resolved. 'Tis an ornament in *prosperity*, a refuge in *adversity*; an entertainment at *home*, a companion *abroad*: it cheers in solitude and *prison*; it moderates in the height of *fortune*, and upon the throne.[102]

---

[101] Walker's last years: Mitchell 1998; Smith: YAS MS 45; Walker and charity: Gibson 1935 and 1937/8; advice on Freeston: Bodl. MS Ballard 5 fo. 56ʳ; Radcliffe and Walker: Hearne i. 85; Walker's grave: Pettis 1715: 22 and YAS 46.

[102] Walker 1677: 117.

11

The Era of Arthur Charlett: 1689–1722

FINDING A NEW MASTER: 1689–1692

Having rid themselves of Obadiah Walker, the Fellows of University College unanimously elected as their new Master the senior Fellow, Edward Farrar, on 15 February 1689. Appointed by the Parliamentary Visitors back in 1651, Farrar offered little beyond age and undoubted Protestantism. Since preaching at the consecration of the Chapel in 1666, he had taken no part in College life, but had been perpetual curate of Flamstead for many years. He was also in poor health: his letters of the 1680s mention pains in his legs and feet, his inability to ride very far, and his complete immobility in winter. Nevertheless, Farrar did what was required. In February 1689, Walker's Catholic Chapel was dismantled—some accounts speak of 'putting up ye Partitions in ye ground chamber of ye Coll.', which must mean the rooms taken over by Walker—and by July all the vacant Fellowships were filled.[1]

Farrar was Master for barely two years. Anthony Wood wrote in his diary for 13 February 1691:

Circa meridiem, died suddenly of an apoplexy Dr. Edward Farrar, master of Univ. Coll., on his clo<se> stool. Much given to bibbing and smoking but to little exercise.[2]

Having tried age, the Fellows now sought youth, and considered Thomas Bennet, last encountered welcoming James II. Bennet had resigned his Fellowship in August 1689 on being appointed rector of the wealthy living of Winwick, Lancashire, by his brother John. He certainly had potential: he was still in his thirties; his selection as Proctor suggested ability; and his living showed that he had connections.[3]

---

[1] Farrar's election: UC:GB3/A1/1 p. 115; his poor health: letters in Pyx Θ fasc. 6 pt. 2; repairs to rooms: UC:BU3/F2/5 fo. 74ᵛ; fresh elections: UC:GB3/A1/1 pp. 117–18.

[2] Wood, *Life* iii. 355 (but Wood disliked Farrar—p. 181).

[3] Resigns Fellowship: UC:GB3/A1/1 p. 119; Winwick: Farrer and Brownhill 1911: 125–9 (Holmes 1982: 99 and 92–4 claims that in the 1720s Winwick was worth about £1,000 a year, while in 1711 the Deanery of Christ Church was worth about £800).

Bennet's election did not go smoothly: William Smith, that dogged peruser of precedents, and John Giles, the senior Fellow, observed that Thomas Bennet had been a Bennet Fellow, and no Bennet Fellow had yet been elected Master. They persuaded themselves that no Bennet Fellow could become Master without a dispensation: the revenues of one of the old Fellowships had long been assigned to the Master, and they feared that Bennet's election would overturn the balance between northern and southern Fellowships. All parties therefore played safe: a dispensation was obtained, and Bennet unanimously elected on 3 March 1691. Insignificant as this little piece of legal pedantry might appear, it assumed alarming significance three decades later.[4]

Tragically a few months after Bennet's election, John Giles, who appears to have been suffering from depression, drowned himself in Christ Church meadow. Worse still, Thomas Bennet himself died on 12 May 1692. According to the Register, he had been suffering from a 'violent cough' (*tussis vehemens*), which might imply consumption, and he died following an attempt to bleed him. He was buried in the Chapel to the south of the altar.[5]

Facing a third Mastership election in as many years, the Fellows could not readily find a successor. George Fleming, an undergraduate at St Edmund Hall, passed on this gossip to his father in June 1692:

There are now great animosities and heats among the Fellows about the election of a Master; Mr. Tod, Mr. Smith, and Mr. Bertie a nobleman, all 3 Fel: have been (as its reported) mentioned; but its generally believed they must be forced to elect one of another house.[6]

Hugh Todd and William Smith could claim scholarship and experience. Albemarle Bertie (m. 1686), elected a Fellow aged 20 in 1689, possessed neither, but he was a younger son of the Earl of Lindsey, whose family held the hereditary title of Lord Great Chamberlain of England.

An impasse was reached, and eventually the Fellows had indeed to seek an outsider. Their gaze settled on a Fellow of Trinity in his late thirties called Arthur Charlett—the same Charlett who had published a counterblast to Obadiah Walker's first publication. Charlett had much to recommend him. As Thomas Hearne said, he was noted 'for the variety of his Correspondents and Acquaintance, as well as magnificent way of Living'. He was a friend of the diarist Samuel Pepys and of Anthony Wood, who made him one of his executors. Charlett had expectations too: a wealthy uncle had given him £1,000, and promised more. A Master not exclusively dependent on his

---

[4] Smith and Giles's concerns: Smith, 327–31.
[5] Giles's death: Wood, *Life* iii. 377, UC:GB3/A1/1 p. 123 and UC:AR2/MS1/11 p. 177 (where William Smith expressed his grief); Bennet's death: UC:GB3/A1/1 p. 124; his burial: UC:AR2/MS1/11 p. 178.
[6] Magrath 1924: 61–2.

THE ERA OF ARTHUR CHARLETT: 1689–1722   221

modest stipend—and offering hopes of benefactions to come—was a promising prospect.[7]

Why might Arthur Charlett be interested in University College? The answer lies in his old college, Trinity, where Ralph Bathurst, Charlett's President, showed how the head of a small college could, through skill and energy, enjoy a high reputation in the university, recruit undergraduates from the best society, and adorn the college with fine new buildings. Charlett could become the Bathurst of University College. On the other hand, Bathurst might prove an undesirable model; the Fellows of Trinity resented his domineering ways.[8]

Several Fellows may have suggested Charlett: according to Thomas Hearne, John Hudson's influence was crucial, but William Smith said that John Boraston (F. 1689–1741) led the campaign. Other friends of the College were involved: Robert Plot supported Charlett, and John Radcliffe's approval was sought. The Visitors were happy to grant the appropriate dispensation for an outsider's appointment. The Fellows, however, set some conditions for the new Master: he could not marry; he would oversee a revision of the statutes within seven years; and he would not attempt to get another outsider elected as his successor. Eventually, Charlett was elected Master on 7 July 1692—but not unanimously. Albemarle Bertie and two other Fellows attended, but pointedly abstained. Charlett and the College were not necessarily guaranteed an easy time.[9]

CHARLETT ASCENDANT: 1692–1698

The next few years generally satisfied the College's expectations of Charlett, and his of it, as he showed himself a patron of scholarship, an energetic university politician, and, within the College, an upholder of its character. 'Patron' is the significant term here. Charlett himself published very little: apart from a letter concerning an explosion in a Newcastle colliery, his only known work after 1692 was *Mercurius Oxoniensis, or the Oxford Intelligencer for the Year of our Lord 1707*, a compilation of useful information about Oxford.[10]

Instead, Charlett eagerly encouraged the work of others, especially within the fields of classics, antiquarianism, and Anglo-Saxon (literature and art seem not to have interested him greatly). His support for classical scholarship first manifested itself in a grand gesture. Since the late 1660s, Deans of Christ

---

[7] Hearne on Charlett: Hearne, i. 214; letters from Samuel Pepys to Charlett: Bodl. MS Ballard 1 fos. 91–121ᵛ; Charlett as Wood's executor: Wood, *Life* iii. 497–9, and Kiessling 2001: xiv (critical of Charlett's treatment of Wood); Charlett's uncle: Smith, 303–4.
[8] Bathurst: Hopkins 2005: 125–62.
[9] Hudson: Hearne, i. 83 (Bodl. MS Ballard 17 fo. 90ʳ shows Hudson lobbying for Charlett); Boraston: Smith, 303; Plot and Radcliffe: Bodl. MS Ballard 14 fo. 53ʳ and 22 fo. 36ʳ; conditions for Charlett: UC:GB3/A1/1 pp. 124–5; the abstainers: UC:AR2/MS1/11 p. 183, where Smith enigmatically commented 'I think that the reason [for their abstentions] should be sought from the two survivors, if they can provide one, and should not be told by me.'
[10] Charlett 1707 and 1708/9.

Church had commissioned editions of Latin or Greek texts with brief notes, for distribution as New Year presents. In 1693, Charlett produced his own New Year present, commissioning John Hudson to edit the historian Velleius Paterculus. Then in 1694 a Freeston Scholar called John Potter (m. 1688) edited two works by Plutarch and St Basil the Great. Charlett's ambition outstripped his finances, for he issued no further New Year Books, but in 1695 and 1696 there appeared in a similar format editions of Cicero's *De Officiis* and *De Oratore*. Both edited by a Bennet Scholar, Thomas Cockman (m. 1691), they were dedicated respectively to Charlett and John Radcliffe. Cockman also produced, in 1699, an immensely successful translation of *De Officiis*, which went into six editions during his lifetime, and was even reprinted in 1894.[11]

John Hudson was perhaps the most important Fellow in 1692. Apart from tutoring more students than anyone else in the 1690s—and tutoring them well, according to Thomas Hearne—he also published major editions of, among others, Thucydides, Longinus, Josephus, and the Greek geographers. His labours were rewarded when in 1701 he was elected Bodley's Librarian. Some claimed that Hudson was more interested in his research than in the Bodleian, but he did solicit donations for the library, and purchased books from abroad through Charlett's contacts. Within College, although Hudson took on fewer pupils after 1701, he served as Catechist from 1701/2 to 1710/11, and as Bursar in 1706/7 to 1707/8. Hudson's scholarly career is interesting because he remained a classicist. Thomas Cockman, who produced no more classical works after 1699, turning instead to theology, was more typical.[12]

Another talented Fellow who had to leave the College prematurely was Joseph Bingham (m. 1684; F. 1689–95). On St Simon and St Jude's day (28 October) 1695, he preached a sermon which, it was claimed, questioned the doctrine of the Trinity, and he was accused of heresy before the Chancellor's Court. Bingham had little choice but to resign his Fellowship. Charlett and the College, however, generously allowed him to retain his stipend for a few months after his resignation. Furthermore, John Radcliffe had already helped out a College man. In 1693 he had acquired the living of Headbourne Worthy (Plate 7), an attractive village just outside Winchester, and earlier in 1695 had installed Bingham as rector, thus giving him the security to work on his *magnum opus*, the *Origines Ecclesiasticae*, an account of the early history of the church which has been called 'perhaps the most learned work of early ecclesiastical history published before the nineteenth century'.[13]

---

[11] Charlett and literature and art: Gillam 1999: 424; New Year Books at Christ Church: Bill 1988: 255; Charlett's books: Carter 1975: 422 and 424; Thomas Cockman's books: Cockman 1695, 1696, and 1699.
[12] Hudson as Tutor: entries in UC:J1/A/1 and Hearne, i. 215; his scholarship: Clarke 1986: 528–30; Hudson as Librarian: Philip 1986: 728–30.
[13] Bingham's sermon: UC:AR2/MS1/11 pp. 190–1, and Hearne, i. 114; his resignation: UC:GB3/A1/1 p. 132; Radcliffe's aid: Guest 1991: 24–5; Bingham's scholarship: Bennett 1986c: 397.

Another kind of scholarship was displayed by Robert Clavering from Lincoln College, elected Fellow in 1697. Clavering became an eminent Hebrew scholar, being appointed Regius Professor of Hebrew in 1715. When in 1708 verses were composed by the university, mainly in Latin and Greek, to mark the death of Queen Anne's husband, Prince George, Clavering composed one in Hebrew which has been especially praised for its technical skill.[14]

Nevertheless, it was antiquarianism and Anglo-Saxon which gained the College most prestige in the 1690s, and which engaged Charlett's enthusiasm most keenly. He had a coin cabinet, and possessed a flint hand-axe (now in the British Museum). He naturally took an interest in King Alfred. Early in the 1690s, a new College benefactors' book was created, and the first benefaction is that of King Alfred, made in c.870 [sic], while William of Durham was merely the re-founder of the College in c.1200 [sic]. The front page is adorned with a picture of Alfred and William side by side (Fig. 11.1). The College even affected Alfred's iconography: a new edition of Asser's life published in 1722 included an engraving of the king by George Vertue based on the portrait commissioned by Thomas Walker in the 1660s. Vertue's engraving in turn influenced portrayals of the King for the rest of the century.[15]

Charlett pulled strings to import two significant antiquarians to University College. The first was William Elstob, a member of Queen's College, who was elected a Fellow in July 1696. The Fellowship, however, had actually fallen vacant in April 1695, and Elstob was not formally admitted a Fellow until January 1698, much later than was customary. The reason for this anomaly, according to William Smith, was that Elstob, too young to be ordained, concealed his age, and so the election and admission had to be delayed until he was old enough. Charlett's hand is clear in this: on learning of Elstob's deception, he could easily have had his election quashed, but instead chose to wait. Fortunately, Elstob became one of the most eminent Anglo-Saxon scholars of his generation, and only his early death in 1715 prevented him from fulfilling his potential.[16]

The second scholar was Humfrey Wanley, who had matriculated from St Edmund Hall in 1695, and come to Charlett's notice. As Thomas Hearne tells it:

Charlett wheedling him, & Wanley being naturally of an unsettled temper, presently left Edm. Hall, having been but at one Lecture with his Tutor, and that was in Logick,

---

[14] Patterson 1986: 537–8 and 547–8, and Clavering's *ODNB* entry.
[15] Charlett's coins: Hearne, i. 175; his flint axe: Piggott 1986: 759; Anglo-Saxon studies in general: Fairer 1986: 807–24, Keynes 1999: 266–8, and Sweet 2004: 189–91; the benefactors' book: UC:BE1/MS1/1; the Vertue engraving: Keynes 1999: 271–2.
[16] Elstob's election: UC:GB3/A1/1 pp. 131–4 and UC:AR2/MS1/11 pp. 191–2 and 194; Elstob's later career: *ODNB* entry (his sister Elizabeth was also an Anglo-Saxon scholar, but is not known to have had any dealings with University College).

FIGURE 11.1 The first page of a Benefactors' Book produced in the 1690s, showing King Alfred and William of Durham side by side.

which he swore he could not comprehend, saying, 'By God, Mr. Milles,...I do not, cannot, understand it', & so came no more, & entered himself at University Coll. [in January 1696], under Dr. Charlett, in whose Lodgings he lay.[17]

Wanley never did return to logic, and so never completed his degree. Instead, under Charlett's patronage, he worked in the Bodleian, becoming arguably the greatest palaeographer of his day. When the Society of Antiquaries was founded in 1707, its earliest members included both Humfrey Wanley and William Elstob.[18]

Another member of the College who revealed his antiquarian worth in the 1690s was William Smith (Fig. 11.2), who was exploring the College's history, and sorting, cataloguing, and transcribing its archives. He proved a brilliant archivist, equal to any of his contemporaries in his palaeography and his ability to interpret and order archival material. All later historians of University College owe him an incalculable debt. Even Thomas Hearne, readily jealous of rival antiquarians, admitted that Smith was 'a severe Student, & is well skill'd in our English Antiquities, particularly those relating to Oxford'. Unfortunately, Smith's research led him to question King Alfred's links with the College, although for now he kept his views largely private.[19]

In addition to creating a distinguished circle of scholars in the College, Charlett found opportunities to support scholarship elsewhere. He was a Visitor of the Ashmolean Museum, and from 1694 a Delegate of the University Press. In the latter post especially, he revealed an energy shared by few of his colleagues. He was eager to publish new works, and also market them,

---

[17] Wanley changes College: Hearne, ix. 161 and UC:J1/A/1 p. 18.
[18] Wanley: *ODNB* entry and Gillam 1999; Society of Antiquaries: Sweet 2004: 84.
[19] Hearne on Smith: Hearne, i. 201.

FIGURE 11.2 William Smith, m. 1668, Fellow 1675–1705, and Rector of Melsonby, 1704–35 (copy made in 1917 of an original portrait in Melsonby Rectory).

regularly circulating leaflets listing the Press's publications. He even revealed artistic ambitions, when he designed the Oxford Almanack of 1703.[20]

Among the scholars whom Charlett patronized was Thomas Tanner, an undergraduate at Queen's and a promising young antiquarian, whom he helped become Chaplain at All Souls, and whom he encouraged, along with a group of other young scholars, to produce a catalogue of the Bodleian's manuscripts. He helped George Hickes get his groundbreaking study of Old English and early German language and history published by the University Press. There was also Thomas Hearne, who devoted his life to publishing medieval texts, and some of whose diary entries we have already encountered. Although Hearne was a member of St Edmund Hall, he knew Charlett, John Hudson, and other members of University College well, and wrote about them to devastating effect in his diary. Charlett regularly discussed antiquarian matters with Hearne, often showing him a new document or curiosity, and the two men enjoyed a complex relationship over many years.[21]

---

[20] The Ashmolean: Macgregor and Turner 1986: 648–9; the Press: Philip 1986: 752–4, and Carter 1975: 150–1, 170, and 177; Charlett's Almanack: Petter 1974: 42.

[21] Tanner: Sharpe 2005: 382–5; Hickes: *ODNB* entry; Charlett and Hearne: Harmsen 2000: 33–92. Several of Charlett's protégés were members of Queen's or St Edmund Hall; John Hudson and Hugh Todd, both former Queen's men, may have drawn these men to Charlett's attention.

Perhaps Charlett's greatest contribution to antiquarian scholarship in the 1690s was to support Edmund Gibson's revision of William Camden's *Britannia*, published in 1695. Gibson, a young member of Queen's, assembled many scholars, including Hugh Todd, who updated the section on Cumberland, and even the aged Obadiah Walker, who contributed notes on early coins. Charlett, however, helped in the background, using his contacts to smooth Gibson's path. When the book was published to wide acclaim, it will have done Charlett no harm that Gibson ended his list of acknowledgements:

But Dr. Charlett, the worthy Master of University-College in Oxford, has been our *general* benefactor; whom this Work (as all other publick Undertakings) has from beginning to end found its greatest Promoter.[22]

Above all, Charlett was the supreme correspondent, as witnessed by his assembled papers, now in the Bodleian Library. Continental scholars could also find Charlett willing and able to help them obtain books published in England, and arrange introductions when visiting, in return for helping him find foreign publications. Charlett also relied for news on friends travelling abroad, such as William Ayerst (Gunsley Scholar 1698–1716), who, when chaplain to the Embassy at Berlin, passed on all the latest court gossip.[23]

Within College, although he could show a certain cheerful informality, Charlett sought to tighten discipline. Rules that all undergraduates and Fellows should take dinner and supper in the Hall were enforced; it became expected that, in Chapel, Scholars should stand when the Master entered. Absentee Scholars were ordered to return to College, or else face expulsion—a sanction not infrequently employed. Charlett also introduced some innovations. University College, unusually, had never created a separate table for Scholars, but instead members sat according to their status as BA, commoner, or servitor. In 1693 Charlett introduced a Scholars' table, despite some Fellows (including William Smith) protesting that this innovation would create ill will between Scholars and commoners. The arrangement became permanent, and by the late 1720s, Buttery Books listed all the Scholars in one group.[24]

Charlett also spent over £200 of his own money on improving the Master's Lodgings. Meanwhile, the Common Room was wainscotted in 1696/7, and given new sash windows, Albemarle Bertie paying for over a third of the costs. The main work of the 1690s, however, was in the Chapel. Not only was its floor paved in marble, but in 1694, to create more seating, Robert Barker, a

---

[22] Camden 1695: Preface to the Reader. The additions by Todd to Cumberland are at pp. 840–6, and Walker's numismatic notes at xci–xcvi, c–cii, and cxxxv–clii. Bodl. MS Ballard 5 contains many letters from Gibson to Charlett concerning *Britannia*.

[23] Charlett's incoming correspondence is now part of Bodl. MS Ballard. Ayerst's letters: Bodl. MS Ballard 27 fos. 25–59 (some of these are published in Doble 1888–9).

[24] Attendance in Hall; Hearne, i. 224; standing for the Master: Usher 1699: 3; absentee Scholars: UC:GB3/A1/1 pp. 133, 147, and 172; the Scholars' table: Bodl. MS Ballard 16 fo. 21^r (letter of William Smith from 1693) and UC:BU4/F/16.

London joiner, dismantled the Chapel's existing screen (barely thirty years old), and erected a magnificent new one further west which halved the Antechapel in size (and separated van Linge's two New Testament windows). Installing the new screen would have required alterations to the Chapel's wainscotting and seating, but it is not known how many existing pews date back to the 1660s, or to this rebuilding. All we know is that the whole project cost over £500. As before, the College looked to its own to find the money: Charlett set an example by giving £20, and other Fellows gave between £5 and £30, but Albemarle Bertie gave £40, the largest donation of all. One undergraduate, Edward Jeffreys (m. 1694), made a special gift. At the east end of the north side is a niche the same size and shape as the windows. Jeffreys paid for a painting here depicting the tale of Lot's wife (a subject which matched the windows' themes of obedience and disobedience). The artist was Henry Cook, a pupil of Salvator Rosa, who also painted a picture above the altar of New College.[25]

Charlett also threw himself enthusiastically into university politics. This was a difficult time: most members of Oxford were Tories, supporting a close union between the Crown and the Church of England, which would repel the twin demons of excessive Parliamentary power, and the toleration of Dissenters and Catholics. James II's Catholicism had proved a terrible dilemma for the Tories, his expulsion a still greater one. For all James's faults, he was a divinely anointed monarch, who could not simply be turned in, as faulty goods, for something better. Some Tories, the so-called 'non-jurors', refused therefore to swear allegiance to William III and Mary II, and retreated from public life. After James II's death in 1701, they turned to James's son, whom they proclaimed as 'James III' (known better to posterity as the Old Pretender), and thus acquired the name of Jacobites. The majority, however, accepted the new regime, with varying degrees of lack of enthusiasm.[26]

The Master and Fellows of University College accepted the change, although their true opinions sometimes slipped out. In 1707, Thomas Hearne, a passionate Jacobite, praised John Nevile (F. 1695–1708) for his 'staunch [i.e. near-Jacobite] principles', and in April 1708, an informant told Charlett:

Somebody or other has given an Account of that very great Indiscretion, which was reported of Dr. Hudson, that he drank the Pretenders Health & Success, which has open'd the Mouths of many against the University.[27]

---

[25] Improvements to the Lodgings: Hearne, i. 215; Common Room: UC:FA3/4/F1/1; Barker's contract and bill for the new screen: UC:FA5/1/F2/2 & 5; benefactions to the Chapel: UC:BE1/MS1/1 pp. 50–5. Cook's painting was painted over, probably in the 1860s, but in 1929 some fragments were rediscovered, which the then Master, Sir Michael Sadler, drew (UC:FA5/3/P2/1-2; also *UCR* 1928/9, pp. 6–7 and *UCR* 1954/5, p. 67).
[26] For the wider Oxford context, see Bennett 1986*a* and 1986*b*.
[27] Nevile: Hearne, ii. 17; Hudson: Bodl. MS Ballard 8 fo. 126^v.

Others were closer still to danger: John Radcliffe had a reputation for Jacobitism; the father of William Standfast (m. 1698; F. 1713–22) was a non-juror, and was briefly imprisoned; and some undergraduates became non-jurors themselves, such as Richard Russell (m. 1698), who, when visiting Oxford in 1717, met his former Tutor (now a loyal Hanoverian) John Hudson, to the latter's discomfiture, and Thomas Hearne's amusement.[28]

Charlett himself, his ambition forbidding him from throwing up his position in Oxford, chose a middle way. He became a major figure in the university, regularly serving as Pro-Vice-Chancellor, and involving himself in Parliamentary elections, often backing the winner (usually a moderate Tory), and occasionally (as in 1701 and 1703) selecting the successful candidate himself. Some preferment even came Charlett's way when, after the 1695 election, he was made a royal chaplain.[29]

But Charlett was playing a double game. Significantly, Anglo-Saxon studies tended to attract non-jurors or Jacobites, like Thomas Hearne and George Hickes. Hickes, indeed, was outlawed for much of the 1690s, and lived in hiding; yet Charlett and Hickes were in correspondence during this time (a fact which could have put Charlett in serious trouble). Hickes and Hearne, however, were outside University College: by keeping his College outwardly loyal, Charlett was trying to have his cake and eat it.[30]

In the 1690s Charlett was in the ascendant. Surrounded by a distinguished Fellowship and many influential friends, he made University College an attractive place again. Admissions rose to heights not seen in decades, climaxing in 1694, when thirty-five undergraduates were admitted (Graph 10.1). To be sure, it had yet to attract many well-born members: in the decade before July 1692, the College's Admission Register shows 54.5 per cent of undergraduates being admitted as commoners, 29 per cent as servitors, and 16.5 per cent as gentlemen commoners or higher, while for the first six years of Charlett's Mastership, the same figures were 61 per cent, 22 per cent, and 17 per cent respectively. Nevertheless, as the College's reputation grew, so might its status.

'THE EVIL SPIRIT THAT HAUNTED THE MASTER': 1698–1711

In 1706, Thomas Hearne commented on Charlett:

At his first coming to ye College, ... he kept up ye Discipline & Exercise of ye House very well, by wch means it flourish'd equally to any House in ye University: but afterwards it declin'd very much partly by ye Remissness of ye Master, & partly by Dr. Hudson's quitting his Pupils when he was made the Bodlejan Library Keeper.[31]

---

[28] Radcliffe: Monod 1989: 280; Standfast: Hearne, iv. 152; Russell: Hearne, vi. 263 and 267.
[29] The 1695, 1698, and 1701 elections: Bennett 1986a: 49, 54–5, and 59; the 1703 election: Bennett 1986b: 71; the wider context: Ward 1958: 11–51.
[30] Jacobite antiquarians: Sweet 2004: 200–2; Hickes's letters to Charlett: Bodl. MS Ballard 12.
[31] Hearne, i. 215.

Two decades later, William Smith observed:

> Dr. *Charlet*...being bred in another COLLEGE, and under different Statutes (where the President in some Cases has a Negative Voice) could not well be inured to govern himself, nor the Fellows by our own Statutes.[32]

How had the high hopes of the 1690s come to this? First of all, Charlett's informality sometimes made him look ridiculous, especially after drinking. Once, Charlett's servant escorted the tipsy Master home from a dinner at New College holding up a silver tankard rather than a lantern. His manner was easy to parody: in April 1711, issue no. 43 of the *Spectator* comprised a pompous and discursive letter from Oxford from one 'Abraham Froth'. Oxford gossip quickly identified 'Froth' as Arthur Charlett: Thomas Hearne thought 'the Letter personates him incomparably well'.[33] These incidents, however, were just embarrassing. Far more alarming was an affair in 1698 which revealed how incapable the Master could be of governing himself.

In May that year a Fellowship fell vacant.[34] There were two leading contenders for the post, William Denison (m. 1693) and Charles Usher (m. 1692); Charlett made it clear that he preferred Denison. Usher was not surprised: he had long suspected that the Master disliked him. Indeed he had already lost one Fellowship election, and John Hudson, his Tutor, had advised Usher to migrate to another college, to try for a fellowship there.[35]

Usher never understood what he had done to Charlett; nor did William Smith, who wrote:

> [Charlett's] Objection to me was, *That he thought him* [Usher] *not so good a Scholar as another Candidate was*: Which upon Examination of both Parties, proved a Mistake. Another Objection was, *That he had* (it may be) *twice or thrice knocked to com in, after the Gates were shut*; Which...used not be looked upon as a very heinous Crime.[36]

No less dangerous for Usher was the antipathy of the College butler, John Pricket. The first College servant to emerge as a character in his own right, Pricket had worked for it at least since 1673/4, when he had been its barber, and he had been appointed its butler in 1683. He had a boisterous, if not dangerous, sense of humour: he was said once to have cut someone's tongue, in order to help him speak French (William Elstob was sufficiently amused to write a poem about it). He also became closely associated with Charlett himself. One gossipy observer, Nicholas Amherst, claimed that Charlett 'was many years directed in all his proceedings, public and private, by his

---

[32] Smith, 260.
[33] The tankard: Hearne, i. 215; 'Abraham Froth': Hearne, iii. 154; another parody of Charlett is given in Money 1998: 280–4.
[34] Much of what follows is drawn from Usher 1699: 2–11.
[35] Fellowship election in 1697: UC:GB3/A1/1 pp. 133–4.
[36] Smith, 271–2.

butler'. This had sinister implications. Charles Usher feared that, after one row too many with the butler, in which Usher allegedly called him 'Pimp Master generall to the Lodgings', Pricket had begun to poison the Master's mind.[37]

In his efforts to block Usher's election, Charlett called in old debts. Humfrey Wanley expressed his support for Denison, and Edmund Gibson willingly engaged himself to lobby wavering Fellows (like Elstob) to support Denison, even advising some that the journey to Oxford was not worthwhile. Usher, however, still commanded a majority, and so Charlett employed blacker arts. On the day before the election, Usher was summoned to the Lodgings where one of the Master's protégés, Richard Wood (m. 1692), claimed that, in his hearing, Usher had said that Charlett 'was as familiar' with John Laurence (m. 1694) as he was with Thomas Tanner, thus hinting that Charlett was homosexual. The next day, Wood went further, claiming that Usher said 'The Master us'd to *Ride such an one.*' Usher admitted that he had heard a joke about Charlett and some unnamed editors which could be construed in that way, but that was all.[38]

The Fellows were suspicious, especially when Charlett claimed that Denison could testify against Usher. When, therefore, the election was held on 16 December 1698, four Fellows (including Albemarle Bertie) voted for Usher, and three abstained. Only the Master and William Smith voted for Denison. Charlett, refusing to admit defeat, appealed to the Visitors (i.e. his colleagues on the Hebdomadal Council), and, with the support of Thomas Bouchier, the Regius Professor of Civil Law, persuaded them to set aside Usher's election. On 23 December a fresh election was held, at which Elstob and Hudson now also voted for Denison. The other Fellows did not participate.[39]

While Edmund Gibson promptly congratulated Charlett on his success, Usher no less promptly appealed to Convocation, as supposedly being the true Visitors of the College, but suddenly found himself accused before the Chancellor's Court of uttering defamatory words against the Master. The case was heard on 18 and 19 January 1699. Humfrey Wanley, Richard Wood, John Pricket, and William Denison were the chief witnesses against Usher, while two Fellows, Albemarle Bertie and John Hinckley, defended him.[40]

The depositions made against Usher are plausible and indeed dramatic, but they do not bear closer scrutiny. The language was now more colourful— Usher was accused of saying that the Master 'did Use to Roger, Clapperclaw

---

[37] College barber: UC:BU3/F2/2; butler: UC:GB3/A1/1 p. 105; Elstob's poem: Hearne, i. 107–9; Amherst on Pricket: Amherst 1754: 65; row with Usher: OUA CC Papers 1699/1: 6.

[38] Wanley: Bodl. MS Ballard 13 fo. 68^r; Gibson: MS Ballard 5 fos. 136–7 and 140^r; Charlett's alleged homosexuality (which remains uncorroborated): Usher 1699: 7–8 and OUA CC Papers 1699/1: 1–12.

[39] The elections: UC:GB3/A1/1 pp. 135–6 and UC:AR2/MS1/11 pp. 195–6.

[40] Gibson: Bodl. MS Ballard 5 fo. 144^r (letter of 27 December 1698); the Vice-Chancellor's court case: Usher 1699: 18–22, UC:GB3/A1/1 p. 135–7, UC:AR2/MS1/11 pp. 195–9, and OUA CC Papers 1699/1: 1–12.

& Ride Tom Tanner'—and of course one witness, Denison, stood to benefit from Usher's defeat. When challenged on this point, Denison demurely replied that 'he was very much surprised' at the charge. Speaking in his defence, Usher tellingly observed that the case was heard when most undergraduates (including several of his supporters) were out of town. Even John Laurence, supposedly libelled by Usher, wrote to say that he remembered no such rumours, and wished 'to free you [Usher] from any aspersions that may be laid on you for any misbehaviour in your discourse to me'. Nevertheless, the Vice-Chancellor found in favour of Charlett: despite a vain appeal to the King's Bench, Usher was expelled from the university.[41]

It took time for the consequences of Charlett's behaviour during these extraordinary weeks to emerge. The ever-supportive Edmund Gibson promised to give Charlett's side of the tale to all who would listen, and another friend spotted Usher looking 'pensive and dissatisfy'd' at a dinner in May 1700. When Usher published a pamphlet defending himself, Charlett and his supporters allegedly tried to buy up and destroy all the copies they could find.[42]

Others were displeased to see Charlett using his patronage of scholars like Gibson and Wanley for such sordid ends. Hugh Todd, now resident in Cumberland, wrote to the Vice-Chancellor in March 1699, regretting that 'things were gone to such Extremities' that compromise was impossible. Five Fellows of the College were listed in Usher's pamphlet as his supporters, and the atmosphere grew unpleasant. Writing to Albemarle Bertie in February 1699, John Hinckley observed 'I shall always be glad to have a finger in any suit commenced against the Master and his Doctors [i.e. the Hebdomadal Council], as hating the tyranny of the one and the usurpation of the other.' Hinckley abandoned Oxford, and in February 1701, when he had been absent without leave for five terms, the Fellows deprived him of his Fellowship.[43]

Reflecting on the Usher affair in 1706, Thomas Hearne claimed that it had resulted in 'the Great amazement of all truely Honest Men in the University & the no small Disgrace of the Master himself.' He was not alone in this analysis: William Smith later confessed that 'I suffered much in my Reputation in the University, for being imagined an Assistant to [Charlett] in his so doing.' After Charlett's death Hugh Todd wrote that he 'was sensible of his Error as long as he liv'd: it put a stop to his Promotion effectually'—and indeed, Charlett appears never to have achieved any preferment after 1699.

---

[41] Colourful language: OUA CC Papers 1699/1:2; Denison: OUA CC Papers 1699/1:7; Usher: OUA CC Papers 1699/1:9; Laurence: OUA CC Papers 1699/1:10; the verdict: OUA CC Papers 1699/1:8.

[42] Gibson: Bodl. MS Ballard 5 fo. 146 (5 January 1699); Usher unhappy: Bodl. MS Ballard 4 fo. 6; buying up the pamphlet: Hearne, ix. 10.

[43] Todd: Bodl. MS Ballard 18 fo. 18ᵛ; Usher's supporters: Usher 1699: 31; Hinckley's letter: uncatalogued papers on the Usher affair (the letter is dated '1699', but the context suggests that Hinckley meant 1699 rather than 1699/1700); his departure: UC:GB3/A1/1 p. 138 and UC:AR2/MS1/11 pp. 201–2.

Meanwhile Humfrey Wanley left Oxford in 1700 on poor terms with Charlett: as late as 1718, Thomas Tanner could write to Charlett of 'that Mr. W. who so basely abused the freedom you gave him of your Lodgings'. Meanwhile Charles Usher himself did not suffer unduly. He entered the law, and, in 1725, Hearne heard that he was a well-respected member of the Council of the City of London.[44]

More prudent men might have questioned the wisdom of yielding to such self-destructive wrath. Prudence, however, was not one of Charlett's virtues, and only two years after expelling Usher he attacked Albemarle Bertie. There was much about Bertie to arouse Charlett's envy: as an Earl's son, he did not need Charlett's patronage; in 1692 he had been considered for the Mastership—William Smith claimed that Bertie 'wanted nothing but Years to have been preferred...before a mere Foreigner'—and had pointedly not voted for Charlett; he had been a generous donor to the College; and when William III visited Oxford in 1695, Bertie led a group of scholars and gentlemen who rode before him. Bertie's support for Usher was the last straw.[45]

Charlett found a subtle weapon. In 1667 John Fell had decreed that Fellows of University College should be ordained deacons within four years of becoming an MA on pain of expulsion. Bertie, MA since 1692, had remained a layman. Therefore, at prayers on 10 July 1701, Charlett suddenly announced to the Fellows that Bertie's Fellowship was vacant because he had not taken orders, and deleted his name from the Buttery Book. No vote was requested. This time Charlett had overreached himself, as the Fellows unanimously appealed to the Visitors. Bertie's defence that, as a Bennet Fellow, he was not bound by a statute applicable only to the older Fellowships proved persuasive: the Visitors reinstated Bertie, on the understanding that he took orders within the next two years.[46]

The result was anticlimactic. Bertie remained a Fellow until he resigned voluntarily in January 1721. He did not take orders, but Charlett let him be. He did withdraw from College life, however, serving instead as an MP for Lincolnshire in 1705–8 and Cockermouth in 1708–10, and as Auditor of the Duchy of Cornwall for 1704–13.[47]

Charlett also played the bully elsewhere. In 1709, Thomas Hearne published the original English text of Spelman's life of Alfred (p. 200), but did not dedicate it to Charlett, who furiously claimed this as an affront to him and the College, and briefly refused to speak to Hearne. On learning that a

---

[44] Hearne: Hearne, i. 116: Smith: Smith, 271; Todd: Bodl. MS Ballard 18 fo. 25ʳ; Wanley: Bodl. MS Ballard 4 fo. 67ʳ and Gillam 1999; Usher in London: Hearne, ix. 10.

[45] Bertie as Master: Smith, 185; meeting William III: Wood, *Life* iii. 494.

[46] Bertie's expulsion: UC:AR2/MS1/11 pp. 204–5 and Smith, 284–5 (the pages of the College Register which might have recorded these events are significantly left blank).

[47] Bertie's resignation: UC:GB3/A1/1 p. 175; his later career: *AO1* (although its claim that he became a fellow of All Souls is untrue).

Fellow had invited Hearne to dine in College, Charlett petulantly said that he would not go to Hall if 'that Person dined there'.[48]

Meanwhile, some Fellows were moving on. William Elstob resigned his Fellowship in 1704, and William Smith did so the following year. Smith had already engineered a happy retirement for himself when in 1692 the College had purchased the living of Melsonby, an attractive parish in Yorkshire, near Richmond and the Great North Road, and close to Smith's home village of Easby. The College would have a different relationship with Melsonby from Arncliffe or Flamstead, because it possessed only the right of presenting a rector, and had no financial claims there, leaving the incumbent free to enjoy all the income from the parish. Livings like Melsonby were therefore enticing prospects for the Fellow in search of preferment or retirement. Smith was deeply involved in the acquisition of Melsonby, and—unsurprisingly—was presented there when it fell vacant in 1704. Thomas Hearne claims that Smith hoped to retain his Fellowship, but his colleagues successfully argued that Melsonby was too wealthy a parish, and Smith had to resign his post in November 1705. He left for Melsonby in June 1706, having completed his work in the archives. He said little about his enforced departure in his history, but he did say of Charlett, that 'whilst I tarried in the COLLEGE, he kept himself, or was kept by others, within some Bounds; but shewed his Temper to the full, when I was once removed from that Society'.[49]

Some retained their Fellowships, but went out of residence, like John Boraston, one of Charlett's former supporters, who withdrew to a small living in Kent. Visiting Oxford in 1700, he found himself present at a Fellowship election where his vote proved to be crucial. Writing to Charlett some years later, Boraston remembered:

You told me that you thought it *unjust* that one who did not live amongst 'em and consequently must be unacquainted with ye Candidates' characters...should vote of any side; & *imprudent* that one who was oblig'd to ye whole Society should make himself a part in opposing any of it.[50]

One can understand why Boraston wished to escape such bullying.

John Hudson, meanwhile, stayed until in 1711 the Chancellor appointed him Principal of St Mary Hall (subsequently incorporated into Oriel College). He resigned his Fellowship gracefully, offering a 'Genteel Treat' to the Master, Fellows, MAs, and gentlemen commoners.[51]

---

[48] Hearne's book: Hearne, ii. 179–83; Charlett's petulance: Hearne, ii. 332.
[49] Purchase of Melsonby: Pyx κ fasc. 1; Smith's presentation: UC:GB3A1/1 pp. 145–6; his resignation: UC:GB3/A1/1 p. 152: Hearne's gossip: Hearne, i. 42, 62, and 260; Smith on Charlett: Smith, 261 (the events of 1698–1701 suggest that his memory was selective).
[50] Bodl. MS Ballard 16 fo. 172[r].
[51] Hearne, iii. 177.

One of the more impressive new Fellows was Thomas Cockman (F. 1700–13), whose publications we encountered earlier. Cockman took his pastoral duties seriously. In the preface to his translation of *De Officiis*, he wrote to his dedicatees, two gentlemen commoners of University College, that the book was 'designed for a Person in your Circumstances, a student in a University, a young Gentleman of great Hopes, one from whom his Country did expect to receive Benefit, and his Friends no small Comfort and Satisfaction'. In 1706, when acting as a private tutor, he wrote to Charlett that his pupil's mother:

very earnestly insists upon my staying & says I doe her Son & family the greatest Service y^t any body can doe; because by a sort of gravity and seriousness of my temper I have some kind of awe over ye young Spark himself & over some company wch he must keep, who as she apprehends...would be glad to spoil him.[52]

Even William Denison turned out fairly well; in 1709, he was appointed public Praelector in Grammar to the university; he served as Proctor for 1710/11; and in the election for the Camden Professorship of History in 1720, he came runner-up. Unfortunately, his relations with Charlett were not always smooth: he became Charlett's curate at the latter's living of Hambledon, but left in 1716 after a quarrel.[53]

On the other hand, there was Francis Rogers (m. 1708; F. 1713–38), who in 1711 published a distinctly mediocre selection of speeches from Latin poetry, dedicated to Charlett. Thomas Hearne was justly scathing—"'tis a most silly ridiculous performance,...done meerly for School-Boys, & yet not done so as to be of use to them'. Nevertheless, Rogers remained in the Master's favour, and two years later was elected Fellow. His academic talents failed to improve: in 1717, Hearne noted that Rogers gave a 'short and poor' sermon, and also that he was 'noted for Shooting'.[54]

Rogers was merely mediocre. More embarrassing was George 'Jolly' Ward (m. 1702; F. 1708–33), the most outrageously Rabelaisian figure whom the College ever elected to a Fellowship. Ward first achieved prominence in 1704, when, after a Scholarship election, there was a drinking party which led to 'arguments and fights'. Whilst the three Scholars-elect were punished by having to wait an extra month before changing status, one existing Scholar was also singled out, losing his emoluments for a month. That Scholar was George Ward.[55]

Gossip recorded Ward's activities with relish. In May 1716, he was caught in his rooms with a 'common strumpet' at the time of evening service, but escaped punishment through the Master's favour. Hearne claimed that Ward had also 'most scandalously debauched the present Young Lord Brooke,...& they

[52] Bodl. MS Ballard 21 fo. 129^r.
[53] Praelectorship: UC:GB3/A1/1 p. 160; Proctor: Hearne, ii.350; Professorship: Hearne, vii. 124–5: quarrel: Hearne, v. 255.
[54] Rogers's book: Rogers 1711: reactions: Hearne, iii. 132–3; Rogers's preaching and shooting: Hearne, vi. 102.
[55] Drunken party: UC:GB3/A1/1 p. 147.

enjoy their Whores (as I am informed) in common'. Ward, it was said, had married an alehouse keeper's daughter, and the Widow Stevens, whom he retained as his bedmaker even after the College dismissed her on account of her louche reputation, was seen emerging from Ward's rooms at unexpected hours of the day. Ward's finances were also scandalous. In 1718 he owed £116 for unpaid lottery tickets, and in 1719 he was ordered to repay a bond worth £322. In 1727 the profits from Ward's Fellowship were being sequestered to pay his debts, and, it was claimed, fear of arrest confined him to the College except on Sundays.[56]

Yet Ward managed to escape punishment because he enjoyed Charlett's favour. Apart from a certain boozy good-fellowship, which attracted him to Professor Thomas Bouchier and his son James, he knew the value of a timely gift. In October 1709, Ward's brother gave a statue of Queen Anne which was set over the entrance to the College. Wits saw through this gesture, and an extempore epigram mocked Charlett's obvious eagerness for preferment:

> O Arthur, Oh! in vain thou tryes
> By merits of this Statue for to rise.
> Thou'lt ne're an Exaltation have
> But that on Prickett's shoulders to the Grave.[57]

Ward's merry carousings in 1704 were not the only corroboration of Hearne's concerns about undergraduate discipline. Thomas Fletcher, a Gunsley Scholar, beat up a Proctor in December 1711, and was expelled from the College outright; and in 1717 John Anderdon (m. 1713), was fined by the Chancellor's Court for going to the house of one Richard Gourdon with some friends, asking loudly for a whore, and, when Gourdon replied that no such people lived there, beating him up.[58]

A more spiteful example of undergraduate misbehaviour had occurred in 1706/7. John Hudson, then Bursar, had the College gardens replanted and repaved. When the work was done, Thomas Hearne claimed that:

No one of the College appear'd at present displeas'd with it but the Master; which perhaps being known to one Robinson (a Commoner of that House, & Nephew to Mr. Smith [William Robinson, m. 1704]) a day or two after it was finish'd with two or three more of the College got into the Garden in the Night time, pull'd up some of the Ews, spoil'd others & did other Mischief, to the no small Grief of the Doctor & the rest of the Fellows.[59]

Not all undergraduates were so delinquent. Michael Ainsworth (m. 1707) was the protégé of the Earl of Shaftesbury, who sent him letters of useful

---

[56] Caught in his rooms: Hearne, v. 228; marriage and the Widow Stevens: OUA CC Papers 1727/29:4; debts: OUA CC Papers 1718/42:1–7 and 1719/52:1–7, and 1727/29:4.
[57] Hearne, ii. 273.
[58] Fletcher: UC:GB3/A1/1 p. 164 and Hearne, iii. 286; Anderdon: OUA CC Papers 1717/74:1–8.
[59] Hearne, i. 223.

advice. Warning Ainsworth at the outset against the 'narrow Principles and contagious Manners of those corrupted Places, whence all noble and *free* Principles ought rather to be propagated', the Earl asked to be kept informed of the books he was reading, giving advice on what to read, and even suggesting walking as the best form of exercise.[60]

A more complex case of undergraduate supervision is that of Henry Harcourt, entered as a gentleman commoner in 1696. Harcourt's father, Simon, hoped that Henry would study for three or four hours a day, and asked Charlett for examples of his work. Unfortunately, in October 1697, Simon Harcourt learned that his son 'refuses to do his Exercise, & if done at all, it is with so much difficulty and trouble to you, that I am ashamed of it'. Grumbling that he had made a mistake in entering his son as a gentleman commoner, he urged Charlett to threaten his son with withdrawal from the College unless he improved. Fortunately, Harcourt junior mended his ways.[61]

Interestingly, Charlett appeared reluctant to tell Simon Harcourt about his son's misbehaviour, and it was left to others to inform him. Henry's status as a gentleman commoner is the key. Jonas Radcliffe, a century earlier, favouring the 'better' above the 'gentler' man, was praised for making all his pupils work, irrespective of their status, but now it was thought inappropriate to work well-born students too hard, lest they acquire a pedantry which ill became them. This could become an excuse for a gentleman commoner to do no work at all.

Unfortunately, Charlett was rather less deferential to his Fellows. In 1711, as William Smith put it, 'the same evil Spirit that haunted the Master before, fell upon him again', as Charlett attacked another Fellow, Thomas Allen. Elected in 1693, Allen had antiquarian interests and was a friend of Thomas Hearne. Although apparently no troublemaker, he somehow aroused Charlett's enmity, and Charlett determined to drive him out. In March 1711, Allen was forbidden from voting in a Scholarship election, because six months had passed since his appointment to a living worth more than the statutory limit, and within two months he was deprived of his Fellowship. There was chicanery here: Fellows were usually granted a year's grace in such circumstances, but Charlett persuaded the Visitors to shorten the term to six months. Hearne and Smith suspected that the statute had been invented to drive Allen out, and rightly so: it was never used again, and in his study of Oxford, John Ayliffe, who used Charlett as a source, claimed that the term of grace required of Fellows of University College was one year.[62]

---

[60] Shaftesbury 1716: 7–8 and 20–4.
[61] Bodl. MS Ballard 10 fos. 97^{r-v} (advice on work), 100^{r-v} (concern at laziness), and 102^{r}–104^{v} (mending ways).
[62] 'Evil Spirit': Smith, 186; Allen's expulsion: UC:GB3/A1/1 pp. 161–2; Hearne's and Smith's reflections: Hearne, iii. 125–6, 167–8, and 186–91 and Smith, 292–3; one year and not six months: Ayliffe 1723: 258.

Charlett's temper may have been affected by his poor health: in 1694 he was visiting Bath for a cure, and in November 1700, a Scholarship election was postponed because the Master was ill with rheumatism. For the rest of his life, Charlett visited Bath regularly (visits which cannot have helped him supervise College life effectively). Meanwhile, his financial expectations were frustrated. He invested half of his uncle's gift of £1,000 in purchasing the advowson of Hambledon, to which he presented himself in 1707, but this use of the money displeased Charlett's uncle, who bequeathed his estate elsewhere. William Smith will have spoken for others when he waspishly wrote that the Fellows 'chose him, in Expectancy of his being a great Benefactor...[but] I think he lived to be his own Heir'.[63]

The Fellows might have derived rueful consolation from the thought that they were not alone in suffering such a Master. Strife between heads of colleges and fellows was common at this time. William Delaune, President of St John's, resembled Charlett in his manner, and in misplaced rumours about his wealth. Francis Atterbury, Dean of Christ Church from 1710 to 1713, created an equally unhappy atmosphere, while Richard Bentley, Master of Trinity College, Cambridge, in 1700–42, was arguably the most despotic and disputatious head of all.[64]

JOHN RADCLIFFE AND JACOBITE SHADOWS: 1712–1722

Charlett's later years as Master were brightened by one piece of good fortune. In November 1714, after an immensely successful career as a doctor to royalty and the aristocracy, John Radcliffe (Fig. 11.3), one of the College's wealthiest and most loyal Old Members, died. Charlett and the College had wooed the unmarried Radcliffe assiduously to profitable effect. Apart from his benefactions to the university, which paid for the Radcliffe Camera, the Radcliffe Infirmary, and the Radcliffe Observatory, Radcliffe made three important bequests to University College.[65]

Radcliffe first gave a large estate in the Yorkshire village of Linton to his executors, from which £600 a year would endow two unusual new Fellowships. Selected by a panel of trustees, these Fellows were to be MAs who wished to study medicine. They would hold their places for ten years, during which time they were expected to travel abroad 'for their better improvement', and they would be attached to University College. Any surplus from the rents would create a fund for the College to purchase advowsons.

---

[63] Charlett's illness of 1694: Bodl. MS Ballard 12 fo. 95ʳ; delayed election: UC:GB3/A1/1 p. 138 (many letters in MS Ballard are addressed to Charlett at Bath); Hambledon and Charlett's uncle: Smith, 303–4; Charlett his own heir: Smith, 260.

[64] Delaune: Costin 1958: 166; Atterbury: Bill 1988: 41–2; Bentley: Trevelyan 1990: 55–69. Mallet 1924–7: iii. 76–86 describes other inter-Collegiate wars from this period.

[65] Radcliffe's will is transcribed in Guest 1991: 478–81.

FIGURE 11.3 John Radcliffe, m. 1666, society doctor and benefactor to University College and the university of Oxford (copy after Geoffrey Kneller).

Radcliffe explicitly asked that Linton would pass to University College itself in due course. His second bequest was a sum of £5,000, to pay for 'building the front of University College down to Logic Lane, answerable to the front already built'. This building would comprise a new Master's Lodgings and accommodation for his new Fellows. Finally, he asked that future incumbents of Headbourne Worthy be selected by a panel including the Vice-Chancellor, the Master of University College, and the Rector of Lincoln—although he gave first refusal to the parish to members of University College (where, needless to say, there was always a willing candidate). Radcliffe's benefaction rivalled Sir Simon Bennet's in its generosity.

Radcliffe's instructions for his new building posed an interesting question: just how 'answerable' should it be to the existing quadrangle, and when he spoke of a 'front', was it enough just to have a single range on the High Street, or did he want a complete quadrangle? The dilemma faced by the project's architect, William Townesend (member of a dynasty which dominated Oxford

FIGURE 11.4 Elevation of a design for a new Master's Lodgings in Radcliffe Quadrangle.

architecture in the eighteenth century), is revealed by his designs, preserved at Worcester College among the collection of George Clarke, Fellow of All Souls, MP for the university, patron of architecture—and, unsurprisingly, acquaintance of Charlett. They all agree that, on the north side, facing the High Street, there should be a range in the style of the 1630s, but some drawings propose that this would have been the only addition in the old style, and that behind it, to the south, should stand a little free-standing classical box to serve as an elegant Master's Lodgings (Fig. 11.4). Other plans, however, propose a two-sided building, to create a whole quadrangle, with northern and eastern ranges. One plan even identifies the functions of each room. The north range includes apartments for the new Radcliffe Fellows and chambers for undergraduates, and the east comprises the new Master's Lodgings, including on the ground floor a parlour, a hall, a 'gallery for books', and a study.[66]

---

[66] Townesend's drawings: Colvin 1964: nos. 53–7, 132, 166–9, and 268 (no. 57 identifies the rooms); Clarke and Charlett (and the former's interest in the new quadrangle): Clayton in Green and Horden 2007: 123–7; the Townesend dynasty: Colvin 2000. The plans show only Staircase XI, as being the entrance to the Lodgings (Staircase XII was only inserted in the 1870s).

It seems likely that Charlett wanted a classical box, and Radcliffe's Trustees a quadrangle. The latter prevailed, to Charlett's annoyance: in December 1717, William Smith commiserated with him that the Lodgings 'fall short of your hopes and expectations'. When the building was completed, just over £300 of Radcliffe's money was left, and Charlett unsuccessfully demanded the money for himself. Rumours spread that Radcliffe's Trustees wished to prosecute Charlett because of his impossible behaviour.[67]

In spite of these problems, the new quadrangle was built in a very short time. The houses adjoining Logic Lane were demolished in 1716, and the old Master's Lodgings in 1717. Already in May 1719 the new tower's High Street façade was ready to accommodate a statue of Queen Mary II. Finally, in November 1719, a statue of Radcliffe himself was erected on the tower's other side. Hearne thought it 'very ridiculous'.[68]

Ever since the additions to New College in the late seventeenth century, Oxford colleges, such as Trinity, preferred three-sided quadrangles, which were thought to encourage airiness and spaciousness. The new quadrangle followed suit. In all other respects, however, Radcliffe's instructions had created an architectural anomaly. Almost every other building erected in Oxford at that time followed the classical style, and the only other major project in the Gothic style, Nicholas Hawksmoor's strange, mannerist quadrangle at All Souls, owed more to the genius of its architect than to earlier tradition. In Radcliffe Quadrangle, however, architectural time stood still, albeit magnificently so (Plate 9). It is easy to underestimate Townesend's achievement. In order to produce a quadrangle whose courtyard was on the same orientation as that of the existing one, he had to contort the outer walls, so that most rooms in the new building are trapezoidal rather than rectangular, with especially narrow rooms at its southern end (one can understand why Charlett hankered after his classical lodgings). The fan-vaulting under the new tower—possibly the last pre-Gothic revival specimen of fan-vaulting in the country—is especially remarkable for fitting so elegantly into an awkward rhomboid space.[69]

Moreover, University College had acquired a brand new quadrangle within just three years. Paradoxically, colleges with a freer hand had a harder time. At Queen's College, an ambitious project to rebuild the college in the classical style, begun soon after 1700, was not completed until the 1760s, and at Magdalen, a still grander scheme to rebuild the college was unveiled in the

---

[67] Smith to Charlett: Bodl. MS Ballard 16 fo. 146ʳ; Charlett and the project: Guest 1991: 73–4; outstanding cash: Guest 1991: 75; prosecuting Charlett: Hearne, vi. 247.
[68] Demolition of houses: UC:E/B6/D2/9; demolition of Lodgings: Hearne, vi. 42: statues of Mary II and Radcliffe: Hearne, vii. 14, 70, and 75.
[69] The wider context: Tyack 1998: 123–61 and Colvin 1986; Hawksmoor at All Souls: Colvin and Simmons 1989: 19–46.

1720s, but was abandoned after only one range (the present New Building) was completed. Radcliffe had made a wise prescription for University College.[70]

Meanwhile, although Radcliffe's first Fellows were elected in 1715, Radcliffe's Trustees were reluctant to make Linton over to the College: both sides were unsure whether the rent would cover the Fellows' stipends. The College finally received Linton in 1744, and administered it separately from the rest of the College's estates. Not only were the two Fellowships the first at University College specifically for non-theologians, but they were unusual in requiring their holders to travel. Merton, Corpus Christi, and St John's had all granted allowances for fellows to travel abroad since the sixteenth century, but travel was obligatory for Radcliffe's Fellows. The only similar examples appear to be at Jesus College which in 1702 created two 'missionary' fellowships, whose holders should travel with the Royal Navy, or else go into 'His Majesty's plantations' to undertake missionary work, and at Magdalene College, Cambridge, which in 1725 received a travelling fellowship, tenable for nine years, intended for fellows in arts. Radcliffe was inspired less by missionary zeal, than by Oxford's poor facilities for the study of medicine, which obliged students to train elsewhere before collecting an Oxford degree: Thomas Cockman's younger brother John (m. 1699) went to Italy to become a doctor.[71]

The Radcliffe Travelling Fellows (as they came to be called) were an anomaly in the College structure. Chosen by an outside panel rather than the Master and Fellows, they did not attend College meetings; they never participated in Fellowship or Mastership elections; and they held no College offices. In the Buttery Books, they were listed, not among the Fellows, but among MA non-Fellows. Furthermore, while they received stipends of £300, the average Fellow at the time received about £70.[72]

Radcliffe's proposal that the surplus from the Linton estate be used to purchase advowsons was more immediately relevant to the College, for attitudes towards livings had changed. Oxford and Cambridge colleges, most of whose fellows were in holy orders, had ceased to regard livings as sources of income for themselves, in the way that Arncliffe and Flamstead had benefited University College. Now they sought livings which, just like Melsonby, could benefit their incumbent—and thus encourage a regular turnover in Fellowships. During this period, many colleges purchased or were given advowsons precisely for this purpose. University College was in especial need of help, because in 1714 its clerical patronage comprised only Arncliffe, Flamstead, and Melsonby. Although it took time for a surplus to

---

[70] Queen's: Hodgkin 1949: 131 and 134–7: Magdalen: Darwall-Smith in Brockliss (forthcoming).
[71] The Linton estate: Guest 1991: 75–6; other fellowships: Highfield 2006: xx (Merton), Stevenson and Salter 1939: 148–9 (Corpus and St John's), Baker 1971: 22–3 (Jesus), and E. Duffy in Cunich and others 1994: 166 (Magdalene); medicine in Oxford: Webster 1986: 683–706.
[72] List of the Radcliffe Travelling Fellows to 1990: Guest 1991: 493–6; stipends: see p. 323.

accrue, the Linton fund was worth waiting for, and the College already had Headbourne Worthy as effectively 'its' living.[73]

Radcliffe's benefactions arrived at a time of political trouble. On the death of Queen Anne in 1714, a very distant German cousin succeeded her as George I. Tories loyal to the concept of a divinely appointed monarch ruling church and state had once again to choose between conscience and expediency, when faced with a monarch whose claim to the throne depended mainly on his Protestantism, and who threw in his fortunes exclusively with the Whigs. Tory Oxford found itself regarded by the government with suspicion and dislike. It did not help that Oxford's celebrations for George I's coronation were muted, nor that in June 1715, its Chancellor, the Duke of Ormonde, was impeached, and fled the country the following month. In September, he resigned as Chancellor, and emerged as an open Jacobite, just when the Old Pretender's supporters rose in unsuccessful revolt in Britain. Troops were even stationed in Oxford.[74]

It remains difficult to judge how widespread Jacobitism was in Oxford. Some clearly wished to replace George I with James III, but others used it merely to express dissatisfaction with the present regime, and some of the undergraduates who drunkenly toasted 'James III' in the streets of Oxford were simply tweaking proctorial noses. The failure of the conspirators of 1715 to rouse England is suggestive.[75]

This was the world of Charlett's last years. University College could not deny its Tory sympathies: back in 1710, when an extreme Tory cleric called Henry Sacheverell was prosecuted for a particularly provocative sermon against religious toleration, University College gave him £32 5s. Charlett and the Fellows swore allegiance to the new regime, but there continued to be embarrassments. On 28 and 29 May 1715, respectively George I's birthday and the anniversary of Charles II's restoration, there were riots in Oxford in support of 'James III', when Whigs were attacked, and nonconformist meeting houses vandalized. Charlett, as the Pro-Vice-Chancellor on duty, was responsible for ensuring discipline. News reached Whitehall, and one of George's chief ministers, Lord Townshend, warned Charlett that the king was 'extremely Surprised' at these events, and that 'your behaviour...has been very remiss upon this extraordinary occasion, and by no means suitable to that Zeal and Duty that Persons in your Station ought to have shewn towards his Majesty and his Government'. Fortunately, Charlett did preserve calm on the day of the Old Pretender's birthday a month later.[76]

---

[73] Other colleges and advowsons: Brooke 1996: 160, Costin 1958: 175, Green 1957: 30, Howard 1935: 81, Jones 2005: 130, and Martin and Highfield 1997: 259.
[74] Coronation: Hearne, iv. 417; Ormonde and troops: *ODNB* entry, and Ward 1958: 57.
[75] See more generally Oates 2003.
[76] Sacheverell's gift: UC:BU5/F2/1 p. 19; riots: Hearne, v. 64, Monod 1989: 182, and Oates 2003: 94–6; Townshend's letter: TNA SP 44/116 p. 293; June 1715: Hearne, v. 65–6.

The last thing the College needed was for its own undergraduates to cause trouble, but on 31 August 1715, when Charlett was in Bath, Benjamin Baynes (F. 1708–22) had bad news:

Our Dinner was just over, and many of the young Gentlemen of our College were got to the Gates, when a Sergeant with four new listed men were bearing their rounds, who, as they approach'd our Gates, made motions with their Swords and grin'd at the Scholars and Turning their Horses heads towards them made their speech; as they were passing off some of *our* Young Gentlemen cried Ormond for ever, upon which the Soldiers turn'd short and fell in with their naked Swords, struck Mr. Jolife Sen. Mr. Whitall and Mr. Wilkinson and miss'd more of 'em.[77]

Rumours circulated about Charlett's loyalty: in January 1716, William Wake, the new Archbishop of Canterbury, was told that Charlett had toasted the Duke of Ormonde's health while dining with the Dean of Christ Church. Charlett certainly lost political ground, being dismissed as a royal chaplain in March 1717, and as a JP in July 1718. Doubts about Charlett may have been reinforced when the Radcliffe Quadrangle was pointedly adorned, not with a statue of George I, but rather the Stuart Mary II. It may not be coincidental that after 1713, admissions to the College fell to their lowest levels since Charlett's election (Graph 10.1).[78]

Whatever his views about George I in sympathetic company, however, Charlett had to appear in public the complete loyalist. In July 1717, when rumours abounded of a proposed government visitation of Oxford, Charlett wrote to the new Chancellor, Lord Arran (Ormonde's brother), that University College was 'intirely devoted and attached to the Illustrious House of Hanover'. Thomas Hearne claimed that the letter was 'much laugh'd at', but we should not underestimate Charlett's anxiety to do something, however hamfisted, to protect himself and the College.[79]

The case of Thomas Hearne exemplifies the dilemmas faced by Arthur Charlett, and indeed John Hudson. Charlett and Hudson had not been unsympathetic towards Hearne's Jacobitism, but in 1716, when Hearne, having refused to submit to the new regime, was deprived of his position at the Bodleian Library, he suspected—probably falsely—that Charlett and Hudson had played a leading part in this. He was especially angry at the apostasy of John Hudson, who in his cups had once uttered Jacobite sentiments, but now seemed ready to take any oath to keep his position. It would be fairer to observe that Charlett and Hudson, desperate to preserve the university's independence (and their own careers), felt that Hearne could

---

[77] Bodl. MS Ballard 38 fo. 213^r.
[78] Wake's letter: Christ Church Library: Wake Letters Vol. 20 fos. 38^v–39^r; loss of chaplaincy: Hearne, vi. 28; dismissal as magistrate: HMC 1901: 239.
[79] Hearne, vi. 75–6. On the predicament of another pragmatic Tory (Delaune of St John's), see Costin 1958: 171–2.

damage Oxford as much as an extreme Whig. Curiously, Charlett and Hearne never quite broke off contact. Hearne, for example, was invited to a private dinner at the Master's Lodgings on St Cuthbert's day in 1716.[80]

After 1717, reports of Jacobite activity in Oxford lessened, as Charlett's brand of resigned pragmatism prevailed, although a whiff of disloyalty persisted for the next few decades. Charlett himself remained a figure of consequence in the university, serving as a Pro-Vice-Chancellor until his death. Perhaps his greatest triumph in these last years was in October 1720, when University College welcomed the young Duke of Beaufort as an undergraduate. He joined through the good offices of William Denison, who, it seems, had tutored him when he had been at Westminster School. The Duke's presence added lustre to Oxford as a whole, to the point that when, in August 1721, an unsuccessful attempt was made to tempt him away to Cambridge, the Vice-Chancellor, Robert Shippen, turned out to greet him on his return to Oxford, bells were rung in several places, and a great dinner held in his and his brother's honour.[81]

Unfortunately, the College's handling of the young Duke (he was only 13 years old) shows all too well the dangers of the prevailing attitudes towards noble undergraduates. In January 1722, Thomas Hearne heard that Denison 'will not let [the Duke] keep any Company proper for him', and had declared that 'the Duke should subscribe to no Books at all'. The College tried to accommodate the Duke's every wish, even wondering whether to move dinner forward by one hour to midday because the Duke preferred it that way.[82] Meanwhile, George Ward tested his own teaching methods on the Duke. On 15 December 1722, Hearne wrote:

Yesterday morning at two Clock, the Duke of Beaufort... rid out of Town with that vicious loose Fellow Mr. Ward (commonly call'd Jolly Ward) of Univ. Coll. It is said that they had sate up 'till that time drinking. Ward was so drunk that he vomited four times between Queen's Coll. Lane & East Gate.[83]

In February 1724, William Stratford, a Canon of Christ Church, reported that the Duke had fallen seriously ill, claiming that it was due to his drinking, for the Duke 'will drink and swear with any cocker [fighter] in England'. He continued: 'It is owing entirely to the company he is brought into by his tutor, who ought to be hanged for it.'[84]

---

[80] Charlett and Hearne's posts: Hearne, v. 283–4, 330, and 336; Hearne and Hudson: Hearne, v. 160 and 200; dinner in 1716: Hearne, v. 184.
[81] Decline in Jacobitism: Oates 2003: 107–11; Tory Oxford: Clark 1985: 153–7; Denison and the Duke: Hearne, vii. 182 and HMC 1901: 280; the Duke tempted to Cambridge: Hearne, vii. 268–70. Nevertheless, von Malaise 1985: 77–8 reminds us that the Beaufort family had strong Jacobite leanings.
[82] Denison's teaching: Hearne, vii. 312; dinner: Bodl. MS Ballard 38 fos. 238 and 241.
[83] Hearne, viii. 24.
[84] HMC 1901: 374. Moralists might note that the Duke's later life included poor health, a messy divorce with accusations of impotence, and an early death (Stone 1993: 117–38).

THE ERA OF ARTHUR CHARLETT: 1689–1722

The education available for a gentleman was clearly failing the Duke of Beaufort. It also failed a gentleman commoner who actually wanted to work. Nicholas Toke (m. 1721), a responsible young man from Kent, wanted to improve his logic by participating in the exercises held in the Hall. Unfortunately, as he wrote to his uncle in January 1722:

Gentlemen Commoners, tho they have many opportunitys of getting improvements of the best Company, lay under this great disadvantage of not improving their learning so much as other inferior gowns in the University. I might indeed go into the Hall to disputations; & should willingly perform all the exercise of an under-graduate; but then I should draw upon me the hatred of all the gentlemen of my own Gown, be guilty of great singularity (which in all places is to be avoided) & be accounted a Person proud of his own performances, & fond of showing his parts.[85]

Eventually Toke paid someone to visit his chamber once or twice a week to practise disputations privately there.[86] A College in which a class of students felt penalized for working, or simply fell into the clutches of 'Jolly' Ward, had fallen far away from the ideals of the early 1690s.

As for Charlett himself, on 24 October 1722, after a dinner at St John's, he suffered a major and incapacitating stroke. He lingered in a semi-conscious state until he died on 18 November. He was buried in the Chapel. Charlett died intestate, so that the College received nothing from him, not even his long-promised collection of books.[87]

Arthur Charlett's Mastership carries a strong sense of failure. Things could have been very different. In the 1690s, Charlett had matched Ralph Bathurst of Trinity as a patron of scholarship, a leading player in university life, the recruiter of a brilliant Fellowship, and the head of a fast growing College. He was also Master during a period of great political tension, and his decision to pursue a pragmatic middle way between extreme Tory and Whig was sensible. Yet it all went wrong: Charlett's energy became self-destructive; his strong leadership declined into a capricious autocracy; his self-important ways were mocked; the College's discipline grew slack; and the quality of the Fellows declined from John Hudson to 'Jolly' Ward.

The last word, however, on this best and worst of Masters should be left to his friend and foe, Thomas Hearne, who in May 1715 set down this surprisingly shrewd sketch of him:

I must therefore do the Dr. this Justice, as to say of him that when he is in the Humour, he is a most generous, friendly & hearty Man, & a great Encourager of good Letters... So that I must ingenuously confess that tho' all that I had before written of him in these Remarks be very true (he having been formerly my deadly Enemy, for

---

[85] Bodl. MS Eng. Th. c. 27 p. 365.
[86] Ibid. 393.
[87] Charlett's last illness: HMC 1901: 338–9; his library: Smith, 260–1.

as he is an excellent Friend where he takes, so he is as great an Enemy when he sets upon it) yet his Kindnesses having been very many (tho' nothing near so many as his Unkindnesses) I must affirm that he does deserve the Character of bonarum litterarum summus fautor [the greatest encourager of literature] in a limited sense; & this is what all that know him will joyn with me in.[88]

---

[88] Hearne, v. 55.

12

Storm and Calm: 1722–1764

Although Arthur Charlett had died intestate, he did make one bequest to University College, namely a bitterly divided Fellowship. The story of the College after 1722 is one of how it was first overwhelmed by and then overcame these divisions to achieve a period of calm, which, if less dramatic to the later observer, would have been preferable to the contemporary participant.

FUNERAL GAMES: 1722–1729[1]

Even as Charlett lay dying, the Fellows of University College began to consider his successor. One figure at least stood out: William Denison was now the senior resident Fellow, and—importantly—the tutor of the Duke of Beaufort. He had powerful friends, including Thomas Bouchier, Charlett's old ally, and his son James (who had succeeded his father as Professor of Civil Law), the current Vice-Chancellor Robert Shippen, and, within College, Charlett's intimates (and his own former pupils), George 'Jolly' Ward and Francis Rogers.[2]

Those Fellows, however, who had not enjoyed Charlett's favour had no wish to see one of his creatures succeed him. Their leader was John Boraston, the senior Fellow. Although long non-resident, he quickly returned to Oxford, and produced as an alternative candidate his former pupil Thomas Cockman. Since we last encountered him, Cockman (Fig. 12.1) had been quietly successful. In 1707 and 1708 he had visited the continent with his brother John, and had been employed as a tutor by the Keyte family of Stratford-upon-Avon, whose patronage had enabled him to marry and resign his Fellowship in 1713. He was now vicar of a parish in Kent. His publications and his character made him a worthy alternative candidate, and indeed barely a week after Charlett's stroke, William Stratford, a Canon of Christ Church, wrote to a former pupil that Cockman was thought 'the best of those named' for Charlett's successor.[3]

---

[1] Much of this section is a shortened (and slightly revised) version of Darwall-Smith 1999.
[2] Denison and the Bouchiers: Bodl. MS Ballard 16 fo. 48[r] and Hearne, viii. 95. Shippen was the son of William Shippen, former Fellow of University College and tormentor of Obadiah Walker.
[3] Cockman's travels: Bodl. MS Ballard 21 fos. 121[r], 130[r], and 133[r]; the Keyte family: Bodl. MS Ballard 21 fo. 136[r]; Stratford: HMC 1901: 338.

FIGURE 12.1 Engraving of Thomas Cockman, m. 1691, Fellow 1700–1713, and Master 1722–45.

There were ten Fellows eligible to elect Charlett's successor. Two others, James Scott and Thomas Heather, had not yet been formally admitted, and so could not vote, but the other ten Fellows were, in order of seniority:

1. John Boraston: m. University 1681; Bennet Fellow 1689.
2. William Denison: m. University 1693; William of Durham Fellow 1698.
3. Samuel Lindsay: m. University 1694; Skirlaw Fellow 1703.
4. Cavendish Nevile: m. University 1698; Skirlaw Fellow 1705.
5. George Ward: m. University 1702; Percy Fellow 1708.
6. John Browne: m. University 1704; Skirlaw Fellow 1711.
7. Francis Rogers: m. University 1708; Percy Fellow 1713.
8. Thomas Cockerill: m. University 1700; Bennet Fellow 1716.

9. Francis Taylor: m. University 1712; Bennet Fellow 1721.
10. Robert Eden: m. Brasenose 1717, and BA from Lincoln College; William of Durham Fellow 1721.

In 1722, University College was unique among the colleges in possessing no single comprehensive set of statutes, but depending still on a patchwork of statutes compiled between 1280/1 and 1561, judgements of the Visitors, and regulations applying to different Fellowships. In a time of consensus, agreement on which statutes to follow was feasible, but in 1722 the College was so fatally divided that the whole rickety system collapsed. The Visitor should have provided impartial protection, but the Hebdomadal Council was currently led by a Vice-Chancellor who openly supported Denison.

A crisis was inevitable: as Dr Stratford recorded early in November, 'the College is equally divided, five and five for Cockman and Denison'. Wiser heads attempted to avert trouble. On Charlett's death the Bursar, John Browne, wrote to William Smith, asking whether Denison could vote for himself, and, if the votes were equal, whether the senior Fellow had a casting vote. Unfortunately, Smith's convoluted reply ignored Browne's questions, but returned to his personal obsessions: recalling the election of Thomas Bennet in 1691, he argued once again that Cockman, as a former Bennet Fellow, required a dispensation to become Master, and also claimed that Convocation, not the Hebdomadal Council, was the true Visitor of the College. Meanwhile, Denison was getting annoyed by the presence of Boraston. On 27 November, Thomas Hearne overheard him grumbling that he, Denison, 'had been all along resident at University Coll., & had not been concern'd in creating any Dissensions in the College'.[4]

The election for the Mastership of University College was held on 4 December. William Denison had laid his plans carefully. The College's only rules for electing a Master, set out in the 1475 statutes, ordered that a Master should come 'from the bosom and company of the College' (*de gremio ac comitiva eiusdem Collegij*) and be chosen 'by canonical election' (*per electionem Canonicam*). Denison and his civil lawyer friends the Bouchiers interpreted this statute as meaning that the election should be held according to the rules of canon law, which ordained that three scrutators should be present, that no one could vote for themselves, and that only a candidate with an absolute majority could win. The last rule would guarantee that no one could win the present election. However, John Boraston (the only Fellow to have elected a Master) could show that, no matter how the Bouchiers interpreted this statute, no recent Mastership election had been conducted thus. Instead each Fellow entered the Antechapel singly to record his vote with the Senior Fellow, who then declared the final result. On

---

[4] Divisions: HMC 1901: 339; Browne and Smith: Smith, 301–8; Denison: Hearne, viii. 18.

election day Denison demanded three scrutators, but Boraston brushed this objection aside. When Denison came to vote, Boraston drily observed that, if Denison wanted an election under canon law, he could not vote for himself. Denison replied that he was not intending to anyway.[5]

When the votes were counted, this was the result:

> Thomas Cockman: 5 votes (from Boraston, Nevile, Browne, Cockerill, and Taylor)
> William Denison: 4 votes (from Lindsay, Ward, Rogers, and Eden)
> George Ward: 1 vote (from Denison).[6]

Cockman—now in Oxford—claimed the Mastership, because he had received most votes, but Denison claimed that, under canon law, the election was invalid, because no candidate had an absolute majority. He also repeated William Smith's opinion that a Bennet Fellow—like Cockman—was not from 'the bosom and company' of the College, and required a dispensation to become Master.

When Cockman first presented himself to Vice-Chancellor Shippen to be ratified as Master, he was told that Denison had registered a complaint about the election. When they met again, on 11 December, Cockman offered to subscribe to the Thirty-Nine Articles, but 'Mr. Vice-Chancellor refus'd to let him subscribe, & told him with some seeming warmth (tho' as yet he had heard nothing judicially about the cause) That if they were Visitors he was no Master'.[7]

Not everyone agreed. Robert Shippen himself was not universally popular, and his reappointment as Vice-Chancellor for a fifth year in 1722 had been controversial.[8] William Stratford, who, as a DD, was one of the Visitors, was unconvinced by Denison's arguments. He and some other Visitors had noted that the 1311 statutes ordered that all disputed elections should be settled within three days. Because this time had elapsed, they refused to have anything more to do with the case. Shippen simply adjourned the meeting to the following day, which was boycotted by the protesters. Shippen therefore declared Cockman's election void, and ordered a fresh one, which was held on 17 December. As Cockman's supporters absented themselves, only five Fellows took part, four of whom voted for Denison, who was declared Master.[9] Hearne was disgusted both by this 'most unpresidented and abominable Act', and by the Duke of Beaufort's celebration of his tutor's triumph:

> There was great ringing of Bells all over the Town, except in Colleges... and against the Duke of Beaufort's Lodgings in University Coll. was a great Bonfire, & abundance

---

[5] These exchanges recorded in Anon. 1723. On the Bouchiers, see Barton 1986: 596–7.
[6] Hearne, viii. 19–20.
[7] Hearne, viii. 22–3, HMC 1901: 342–3, and UC:MA34/MS2/2 (source of quotation).
[8] Shippen's unpopularity: HMC 1901: 335 and Ward 1958: 114–16.
[9] Hearne, viii. 24–5, HMC 1901: 342–3 and UC:MA34/MS2/2.

of Ale in the Street, the Duke looking on all the time out of a Window, & encouraging the Mob, & being at the Charge of all these vile, rascally doings.[10]

Thomas Hearne heard what happened next from his friends Francis Taylor and Cavendish Nevile: Denison was installed as Master; he had the Master's stall in the Chapel broken open, in order to sit in it; and the Duke of Beaufort and George Ward tried to occupy the Master's Lodgings, but the servant left there by Cockman refused their bribes.[11]

This might have been the end of the story, for what could Thomas Cockman do against the Visitors of his College? In 1726, following an equally bitter election at Balliol, the Visitor there would impose his nephew as Master, and the Fellows could do nothing. Cockman's friends, however, took part in mischievous displays of defiance. When John Boraston returned to Kent, he took the College seal with him, so that no official College orders could be promulgated. In late February, John Browne, when preaching in the university church in the presence of Robert Shippen, prayed openly for Cockman as Master of University College. William Stratford noted that the congregation immediately looked at the Vice-Chancellor, who was 'in some confusion'. In March 1723 Cockman visited Oxford and took Sunday prayers in Chapel (in Denison's absence). He also had plans for a counter-attack.[12]

Cockman's problem was that the College's Visitor was clearly partial. What, therefore, if he could find a more impartial one? It could be argued that if, as was generally agreed, King Alfred had founded University College, then it was a royal foundation, and therefore the Crown, and not the Chancellor of Oxford as represented by the Hebdomadal Council, should be its Visitor. This was a daring proposition. Cockman and his team were no less Tory than Denison and his friends, and yet they would have to accept George I and his Whiggish ministers as their new Visitors. Stratford, for one, was terrified by such a prospect. He urged Cockman to delay for a while, 'that our mad men might have leisure if they pleased to come to their senses'. His appeal was vain: Cockman's party formally appealed to the Crown. Careful overtures had evidently been made, for in March 1723 Cockman's petition was received by the King 'very graciously'.[13]

Denison's supporters fought back. In the same month, Richard Newton, Principal of Hart Hall, published a pamphlet defending the arguments for a 'Canonical Election', and the peculiar status of Bennet Fellows (Fig. 12.2). It only hardened existing divisions. For Stratford, the pamphlet's facts and

---

[10] Hearne, viii. 25–6.
[11] Hearne, viii. 26, 27, and 29.
[12] Balliol: Jones 2005: 155–8; Boraston and the seal: Hearne, viii. 24; Browne's sermon: HMC 1901: 346; Cockman in College; Hearne, viii. 54.
[13] Stratford's appeal: HMC 1901: 349–50; receipt of petition: HMC 1901: 350.

FIGURE 12.2 Title page of *The Proceedings of the Visitors of University College*, 1723.

argumentation were 'false from the beginning to the end', and Hearne thought it 'the Result of Tittle Tattle at Tea Tables'. Cockman's team issued a counterblast.[14]

Cockman, however, could trust in more than a mere pamphlet, for in April the Attorney-General summoned all parties to London. It was not a good day for Denison: when he expressed ignorance as to whether King Alfred's arms hung in the College, and whether he was prayed for as its founder, he was reminded that he had once given a speech on an occasion when just such prayers had been made. The Attorney-General concluded that the Crown appeared to have the right to visit the College, and that Denison's side had to prove otherwise. Instead of any proof, however, an anonymous letter was sent to the Attorney-General claiming that Cockman's supporters 'are the most Knowne & notorious Jacobites in the whole University', and reminding

---

[14] Newton 1723; reactions: HMC 1901: 352 and Hearne, viii. 57; counterblast: Anon. 1723.

George I of the consequences of James II's intervention in Magdalen College. This defiance, however, concealed an anxiety that Denison's scheme was not working well. When old Thomas Bouchier died in May 1723, Hearne claimed that he 'was mightily troubled... that he had not baffled Mr. Cockman... [and] would sometimes cry out, *This Cockman hath killed me*.'[15]

In October 1724, the Attorney-General and Solicitor-General issued a memorandum on Cockman's petition. Their conclusion was simple: if University College had been founded by King Alfred, then the Crown was its Visitor. It had to be decided, therefore, in a court of law, whether Alfred had founded the College. Until then, the College was in stalemate, with two Masters, each refusing to acknowledge the other, with the hapless James Scott and Thomas Heather still not yet admitted to their Fellowships. Even they were divided: Scott, a Percy Fellow, supported Cockman, and Heather, a Bennet Fellow, Denison.[16]

During this strange time the Master's Lodgings remained in Thomas Cockman's possession, although Cockman himself stayed away, presumably considering it prudent to avoid causing trouble by his presence. His fears were reasonable, as shown in Hearne's account of a visit made by Cockman to the College in 1726:

Mr. George Ward (commonly call'd Jolly Ward) of University Coll. sent to the Master, Mr. Cockman, that he would speak with him. The Master let him know that he was at home. Upon which Ward went to him, & ask'd him by what Authority he took Possession of the Lodgings, and acted as Master, when he knew 'twas another Man's Right, adding that in a Little Time he would be called before his Betters.[17]

Meanwhile, Thomas's brother John Cockman, now an eminent doctor in Maidstone, sometimes stayed in the Lodgings, and Thomas Hearne was regularly granted access to examine Charlett's papers, which were being sold off.[18]

Denison also lived outside the College, renting a house in High Street. In May 1724 he married Anna Maria Bouchier, James's sister, and had two sons in 1725 and 1728. His marriage shows his continuing confidence, for now if he lost the Mastership, he would lose his Fellowship too.[19]

We do not know how such spaces as the Chapel, the Hall, and the Senior Common Room functioned. Meals had to be eaten, and services held, but

---

[15] The Attorney-General: Hearne, viii. 70; anonymous letter: BL Add. 35584 fo. 310ʳ and Hearne, viii. 89; Bouchier's death: Hearne, viii. 102.

[16] The report: Smith, 311–14. In Darwall-Smith 1999, I assigned the wrong Fellowships to Heather and Scott.

[17] Hearne, ix. 90.

[18] John Cockman in the lodgings: e.g. Hearne, viii. 50, 83, and 101; Charlett's papers and books: Hearne, viii. 130–1, 142, and variously in 158–88 (and also Gillam 1952).

[19] Denison's lodgings: Hearne, ix. 371–2; his wife and children: Shipton-under-Wychwood marriage registers, and Hanborough baptism registers (both at Oxfordshire Record Office).

how the opposing parties achieved any kind of *modus vivendi* is not known. The Treasury stayed with Cockman, because John Browne remained as Bursar. The finances of the College, however, were in trouble. Browne compiled official accounts for 1722–9, but they appear all to have been written after 1729: they read all too easily and contain some elementary slips. A closer examination reveals the sad truth. No College feasts were held, and few repairs took place. Worse still, no new leases had been drawn up since 1722, and thus no entry fines received (so that the Fellows themselves suffered financially). Some College tenants exploited the confusion: an anonymous Fellow lamented that 'Several Tenants & others retain rents & debts in their hands to the value of about 1000 pounds, pretending that they can't have a legal discharge, so long as this Dispute about the Headship continues.'[20]

Surprisingly, undergraduates continued to matriculate from the College. Ten freshmen a year on average came up in 1723–9—the same average as 1715–22. There were two bad years, 1723 and 1727, when only six men came up, but 1725 saw thirteen admissions, including the Duke of Beaufort's younger brother, Lord Charles Noel Somerset. However, Francis Rogers and George Ward were accused of neglecting their duties as Dean and Praelector in Greek respectively, and Ward of encouraging undergraduates not to attend lectures given by his opponents. For his part, Ward claimed that when in 1723 he tried to hold elections for College offices, Browne, Cockerill, and Taylor refused to participate. Curiously enough, though, our only known undergraduate witness from this period, the hard-working Nicholas Toke, says almost nothing in his letters about the dispute, but instead writes about his current reading.[21]

In May 1726, Cockman received news of an encouraging precedent: the Provost and the Fellows of Oriel had also gone to law over the identity of their Visitor, after an equally bitter dispute, and judgement was now given that the Crown was their Visitor. Exactly a year later, in May 1727, the case of University College was heard at last, and a similar conclusion reached: Alfred was the Founder of University College, and the Crown was therefore its Visitor. The actions of the Hebdomadal Council against Thomas Cockman were void, and Cockman's election was therefore valid.[22]

It is easy, but unfair, to smile at this judgement today. Educated opinion had long accepted that King Alfred had founded University College—was this not proved by genuine (if mendacious) documents from the 1380s? The lack of ninth-century material was not a problem: Cockman himself

[20] Accounts for 1722–9: UC:BU2/F1/3 fos. 66^v–102^r and the so-called *Billa Bursarii* (UC:BU5/F2/1 pp. 77–102); no new leases: UC:EB2/F/1 p. 46; defaulting tenants: UC:MA34/MS2/6.
[21] Arguments: UC:GB3/A1/2 fos. 1–27.
[22] Oriel: Varley 1941; University College: Heane, ix. 314.

suggested that, even if Alfred had used a foundation charter (itself a debatable point), it would have been lost when the Danes sacked Oxford in the early eleventh century.[23] By declaring Alfred the founder of University College, the High Court merely gave legal backing to a long-established belief, and corrected the anomaly that a Royal foundation lacked a Royal Visitor. The fact that the College was also released from the jurisdiction of a 'Visitor' which had so misused its powers might have had a bearing on the result.

On 8 June 1727, Thomas Cockman returned to University College as undisputed Master—or so he thought. On the following Sunday, he went to the Chapel to read prayers, but as he entered, he found George Ward already sitting in the Master's seat reading the prayers as Denison's deputy. Ward then ordered that Cockman's name be struck from the Buttery Book, and that the Master's Chair be taken out of the Hall, so Cockman could not use it. Denison and his supporters would not admit defeat.[24]

Ward enjoyed tormenting Cockman. He was in the Master's seat in Chapel on the following Sunday, and told Cockman that he would only recognize him as Master if he was shown something signed by the King or the university to prove it. A few days later, he ordered the College servants not to obey Cockman, as he was only an intruder. In October, Ward formally admitted Thomas Heather as Fellow—at last—and, when Cockman protested that he could do this himself, Ward told him that he had no business there. Heather likewise refused to acknowledge Cockman as Master (whereas James Scott was promptly admitted by Cockman).[25]

Scott suffered for supporting Cockman. Back in March 1727, during an argument with Ward, Scott had exclaimed that Ward encouraged vice and immorality in the College. Ward, all injured innocence, promptly sued him for defamation before the Chancellor's Court, claiming £50 compensation. Unfortunately James Bouchier was presiding in court that day. Bouchier, touched by his friend's heart-rending appeal, was prepared to be fair: Scott, he ordered, need only pay Ward £30.[26]

Ward's behaviour was not unique. On 29 June, Cockman attended a service at the university church, and took his place among the seats reserved for heads of houses. Unfortunately, the Pro-Vice-Chancellor present that day was Shippen. After the service, Shippen sent his Bedel to Cockman, ordering him to sit among the MAs and not among the heads of house. Cockman had the presence of mind to jot this rude message down on a scrap of paper for further reference.[27]

---

[23] UC:MA34/MS1/24.
[24] Hearne, ix. 314–15.
[25] Ward in Chapel: Hearne, ix. 319; the servants: Hearne, ix. 322–3 and UC:MA34/L1/6; swearing in Heather and Scott: Hearne, ix. 354–5.
[26] OUA CC Papers 1727/27:1–18. Scott appealed, but, on account of the poor condition of the documents, it is unknown whether he was successful.
[27] Cockman and Shippen: Hearne, ix. 332–3 (Cockman's note is preserved as UC:MA34/L1/5).

In describing these remarkable events, Thomas Hearne claimed that no sensible person took Denison and his supporters seriously. Maybe so: but as Cockman endured these humiliating scenes, University College remained ungovernable. Perhaps the Crown had not wished to test its new powers too far, to avoid comparison with James II, but by autumn 1727 its intervention was clearly essential. Cockman, having petitioned for a visitation, withdrew again to Kent, leaving his supporters to protect the Lodgings, and the College returned to its state of suspended animation.[28]

The next development in the case came as a complete surprise. In April 1728, Thomas Hearne received a visit from Charlett's old friend Thomas Tanner, with news that 'old Mr. William Smith had printed a Book in 8vo of about 400 pages against Mr. Cockman, but that 'tis stupid and frivolous.'[29] Like some long-dormant volcano, William Smith had been provoked by the court's verdict to break his silence on the origins of University College, pouring into his book *The Annals of University College* the fruits of decades of research and thought. The result was astonishing: Smith (who had taken all his volumes of transcripts up to Melsonby with him) blew away the legend of King Alfred as a concoction of the 1380s, and revealed William of Durham as the College's true founder. With its admirable disentangling of truth and legend, and its rigorous archive-based methodology, Smith's is the first truly scholarly history of any Oxbridge College, and, as readers of earlier chapters will have seen, all later analyses of this College's early history are indebted to it. Although the book arrived too late to affect the court's decision, it was not impossible that it could help with an appeal.

Unfortunately, *The Annals of University College* is an appalling book to read. Written in haste, the narrative is at times as incoherent as *Tristram Shandy*: promises of topics to be discussed later are left unfulfilled, and digressions meander until the narrative thread is broken. Smith could not resist settling old scores, attacking Boraston for 'intermeddl[ing] in so bad a Cause as he had done'.[30] He also damaged his case by continuing to maintain that the College's true Visitor was Convocation, not the Hebdomadal Council—and certainly not the Crown. It is debatable whether Smith's interpretation was correct as regards the medieval College, but it was utterly irrelevant now, and guaranteed to annoy both sides. Finally, at a time when Alfred's links had just been upheld in law, even an elegantly written and clearly argued demolition of his claims would have made little headway; such a crabbed and disorganized work did not stand a chance, especially among Cockman's friends. On reading the book, Thomas Hearne dismissed it as 'a meer injudicious Rhapsody, and full of lyes throughout', while Stratford, recalling

---

[28] Mockery: Hearne, ix. 315; Cockman's absence: see, for example, UC:MA34/MS2/13; his petition: TNA PC 1/4/88.
[29] Hearne, x. 9.   [30] Smith, 299.

Smith as 'the common plague of the whole society', thought that he 'slandered in it every one that he ever knew'. One anonymous Fellow of University College asked 'which ought most to be relyed upon, the Determination of a full bench of excellent Judges & a Jury of impartial gentlemen... or the private opinion of a partial disgusted old man, who was always famous, as you remember he was, for opposition & confounding things.' Others were more impressed: in December 1728, copies of Smith's book were sent anonymously to every Common Room in Oxford (Hearne suspected that Denison's party was responsible).[31]

Unfortunately for Denison, his cause had suffered a major reverse in May 1728. The Chancellor, Lord Arran, presented to the heads of houses a draft letter, supposedly written at the instance of Denison, Shippen, and Bouchier, which protested to the King at the university's losing its Visitorship of University College. The letter was rejected by a majority of two to one. Stratford wisely observed that 'I am afraid that Mr. Cockman owes this success to the general hatred of Dr. Shippen as much as to the goodness of his cause.'[32]

Finally, on 19 April 1729, a Visitation of University College opened in London. Its seven Commissioners, carefully selected, included two former members of the College, Robert Clavering and John Potter, now respectively Bishops of Peterborough and Oxford, as well as Thomas Tanner, who knew the College well. The Fellows were summoned; the old arguments were heard again; and on 1 May 1729, the Commissioners gave their verdict. Thomas Cockman was the true Master of University College, and William Denison's Fellowship was declared vacant, on account of his having a benefice. Samuel Lindsey, Cavendish Nevile, Thomas Cockerill, and Thomas Heather, who had all married or acquired wealthy livings, also lost their Fellowships. Denison had finally lost.[33]

He did not give way gracefully—even in October 1729, Francis Taylor told Thomas Hearne that Denison, Ward, and Rogers 'do what they can to prejudice their College by insinuating still that K. Alfred was not their Founder'—but eventually he admitted defeat. His movements from 1729 to 1745 have yet to be traced. He had two parishes in Hampshire, and the Duke of Beaufort may have found a means of rewarding Denison for his loyal service—he certainly rewarded Thomas Heather, making him a domestic chaplain some time before 1731. Finally, in 1745 (just after Cockman's death), Lord Arran found some Oxford preferment for Denison, when he appointed him Principal of Magdalen Hall (now Hertford College), a post Denison held until his death in 1756.[34]

---

[31] Reactions: Hearne, x. 27, HMC 1901: 466, and UC:MA34/MS2/10; circulation of the book: Hearne, x. 76.
[32] HMC 1901: 463.
[33] The Visitation is recorded at UC:GB3/A1/2 fos. 1–27.
[34] Final murmurings: Hearne, x. 183; Heather and the Duke: OUA CC Papers 1731/13:15.

Controversy kept Denison company to the end. Soon after arriving at Magdalen Hall, he sacked the manciple of the Hall over an argument about responsibility for settling the Hall's bills. It is clear, too, that he could not forget the events of the 1720s. He was buried at Hanborough, Oxfordshire, and his epitaph, while commemorating his links with the Dukes of Beaufort, referred to 'the deceit of traitors' and 'the attacks of his enemies' failing to deprive him of academic privilege. Even thirty years on, Denison and his family wanted to put the record straight.[35]

William Smith likewise now fades from the scene. Although he was in his late seventies, and supposedly in poor health, his last years were contented ones. He seems to have come into money, for, in addition to building a handsome rectory house at Melsonby, he built in his home town of Easby a fine new house, Easby Hall, in about 1729, and then, in 1732, he endowed a hospital there. He died in 1735, three decades after leaving Oxford.[36]

Thomas Cockman himself said little in public about his victory, but his friends may have been less reticent. In 2007 the College acquired from the Toke family (the descendants of Nicholas Toke, John Cockman's son-in-law), a portrait attributed to Benjamin Ferrers of seven men, all wearing gowns (Plate 10). They are seated in a room adjoining a library, around a table on which lie some pipes and a silver cup. In 1949, the cup was tentatively identified with one owned by the College and the room, as being situated somewhere in the Master's Lodgings in the Radcliffe Quadrangle. The central figure and the one on the far left both wear mortar boards, and resemble each other. It was therefore suggested that they represent, respectively, Thomas and John Cockman, sitting in the Master's Lodgings. If this identification holds good (and the portrait's provenance supports it), one can go further. There are five other figures in the portrait: five Fellows supported Thomas Cockman. Does this group portrait then represent Thomas Cockman celebrating his Mastership, alongside his brother and his supporters?[37]

It may now seem incredible that a dispute in a small college assumed such importance. Its vehemence is something of a back-handed compliment to Charlett, in that a post, which in 1692 had been so difficult to fill, was now something worth fighting for. Moreover, the headship of an Oxford College was, in the 1720s, one of the few pieces of non-parochial preferment readily available to a Tory. Carr suggested that the dispute arose from tensions between northern and southern Fellows.[38] However, although the admitted Bennet Fellows supported Cockman, he did attract northerners, including John Browne; and, of the unadmitted Fellows, it was the Bennet Fellow,

---

[35] Denison and the Manciple: Anon. 1748 and Edwards 1749.
[36] Smith's hospital has been turned into private housing. I am most grateful to the owners of Melsonby Rectory and Easby Hall for letting me visit their houses in September 1999.
[37] Correspondence from 1949: UC:P171/C1/1–8.
[38] Carr, 172–3.

Thomas Heather, who supported Denison. Carr's explanation also disregards the fact that much of the university took sides. We cannot talk either of a dispute between Whigs and Tories, for there were Tories on both sides—and worse, as the Jacobite Thomas Hearne found himself supporting the Hanoverians as the College's rightful Visitors.

Instead we should summon up the malevolent ghost of Arthur Charlett. Denison's supporters included Charlett's favourites Francis Rogers and George Ward, and non-College cronies like Shippen and the Bouchiers, whereas Cockman's party included John Boraston and others who had not enjoyed Charlett's favour. The division was not clear-cut—Cockman's supporters included a relative of Charlett, Francis Taylor, and a long-standing friend, William Stratford—but Denison clearly stood at the centre of a Charlett clique, albeit not necessarily to his advantage. Powerful as Robert Shippen was, he was also divisive, to the point that Denison and Cockman's support within Oxford mirrored some of the divisions which tore the Tories apart in the 1720s. Meanwhile, the government could look on with a certain satisfaction, for, while their Tory opponents fought amongst themselves, they had acquired a piece of Oxford patronage.[39]

Whatever caused the great Mastership dispute, its effects are clear enough. University College was in a wretched condition: its Fellowship was divided; its finances were wrecked; its members' antics had given it an unwelcome prominence; and any trace of the reputation it had enjoyed during Charlett's early years had long gone. The challenges facing Thomas Cockman were immense.

THOMAS COCKMAN AND THE RETURN TO NORMALITY: 1729–1745

Cockman's return to University College as undisputed Master on 10 May 1729 set the tone for his rule. Bonfires and bells had attended Denison's election, but Cockman came at night, 'very privately'. Almost at once he began to restore normality, starting with the College's estates: fresh leases were drawn up, and on 14 May the first entry fines in seven years were received. Some scores were settled: two tenants were given large fines, because the College felt that they had been 'ill us'd' by them. A fortnight later the five Fellowships declared vacant by the Commissioners were filled. No less significantly, on 18 May Cockman met Thomas Hearne to seek his expert advice in framing a new set of College statutes. Back in 1692, Charlett had been elected on the understanding that he would do this, but the statutes remained unrevised, and the chaos of the 1720s resulted. Meanwhile, in addition to the expense of the Visitation (at least £90), the College had to pay for seven years' neglect of its fabric, so that its expenses in 1729/30—just

[39] Some of the relationships between the parties are unravelled by Ward 1958: 114–16.

over £1,200—were the largest until the 1780s. Furthermore, William Denison sought repayment for some debts, and the College had to give him over £80. More happily, on SS Simon and Jude's day 1729 the College celebrated its first feast since 1722, and Cockman made a conciliatory gesture by inviting Robert Eden, one of Denison's former supporters, to preach at the preceding service.[40]

There remained the matter of how to handle the Fellowship. Fortunately, Cockman had an easier time than he might have feared. John Boraston was appointed Catechist in May 1729, and resided in College for the first time in three decades, undoubtedly to support his old pupil. Of the other remaining Fellows in 1729, only three, Ward, Rogers, and Eden, had been Denison's men. Rogers withdrew almost completely from College life until his death in 1738, Eden reconciled himself to Cockman, and Ward, potentially the most recalcitrant of them all, evidently accepted the inevitable, and instead harried Thomas Hearne over a newly discovered document composed by the latter some years earlier in which he seemingly admitted the possibility of conforming to the Hanoverians. In any event, Ward died in August 1733, barely four years after the Visitation. One feels that the College was purified by his absence.[41]

Some Denison sympathizers made their feelings rather clearer: Lord Charles Noel Somerset left University College, and entered himself on the books at Brasenose (Shippen's college), and his elder brother, the Duke of Beaufort, in his will of 1744 endowed four Scholarships at Oriel College—not University College under Cockman. Some other promised benefactions also failed to mature. Others, however, welcomed the new regime. Thomas Allen, edged out of his Fellowship back in 1711, gave University College £50 in 1730. Cockman's College also enjoyed one significant benefaction. In 1737, William Lodge (m. 1686), a Lincolnshire rector, left property in York and the nearby villages of Healaugh and Wighill, to endow three Scholarships open only to servitors. Lodge's benefaction, however, was rather old-fashioned, because, as will be seen in Chapter XIV, few undergraduates now wished to matriculate in so lowly a status.[42]

Thomas Hearne showed his support in a characteristic manner by publishing in 1730 *Vindiciae Antiquitatis Academiae Oxoniensis*, an edition of Thomas Caius' original 1566 treatise, John Caius' reply with Thomas's indignant annotations, and the previously unpublished text of Thomas's riposte (p. 107). Although Hearne did not allude to contemporary events,

---

[40] Cockman's return: Hearne, x. 129; renewed leases and punished tenants: UC:EB2/F/1 pp. 46–7; Fellowship elections: UC:GB3/A1/2 fos. 27^r–28^v; new statutes: Hearne, x. 132; College expenses: UC:BU5/F2/1 p. 111 and UC:BU2/F1/3 fo. 105^v; Denison's repayments: UC:BU5/F2/1 p. 118; SS. Simon and Jude's day: Hearne, x. 193 and UC:BU2/F1/3 fo. 106^r.

[41] Information on Fellows taken from UC:GB3/A1/2; Ward and Hearne: Hearne, xi. 476–9; Ward's death: UC:GB3/A1/2 fo. 33^r.

[42] Lord Charles Noel: Hearne, xi. 231; Duke of Beaufort (of whom Oriel also possesses a fine portrait): information from Robert Petre, Archivist of Oriel College; one failed benefaction: UC:MA34/C1/4–7, 15 and 17; Thomas Allen: Hearne, xi. 148; Lodge's will: UC:BE1/MS2/2 p. 497.

FIGURE 12.3 The Oxford Almanack for 1735, showing University College and its benefactors. From left to right, the benefactors are John Radcliffe, Henry IV (with allegorical attendant), Alfred the Great, William of Durham, Walter Skirlaw, Sir Simon Bennet, Henry Percy, Earl of Northumberland, Robert Dudley, Earl of Leicester, and Charles Greenwood.

the timing of this defence of Alfred is suggestive. Cockman's College also showed gratitude to its now-official Founder: when a view of University College appeared on the Oxford Almanack of 1735 (Fig. 12.3), the then customary assembly of College benefactors gathered in the foreground showed an enthroned King Alfred in the centre, with—significantly—William of Durham kneeling humbly before him, clearly knowing his place. The College itself contributed £6 10s. towards the engraving.[43]

Unfortunately, the fires of the 1720s had not been completely extinguished. In May 1729, John Browne stepped down from his long tenure of the Bursarship in favour of Francis Taylor. Taylor fell out with two new Fellows, Thomas Kay and Henry Tennant, deleting their names from the Buttery Book for not paying their batells bills. The other Fellows were angry, and demanded an apology. Taylor went into what can only be described as a sulk, refusing to

[43] 1735 Almanack: Petter 1974: 59–60; paying for the same: UC:BU5/F2/1 p. 144.

submit accounts, or enter College. The Fellows repeatedly summoned him to appear, and eventually deprived him of his stipend for several months. Only in December 1730 did Taylor finally submit his accounts, and apologize to Kay and Tennant. Even then, Taylor had not settled all his debts, and in 1732–5 the College regularly summoned him before the Chancellor's Court. As Taylor refused even to appear in court, the money was sequestered from his stipend. Taylor was evidently deeply hurt: he took no further part in College life until after Cockman's death, when he served as Librarian in 1745/6.[44]

Some might ask whether Taylor had been hounded out of College by opponents who, if they could not touch Cockman, could at least attack one of his allies. However, the facts do not support this: there is no hint that the Fellowship was anything other than united in this affair. We do not know the affiliations of the new Fellows, but they are unlikely to have been supporters of Denison. A more plausible interpretation is that Cockman wished to display his even-handedness. While Charlett had stood by his disreputable friends, Cockman reprimanded Taylor for overstepping the mark.

This behaviour is consistent with Cockman's general demeanour. During the whole of the Mastership dispute, no matter what indignities he suffered, Cockman appears never once to have lost his temper, and, in his final victory, he made no public show of triumph. He also continued to take his duties towards undergraduates seriously. In a dedicatory note 'To the Younger students in the two Universities' to a pair of sermons preached in Oxford in January 1732, he advised his audience:

You are now just entering, Gentlemen, upon the Journey of Publick Life, and your Happiness and Success in it, with Regard both to this and another World, will in great measure depend upon your setting out right at first; *that is*, in the Ways of true *Virtue and Religion*, which alone can... render you a Blessing and an Honour to yourselves, your Families, your Country and your Religion here, and make you everlastingly happy in a Life to come hereafter.[45]

Cockman encouraged good behaviour within College. In the 1730s it is recorded for the first time that misbehaving junior members had to apologize publicly in Hall at dinner. Presumably this was thought a greater deterrent than any financial penalty. The preface to a posthumous edition of Cockman's theological writings recalls his behaviour as Master:

He adorned the Province, which he had gotten, by his prudential Government, his well directed Studies, and unblemished Morals. His regular Conformity to all the Parts of statutable Discipline, his constant Attendance at Divine Worship, his faithful Discharge of his Trust towards the younger Students, with Regard to their Manners and Literature, gave Weight and Spirit to his Instruction, and a Grace to his

[44] Taylor's dispute: UC:GB3/A1/2 fos. 30^v–32^v and UC:MA34/C1/10; pursuing Taylor: OUA CC Papers 1732/54:1–5, 1733/24:1–5, 1734/1:1–4, and 1735/5:1–6.
[45] Cockman 1732: preface (unpaginated).

Reproofs... He did not content himself with the ordinary Care of the Master in a general Inspection, but attended on them frequently at their Chambers, giving his private Instructions, directing their Studies, and aiding them in the Prosecution of them.[46]

This picture is corroborated by an unexpected source, namely a pamphlet of 1747, which, after attacking Oxford for its members' bad behaviour, singled out Thomas Cockman to show what a really good head of house could achieve:

> All those who had the Pleasure of being under his Jurisdiction took more Pride in receiving his Applause, than they would have done on an unexpected Coronet devolving on them; and were in greater Fear of doing any thing to excite a Rebuke from him, than of being expelled the University.[47]

Cockman's conscientious approach to his duties paid dividends: undergraduate admissions in the 1730s were significantly better than those of the last two decades (Graphs 10.1 and 12.1). Indeed Thomas Cockman himself provides a corrective to depictions of Georgian Oxford which tend to overemphasize entertaining but dangerous characters like George Ward.

The same holds true of several Fellows from the 1730s. Perhaps the most interesting is Robert Eden, who along with Francis Walwyn served as Tutor for most of the 1730s (Eden's appointment to this office shows that he and Cockman were reconciled). Eden took the College's undergraduate teaching in a new direction when he and Walwyn began to teach civil law. As Chapter XIV will show, some individual undergraduates were already studying civil law, but Eden systematized its teaching by writing a textbook on civil law, which was published in 1744, after he had left Oxford and had become Archdeacon of Winchester and rector of Headbourne Worthy. Eden explained in his preface that he and Walwyn had thought that it would be useful to teach civil law, but, because there were no suitable textbooks, he had written one himself. Although Eden's book was never reprinted, it did form part of the regular reading for students studying for the BCL degree. Eden and Walwyn evidently concluded that those pupils who were not going to enter the church could benefit from learning the rudiments of law, whether or not they wished to take a law degree (for in 1689–1722, only 3 per cent of members of University College are known to have taken either a BCL or DCL; in 1723–64 the proportion rose only to 5 per cent).[48]

We can learn something of the life of one of Eden and Walwyn's pupils from an account book kept by Charles Yarburgh (m. 1735; Freeston Scholar 1739–44). He bought many classical texts, including Herodotus, Theocritus, Caesar, Cicero, Pliny, Tacitus, and Suetonius (although it is not clear whether he was buying translations or original texts), a collection of John Locke's

---

[46] Silvester 1750: preface (unpaginated).
[47] Anon. 1747: 23–4.
[48] Eden's textbook: Eden 1744; assessments: Barton 1986: 599 and Bourguignon 1987: 37. Many DCL degrees were only honorary anyway.

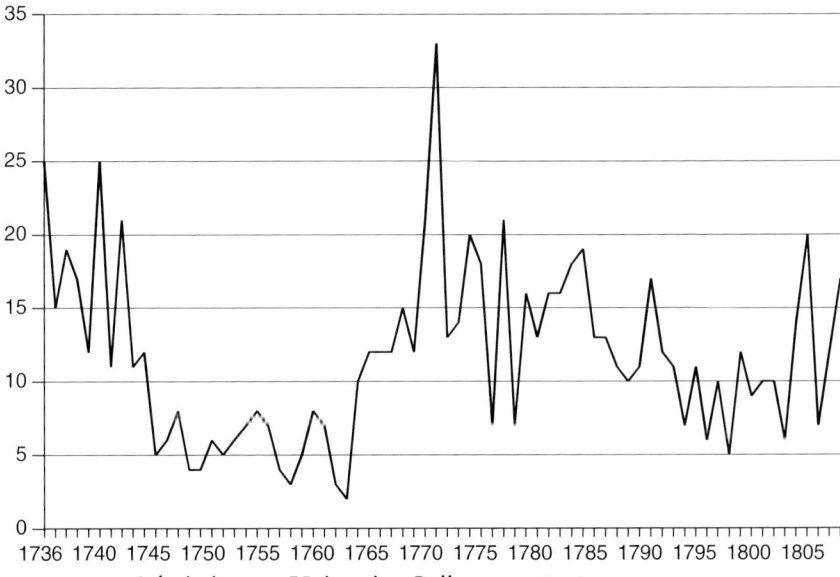

GRAPH 12.1 Admissions to University College, 1736–1807.

essays, and treatises on logic and rhetoric. There were necessary College expenses, such as Christmas boxes for College servants. Off duty, Yarburgh bought the enticingly titled *History of the Buccaneers* and *Gulliver's Travels*, but also the works of Alexander Pope, and he also purchased fishing tackle and hired a boat on the river. He took up bowling and cricket, and sometimes hired a horse to explore the countryside. His accounts also reveal a fondness for chocolate, and trips to local inns, coffee houses, and the local cockpit. Once or twice he lost a little money at cards. He took up dancing lessons, and joined a catch club, enjoyed seeing such curiosities as a magic lantern show or 'the little Man without Feet', and cheered up his rooms by buying singing birds. Yarburgh's accounts are fascinating for their very ordinariness. He did enough work to merit a Scholarship, but he also enjoyed his recreation. When he ended one letter to his brother 'Univ. Coll Oxon 11 a Clock at night 3 parts drunk', it is difficult to be too censorious.[49]

Other undergraduates kept the waning antiquarian tradition alive, such as Charles Lyttleton (m. 1732), later Bishop of Carlisle, one of the first Britons to attempt a more systematic study of Saxon and Gothic architecture. A young baronet who matriculated in 1736, Sir Roger Newdigate, also became fascinated by the Gothic style, an interest which would later influence his old College.[50]

---

[49] Yarburgh's account book: Borthwick Institute, YM/AB/13; letter: Borthwick Institute YM/CP/2.
[50] Sweet 2004: 205, 248–50, and 453, and Lyttleton's *ODNB* entry.

In the wider world, Cockman was no fixer: he did not involve himself in university or national politics, but concentrated his attentions on his College. In any event, his early dealings with a Hebdomadal Council newly shorn of its Visitatorial powers might not have been easy. Cockman did occasionally preach to the university on important occasions, such as on 30 January 1733, the anniversary of Charles I, King and Martyr, and more significantly, in July 1733, when he gave one of the two main sermons at the last revival of the University Act (the forerunner of today's Encaenia). Unfortunately even the sympathetic Thomas Hearne thought that Cockman was outshone by the other preacher.[51]

Cockman's concentration on domestic matters makes it appropriate that the most significant event of his Mastership was the promulgation of University College's first comprehensive set of statutes. After four years' work, a new set was almost ready by 1733, but it was only in 1736 the new statutes were completed and approved by its new, Royal, Visitor.[52]

Many of the new statutes merely codified existing ones, and sometimes just paraphrased them (the rules concerning the smooth running of the College drew heavily on the statutes of 1292), but some modifications were made in the light of recent events. Any Fellow or Scholar of the College could now be Master—even a Bennet Fellow—and, if no candidate had an absolute majority, then the Senior Fellow had a casting vote. The confusion of the 1720s could thus never be repeated. Furthermore, the Master's powers were carefully defined: although Fellows had to obey the Master's authority, a Fellow could only be removed by a vote of the Master and a majority of Fellows, and decisions taken by the Master and Fellows could only be rescinded by a two-thirds majority. Such rules would have kept Arthur Charlett better within bounds.

As for the statutes regarding Fellows, although certain general regulations could be made concerning their private means, the manner of their election, and the like, it was felt that the wishes of founders of individual Fellowships should still be respected. Therefore William of Durham, Skirlaw, and Percy Fellows should continue to study theology, and come from north-east England. On the other hand, the only restrictions placed on Bennet Fellows were that they should first have been Bennet Scholars, and should definitely not come from north-east England. All Fellows were expected to enter holy orders within four years of taking their MA, but two Bennet Fellows could remain laymen, studying Medicine or Jurisprudence. The statutes also established the duties of College officers, including the Catechist, the Dean, the

---

[51] Preaching on Charles I's day: Hearne, xi. 153; Act Sermon: Cockman 1733 and Hearne, xi. 227, 231, 238–9, and 241. Today the 1733 Act is best remembered for the concerts given then by Handel.

[52] Delay of 1733: Hearne, xi. 278; official copy of these statutes: UC:GB1/L3/2 (Cox 1971*b* provides a detailed summary of their contents).

three Praelectors, the Librarian, the Moderator of the BAs, and the Registrar, and formally created the post of Vice-Master, which should come into being only when the Master was absent.

With regard to the Scholars, an important loophole was closed. Although existing statutes were clear enough concerning the selection of Scholars, they said little about their tenure. As a result, some Scholars held their awards for preposterously long terms. Gunsley Scholars were the worst offenders: two members of the Ayerst family, both called William, held their awards respectively in c.1662–91 and 1698–1716, but the most tenacious of all was John Bateman. Appointed a Gunsley Scholar in April 1678 whilst still a pupil at Maidstone, he matriculated from University College in 1683, and retained his Scholarship until his death in 1749—a total of seventy-one years, and the longest time that any College member has held an award. But, under the old statutes, nothing could be done. Now all new Scholars had to resign their awards two years after taking their MA.

The new statutes—and, indeed, the new Visitor—marked a new start for University College. No longer was the College dependent on the whim of the Hebdomadal Council: no longer did it have to submit newly elected Fellows for its approval, and the Vice-Chancellor no longer signed its accounts. On the other hand, the College still needed Visitatorial advice: the statutes concerning Fellowships led to continuing problems of interpretation. In 1735, 1740, and 1768, Fellowship elections were set aside by the Visitor on the grounds that the Fellows had passed over someone from the correct geographical background.[53]

Thomas Cockman died in the Master's Lodgings on 1 February 1745, and was buried at the east end of the Chapel, under the communion table, 'as if', wrote Carr, 'to make sure that after death none should disturb his rest'.[54] Cockman was not a 'great' Master: he made no original contribution to scholarship; he was no grand patron; he took no part in university or national politics. Yet he is also one of the most sympathetic characters in this whole history. He inherited a College divided, shamed, and short of money, and with an unassuming mixture of kindness and firmness healed its wounds and restored its stability.

JOHN BROWNE AND THE HUTCHINSONIANS: 1745–1764

The first election under the new statutes passed quietly. A month after Cockman's death, all twelve Fellows—including even Francis Taylor—

---

[53] Independence from Hebdomadal Council: UC:GB3/A1/2 fo. 29; disputed elections: UC:GB3/A1/2 fos. 34^v–35^v, 42^r–45^v and 76^v–80^v. The first half of the eighteenth century saw other Colleges having their statutes on the election of Fellows reinterpreted in a stricter manner, as for example at Magdalen (Darwall-Smith in Brockliss (forthcoming)) and at All Souls (Davis in Green and Horden 2007: 233–8).

[54] UC:GB3/A1/2 fo. 48^v and Carr, 181.

unanimously elected John Browne Master, and a few days later the result was confirmed by the Lord Chancellor. We last encountered this new Master as a supporter of Cockman in the 1720s. Since then his had been a quieter life: in 1738 he had become Archdeacon of Northampton, and he resigned his Fellowship the following year. In 1743 he became a Canon of Peterborough Cathedral. Now aged about 60, Browne's seniority and authority made him an obvious choice.[55]

John Browne, however, remains the most obscure eighteenth-century Master of University College. No collection of his papers exists; no diarist or writer of memoirs is known to have alluded to him; and no portrait survives. Although he served as Vice-Chancellor in 1750–3, personally he did little of note. Nevertheless, some clues remain. Someone capable of praying for Thomas Cockman as Master in the presence of his opponents evidently had fire in his belly. Moreover, one observer of his Vice-Chancellorship referred to Browne as entering 'upon the plan of reformation which his predecessors had begun...[hoping] to make such a progress therein, by the meeting of Parliament, as what may reasonably stop the mouths of our enemys, and open those of our friends'. This suspicion of Parliament—and his very appointment as Vice-Chancellor—implies that Browne's politics were solidly Tory.[56]

Nevertheless, Browne was not particularly active in politics, as seen in the Parliamentary election of January 1751. This was an exciting event, because one of the candidates was an Old Member, Sir Roger Newdigate. Newdigate is an interesting character: an independent Tory and a country gentleman, he was also a progressive landlord, who invested in coalmines, canals, and turnpikes. He was a connoisseur of art, collecting marbles and vases in Italy, and a discerning patron of architecture. He also endowed the Newdigate Prize for poetry. Newdigate's politics appealed to members of the university, and he was duly elected, retaining his seat until he retired in 1780. Arthur Charlett would have relished the opportunity to support such a candidate enthusiastically, but John Browne appears to have done nothing apart from leading all seven College members who voted into Newdigate's camp. A letter from Newdigate to Browne, written after the election, thanks him for his friendship, but makes no mention of actual positive assistance. Even afterwards, Browne made little effort to cultivate such an important Old Member.[57]

The political torpor of the College was perhaps advantageous. The Jacobite cloud had still not quite lifted from Oxford, as occasional displays of Jacobite enthusiasm were suppressed. However, in 1745, Jacobitism became more than an idle threat when Prince Charles Stuart, the Young Pretender, led a

[55] Browne's election: UC:GB3/A1/2 fos. 49^r–50^v; his career: Le Neve 1996: 123 and 130.
[56] Browne as Vice-Chancellor: quoted in Ward 1958: 187.
[57] Newdigate's character: *ODNB* entry; his election: Langford 1986: 125–6, the Poll Book of the election, and White 1995: 44–51 (the letter to Browne is on 49–50).

rebellion which proved far more dangerous than his father's. Some of the College's former members came out in support: Bryan Faussett (m. 1738), now a Fellow of All Souls, tried to raise a volunteer corps in support of Prince Charles, and Charles Noel Somerset, now Duke of Beaufort, met the Prince when he secretly visited London in 1750. Within the College, however, there is no record of any trouble. Whatever John Browne's personal views, his College remained outwardly loyal.[58]

Nevertheless, during Browne's Mastership the membership of University College fell to its smallest levels since the Civil War (Graph 12.1). Twelve undergraduates came up in 1745, but between 1746 and 1763, admission totals remained in single figures, reaching their lowest in 1762 and 1763 when just three and two undergraduates came up. It was not until 1764 that numbers rose again. The low numbers caused problems: in 1747–56, several Scholarship elections were postponed or cancelled because there were no suitable candidates. Browne's College, however, was not alone: the eighteenth century witnessed a general decline in undergraduate admissions at Oxford and Cambridge which reached its nadir in the 1750s. Various reasons have been suggested: parental anxiety about Oxford's Jacobite leanings; concern that undergraduates fell into bad habits; and the great expense of a university career. This lack of numbers had one happy result for those who did come up: greater privacy. With less demand for accommodation, a member of University College in the 1750s could have two or three rooms to himself. The drawback was that the stipends of individual tutors would suffer, as would the salaries of servants who depended on tips from members of College.[59]

Political inactivity and low numbers might suggest that University College was in a state of hibernation under John Browne, but this was not quite the case. It still basked in King Alfred's glory. When John Browne, as Vice-Chancellor, could choose the design of the Oxford Almanack for 1753 (Fig. 12.4) he settled for King Alfred standing in front of the Radcliffe Quadrangle to welcome allegorical figures representing the arts and sciences to his foundation. More significantly, now that the College was in possession of the Linton estate, it could use the surplus from its funds as John Radcliffe had stipulated, and purchase advowsons. Thus it acquired the livings of Tarrant Gunville near Blandford Forum in Dorset (1747), North Cerney near Cirencester in Gloucestershire (1753; Plate 8), Elton near Peterborough in Huntingdonshire (1760/1),

---

[58] Jacobitism in Oxford in the 1730s and 1740s: Monod 1989: 275–8; Bryan Faussett: *ODNB* entry; the Duke of Beaufort: Monod 1989: 207–9.
[59] Unfilled posts: UC:GB3/A1/2 fos. 52^v–53^r, 53^v, 59^r, and 60^v–61^r; decline in admissions: Green 1986a: 309–16 and Searby 1997: 12 and 62; extra space: Colvin 1986: 843–5 and Tyack 1998: 129–31. Numbers were falling in other European universities in the eighteenth century (Di Simone 1996: 304–11).

FIGURE 12.4 The Oxford Almanack for 1753. King Alfred welcomes the arts and sciences to 'his' College.

and, just after Browne's death, Checkendon in south Oxfordshire (1765/6; Fig. 14.2). Soon there would be some real preferment for the Fellows.[60]

Signs of intellectual life in the mid-century College appear in a biography of George Horne (m. 1746), Bishop of Norwich, by his undergraduate friend William Jones (m. 1745).[61] Both were Scholars: Jones (usually called 'William Jones of Nayland', to distinguish him from another—unrelated—William Jones whom we shall meet later) first became aware of Horne when their Tutor Henry Hobson (F. 1740–77) asked them both to rewrite a poem by the Roman philosopher and poet Boethius in a different metre. The contest united the two young men in a lifelong friendship.[62]

Horne took his studies seriously—Jones recalls him studying 'Oratory, Poetry, Philosophy, History, and ... well acquainted with the Greek Tragedians, of which he was to become a great admirer'—almost in spite of his tutors: Jones thought

[60] The 1753 Almanack: Petter 1974: 67, and Keynes 1999: 323 (Petter 1974: 13 shows that by now almanack designs were selected by the Vice-Chancellor); purchases of advowsons: UC:BU5/F2/1 p. 256, UC:BU5/F2/2 fos. 15ʳ, 41ʳ, and 60ᵛ. See too Appendix V.
[61] Jones 1795.
[62] Friendships: Jones 1795: 19.

the College's lectures in geometry and natural philosophy 'not very deep'. However, University College did support Horne when it mattered. As a southerner and a Gunsley Scholar, Horne's prospects of a Fellowship in his own College were small, but in 1750, a Fellowship at Magdalen College open to men from Kent fell vacant, and there was no internal candidate. Jones recalled the (unnamed) Senior Fellow of University College rushing to Magdalen to tell them of the 'extraordinary young man they might find in University College'; on his recommendation Horne was promptly elected. Horne fully justified his promise: in 1768 he was elected President of Magdalen, and he ended his days as Bishop of Norwich. He was also remembered as much for his goodness as his learning. One memoirist, growing up in the 1790s, recalled phrases like 'true as George Horne' or 'sweet-tempered as George Horne' still in regular use.[63]

The young Horne attracted like-minded friends at Oxford, including Charles Jenkinson (m. 1746; Leicester Scholar 1751), whom Jones remembered as 'a gentleman who...always promised to *do* something, and to *be* something, beyond other men of this time'.[64] Jenkinson, indeed, was remembered as a particularly diligent student. Thomas Maurice, whom we shall meet later, heard tales of Jenkinson's undergraduate years:

[Jenkinson's] pursuits were rather out of the common line, and somewhat perplexing to his contemporaries in college, as, without wholly neglecting his classical studies, he seemed immersed in abstruse researches of a political nature, and his table was constantly covered with judicial tracts and collections of ancient statutes, treaties &c., while the works of Grotius, Puffendorf, and other renowned civilians were for ever in his hand.[65]

It will become clear that Jenkinson justified the hopes placed in him—or at least encouraged his friends to believe that they had spotted his potential.

Jones's biography, however, shows that it was in religion, rather than law, that University College achieved an especial vitality. The modern reader might be justified in thinking here of the growth of Methodism under the inspiration of a Fellow of Lincoln College called John Wesley, which remains the best-known religious movement in mid-Georgian Oxford. However, with the exception of Thomas Broughton (m. 1731), later secretary to the Society for Promoting Christian Knowledge, who joined Wesley's disciples while an undergraduate, Methodism put down no roots at University College.[66]

Instead, University College became infused with a very different set of beliefs called Hutchinsonianism, inspired by the Yorkshireman John

---

[63] Horne as a student: Jones 1795: 21 and 24; his fellowship: Jones 1795: 20; his good nature: Cox 1870: 163; Horne at Magdalen: Darwall-Smith in Brockliss (forthcoming).
[64] Jones 1795: 165.
[65] Maurice 1819–20: ii. 191–2.
[66] Green 1986*b*: 442, and Thomas Broughton's *ODNB* entry.

Hutchinson (1674–1737). This 'somewhat freakish movement', as Vivian Green called it, requires some explanation, both because it is comparatively little known today, and because it exerted a considerable influence in Oxford even into the early nineteenth century. At its simplest, Hutchinsonianism was a reaction to rationalism, which, it was feared, had dethroned divine revelation in favour of human reason. Hutchinson himself believed that the scientific revolution of his day, especially as represented by Newton, conflicted with revealed religion. He therefore attempted to disprove Newtonian physics, and created a so-called 'physico-theology', ambitiously attempting to explain science with the aid of religion.[67]

Hutchinson proposed a novel interpretation of the Hebrew language, claiming that each character of the alphabet had a particular spiritual meaning, and that the book of Genesis, when read aright, provided a full account of natural philosophy and religion. He even created an alternative model of the universe, which denied the existence of a vacuum, and attempted to explain Newtonian physics in a more spiritual way. Hutchinsonians also believed in the divine appointment of kings and the priesthood, and the importance of the Church as a repository of revelation and tradition. Although Hutchinson's physics were gradually set aside, his theology remained attractive, if still controversial: John James, an undergraduate at Queen's in the 1770s, mocked the Hutchinsonians' 'laboured interpretations of certain passages in the Bible'.[68]

William Jones was first exposed to Hutchinsonianism by Alexander Catcott, a member of Wadham College, but a far greater influence was a charismatic—and Hutchinsonian—Fellow of University College called George Watson (m. 1740; F. 1747–54). Jones's description of Watson is worth quoting, because he clearly wished to show Watson as the perfect Fellow and Tutor:

> He was a classical scholar of the first rate,...remarkable for an unusual degree of taste and judgement in Poetry and Oratory; his person was elegant and striking, and his countenance expressed at once both the gentleness of his temper and the quickness of his understanding. His manners and address were those of a perfect gentleman:...his benevolence was so great, that all the beggars in Oxford knew the way to his chamberdoor: upon the whole, his character was so spotless, and his conduct so exemplary, that, mild and gentle as he was in his carriage toward them, no young man dared to be rude in his company.[69]

Not unlike the eulogist of Thomas Cockman, Jones praised Watson for matching his morals and learning with an elegant outward appearance.

Jones first met Watson when they shared the same staircase. Jones became aware of Watson's Hutchinsonianism—for all his discretion on the subject.

---

[67] 'Freakish': Green 1986b: 456–7. For some accounts of Hutchinsonianism, see Kuhn 1961, Clark 1985: 218–27, Aston 1993, Nockles 1994: 45–6 and 211, and Young 1998: 136–51.
[68] Evans 1887: 199.
[69] Jones 1795: 23–5 (Catcott) and 25–6 (Watson).

Watson was willing to teach Jones Hebrew, and then, on Jones's recommendation, also taught Horne.[70] Horne, however, was initially unconvinced by Hutchinsonianism. Jones wrote:

> How it was objected to, and how it was defended, I do not now exactly remember; I fear, not with any profound skill on either side; but this I well recollect, that our disputes, which happened at a pleasant season of the year, kept us walking to and fro in the Quadrangle till past midnight.[71]

This picture of undergraduates eagerly debating into the small hours has a refreshingly timeless feel. It reminds us, too, that we do Georgian Oxford a disservice if we ignore people like Jones and Horne, even if they are less immediately glamorous than the reprobate or the rebel.

Hebrew and Hutchinsonianism proved an exciting mixture, and Horne was eventually won over. In a poem dedicated to Watson, Horne records how his teacher's revelation of the true way dispelled his despair at rationalist approaches to the world:

> For Wisdom then to Moderns I apply'd,
> And on Divines and Moralists rely'd.
> But [then] I found (may black Oblivion veil
> From future Times the guilty horrid Tale)
> Reason enthron'd in Revelation's Place
> Dull Metaphysicks Substitutes of Grace,
> A Saviour's Merits cast neglected by
> And God's blest Word in tenfold darkness lye.[72]

Others came under Watson's spell, including Nathan Wetherell, a BA of Lincoln College who was elected a Fellow in 1750. Wetherell collaborated with Horne, after the latter's move to Magdalen College, in an (eventually abortive) attempt to compile a new Hebrew lexicon. Wetherell, however, remained interested in Hutchinsonianism, especially in regard to the role of monarchy. In January 1756, on the anniversary of Charles I's execution, he preached a provocative sermon in the university church praising the doctrine of passive obedience to a monarch, a doctrine which, since 1689, had been thought to savour of Jacobitism. By 1756, however, Jacobitism was a spent force, and Wetherell should rather be seen as choosing to reveal his High Tory affiliations in a self-consciously arresting manner.[73]

Some may wonder at this point why the Hutchinsonians deserve such attention here. The reason lies in the people who were drawn to it: in the later eighteenth century, although William Jones of Nayland remained somewhat closer to his Hutchinsonian roots than George Horne, both men—especially

---

[70] Jones 1795: 26–7.   [71] Jones 1795: 25.
[72] 'A Letter to the Revd. Mr. Watson': MCA MS 473 no. 12.
[73] The Hebrew lexicon: Jones 1795: 46–7; Wetherell's sermon: Kennicott 1756: 15–16.

Horne—became eminent exponents of a High Church and Tory theology. Their writings remained influential after their deaths, for the young theologians of the Oxford Movement in the 1830s and 1840s took a great interest in them. Nathan Wetherell never became such an eminent theologian, but achieved significant influence in other ways. A hint of this came in June 1761, when another BA of Lincoln College, Robert Chambers, was also elected a Fellow of University College. Chambers was a kinsman of Wetherell (his aunt married Wetherell's brother), but he was also remarkably well connected: during the summer of 1754, when he had been studying at the Middle Temple, he had attracted the friendship of Samuel Johnson. The next chapter will reveal how skilfully Wetherell exploited such links of kinship and friendship. In short, George Watson's Hutchinsonian protégés achieved a significance quite out of proportion to their numbers.[74]

It is characteristic that nothing is known of John Browne's views on Hutchinsonianism: George Watson's reluctance to reveal his beliefs implies an unsympathetic Master, but Nathan Wetherell nevertheless served as Dean in 1757/8–1758/9 after his controversial sermon. By now John Browne was well into his seventies, and on 7 August 1764 he died at Long Compton, a Warwickshire parish where he had been vicar since 1714. In his will, Browne bequeathed his library 'to be used and enjoyed by the Master of the said College for the time being and to be kept in his Lodgings and to be esteemed and go with them as and in the manner of Heir looms' (the Browne Library still remains in the Master's Lodgings). However, his main bequest was an estate in Marlow, Buckinghamshire, and a house in Oxford, situated directly east of Logic Lane (the current site of Durham Buildings), the income from which would fund College Scholarships—but not in the usual way. Browne created two new Scholarships worth £20 a year, open to Yorkshiremen, but he assigned other sums to augment existing awards. Many College Scholarships were now almost worthless, since their stipends had remained unchanged for so long. The Leicester Scholars did well, receiving £20 a year, and the Gunsley Scholars were not so badly off, at £15, but Freeston junior Exhibitioners and Hunt Scholars each received £5, while Browne Scholars received a paltry £2 12s. John Browne augmented the Freeston, Browne, and Hunt Scholarships, so that they were all worth £20 a year.[75]

As well as showing his affection for the College which he had known for sixty years, John Browne's will provides the clearest insight into his character, for his bequest to the College reveals an unassuming good sense. Like

---

[74] Jones and Horne's influence: Aston 1993 and Clark 1985: 218–27 and 247–8; Chambers's kinship with Wetherell: Curley 1998: 6 and 54; Chambers and Johnson: Redford 1992–4: i. 86, Boswell 1980): 372 and 387, and Curley 1998: 19.
[75] Browne's death: UC:GB3/A1/2 fo. 70ᵛ; Browne's will: copied in accounts for Dr Browne's Trust, 1764–1813 (uncatalogued). Due to some life interests in his will, Browne's Scholarships, and augmentations only came into effect in 1781 (UC:GB3/A1/2 fo. 97ʳ).

Thomas Cockman, Browne was not a grand fixer or patron, but rather presided over a generally peaceful College, which, if not outstanding, could still encourage scholarship and learning. Moreover, whether through luck or judgement, he left it with members who would, in the following two decades, lead it into one of the most brilliant periods in its history.

13
Glory and Decline: 1764–1807

THE GREAT AWAKENING: 1764–1772

Finding a successor to John Browne proved contentious. There were two candidates, the Hutchinsonian Nathan Wetherell and Joseph Betts, Fellow since 1741, who had regularly held at least one College office for two decades, and been a Tutor since 1747. Betts thought that the election was his, but Henry Tennant, the senior Fellow, and his supporters suddenly transferred their votes to Wetherell. As a result, on 28 August 1764, seven Fellows voted for Wetherell, and four for Betts. Wetherell himself, with typical subtlety, was present but abstained. Betts was bitter at his treatment—in November 1764, he wrote to Charles Jenkinson that his enemies had used 'the dirtiest & lowest devices the meanest Heart can invent' on him—and resigned his Fellowship a year later, on being elected Savilian Professor of Geometry, but died only a few months afterwards.[1]

Betts was the more senior Fellow, and most of his supporters had been Fellows for twenty years or longer, but Wetherell attracted the votes of the younger Fellows (including his kinsman Robert Chambers). Perhaps Betts was too old-fashioned; one tale suggests as much. In March 1764, University College welcomed a young Harrovian called William Jones (no relation of William Jones of Nayland) who had won such a formidable reputation as a schoolboy that his headmaster claimed that Jones knew more Greek than he did. Jones's Tutors at University College were John Betts and John Coulson, a Fellow since 1744, one of Betts's supporters, and something of an eccentric. Jones was unimpressed: he found the public lectures meaningless, and later grumbled 'that he was required to attend dull comments on artificial ethics, and logic detailed in such barbarous Latin, that he professed to know as little of it as he then knew of Arabic'. One suspects that Betts and Coulson were not very inspiring teachers. The Fellows, therefore, who preferred Wetherell to Betts were seeking a change.[2]

---

[1] The election: BL MS Add. 38649 fo. 111^r (part of the text of this letter is missing, but it shows that Tennant's action was crucial) and UC:GB3/A1/2 fo. 71^r; Betts' anger: BL MS Add. 38649 fo. 115^v.
[2] Jones at Harrow: Tyerman 2000: 118–23; Jones's teachers: Teignmouth 1804: 31.

FIGURE 13.1 William Jones, m. 1764 and Fellow 1766–83, by John Linnell after a portrait by Joshua Reynolds.

FIGURE 13.2 Robert Chambers, Fellow 1761–75, by Robert Home.

Although John Browne's College had nurtured the likes of George Horne, it was not a very brilliant institution. This changed under Nathan Wetherell. First of all, there was young William Jones (Fig. 13.1). There are several cases in Georgian Oxford of a potential genius coming up to a college unable to handle him, such as Jeremy Bentham at Queen's, or more infamously, Edward Gibbon at Magdalen. This did not happen at University College. In October 1764, Jones was elected to a Bennet Scholarship. Betts and Coulson then exempted Jones from attending their lectures, 'alleging with equal truth and civility, that he could employ his time to more advantage'. Such a dispensation could not be granted without the Master's approval. Jones repaid Wetherell's trust: left to his own devices, he read 'all the Greek poets and historians', and taught himself Arabic and Persian.[3]

Jones knew his scholarly worth. His first biographer claims that he desired a Fellowship to support his family, and in 1765, despairing of obtaining one, became private tutor to a young aristocrat, Viscount Althorp, later Earl Spencer. This tale, however, is not quite what it appears. Jones was only 18 years old, and would have known that he would have to wait for a Bennet Fellowship to fall vacant. More probably he was hinting that the College

---

[3] Bentham: Hodgkin 1949: 149–53; Gibbon: Darwall-Smith in Brockliss (forthcoming); Jones's exemption: Teignmouth 1804: 32–4. Another exceptional student, Robert Southey (m. Balliol 1793), was similarly exempted from attending lectures (Jones 2005: 175).

might lose its brilliant student. Wetherell took no chances: Joseph Betts resigned his Bennet Fellowship in November 1765, but in February 1766 the election of his successor was postponed until further notice, 'on account of the youthful years of the candidates'. When the election was held in August 1766, Jones was elected, although he was still in his teens, and had still to take his BA, making him the first known Fellow of University College to have been elected while still an undergraduate. The hand of Nathan Wetherell is easily detectable, especially because Jones was elected only by Wetherell and two Fellows.[4]

Wetherell's plans for Jones worked perfectly. To be sure, Jones never held any College office during his seventeen years as a Fellow: he had young Viscount Althorp to teach, and thereafter he pursued a legal career. This use of a stipend to subsidize the latter career was not unusual, but Jones combined his legal work with scholarship. He enjoyed having in Oxford 'access to extensive libraries, rare manuscripts, the company of learned men, and all... that his heart could wish', and usually stayed in College over Christmas and in August to pursue his research, calling in at other times when passing through on legal business.[5]

Jones would become one of the most remarkable Fellows of University College at any time in its history. A consummate linguist, he once reckoned that he had studied eight languages 'critically' (including Arabic, Persian, and Sanskrit), eight 'less perfectly, but all intelligible with a dictionary' (including Portuguese, Hebrew, and Hindi), and twelve more 'least perfectly, but all attainable' (including Tibetan, Welsh, and Chinese). With a certain insouciance, he wrote to a friend in January 1771 that the 'Persian' manuscript he had sent him was a Chinese one, but no matter: as Jones said, 'I shall be able to make [it] out, when the weather will permit me to sit in the Bodleian.'[6]

The fruits of Jones's terrifying productivity soon emerged. In 1770, he produced, at the request of the King of Denmark, a French translation of a Persian history of Nadir Shah; in 1771 he published three volumes, including a dissertation on oriental literature and a Persian grammar; in 1772 he produced a volume of poetry 'consisting chiefly of translations from the Asiatick languages'; and in 1774 a treatise on oriental poetry. He then published a translation and commentary of the Greek orator Isaeus in 1779 and an *Essay on the Law of Bailments* in 1781. Not only did he publish more than any other eighteenth-century Fellow of University College (apart,

---

[4] Jones's tutorship: Teignmouth 1804: 34; his election: UC:GB3/A1/2 fos. 73^r–75^v; Jones's status: some Fellows appointed after 1648 lacked degrees, but the Civil War had interrupted their academic careers.

[5] Working in Oxford: Teignmouth 1804: 36; his periods of residence can be deduced from the addresses of his letters in Cannon 1970.

[6] Jones's languages: Teignmouth 1804: 376; working in the Bodleian: Cannon 1970: i. 79 (the Bodleian, obeying its Founder's injunctions against kindling flames, remained unheated in winter).

possibly, from John Hudson), but, as 'Oriental' Jones, he was more or less the only one to win international fame. His achievement lay in the breadth of his appeal. Scholars could explore the languages which he uncovered, while his stylish translations of oriental literature provided such inspiration to poets and men of letters, that Jones can be hailed as a forerunner of the Romantic movement. Even Goethe admired his work.[7]

While William Jones was single-handedly transforming the College's scholarly reputation, Wetherell oversaw no less remarkable a transformation in its teaching. He himself took an active role in teaching undergraduates, acting as Catechist in 1767–88, with only one year's gap. No previous Master is known to have held a teaching post. For Wetherell, it was an excellent means of getting to know his undergraduates—and vice versa. One remembered him as 'a man of great urbanity of manners, rigid in general discipline, but kind to the inexperience of youth and lenient to the failings of genius'. He certainly knew their ways: John Scott, later Lord Eldon, recalled that William Windham (m. 1767) sketched a doodle of the Master during one of his lectures, only to find Wetherell, expressing pleasure that Windham was keeping such careful notes, asking to see them.[8]

Wetherell also chose College Tutors carefully. John Betts ceased to be a Tutor in 1764, and John Coulson took his final pupil in April 1766, but Robert Chambers (Fig. 13.2) began to work as a Tutor in October 1764. Wetherell also spotted talent outside the College. In December 1764, the Fellowship vacated by Wetherell's promotion was filled by a young BA from Corpus Christi, a Newcastle man called William Scott (Fig. 13.3). Scott accepted his first tutorial pupil in September 1765, when he was still not yet 20, and soon he and Chambers were in complete charge of the College's tutorial responsibilities.[9]

Young William Scott acquired a legendary reputation as a tutor, eliciting a remarkable tribute from Edward Gibbon. In his autobiography, having damned the Oxford of his own time, Gibbon admitted that matters had since improved, and that 'many students have been attracted by the merit and reputation of Sir William Scott, then a tutor in University College...my personal acquaintance with that gentleman has inspired me with a just esteem for his abilities and knowledge'. This assessment is supported by the testimonies of two pupils of William Scott. The first, Walter Stanhope, a Yorkshire gentleman, came up in 1766. Like George Radcliffe a century and a half earlier, he had been brought up by a widowed mother, and he wrote regularly both to her and to two doting uncles. Stanhope possessed a good sense of

---

[7] Jones's books: Cannon 1990: 14–16, 35–40, 47–52, 63–6, 150–2, and Marshall 1986: 562–3; his reputation in his lifetime: Cannon 1990: 16–17, 40, 313, and 343–4.

[8] Enforcing discipline: UC:GB3/A1/2 fos. 77^{r-v}, 84^{r}–85^{v}, 89^{v}, and 102^{r}; Wetherell's teaching: Maurice 1819–20: ii. 20: Windham's doodles: Twiss 1844: i. 54–5.

[9] Changes in Tutors are detectable in UC:J1/A/2; Scott's election: UC:GB3/A1/2 fo. 72^{v}.

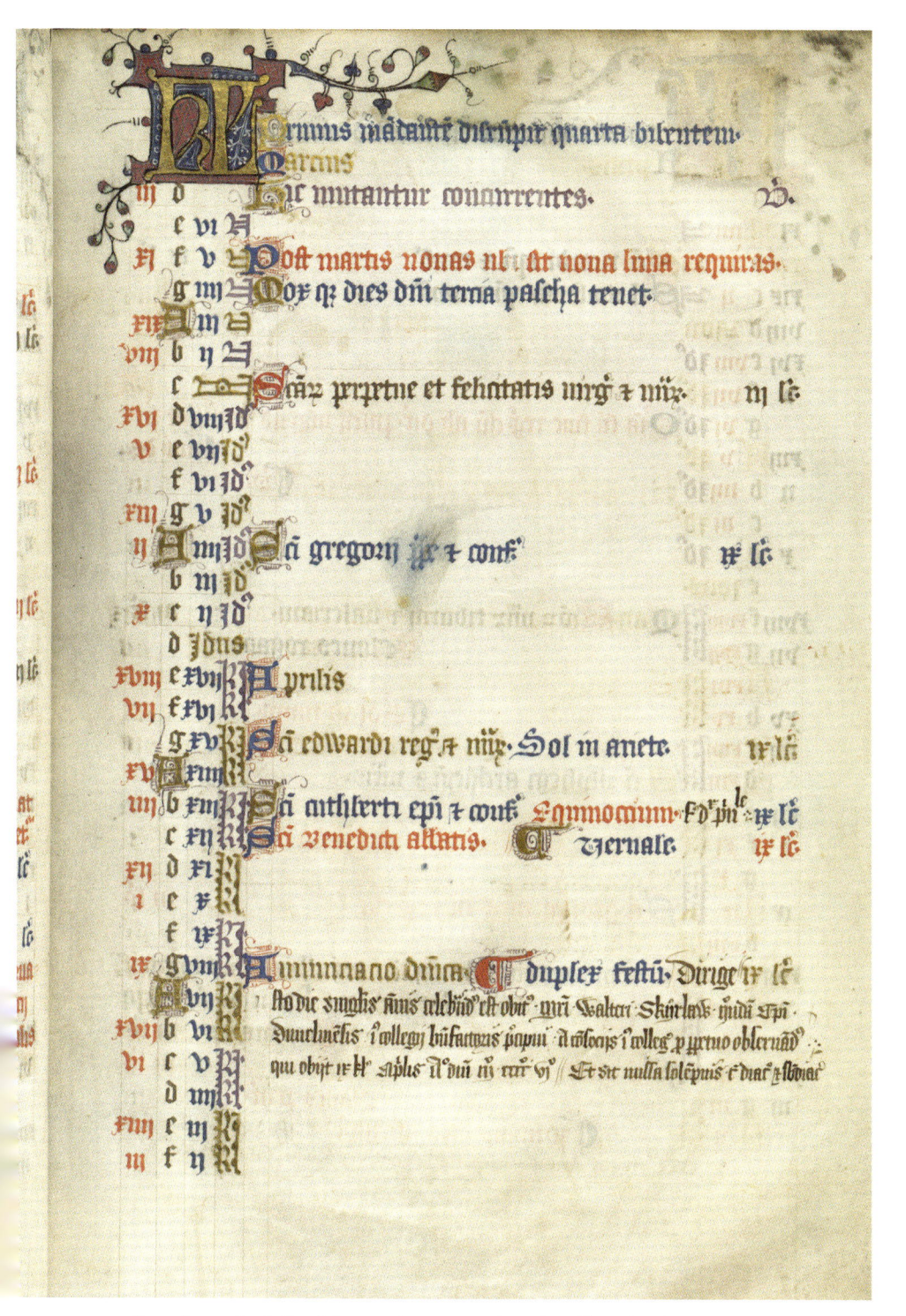

PLATE 1: Page from the Missal (c. 1400) once used in the Chapel of University College, showing saints days and feasts to be observed in March. St. Cuthbert's Day is on 20 March. A note to commemorate Walter Skirlaw on 25 March has been added.

PLATE 2: St. Oswald's Church, Arncliffe, Yorkshire, whose rectory was given to University College by Henry Percy, Earl of Northumberland, in 1443.

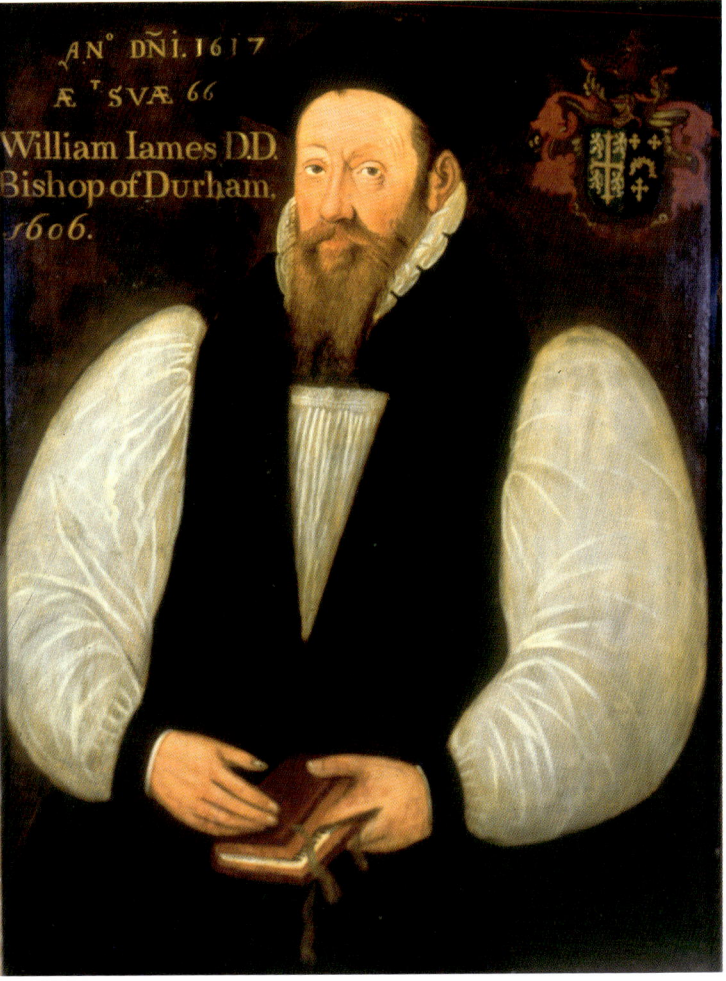

PLATE 3: William James, Master 1572–84, by an unknown artist.

PLATES 4 & 5: Two of the windows designed for the College Chapel by Abraham van Linge in 1641, showing the tales of Abraham and Isaac (l.) and Jonah and the whale (r.).

PLATE 6 Illustration from a twelfth-century manuscript of Bede's *Life of St. Cuthbert* given to the College by William Rogers in 1670, showing an angel curing St. Cuthbert's diseased knee.

PLATE 7: St. Swithun's Church, Headbourne Worthy, Hampshire, whose advowson was acquired by John Radcliffe in 1693, and bequeathed to trustees who should give first refusal on it to members of University College.

PLATE 8: All Saints' Church, North Cerney, Gloucestershire, whose advowson was purchased by University College in 1753.

PLATE 9: The Radcliffe Quadrangle, built 1716–19.

PLATE 10: Group portrait attributed to Benjamin Ferrers showing Thomas Cockman in the middle and his brother John on the far left, along with what are possibly his supporters in the Mastership dispute of 1722–9.

PLATE 11: James Griffith's unbuilt design for a new Master's Lodgings, intended for the site of Deep Hall, *c.* 1798 (now the site of the Shelley Memorial).

PLATE 12: James Griffith's executed design for altering the façade of the south range of the Front Quadrangle, *c.* 1799.

PLATE 13: Miniature of James Griffith, Fellow 1782–1808 and Master 1808–21, by de la Roche.

University Boat 1827.

PLATE 14: University College's first rowing crew, participating in Eights Week, 1827.

PLATE 15: Conversation piece by F. H. S. Shepherd of Sir Michael Sadler and the Fellows of University College, 1934. The sitters are (back row) David Lindsay Keir, Ernest Ainley Walker, A. D. 'Duncs' Gardner, G. D. H. Cole, John Maud, Arthur Goodhart, and John Wild, and (front row), Edmund Bowen, Arthur Poynton, Sir Michael Sadler, A. S. L. Farquharson, Edgar Carritt, George Stevenson, and Kenneth Leys.

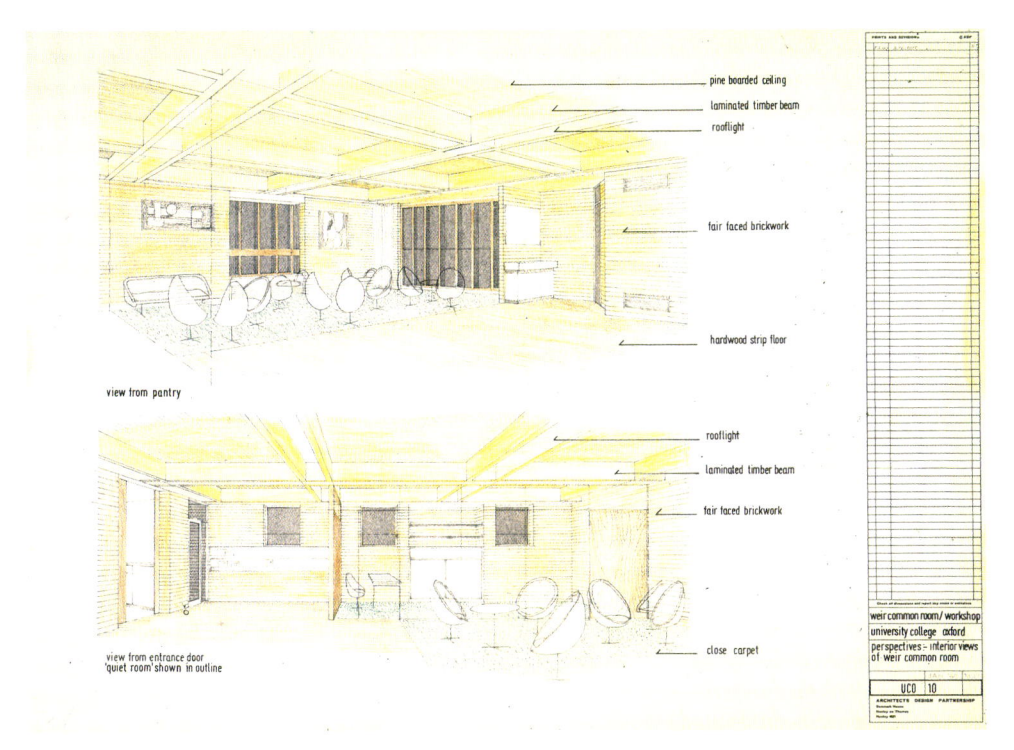

PLATE 16: Design by John Fryman of the Architects Design Partnership of the proposed interior of the Weir Common Room in the Mitchell Building.

PLATE 17: A typical room in the Staverton Road Annexe ('Stavertonia'), designed by Sir Philip Dowson (matr. 1943) of Arup Associates.

PLATE 18: Lord Butler of Brockwell, Master 1998–, and Lady Butler by Benjamin Sullivan. This is thought to be the first official painting of the head of an Oxford or Cambridge college to include his or her spouse.

FIGURE 13.3 William Scott, later Lord Stowell, Fellow 1764–82, by John Hoppner.

FIGURE 13.4 John Scott, later Lord Eldon, m. 1766 and Fellow 1767–73, by William Owen.

humour and a certain irreverence, so that his letters still make excellent reading. The second, Thomas Maurice, migrated to University College from St John's in 1775, and forty years later wrote about his Oxford years in his memoirs. His account, while it is coloured by the passage of time, and gushes somewhat, is nevertheless valuable.[10]

University College was filling up when Walter Stanhope arrived. As he wrote to one of his uncles, 'the College is so very full, that all the Members of above four Years standing were oblig'd to be turn'd out of their Rooms'. He was impressed with Chambers and Scott—'Their learning', he said, 'is deep, liberal & not pedantic'—but reserved especial praise for Scott: 'He is just 21 & there scarce ever was a better Classical Scholar, or indeed one more learned in any other Branch of Literature.' Scott exercised a similar spell over Thomas Maurice. For Maurice, Scott, 'the most enlightened tutor, at that time, in Oxford...spurn[ed] the dull monotonous routine of studies generally pursued in other Colleges, encouraging his pupils to launch forth into the investigations of nobler objects of

---

[10] Gibbon: Gibbon 1796: i. 51 (an edition which Scott could have read himself); Walter Stanhope's letters survive in the Spencer Stanhope collection in WYAS (B), but extensive extracts are printed—albeit not always accurately—in Stirling 1911 (I therefore give Stirling's page references); Maurice's memoirs: Maurice 1819–20.

scientific inquiry, than the dry metaphysics and frivolous disputations of the Aristotelian school.' Maurice also noted approvingly that Scott 'was not sparing of good dinners to benefit the constitution of his pupils'.[11]

Stanhope, however, became disillusioned with Chambers. During his undergraduate years, Chambers had laid the foundations for a legal career, being admitted to the Middle Temple back in 1754. When a bequest from Charles Viner endowed the first posts in Oxford for the study and teaching of common, as opposed to civil, law, Chambers took immediate advantage. He became a Vinerian Scholar in 1758, a Vinerian Fellow in 1761, and then the second Vinerian Professor of Law in 1766. In December 1766 he was also appointed Principal of New Inn Hall, a sinecure which came with a house and no duties, and which he could hold in conjunction with his Fellowship. Chambers's legal ambitions affected his teaching: Stanhope grumbled that Chambers was only giving his pupils half his promised course of lectures, while still demanding a 'handsome Salary', and claimed that he was gaining a bad reputation within Oxford for neglecting his pupils, and 'by being so *great* a *little* Coxcomb'.[12]

Nevertheless Scott and Chambers kept Stanhope well occupied. Stanhope may have come up as a gentleman commoner, but in Wetherell's College (unlike Charlett's) everyone had to study, irrespective of status. In 1766, Stanhope wrote with evident astonishment that 'Our Peer [Jacob, Lord Folkestone, later Earl of Radnor (m. 1767)] is very regular, & as well as the Gent. C^r [William Windham], does as much exercise as a Servitor.' Stanhope provides valuable information on what he studied. In December 1766 he listed the books in his rooms for one of his uncles. He owned many canonical classical texts—Homer, Virgil, Horace, Cicero, Terence, Ovid, and Plato, for example—but also textbooks on logic, some modern books on ancient history, and some religious works. For recreational reading, he had the *Spectator*, editions of Milton and Gay, and—more daringly—Smollett's *Peregrine Pickle*. Later, in February 1767, Stanhope described his weekly round of lectures—the first such timetable known for the College since the 1660s. On Mondays, Wednesdays, and Fridays, he endured 'a dry tedious Lecture in Metaphysicks', to which he brought written answers to questions given during the previous lecture. On Tuesdays and Saturdays he had lectures on Sophocles, whom he considered 'difficult, tho' sometimes not unpleasant'. These were private lectures given by Scott exclusively for his pupils. On Thursdays there were lectures on Plato, and disputations were held twice a week. Chambers was in London, but meanwhile he set his pupils to read a textbook on ancient history, and requested that they learn French. On top of all this, Scott set Stanhope to translate a hymn of Callimachus. Stanhope joked that 'This College is now

---

[11] Stanhope: WYAS (B) SpSt/6/1/105 (rooms in College) and SpSt6/1/90 (his tutors), reprinted in Stirling 1911: i. 195, 200, and 205; Maurice: Maurice 1819–20: ii. 9–10 and 26.

[12] Chambers's Vinerian posts: Barton 1986: 601–5, and Curley 1998: 32, 43, and 69; New Inn Hall: Curley 1998: 71; Stanhope's criticisms: WYAS (B) SpSt/6/1/90 (Stirling 1911: i. 205).

call'd University-School, & yet (would you think it) they are fabricating new Regulations, & infinitely more burthensome Exercises.'[13]

The tale of these 'burthensome Exercises' is an extraordinary one. Only recorded, it seems, in Stanhope's letters, it shows Wetherell's eagerness to tighten academic standards—and marks the College's earliest known student protest. The new regulations, Stanhope explained, comprised daily undergraduate disputations, twice weekly Greek lectures, and the composition of a sample of Latin verse or an English Essay every week.[14] Some might comment that it was slightly hypocritical of the Master and Fellows to impose this demanding regime precisely when Robert Chambers was being let off his tutorial duties. The result was a threat of industrial action. In April 1767 or 1768 (the dating is uncertain) Stanhope wrote to one of his uncles:

> The Master...determin'd to gall us with disputations six times a Week (tho,...he only carried it by his *casting Vote*), this every Undergraduate Member independent of the College, & then resident, resolv'd not to comply with. Accordingly we went to ask them off, & at last gain'd our Point; if we had not, we should have threaten'd, and even, if driven to Extremities, should have actually left the College.[15]

The College backed down. Significantly, William Scott was 'much against' the change, less, one suspects, out of a concern for his pupils' workload, than for the narrowness of the new syllabus, for the young Tutor was a polymath, keeping a notebook on chemistry and mineralogy, and encouraged his pupils to range widely. In February 1768 Stanhope attended lectures in 'Experimental Philosophy' (i.e. science) and civil law, and Thomas Maurice studied mathematics, astronomy, and physics. There were other signs of the College's intellectual vitality: all but one of the Chancellor's Prizes for English Essays awarded in 1768–72 went to members of University College, including William Scott's younger brother, John.[16]

Scott won recognition when in 1773, aged 28, he was appointed Camden Professor of Ancient History. With characteristic application, Scott—unusually for that period—actually gave professorial lectures, and good ones too. Thomas Maurice recalled Scott's 'incomparable Lectures' and praised their 'eloquent manner'.[17] A slightly less reverent, but still complimentary, assessment of Scott comes from John James, an undergraduate at

---

[13] These three letters are in WYAS (B) SpSt/6/1/90 (Stirling 1911: i. 191 and 203–4 quote the passages on hard-working aristocrats and lectures). The last letter is also transcribed in Mitchell 2002: 87.
[14] WYAS (B) SpSt/6/1/90 (Stirling 1911: i. 204–5).
[15] WYAS (B) SpSt/6/1/105 (Stirling 1911: i. 206).
[16] Scott's protest: WYAS (B) SpSt/6/1/90 (Stirling 1911: i. 204); Scott and the sciences: Bourguignon 1987: 34; Stanhope and Maurice: WYAS (B) SpSt/6/1/106 (see Mitchell 2002: 89) and Maurice 1819–20: ii. 20 (compare Hodgkin 1949: 116–18); essay prizes: Twiss 1844: i. 58.
[17] Scott as professor: Clarke 1986: 516 and Maurice 1819–20: i. 107.

Queen's in the late 1770s. Noting Scott's friendship with Samuel Johnson (of which more shortly), James wrote:

[Scott] has a good deal of the Doctor's manner: elevated stile, pointed antithesis, rounded periods, moral and penetrating remarks. Sometimes, however, he copies the Doctor's faults, such as... that care to avoid the mention of anything mean or familiar by its common name.... Describing the houses of the Athenians, he acquainted his audience 'that they had no convenience by which the volatile parts of fire could be conveyed into the open air.' How would a bricklayer stare at being told that he meant no more than that the Athenians had no chimneys!...Take him however, 'all in all', and I am afraid the university will seldom 'look upon his like again.'[18]

From today's perspective, William Scott is an undoubted phenomenon. It was not only that he was so young, or that he taught such a wide range of subjects, he was also remarkably influential. Of about 175 undergraduates who matriculated from University College between September 1765 and December 1775, only thirteen were not tutored by Scott either exclusively or in collaboration with another Fellow. Moreover he and Chambers clearly enjoyed Wetherell's full support. Chambers, as a Percy Fellow, and William Scott, as a William of Durham Fellow, ought, under the 1736 Statutes, to have taken holy orders and studied theology, but Wetherell allowed them both to remain laymen and study law.[19]

William Scott, however, had an equally remarkable younger brother, John (Fig. 13.4). John Scott matriculated in 1766 from his older brother's College ('Send Jack up to me', William had said to their father, 'I can do better for him here'), and was taught by him. John had all his brother's abilities, as Wetherell was quick to appreciate. In July 1767, he was elected a Percy Fellow when aged just 16 years old, and, like William Jones, still an undergraduate. In this election, however, Wetherell felt confident enough to dispense with postponing it on the grounds of youth, and John Scott remains the youngest known Fellow of University College.[20]

Rather unfortunately, John Scott did not long remain a Fellow. In 1772, when only 21, he eloped with a Newcastle beauty in the best romantic tradition, with a ladder up to a first-floor window, and a speedy ride to Scotland; he had to resign his Fellowship the following year. Nevertheless, Wetherell did what he could: John Scott served as Tutor in 1774–5—the only Georgian Fellow allowed to do this after his resignation—although Scott admitted that he 'never did more as a tutor than attend to some members of the College, as his law pupils'. Robert Chambers also helped. In 1773, when he was planning to leave for a judicial post in India, he could still retain his post at New Inn Hall. He therefore offered his lodgings to Scott and his wife.

---

[18] Evans 1887: 92–3.
[19] Scott had joined the Middle Temple in 1762 (Bourguignon 1987: 35).
[20] John Scott at Oxford: Twiss 1844: i. 48; his election: UC:GB3/A1/2 fo. 76^r.

In 1774–7 Scott also deputized for Chambers as Vinerian Professor, and delivered his lectures on his behalf—although not always with enough preparation. Scott never forgot the embarrassment, in his first lecture, of finding himself reading about a statute which censured young men running off with women, and observing his audience giggling.[21]

Wetherell's revolution was noticed: applications to University College increased drastically (Graph 12.1), culminating in 1771, when thirty-three undergraduates came up, the largest annual intake since 1694. Both Stanhope and Maurice observed the resulting pressure for accommodation: indeed Maurice first had to take lodgings in High Street, because there were no College rooms free. One quick solution was found, when in 1773 the College purchased from Christ Church a house once called Deep Hall, but also known as 'The Principality'. Situated between the Main Quadrangle and Stanton Hall, Deep Hall offered possibilities for expansion, although for now it was just used as a student annexe: the Bursar's Book for 1779/80 notes some undergraduates as occupying 'Chambers of Deep Hall'. However, it also has a section titled 'Borrowed rooms', which suggests that Deep Hall was not big enough, and that the College had to rent rooms elsewhere for its students.[22]

There was something else about Wetherell's undergraduates, in particular the high achievers among them. About forty of the Fellows and undergraduates who came to the College under Wetherell appear in the 2004 edition of the *Oxford Dictionary of National Biography*, which is slightly more than all the people in it who came up between 1689 and 1764—and several from this latter group, such as Robert Chambers and William Jones, only realized their potential under Wetherell. Furthermore, while twenty-five Old Members from 1689–1764 became MPs, thirty-seven of Wetherell's members did so (including Walter Stanhope). It is agreeable to glory in Wetherell's 'great' Old Members—government ministers, such as William Windham (m. 1767), colonial governors such as Sir William Young (m. 1768), a Master of the Rolls, Thomas Plumer (m. 1771; F. 1780–94), a soldier and administrator like Francis Rawdon, later Earl of Moira and Marquess of Hastings (m. 1771), and scholars like William Jones and Thomas Maurice—but self-indulgent. Merely to list them thus avoids the awkward question of the part played by University College in their distinction. This question always needs asking, but perhaps most pointedly in this hour of the College's greatest glory. We will return to this important matter in the next chapter.

---

[21] Scott's elopement: Twiss 1844: i. 74–6 (many years later Scott was displeased when one of his daughters similarly eloped (Twiss 1844: ii. 298)); Scott and Chambers: Twiss 1844: i. 86–9; Scott's lectures: Barton 1986: 605 and Twiss 1844: i. 91.

[22] Accommodation shortages: Maurice 1819–20: ii. 25; purchase of Deep Hall (the house once occupied by Robert Boyle—p. 180): UC:E/A8/D/4; undergraduate accommodation at Deep Hall and elsewhere: UC:BU3/F3/5 pp. 189–91.

There is little doubt, however, of the bond between the College and Robert Chambers, William Jones, and the Scott brothers. This remarkable quartet would have stood out in any age, and it is a great tribute to Wetherell that he could harness their differing gifts. Their later careers more than fulfilled their early promise.[23] Robert Chambers was appointed a Judge in the court at Bengal in 1774, resigned his Fellowship the following year, and spent twenty-five years in India, becoming Chief Justice of the Supreme Judicature at Bengal in 1791, and performing a vital role in creating an Anglo-Indian corpus of law. William Scott resigned his Fellowship in April 1782, upon his marriage, but retained his Professorship until 1785. His having taken his DCL in 1782, showed that he had legal ambitions. He succeeded admirably: he became Judge of the High Court of the Admiralty in 1798, and was ennobled as Baron Stowell in 1821, winning a high reputation for his judgements on naval and international law. He also served as MP for Oxford University in 1801–21. John Scott climbed higher still, serving successive governments as Attorney-General in 1793–9 and then as Lord Chancellor in 1801–6 and 1807–28. In 1799 he became Lord Eldon, and, as Lord Eldon, the friend of both George III and George IV, he became admired and loathed in equal measure for the firmness, if not rigidity, of his opposition to almost any kind of reform, judicial or political.

Finally there was William Jones. In 1783, he followed Chambers to Bengal to sit as a judge alongside him. Unsurprisingly, he was not content simply to perform his judicial duties. He attempted to produce a digest of Muslim and Hindu law, and became fascinated by Indian culture, exploring all aspects of it, and disseminating the fruits of his labours. Yet again, Jones appealed to a wide audience: his translations of Indian literature proved even more influential than his earlier literary work, and his investigations into Sanskrit, while not the first made by a European, led him to far-reaching conclusions about the origins of language which laid the foundations for the modern study of philology. He respected deeply what he found in India, and later British administrators might have done well to follow his example. Jones died exhausted in 1794, aged only 46, yet his scholarly and literary legacy remains astonishing in its scope and quality.

WETHERELL'S WEB: ARCHITECTURE, LITERATURE, POLITICS, AND THE VICE-CHANCELLORSHIP

In the 1760s and 1770s, Wetherell and his brilliant young Fellows had transformed University College, but Wetherell also created a remarkable network outside the College which gave him and it an influence quite out of proportion to its size. He was a smooth operator—he has been described

---

[23] The later careers of all four men can best be explored in Curley 1998, Bourguignon 1987, Melikan 1999, and Cannon 1990.

as 'full of oily obsequiousness to the great'[24]—and enjoyed a success which Arthur Charlett would have yearned for.

To set Wetherell's activities in context, it is as well to consider his political views. Although nothing is said of his Hutchinsonianism after the 1750s, he always retained a Hutchinsonian respect for Church and State, as a wholehearted Tory. Eighteenth-century Toryism tends to be associated with a determined hostility to change, as seen in Lord Eldon, so that Wetherell's reforming spirit might appear surprising. It is, however, not so unreasonable: if Oxford was to produce right-thinking leaders of Church and the State, then they needed to be well educated. In that spirit, Cyril Jackson, Dean of Christ Church in 1783–1809, also worked his undergraduates hard, irrespective of status, and William Powell, Master of St John's Cambridge in 1765–75, introduced examinations for undergraduates but opposed alterations to the regulations on subscription, while Balliol's rise to academic glory began under John Parsons, Master in 1798–1819, who like Jackson and Powell combined strong Tory beliefs with a reforming zeal.[25]

Among the first people whom Wetherell cultivated was the university's MP, Sir Roger Newdigate. The two men were apparently first drawn together by an architectural project: in October 1764, shortly after Wetherell's promotion, Newdigate was proposing to the College that it rebuild its Hall. The origins of this project may have lain in Newdigate's love of Gothic architecture, for at this time Arbury Hall, his country residence, was being Gothicized by the architect Henry Keene. Newdigate and Keene now audaciously suggested to University College that the Hall's hammerbeam roof of the 1650s be hidden by a plaster 'Gothic' fan-vaulted ceiling. Unlike the fan-vaulting in the porch of Radcliffe Quadrangle, Keene's vaulting was entirely decorative, and performed no structural function. He also installed appropriately Gothic wainscotting, and in the centre of the south wall placed a stone fireplace with a roundel showing King Alfred in profile. The College looked to its members to find the money, not entirely successfully. In 1767, the money raised was £250 short of the total. Newdigate helped where he could: Lady Newdigate painted an ornamental shield for the Hall, and he himself gave some fine chairs for High Table (still in use today). Paradoxically, whereas the Gothic of the Radcliffe Quadrangle had been a last flourish of the traditional style, the Hall ceiling, completed in 1766 (Fig. 13.5), was the very height of fashion—indeed the first major example of the Gothic Revival style in Oxford.[26]

---

[24] Ward 1958: 231.
[25] Jackson: Bill 1988: 64–84; Powell: Miller 1961: 64–8, and Howard 1935: 91 and 95–102; Parsons: Jones 2005: 177–9.
[26] Newdigate and University College Hall: White 1995: 136 and UC:FA4/1/C1/1–2; Arbury Hall: Sweet 2004: 453; Keene's designs: UC:FA4/1/Y1/2; shortage of money: UC:BU5/F2/2 fo. 63ᵛ; subscribers: BL MS Add. 38205 fo. 37ʳ (an incomplete list) and BL MS Add. 38305 fo. 19ᵛ

FIGURE 13.5 Engraving by J. Hall after Auguste Pugin of the Hall of University College in 1814, showing the alterations made by Henry Keene in 1766. The portrait nearest to the viewer on the left is that of Robert Chambers; that to the right is of either Lord Eldon or Lord Stowell.

Newdigate and Wetherell remained on friendly terms for the rest of their lives. When Newdigate left Parliament in 1780, he thanked Wetherell and the College 'for the great and repeated favors continued to me in the course of many years since I first became a member of [the College]... no time can obliterate the gratitude I feel, or abate the fervor of my zeal for the prosperity of the University of Oxford and of University College in particular.' They also shared a shrewd business sense, for they invested in the building of a canal linking Oxford with the Coventry Canal. Work started in 1768, and although progress was slow—the canal only reached Oxford in 1789—their investment was eventually well repaid.[27]

(donation of £10 from Charles Jenkinson); Lady Newdigate: White 1995: 146–7; chairs: WRO CR136/B2327; appraisals: Tyack 1998: 181–2 and Colvin 1986: 848, who calls it 'a charming example of the Georgian rediscovery of gothic as a decorative style'.

[27] Newdigate's resignation: White 1995: 226; the Oxford canal: *VCH Oxon.* iv. 208–9 and 293–4, and White 1995: 145 and 158.

Another Old Member who attracted Wetherell's interest was Charles Jenkinson, George Horne's contemporary and friend, who had now emerged as a powerful but discreet politician. In 1760 he became private secretary to Lord Bute, George III's tutor and first favourite, and he held government posts for most of the next four decades, acquiring a reputation as an *éminence grise*. When in 1768 Jenkinson stood as a Parliamentary candidate for Oxford University, Wetherell enthusiastically supported him (as did George Horne, now President of Magdalen). His letters to Jenkinson in 1768 reveal a shared taste for political intrigue, as he went about Oxford calculating who supported whom, and whether he could change anyone's mind. Unfortunately Jenkinson was seen as too close to the government, when the university wanted someone of Newdigate's independent cast of mind, and he lost heavily. It was a significant education for Wetherell in the arts of political management. Nevertheless, there were no hard feelings: when Wetherell had a son in February 1770, he named him Charles, and Jenkinson was the boy's godfather.[28]

Arguably the greatest lion bagged by Nathan Wetherell was Samuel Johnson. Johnson was linked to the College through Robert Chambers, whom he had befriended back in the 1750s; John Scott remembered Chambers's and Johnson's easy familiarity. The three men were once walking in New Inn Hall garden, when Chambers was gathering snails and throwing them into his neighbour's garden. Johnson rebuked him, but, on being told that the neighbour was a dissenter, replied, 'Oh! If so, Chambers, throw away, throw away, as hard as ever you can.' More seriously, when Chambers was experiencing writer's block in completing a series of lectures after his election as Vinerian Professor, Johnson came down to Oxford and helped him finish the task. The debate about the extent of his contribution has remained unresolved ever since.[29]

Through Chambers, Johnson made several friends in the College, and derived considerable happiness from them, regularly enjoying the good fellowship there: he once said to Boswell that 'I have drunk three bottles of port without being the worse for it. University College has witnessed this.' Indeed it is fair to say that in the 1760s and 1770s University College was Johnson's favourite Oxford haunt, even more so than Pembroke, his undergraduate college. Johnson became especially close to William Scott, William Jones, and William Windham; all three men, along with Chambers, were elected members of the Literary Club, which Johnson had founded in the 1760s so that he and some chosen friends could meet regularly. In the literary world of the time, there could be few clearer signs of the College's eminence. Nathan Wetherell himself and Johnson had similar views on politics and

---

[28] Jenkinson: *ODNB* entry; the 1768 election: Sutherland 1986a: 155–60, Ward 1958: 226–38, and BL MS Add 38457 *passim*; George Horne: Jones 1795: 165, remembered Horne and Wetherell reminiscing good-humouredly about the election; Wetherell's son: BL MS Add. 38206 fo. 214[r].

[29] The snails: Lincoln and McEwen 1960: 17–18; the lectures: Curley 1998: ch. III.

religion, even down to a certain Jacobite posing. Wetherell had more or less knowingly caused a sensation with his sermon of 1756, and James Boswell observed Johnson's 'affectation of more Jacobitism than he really had'. Boswell himself once observed Johnson among his University College friends when they both visited in Oxford in March 1776, and were made guests at that year's St Cuthbert's Day Feast. Johnson's happy relationship with the College is recalled by a mezzotint of him, a gift of William Scott which still hangs in the Senior Common Room (Fig. 13.6).[30]

Johnson's involvement with University College is illustrated in the case of George Strahan (m. 1764; F. 1767–73), the son of Johnson's acquaintance, the printer William Strahan. George had been apprenticed to a bookseller, but, by the time he was 18, realized that the work was not for him. Johnson, with Robert Chambers's help, arranged for George to receive two years' intensive coaching, and in October 1764 he was entered at University College. Johnson wrote to George's father that 'I think I have pretty well disposed of my young friend George', for 'The College is almost filled with my friends, and he will be well treated.' The Master, aware of Strahan's unusual background, suggested to Johnson that one of the College's servitors might teach him Greek. Strahan fulfilled all the hopes placed in him: within a few days, he was elected to a Bennet Scholarship, and in 1767 he became a Bennet Fellow. Later he became vicar of Islington. He became 'one of [Johnson's] great favourites', and looked after him in his last illness.[31]

Needless to say, Johnson's visits impressed themselves on the memories of undergraduates: Thomas Maurice remembered Johnson exercising for his asthma by swinging the lead handle of the College pump. He was a passionate admirer of Johnson's work, as William Scott knew; and when Scott showed Johnson one of Maurice's poems, Maurice, on hearing of the great man's approval, 'seized a Rambler, three times I devoutly kissed the honoured page, nor rose from my desk till my gratitude had completed a poem of 50 lines in honour of the good Doctor'. When Maurice at last met Johnson, he observed that 'uncouth as are his figure and manners, I could not but be deeply affected with the beneficent expressions uttered, and the obliging attention paid me by so distinguished a character'. In turn, Johnson graciously humoured his young admirer: he encouraged Scott and Maurice to suggest names for inclusion in his *Lives of the Poets*, then in progress.[32]

---

[30] Boswell 1980: 911 (drinking port), 338–9 (the Literary Club), 442 and 530 (William Jones), 327, 453, and 924–9 (William Scott), 585 and 1239 (William Windham), 304 (Johnson the Jacobite) 690–6 (the 1776 visit); the mezzotint: Sadler 1933: 10–11.

[31] Redford 1992–4: i. 209–11, 217–21, 224–5, and 234–5 (letters to George Strahan), and i. 244–5 (letter to Strahan's father); Strahan's later career: Boswell 1980: 1390–1 and his father's *ODNB* entry.

[32] Maurice 1819–20: ii. 21 (Johnson's exercises); ii. 26 (poem to Johnson—which reflects Maurice's sincerity, if little else—and meeting Johnson); ii. 29–30 (discussing poets).

FIGURE 13.6 A mezzotint of Samuel Johnson by Charles Townley based on a portrait by John Opie, which was presented to the College by William Scott.

Walter Stanhope was less easily impressed. On meeting Johnson, he wrote to one of his uncles:

[Johnson] seems to be a Man of very strong Sense, & deep Judgement, but not remarkably bright, or of quick Apprehension; he is also fond of Sarcasm, which has a double Portion of Gall, flowing from the most disgusting Voice, & Person you almost ever beheld.[33]

Some of Johnson's London circle also came to know the College. In 1769, Charles Burney, the great musicologist, came to Oxford to take his Doctorate in Music, and matriculated from University College to do so. Until the 1860s music graduates merely had to submit a composition and have it publicly performed, and so they would matriculate, take their degree, and leave, all within a few days. Thus Burney appears to have had no dealings with the College after 1769. Nevertheless, he was one of only two musicians before 1800 to graduate from University College: musicians tended to join more obviously musical colleges like Magdalen. However, Burney was a friend of Dr Johnson, and perhaps this affected his choice of college. Burney's name added lustre to Wetherell's College: not only did he become arguably the most important musical historian of his age, but the anthem submitted for his

[33] WYAS (B) SpSt/6/1/105 (Stirling 1911: i. 208).

degree has been hailed as the finest exercise of the century: C. P. E. Bach, no less, saw fit to perform it in Hamburg.[34]

Johnson's close friend Hester Thrale also came to know University College. She had her own links to the College, as her husband Henry had matriculated from here in 1744. In September 1774 Johnson and the Thrales visited Oxford after a tour of Wales, and in her journal of the holiday, Mrs Thrale records visiting University College. According to her journal, she even dined in the Hall and visited the Senior Common Room—the first woman known to have done so:

> We dined in the Hall at University College, where I sat in the seat of honour...Mr. Colson entertained us with liberality and with kindness...We drank tea in the Common room, had a world of talk, and passed the evening with cheerfulness and comfort. I liked Mr Coulson much and pressed him to come to Streatham.[35]

John Coulson, one of William Jones's uninspiring tutors, was one of Johnson's more unexpected friends in the College (although Coulson, a Fellow since 1744, would have remembered Henry Thrale as an undergraduate). One suspects, however, that Coulson amused, rather than impressed, Johnson. In June 1775, he wrote to Mrs Thrale:

> Such is the uncertainty of all human things that Mr. Colson has quarrelled with me. He says, I raise the laugh upon him, and he is an independent man, and all he has is his own, and he is not used to such things.[36]

Coulson was something of a College character: both William Scott, who remembered him as 'very eccentric', and Walter Stanhope recalled an ingenious practical joke at his expense. Coulson, known for his considerable lack of personal hygiene, used to hang his breeches out of his window to air. The undergraduates grew exasperated at this slightly offensive eccentricity, and so on one day when the breeches appeared, they all hung from their own windows breeches, carpets, quilts, and other suitable material. Dr Johnson was visiting Oxford, and, hearing that something was happening at University College went to see for himself. According to Stanhope, as Johnson saw the front of the College thus decorated, he clung to some railings for support, and 'laughed like a rhinoceros' at the sight. Drawn by the great man's mirth, others came to admire the view, and the episode became called the 'famous University College Illumination', in parody of the occasions when candles were put in the windows of the College. It is not recorded whether Coulson took the hint.[37]

---

[34] Burney: Wollenberg 2001: 15–19. The College's other musician was Thomas Deane (D.Mus. 1731).
[35] Broadley 1910: 216.
[36] Redford 1992–4: ii. 217. The quarrel was soon settled.
[37] Scott told this to John Wilson Croker, who included it in Boswell 1831: iii. 159, and Stanhope's version (apparently transmitted orally in his family) is in Stirling 1911: i. 209–10.

Yet Coulson was more than an unhygienic eccentric. While Wetherell and the younger Fellows brought unprecedented glory to the College, Coulson made a valuable contribution in the background. In addition to his tutorial duties from 1745 to 1766, he held at least one College office—sometimes two or three—every year from 1745 until 1780, when he resigned. No other Georgian Fellow was so conscientious. Yet there is something slightly lonely about Coulson. When William Jones made his summer study visits to Oxford, he often found Coulson the only other person resident in College, as if he had nowhere else to go apart from the College to which he had given so much. Eventually, however, Coulson had his reward, for he retired in 1780 to Checkendon, the richest living in the College's gift.[38]

Wetherell's networking skills and ambitions united to spectacular effect when in 1768–72 he served as arguably the ablest and most active Vice-Chancellor of the century. In 1769 the Bodleian statutes were reformed; in 1770, BA regulations were tightened up, and academic dress was reformed, to remove some of its more demeaning aspects (servitors, for example, no longer had to wear the round caps which broadcast their status). Wetherell's Vice-Chancellorship also witnessed an unusual example of cooperation between university and city. In 1771, he helped draw up the Oxford Improvement Act, which created a team of Paving Commissioners who supervised paving, cleansing, lighting, and other general improvements to the city. The new act also provided for a new Magdalen Bridge, a turnpike along St Clements, and a new covered market. The Commissioners were given compulsory purchasing powers; several buildings were demolished, including the old north and east gates, and market stalls and protruding shop signs done away with. The impact of the Improvement Act was thus considerable. It brought into existence landmarks like Magdalen Bridge and the Covered Market, and the wider streets of the city centre; so that Wetherell arguably helped create modern Oxford.[39]

Typically for Wetherell, this activity benefited both himself and the College. Among the properties purchased for the new Covered Market were three houses owned by University College—the very same properties fiercely fought for by John Gonwardby's heirs four centuries earlier. They were sold for £800, which the College invested in government funds—the first time that they had used money for this purpose—and the result was encouraging. The three houses had yielded an annual rent of about £5 10s. (along with regular entry fines), but the dividends from the funds yielded a regular annual income of £24. When, therefore, in 1787 the College sold its

---

[38] Coulson's run of service is traced in UC:GB3/A1/2; Coulson alone: for example, Cannon 1970: i. 33.
[39] Wetherell as Vice-Chancellor: Sutherland 1986c: 219–25; academic dress: Green 1986a: 323–7; the Oxford Improvement Act: VCH Oxon. iv. 188–9 and 232–3.

house on the corner of Carfax for £100 to the Paving Commissioners, to widen the road, this money was likewise invested in government funds.[40]

Wetherell also sought some preferment as a personal souvenir of his Vice-Chancellorship, and asked Charles Jenkinson to put in a good word with Lord North, Prime Minister from 1770. He did not want a parish, because he could not manage this in conjunction with the College, but would appreciate a non-residential post in his native Durham, if possible. Jenkinson obliged, and in 1771 Lord North appointed Wetherell Dean of Hereford, a post which to Wetherell's delight brought a stipend of almost £300 a year. His concerns about a conflict of interest were allayed: two of his recent predecessors had been largely non-resident, and so at first Wetherell visited his cathedral but rarely, leaving its administration to the resident canons. Wetherell received further preferment in 1775 when he became a canon of Westminster Abbey.[41]

Wetherell's Vice-Chancellorship reached its apogee in the summer of 1772 when the Chancellorship fell vacant. Four years after his failure with Jenkinson, Wetherell was now a master of the political arts, and he determined that Lord North should be elected. This was a daring move: for many decades Oxford had been at best independent of, at worst hostile towards the government—Jenkinson had, after all, failed in 1768 because of his government connections—but now Wetherell wanted the current Prime Minister to be the head of the university. Politics, however, had changed. Lord North was indeed a Whig, but the Whigs of 1772 were very different from those of the previous generation, and Oxford's Tories much less hostile to the Hanoverians. Therefore, even before the old Chancellor was dead, Wetherell and Jenkinson were starting to plan their campaign.[42]

Unsurprisingly, not everyone wanted a Prime Minister as Chancellor, and some favoured an independent candidate. Awkwardly for Wetherell the independents' first choice was an Old Member of University College, William Bouverie, Earl of Radnor (m. 1743); and Radnor's 'campaign manager', so to speak, was William Scott. However, the independents were soon divided: the current Duke of Beaufort (an Old Member of Oriel College) also attracted a party. Wetherell lobbied furiously to save Lord North the indignity of a contested election; his tactics can be seen at their silky best in his account to Charles Jenkinson of a useful conversation with William Scott:

Scott came to Town last night & was with me the whole Evening alone. After much *friendly* conversation he promised me to do the utmost in his power to prevent any opposition whatever; if that point cannot be carried, & a Candidate must be set up; If

---

[40] The High Street houses: UC:BU2/F1/4 fo. 184^v–185^r; the Carfax house: UC:BU2/F1/5 fo. 37^r.
[41] Wetherell's petitions: BL MS Add 38206 fos. 304^r, 306^r, 319^r, 384^r, and 397^r; his promotion to Hereford: Mitchell 1986: 164–5 and BL MS Add. 38207 fo. 41^r; the Deanship's stipend: BL MS Add. 38207 fo. 47^v; Wetherell as Dean: Tomlinson 2000: 128 and 149–51; Wetherell as Canon: Le Neve 1992: 93.
[42] The election: BL MS Adds. 38470 fos. 43–95, Mitchell 1986: 169–71, and Ward 1958: 256–60.

the candidate is the D. of Beaufort, he will come over to Lord North, and influence as many people as he can in his Lordship's favour - If Ld Radnor is to be the Candidate, his connections & the part he has already taken will oblige him to carry the matter so far till he can make a handsome retreat.[43]

Wetherell won round the heads of most of the colleges, and Scott and other independents admitted defeat. Their candidates withdrew, and Lord North was triumphantly elected Chancellor unopposed. It was Wetherell's finest hour: he had helped lead the university back into an alliance with the political establishment. Oxford was no longer in the wilderness.

The timing could not have been better. In 1771–3 several attempts were made in Parliament to abolish the subscriptions to the Church of England demanded of all Oxford matriculands, so that the university could be opened up to dissenters. Wetherell, totally opposed to this proposal, used Charles Jenkinson and Sir Roger Newdigate to save Oxford from it. Newdigate played an especially prominent part in Parliament in defeating the bill. By having his friends settle the matter thus, Wetherell had saved Lord North from an awkward conflict of interests, as both Prime Minister and Chancellor of the University.[44]

These happy times were marred by one unforeseen incident. The Encaenia of 1773 would be the first one attended by the new Chancellor, and the natural choice of speaker was University College's most eminent scholar, William Jones. But there was a problem: Jones was now a radical Whig, with a passionate belief in liberty of thought and justice, and his proposed speech revealed his politics all too clearly. The speech was never delivered: as Jones later commented, 'they expected a very different kind of speech from what I intended to give them, which determined me not to speak at all'.[45]

The events of 1773 foreshadowed more serious ones in 1780, when Wetherell faced an exceptional challenge to his political skills.[46] Sir Roger Newdigate resigned his Parliamentary seat, and Wetherell found a suitable successor in Sir William Dolben, a stolid country gentleman whose politics resembled Newdigate's. Unfortunately, both William Scott and William Jones then put their names forward, Scott as an independent, and Jones as a Whig, Jones placing his hopes both in a split in the Tory vote between Scott and Dolben, and in sufficient non-resident members coming to Oxford in his support. Samuel Johnson saw the true picture far more clearly than his

---

[43] BL MS Add. 38470 fo. 79^r.
[44] The subscription debate: Mitchell 1986: 166–8 and 175–7, and Ward 1958: 260–8: Newdigate: White 1995: xxxviii and 172–4; Jenkinson: BL MS Add 38207 fos. 85^r, 90^r, 100^r, 184^r, 190^r, 197^r, and 239^r.
[45] Teignmouth 1804: 110–111 and Cannon 1970: i. 131.
[46] The 1780 election is described more fully in Mitchell 1973, Mitchell 1986: 181–3, and Ward 1958: 274–9. See too Cannon 1970: i. 358–436.

friends, writing to Mrs Thrale in May 1780 that Scott and Jones 'are struggling hard for what others think neither of them will obtain'.[47]

University College cannot have been a happy place that summer, with a Master and two Fellows campaigning against each other. Jones's sympathies towards the American colonists would have been especially embarrassing for Wetherell, because several Old Members were leading officers in the British Army in America, including Francis Rawdon, John Dyke Acland (m. 1765), and Banastre Tarleton (m. 1771), the last of whom was at that very moment besieging the rebel stronghold of Charleston. Wetherell's luck held: after the Gordon Riots had ravaged London in June 1780, Jones accepted that, although they actually arose from anti-Catholic demonstrations, Oxford voters would nevertheless see them as the inevitable results of excessive liberty, and thus taint his own cause. He therefore withdrew his candidacy in August. Scott likewise withdrew, leaving Dolben as sole candidate.

Jones—who ought to have anticipated such a result—was wounded by his experiences. When informing Wetherell of his withdrawal, he could not conceal his bitterness:

If I have not been able to *prove* my attachment to my fellow-collegiates, it is because they never called for my service; if they had, they should have found that no man would have exerted himself with more activity to serve them... I am conscious of having deserved very well of the college; and if any of its members are so unkind as to think otherwise, I will shew my sense of their unkindness by persisting till my last hour in deserving well of them.[48]

He wrote to the Master of Pembroke in more scathing terms in September 1780:

I shall hear without pain that Dr. Wetherell charges me with wishing to *overturn that constitution*, to *preserve* which I would sacrifice my peace of mind or even my life, but which he certainly does not understand or does not regard.[49]

There were other losses: Jones had written in May 1780 that 'I shall be grieved, if this competition should extinguish the intimacy between Dr. Scott and me',[50] but the election did just that. In January 1781, he wrote of Scott:

The real truth is, that there *never* subsisted between us any of that *cordial* friendship, which a similarity of opinions on important points can alone inspire and improve. I knew twelve years ago, that his notions of *power* were too high for general freedom; and perhaps, he might think that my notions of freedom were too large for publick order and due subordination.[51]

---

[47] Redford 1992–4: iii. 254. [48] Cannon 1970: i. 433.
[49] Cannon 1990: 366. [50] Cannon 1990: 364. [51] Cannon 1970: ii. 456.

The Parliamentary election of 1780 reveals the sad fact that William Jones was now an anomaly in Wetherell's College. He was its only serious scholar, and his radicalism set him apart from Wetherell, the Scott brothers, and most members of the College. There were other radicals, such as Thomas Cooper (m. 1779), who in the 1790s expressed such public support for the French Revolution that he eventually had to flee to America; but they were greatly in the minority. Jones was certainly admired within the College for his learning, as the presence of Flaxman's great monument in the Chapel eloquently shows, but eventually he did not quite fit in. The man who truly embodied the values of Nathan Wetherell's College was actually John Scott, Lord Eldon. When, in the 1820s and 1830s, he would lead last ditch resistances against Catholic Emancipation and the Reform Bill, he was merely staying true to the principles which he had absorbed at University College in the 1760s, and it was only appropriate that he became High Steward of Oxford in 1801.[52]

DECLINE: 1780–1807

The bitter election campaign of 1780 marks a watershed in the history of University College. William Scott and Jones resigned their Fellowships in 1782 and 1783 respectively to pursue their legal careers, and the College's good friend Samuel Johnson died in 1784. In their absence, a College which had seen over a decade and a half of unparalleled activity and success declined into an amiable and drowsy mediocrity.

By the mid-1780s, Wetherell had two other major calls on his time. The first one was his Deanery at Hereford, for events there now demanded even his attention. On Easter Monday (17 April) 1786, after centuries of neglect, the west front of Hereford Cathedral suddenly collapsed. Although wiser heads observed that little could honestly have been done to prevent the disaster, it nevertheless occurred on Wetherell's watch, and he and the Chapter were heavily criticized. Wetherell now made up for his neglect, usually residing in Hereford from August to November every other year.[53]

Secondly, Wetherell had a growing family to provide for. He had six sons, to whom he wished to give a good start in life. Three of them, Nathan Croke, Charles, and Richard, matriculated from University College in 1784, 1786, and 1791; two, Robert and James, from New College in 1784 and 1805; and one, Henry, from Magdalen in 1791. Robert and James Wetherell also became Fellows of New College, and Henry and Charles Demies at Magdalen (where Wetherell's friend George Horne was President until 1791), while Nathan Croke was elected a Fellow of University College in 1788. Henry

---

[52] Cooper: Mitchell 1989 and *ODNB* entry.
[53] The collapse of the west front: Tomlinson 2000: 136–9 and Whitehead 2000: 257–9; Wetherell's increased commitment: Tomlinson 2000: 149–51.

Wetherell's career was especially unusual: having resigned his Demyship in 1799, he migrated to University College, signing the admissions register there on 2 March 1802. He was never actually a Fellow of University College, but shortly after his migration he was appointed Junior Proctor for the following year. The reaction of the College's Fellows on seeing the Master's son—who was not even one of their number—thus promoted over their heads is unknown.[54]

Of Wetherell's sons, Charles at least had some ability: he entered the law, briefly becoming Attorney-General in 1826, and attained a certain measure of renown for his extreme High Tory views. Nathan Croke Wetherell, however, disappeared into obscurity. Fellow of University College for over half a century from 1788 to 1840, he was almost continuously non-resident. This may have been due to ill-health: in 1797, 'having of late given proofs of a very disturbed & extravagant state of mind', he appears to have suffered temporarily from mental illness. His father's reaction reveals his slightly chilly character. Wetherell had been petitioning Jenkinson (now Earl of Liverpool) to make Nathan Croke a Commissioner of Bankrupts. While his eldest son's recovery looked hopeless, Wetherell suggested that Liverpool now help his younger son Charles—but as soon as Nathan Croke had recovered, he suggested that the elder brother be favoured once again.[55]

While the Master had other interests, his Fellowship was young and inexperienced. For most of the eighteenth century, their number had usually included one or two Fellows of long standing, such as John Coulson; but by the mid-1780s, only one Fellow (Samuel Swire) had been elected before 1770. Just as elsewhere in Oxford, the Fellowship was also largely an absentee one, with most Fellows treating their stipend as an aid to setting themselves up in a career. The Buttery Books suggest that, in the middle of the century, four or five Fellows were normally resident, but by the 1780s and 1790s this had dropped to two or three. One or two might take up residence intermittently, and the rest never appeared at all: indeed, when Nathan Wetherell died, only one Fellow appears to have been in residence. Fewer Fellows, therefore, were available to hold College offices. Under Charlett and Cockman, between six and eight of the twelve Fellows performed these tasks, but by the late 1750s, this had decreased to an average of five a year. Nathan Wetherell started well, taking the post of Catechist until 1787/8, and between five and six other Fellows helped him out, but from 1775/6 until his death usually just three Fellows performed all the College offices between them, two of them also acting as Tutors. Fellowship elections were affected: while as many as ten

---

[54] Henry Wetherell: Bloxam 1853–85: vii. 122 (*AO2* wrongly says that he was elected a Fellow of University College). Such nepotism was not uncommon: see, for example, Martin and Highfield 1997: 242.
[55] Charles Wetherell: *ODNB* entry; Nathan Croke Wetherell and the Earl of Liverpool: BL MS Add. 38321 fos. 213^r and 256^r.

Fellows attended elections under Charlett, Wetherell was usually joined by between two and four. There was a danger here that too many Fellows would feel disengaged from the College.[56]

Even more unfortunately, the College could not find worthy successors to the Scott brothers and William Jones. None of the new Fellows were actively incompetent or corrupt—and Thomas Maurice said of one, Philip Fisher (F. 1770–88) that 'no sounder classic, or more polished gentleman, existed in the whole University'—but a depressing glimpse into their lives comes from the Common Room Betting Book for 1785–1810. Such betting books, in which Fellows recorded wagers, usually for bottles of port, became popular in Oxford Common Rooms at this time. Some bets related to local matters: will one Fellow get married before another? Will the Master have another child? Did the Magdalen College Bells ring quarter of an hour early this evening? Others are political: will Pitt still be Prime Minister in two years' time? Will he be Prime Minister again before the Gaudy of 1803? Some are more general: is there a mail coach direct from Birmingham to Bristol via Oxford? Are there any wild lions in America? Some are simply flippant: is Griffith taller than Hooper? Did Moises really leap over the ditch in Christ Church meadow (he did)? Will Durrell sneeze in the next five minutes? Some Fellows were more enthusiastic betters than others. Hugh Moises (F. 1786–1813) was one such—although he also lost more bets than almost anyone else.[57]

We should not judge this conduct too harshly: we are seeing the Fellows off duty, when released from their lecturing or teaching duties, and Fellows of earlier generations had also relaxed. According to John Scott, even William Jones enjoyed excruciating puns: when asked whether Nebuchadnezzar and Nebuchadonosor were the same person, he replied. 'Nay by G—d I don't know, Sir.'[58] Nevertheless, the Betting Book conjures up a somnolent picture of a group of Fellows snug in their Common Room, with little to do, and seeking ways of amusing themselves. It is a friendly enough world, but rather dull. One also suspects that the conversation of the Common Room in the 1760s and 1770s, not least when Dr Johnson was visiting, would have been somewhat livelier.

Some Fellows were not so much dull as unfortunate, such as the feckless William Couture (m. 1771). Elected a Bennet Fellow in November 1777, he revealed a great talent for landing himself in debt, as revealed pitilessly in his

---

[56] Absent Fellows: figures taken from the Buttery Books for every ten years from 1748/9 to 1798/9 and then 1807/8 (UC:BU4/F/23, 28, 38, 48, 58, 68, and 77); elsewhere in Oxford: Doolittle 1986: 239–41 (and, for Cambridge, Searby 1997: 101–2); Fellows criticized for holding several offices at once: Mallet 1924–7: iii. 129–30.
[57] Fisher: Maurice 1819–20: ii. 20; the Betting Book: UC:O1/A1/1, and Bayley 1952 and 1954a.
[58] Lincoln and McEwen 1960: 33.

letters of the early 1780s to the then Bursar, Robert Clarke. 'There is', he confessed in the spring of 1780, 'a trifling Ballance due to those who have threatened an Attack upon my Fellowship, I allow; but their just Demand which remains to be settled, I am convinced is so slender as not to warrant the ungrateful Steps they have pursued to obtain it.' In April 1780 he was summoned before the Chancellor's Court to pay debts amounting to £34 13s.[59] His worst moment came in October 1780, when he wrote to Clarke from the Maidenhead Inn at High Wycombe:

> Yesterday I was arrested for £12 & not being able to settle it, I was conducted to this House by the Officer who is the Landlord of it & in whose Custody I now am. The contingent Expenses both in Town & County with the extravagant Extortions of such a Place as this where every inhuman Advantage is taken, will swell the sum little short of Twenty Pounds —Unless it is quickly discharged, I shall have no other Prospect before me than the gloomy one of a Prison.[60]

Clarke accepted the inevitable, and scribbled at the bottom of the letter: 'Sent to Mr. Couture two ten pound Bank Notes.'

As a non-resident Fellow, Couture had to supplement his income from elsewhere, which in his case meant seeking a church appointment. His letters to Clarke show him scratching a living by standing in for a priest for a few months at a time. Eventually Couture's luck changed. In 1788, on the death of John Coulson, the valuable living of Checkendon fell vacant, and Couture, now the senior Fellow, had first refusal. He did not refuse. Unfortunately the living's ample stipend did not solve his financial problems: he was summoned before the Chancellor's Court in 1796 and 1799 for yet more debts, and in April 1801 the Fellows took the extreme step of removing Couture's name from the College books, because he had not settled his batells bills, and had not replied to any letters asking him to pay. When he died in 1820, the College had to agree upon a procedure to follow when the incumbent of a College living died insolvent.[61]

Wetherell's later years saw two major architectural projects. The first was a new Master's Lodgings on the site of Deep Hall, next to the Main Quadrangle, and the conversion of the existing Lodgings into student accommodation. In November 1798, Wetherell and the Fellows agreed that there were 'no good habitable apartments in the Lodgings', that they lacked both a kitchen and proper servants' quarters, and that Deep Hall was now in 'so ruinous a condition' that it should be demolished. They hoped that the Court

---

[59] Couture's letters to Clarke: UC:S17/C3/1–23; letter of 1780: UC:S17/C3/1; in the Chancellor's Court: OUA CC Papers 1780/23. Couture's hapless career is described in more detail in Mitchell 2007.
[60] UC:S17/C3/10.
[61] Couture's fresh debts: OUA CC Papers 1796/10 and 1799/22; struck off the College books: UC:GB3/A1/2 fo. 129^v; death: UC:GB3/A1/2 fos. 157^v–158^r.

of Chancery would release some of the surplus in the Linton Fund for this project. The Senior Fellow, James Griffith (F. 1782–1808), an enthusiastic amateur artist and architect, produced a design for the new Lodgings (Plate 11). It is in the pasteboard 'Gothick' of the time, in which a Gothic veneer fails to conceal a classically symmetrical core, but Griffith would have certainly given Oxford's High Street a striking new building. This project, however, foundered, presumably because the funds could not be released.[62]

The second project was a new façade for the south range of the Main Quadrangle. Its sub-classical entrances to the Hall and Chapel had always presented a somewhat incongruous aspect, and so in November 1799, it was decided to Gothicize the whole thing, again to the designs of James Griffith (Plate 12). The gables above the Hall and Chapel were replaced with castellations, and buttresses were attached, while the structure above the central entrance was replaced with a bow window. The Chapel roof was also apparently replaced. Although no sources within the College refer to this, the antiquarian James Ingram, writing in the 1830s, wrote that a new roof was erected in 1802, 'the original ceiling of oak panel-work having become decayed'. No evidence survives for the appearance of this second roof.[63]

Wetherell evidently liked the 'Gothick' style, for it is employed in all the projects with which he was involved, beginning with the redecoration of the Hall in the 1760s. At Hereford, the architect chosen to replace the west front of the Cathedral was James Wyatt, the master of this style. Wyatt's front, completed in 1795, was either elegant and simple or insipid and shallow, according to taste, and was later replaced by a generation seeking a more historically informed version of Gothic.[64]

Meanwhile, the effects of the French Revolution and its wars were being felt even by a sleepy College. In 1798/9 University College purchased uniforms for the Volunteer Corps for College servants. Even the Fellows' Betting Book took a more serious turn: in May 1802 and November 1803, there were bets 'that Buonoparte is alive this day twelvemonth', and 'that the King, in case of actual Invasion, has the power of calling out to bear arms every man in the country, not excepting clergymen'. The College also shrank, as admissions fell in the 1790s to numbers not seen since the 1750s (Graph 12.1).[65]

Events in France may have influenced Oxford in another way. In 1800, a university statute was passed which provided for an optional but searching oral examination, for which candidates would be marked and given honours accordingly. For the first time in Oxford's history, people could be awarded a

---

[62] A new Lodging: UC:GB3/A1/2 fos. 123^v–124^v.
[63] Griffith's façade: UC:GB3/A1/2 fo. 127^{r-v}; contract: UC:FA3/2/L1/1; Chapel roof: Ingram 1837: i.14.
[64] Tomlinson 2000: 140–2 and Whitehead 2000: 261–5.
[65] The Volunteer Corps: UC:BU5/F2/2 fos. 196^r, 200^r, 204^r, 207^v, and 215^r; the Betting Book: UC:O1/A1/1.

degree solely on the basis of a single set of examinations, mainly on classical literature and philosophy (admittedly, Cambridge had been holding similar examinations since the 1740s, though only in mathematics). The first examinations, sat by only two students, were held in 1802. The statute's promoters, Cyril Jackson, Dean of Christ Church, John Eveleigh, Provost of Oriel, and John Parsons, Master of Balliol, were stout Tories all, who, observing the terrible events in France, evidently determined to save Britain from this fate by producing a properly educated Tory elite. Wetherell is not known to been involved in this statute, but he clearly approved: one of the four people who sat the 1803 examinations, George Rowley (m. 1799), was from University College, as was one of the three candidates in 1806, Nathaniel Ellison (m. 1802). These men would hardly have taken the exam without Wetherell's approval.[66]

Wetherell involved himself in politics to the end. When the (Whig) Duke of Portland was elected as the new Chancellor in 1792, Wetherell made sure that University College played its part: the outside of the College was painted in honour of Portland's installation, and the cook was paid £30 for dinners and wine 'for the High Table during the time of the Duke of Portland's Installation'. Wetherell's political beliefs, however, remained unchanged, even at the cost of old friendships. In 1801, William Pitt's government fell when his plans for Catholic Emancipation were frustrated. Among the ministers who supported this measure and resigned with Pitt was William Windham. In this same year, when it was rumoured that one of the university's Parliamentary seats might become vacant, Windham wrote to Martin Routh, the President of Magdalen, wondering how to start canvassing, 'a point more difficult to settle', he observed, 'in consequence of the part taken, as you know, by Dr. Wetherell'. In 1805, following similar rumours, Windham wrote to Wetherell himself seeking his backing. Wetherell, remembering Windham's earlier apostasy, replied with surprising vehemence that he would not endorse a supporter of Catholic Emancipation, because he considered 'that expedient for reconciling the differences & animosities in Ireland as pregnant with inevitable evils of the greatest magnitude both to Church & State'.[67]

By now Wetherell was in his late seventies; he had been a member of University College since 1750, and his tenure of forty-three years remains the longest Mastership in its history. At last, on 29 December 1807, he died, and was buried in the College Chapel. He died wealthy: Martin Routh wrote in January 1808, 'The old Master of University has slipt out of the World, and left £150000, I have not mistaken the number of noughts, and all its cares

---

[66] The examination statute: Green 1986c; Cambridge's exams: Searby 1997: 158–9.
[67] Welcoming the new Chancellor: UC:BU2/F1/5 fos. 74^r and 81^v, and Mitchell 1986: 187–8; Windham and Routh: MCA MS 475 (ii) no. 67; Wetherell's rebuke: BL MS Add. 37909 fo. 38^r.

behind him.' Others thought the sum nearer £100,000. University College did not benefit from his will; the Master had a large family to provide for.[68]

When one looks back over his long Mastership, Wetherell emerges as an ambiguous figure. In the 1760s and 1770s, University College became briefly the most intellectually exciting college in Oxford, but by the late 1780s it had sunk into comparative mediocrity. The College was undoubtedly lucky in the 1760s, but the young Wetherell had made his own luck by helping William Jones and John Scott to their Fellowships, by head-hunting William Scott from Corpus Christi, and by weaving a network of influential friends elsewhere. Where did it go wrong?

There seems, after all, to be a certain chilly selfishness about Nathan Wetherell. What drove him, one wonders, apart from a ceaseless ambition to better himself and his family, and an enjoyment of the grand political game? Wetherell was the success which Arthur Charlett could so nearly have been, but there is one big difference between them: Charlett, for all his faults, loved scholarship, and enjoyed encouraging his protégés in their latest projects, whereas Wetherell exhibited no such interest. He was not insensible of the glory which William Jones brought upon his College, but he seems to have taken no active interest in Jones's achievements. Neither did he display much interest in theological matters after his election as Master. His true soulmate was Charles Jenkinson, another ambitious grey eminence.[69] Having transformed the College, Wetherell by the early 1780s had no worlds left to conquer: he had been a brilliant Vice-Chancellor; as a Dean and a Canon, he had won high preferment; he had direct links with the Prime Minister; his finances were prospering. What else remained for him now except to ensure that his children were properly looked after? And thus his concentration lapsed, and his achievements unravelled, to the point that arguably the College was in worse intellectual shape in 1807 than it had been in 1764. Like some great firework, Wetherell's brilliant College had burnt itself out.

---

[68] Wetherell's wealth: MCA MS 462 no. 23 and Bloxam 1853–85: vii. 107; his will: TNA PROB/11/1473.

[69] It is somehow appropriate that no likeness of Wetherell is known.

14
The Workings of a Georgian College

In spite of the bad publicity surrounding eighteenth-century Oxford in general, this century was arguably the most exciting in the history of University College. The preceding chapters have shown that not only did it enjoy (or suffer) periods of great drama, but its intellectual achievements in the early years of Arthur Charlett's and Nathan Wetherell's Masterships remain unsurpassed until the later twentieth century. We can now turn to some themes which run through the century, namely the members of the College, their work and their play, their careers, the finances of the College and its Fellows, and the relationship between Old Members and their College.

CLIMBING THE ACADEMIC LADDER

Between 1689 and 1807 1,472 people were attached to University College, of whom 460 came up in 1689–1722, 432 in 1723–64, and 580 in 1764–1807. By now, almost all of them were admitted as undergraduates: mature commoners who were admitted with at least one degree had effectively disappeared by the 1720s. We rarely know what attracted undergraduates particularly to University College, and frustratingly little is known about their earlier education. Occasional glimpses suggests that a particular school under a successful master could create a happy relationship with the College. Hugh Moises, for example, Master of Newcastle Grammar School in 1749–87, was a particularly gifted headmaster whose pupils at University College included Robert Chambers and the Scott brothers—and his son, another Hugh (m. 1781; F. 1786–1813).[1]

As in the seventeenth century, the College lay at the centre of various networks of families and friends. Thus the studious gentleman commoner Nicholas Toke married the daughter of John Cockman (becoming Thomas Cockman's nephew by marriage), and sent two of his sons, John and Nicholas, to University College in 1756 and 1759. His grandson Nicholas followed them in 1782. A more complicated network surrounded William and John Scott. Their cousin, Henry Utrick Reay, matriculated in 1768, and was a

---
[1] Hugh Moises: *ODNB* entry.

Fellow in 1774–86. Slightly more surprisingly, John Scott's brother-in-law, Matthew Surtees, matriculated from University College in 1773, a year after Scott's elopement—and William Scott was Surtees's tutor. Surtees himself became a Fellow in 1780, and rector of North Cerney in 1793. Hugh Moises, the Scotts' headmaster, married the sister of Matthew Ridley of Heaton Hall, and two of Ridley's sons, Nicholas and Henry (who married another sister of Matthew Surtees), matriculated from University College in 1767 and 1770, as did his grandson Richard in 1799, while the College's Newcastle house was leased from 1732 onwards to successive members of the Ridley family.[2]

Such dynasties could benefit the College's members. William Bouverie, created Earl of Radnor in 1765, matriculated from University College in 1743. He sent three sons there in 1767, 1771, and 1772, and all three had William Scott as their tutor. The Bouveries did not forget their tutor, nor he them. When William Bouverie tried to stand as Chancellor of Oxford in 1772, Scott had canvassed for him, and in 1790–1801 Scott was MP for Downton, a Bouverie pocket borough.[3]

None of the next generation of Bouveries, however, came to University College, preferring smarter colleges like Oriel and Christ Church. Such 'trend-seeking' was not uncommon, as can be seen from the sons of the members who achieved eminence at the College in the middle of the century. The Scott brothers sent their sons to University College, while Robert Chambers sent his elder son to University College in 1797, and his younger to Christ Church in 1803, but Charles Jenkinson sent both his sons, including the future Prime Minister, the second Lord Liverpool (under whom Lord Eldon would serve as Lord Chancellor), to Christ Church in 1787 and 1801. The Acland family were especially good at sniffing out the 'right' college. The soldier John Dyke Acland (m. 1765) came up to University College, as did his brother, Thomas (m. 1770), and his cousin John (m. 1774). Their fathers, however, had both matriculated from Balliol in the 1740s, their own sons matriculated from either Oriel or Christ Church in the early nineteenth century, and all their grandsons went to Christ Church. When University College lost eminence, it could not count on the loyalty of all its old members.[4]

Undergraduates were now generally a little older (see Appendix IV), as their average age on coming up during the eighteenth century rose to between 17 and 18. There were also slightly more 19-year-olds, while the proportion of youths who came up aged 15 or younger gradually fell away to insignificance. This slow rise in age can be seen elsewhere: at Christ

---

[2] Nicholas Toke's Cockman wife: Bayley 1959b: 257; Hugh Moises's family: *ODNB* entry; the Newcastle house: UC:E5/2/D7/14–15; Henry Ridley: *Gentleman's Magazine* Nov. 1825, p. 473.
[3] Mitchell 1970: 355 and Bourguignon 1987: 39.
[4] My thanks to Peter Gilliver for helping to disentangle some of these genealogies.

Church, half of all commoners who came up in 1660–1702 were aged 16 or 17, but by c.1750 their average age had gone up to 17 or 18.[5]

The status of undergraduates—at least in their own descriptions—changes over the century. Appendix IV also shows that the proportion of undergraduates describing themselves as the sons of esquires increases dramatically through the eighteenth century, while the number of sons of gentlemen declines slightly, and the number of sons of plebeians collapses. Meanwhile, the College's Admission Register classed 61 members as gentlemen commoners, 224 as commoners, and 131 as servitors in 1689–1722, while the respective figures for 1723–64 were 59 gentlemen commoners, 239 commoners, and 95 servitors, and in 1764–1807 65 gentlemen commoners, 452 commoners, and a mere 26 servitors.

At first glance, these figures suggest a College excluding those of lower birth; but throughout Oxford and Cambridge the number of servitors and sizars (the Cambridge term) collapsed in the eighteenth century. This could be seen as unfortunate: the servitor system, demeaning as it appears today, could offer opportunities. When George Richards matriculated from University College as a servitor in 1733, Thomas Hearne observed that his grandfather had been cook of St Edmund Hall, and that his father (now a parish priest in Kent) a servitor at St Edmund Hall. A spectacular example of a servitor making good is John Potter (m. 1688), who won a Freeston Scholarship in 1691, and was elected a Fellow of Lincoln College in 1694. He entered on a successful career in the church, becoming Archbishop of Canterbury in 1737.[6]

This decline in poor students, however, may be in part more apparent than real: undergraduates were more inclined to overstate their status. For example, the architect John Wood the Younger (m. 1747), who built the Royal Crescent and the New Assembly Rooms in Bath, calls his architect father, John Wood the Elder, an esquire. A century earlier, he might well not have described him thus. By the 1760s, just about the only servitors at University College were the recipients of Lodge Scholarships—which, under their benefactor's instructions, could only be awarded to servitors. It may well be the case that eighteenth-century Oxford was less welcoming to undergraduates from poorer backgrounds, but the sources make this difficult to prove.

Data about members' geographical origins is, fortunately, more reliable.[7] First of all, although more undergraduates still came to University College from Yorkshire than from any other county, their proportion decreased. In 1689–1764, almost a fifth of all undergraduates came from Yorkshire, but this

---

[5] Bill 1988: 172.
[6] Servitors at Oxford: Davies and Garnett 1994: 40, and Bill 1988: 191–4; Sizars at Cambridge: Twigg 1987: 192–3, Miller 1961: 59–60, and Searby 1997: 71; Richards: Hearne xi. 187; Potter: *ODNB* entry.
[7] This information is now taken from the College's Admission Registers.

proportion decreased to 13.7 per cent in 1764–1807. On the other hand, whereas in 1689–1764 there were just six undergraduates from Durham and twenty-four from Northumberland, in 1764–1807 fourteen undergraduates came from Durham and no less than thirty-seven from Northumberland.

Nathan Wetherell came from Durham, and William Scott from Northumberland, and the origins of a Master or charismatic tutor could affect the College's admissions. During the Mastership of Arthur Charlett, a Worcestershire man, the second most popular county of origin after Yorkshire was Worcestershire (39 undergraduates). Meanwhile, although Kent had long been a popular county, thanks to the Gunsley Scholarships (31 undergraduates came from Kent in 1689–1722, and 39 in 1764–1807), no fewer than 56 undergraduates came from there in 1723–64—but then Thomas Cockman came from Kent. Also in this period, 26 undergraduates came from Warwickshire, where John Browne had a parish.

Many undergraduates now came from London—32 in 1689–1722, 25 in 1723–64, and 78 (only two fewer than the total of Yorkshiremen) in 1764–1807—but to say that one came from London simply meant that one's family had moved there. For example, when John Scott's eldest son, another John, signed the Admissions Register in 1792, he recorded that his father lived in London. But John Scott himself came from Newcastle, as did his wife. To say that John Scott the younger was a Londoner is to ignore his northern roots.

During the eighteenth century, University College accepted its first undergraduates from British colonies overseas. The first of them came from the Caribbean, of whom the earliest, Wardell Andrews of Barbados, matriculated in 1697. Over the next century, at least two or three overseas undergraduates came up each decade. The first from North America was John Lawrence (m. 1741), from Philadelphia, and two more, Thomas Richardson from Maryland (m. 1759) and Charles Martyn from South Carolina (m. 1780), matriculated before the Treaty of Versailles recognized the United States of America.[8]

Once they had come up to Oxford, undergraduates still sometimes changed Colleges. Between 1689 and 1807 just 41 undergraduates who had matriculated elsewhere migrated to University College, but 146 members of University College went elsewhere to take their BA or MA. Most 'exports' left in search of scholarships or fellowships, such as George Horne, lost to Magdalen in 1750, John Potter, lost to Lincoln in 1694, or Edmund Cartwright (m. 1760), generally credited with inventing the power loom, who in 1762 became a Demy and then a Fellow of Magdalen.[9]

We now move up the academic ladder to the College's Scholars; 274 men are known to have been elected to Scholarships at University College between 1689 and 1807. Over two-thirds of them were elected one year or less

---

[8] On these early members from abroad, see further Darwall-Smith 2003.
[9] Cartwright: *ODNB* entry, and Bloxam 1853–85: vi. 327–38.

after matriculation and most of the rest did not have to wait any longer than three years (Gunsley Scholars were unusual in being selected before matriculation). Their geographical backgrounds were affected by the rules concerning their selection. Out of the 274 Scholars of 1689–1807, 118 came from Yorkshire and 52 from Kent. Apart from London, there were fewer than a dozen Scholars from any other single county.

Because the selection procedure for each set of Scholarships depended upon the whim of its founder, the standard of Scholars varied greatly. Whereas Freeston and Bennet Scholarships tended to go to worthy recipients, the same was not always true in other cases. In regard to Gunsley Scholarships, for example, preference had to be given to members of the Ayerst family, kinsmen of Robert Gunsley himself. William Smith expressed his unhappiness at this to Arthur Charlett in November 1692:

> We are debarred from making the choice within the College, & must... send some of the Society into Kent to chuse out of the Scholes of Rochester & Maidstone, but the choice will this turne fall... on a child as the last did under ten years old, upon the pretence of relation to the founder, by a benefit of which Mr. Ayerst who resigned last year had been scholar of the college before any that are now of it had been born into the world.[10]

Five Gunsley Scholars elected after 1689 were members of the Ayerst family, of whom only William Ayerst (Gunsley Scholar 1698–1716), who travelled abroad in the service of the Earl of Stratford, and produced an edition of the works of Sallust, had any merit. Few of the other Gunsley Scholars fulfilled their promise. Only two, Thomas Allen and Francis Walwyn, were elected Fellows of University College, and only one is known to have become a Fellow elsewhere—although this was George Horne.[11]

At least the College had some say in the selection of most Gunsley Scholars; Leicester Scholars were nominated exclusively by the Earls of Leicester and, later, their descendants. Thomas Coney (Leicester Scholar 1692–9) later confessed to Thomas Hearne that he 'gave 3 score Pounds to come in Leyrcester [sic] scholar of University College, which money, besides five Pounds more for a Procuress, was to be given to one of the Lord Leyrcester's whores. This usual.'—although Hearne did concede that Coney was 'a man of a fair Character'. Out of the thirty-one Leicester Scholars appointed in 1689–1800, only one, George Shepherd (Leicester Scholar 1788–93) became a Fellow at University College. Another, the politician Charles Jenkinson (Leicester Scholar 1751–4), certainly attained eminence in later life, but the remainder brought little glory to the College.[12]

---

[10] Bodl. MS Ballard 16 fo. 17ʳ. 'Mr. Ayerst' was William Ayerst, who matriculated in 1662, and resigned his Scholarship in 1691.
[11] William Ayerst's career: Hearne, iv. 170 and his entry in *AO1* (and p. 226 for his correspondence with Charlett).
[12] Coney's election: Hearne, iv. 132–3; his character: Hearne, ii. 69 and iii. 21.

Scholars with academic pretensions had a problem, because they might have to wait some time for a vacant Fellowship. Some spent time elsewhere, making a living as a curate or teacher. From time to time, therefore, the College had to order its Scholars to appear in Oxford, and occasionally even deprived them of their awards for being absent without leave.[13] Unlike at other Colleges, Scholars could not always count on receiving preference in Fellowship elections. In 1689–1764, 34 of the 41 Fellows with prior links to University College had been Scholars; but in 1764–1807, the proportion had fallen to 19 out of 28. On the other hand, between 1689 and 1807, at least 23 Scholars are known to have been elected fellows of other colleges. Not all Scholarships were equal in value, especially before 1781, when John Browne's benefaction to augment existing awards at last came into effect.[14] Sometimes, therefore, a Scholar might move from a poorer Scholarship to a wealthier one: one-sixth of all Scholars elected in 1689–1807 are known to have held two awards either successively or concurrently.

Higher still on the academic ladder stood a Fellowship. Standards were maintained in their selection: after 1689 all candidates for Fellowships sat examinations—although it is uncertain whether this was merely the first time that an existing practice was recorded. No examination papers survive, but there are some clues to their content. Those held in June 1689 required translations from English (presumably into Greek or Latin), essays on a given subject, and questions on unspecified philological and philosophical subjects. The Fellowship examinations of July 1701 demanded tests in Greek and Latin literature and philosophy, and translations from English into Latin, but those held in March 1735 and May 1740 gave unspecified scope for candidates to show their ability at theology. The 1740 exams at least also included a written element: when this election was contested, the Lord Chancellor examined the 'written exercises' of the rival candidates. University College was not unusual in holding examinations: Merton and All Souls are known to have done this too.[15]

On occasion a candidate might be exempted from examinations, most commonly because he had been awaiting a Fellowship for some time, and had already shown his worth to the College. Thus Thomas Cockman, who had been acting as a Tutor since 1699, was exempted from the exams of 1700, and Thomas Cockerill (m. 1700) from those of 1716. Albemarle Bertie, however, was exempted from the 1689 examinations because (according to

---

[13] For example, UC:GB3/A1/1 pp. 126 and 128.
[14] First elections of Dr Browne Scholars and Scholars with Dr Browne's augmentations: UC:GB3/A1/2 fo. 97. The College Register used this nomenclature to prevent confusion with the existing 'Browne Scholarships' (p. 118).
[15] UC:GB3/A1/1 pp. 117 (1689) and 139 (1701), UC:GB3/A1/2 fos. 35^v (1735) and 45^r (1740). Other colleges: Martin and Highfield 1997: 241, and Doolittle 1986: 234–5.

the College Register) of his natural talents—and presumably because his father was the Earl of Lindsey.[16]

When a Fellowship fell vacant, candidates' friends regularly lobbied the College; the unhappy election of William Denison was only an extreme example of this practice. Elections might also be delayed to keep a candidate out. In January 1708 Benjamin Baynes (m. 1701) was elected Percy Fellow over Edward Middleton (m. 1702), but this Fellowship had been vacated in March 1707, and the election postponed several times. Thomas Hearne thought he knew why: Dr Radcliffe, he claimed, supported Baynes, and, because Middleton was consumptive, the election was delayed until he was past recovery, and had retired to the country. Nevertheless, University College continued to favour its own, for of the 91 Fellows elected in 1689–1807, 74 were already members.[17]

For much of this period, there was something of a log-jam among the Fellowship, which left would-be Fellows stranded for several years. The problem was not new: John Hinckley (m. 1669) had had to wait twenty years for his Fellowship. In particular, two Bennet Fellows elected in 1689, Albemarle Bertie and John Boraston, retained their Fellowships until 1721 and 1741 respectively, and almost three-quarters of the Bennet Fellows elected in 1689–1722 had to wait at least a decade from their arrival in the College until their election. Indeed, Fellows of University College retained their posts for unusually long periods: the average tenure of Fellows elected between 1689 and 1764 was between nineteen and twenty years, whereas Fellows elected at Queens' College Cambridge in 1660–1778 remained in post for an average of twelve years, as did Students of Christ Church elected in 1660–1800, and eighteenth-century Fellows at St John's Cambridge stayed for an average of fifteen years. It therefore says something about Wetherell's useful links—to say nothing of the College's new livings starting to fall vacant—that in 1764–1807 the average tenure of a Fellowship went down to 14.4 years.[18]

Some other changes in the Fellowship became apparent during the century. First of all, the proportion of Yorkshiremen fell. In 1689–1722, 13 of the 28 Fellows elected came from Yorkshire, 3 from Northumberland, and none from Durham, but of the 24 Fellows elected in 1723–64, 7 came from Yorkshire, 6 from Northumberland, and 2 from Durham. Under Nathan Wetherell (a Durham man), the balance shifted further: of the 39 Fellows elected in this period, 10 each came from Yorkshire and Northumberland,

---

[16] UC:GB3/A1/1 pp. 117 (1689), 139 (1700), and 169 (1716).
[17] Letters of recommendation: Bodl. MS Ballard 9 fo. 37^r, 10 fo. 50^r, and 15 fo. 17^r; Baynes's election: Hearne, ii. 87–8 and UC:GB3/A1/1 pp. 155–6.
[18] Other colleges: Twigg 1987: 187; Bill 1988: 139; Miller 1961: 51–2. The arcane regulations about eligibility to Magdalen fellowships created serious log-jams there in the eighteenth century (Darwall-Smith in Brockliss (forthcoming)).

and 6 from Durham. During Wetherell's Mastership there was also a change in the status of Fellows at the time of their election. In 1689–1722, 17 Fellows were MAs, and 11 BAs; in 1723–64 the respective figures were 16 and 8. Wetherell, however, liked a younger Fellowship: 23 Fellows elected in 1764–1807 were BAs, and 5 (including William Jones and John Scott) were elected while still undergraduates.

TUTORS, PUPILS, AND LIBRARIES[19]

The central relationship in an undergraduate's life still remained that with his tutor or tutors. However, the relationship in some respects matters more than ever in this period. It has been written of Cambridge that 'between the Restoration and the mid-eighteenth century there scarcely was such a thing as an undergraduate syllabus in the sense in which we use the term', and the same held true at Oxford.[20] Instead almost everything depended on the ability of one's tutor: one need only weigh up the prospects of being taught by John Coulson or William Scott to realize what this could mean. The demands made of responsible College Tutors were great: Walter Stanhope may have grumbled at his workload under William Scott, but Scott's demands of his pupils imposed a huge workload on himself.

In the early eighteenth century, undergraduates at University College had some freedom in their choice of Tutor: the Admissions Register for 1701–5 shows almost half the Fellows acting as Tutors. By the second half of the century, however, there were usually just two, or occasionally three, Fellows who handled all tutorial duties, a reduction mirrored elsewhere in Oxford and Cambridge. Other Fellows could encounter undergraduates through lectures and disputations: Robert Chambers called William Jones 'the most laborious student I ever knew', although he was never Jones's tutor. He did, however, hold various College lectureships during 1762–6, and so could have experienced Jones's brilliance that way. Some Fellows might offer extra-curricular coaching, as when George Watson taught Hebrew and Hutchinsonianism to George Horne and William Jones of Nayland, despite not being their official Tutor. The wealthy student or schoolboy could even have a tutor all to himself. Thus William Jones and Thomas Cockman were both employed as private tutors.[21]

Although we know a fair amount about what people were studying in Georgian Oxford, it is harder to establish how this knowledge was transmitted. Stanhope and others talk of lectures, but these may not have consisted of much more than reading over a text together. Some questioned this method:

---

[19] A detailed study of this subject can be found in Bill 1988: chs. IV–V. See too Clarke 1986: 517–25.
[20] Cambridge: Morgan 2004: 511; Oxford: Bill 1988: 242–3.
[21] Tutoring at Cambridge: Bendall and others 1999: 300, Miller 1961: 57, and Twigg 1987: 189; Chambers on Jones: Curley 1998: 63–4.

Samuel Johnson once said to William Scott 'Lectures were once useful; but now, when all are read, and books are so numerous, lectures are unnecessary'—and Scott agreed.[22]

Latin and Greek dominated undergraduate studies (unlike Cambridge, which set more store by the study of mathematics), but there was a change in emphasis during the century. Although, to judge from the books they possessed, Nicholas Toke and Charles Yarburgh in the 1720s and 1730s certainly knew Greek, they read more Latin literature, whereas Walter Stanhope in the 1760s studied such challenging Greek authors as Sophocles and Callimachus, which Toke and Yarburgh were spared. This greater interest in Greek can be matched elsewhere. The College also offered opportunities to study subjects outside the basic curriculum, such as Hebrew. Until 1740/1, payments are regularly made to the most eminent coaches in Oxford—Rabbi Isaac Abendana, Rabbi Philip Levi, and Jean Gagnier—for teaching Hebrew, although this may have been offered only to those who had taken their BA, and not to undergraduates. Then in the 1730s Robert Eden and Francis Walwyn began formally to teach civil law. This became something of a College speciality: Thomas Maurice wrote of the 1770s that 'the members of University College, in particular, had the additional advantage of hearing some admirable lectures on the study of the CIVIL LAW, which were attended with as much delight as improvement by the students.'[23]

The College, however, provided surprisingly little help in theology. Although at least a quarter of all members of University College in the eighteenth century took holy orders, the actual study of theology remained the preserve of those who had reached the rank of MA. Undergraduates would have come to know the Bible and the liturgy from Chapel services, and the Catechist's lectures were supposed to instil some basic theological knowledge. They also had the opportunity to hear university sermons, but that was more or less all. In the early part of the century those who wished to enter holy orders merely had to be of BA status, present a testimonial from their College, and then pass an oral examination by the chaplain of the Bishop who would ordain them (such examinations depended greatly upon the chaplain). Later in the century, ordinands were also expected to have attended a course of lectures given by the Regius Professor of Divinity. Admittedly, a responsible head of house could take the writing of a testimonial seriously: Arthur Charlett once sought the advice of Joseph Bingham on the granting of testimonials, and Bingham wrote a long and considered reply. Nonetheless, some contemporaries did question the preference for classical

---

[22] Boswell 1980: 1136.
[23] Cambridge: Searby 1997: 154–63; study of Greek: Quarrie 1986: 494–7 and Darwall-Smith in Brockliss (forthcoming); payments for Hebrew teaching are regularly recorded in UC:BU2/F1/2 and UC:BU5/F2/1; Hebrew teachers: Patterson 1986: 541–2; civil law in the 1770s: Maurice 1819–20: ii. 137–8.

over theological training at undergraduate level. George Horne expressed his anxiety that 'while the heads of boys are filled with tales of Jupiter, Juno, Mars, Bacchus and Venus, the Bible is little heard of; and so the Heathen creed becomes not only the first, but the whole study', and that students would learn 'a system of Ethics, which teaches morals without religious data'.[24]

It is possible to understand something of the reasoning behind the range of subjects which the assiduous undergraduate might study. One such student, Nicholas Toke, is particularly informative. Like Yarburgh and Stanhope, his studies ranged widely. In his first months at Oxford, he read books on modern history, including Walter Raleigh's *History of the World*, as well as classical texts (although more in Latin than in Greek), and treatises on logic. He also began to study philosophy and geography. He even wanted to explore natural philosophy, and planned to attend a course of lectures in anatomy. By the end of 1722, he was learning French and Italian, and in 1724 he was studying mathematics, and reading Euclid and an English translation of Willem Gravesande's *Mathematical Experiments of Natural Philosophy*, an early attempt to explain Newtonian physics to a wider audience. In 1725, he had moved on to civil law. Although Toke does not reveal how much advice he had from his tutor, Thomas Cockerill, he received a well-rounded education, in which he progressed from the study of classical literature and history to more applicable subjects, like mathematics and civil law. This breadth of reading can be matched at other colleges in Oxford.[25]

Toke himself valued this varied curriculum:

> I would obtain in that part of the character of a Gentlemen [*sic*] viz. of being Aliquis in omnibus [something in everything]; ... I shall never be content to bury my self in a Country Seat, & trifle away my life with a pack of Hounds all day, & an overflowing bowl at night. Neither can I be reconciled any more to those who cloyster themselves up all their lives in a study, then who live in a continued course of idleness. For I have as bad a notion of what we call mere Scholars, as of those, who are no Scholars at all. The former make a wretched appearance abroad in the World, tho' they may be great men in their studys at home; & the latter do sometimes indeed betray their ignorance, but for all that we may very frequently discern a great Genius in 'em, tho' for want of learning tis darken'd & eclips'd.[26]

Both Thomas Cockman (Toke's future uncle by marriage) and George Watson were praised because they matched their scholarship with an outward

---

[24] Theological training in colleges: Greaves 1986: 403–6 and Green 1986b: 432–3; entering holy orders: Virgin 1989: 132–3 and 137–8, and Bennett 1986c: 388–9; Bingham on testimonials: Bodl. MS Ballard 15 fo. 20^r; Horne's concerns: Jones 1795: 33–4.
[25] Toke's early studies: Bodl. MS Eng. Th. c. 27 pp. 269–70 (transcribed in Bayley 1959b: 259–60), 337–8, 365–6, and 393; French and Italian: Bodl. MS Eng. Th. c. 28 p. 121 (transcribed in Bayley 1959b: 262); mathematics: Bodl. MS Eng. Th. c. 28 p. 245; Gravesande's treatise (first published in English in 1720): Brockliss 1996: 586; civil law: Bodl. MS Eng. Th. c. 29 pp. 23–4 and 43–50; other colleges: Bill 1988: 275–97 and Evans 1887: 49–52 and 66–8.
[26] Bodl. MS Eng. Th. c. 27 pp. 365–6.

elegance of manner. Cockman himself, urging his pupils to read Cicero, not for the sake of scholarship, but so that active benefit might be derived from its lessons, would have understood this attitude which would certainly not encourage a rigorous, specialized, reading of a text, but could give the works of Cicero, say, a contemporary quality which they may have lost.[27]

Samuel Johnson also approved of sensible moderation. In May 1765, not long after his protégé George Strahan had matriculated from University College, Johnson advised him not to 'tire yourself so much with Greek', but divide his day between Greek, Latin, and English. Strahan should also learn some French, and take a literary journal, which would 'inform you what learning is going forward in the world'.[28]

Georgian Oxford, then, possessed an educational ideal which is not unworthy of our respect. Unfortunately, it was easy to abuse. In particular, if there was concern that a gentleman commoner or nobleman might become a pedant through excessive study—and, as Nicholas Toke found, run the risk of arousing jealousy for combining intellectual and social excellence—then he might end up studying nothing, and turning out like the Duke of Beaufort.

There was also still no means of assessing students. Until 1800, Oxford's examinations still held to the medieval idea, preserved in the Laudian statutes of 1636, that they should be less a searching test than a ceremony one went through when one's teachers thought one was ready for it, which involved not tests, but a series of exercises. By now, however, the content of these exercises had become almost meaningless. In order to take his BA, William Jones had to hold four disputations in the Schools, each one lasting three hours, which he described to his pupil Viscount Althorp as a 'silly ceremony'. There is also the most notorious examination of Georgian Oxford, that of John Scott, Lord Eldon. Recalling his examination for Hebrew and History (he did not say whether it was for his BA or MA), Eldon claimed it went as follows: '"What is the Hebrew for the place of a skull?"—I replied, "Golgotha."—"Who founded University College?"—I stated... "that King Alfred founded it."—"Very well, sir," said the examiner, "you are competent for your degree."' This story, however, is not all that it seems. Not only did Eldon have a penchant for embellishing amusing tales, but he had also been a Fellow since the age of 16. The examiners may well have concluded that a Fellow did not need detailed questioning for his degree, but that something should be done for form's sake.[29]

There are better ways of seeing University College at work, one of which is its Library—or rather, 'Libraries'. The *Gentleman's Magazine* of 1786 included a letter which, in describing University College, recorded that 'Over

---

[27] Attitudes to classics: Bill 1988: 14.
[28] Redford 1992–4: i. 248
[29] Jones: Cannon 1970: i. 24: Eldon: Twiss 1844: i. 57.

the gateway within side the old quadrangle, between the windows of the under-graduates' library, is a good statue of King James II.' This casual reference suggests that the current Estates Bursary was once a Library for undergraduate use separate from the main one, and indeed in 1791/2 new windows were installed in the 'Treasury and Junior Library'. We do not know when the College created it: in 1732/3 some money was spent on a room called the 'Fellows' Library', suggesting the presence of at least two Libraries in the College. Some other colleges, such as Christ Church, Trinity, Magdalen, and Queen's had similar undergraduate libraries, but it was still an unusual development.[30]

There survives a catalogue for University College's undergraduate Library, compiled in the early 1730s. It reveals a fairly structured collection: there is a comprehensive selection of Latin and Greek literature—although unsurprisingly, given its date, the Latin section is stronger than the Greek (there is no edition of the plays of Aeschylus, for example)—many works of theology, including both recently published sermons and the works of Albertus Magnus and St Thomas Aquinas, and books on law. There are scientific texts, including Galileo's *Starry Messenger* and Newton's *Optics* and *Principia* (as well as a copy of Gravesande for those daunted by Newton himself), as well as many books on British and European history. There are works by English authors, including Pope and Addison, as well as such French writers as Corneille, Racine, and Scarron, and even, for those with Italian, a copy of Boccaccio's racy *Decameron*. The collection provides an interesting contrast with a catalogue compiled at this time for Magdalen's undergraduate Library. Magdalen's undergraduates enjoyed rather lighter reading, for there are more works about cookery, gardening, hunting, and the acquisition of good manners. University College's undergraduates received rather more demanding fare. On the other hand, many of the editions of classical texts in University College's library are very old ones: the copies of the works of the poet Statius, the biographer Suetonius, and the tragedian Sophocles date respectively from 1475, 1535, and 1603, and the only edition of Virgil was published in 1618. Magdalen's library seems to have had rather newer books. One may reasonably ask whether University College's undergraduate Library was stocked in part by hand-me-downs from the main Library. It also appears from such evidence as Charles Yarburgh's accounts, that undergraduates also purchased many textbooks themselves.[31]

Meanwhile, the main College Library began the century with many of its books still chained. The last payment for chains, however, is recorded in 1739/40, and in 1744/5, 4 guineas were spent on cleaning and replacing

---

[30] An undergraduate library: *Gentleman's Magazine*, 56 (1786), 7, and UC:BU2/F1/5 fo. 65ᵛ; the Fellows' Library: UC:BU2/F1/3 fo. 124ʳ; other colleges: Philip 1986: 749–52.

[31] Magdalen's undergraduate library catalogue: Ferdinand 2006.

books, and a carpenter received £1 11s.3¼d. 'for Work done in the Library'. The likeliest explanation for these large sums is that it had been decided to unchain the books.[32]

Undoubtedly the Library continued to receive gifts and bequests, but no record of these was kept after the 1670s. Rather more, however, is known about books bought with College funds, many of which are named in the accounts, and they show a certain overlap with the undergraduate Library. Several theological texts were acquired, including an edition of the Hebrew Bible, a history of the Popes, and collections of sermons; there were books on classics and archaeology, including Thomas Major's magnificent engravings of the ruins of Paestum, and books on British history, including Clarendon's *History of the Rebellion*, Leland's *Itinerary*, and Antony Wood's history of Oxford. Maps were acquired as well as a copy of Newton's *Principia* in 1744/5. The Library also had its own collection of works of English literature, including Milton, and Johnson's edition of Shakespeare. The College purchased Johnson's dictionary in 1755/6, almost as soon as it came out—and long before its members came to know the great man for himself. The books bought for the main Library are rather more expensive—and newer—than those in the undergraduate one, and many of them would have been beyond the means of most Fellows or undergraduates.[33]

As for which of these expensive books were actually used, we are fortunate in having a register of books borrowed from the Library for the years 1766–84.[34] This shows that the main Library was not exclusively for Fellows. Scholars, gentlemen commoners, and ordinary commoners are found signing books out alongside Fellows. Among those borrowing books were Robert Chambers, William Scott, John Coulson, George Strahan, William Windham—and even Walter Stanhope. William Scott certainly used the Library for teaching purposes—in 1766 he borrowed Polybius and Callimachus, just when he was teaching the latter to Walter Stanhope—but people also used the Library for recreation. Books on geography and modern history were popular, as was Johnson's edition of Shakespeare. Rather more unexpected was the popularity of Cowper's *Anatomy of Humane Bodies*, an extensively illustrated anatomical textbook first published in 1698. It was regularly borrowed, even by people with no medical training. Unfortunately, not

---

[32] Money for chaining books: UC:BU5/F2/1 pp. 8, 69, and 132, and UC:BU2/F1/3 fos. 157^v and 162^v; their possible unchaining: UC:BU5/F2/1 pp. 228–9. Other colleges held out longer: Magdalen did not unchain its books until 1799 (Darwall-Smith in Brockliss (forthcoming)).

[33] Theology books: UC:BU5/F2/1 pp. 132 (Hebrew books), 256 (Hebrew Bible and the history of the Popes), UC:BU5/F2/2 fos. 26^r and 30^v (sermons); classics: UC:BU5/F2/1 pp. 174 and 200; Paestum: UC:BU5/F2/2 fo. 61^r; British history: UC:BU5/F2/1 pp. 6 (Clarendon), 218 (Leland), and UC:BU5/F2/2 fos. 127^r and 146^r (Wood); maps: UC:BU5/F2/1 pp. 77 and 174; Newton's *Principia*: UC:BU5/F2/1 p. 228; English literature: UC:BU5/F2/1 p. 270 (Milton), UC:BU5/F2/2 fos. 60^v (Johnson's edition of Shakespeare) and 22^v (Johnson's Dictionary).

[34] UC:L1/A1/1.

everyone returned books, and in September 1771, a list of overdue books had to be drawn up. Robert Chambers was a particular offender.

SOCIAL LIFE

In considering what members of College did outside their working life, it is easy to forget the significance of religious observance. Every day began with compulsory Chapel, usually held at 6 a.m. in the summer and 7 a.m. in the winter. Visitors were expected to attend: Dr Johnson, staying at University College in June 1775, found getting up at 6 a.m. hard work. These services, however, would have been fairly colourless affairs. As was typical with small colleges, the Chapel had no organ, and there was no music.[35]

Members of the College would have had breakfast after Chapel, and then, after a morning of lectures and work, the main meal of the day was dinner in Hall. In 1720, this took place at 11 a.m., and there were suggestions that it be moved forward an hour to please the Duke of Beaufort. As the century drew on, so the hour of dinner at Oxford moved forwards, until it was held at 3 p.m. or 4 p.m. in most colleges. In the evening there would be a light supper.[36]

Social divisions among junior members remained clearly defined. The College's Buttery Books continued to divide members into Fellows and noblemen at the top and servitors at the bottom, and each class had its own seats in Hall and Chapel. These divisions influenced one's choice of friends: the poet William Shenstone (who matriculated from Pembroke) had a schoolfriend at University College called Richard Jago (m. 1732). Unfortunately Jago, the son of a poor clergyman, matriculated as a servitor. This presented problems when Shenstone wished to see his friend: because as his first biographer wrote, 'it [was] then deemed a great disparagement for a commoner to appear in public with [a servitor]', he could only visit Jago in private.[37]

Some evidence survives for the cost of being an undergraduate. When George Strahan came up to Oxford in 1764, Samuel Johnson estimated that Strahan, already in receipt of £10 from his Bennet Scholarship, would require an annual allowance of about £100, with slightly more in his first year, for his matriculation fees and caution money. With that allowance Strahan might 'live with great ease to himself'. There was, however, another cost for freshmen. When an undergraduate moved into his rooms, there was an arrangement called 'thirds', by which he bought his predecessor's furniture: as Johnson described it, an undergraduate 'enters upon a room pays two

---

[35] Chapel at 6 a.m.: Redford 1992–4: ii. 215; Chapel at 7 a.m.: Bodl. MS Ballard fo. 163^r; times at other colleges: Bennett 1986c: 387, and Green 1986b: 428.

[36] Dinner in 1720: Bodl. MS Ballard 38 fos. 238^r and 241^r; dinner in later decades: Green 1986a: 333–4, Jones 2005: 143, and Green 1957: 37. No evidence survives for dinner times at University College, but they must have moved forward similarly.

[37] Different seats: in the 1742/3 accounts cushions are purchased for the servitors' seats in the Chapel (UC:BU2/F1/4 fo. 14^v); Robert Jago: Graves 1788: 27 and 29 and *ODNB* entry.

thirds of the furniture that he finds and receives from his Successor two thirds of what he pays. So that if he pays 20£ he receives 13-6-8.' On the other hand, when Walter Stanhope came up in 1766, he spent £100 in 'thirds' for his rooms. This was equivalent to a Fellow's annual stipend, and shows how much money could be spent by a wealthy undergraduate.[38]

College life became more gracious during the eighteenth century. The garden had a summer house by 1710/11, and Arthur Charlett had a separate one of his own. In the 1740s, lanterns provided light in the quadrangle after dark. Originally the quadrangles had gravel paths, but in the 1790s these were replaced with paving stones. The Senior Common Room became more comfortable: by the early 1760s, Fellows were subscribing to magazines, had purchased a decanter and glasses, and were hanging almanacks on the walls. Noblemen and gentlemen commoners had long been permitted to use the Senior Common Room, but in 1777 the College reconsidered the status of such members. A College order that year decreed that gentlemen commoners could no longer dine on high table or be admitted to the Fellows' Common Room until they had worn a gown of that order for three years, and in 1795, the rules were tightened further: now gentlemen commoners would not be allowed these rights until they had taken their degrees.[39]

Outside working hours, there were hardly any organized sporting activities as we would understand them. Francis Yarburgh enjoying walking, riding, boating, and playing cricket—all typical recreations of the day—and William Jones used to ride as a diversion from his academic work. In the winter, undergraduates and Fellows skated. Lord Eldon remembered getting a soaking in Christ Church meadow when some thin ice gave way beneath him, while William Jones rediscovered with delight the pleasures of skating in January 1780.[40]

Of course, undergraduates were enticed into local inns and pubs, just like Francis Yarburgh. The diarist James Woodforde, serving as pro-proctor in 1774, encountered a Gunsley Scholar called Joseph Hawkins (m. 1773) in an inn in George Street, 'carousing with some low-life People'. As Woodforde hauled him home, 'he was terribly frightened & cried almost all the Way to his Coll:.' Undergraduates also fell into debt. Some may have fallen the prey of unscrupulous tradesmen, such as Edward Burton Barker (m. 1791), who was sued for debt in 1795, but acquitted because his note of hand had been extorted through fear of a debt which was not strictly due. Other undergraduates,

---

[38] Strahan: Redford 1992–4: i. 245; Stanhope: WYAS (B) SpSt/6/1/100.
[39] Summer houses: UC:BU2/F1/3 fo. 19ᵛ and UC:BU3/F1/3 fo. 41ʳ; lanterns: UC:BU2/F1/4 fos. 3ʳ, 8ᵛ, and 50ʳ; gravel: UC:BU2/F1/4 fo. 117ᵛ–8ʳ, when £14 7s. 6d. was spent on gravel in 1759/60; paving stones: UC:BU2/F1/5 fos. 73ᵛ, 79ʳ, 85ʳ and 106ʳ; beautifying the Senior Common Room: UC:BU3/F3/2 pp. 57–8 and UC:BU3/F3/4 fos. 109ʳ–10ʳ; use of the Senior Common Room: UC:BU3/F3/4 pp. 109–10; restrictions on gentlemen commoners: UC:GB3/A1/2 fos. 92ʳ and 119ʳ.
[40] Recreations: Green 1986a: 339–41; Jones: Cannon 1970: i. 115 and ii. 484; skating: Lincoln and McEwen 1960: 84, and Cannon 1970: i. 337.

however, drew their troubles upon themselves. Two members of University College whom the Chancellor's Court came to know rather well were John Barnett (m. 1804), summoned ten times in 1807–9 for debts (mainly for clothes) amounting to about £80, and Henry Torre (m. 1798), summoned twelve times in 1801–4 for debts from various tradesmen amounting to over £90.[41]

There were other diversions. One undergraduate, Hildebrand Jacob (m. 1736), scratched on a window looking out onto High Street a quotation from Ovid which translates as 'My soft (*molle*) heart is susceptible to the shafts of love', and which could have been a pun on a girl called Molly who had caught his eye. This reminds one of a difficult aspect of College life, the fact that all its members, apart from the Master, still had to remain unmarried. It was very romantic of John Scott to throw up a Fellowship for love, but it was also very risky, while his prospects were not secure. His wife recalled that he was prepared to consider (reluctantly) taking orders, if a College living fell vacant. Wisdom, however, prevailed, and, during the year of grace after his marriage, Scott devoted himself to legal studies.[42] More prudent Fellows endured protracted courtships. In the year of his election as Fellow, William Jones met the daughter of the Dean of Winchester, Anna Maria Shipley, and was at once struck by her. Some years later, he wrote:

I have long and constantly admired the good sense, sweet disposition, and pleasing manners of Miss Shipley, and my admiration would long ago have ripened into the purest affection, if my own suspected and singular situation, neither judge nor advocate, Asiatic nor European, dependent nor independent, had not made me despond, as I have often hinted to Lord Althorp, of connubial happiness.[43]

It was not until 1783, when Jones was appointed a Judge in India, that he was at last able to marry Anna Maria.

A few Fellows lacked both patience and prudence. George Ward cheerfully—and unsurprisingly—disregarded the rules concerning celibacy. Rather more unexpectedly Thomas Hearne claimed that William Smith had been married for some years before he resigned his Fellowship, keeping his wife and their child in secret at Windsor, and that William Greenwood (F. 1700–7) had fathered a bastard child on 'Brown the Coffee-man's Daughter'. Even Robert Chambers was rumoured to have fathered an illegitimate daughter in about 1764.[44]

---

[41] Woodforde: Hargreaves-Mawdsley 1969: 218; Barker: OUA CC Papers 1795/5; Barnett: OUA CC Papers 1807/1, 1807/2, 1807/3, 1807/7, 1808/5, 1808/27, 1808/35, 1808/36, 1809/4, and 1809/5; Torre: OUA CC Papers 1801/4, 1801/24, 1801/29, 1801/35, 1801/36, 1801/37, 1801/38, 1801/44, 1803/34, 1804/29, 1804/30, and 1804/31.
[42] Inscription: Bowen 1932/3; Scott: Twiss 1844: i. 83–4.
[43] Cannon 1970: ii. 585. See too Teignmouth 1804: 37.
[44] Smith and Greenwood: Hearne, iii. 126 (Smith certainly married Mary, the widow of Gerard Langbaine (m. 1672), but it is not known when the marriage took place); Chambers: Curley 1998: 157–8.

Some undergraduates were tempted. In May 1721, Odiam Hooper (m. 1720) married Anne Cox, daughter of an alehouse-keeper in the parish of St Peter in the East. Hearne caustically wrote 'This Hooper, who is look'd upon as a soft Man, is Heir to a good Estate, whereas the Girl (who is about 17 years of Age) hath neither Fortune nor Beauty.' Nicholas Toke noted that Hooper was at least able to win his father's pardon for his action. There was also the case of one Docea Jordon, who died in 1724, and, who, rumour had it, had been the illegitimate daughter of 'a Gentleman of University-College'.[45]

The only woman who was allowed to live in the College and who was not a servant was the Master's wife. Of the College's Georgian Masters, only Thomas Cockman and Nathan Wetherell married, but neither Mrs Cockman nor Mrs Wetherell took part in College life. Mrs Cockman, who kept away from Oxford during the dispute of the 1720s, only appears in official records in 1745/6, when, after her husband's death, the College paid her for some marble chimney pieces and other fittings which were to be left in the Lodgings when she moved out. During her widowhood, she preserved her husband's memory by encouraging an edition of Cockman's theological works. It remained the case, therefore, that a married Master kept his College and personal lives strictly separate. This segregated life makes the appearance of Mrs Thrale both in Hall and in the Senior Common Room in 1774 all the more surprising.[46]

SERVANTS

The College's servants start to emerge from obscurity during the eighteenth century. There remain difficulties: servants are identified in the General Accounts by their functions, rather than their names. Furthermore, some servants are not listed. Bedmakers, for example, were paid not by the College, but the individuals who employed them, and so go largely unrecorded. In addition to employing people within Oxford itself, University College also began to employ local people to manage its more distant estates, such as a Mr Crowder, whose salary was increased to 30 guineas in 1798, for his work with the College's Yorkshire estates.[47]

Nevertheless, some information can be gathered about individual servants. We have already met John Pricket, Arthur Charlett's butler and henchman. A more benign figure was Samuel Wright, the head cook, who died in 1726, and whom Thomas Hearne described as 'a Person of great skill in his

---

[45] Hooper: Hearne, vii. 244 and Bodl. MS Eng Th. c. 27 pp. 269–70; quoted in Bayley 1959*b*: 260; Jordon: Hearne, viii. 266.
[46] Payments for Mrs Cockman: UC:BU5/F2/1 p. 239; publishing her husband's work: Silvester 1750: preface (unpaginated).
[47] UC:GB3/A1/2 fo. 121ᵛ.

business, and of an excellent facetious Temper, which made his Company much desired, he being, withall, an honest Man'.[48]

By the early eighteenth century, more women were working in the College, mainly as bedmakers. We have already encountered George Ward and the Widow Stevens; Thomas Hearne encountered another female bedmaker, Mrs Grimage, who looked after the rooms of his friend Thomas Allen. When in 1711 Allen had been forced out of his Fellowship, he asked Hearne to check something in his rooms, and Grimage was reluctant to let Hearne in. Hearne, inevitably, suspected that his (and Allen's) old adversaries William Denison and George Ward had persuaded Grimage to let them rifle around Allen's rooms.[49]

Georgian bedmakers performed other duties for their charges. Robert Clarke (F. 1777–82) paid his bedmaker extra to bring him bread and milk, and to clean his shoes. There were some perks: Charles Yarburgh's account book shows that undergraduates contributed to Christmas boxes for their servants. Furthermore, successive members of the same family sometimes worked for the College. We have met the Mrs Grimage who was a bedmaker at the College in 1711; another Mrs Grimage was a bedmaker in 1787/8.[50]

However, the most significant evidence for servants' lives is a pamphlet published c.1791 by John Briggs, the Porter of University College, about a journey to Newcastle (Fig. 14.1). It is a plain document, containing little observation of the places he visited—he does not even explain why he made the journey—but Briggs identified the people whom he visited, who included almost twenty present or former members of the College, or their relatives. Although Briggs belonged to the servant class, and he was meeting people of the professional class, mainly clergymen and lawyers, he was nevertheless warmly welcomed everywhere: John Francis Allen, a non-resident Fellow 'entertained [me] extremely well'; Samuel Swire, now resident at Melsonby, insisted on showing him the new extension to his rectory; George Abbs (m. 1787) and his father, who lived at Monkwearmouth, took him for a walk along the sea to show him the harbour; and William Carr (m. 1781) showed him around the ruins of Bolton Abbey. Briggs was always eager to praise his hosts' generous condescension, but the point remains that he was treated very well. It is not too fanciful, when one looks at Briggs's experiences, to see something of the special relationship between College servants and Fellows or undergraduates, which will become a much more significant theme in College life from the middle of the nineteenth century.[51]

---

[48] Hearne, ix. 139.
[49] Hearne, iii. 209–10.
[50] Clarke's bedmakers: UC:S17/F1/127–48; Yarburgh: Borthwick Institute, YM/AB/13; the Grimage dynasty: UC:BU2/F1/5 fo. 41ᵛ records a robbery at the second Mrs Grimage's house.
[51] Briggs c.1791: 7 (Allen), 8 (Swire), 10 (Abbs), and 13 (Carr).

FIGURE 14.1 The title page of *A Tour from Oxford to Newcastle upon Tyne in the Long Vacation of the year 1791*, by John Briggs, Porter of University College.

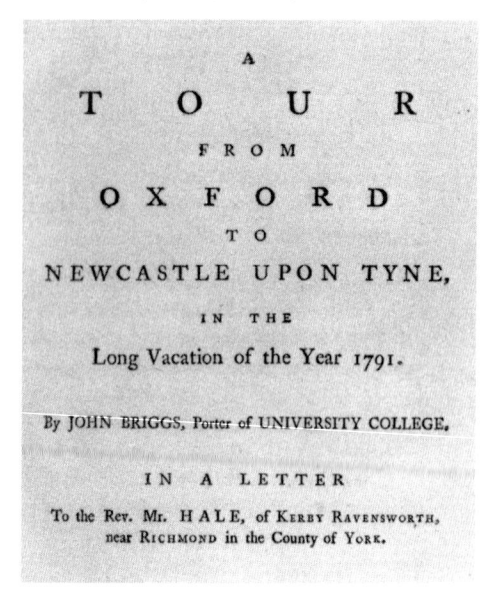

THE FINANCES OF THE COLLEGE AND ITS FELLOWS[52]

It is not really possible to draw a complete and accurate picture of the finances of University College or its Fellows in the eighteenth century. Graphs based on the General Accounts (Graph 14.1) do provide a broad outline of the College's fortunes if they are read with care. For example, they never include income from the Linton estate, which was always managed separately, and which was considerable: in the early 1760s, the College received about £700 a year from Linton, and by 1779/80 it received over £1,300. Of this money, £600 always paid the stipends of the two Radcliffe Fellows, and the surplus went into the advowsons fund. Another account managed separately was the so-called *Billa Bursarii*, or Bursar's Bill, which recorded stipends from vacant Fellowships or Scholarships, and receipts to and payments from the Treasury. The receipts include one-off gifts, the Treasury's dividends from fines, admission and degree money, and caution moneys received. The payments include caution moneys paid out and such miscellaneous expenses as books, repairs to college fabric and pictures, and travel expenses. The *Billa* was also the only account which recorded transfers from the Treasury for the purchase of land, or income arising from its sale. From 1794/5 onwards, the totals for income and expenditure in the *Billa*

---

[52] For the wider context see Dunbabin 1986.

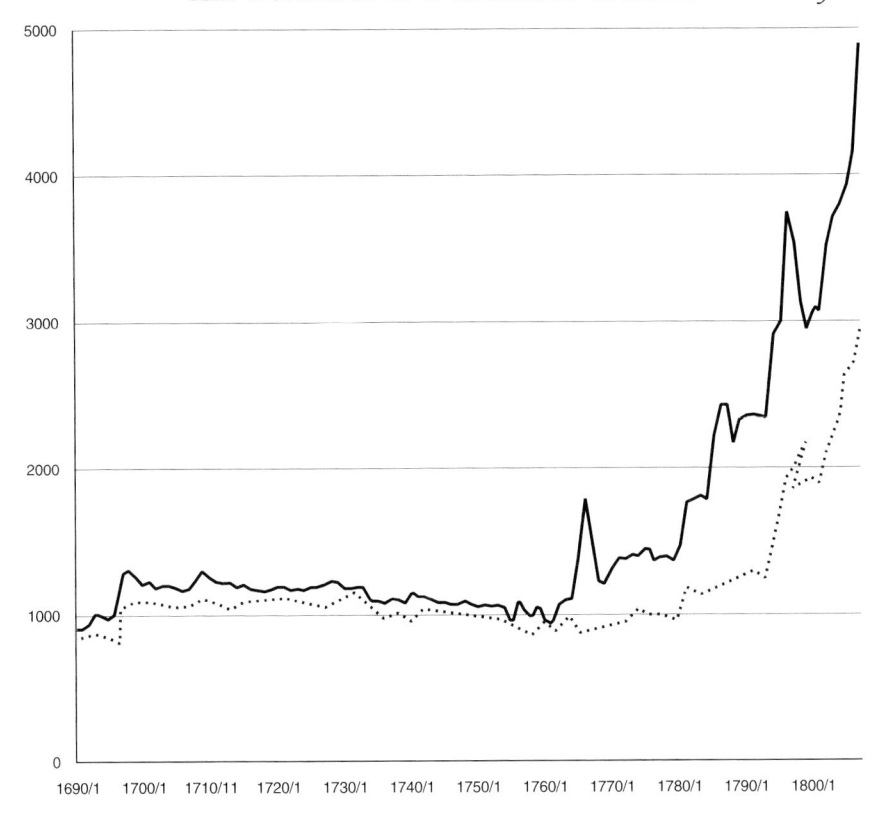

GRAPH 14.1 Income and Expenditure of University College 1690/1–1807/8.

Bursarii are recorded in the General Accounts, and the effect on the latter is immediate. Finally, it is not possible to know how much money was kept in the Treasury, for this was not recorded: all we have are notes indicating when money was transferred from it.[53]

Nevertheless one can draw some conclusions about the College's financial health during the eighteenth century. For most of the first half of this period, the College's income remained fairly static at between £1,000 and £1,200 a year, slightly falling off in the late 1730s and 1740s. Almost inevitably, things changed under Nathan Wetherell. He cashed in some of the College's assets:

---

[53] The Linton Fund: UC:BU3/F3/2 pp. 162–3 and UC:BU3/F/3 fos. 82ᵛ–83ʳ (1760s), and UC:BU3/F3/5 pp. 155–6 (1779/80); money transferred from the Treasury to the General Account and *Billa Bursarii*: UC:BU2/F1/5 fo. 65ᵛ and UC:BU5/F2/2 fos. 14ᵛ or 40ʳ.

in 1765–8 the College sold considerable quantities of timber from its estates in Yorkshire, Wales, and Handley Park. As a result, the College's income rose to almost £1,400 in 1765/6, £1,800 in 1766/7, and £1,500 in 1767/8, before coming back to just over £1,200 in 1768/9. The College's income quadrupled during the forty-three years of Wetherell's Mastership. This was as well: prices remained stable between the 1730s and 1780s, but almost doubled during the Napoleonic War.[54]

Wetherell effected other changes to the management of the College's accounts and its estates. For the first time money was invested in government stocks rather than land. Wetherell and the Fellows also began to move away from the old system of beneficial leases in favour of leasing some of the College's larger properties on so-called rack rents, whose amounts were recalculated each time that a lease was renewed, and which were thus inevitably 'racked' upwards. In return, no entry fine was demanded, and the College took a greater responsibility for the upkeep of the property. It was a tricky balance to strike: although the College could be assured of a rent which could be regularly reassessed to take account of inflation, it could receive large bills for the repair of a rack-rented property. Several colleges, however, were starting to act similarly: Balliol began to allow its beneficial leases to run out in the 1750s, while St John's Cambridge and St Catharine's Cambridge did so in the 1770s, and Gonville and Caius in 1816.[55]

The results were immediate. In 1781/2, the annual income from Handley Park, Northants., rose from £350 to £595, after a lease drawn up in the new way took effect. Then, in 1785/6, the rent from Eastwick Farm rose from £21 8s. 4d. the previous year to £140, and the income from Marks Hall rose £49 6d. to £200. Thanks to these increases, the College's gross rent rose this year from just over £1,500 to almost £1,900. By 1799 Handley Park, Marks Hall, Hailey, Edgiock, and some houses in Oxford were all leased at rack rent. This had implications for the Fellows, whose stipends were still augmented by their annual dividends from entry fines. In order, therefore, to protect the Fellows, a system of 'virtual' fines was created: when a lease was made on a rack rent, the Bursar would draw an amount similar to the fine from the College Treasury, and divide that among the Fellows instead.[56]

As the College altered the method of collecting its rents, so it changed the method of administering its properties. College tenants had been allowed to sublet their properties, and so at Pontefract the College used to lease several

---

[54] Selling timber: UC:BU2/F1/4 fos. 151^r, 156^r and 161^r; colleges whose rent rose in the Napoleonic War: Bendall and others 1999: 333 (Emmanuel) and Howard 1935: 109 (St John's Cambridge); price rises in the eighteenth century: Phelps Brown and Hopkins 1956.

[55] Other colleges: Bendall and others 1999: 338–9 and 369, and Howard 1935: 115.

[56] Handley Park: this arrangement had been made in a lease of 1772 (UC:EB1/A/4 pp. 142–3); Eastwick Farm in 1785/6: UC:BU2/F1/5 fos. 25^r–6^r; leases in 1799: UC:GB3/A1/2 fo. 125^v; 'virtual' fines: at UC:EB2/F/1 pp. 82, 85–6, and 92.

houses to one tenant, who then sublet them at a profit. In 1789/90, however, the Pontefract property was split up, so that each house was now leased directly to its occupant. As a result the rent from Pontefract rose from £74 18s. to £222 4s.—although the College did have to spend £62 19s. 4d. on repairs there in 1790/1. The Fellows, however, had more ideas for their Pontefract estates: in 1793, when fresh leases were due, they agreed that, in order 'to encourage Building... as well as to substantially repair', they would offer leases lasting forty years, with no fine on renewal, and with a modest rent for the first few years, to be increased subsequently to the market rate. Nevertheless, the tenants did pay an advance on the increased rent, which was almost like an entry fine. We will encounter such 'building' leases more frequently in the nineteenth century.[57]

This responsible attitude extended to the management of the College's timber. Although Wetherell did oversee the sale of timber from College property, he and the Fellows managed its woodland carefully: for example, in 1765, it was thought appropriate to reduce an entry fine on property in Wales, 'if the Woods [there] be shut up in order to encourage the Growth of Timber'. The College also tried to maintain friendly relations with its tenants: dinners, or, at the very least, wine, were arranged for those tenants who could travel to Oxford to pay their rents.[58]

Meanwhile it is at last possible to gain a clearer idea of what the Fellows of University College were earning. A Fellow relied on several sources: there was his official stipend, which remained unchanged from the 1660s until the start of the nineteenth century; there was his dividend from that year's entry fines; he received small stipends for holding College offices; he would be paid more if he became a Tutor; and he also received money from room rents. In the days of the old quadrangle, Fellows had pupils living in or above their rooms, and received rent for this. When the new quadrangle gave undergraduates their own rooms, it seems to have been agreed that, by way of compensation, the rents from some rooms would go to Fellows rather than the College. Thus an extant list of rooms from 1769/70 notes which room rents go to which Fellows, and which ones to the College.[59] This custom survived well into the nineteenth century. Furthermore, Fellows were not charged for their rooms, and appear to have received an allowance for their food.

Extant Bursars' Books show that in 1698/9, for example, the Master's total stipend was just over £100, William Smith, the Senior Fellow, received just

---

[57] Pontefract rents in 1789/90: UC:BU2/F1/5 fo. 49^v; repairs to Pontefract property: UC:BU2/F1/5 fo. 59^r; special terms in the leases of 1793: UC:EB2/F/1 p. 97.

[58] Welsh woodland: UC:EB2/F/1 p. 79; St John's Cambridge exploiting its timber: Howard 1935: 121; entertaining tenants from the 1740s to the 1780s: UC:BU2/F1/4 fos. 50^v, 63^r, 82^r, 225^r, and UC:BU2/F1/5 fo. 16^r.

[59] Pasted into the front cover of UC:BU3/F3/4.

over £40, and other Fellows about £30. In 1761/2 the Master's total gross stipend had risen to £128 a year, and Fellows' to about £50, but by 1769/70 the Master's gross stipend had risen to over £300, and that of most Fellows to £60–£75. In 1779/80 the Master received almost £380, and the Fellows £80–£100, and by 1807 it was thought that a Fellowship was worth about £150. These sums fail to take account of payments in kind: in 1719 George Ward's gross stipend was reckoned at £72 16s., and in 1782 William Jones reckoned that, although he received about £100 in cash from his Fellowship, when his lodgings were taken into account, its true value was closer to £300 a year. These figures appear not atypical of smaller colleges, at least for Fellows—a Fellow at Lincoln in the 1720s thought his Fellowship worth about £60 a year—but at wealthy Magdalen a senior Fellow could expect to receive £64 in 1697, £65 in 1751, and £564 in 1810.[60]

Very little evidence survives to reveal how much Fellows earned as Tutors. Once again, some assistance comes from Charles Yarburgh's account book, which shows that between May and November 1739 he paid Robert Eden 3 guineas for teaching him, suggesting that Eden charged Yarburgh 6 guineas a year. In 1735, when Yarburgh matriculated, Eden had accepted almost twenty pupils. Eden might therefore have expected to receive well over 100 guineas a year from one year's intake alone. In the 1730s, therefore, Eden could have earned at least 300 guineas a year from all his undergraduates. Evidence from Christ Church that a Tutor there in the 1750s could earn £400 a year suggests that this is a reasonable estimate: the greater the number of pupils, the more money one could earn. In 1772, a French visitor to Oxford, André Morellet, claimed that a 'M. William' at University College (who can only be William Scott), made more than 1,000 guineas a year as a Tutor. Morellet might have been exaggerating: in 1772, Scott was Tutor to about sixty undergraduates, implying that he charged them about 15 guineas a year, which seems a little excessive. Nevertheless, even on the basis of Eden's fees, William Scott could easily have earned well over £350 a year—equivalent to the stipend from a comfortable parish living.[61]

Fellows could earn limited amounts of money from other sources. Some were allowed to be incumbents of small parishes, and some layman Fellows, like William Jones, combined their Fellowships with working as a lawyer. Some, like George Croft (F. 1772–80), Master of Beverley School, took up teaching posts. Others adopted more unusual shifts: William Standfast (Bennet

---

[60] Fellows' gross stipends: UC:BU3/F3/1 pp. 150–75 (1698/9), UC:BU3/F3/2, pp. 125–50 (1761/2), UC:BU3/F3/4 pp. 125–50 (1769/70), UC:BU3/F3/5 pp. 119–44 (1779/80), and UC:GB3/A1/2 fo. 136^r–137^v (1807); Ward's stipend: OUA CC Papers 1719/52:7; Jones's calculations: Cannon 1970: ii. 599; other colleges: Green 1979: 327, Darwall-Smith in Brockliss (forthcoming), and Doolittle 1986: 238–9.

[61] Yarburgh's account book: Borthwick Institute, YM/AB/13; Christ Church: Bill 1988: 231; Scott's income: Merrick 2003: 37.

Scholar 1700–13) practised as a doctor, but, finding it unprofitable, took divine orders and returned to Oxford, to be elected a Fellow in 1713. John Alleyne (m. 1749; F. 1754–80) had been a Chorister at Magdalen College in 1738–49, and retained strong links with his first College: not only did he have friends there, but from 1763 he was Magdalen's Steward, which required him to draw up fair copies of Magdalen's annual accounts. He held this post until 1785, five years after he had exchanged his Fellowship for the parish of North Cerney.[62]

LIFE AFTER OXFORD

The later careers of members of University College from the eighteenth century are, unfortunately, not always easy to trace, but certain trends can be observed. First of all, increasing numbers of undergraduates chose to take a degree: 55.5 per cent of undergraduates matriculating from University College in 1689–1722 obtained at least a BA. This proportion rose to 61.7 per cent in 1764–1807. Those who took degrees were increasingly interested in obtaining an MA or a higher degree: just over half of those matriculating between 1689 and 1764 who took a degree ended up with an MA or a higher degree, but almost three-quarters of those matriculating in 1764–1807 did this. We shall see, however, that there was a good reason for so doing.

Nothing is known about the later lives of half the College's members from this period. Roughly half of those about whom something is known entered holy orders, and all but a handful of these ended their days as parish priests—a proportion which is mirrored elsewhere.[63] Nevertheless, there are interesting developments in the second half of the century concerning the College's highest achievers, something alluded to briefly in the last chapter. In 1689–1722, 18 Old Members achieved higher preferment in the Church, 9 became MPs, 6 became baronets, and 2 became peers. In 1723–64, although only 6 Old Members achieved higher preferment, 4 of them did become Bishops, and there were also 16 MPs, 16 baronets, and 9 peers. In 1764–1807, however, 16 Old Members achieved church preferment, no fewer than 37 became MPs, 17 became baronets, and 6 became peers.

The fortunes of Fellows improved. In 1689–1722, 13 Fellows became parish priests, but only 3 achieved preferment in the church (one of whom, Robert Clavering, became a Bishop), and 8 died in office. In 1723–64, 11 became parish priests, 4 died in office, and just one achieved preferment, although one (Robert Chambers) became a judge. Under Wetherell, 8 Fellows died in office, and 9 became parish clergy, but no less than 8 of them

---

[62] Permission to take up a living: Bodl. MS Ballard 21 fo. 109ʳ (John Browne) and UC:GB3/A1/2 fo. 134ʳ (Hugh Moises); pluralists at St John's Cambridge: Miller 1961: 52–3; Standfast: Hearne, iv. 206; Alleyne: Bloxam 1853–85: i. 160–1 and Hargreaves-Mawdsley 1969: 212, 241, and 281 (Alleyne encountered at dinners at Magdalen).

[63] Searby 1997: 76 shows that roughly half of Cambridge alumni from 1752 to 1886 whose later career is known went into the church.

won preferment in the church, and 5 became judges. Wetherell's network of influential friends evidently had its effect on his Fellows.

Although the church remained the likeliest career for anyone coming up to University College, it was a risky choice, because the apex of the clerical hierarchy was tiny. There were barely two dozen Bishoprics, the same number of Deaneries, and just sixty archdeaconries. Below that were many hundred parishes which varied wildly in their value. Members of University College who took orders had to take their chances along with everyone else. This could lead them into unexpected places: in 1741, a Bennet Scholar, Edwin Alcock, was deprived of his award, because he had been absent for more than a year working as a minister in St Helena.[64]

Some members of the College lost the clerical battle. In January 1723, Hugh Todd lamented that John Boraston 'should pine away in a poor Curacy for near 40 years', and indeed Boraston never won good enough promotion to let him resign his Fellowship. An unhappier tale is that of John Bateman, whose tenure of a Gunsley Scholarship in 1678–1749 we have already encountered as an example of the abuses which the 1736 statutes tried to eliminate. Thomas Hearne happened to know Bateman slightly: he noted that he was interested in botany, and 'what spare time he has from his Divinity Studies he lays out that way, much to his Commendation and Credit'. In 1716 Bateman was acting as Arthur Charlett's curate at Hambledon, and Hearne takes the opportunity to call him 'a weak man'. A little later he calls him 'a Man of very ordinary parts'. He appears never to have obtained a living, but only ever worked as a curate. His stipend from his Gunsley Scholarship therefore made all the difference, and he had every incentive to retain it.[65]

Such cases explain the College's great interest in purchasing the rights to livings. They chose carefully: although most College livings have a rural appearance, they are situated near a large town or a main road, or both. When a living was purchased, one also had to make a delicate calculation as to how long the College might have to wait for a vacancy. Sometimes, the incumbent did the right thing and did not outlive the sale too long; thus Melsonby, purchased in 1692, became vacant in 1704, and Checkendon (Fig. 14.2), purchased in 1765/6, became vacant in 1776. At North Cerney (Plate 8) and Elton, however, the College had to wait for a quarter of century. Worst of all was Tarrant Gunville, purchased in 1747, but not vacant until 1797.

There was a definite hierarchy of College livings. The senior Fellow had first refusal on any living which fell vacant, after which it was offered to the next senior, and so on. Between April 1778 and September 1779, four College livings became free, and when one looks at the seniority of the Fellows who

---

[64] The clerical pyramid: Holmes 1982: 88; Alcock: UC:GB3/A1/2 fo. 46ᵛ.
[65] Boraston: Bodl. MS Ballard 18 fo. 25ʳ; Bateman: Hearne, i. 231, and v. 255 and 279.

FIGURE 14.2 St Peter and St Paul's Church, Checkendon, Oxfordshire whose advowson was purchased by University College in 1765/6.

filled them, then it would appear that the most desirable living was Checkendon, followed by North Cerney, Headbourne Worthy, and Arncliffe. A list of College livings and their incomes compiled in 1790 shows that, while Checkendon was worth £400 a year, Tarrant Gunville £300, North Cerney £294, Elton £270, and Melsonby £257, Headbourne Worthy only brought in £165 a year, and Arncliffe a mere £80.[66]

Unsurprisingly Arncliffe proved a difficult living to fill. In 1681, it was given to a 22-year-old graduate of the College called Miles Tennant, who remained there until his death in 1732. He actually came from the parish of Arncliffe, and was a servitor, so that one suspects that he had been groomed for this post. For someone of Tennant's condition, even a poor living like Arncliffe gave him a chance to better himself and his family, for he sent his son Henry to University College in 1722, and saw him elected Fellow there in 1729. Nevertheless, Tennant found it hard to make ends meet, and, amidst criticism of neglect from parishioners in the two valleys he was required to serve, chose to save money by not employing a curate at the chapelry of Hubberholme, in the

[66] This ecclesiastical horse-trading can be traced in UC:GB3/A1/2 fos. 93^r–95^v; valuation of livings in 1790: Linton uncatalogued papers.

neighbouring dale, but managed both churches himself, in spite of the difficult journey which he regularly had to make over a steep ridge between them. After one Fellow had held the living for just three years, before escaping to the lusher pastures of Melsonby, another non-Fellow, John Chapman, held it. On his death in 1764, Miles Tennant's son, Henry, became vicar of Arncliffe, but, unlike his father, he was largely non-resident. Worse followed under George Croft, vicar from 1779–1809. Croft was also non-resident, and in the 1790s Arncliffe church, long neglected, was demolished and rebuilt cheaply and shabbily. Croft, who was more interested in his teaching career, had no compunction in refusing to live in Arncliffe, while taking from it what money he could. Even to parishioners, he complained that the income from Arncliffe was poor and that he had every excuse for non-residence, but that, if Arncliffe could only bring in enough money, then he would not have to do any teaching. Such were the disparities between the College livings that in the 1790s, with the assistance of John Scott, the College obtained permission to use part of the surplus of the Linton Fund to augment the poorer parishes, so that every living was worth at least £300 (Wetherell also ensured that the Fund would increase the Master's stipend by £330).[67]

AN OLD BOY NETWORK?

In the last chapter, an awkward question was asked. It is all very well for a College to glory in lists of famous alumni, but how much did such alumni feel that they owed to their College? At University College some eighteenth-century alumni certainly did feel a debt of gratitude. Sir Roger Newdigate was proud to identify himself as an Old Member of University College, while William Windham's first biographer wrote that 'he always retained feelings of gratitude towards his *Alma Mater*'. In later life, Windham liked to stay in College: he rented a room there for part of 1779, and in October 1782 William Jones was glad to have his solitary stay in Oxford pleasantly interrupted by the arrival of Windham. Another pair of Old Members who liked revisiting old haunts were William and John Scott. Lord Hewart (m. 1887) was told by an Old Member, who had matriculated in 1872, that an old College servant had told him that 'Lord Stowell and Lord Eldon used to come back to Oxford every now and then, for a little jaunt. He had waited on them in Common Room, and they always had a beefsteak pudding with oysters and *several* bottles of port—I forget the number.' Even in his eighties,

---

[67] Arncliffe in general: Darwall-Smith 2006: 89–93; Miles Tennant's death: memorial in Arncliffe Church; Croft: Shuffrey 1903: 160 and 165, and Croft's *ODNB* entry; John Scott's advice and a report on the Linton Fund of 1790: Linton uncatalogued papers and UC:GB3/A1/2 fos. 105ᵛ–106ᵛ; agreement in Chancery of 1792: UC:E4/2C/11; St John's Cambridge also supplemented the values of its poorer livings (Howard 1935: 140).

Lord Eldon told his niece that, on her next journey to Oxford, she should visit University College.[68]

The most remarkable expression of fellow-feeling among Old Members was the University College Club, founded in 1792 at the suggestion of the 2nd Earl of Radnor (m. 1767) for Old Members who had matriculated in the 1760s and 1770s. Members dined together on the first Saturdays of February, March, April, and May, at the Crown and Anchor Tavern in the Strand. In 1804, William Scott, as President, commissioned an engraving listing all thirty-three members of the Club, with Nathan Wetherell an honorary member (Fig. 14.3). There could be no better testimony to the remarkable achievement of the College in these two decades: the list includes four judges, ten MPs, two Lord Lieutenants, at last half a dozen current or former government ministers, and the Commander in Chief for Scotland.[69]

There was, however, a little more to this club than a collection of Old Members assembling to rekindle old times, for many of its members were of a strong Tory inclination. Among notable absences were at least two Whig MPs, Norman Macleod (m. 1770) and the former soldier Banastre Tarleton (m. 1771). Sir William Jones, for all his Whiggish ways, at least was a member—but then, when the Club was founded, he was safely out of the way in India. The fact that the Club was founded in 1792, just when the French Revolution was starting to become more violent, suggests that it was as much a place for like-minded people to discuss politics as to remember their Oxford days.

In return, the College took public pride in its Old Members. In July 1806, just before his death, Sir Roger Newdigate was asked to give a portrait of himself to the College, and this was not unusual. A portrait of Sir Robert Chambers was given by his widow after his death in 1803, and portraits of Lord Eldon and Lord Stowell were certainly owned by the College by 1844. In an engraving of the Hall in 1814 (Fig. 13.5) the portrait of Sir Robert Chambers is clearly visible, as is that of one of the Scott brothers. More memorials were also erected in the Chapel at this time: the magnificent monument by Flaxman to Sir William Jones in the Antechapel (Fig. 14.4), originally intended for Calcutta, was given to the College by his widow. Smaller, but no less fine, monuments again by Flaxman to Sir Robert Chambers and Wetherell himself, were also erected in the Antechapel, the former apparently thanks to Chambers's widow.[70]

---

[68] Windham: Amyot 1812: i. 5; Windham in College: UC:BU3/F3/5 p. 185, and Cannon 1970: ii. 576; the Scott brothers: Hewart 1936: 21 and Twiss 1844: iii. 268.

[69] The University College Club: Mitchell 1970 (not least for his analysis of the membership and its politics) and Twiss 1844: i. 487–9.

[70] Newdigate: White 1995: 320; Chambers's portrait: Curley 1998: 515 and 540; the Scott brothers: Twiss 1844: iii. 313 (Waterhouse 1986: 863–4 shows that the presentation of portraits was becoming common in Oxford); Jones: Teignmouth 1804: 494; Chambers's memorial: Curley 1998: 540.

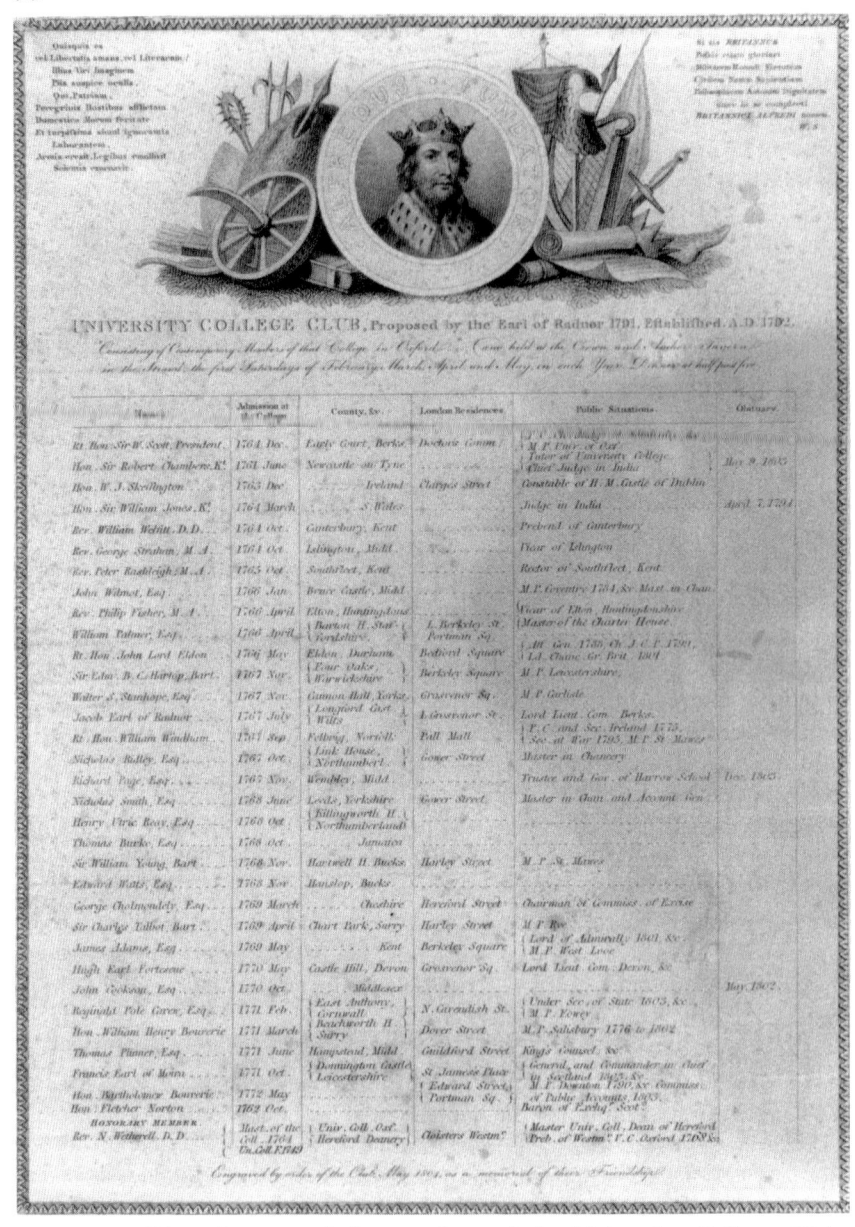

FIGURE 14.3 List of names of the members of the University College Club, printed in 1792, with updates to 1804.

It is one thing to indulge in such charming gestures of mutual affection, but Old Members in influential positions were also willing to help people from their College. In 1766 Sir Roger Newdigate told Wetherell that he had recommended Robert Chambers to the Lord Chancellor, and hoped that 'he will succeed in his [unspecified] application'. William Scott's successor as judge of the Admiralty Court, Sir Christopher Robinson (m. 1782) owed his initial success as a lawyer to Scott's support. Within Oxford itself, in 1761–1800, more Demies at Magdalen came from University College than from any other Oxford college—but then George Horne (m. 1746), had been a Fellow of Magdalen in 1750–68 and President in 1768–91, and we should not forget John Alleyne's links there. Help also came from the College's friends. In June 1779, Samuel Johnson offered the curacy to a friend's living to a member of University College, asking that Thomas Maurice be given first refusal. Although Maurice turned it down, Francis Simpson (m. 1774; F. 1781–98) was happy to take up the offer.[71]

No patron, however, could compete with John Scott, Lord Eldon. Lord Chancellor for almost three decades, Eldon had an unparalleled store of patronage at his disposal, and he did not forget members of his old College. His friends George Strahan and Philip Fisher became prebendaries at Rochester and Norwich; preferment was found both for his old headmaster, Hugh Moises, and his son, and for Thomas Maurice. When Eldon's workload as Lord Chancellor grew too much, and the post of a Vice-Chancellor was created in 1813, it went to Thomas Plumer (m. 1771; F. 1780–94). Nor did Eldon forget College friends who had not achieved greatness. One such was Samuel Swire, Fellow from 1766–88, and then vicar of Melsonby (and recipient of several affectionate letters from Eldon). Eldon offered Swire a valuable living some distance from Melsonby, but Swire, to his credit, declined, saying 'that he could not prevail upon himself to shear a Flock, which he could not feed'. Eldon, equally to his credit, respected his friend's decision. James Griffith declined a similar offer, but Eldon was able to arrange a prebendal stall for him, first at Bristol, and then at Gloucester.[72]

University College itself had one piece of patronage all its own. By the late 1720s, there is a trend for former members of the College to keep their names on the Buttery Books, paying a modest fee for doing so. Keeping one's name on the books meant that one did not reclaim one's caution money, and, for those who could afford it, it was a means of making a discreet benefaction (the College, clearly aware of this, ordered in 1797 that Old Members could only leave their names on the books if they left caution money of at least £10).

---

[71] Newdigate: White 1995: 142; Robinson: *ODNB* entry; Magdalen: Darwall-Smith in Brockliss (forthcoming); Johnson: Redford 1992–4: iii. 170–1.

[72] Twiss 1844: i. 58 (Strahan and Fisher), i. 387 (Hugh Moises, father and son), iii. 466 (Maurice), ii. 240–2 (Plumer), i. 371, 407, and 495–6, and ii. 4–5, 62–4, 196–8, and 256–7 (Swire), and ii. 612–13 (Griffith); also on Swire: Lincoln and McEwen 1960: 54 (although his name is wrongly transcribed); on prebendaries, see p. 4.

FIGURE 14.4 Monument by John Flaxman to Sir William Jones in the Chapel of University College.

There arose, however, a better reason for doing this. In the middle of the century, there was a dispute about who could be a member of Convocation, something left unresolved in the Laudian statutes of the 1630s. This mattered: members of Convocation had the final vote in matters of university policy, and also voted for Chancellors, and the university's MPs. In 1759 it was decided that any MA who had his name on their college's Buttery Books could be counted a member of Convocation. This ruling made it attractive for Old Members to keep their names on the college's books indefinitely. The Buttery Book for 1768/9 listed twenty-five gentlemen commoners and MAs; that for 1778/9 had forty-one; and by 1807/8 there were almost fifty. The effects of this change are visible in the poll books for two elections. In 1751, when Sir Roger Newdigate was elected, University College furnished a mere seven electors, but in November 1806, when Sir William Scott stood for re-election as MP, the Master, three Fellows, and two Scholars were joined by eighteen MA Old Members, some of whom, like George

Croft, had matriculated over forty years earlier. The Buttery Book for 1806/7 names forty-five MAs on the College's books. In the weeks before and after the election, just six of these appear to have been resident, but in the week of the election seventeen more turned up, voted, and went on their way again. As transport links with Oxford improved, so it became easier for the College to draw on its backwoods alumni.[73]

THE PROBLEM OF GEORGIAN OXFORD

However exciting a place University College sometimes was in the eighteenth century, it is difficult not to end this part of the journey with a sense of frustration, having seen the College's rise to glory in the 1760s and 1770s be succeeded by a dismal decline. In the last chapter some blame for this was laid at Nathan Wetherell's door, but in fairness to Wetherell, larger factors were at work.

For those who really wanted to teach or work, Georgian Oxford could prove an exhilarating experience. The lack of an official syllabus gave a charismatic tutor like William Scott the chance to introduce new and unexpected subjects, and an assiduous undergraduate like William Jones the opportunity to explore far more widely than modern students, whose work is circumscribed by the tramlines of their subjects. Unfortunately, this very freedom also meant that there was no obvious method of spurring on the lazy tutor or pupil.

Moreover a liberal education offered little support for thorough specialist scholarship. The most important works of scholarship to emerge from University College at this time did not come from Fellows who followed the usual career paths. William Jones is the most remarkable such example, but there was also Samuel Musgrave. Elected Radcliffe Travelling Fellow in 1760, Musgrave duly travelled abroad, but he became less interested in medicine, and more interested in the plays of Euripides, spending his time collating manuscripts all over Europe. His edition of the plays, published in 1778, is still regarded as an important contribution to the textual criticism of the tragedian. Yet Musgrave had accomplished this almost in spite of his Fellowship. University College could certainly produce decent clergymen and well-rounded gentlemen, but one may reasonably ask whether a university should not be something more than a mixture of seminary and finishing school. Scottish universities, for example, notably Edinburgh and Glasgow, with their lectures given in English, their creation of taught courses in law and medicine, their accessibility to nonconformists, and their greater openness to the values of the Enlightenment, showed a different way, while in the

---

[73] Caution money: UC:GB3/A1/2 fo. 121^r; membership of Convocation: Sutherland, 1986*b*: 194–202; names on the books: UC:BU4/F/38, 48, and 77; the 1806 election: UC:P3/N1/1 (poll book) and UC:BU4/F/76 (Buttery Book).

Hanoverian monarchs' other realm, the university of Göttingen, founded in the 1730s by George II, quickly became another centre of Enlightenment values, and in both it, and other German universities, there arose a new culture, in which academics were expected to carry out research and publish the results.[74]

Finally, University College—and Georgian Oxford—had a problem in recruitment and retention. The College's greatest Tutor of the century, William Scott, became worn out and unhappy from his labours. Writing to his father in 1772 about his brother's love affair, he thought that John's happiness 'would not [be] promoted by a long continuance in college. The business in which I am engaged is so extremely disagreeable in itself and so destructive to health (if carried on with such success as can render it all considerable in point of profit), that I do not wonder at his unwillingness to succeed me in it.'[75]

For those who lacked Scott's or Jones's dynamism, the problem was less exhaustion than stagnation. André Morellet, the Frenchman who had met William Scott in 1772, found life at Oxford 'truly monastic' (*vraiment monastique*), and thought that 'a man who has a fellowship is easily tempted to do nothing' (*Un homme qui a une place de fellow est bien tenté de ne rien faire*). In fairness, Fellows had next to no statutory duties beyond ensuring that the administrative and teaching duties of the college were discharged, and that they themselves studied theology or, when permitted, medicine or law. The idea that Fellows were expected to carry out research, let alone publish, was quite foreign to eighteenth-century Oxford. However, Morellet had a point, which Hugh Moises the younger also understood. Moises' father wrote to Lord Eldon that his son 'is, I believe, heartily tired of the insipidity, the uselessness, the insignificance, of a college life without employment; and his prospects of preferment from thence are so distant and so dim'.[76]

Even Samuel Johnson, stout friend of Oxford in general and University College in particular, perceived another problem for the Georgian university. 'Our fellowships', he once said to Boswell, 'are only sufficient to support a man in his studies to fit him for the world, and accordingly in general they are held no longer than till an opportunity offers of getting away.' 'In the foreign Universities', he continued, 'a professorship is a high thing.... Our Universities are impoverished of learning, by the penury of their provisions. I wish

---

[74] Musgrave: Clarke 1986: 527 and 532; Scotland and Göttingen: Hammerstein 1996a: 138–40 (and also Anderson 2006: 17–20) and Hammerstein 1996b: 626–31, 633, and 637; German universities: Clark 2006.

[75] Twiss 1844: i. 74.

[76] Morellet: Merrick 2003: 37; Moises: Twiss 1844: i. 470. Compare Hodgkin 1949: 150–60, and Trevelyan 1990: 75–6, on the lack of incentives for Fellows.

there were many places of a thousand-a-year at Oxford, to keep first-rate men of learning from quitting the University.' Undoubtedly Johnson was thinking of the experiences of the Scott brothers, Chambers, and Jones, four brilliant men whom University College was unable, in the long run, to retain. It would be the responsibility of the nineteenth-century College and university to find a solution to these problems.[77]

[77] Boswell 1980: 726–7.

15

From Shelley's Oxford to Stanley's Oxford: 1808–1850

JAMES GRIFFITH AND PERCY SHELLEY: 1808–1821

On 22 January 1808 a mere five Fellows assembled to choose as their new Master James Griffith, the designer of the new Chapel and Hall façade. Unlike Wetherell, Griffith (Plate 13) took little interest in university politics, as architecture and art continued to dominate his life. He designed a new vestry for Melsonby Church in 1811, and in 1819 joined a Delegacy which advised on developing the site of Hertford College as a new home for Magdalen Hall. He was also skilled in 'pokerwork', the curious art of sketching pictures on wood with a red-hot poker. One of his works, an image of Christ holding a cup, stood behind the altar in Chapel.[1]

There survives an account of Griffith's life within the Master's Lodgings—the first such account so far encountered for University College. On his election, Griffith married a cousin, Mary Ironside, and in 1810 two of her nieces came to stay with them, one of whom, Elizabeth Grant, later wrote some memoirs. Elizabeth was a sharp-eyed little girl—before Griffith's marriage, she noticed that he 'contrived to spend a good deal of time with us...particularly if Aunt Mary was to be met with'[2]—and her descriptions of Griffith and his College are valuable and entertaining.

Grant adored her uncle. Whilst she recalled gratefully the careful religious instruction which he gave her and her sister, she also remembered his 'immensity of fun'. Their aunt insisted that the girls walk elegantly—and uncomfortably—in a ladylike manner, but uncle James let them race up Headington Hill, and showed them round the colleges.[3] She did not, however, like the Master's Lodgings, whose rooms she thought poorly planned,

---

[1] Election: UC:GB3/A1/2 fo. 140^{r-v}; Melsonby: plaque in church; advice on Magdalen Hall: MCA MC:FA10/3/1MS/1; examples of his pokerwork (including the image of Christ) still survive.

[2] Grant: *ODNB* entry (under her married name of Smith); Griffith and her aunt: Grant 1992: i. 55.

[3] Grant 1992: i. 157–8.

all opening one into another, and she especially disliked the Master's library (now the ground-floor rooms to either side of Staircase XII), where she and her sister endured their lessons. The library where Arthur Charlett had shown off his books and which John Browne had enlarged was now a grim place without curtains or carpets, filled with dusty and unread old books, and whose furniture comprised three chairs, a table, and a pianoforte.[4]

The neglected library was not all that Grant found amiss. She gradually noticed that her uncle's kindness was largely confined to his Lodgings. Heads of houses, she claimed, 'conversed with [their undergraduates] never, invited to their homes never, spoke or thought about them never. A perpetual bowing was their only intercourse.' Grant herself was not allowed to mix with the undergraduates, although there were some unofficial meetings. There was the curly-headed lad who played the French horn to them from his window overlooking the Master's garden; and there was 'a very tall young man from Yorkshire', who occupied rooms at right-angles to the girls' bedroom, and mock-heroically declaimed to them from the book he was reading, although in each case the vigilant Dean, George Rowley, put a stop to further dealings.[5]

Grant was also scathing about the College's religion, which appeared 'to consist in honouring the King and his *ministers*, and in perpetually popping in and out of chapel,' and its teaching:

There were rules that had in a general way to be obeyed, and there were Lectures which must be attended, but as for care to give high aims, provide refining amusements, give a worthy tone to the character of responsible beings, there was none ever even thought of.[6]

Grant had picked up on the somnolent world of the Senior Common Room's Betting Book, where the range of subjects remained unchanged—university politics, national issues, and jests—although in 1814 and 1815 there were an unusual number of bets about Napoleon. The Master's nieces came among the Fellows as a breath of fresh air: Hugh Moises, the supposed life and soul of the Senior Common Room (p. 297), once observed that 'the two little girls in white frocks were the only live creatures that looked *real* amongst them all'.[7]

Grant, however, was not being wholly fair. In particular, the introduction of optional examinations in what became known as 'Literae Humaniores' in 1800 inspired a rethinking of the university's methods of assessment. In 1807 similar examinations in mathematics and physics were instituted, but all tests

---

[4] Ibid. 152 and 156–7.
[5] Ibid. 162 (heads of houses, on which compare Thomas Cockman (pp. 262–3)) and 164–6 (undergraduates).
[6] Ibid. 161 (religion) and 162 (teaching).
[7] Betting Book: UC:O1/A1/2; Moises: Grant 1992: i. 163.

for the MA degree abolished. Then in 1808 all undergraduates seeking a BA had to sit a preliminary examination in Greek, Latin, and logic called Responsions at the end of their first year or the start of their second, and then a final one in divinity, classics, and philosophy at the end of their third or fourth year. Although less demanding than those for the honours degree, these examinations were compulsory.[8]

Griffith and the Fellows supported these changes: during 1811 and 1812 they instituted time limits for undergraduates to sit Responsions and Finals, and penalties for poor performances in examinations. In any event, there were undergraduates who wanted to work, such as Thomas Maude (m. 1819), whose exercise book survives. This contains his very thorough notes on works of Greek literature (mainly tragedies), which—as was typical of the day—are largely concerned with textual criticism, the exact meaning of a phrase or word, or comparisons with other texts. Unfortunately the colleges' teaching system, which had to cope with a group of undergraduates of decidedly mixed abilities, had to work with the lowest common denominator, so that early nineteenth-century undergraduates who sought an honours degree found such teaching hopelessly substandard, and sought private tutors for extra coaching. A flourishing industry grew up: one former member of University College, Robert Lowe (m. 1829), later Chancellor of the Exchequer under Gladstone, proved a particularly good private tutor in his youth.[9]

Griffith's College also witnessed the disappearance of gentlemen commoners and servitors. Only five gentlemen commoners were admitted in 1810–13, and none after that, except for the special case of Francis Trithen, admitted gentleman commoner in 1848 when he was elected Taylorian Professor in modern European languages. Meanwhile only two servitors—both Lodge Scholars—were admitted after 1807.[10]

There were also interesting developments in relation to the College's property in north Oxford. For centuries University College had leased out a block of land, which now comprises the north side of Little Clarendon Street with parts of Walton Street and Woodstock Road, as one big portion, along with the common fields in St Giles. In 1808 the common fields were leased separately, and the single portion divided into ten parts for building purposes, each tenant receiving a forty-year lease of two pepper corns for the first fourteen years, and then £3 a year. During the next few decades these plots were repeatedly subdivided, until almost every property was let

---

[8] See further Curthoys 1997b: 342–52.
[9] General context: Brock 1997: 20–2; new rules: UC:GB3/A1/2 fos. 147^r, 148^v, and 149^v (see Green 1957: 80 for similar ones introduced at Lincoln in 1819); Thomas Maude's notebook: UC:P202/MS1/1.
[10] Trithen: Barber 1997: 635. In contrast, Trinity College, having admitted 26 gentleman commoners in 1821–35, only ever admitted one more afterwards (Hopkins 2005: 226).

individually, in most cases for business purposes. In 1832 the common fields in St Giles were enclosed, and University College was allotted two pieces of land, one adjoining what is now the Old Parsonage Hotel, the other, situated further north, on the site of what is now part of St Hugh's College. The northern allotment was leased as a site for a single residential building, and the southern one became a residential block called 1–9 Park Villas. The role played by St John's College in the development of North Oxford is well known, but this only began in the 1860s. University College was exploiting the financial possibilities of its, admittedly smaller, sites several decades earlier.[11]

Griffith's Mastership, however, is overshadowed by two events. The first was in autumn 1809, when the Chancellor, the Duke of Portland, died, and a successor was sought. Lord Eldon was an obvious candidate, but there was no Nathan Wetherell to ensure a smooth transition. In an acrimonious contest, a rival candidate split the Tory vote, so that Eldon lost to the Whig Lord Grenville by just thirteen votes. It was a terrible embarrassment for the College, made worse by Grenville's support for Catholic emancipation, a subject abhorrent to Eldon. One contemporary witness claimed that, a year later, University College was still 'deformed' by bitter feuds over the election and 'by angry and senseless disappointment'.[12]

The second unfortunate event would have seemed at the time merely an irritating disciplinary matter. In autumn 1810, there came up a new Leicester Scholar, called Percy Bysshe Shelley. He received his Scholarship solely because he was related to the person who then had the right of nomination (just like his father Timothy, appointed a Leicester Scholar in 1774).[13] Another undergraduate, Thomas Jefferson Hogg, found himself seated one afternoon in Hall next to the new Scholar, who discussed German and Italian literature with him so animatedly that they adjourned to Hogg's rooms for the rest of the evening.[14] Hogg and Shelley recognized in each other kindred spirits, and became inseparable friends.

Shelley cut an unusual figure. Elizabeth Grant remembered him as 'slovenly in his dress, neither wearing garters nor suspenders', while Hogg recalled that Shelley wore his hair long, when short hair was in fashion. Shelley's rooms on the first floor of Staircase I were as extraordinary as

---

[11] Leases of the St Giles properties: UC:E2/9/5D–14D; deeds for the northern allotment: UC:E2/9/17D/1–10 and UC:EB1/A/7 pp. 431–3 (the house built here, called 'The Mount', was leased in the 1890s to St Hugh's College, who purchased it in 1927); deeds concerning the southern allotment: UC:E2/9/34D/1–3; St John's and North Oxford: Hinchliffe 1992.

[12] The Chancellorship election: Twiss 1844: ii. 107–15, Ward 1965: 30–6, and Mitchell in Albery and others 1992: 26–7; its aftermath: Hogg 1906: 154.

[13] The two Shelleys' nominations: UC:GB3/A1/2 fos. 88^r and 145^v. The classic account of Shelley's time at Oxford, for all its faults, remains Hogg 1906: 42–197, but Gilmour 2002: 119–45, and Albery and others 1992, provide important modern reassessments.

[14] Hogg 1906: 44–5.

their occupant. Hogg memorably described their chaotic state, with plates, bottles, books, and papers scattered over the floor, and strange chemical apparatus on the tables, with which Shelley conducted experiments of various degrees of riskiness. Shelley also read extensively, and published a collection of poems and a novel while at Oxford. There was little set work for him to do: Hogg claimed that the undemanding College lectures were easier than lessons in school, and, although written exercises were occasionally required, he suspected that they were never read. He also recalled an atmosphere of 'unceasing drunkenness and continual uproar' in the evenings. Hogg's account, however, must be treated carefully. For example, he claimed that Shelley avoided dining in Hall, and took little interest in food and drink, whereas the relevant Buttery Books reveal Shelley's bills for food and drink to be amongst the highest of any resident undergraduate. More seriously, Hogg, who in later life renounced the advanced opinions of his youth, played down Shelley's advanced views on politics and religion.[15]

From the first, Shelley was a difficult undergraduate. Elizabeth Grant, presumably remembering her uncle's comments, described Shelley as 'very insubordinate, always infringing some rules...and when spoken to about these irregularities, he was in the habit of making such extraordinary gestures, expressive of his humility under reproof, as to overset first the gravity, and then the temper, of the lecturing tutor.' Then there were Shelley's politics. His father was a Whig MP, and father and son had supported Lord Grenville's election as Chancellor. This was quite bad enough for Lord Eldon's College, but Shelley went further, expressing his disapproval of the monarchy and his support for the ideals of the French Revolution, if not its violent excesses. In addition, partly under Hogg's influence, Shelley became an atheist.[16]

Shelley and Hogg combined their radicalism with a wicked sense of humour, writing letters, sometimes under pseudonyms, to chosen victims, alarming them with their atheistic views, and drawing them into exchanges of letters, in which Shelley and Hogg produced dazzling displays of ingenuity remarkable in a pair of first-year undergraduates.[17] Insubordinate students were hardly new in Oxford, but Shelley and Hogg's insubordination was different. It was one thing to drink too much and say something unwise to the Dean, but quite another to become an intellectual rebel, questioning and mocking the very foundations on which Oxford then rested. Indeed one

---

[15] Appearance: Grant 1992: i. 167 and Hogg 1906: 46; position of room: UC:BU3/F3/7; condition of same: Hogg 1906: 53–6; literary activity: Gilmour 2002: 128–33; College life: Hogg 1906: 157 and 173–4; expenses in College: Hogg 190: 62 and 86–7 and UC:BU4/F/80–1 (also Gilmour 2002: 127–8).

[16] Behaviour: Grant 1992: i. 167 (for another memory of Grant's, see Bayley 1964); politics: Mitchell in Albery and others 1992: 15–30: atheism: Gilmour 2002: 123–4.

[17] Hogg 1906: 163–4. Two such correspondences are discussed in Barker-Benfield 1991 and Darwall-Smith 2005*b*.

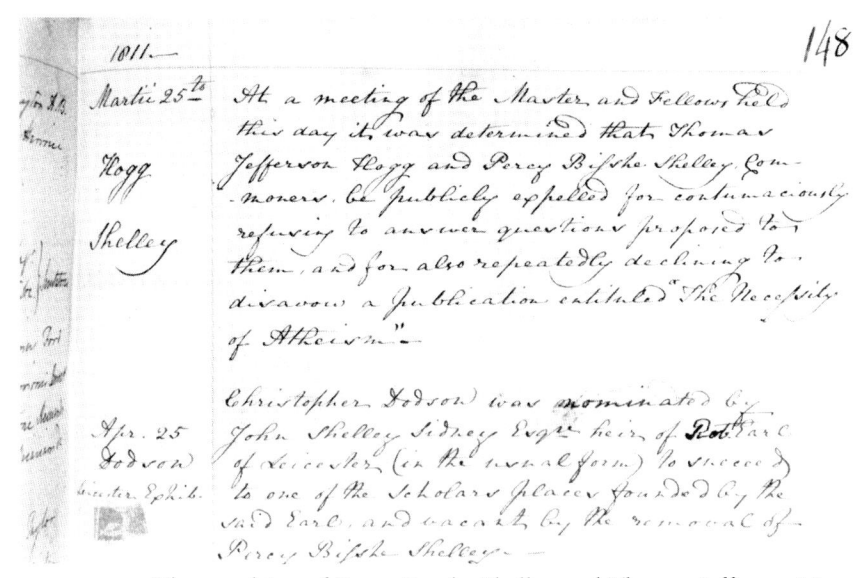

FIGURE 15.1 The expulsion of Percy Bysshe Shelley and Thomas Jefferson Hogg on 25 March 1811, as recorded in the College Register.

observer has even described Shelley as the first modern undergraduate, with his mixture of 'idealism, the special prominence accorded to being young, a sense of estrangement from an incomprehensible adult world and a desire to challenge authority'.[18]

Had Shelley and Hogg kept such radical opinions private, that would have been acceptable. Instead Shelley wrote, with Hogg's help, and printed early in March 1811 a pamphlet titled *The Necessity of Atheism*, sending some copies to heads of houses and others in Oxford, and placing the rest in an Oxford bookshop. The bookshop was persuaded to destroy its copies, and the College hoped that the matter would rest there. However, Edward Copleston, a Fellow of Oriel who had defended Oxford against attacks made on it in the *Edinburgh Review*, did not want this insult to the university ignored, and asked the Master and Fellows to intervene.[19]

Intervene they did. The College Register had this terse entry for 25 March 1811:

At a meeting of the Master and Fellows held this day it was determined that Thomas Jefferson Hogg and Percy Bisshe Shelley, Commoners, be publicly expelled for contumaciously refusing to answer questions proposed to them, and for also repeatedly declining to disavow a publication entituled 'The Necessity of Atheism'.[20] (Fig. 15.1)

[18] Rothblatt 1997: 299.
[19] Gilmour 2002: 141–3. Shelley certainly thought Copleston's role crucial (Ingpen 1912: i. 220).
[20] UC:GB3/A1/2 fo. 148^r.

Thomas Hogg later claimed that Shelley defied the Fellows, refusing to answer their questions, until the Master, losing his temper, ordered his expulsion, and then Hogg himself, furious at his friend's maltreatment, demanded that he should answer to the same charge and receive the same treatment—and so was also expelled. Shelley himself in a letter of January 1812, gave a more sober version: 'I was informed, that in case I denied the publication, no more would be said. I refused, and was expelled.' A contemporary, Charles John Ridley (m. 1809; F. 1813–54) understood that Shelley was simply asked 'if he could or would deny the obnoxious production [the pamphlet] as his'. Shelley gave no direct reply. Hogg then claimed that, 'if Shelley had anything to do with it, he (Hogg) was equally implicated', and should receive a similar penalty—and he did.[21]

Ridley shows how more conventional undergraduates viewed Shelley and Hogg:

[Shelley and Hogg] had made themselves as conspicuous as possible by great singularity of dress, and by walking up and down the centre of the quadrangle, as if proud of their anticipated fate. I believe no one regretted their departure; for there were but few, if any, who were not afraid of Shelley's strange and fantastic pranks, & the still stranger opinions he was known to entertain; but all acknowledged him to been [sic] very good humoured and of kind disposition. T. J. Hogg had intellectual powers to a great extent, but unfortunately misdirected. He was most unpopular.

It is easy now to take Shelley and Hogg's side, but Shelley and Ridley's accounts, to say nothing of the delay in the investigation, suggest that Shelley was given every opportunity to escape punishment. Furthermore, all members of Oxford still had to subscribe to the articles of faith of the Church of England: people who refused to deny charges of atheism were asking for trouble. Contemporaries generally supported the College: George Cox, the Esquire Bedell in law, recalled that 'like most residents in Oxford, I never heard of [the expulsion] till long after', and felt that the College could not 'keep such a rotten sheep in their fold'. Even in the 1850s, official eyebrows were raised at undergraduates who expressed an interest in Shelley's works. It was not until much later, when Shelley's reputation was well established, that the College would begin to ask whether it might have handled matters differently.[22]

GEORGE ROWLEY AND TRAVERS TWISS: 1821–1836

James Griffith never knew of Shelley's later fame, for he died in May 1821, and was buried in the Chapel. The new Master was the Dean, George Rowley. Rowley was the obvious choice. Of humble origins (he had come

---

[21] Hogg 1906: 168–70; Ingpen 1912: i. 220; Ridley's account is preserved in UC:GB3/A1/2.
[22] Cox 1870: 72; disapproval of Shelley in the 1850s: *UCR* Vol. IV no. 5 (1965), 325.

up as a bible clerk), he had been the first member of University College to take an honours degree, and was elected a Fellow in 1807. During Griffith's Mastership, he became a central, if not overbearing, figure in the College, serving as Dean and Tutor continuously from 1808, and regularly as Bursar—but also appearing very frequently in the Fellows' Betting Book.[23]

Elizabeth Grant disliked Rowley—'such a little ugly and pompous man', 'always prowling about'—and remembered with great amusement one prank played on him by the undergraduates:

> Mr. Rowley having made himself disagreeable to some of his pupils who found it suited their health to take long rides in the country, they all turned out one night to hunt the Fox under his window. A Mr Fox, in a red waistcoat and some kind of skin for a cap, was let loose in the middle of the quadrangle, with the whole pack of his fellow students barking around him. There were cracking whips, shrill whistles, loud hallows, and louder harkaways, quite enough to frighten even the dignitaries. Mr. Fox, I remember, was found quietly reading in his rooms, undisturbed by all the tumult, although a little flurried by the very authoritative knocks which forced him, at that hour of the night, to unlock his door.[24]

George Cox, a contemporary of Rowley, who served successively as Bedel in law and Bedel in arts and medicine, was more generous:

> By dint of hard work and steady application...he had worked his way up from the bottom to the top of the College-ladder...Dr. Rowley married and had a family, living generally in a quiet domestic manner; working hard, at his leisure hours, in his garden, and taking long country-walks.[25]

William Carr dismissed Rowley's Mastership as 'in no way remarkable in the history of the College', and, to be sure, the College remained a rather sleepy place. Annual admissions remained at about fifteen a year, only slightly better than in the late eighteenth century (Graph 15.1). As for the teaching, Ashton Oxenden (m. 1827), thought his college lectures 'of the driest and most unattractive kind', and William Rooper (m. 1825), remembered:

> The number of undergraduates was only forty, and most of them were sons of north country gentlemen. The college was more famous for the prowess of its members in the hunting field than for hard reading.[26]

Life could be pleasant enough. Undergraduates wore evening dress and a white neckcloth for dinner in Hall (now moved forward, in common with

---

[23] Election: UC:GB3/A1/2 fos. 158ᵛ–160ʳ; Rowley's career: Cox 1870: 212. A Francis Rowley, chorister at Magdalen College 1795–1803, may be a younger brother (see Bloxam 1853–85: i. 206).
[24] Grant 1992: i. 170 and 166–7.
[25] Cox 1870: 212–13.
[26] Carr, 198; Oxenden 1891: 18; Rooper 1893: 23–4 (Rooper's estimate of numbers is supported by contemporary Buttery Books).

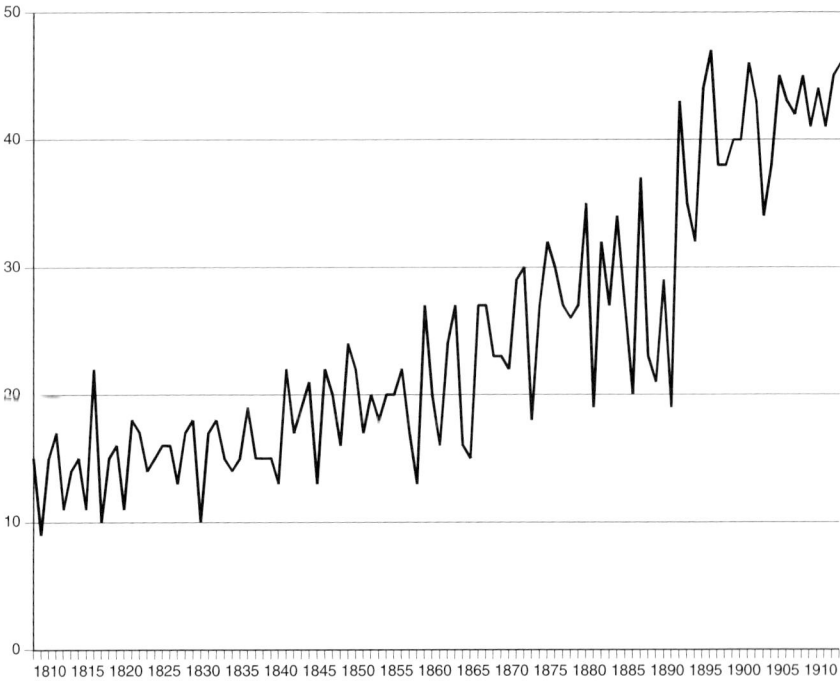

GRAPH 15.1 Admissions to University College, 1808–1913.

other colleges, to 5 p.m.), and dined at separate tables, each set for eight persons, while inventories from the 1830s show undergraduates' rooms fitted with rolling blinds, sofas, dining tables, reading tables, carpets, rugs, and other gracious amenities.[27]

College and Master remained strongly Tory. When, in 1829, Robert Peel, then MP for Oxford University, offered himself for re-election after helping to steer a bill for Catholic Emancipation through Parliament—to the horror of many in Oxford—an advertisement appeared in *The Times* on 16 February 1829 above the names of seventy members of Convocation who declared that Peel was 'unfit to be re-elected at the present crisis' and that they had 'resolved to adopt such measures as may appear most effectual to secure the election of a proper representative for this University'. Rowley's name appears fourth on the list, and two Fellows, John Watts and William Glaister, also signed up. When the election was held in the week of 20 February 1829,

---

[27] Dinners: Rooper 1893: 24 (and Curthoys and Day 1997: 271 for elsewhere); rooms: UC:FA1/3/MS3/11, 19 and 21.

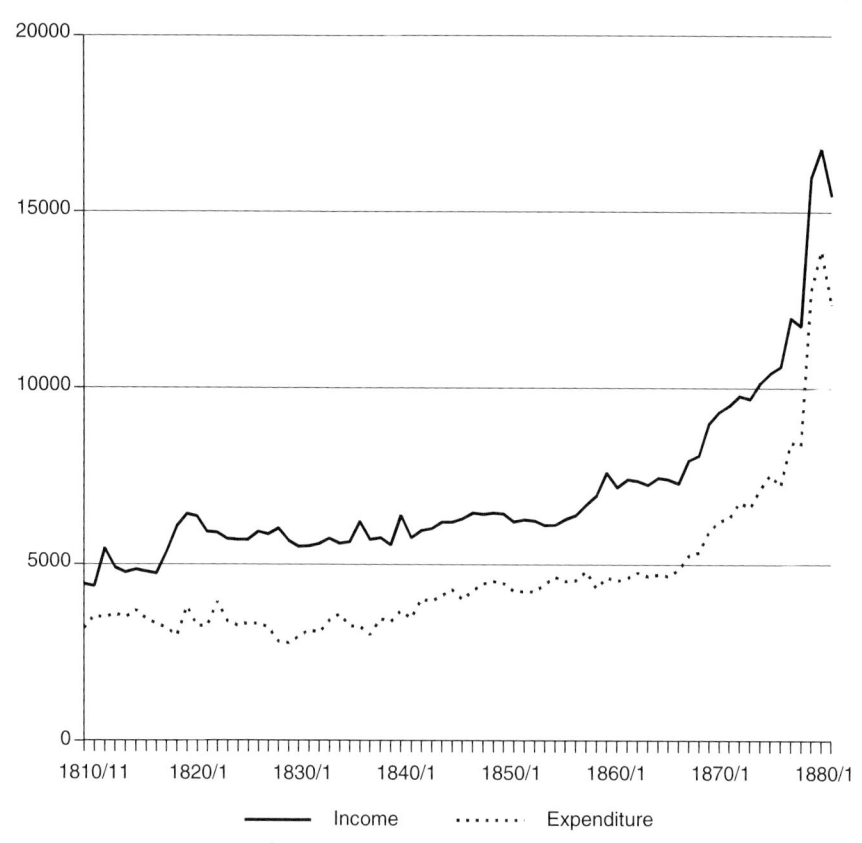

GRAPH 15.2. Income and Expenditure of University College, 1808/9–1881/2.

all but two of the non-resident Fellows turned up to vote, as did over two dozen Old Members—and Peel lost his seat.[28]

In financial terms, Rowley's College remained in a fairly comfortable position during the early nineteenth century, for its income continued to rise (Graph 15.2), even as prices fell after the end of the Napoleonic Wars. Increases in properties let at rack rent, such as at Handley and Flamstead, helped University College prosper (and there was also between £1,000 and £1,500 extra coming from the Linton Estate). The College was prepared to be hard-headed about ancient estates which were not providing a decent return. The Crown Inn estate in Cornmarket Street had fallen into such a ruinous state that in 1827 the College concluded it made better financial sense to sell it outright and invest the proceeds, than to restore the buildings, in the hope of

[28] Peel's defeat: Ward 1965: 71–5; Old Members returning; UC:BU4/F/98.

getting more money from increased rents. Other sales were affected by outside circumstances. The College sold almost all its islands in the Thames in 1824 for the rebuilding of Folly Bridge, and in the 1840s they also had to sell some lands to the railways, especially in the south of Oxford.[29]

The good financial health of the College extended to the Master and Fellows. Although their dividends could vary greatly—in 1811/12, during the Napoleonic Wars, each Fellow received a dividend of £114 1s. 10d., but by 1817/18, this had risen to £289 12s., while in 1832/3, it was only £179—nevertheless, someone like the non-resident Nathan Croke Wetherell regularly received between £200 and £300 a year during the 1820s and 1830s for doing absolutely nothing. Resident Fellows could expect more. If one held several College offices, for example, this brought in an extra £80 or £90. However, it was the Tutorships which brought the greatest financial rewards. In 1811/12, Matthew Rolleston (f. 1809-17) received almost £200 as Tutor, which effectively doubled his stipend; in 1817/18, George Rowley received over £400 for the same duties, and by the 1840s Tutors could earn up to £800 a year. Nevertheless, these amounts could readily be exceeded in the major public schools. At Eton in 1860 a Classics Master teaching forty pupils and receiving thirty boarders could enjoy an income of £2,000, and at Harrow in the 1850s, where the basic salary of an assistant master in the 1850s was £150, a successful housemaster could receive up to £5,000 or £6,000 a year. No Oxford tutor could earn sums comparable with these.[30]

Significant changes in undergraduate life during this period took place neither in the lecture room nor on the hunting field. Ever since we first encountered them, University College undergraduates have been enjoying sport, but only such non-competitive or individual ones as riding, hunting, fencing, or skating. Even rowing was little more than boating on the river for fun. From the 1820s onwards, however, team sports became more popular, especially cricket and rowing.[31]

Cricket had been played at Oxford in the eighteenth century, but it was now taken more seriously: the first Oxford–Cambridge match took place in 1827, and included a member of University College, John Papillon (m. 1825).[32] The idea of racing in eight-oared boats appears to have originated at Eton, and the first inter-collegiate race was held between Brasenose and Jesus in 1815. Although University College did not immediately field a

---

[29] Sale of Crown Inn: UC:EB2/F/2 fo. 4ᵛ and UC:EB1/A/5 pp. 125–49; sale of islands: UC:EB1/A/5 p. 89; sale of land in 1845 to the Great Western Railway: UC:E2/10/2M/1 and UC:E2/10/2MS/1. General context: Howard 1935: 109–12 and Dunbabin 1997: 381.

[30] Dividends: UC:BU3/F3/7, 9 and 15; Tutors' stipends: UC:BU3/F3/7 fos. 56ᵛ–57ʳ (Rolleston) and UC:BU3/F3/9 fos. 54ᵛ–55ʳ (Rowley; a Tutor at Lincoln College in the 1850s could earn over £300 a year (Green 1979: 573)); public school masters' income: Card 2001: 174 (Eton) and Tyerman 2000: 265–6 (Harrow).

[31] See further Chandler 1988 and Curthoys and Day 1997: 273–7.

[32] Bolton 1962: 1–6. Matches were then played in Cowley Marsh and Bullingdon Green.

boat, some of its members were already interested in rowing: Thomas Musgrave (m. 1819) unfortunately drowned when attending a picnic at Nuneham after the 1822 Eights. Eventually in 1827 it was decided to form a University College eight. William Rooper held a meeting in his room, at which it was agreed to raise over £100, build a boat, and select a crew. University College's first eight, with Rooper as bow, came third in the 1827 Eights (Plate 14). It appears not to have competed in 1829 or 1832–8, but otherwise appears to have done so almost continuously ever since, first going Head of the River in 1841. Meanwhile, a second series of races, known as 'Torpids', had been held since the late 1830s. Originally these appear to have been intended for a crew inferior to that which rowed in Eights Week, and were held at around the same time, until they were moved to Hilary Term in 1852. A University College eight first took part in Torpids in 1841, but its first Torpid only went Head of the River in 1869.[33]

Cricket and rowing were originally dominated by undergraduates from such schools as Eton and Harrow, but this gradually ceased to be the case, more quickly with rowing than with cricket: although rowing made great physical demands, its rudiments could be learned more quickly than cricket, so that lack of experience before coming up was not a disadvantage. One should also not underestimate the attraction of a novel sport like this to the new undergraduate. It would not be until the second half of the century that team sports supplanted other forms of recreation, but the foundations were being laid.[34]

Meanwhile, although barely half the Fellows performed all the College offices, two of them acting as Tutors, efforts were made to accommodate new subjects: in June 1831, a new lectureship in mathematics was created. Common Room culture was changing, as the Betting Book fell from fashion: just three bets were recorded in 1831, one each in 1832 and 1833, and no bets at all in 1839–48.[35]

The College bought more advowsons—Beckley in Sussex in 1817 and Kingsdon in Somerset in 1829—and Fellows in College livings were treating their parish work differently. Arncliffe, beautiful but remote and ill-paid, had endured absentee vicars for decades. In 1835, however, the living fell vacant, and the most junior Fellow, William Boyd, was packed off to assess the parish. After a long and difficult journey Boyd discovered the vicarage house being used partly as a poorhouse and partly to store wool. On his return he reported on Arncliffe in such terms as to put everyone off; but

---

[33] Early years on the river and Thomas Musgrave: Sherwood 1900: 7–11 (there is a memorial to Musgrave in the College Chapel); creation of a University College eight: Rooper 1893: 26; performance of same: Sherwood 1900: 43–6 and 147.

[34] Chandler 1988: 16–17.

[35] The number of Tutors was typical of the age: Curthoys 1997a: 165; lectureship in mathematics: UC:GB3/A1/2 fo. 170.

almost at once Boyd was so conscience-stricken that he decided to accept the living himself. Fortunately the tale had a happy ending. Assisted by a private income (he came from a family of Newcastle bankers), Boyd devoted himself to his parishioners, rebuilt the church and vicarage, had the road to the village remodelled, and remained at Arncliffe until his death in 1893, known affectionately throughout the region as the 'Patriarch of the Dales'.[36]

Another good parish priest was John Watts (F. 1817–29), rector of Tarrant Gunville, Dorset, in 1828–72, who oversaw a major restoration of his church in 1845. However, Peter Hansell (F. 1829–36), the first College appointment at Kingsdon, proved rather more embarrassing. Caught in 1844 having an affair with his children's governess, and suspended from his living for seven years, he spent a long exile in France before returning to his parish in the 1870s.[37]

The most significant development of Rowley's Mastership was brought about by a lay Fellow, Travers Twiss (m. 1826; F. 1830–63; Fig. 15.2). Not only did Twiss hold most major College offices in the 1830s and early 1840s, and act as Tutor in 1836–43; he was also a remarkable polymath. The College's first mathematics lecturer, he was also public examiner for the university in both classics (1835–7) and mathematics (1838–40), and Drummond Professor of Political Economy in 1842–7. One of the few Oxford men of his day who knew German, he published in 1836 a concise version of Barthold Niebuhr's *History of Rome*, a book whose modern approach revolutionized its subject. He also travelled widely, becoming a friend of Prince Metternich. In the late 1830s he was also studying law, which would become his major interest; he campaigned for the improvement of law studies in Oxford, and in 1855 was appointed Regius Professor of Civil Law. He became a recognized expert in international law, as well as in the ecclesiastical and admiralty courts.[38]

Half a century later Twiss explained his reforms in University College thus: 'as Dean and Tutor of University College I had prevailed on the Master and Fellows to adopt a liberal interpretation of the College statutes and to allow to county candidates only a preference *ceteris paribus*.' His legal language conceals something very radical. Generations of candidates from Yorkshire, Durham, and Northumberland had assumed that the north-eastern Fellowships were open only to them. On re-examining the statutes Twiss observed those concerning most of these Fellowships merely gave preference to north-easterners, all other things being equal. His reinterpretation there-

---

[36] Beckley: uncatalogued conveyance; Kingsdon: UC:GB3/A1/2 fo. 171ʳ; Boyd at Arncliffe: Boyd and Shuffrey 1893: 2–3, Boyd Carpenter 1911: 216–19, Shuffrey 1903: 247–8, and Darwall-Smith 2006: 93–6. This growing seriousness in religious matters can be traced elsewhere in Oxford (see Nockles 1997: 199–200).
[37] Watts: information from a visit to Tarrant Gunville in March 2007; Hansell: my thanks to Jim and Sally Smith of Kingsdon for sharing their information on him with me.
[38] Twiss's life: *ODNB* entry; knowledge of German: Jenkyns and Murray 1997: 533.

FIGURE 15.2 Travers Twiss, m. 1826 and Fellow 1830–63.

FIGURE 15.3 Frederick Plumptre, m. 1813, Fellow 1817–36, and Master 1836–70, by E. U. Eddis.

fore enabled the College to head-hunt talented candidates from any county who could surpass local candidates in academic excellence. Twiss does not date his reform, but the *Oxford University Calendar* supplies a clue. The calendars up to 1835 state that William of Durham, Skirlaw, and Percy Fellowships are open only to north-easterners; but the calendar for 1836 (compiled, of course, late in 1835) says that the William of Durham and Percy Fellowships are only open 'with a preference, *ceteris paribus*' for north-easterners. This reform, therefore, took place during the Mastership of George Rowley, and indeed in February 1836 the new rules were applied for the first time when Piers Claughton, a Lancashire man, was elected to a William of Durham Fellowship.[39]

Rowley was now at the height of his career: he had been appointed Vice-Chancellor in 1832, and two years later oversaw the unopposed election of the Duke of Wellington, hero of Waterloo, as Chancellor of the university. The installation of the new Chancellor was a grand occasion for Rowley's College, in particular because its members could honour Lord Eldon, now in his eighties, for one last time. As High Steward of the university, Eldon attended the installation, and received almost as much applause as the Duke. He then attended a dinner in the Hall, and thought he saw 'thirty

---

[39] Letter from Twiss to the *Times*, 3 April 1885 (although he was neither Dean nor Tutor in 1835); Claughton's election: UC:GB3/A1/2 fo. 172ᵛ. See too Curthoys 1997a: 169.

Peers or more' there. James Barmby, a former Fellow and now rector of Melsonby, recalled the ecstatic reception accorded the Duke and his own chance to shake Eldon's hand (he thought him 'very old and feeble indeed').[40]

The old Duke's installation was not without incident. George Cox remembered that 'he was occasionally choked and bothered by the Latin formulæ; turning round for help to his prompter, the Vice-Chancellor'. Sixty years later, an anonymous source offered a different reason for the Duke's slips. Describing Rowley as 'the most unlucky V. C. they could have had', who 'became afterwards a sot', he claimed that the Duke had been unable to read Rowley's handwriting.[41]

It is not hard to imagine what it meant for a man of Rowley's origins to find himself corresponding with arguably the most famous Briton of the day, advising Wellington about the role of College Visitors, or seeking his support to repel yet another attempt to admit dissenters to Oxford.[42] Unsurprisingly Rowley's nerves occasionally got the better of him. In January 1835, Wellington, in a hurry, had his secretary write to Rowley in the third person, rather than write to him directly as usual. Rowley, aghast at this sudden formality, feared that he had offended the Duke, and wrote in profuse apology ('I regret most sincerely that any thing in my communication of the 7th should have incurred your Grace's displeasure...'). Wellington wrote a prompt—and rather surprised—letter of reassurance ('I never was more surprised than by yr letter recd this morning... You gave me exactly the answer which I expected; & I cannot conceive what can have induced you to believe that it excited Displeasure...'), and the matter was closed.[43]

Unfortunately, Rowley's Vice-Chancellorship coincided with a particularly turbulent period in Oxford life, connected with the rise of the Oxford Movement.[44] The origins of the movement are traditionally dated to 1833, when John Keble, a Fellow of Oriel, preached a sermon at the Oxford Assizes condemning the suppression of some Irish bishoprics. Keble was one of a group of Oxford men (who included another Fellow of Oriel, John Henry Newman) who wished to refresh the spirituality of the Anglican church by reviving older traditions and emphasizing the importance of doctrine (which later members of the movement extended towards the revival

---

[40] Eldon at the installation: Twiss 1844: iii. 226–33. A list of those attending the dinner (UC:GB3/A1/2 fos. 171^v–172^r), who included the King's brother, the Duke of Cumberland, and the Archbishop of Canterbury, shows that Eldon's estimate was correct. Extracts from Barmby's diary are published in Anon. 1934.

[41] Cox 1870: 272 versus Daniel 1888–95: no. 13, p. 79. Falconer Madan's copy of the latter in the Bodleian identified the writer as John Ffoulkes (m. Jesus 1831). In fact Rowley's handwriting is usually very legible.

[42] Correspondence between Rowley and Wellington can be found in SUL Wellington Papers 2/244–247.

[43] The exchange is in SUL Wellington Papers 2/246/2–8.

[44] Nockles 1997: 202–27 provides an introduction to the Oxford Movement.

of ritual). Although they resembled High Church men—indeed George Horne was among the few Georgian theologians whom they respected—members of the Oxford Movement, who acquired the nickname of 'Tractarian' from the tracts which they published, saw themselves as distinct from old-fashioned High Church men, whom they dismissed as 'Zs'.[45]

The young Tractarians cared little for the authority of the Vice-Chancellor and the heads of houses, and were capable of rounding up support against them concerning matters which they believed touched upon the links between church and university. The most acrimonious confrontation occurred in 1836. In February that year a new Regius Professor of Divinity, Renn Dickson Hampden, was appointed by the Whig Prime Minister. Hampden, a theologian with known liberal tendencies, was anathema to the Tractarians, and a motion to deprive the new Professor of certain powers, such as the right to appoint select preachers, was hauled through Convocation in May, in defiance of the Hebdomadal Council—and of Vice-Chancellor George Rowley. George Cox heard that the Vice-Chancellorship 'was said to have told unfavourably upon his [Rowley's] constitution'. Whether or not this was true, on 5 October 1836, only a few days before his Vice-Chancellorship was due to end, Rowley died after a few weeks' illness, and was buried in the Chapel.[46]

FREDERICK CHARLES PLUMPTRE AND ARTHUR STANLEY: 1836–1850

Frederick Charles Plumptre (Fig. 15.3) was elected the new Master on 25 October 1836. A former undergraduate (m. 1813) who had achieved a Second in Literae Humaniores in 1817, Plumptre was elected a Fellow that same year, and had been to Rowley what Rowley had been to James Griffith, acting as Dean and Tutor continuously from 1821, and holding other major College offices along the way. However, whereas Rowley's origins had been humble, Plumptre's academic pedigree was astonishing: six previous generations of Plumptres had gone to Cambridge, some of them becoming Fellows, and his great-uncle Robert had been President of Queens' College. Plumptre himself probably broke with tradition because his father had a living in Durham, and University College, with its eight north-eastern Fellowships, was more tempting than anywhere at Cambridge.[47]

Plumptre is a difficult Master to sum up. He lived through some of the greatest changes which University College has ever undergone, some of which he evidently supported, and yet he presented a conservative face to

---

[45] Tractarian admiration for George Horne: Nockles 1994: 4, 45–6, and 57–8.
[46] Rowley's turbulent Vice-Chancellorship: Ward 1965: 80–103; its effects: Cox 1870: 213; Rowley's death: UC:GB3/A1/2 fo. 173^r and SUL Wellington Papers 2/247/84–5.
[47] Plumptre's election: UC:GB3/A1/2 fos. 173^v–174^r; his ancestors: Twigg 1987: 180–1 and 461 (a remarkable family tree of his Cambridge relatives).

the world. He was not an easy man to know well: unusually tall (well over six foot high), he was also shy. Ashton Oxenden remembered Plumptre before he became Master, when he was nicknamed 'the Long Dean', on account of his height and thinness, and praised him as 'the kindest and most courteous of dons', but could never forget the difficulty with which Plumptre nervously once attempted to encourage him to hunt a little less, and to read a little more.[48] Less to Plumptre's credit, he was Tutor for much of the 1820s, precisely when the standards of undergraduate tuition were criticized especially harshly.

In later years, Plumptre hid his shyness under a carapace of dignified imperturbability, if not pomposity. He hosted breakfast parties for his undergraduates, which were remembered as heavy affairs. The philologist Friedrich Max Müller remembered him as 'a tall stiff, and to my mind, very imposing person'. So dignified and immovable were Plumptre's features, that Max Müller could believe it when someone joked that the Master slept in starched sheets.[49]

There was more to Plumptre, however, than his stiff exterior. In the first place, he took a considerable interest in architecture and architectural history. He published learned studies of All Saints' Church, Bakewell, and of Dover Abbey, and served three terms as President of the Oxford Architectural Society. He was deeply involved in the restoration of two Oxford churches (St Mary Magdalen and St Ebbe) and the building of two new ones (Holy Trinity—now demolished—and Headington Quarry). Unsurprisingly, therefore, Plumptre had a greater influence on the architecture of University College than any Master since Arthur Charlett. Despite the artistic leanings of James Griffith, the College had seen next to no architectural activity since the rebuilding of the Chapel and Hall façade at the turn of the century. In about 1810, Deep Hall was demolished, and the site turned over to the Fellows' Garden, and in 1818, a floor was inserted into the middle of the Library (still situated above the kitchen) to create a separate storey in the roof section, which was converted into bedrooms, but that was all.[50]

This changed under Plumptre. In June 1840, the College agreed to refit the Library with new bookcases and a new staircase, to convert a room on the ground floor of Staircase II into a second Common Room, and to demolish the house to the west of Deep Hall, once known as Stanton Hall, and to ask the eminent architect Charles Barry (already at work on the new Houses of Parliament) for a new building, 'as nearly as possible in keeping with that of

---

[48] Oxenden 1891: 19.
[49] Breakfast parties: Hare 1896–1900: i. 440–1; Max Müller 1901: 206–7.
[50] Plumptre's treatises: Plumptre 1847 and 1861; his work on the Oxford city churches: UC:MA40/L1–L4; the Fellows' Garden: Sturdy 1988: 59–62; alterations to the Library: UC:FA3/3/F1/1. This was, however, a quiet period in Oxford architectural history generally (Howell 2000: 729–32).

the College'. The Senior Common Room had originally just been the room on the right hand of Staircase II, but now the Fellows annexed the room opposite, turning it into a space variously called a Smoking Room or Coffee Room, and having it fitted out with new panelling. They also had a door opened up into the Fellows' Garden.[51]

The simple but serviceable building erected on the site of Stanton Hall provided the first new accommodation within the College since the Radcliffe Quadrangle. Charles Barry's designs for the New Building, as his only work in Oxford was—and still is—called, were accepted later in June 1840; work progressed fast, and its rooms were ready for occupation by March 1842. It cost almost £8,000 to build, rather more than expected, and Plumptre himself lent £3,000 to help cover costs. Eventually, in March 1850, the College created a fund for College buildings, and demanded a levy from members of the College to support it. The College benefited from its more generous accommodation, and admission numbers rose in the 1840s, although University College remained one of the smaller colleges, bigger than Jesus or Lincoln, but far behind Balliol, Brasenose, and Exeter.[52]

Plumptre also took considerable pains over the admission of undergraduates, keeping notebooks recording applicants to the College. These show that, in spite of its size, places at University College were almost as keenly contested as those at Balliol, Christ Church, and Oriel: Plumptre was receiving applications from candidates two or three years before they were expected to come up, and, by the late 1840s, even four years before. The College also appears to have been socially quite exclusive, to judge from the schools his undergraduates attended. For example, of the 55 undergraduates admitted in 1843–7 whose schooling is known (out of a total of 95), 6 were privately educated, and 49 came from fourteen schools. No fewer than 37 attended either Eton (12), Harrow (6), Winchester (6), or Rugby (13). Of other major public schools, Charterhouse sent just four boys, and Shrewsbury three. There was one Gunsley Scholar from Maidstone Grammar School. One undergraduate came from Rossall, a school only founded in 1844—but its first Headmaster, John Woolley, was a former Fellow of University College. Plumptre's notes show that he took careful account of school reports, especially character references—'well spoken of' is a frequent term of praise—but also applicants' family backgrounds.[53]

---

[51] Building projects: UC:GB4/A1/2 p. 8; specification for Common Room work: UC:FA3/4/F2/6.

[52] Barry's plans (none of which survive): UC:GB4/A1/2 p. 9; rooms in the New Building: UC:BU3/F3/21; costs: UC:MA40/F1/1 fos. 184^v–185^r and UC:GB4/A1/2 pp. 21–2; sizes of colleges: Curthoys 1997a: 159.

[53] Plumptre's notebooks: UC:J4/A1/1–6; the College's popularity: Curthoys 1997a: 147, and Curthoys 1997c: 483 and 504. The heavy Rugbeian presence probably owes much to a Rugbeian Fellow, Arthur Stanley, of whom more later.

Roughly half the names in Plumptre's books were not admitted: in May 1869, for example, only seven out of twelve applicants for College places were accepted. By the 1850s, at least, applicants had to show knowledge of certain Greek and Latin texts, be 'well grounded' in Greek and Latin grammar, translate from English into Latin, and have some knowledge of geometry, arithmetic, and divinity. Also, as Augustus Hare (m. 1853) remembered, they had to endure not only a written examination, but also an interview with Plumptre (whom he described as 'very cold, very stern, and *very* tall').[54]

Better provision was made for Scholars: in November 1837, only a year after Plumptre's election, the College agreed to give all existing Scholars an allowance for their room rent, and to endow from its own resources two new Scholarships, each worth £30, with no restrictions on eligibility, and tenable for four years. Although University College still lagged behind other colleges in the number and worth of its Scholarships, it still attracted decent applicants: Plumptre wrote in July 1838 'there has been much competition for our Scholarships and the nature of the examinations for them requires that a young man should possess decided ability in order to obtain one'.[55]

The early years of Plumptre's Mastership witnessed the first enlargement in the Fellowship for over a century. In 1837 University College received a bequest of £4,000 from Marianne, Viscountess Sidmouth, to be invested to endow a Fellowship in honour of her father, William Scott, Lord Stowell. The new Fellowship, however, differed from other Fellowships, for the Stowell Law Fellow could only study Civil Law, and was expected both to take his BCL and be called to the Bar during his tenure. He could also hold his Fellowship for only seven years, and would not be allowed to participate in the administration of the College, although he was entitled to rooms in College.[56]

Plumptre reaped the benefits of Travers Twiss's reinterpretation of the statutes concerning Fellowships. His own role in this reform is unknown, but he did oversee the election of some Fellows, several of them imported under the new rules, who led the College in a strikingly liberal direction. The first such Fellow was, however, a Yorkshireman. William Donkin (Fig. 15.4) had moved from St Edmund Hall to a Scholarship at University College in 1834, and in Easter 1836 achieved Firsts in both Literae Humaniores and mathematics and physics—the first member of University College to win a 'Double First'. His election to a Fellowship in December 1836 was a

---

[54] The 1869 applicants: UC:J4/MS1/5; Academic standards: UC:P167/P1/1 fos. 48^v–49^r and UC:J4/MS1/7; Hare's entrance exam: Hare 1896–1900: i. 405–6.

[55] Scholarships enlarged: UC:GB3/A1/2 fos. 177^{r-v}; competition from elsewhere: Curthoys 1997*a*: 170; Plumptre in 1838: UC:MA40/C2/3.

[56] Sidmouth's bequest (the College's first major donation made in stocks rather than property): UC:BU2/F1/6 fo. 135^r; regulations for new Fellowship: UC:GB3/A1/2 fos. 177^{r-v}, election in November 1837 of George Tickell, first Stowell Law Fellow: UC:GB3/A1/2 fo. 177^v.

FIGURE 15.4 William Donkin, Fellow 1836–43.
FIGURE 15.5 Arthur Stanley, Fellow 1838–51.

formality: even the waspish Mark Pattison, of whom more later, said of Donkin that 'no one more fitted by science and accomplishments to be a fellow of a college existed at that time in the University'. Indeed Donkin was the first Fellow of the College to devote himself exclusively to the sciences, being appointed Praelector in mathematics within weeks of his election, and in 1842 he became Savilian Professor of Astronomy. He was a supporter of university reform, but was also an enthusiastic amateur violinist and pianist, at a time when it was frowned upon for members of the university to be musical. Friedrich Max Müller remembered Donkin's Oxford home (where he and Donkin would perform together at evening parties) as one of the few congenial social centres for members of the university. Donkin's shy good nature also made him well liked.[57]

Donkin planned to combine his two loves in a treatise on theoretical and practical acoustics, but he never quite fulfilled his potential on account of his poor health and innate diffidence. In later years he had to spend much time abroad, and he died in 1869, aged only 55. Only the first of a three-volume treatise on acoustics was complete enough to be published posthumously. Donkin's shyness made it difficult for him to fight for his corner: it is said that, when asked what office space he would like in the new University

---

[57] Donkin's character: Pattison 1988: 88; his liberalism: Abbott and Campbell 1897: i. 95. his music-making: Tuckwell 1900: 69–70 and Max Müller 1901: 237.

Museum, he replied that a hut in the grounds would be sufficient.[58] Nevertheless, something of how he struck his contemporaries can be seen in a tribute paid in 1872 to:

> the keen subtle intellect, the noble soul of the Professor Astronomer... who, had his outward health been at all equal to his inward powers, would have left a foremost mark on Oxford and his time.[59]

The writer of those words was Arthur Penrhyn Stanley, who had been elected Fellow on 4 July 1838. Stanley (Fig. 15.5), a favourite pupil—and future biographer—of Thomas Arnold at Rugby, had enjoyed a brilliant undergraduate career at Balliol. Unfortunately, the theological beliefs which he shared with Arnold were deemed dangerously liberal, and hints were dropped that, should he seek a Fellowship at Balliol, his success could not be guaranteed, and that he should look elsewhere. Travers Twiss, it seems, knew of Stanley's plight, and, as Stanley happily admitted, persuaded him to apply for a vacant William of Durham Fellowship.[60]

The following election was the first major test of the College's new policy concerning its northern Fellowships, for their effective opening up could well aggrieve north-easterners who saw them as their exclusive right. One such was a Yorkshireman at Oriel called Mark Pattison, later Fellow and Rector of Lincoln. When writing his memoirs in the 1880s, he still remembered his horror when, assured that there was no strong internal candidate, he strode confidently into the Hall at University College, sat down, looked around at the other candidates—and saw Arthur Stanley. Pattison suspected at once that Twiss had invited Stanley to stand as a preferred candidate, and was furious at enduring this charade of an examination. Twiss was still alive when Pattison's *Memoirs* were published, and in a letter to *The Times* of 3 April 1885, apart from proudly admitting responsibility for opening up the College's Fellowships, he claimed that Pattison, at the end of the first day, had written to two Yorkshiremen among the Fellowship urging them not to admit an intruder. Needless to say, the Fellows showed the letters to the rest of the Governing Body—and the Provost of Oriel. Pattison's chances were dashed, and Stanley's election secured.[61]

Speaking at the 'Millenary Dinner' of 1872 (p. 390), Stanley reflected happily on his time at University College:

---

[58] Acoustics: Simcock in Fox and Gooday 2005: 146; diffidence: Fox in Fox and Gooday 2005: 53 and Hannabuss 2000: 447.

[59] *Guardian*, 19 June 1872.

[60] Stanley's election: UC:GB3/A1/2 fo. 178ᵛ; enforced departure from Balliol: Prothero and Bradley 1893: i. 191 and 195: Twiss's influence: Prothero and Bradley 1893: i. 198, and the *Guardian* of 19 June 1872.

[61] Pattison 1988: 96–7.

First, let me speak of the advantage I gained from having to govern and lead that sometimes unruly, sometimes docile flock—learning lessons from the patience of one, the fortitude of another, the high principles and devotion of a third... Secondly there was the Common Room. There, amid the utmost divergence of opinion, the good temper and good humour which prevailed were an excellent preparation for the conflicts of opinion in which it has been my lot to be engaged ever since.[62]

In fact Stanley spent his first months at University College pining for his beloved Balliol: the food was awful, the Common Room dull, and his teaching duties tedious. 'The only unpleasant part,' he wrote, 'I find in my lectures is the total absence of any expression of feeling in the faces of my twelve auditors.'[63] In fairness to Stanley, the College in the early 1840s was still not very academic. George Granville Bradley (m. 1840), another Rugbeian pupil of Arnold, was not impressed by the atmosphere he encountered:

There was much idleness in the usual sense of the word;...men were regular at lectures but *read little*. There was much vigorous athletic life...great recent successes on the river were filling us all with unbounded delight; some few of us, a very few, read hard and discussed our favourite authors in private; but as a rule such...found little favour.[64]

Matters eventually improved. Stanley was touched by Travers Twiss's kindness, and he warmed to the sense of humour of William Donkin, whom he found 'shy and silent, but very gentlemanlike'. Indeed, when Stanley returned to Oxford in 1841 from a visit to Greece, his first evening in College was spent 'being let loose in an endless gallery of friends', before ending with a long conversation with 'dear Donkin'. He began to win over his pupils: as he wrote, 'You will be glad to hear that my audience has at last given signs of human feeling by a burst of laughter at a ludicrous story. I was quite alarmed at the effect of my own wit.'[65]

Undergraduates were drawn to this shy but somehow charismatic young man. George Bradley tried to explain Stanley's special qualities:

It is impossible for me to describe to you...the feeling which he inspired in a circle, small at first, but with every fresh term widening and extending. The fascination, the charm, the spell, were simply irresistible; the face, the voice, the manner; the ready sympathy, the geniality, the freshness, the warmth, the poetry, the refinement, the humour, the mirthfulness and merriment, the fund of knowledge, the inexhaustible store of anecdotes and stories, told so vividly, so dramatically.[66]

---

[62] *Guardian*, 19 June 1872.
[63] Prothero and Bradley 1893: i. 211, 215, and 309.   [64] Bayley 1963: 185.
[65] Twiss and Donkin: Prothero and Bradley 1893: i. 216; return from Greece: Prothero and Bradley 1893: i. 296–7; pupils: Prothero and Bradley 1893: i. 310.
[66] Prothero and Bradley 1893: i. 356. See too Curthoys 1997a: 158.

Although Bradley conceded that Stanley was no philosopher, and was uninterested in the minutiae of philology, yet Stanley's divinity lectures were so popular that his pupils obtained permission for friends from other colleges to attend them. Bradley even claimed that:

> The first germ of those inter-collegiate lectures which have revolutionised Oxford teaching is to be found in those close-packed chairs that crowded the still damp ground-floor rooms in the then New Buildings.[67]

Likewise, some members of University College received informal instruction elsewhere, such as John ffolliott (m. 1844). Through an acquaintance at Balliol, he came to know Stanley's great friend Benjamin Jowett, and, although never formally taught by Jowett, he became a lifelong member of Jowett's inner circle of admiring current and former pupils.[68]

Most unusually, some evidence for Stanley's teaching methods survive in his heavily annotated editions of the *History* of Herodotus, the *Politics* of Aristotle, and the *Verrine Orations* of Cicero.[69] They show how Stanley would take a class through a text line by line, pointing out matters of interest. To judge from such witnesses as Mark Pattison and, rather less reverently, the novelist 'Cuthbert Bede', this was the basic method of undergraduate tuition during the early nineteenth century—as it had been during the eighteenth.[70]

A little quirk of Stanley's was recalled by his pupil Arthur Butler (m. 1850), a future Fellow of Oriel and Headmaster of Haileybury:

> In treating a difficult and complex book like the 'Politics' of Aristotle, he [Stanley] would recommend us carefully to note peculiarities with three varieties of coloured pencils under the following heads: truths for all time, red; truths for the time of Aristotle, blue; and the, with a humourous twinkle of his eye, truths for the schools, black.[71]

Stanley's notes in his Herodotus are indeed colour-coded, although not quite as Butler remembered. A key on the title page identifies texts with black lines as 'philological', with red ones as 'historically important', with blue ones as 'religiously important', and so on. The texts bear witness to the pains which he took in his teaching. In addition, Stanley, like Travers Twiss, was aware of German work in ancient history.[72]

Stanley became a central figure in College life in the 1840s—he was Praelector in Latin in 1842–4, Praelector in Greek for 1844–6, simultaneously Dean and Catechist in 1846–1851, and Tutor in 1843–51—and he does seem to have had some impact on academic standards, as reflected in the number of

---

[67] Prothero and Bradley 1893: i. 355–6.
[68] Abbott and Campbell 1897: i. 129, 136, and 168–71.
[69] UC:S16/MS1/1–6.
[70] See too Curthoys 1997a: 149–50.
[71] Prothero and Bradley 1893: i. 359. [72] Jenkyns and Murray 1997: 529–30.

undergraduates who sat for honours degrees at this time. Only 4 per cent of men matriculating between 1799 and 1805 had obtained an honours degree, and just over one-fifth of those who came up in 1806–25. From 1826 there was a slight increase, but just over one-third of undergraduates who came up in 1846–50 sat for honours degrees—the highest proportion yet.[73] Indeed 1844 was something of an *annus mirabilis* for Stanley and the College: two of the four Firsts and three of the fifteen Seconds awarded in Literae Humaniores that Easter term went to University College men. One First went to George Bradley, the other to Edward Plumptre (m. 1840), a nephew of the Master, who distinguished himself further by also winning a First in mathematics and physics—the only one awarded that term. In the early 1850s, Stanley described what his pupils studied. There were separate courses in classics and philosophy for undergraduates reading for honours and for an ordinary degree, but extra lectures were laid on for undergraduates reading mathematics, although there were only two or three takers. There were also compulsory lectures on the Old and New Testament, and on the Thirty-Nine Articles.[74]

Stanley appears to have introduced another innovation into College life. Surprising as it may appear, sermons had apparently not been preached in services in the College Chapel (the lectures of the catechist may have been thought sufficient). Stanley, however, began to preach occasional sermons, with great success.[75]

A very different Fellow from Stanley and Donkin—and indeed from the rest of the Fellowship—was Frederick William Faber (Scholar 1834; F. 1837–44), University College's only prominent early member of the Oxford Movement. It is a curious fact that, although university life at this time was dominated by the vicissitudes of the Oxford Movement—until a series of sensational conversions to Rome in 1845, including that of John Henry Newman, calmed the worst tensions—University College seems to have been unaffected by serious strife. Plumptre's own character may have played a part, for his religion was typical of him: a traditional High Church man, he was neither Evangelical nor Tractarian. Indeed, he evidently became quite hostile to those of the latter tendency. When an alliance of Evangelicals and High Church men planned a Memorial to the Oxford Martyrs as a reaction against the perceived 'Romish' character of the Oxford Movement, it was Plumptre, no less, who as Chairman of the Committee of Management laid the foundation stone for the Martyrs' Memorial in May 1841. He could have made no clearer statement of his feelings.[76]

---

[73] The proportion of undergraduates taking honours degrees had been roughly in line with other colleges, but in the 1840s it was above average (Curthoys 1997*b*: vi. 360).
[74] The syllabus: Anon. 1852: Evidence, 305–12.
[75] Sermons: Prothero and Bradley 1893: i. 365–7.
[76] The Martyrs' Memorial: Nockles 1997: 235–7; Plumptre and the foundation stone: *Times*, 24 May 1841.

Faber's religious beliefs, then, set him apart. Indeed, he would have stood apart in many respects: he was a handsome man of great personal charm, and well regarded as a poet. When he first came up to Oxford, Faber was a devout Calvinist, a serious youth with anxieties similar to those of George Horne about the perils of exposing someone brought up in the Christian faith to 'Horace's Odes, where all sorts of enormities are dressed up in all the felicities of melody and diction'. Early in 1836, Faber attended a sermon preached by Dr Edward Pusey on 'Sin after Baptism', and was at once converted to the views of the Tractarians. A year later, he was elected to his Fellowship, and Newman felt confident enough to single out University College as one of the colleges where a nucleus of sympathizers was forming.[77]

Newman's confidence proved to be misplaced. In particular Faber had little influence at University College. He held next to no College offices, and was largely non-resident. Religious matters of course interested thinking undergraduates deeply—George Bradley recalled 'much tension and interest among thinking men' about religion[78]—but the offices which brought Fellows into close contact with undergraduates, namely Tutorships (still in the personal gift of the Master) and Praelectorships, were bestowed on moderates and liberals like Twiss and Stanley. Faber, meanwhile, began a difficult spiritual journey of his own. After a visit to Italy in the early 1840s, he began to wonder, like Newman, whether his true home might be in Roman Catholicism. However, he remained Anglican enough to take the College living of Elton in 1843. He proved an excellent parish priest: his predecessor but one, Philip Fisher, rector since 1787, had spent most of the previous four decades living in London, where he was Master of the Charterhouse, or in a charming villa in Kingston-upon-Thames, while, according to Faber's first biographer, Elton 'was in evil repute among its neighbors, and as his predecessor had done little or nothing for its reformation, it had become almost a byword for its intemperance and profligacy'. Local rumour had it that the next rector, Piers Claughton, promptly resigned on seeing the state of the rectory, leaving Faber to take over. Faber, on the other hand, devoted himself to parish work as enthusiastically as William Boyd in Arncliffe, and with equal success.[79]

Nevertheless, Faber's religious doubts could not be stilled, and in November 1845 he followed Newman to Rome. With a certain theatrical flair, after preaching his last sermon, 'he hastily descended the pulpit stairs, threw off

---

[77] Faber's character: Pattison 1988: 89, and Selborne 1896: i. 136–9; Faber on Horace: Bowden 1869: 49; his conversion: Selborne 1896: i. 213–14; Newman's optimism: Nockles 1997: 232.

[78] Bayley 1963: 185.

[79] General context: Clark 2007: 195–215 and (on Claughton) 295; Fisher: Quick 1990: 51–2; Faber: Bowden 1869: 209–17 and Prothero 1895: 93–4.

his surplice, which he left upon the ground, and made his way as quickly as possible through the vestry to the rectory'.[80] Piers Claughton, reappointed as rector, found Faber a tough act to follow. As he explained to Arthur Stanley, Faber had shared his teachings with his parishioners, several of whom converted with him. Claughton was rather perplexed to encounter 'young farmer boys talking of "The Church of St. Peter, out of which there is no salvation." ' Stanley himself commented of Faber that 'I think he must have gone to the verge of what was right, if not beyond it, in Romanising the people, while he was still himself doubting what he should do.'[81]

University College produced a few other converts to Rome, including George Tickell, elected as the first Stowell Law Fellow in 1837, who became a Jesuit, and George Ranken (m. 1845), later a privy chamberlain to Pope Leo XIII, but Faber was the College's most eminent Catholic convert.[82] He joined the Congregation of the Oratory, creating the London Oratory, and he won a considerable reputation for his writings, especially his hymns, for which he is best remembered. In addition, he became a keen advocate of Ultramontanism, that movement which supported the claims of a strong central papacy.

At University College, meanwhile, Faber had been a somewhat marginal figure. Arthur Stanley was far more central to its life in the 1840s through his teaching and example. Stanley, however, had grander ideas for the reform of the university. At this time there was no single programme for the reform of Oxford: its nature—and, indeed, its speed and method—were all keenly debated. Some dons wanted a wider range of subjects to be taught, especially among the sciences; others wished to end the clerical domination of Oxford; others sought a greater role for professors and for research. An especially controversial question was whether the university could reform itself, or whether it was so far beyond self-help that Parliamentary aid was needed. Frederick Plumptre himself, who had overseen considerable internal reforms within his College, believed that Oxford should be left alone: in 1850, he was reported as describing the buildings of Oxford as memorials to a history of independence from external interference.[83]

Stanley, Twiss, and Donkin identified themselves with the more radical reformers, and sought allies in other colleges. At Queen's College it was remembered how, on wet afternoons, Stanley would pace up and down its cloisters with George Johnson, a like-minded Fellow there, and discuss university reform. Stanley's most important ally, however, was his best friend from Balliol, Benjamin Jowett, now a Fellow there. From 1841 Stanley and

---

[80] Bowden 1869: 233.
[81] Prothero 1895: 93–4. Claughton's second tenure at Elton proved more successful; it is said that he invented the harvest festival there (*ODNB* entry).
[82] See further Firth 1972.
[83] Curthoys 1997a: 146, quoting from the *Herald* of 22 June 1850.

Jowett were members of a small discussion group called the Decade, which met in each other's rooms to discuss an agreed topic.[84]

Stanley, Jowett, and their allies looked abroad for inspiration. During the previous half-century universities elsewhere in Europe had undergone enormous change. In France, universities had been abolished in 1793, and then recreated under Napoleon in a different, highly centralized, guise, very susceptible to government influence, and consisting of a single 'university' with many faculties all over France. Meanwhile, in Germany, a different—and far more influential—model was created, best exemplified in the foundation of Berlin University in 1810. The German model centred on a professorial system (with high salaries for the professors), and the belief in a unity of teaching and research, where researchers could transmit the fruits of their work to their pupils. Emphasis was also placed on the unity of scholarship, so that there were no specialized schools as there were in France. Furthermore, teachers had freedom of teaching and learning, and there were far fewer religious restrictions on students. Nearer to home, there was the example of the Scottish universities, still excelling in the teaching of medicine and law, especially the former. English reformers were greatly taken with the German model of a liberal university, and Stanley, eager to see this new world for himself, visited Germany in 1839 and 1844, accompanied on his second visit by Benjamin Jowett. Although Jowett, for one, would eventually oppose (successfully) the attempts of Mark Pattison and others to import the German professorial system into Oxford, he and Stanley appreciated the freedom of thought which they encountered: in 1844, Stanley declared that 'we ought to study German as well as English theology,' and he and Jowett, practising what they preached, joined the small number of Oxonians of the day who learned German.[85]

Stanley's great advantage in his campaign was his charm. Even those who disagreed vehemently with him conceded that he never let differences over policy affect personal relationships, and the Common Room at University College evidently benefited. One of the Fellows elected in the later 1840s was William Bright (m. 1843, F. 1847–69), a Rugbeian pupil of Arnold who, unlike Stanley and Bradley, became a prominent High Church man. When Bright was appointed Professor of Ecclesiastical History many years later, Stanley immediately wrote to congratulate him, and Bright gratefully replied:

---

[84] Stanley and Johnson: Hodgkin 1949: 172; Stanley and Jowett: Abbott and Campbell 1897: i. 81.
[85] Other universities: Anderson 2004: 34–5 (Scotland), 39–49 (France), 53–61 (Germany), and 66–8 (religious freedoms), and Brockliss 1997; Stanley in Germany: Prothero and Bradley 1893: i. 325; studying German: Abbott and Campbell 1896: i. 90.

I will never encourage—I will always discourage the temper of hard and unfair partisanship which would sacrifice truthfulness to the supposed interests of a cause. These are lessons which I learned from Arnold at Rugby, and from you at Oxford.[86]

Stanley had won Bright's friendship, if not his discipleship. Two other young Fellows, however, were definitely on Stanley's side. 'Refugees' from Magdalen College, John Conington and Goldwin Smith were unwilling either to take holy orders or to wait for fellowships to fall vacant under Magdalen's particularly arcane statutes. In both cases, Magdalen's loss was University College's undoubted gain.[87]

John Conington had actually matriculated from University College in 1843, but almost at once won a Demyship at Magdalen. Because of the restrictions at Magdalen, however, he returned to his original College, and was elected a Scholar in May 1846. A year later, having achieved a brilliant First in Literae Humaniores, Conington was elected to a William of Durham Fellowship. Just as with Arthur Stanley's election a decade earlier, however, there was a disgruntled runner-up, a Freeston Scholar called Joseph Moorsom (m. 1839). Whereas in 1838 Mark Pattison had eventually accepted defeat, albeit with a bad grace, Moorsom appealed to the Visitor to have the election set aside on the grounds that, as a Yorkshireman, he was more eligible for a William of Durham Fellowship than Conington, a Lincolnshire man. A victory for Moorsom would have swept away the reforms of the last decade; fortunately the Lord Chancellor upheld the interpretation which only granted preference to north-easterners, 'all other things being equal'. Since Moorsom had got a Second in his Finals, and Conington a First, the conclusion was obvious: academic merit won, and Moorsom lost his appeal.[88]

Conington's appearance was bizarre—one observer recalled his 'extraordinary visage, with its green-cheese hue, gleaming spectacles, quivering protusive lips'[89]—but even Mark Pattison was in awe of his intellect:

the most distinguished scholar whom the University had turned out, but [he] was, much more than a scholar, a man whose words and opinions came with weight as from a full and powerful mind.[90]

Conington's scholarship was rewarded when in 1854 he was appointed the first Corpus Professor of Latin. He published commentaries on two plays of Aeschylus and on the *Satires* of Persius, and before his early death had completed most of a commentary on the works of Virgil, which, as

---

[86] Prothero and Bradley 1893: ii. 372–3.
[87] Magdalen's fellowships: Darwall-Smith in Brockliss (forthcoming).
[88] Conington's elections as Scholar and Fellow: UC:GB3/A1/3 pp. 11 and 14; Moorsom's appeal: UC:GB3/A1/3 pp. 16–20.
[89] Tuckwell 1900: 104.
[90] Pattison 1988: 127.

completed by his successor as Professor, Henry Nettleship, remains an important work.[91] When elected a Fellow, he was ranked among the liberals, but in the summer of 1854, shortly before moving to Corpus Christi, he underwent a spiritual crisis, as a result of which he renounced his liberal past, and became conservative in both religion and politics. Pattison claimed that Conington's crisis arose 'not by the seduction of piety, but by the terrors of hell'.[92] The writer John Addington Symonds knew Conington in the later 1850s, after his spiritual crisis, and hints at the reasons behind Conington's struggle:

> The association with Conington was almost wholly good. It is true that I sat up till midnight with him nearly every evening, drinking cup after cup of strong tea in his private lodgings above Cooper's shop near University [83–4 High Street]. This excited and fatigued my nerves. But the conversation was in itself a liberal education for a youth of pronounced literary tastes. Now and again it turned on matters of the affections. Conington was scrupulously moral and cautious. Yet he sympathized with romantic attachments for boys.[93]

University College's other Magdalen import, Goldwin Smith (Fig. 15.6), had been elected a Demy there in 1842. He and Conington became rivals and friends, but again there were no vacant fellowships at Magdalen for which Smith was eligible, and so in 1846 he found, as he remembered, 'a more congenial home at University College'.[94] Smith's refuge was a Stowell Law Fellowship. Because this Fellowship lasted only seven years, Smith sought something permanent: in 1846, he applied unsuccessfully for a fellowship at Oriel, and then in 1849 stood for one at Queen's. This latter election achieved some notoriety: in a contest remarkably like that between Conington and Moorsom, Smith, from Berkshire, had won a First in his Finals, while his main opponent, from Cumberland, had a Fourth in Classics and a Second in Mathematics. Queen's, however, decided to observe its Founder's Statutes to the letter, although this meant valuing birthplace over intellect, and Smith lost by a slim margin. Some saw this fiasco as a turning-point. Moderates like Plumptre had hoped that the university and its colleges could reform themselves, but many waverers were now convinced that reform from within was impossible, and that outside assistance was needed. Smith in particular despaired. Writing to a friend from his Magdalen days, Roundell Palmer (later, as Earl of Selborne, Lord Chancellor in Gladstone's Cabinet), shortly after the election he felt that 'no progress has been made anywhere'.[95]

Plumptre and the Fellows of University College decided to retain Smith permanently, and showed what could be done with an elegant manipulation of their statutes. In March 1850, when Smith resigned his Stowell Fellowship

---

[91] Jenkyns 2000: 330. [92] Pattison 1988: 129.
[93] Symonds 1984: 109. [94] Smith 1910: 73.
[95] Oriel: Pattison 1988: 56; Queen's: Hodgkin 1949: 175; Smith: Selborne 1896: ii. 195–6.

FIGURE 15.6 Goldwin Smith, Stowell Law Fellow 1846–50 and Fellow 1850–68.

he was elected a Bennet Scholar: an apparent loss of status, but with a purpose. One of the Bennet Fellows, George Bradley (now a promising teacher at Rugby) had just married, and his year of grace was due to expire. On 28 October 1850, therefore, an election for his successor was held. By statute only a Bennet Scholar could be a Bennet Fellow, and so the new Bennet Fellow was none other than the newest Bennet Scholar.[96]

Goldwin Smith, described by one observer as 'tutor, journalist and prophet', was perhaps the most controversial Fellow of the mid-century College, not least because of his readiness to express himself in print, be it on university reform, an end to the religious tests in Oxford and Cambridge, or appealing for a smaller British empire. He was not universally liked: Benjamin Disraeli memorably called him 'a wild man of the cloister', and another observer said of him 'We all saw in him the coming man; but he married, settled in America, and never came.'[97]

[96] Smith's elections: UC:GB3/A1/3 pp. 24–6.
[97] Characterization: Ward 1997: 309; attacking the empire: Symonds 1986: 80–3; Disraeli: Brock 2000a: 42; 'coming man': Tuckwell 1900: 104.

Yet Goldwin Smith was more complex than his political activities might suggest: he was President of the Oxford Architectural and Historical Society in 1863–6, and he participated in the College life in various ways. Furthermore his eagerness for a secular university did not mean that he lacked any belief. Far from it: in a letter of 1850 to Roundell Palmer, Smith declared 'As to the clerical order... to hate them would be to hate men whom I regard as the guides of my life. But their exclusive ascendancy here is, as is felt by some of the best of themselves to be, an evil both to the University and to themselves.'[98]

Men like Goldwin Smith and Arthur Stanley now ceased to believe in the internal reform favoured by Frederick Plumptre. It would just take enough members of the university, and a sympathetic ear in government, for outside intervention to be brought in to achieve what Oxford could not. Hopes were raised among the reformers in 1846 when a new government was formed under Lord John Russell, a Prime Minister who had been, not to Oxford or Cambridge, but to Edinburgh, and it became clear that he might be persuaded to intervene in Oxford. Indeed, in the winter of 1847/8, a petition for a university commission was presented to him, although it came to nothing. George Bradley was among the signatories.[99]

In 1850 the reformers tried again, this time successfully, and, according to Goldwin Smith, their plan was hatched within University College itself:

Mr. James Heywood, a Nonconformist Member of Parliament, was bringing forward an annual motion for inquiry into the Universities mainly with a view to the abolition of religious tests. His motion was regularly negatived... A few of us, Mark Pattison and Jowett among the number, met in the rooms of Arthur Stanley at University College and addressed to Lord John Russell... a request that he would not allow the occasion of Heywood's motion again to pass without holding out hope of assistance to University reform. In compliance with this request Lord John Russell announced a Commission of Inquiry into the Universities and their Colleges.[100]

Stanley's rooms (on the first floor of Staircase III and Staircase IV) were thus the setting for a momentous event in Oxford's history.[101] By inviting the government to reform Oxford, Stanley, Smith, and their colleagues had unleashed a power whose effects none could guess at.

---

[98] Selborne 1896: ii. 196.
[99] Russell: Ward 1997: 306–9; 1847/8 petition: Ward 1965: 137.
[100] Smith 1910: 101–2. See too Ward 1965: 152–5.
[101] Stanley's rooms in 1850: UC:BU3/F3/29–30.

16

The College Transformed: 1850–1881

In 1850, University College was still an institution open only to members of the Church of England, most of whose Fellows were in holy orders, and most of whose Fellowships and Scholarships were restricted to applicants from the north-east or Kent. Undergraduates could only study classics or mathematics, and anyone with academic ambitions required private coaching. In 1881 the Mastership was offered to an eminent agnostic; most Fellows were laymen; Fellowships and Scholarships were open to all comers; the range of subjects available for study now included science, law, and modern history; and College teaching could now cater for all abilities. In short, during these thirty years University College underwent some of its greatest changes.

THE GREAT COMMISSION, 1850–1857[1]

When a Royal Commission was set up in 1850 to investigate the University of Oxford, University College was in the midst of the ensuing controversy: Arthur Stanley was appointed the Commission's Secretary and Goldwin Smith its Assistant Secretary, while Frederick Plumptre, Vice-Chancellor since 1848, led a Hebdomadal Council which refused to cooperate with the Commission or furnish any information about University College. Matters were not helped when the notoriously absent-minded Stanley placed important letters to the Chancellor and Vice-Chancellor in the wrong envelopes.[2]

Stanley and Smith did not abuse their position by providing the Commission with confidential information about the College, but other means were found of offering help. Stanley gave evidence to the Commission, as did two other Fellows (Travers Twiss and John Conington), as well as some former members, including Robert Lowe and William Donkin. Robert Lowe—a former pupil of Plumptre—gave a damning critique of the College tuition

---

[1] Fuller accounts of the Oxford Commission are in Ward 1965: 165–79 and Ward 1997: 315–20. Cambridge faced a separate Commission at the same time (Searby 1997: 507–44).

[2] The Council's and Plumptre's refusal: Anon. 1852: Evidence, 3–4 and 305 (Plumptre's opposition is also clear in his correspondence with the Duke of Wellington: SUL Wellington Papers 2/256); Stanley's letters: Prothero and Bradley 1893: i. 422.

of his own time; John Conington condemned both the 'the utter inexpediency of all local restrictions on Fellowships', and the rules on celibacy and on holy orders; while Travers Twiss praised the 'more beneficial interpretation' of their statutes adopted by some colleges (like University College). Smith himself, intent on writing a history of the university, had been mining Oxford college archives, and had already assembled some useful information when most of them were closed to the Commission. The Commissioners therefore learned much about University College without needing to ask it directly.[3]

The Fellowship somehow held together—Goldwin Smith remembered a congenial atmosphere in the Senior Common Room in the 1850s, with the Fellows chatting around the fire after dinner—and even tried to achieve Plumptre's goal of reforming itself without outside help. In 1851, a College meeting (attended by Stanley and Smith) created a Committee including the Master and Twiss 'to examine the Statutes of the College and report upon any alterations which may seem to be desirable'.[4]

The Committee never reported back; but when in 1852 the Commission produced its own report, it was generous to University College: 'This College has, since the appointment of its present Master, made great efforts to free itself from the restrictions which Statute or custom had imposed upon its elections.' It was especially commended for relaxing the rules on geographical restrictions, and the requirement to take orders, which reforms, the Commissioners felt, had ensured great successes in examinations. The Commissioners therefore had few recommendations, except to extend existing reforms, and codify them in new statutes.[5]

One of the MPs for the university, W. E. Gladstone, now steered a bill through Parliament to act on the report's recommendations. University College, anticipating the worst, revived its statutes committee in March 1854, now co-opting Goldwin Smith. This was wise: a few months later, Gladstone's bill completed its journey through Parliament. Apart from introducing changes to the structure of the university's administration, it created a fresh Commission to draft new sets of statutes for all the colleges—with powers of enforcement if necessary—and Goldwin Smith was appointed joint secretary.[6]

While the new statutes were being written, the Commissioners told the College what was expected of it. In December 1855, they decreed that in future Fellowship elections, 'no preference shall be given to any person in

---

[3] Evidence from members of the College: Anon. 1852: Evidence, 12–13 (Lowe), 106–10 and 260–2 (Donkin), 115–19 (Conington) 154–7 and 293–5 (Twiss), 305–12 (Stanley); Smith's research: Smith 1910: 102.
[4] SCR atmosphere: Smith 1910: 75; Statutes Committee: UC:GB3/A1/3 p. 31.
[5] Anon. 1852: Report, 185–7.
[6] Statutes Committee: UC:GB3/A1/3 p. 39; the 1854 Act: Ward 1997: 330–6 and Harvie 1997: 699–700.

respect of a place of birth or of his being or having been a Scholar on any foundation of the College.' When the Commissioners' new statutes for University College were published in March 1857, they followed the guidelines laid down in 1852: the Master no longer had to be a member of the College, but could be an outsider (Section 1); the order of December 1855 for Fellowship elections was upheld (Section 5); and only six Fellows needed to be in holy orders (Section 18). All restrictions on birthplace or kinship on Scholarships were lifted—but not those relating to schools, so the Gunsley and Freeston Scholarships remained unaffected. There were some novelties: colleges could now elect Honorary Fellows, and in March 1858 University College exercised this right for the first time, selecting William Donkin. In 1864 the same honour was conferred on Travers Twiss and Arthur Stanley. Such changes were common to colleges in both Oxford and Cambridge.[7]

THE LATER YEARS OF MASTER PLUMPTRE, 1857–1870[8]

Plumptre's reaction to the new statutes remains unknown. Although he may have regretted the loss of much of the Oxford he knew, yet he had already moved the College in many of the directions indicated by the Commissioners. Furthermore, by working with the Commissioners, he had avoided the fate of St John's College, which stubbornly refused to cooperate, and had a set of statutes forced on it far more liberal than the ones originally proposed. Furthermore, despite the efforts of Goldwin Smith and others to abolish religious tests completely, members of Oxford above the rank of BA still had to subscribe to the articles of the Church of England.[9] Plumptre himself expected similar of undergraduates, as shown at a College meeting of 21 October 1868:

The matter of the admission of Mr. Powell, who had expressed sceptical opinions in the matriculation examination, having been laid before the meeting by the Master, and those present having expressed various opinions on the subject, the Master expressed his determination to refuse to grant his consent to this admission.[10]

By the mid-1850s, many figures of the previous generation had either resigned, like Arthur Stanley (who inherited his family fortune in 1851) and John Conington (promoted to a professorship in 1854), or become involved in other activities—Travers Twiss was appointed Regius Professor

---

[7] Rules on elections: UC:GB3/A1/3 pp. 42–4 (the first Fellows under the new rules were elected in June 1856); Honorary Fellows: UC:GB3/A1/3 pp. 48 and 61; other colleges in general: Engel 1983: 56–7; individual cases: Bury 1952: 52–3 (Corpus Christi, Cambridge), Hopkins 2005: 239–40 (Trinity, Oxford), Baker 1971: 56–7 (Jesus), and Magrath 1921: ii. 183 (Queen's). Magrath believed that Goldwin Smith, perhaps with a certain satisfaction, himself drafted the new Ordinances for the College which had rejected him in 1849.
[8] Harvie 1997 provides a university-wide view of the years after 1854.
[9] St John's: Costin 1958: 257–78; Smith on the tests: Smith 1864, for example.
[10] UC:GB4/A1/2 p. 101. Powell was not admitted.

of Civil Law in 1854 and Goldwin Smith Regius Professor of Modern History in 1858. Smith's departure from Oxford was an unhappy one: personal grief on the suicide of his mentally ill father and frustration at the lack of further reforms persuaded him in 1868 to take the dramatic step of emigrating to America as one of the founding professors at Cornell University.

The newer Fellows reflected the mixture of change and stability which marked Plumptre's later years. Two, William Bright (p. 362) and Peter Goldsmith Medd (m. 1848; F. 1852–77), were members of the later, post-Newman, generation of Tractarians, who stayed true to the traditional, clerical, vision of Oxford.[11] They took an especial interest in liturgical scholarship: Bright edited collects and wrote hymns, and he and Medd jointly translated the Book of Common Prayer into Latin. Medd was also involved in founding Keble College, and served on its council. Bright and Medd acted as Tutors in the late 1850s and 1860s, and Bright was remembered affectionately, as in this tribute from an unnamed pupil:

> It was a delight to read Virgil with him. To those who had been accustomed merely to verbal criticism, it was a revelation to find the *Æneid* full of character. Æneas, for instance, he could never forgive, not only for his conduct to Dido, but for his constant timidity. 'Stupid fellow! of course up goes his hair on end again!' and so forth. It is needless to say what his Divinity Lectures were. His notes are still among my treasured possessions.[12]

Medd, however, appears to have been less popular, undoubtedly because he was Dean for most of the 1860s. A poem of 1864 called 'Alfred's Avatar' by an undergraduate, Richard Crawley (m. 1861), mocked him as:

> Awkward at ease, contemptible in state,
> Marble to little crimes, but wax to great,
> Stern when a hermit steps upon the grass,
> Forgiving when a drunkard dubs you 'Ass'.[13]

According to J. R. Magrath, Provost of Queen's in 1878–1930, Bright and Medd turned their interest in ceremony and custom on University College, persuading it to abandon three customs unique to it. The first and most bizarre one, which was ended in 1864, was 'chopping the block'. On Easter Sunday the kitchen staff decorated their chopping block with flowers, and placed it in a passageway for members of the foundation to strike at with a cleaver. After each member struck the block, he tipped the cook. Some claimed that guests could also chop the block, and even that, if a guest chopped the block right through, he could claim a large part of the College's

---

[11] See too Kidd 1903 (Bright) and Whale 1983 (Medd) and both men's *ODNB* entries.
[12] Kidd 1903: xiv–xv.
[13] UC:P167/P1/1 fos. 7^v–8^r (reprinted in Crawley 1983).

estates. The second custom was that a loving cup would go round High Table every day at dinner. The third was another curious one: after Communion Services, the remains of the bread and wine, instead of being consumed by the celebrant, were brought down by the bible clerk to the Antechapel where the Master and Fellows, standing in a circle, consumed them. The last custom would have especially displeased Bright and Medd, being contrary to the rubrics of the Book of Common Prayer.[14]

There was another significant change in the conduct of dinner: in 1868, the Governing Body agreed that 'the grace hitherto used after dinner be said before dinner'. This is the earliest known reference to the College grace, apparently the longest one regularly used in Oxford or Cambridge. It is not known when it was adopted—nor what grace had been said before dinner— but it was not unusual: its wording is very similar to the after-dinner grace at Queen's (which is still used at Gaudies), and Balliol's long after-dinner grace, abolished by Benjamin Jowett in 1870, has a similar format but very different words. No reason is given for moving University College's grace, but it would not have displeased the likes of Bright and Medd for dinner to open in this solemn manner.[15]

As Bright and Medd tried to keep the College true to its religious roots, two other Fellows were travelling in a different direction. The first, Charles Stuart Parker (F. 1854–69), served as a Tutor in 1858–65. Parker resembled Goldwin Smith both in his liberal politics and his journalistic leanings, and enjoyed introducing eminent visitors from the outside world to his pupils. He later became a Liberal MP.[16] The second, Charles Faulkner, was one of the first two Fellows elected in 1856 under the new regulations (Fig. 16.1). A graduate of Pembroke, he was not a classicist, but a scientist, getting a First both in mathematics and physics, and in natural sciences. Faulkner was remembered for his devotion to mathematics and science, and his lack of interest in theology. Although he made no major discoveries and published nothing, he was an assiduous lecturer, helping to establish inter-collegiate lectures in mathematics, and a capable teacher to those who wished to learn. One pupil, Edwin Lendon (m. 1866), remembered him as being 'most kind to me'. Unfortunately, some claimed that 'the Fogger' never wholly lost 'his ancestral Mercian speech', and Lendon claimed that the College 'bloods' mocked his 'Birmingham boots'.[17]

Faulkner, however, had wider interests. He was passionate about art, and was a capable, if unoriginal, draughtsman. While an undergraduate, Faulkner

---

[14] The customs: Carr, 226; their ending: UC:GB4/A1/2 p. 63 and *UCR* 1929/30, p. 4.
[15] The grace: UC:GN4/A1/2 p. 100; Queen's: Magrath 1921: ii. 239; Balliol: Abbot and Campbell 1897: ii. 4 and 21–2.
[16] Parker's *ODNB* entry.
[17] Faulkner: *ODNB* entry, Anon. 1930/1 (which includes Lendon's memoir), and Hannabuss 2000: 453.

FIGURE 16.1 Charles Faulkner, Fellow 1856–92.

came to know William Morris through his childhood friend Edward Burne-Jones, and they became good friends, Faulkner being best man at Morris's wedding to Jane Burden. When, in 1857/8, William Morris and other Pre-Raphaelites decorated the Oxford Union, Faulkner drew in 'all kinds of quaint beasts and birds', as Burne-Jones observed. In 1860, Faulkner helped decorate Morris's Red House, and in 1861 he joined the firm of Morris, Marshall, Faulkner & Co. Business did not agree with Faulkner, and in 1864 he resumed his College work. He remained close to Morris, holidaying with him in Iceland in 1871, and came to share his political beliefs. Faulkner's artistic interests had other consequences: Edward Burne-Jones sent his son Philip to University College in 1880, although Philip Burne-Jones preferred to follow his father's calling, and left without a degree—not before having painted an owl in his rooms in Kitchen Staircase.[18]

Faulkner sometimes clashed with his clerical colleagues. Edwin Lendon, who won a First in natural science, remembered:

[18] Faulkner's friendship with Morris: MacCarthy 1994: 60–5, 131, 151, 159, 166–76, 279–309, and 330–4; Philip Burne-Jones: Moore 1954: 3.

Once at Collections, when I was busy at the Museum and deep in 'Evolution', Dr. William Bright...had made an onslaught on me because I did not know any miracle in one of the Gospels. I remember C. J. Faulkner speaking up for me, and saying that he was quite satisfied with my work.[19]

The Fellowship, however, was changing in Faulkner's direction. Although change did not occur overnight—Peter Medd, the last Fellow elected under the old statutes, only resigned in 1877—it was detectable. First of all, the Fellowship became ever less clerical. The 1857 statutes reserved six of the College's twelve full Fellowships for men in holy orders, but this minimum was reduced to four in 1863, and to two in 1871. Secondly, whereas roughly three-quarters of the Fellows elected in 1808–54 were former undergraduates of the College, this proportion dropped to a quarter in 1856–1914. On the other hand, members of University College could apply for Fellowships all over Oxford. One such was Alfred Robinson (m. 1860), who in 1864 became one of the first non-Wykehamists to be elected a Fellow of New College, where he was Bursar for twenty years and was described by one contemporary as 'the most important person in the College'.[20]

Relations with the College's livings also changed. As fewer Fellows took holy orders, so fewer of them desired a College living: as early as 1860, a rector with no College links had to be appointed to Elton. The last Fellow to move directly to a College living in the traditional way was Peter Medd, instituted at North Cerney in 1876. Only three Fellows later took College livings, the last of them, Vernon Storr (F. 1895–9 and 1905–13), going to Headbourne Worthy in 1910. Medd's move to North Cerney was especially symbolic: he was succeeded as Fellow by Lazarus Fletcher, a Balliol scientist who became Director of the Natural History Museum. In March 1870, a proposal from Plumptre to purchase another living was defeated, and in 1884 the College sold the livings of Elton and Kingsdon (where Peter Hansell was still incumbent).[21]

The College's building activities during the 1850s and 1860s comprised a new Library and buttery, and a dramatic restoration of the Chapel (Figs. 16.2–16.3). The first project, the Library, owed its origins to a pair of unwanted statues. In 1840, the second Lord Eldon had commissioned a pair of statues of his grandfather and Lord Stowell, intending to offer them to New College. The project was dogged by ill-luck: four sculptors (Sir Francis

---

[19] Anon. 1930/1: 20–1. The College Library had acquired a copy of Darwin's *Origin of Species* by July 1870, when Faulkner borrowed it (UC:L1/A1/3).
[20] Reduction in clerical Fellows: UC:GB3/A1/3 pp. 56–9 and 91–4; import and export of Fellows: Appendix II; Alfred Robinson: George 1906: 7.
[21] Information on incumbents of livings taken from lists in the relevant churches, and references in UC:GB3/A1/3; Fletcher's election: UC:GB3/A1/3 p. 134; not purchasing another living: UC:GB4/A1/2 p. 107; selling existing ones: UC:GB4/A1/4 fos. 121[r], 132[r], and 145[r], and UC:EB1/A1/6 pp. 260–1 and 271–2; other colleges selling livings: Green 1957: 231–2 (Lincoln) and Hopkins 2005: 302–3 (Trinity).

THE COLLEGE TRANSFORMED: 1850–1881

FIGURE 16.2 The interior of George Gilbert Scott's Library at University College, in its original form.

FIGURE 16.3 The east end of the College Chapel, as seen after the alterations of George Gilbert Scott.

Chantrey, Allan Cunningham, Musgrave Lewthwaite Watson, and George Nelson) successively worked on the piece, either dying or breaking down along the way. The statues were displayed in the Great Exhibition in 1851; New College now indicated that they had no room for them, and so Lord Eldon turned to University College, although he died in 1854 before negotiations had progressed further. In the spring of 1858 his trustees offered the College £5,000 for a new Library, on condition that the statues be placed in it. The College gladly accepted.[22]

As with the New Building, Plumptre employed an architect of national reputation. George Gilbert Scott would have been known personally to him, having designed the rebuilding of St Mary Magdalen church, the new church at Headington Quarry, and the Martyrs' Memorial, all projects in which Plumptre had been involved. A site was chosen in the Fellows' Garden, on Scott's advice, and work had started by 1859. The addition of extra galleries pushed the final costs over £5,000, but Plumptre made up much of the difference himself. Meanwhile, unfortunately, the old Library was gutted and the space converted into student rooms by 1863/4. George Cox called the new Library 'splendid and tasteful', but in 1895 Goldwin Smith dismissed it as 'more like a mediaeval Chapel than a Library', and the statues, praised by contemporaries, were thought 'very cold' by Nikolaus Pevsner.[23]

Having brought Scott into the College, Plumptre decided to keep him. The area between the Hall and the Chapel was reconfigured: Scott designed a new buttery adjoining the Chapel to the south, and the passageway from the Main Quadrangle to the Library evidently assumed its current form around now, with a new screen and entrance way into the Hall.[24]

However, Scott's most significant work outside the Library—and his most controversial—was in the Chapel. Already, in 1853–5 some new oak desks had been installed there to accommodate the increased membership, but a more serious problem was posed by Henry Gyles's east window, now in sorry condition. In 1924 Harvey Gem (m. 1856) remembered that 'it had quite lost its meaning, [and] the colours had faded'. In October 1859, therefore, Goldwin Smith (whose role in this episode belies his secularist reputation) and William Hedley (F. 1844–63) proposed an appeal to Old Members for the restoration of the Chapel, starting with the east window. The style of the mid-seventeenth century had fallen out of fashion, for the Fellows asked

---

[22] The statues: Bayley 1959a; the Eldon Trustees' gift: UC:FA8/1/C1/1–2.
[23] Scott in Oxford: Howell 2000: 737–47; site of the Library: UC:GB4/A1/2 p. 38; costs as of March 1863: UC:GB4/A1/2 p. 56; rooms in Kitchen Staircase: UC:BU3/F3/42 fo. 34ʳ; opinions of the Library and statues: Cox 1870: 277, Smith 1895: 147–8, and Sherwood and Pevsner 1974: 212.
[24] Bills for this work: UC:FA1/F8/1 nos. 17–18; estimated cost (just under £650): UC:GB4/A1/2 p. 57.

'for aid in putting the Chapel into a better condition, and one more in accordance with the improved taste and feeling of the present day'.[25]

In 1862 the College approved Scott's plans for a marble and stone reredos and arcading on the east wall of the Chapel, and Plumptre agreed to pay for the new east window, designed by Clayton and Bell. Scott also installed a new roof. The Fellows were so pleased that in 1864 they asked Scott to extend his arcading along the north and south sides of the Chapel to meet the oak pews. Meanwhile the old communion table was given to Hubberholme Church, and the old panelling at the east end, with James Griffith's pokerwork picture of Jesus, put into storage. Finally, in March 1866 an Old Member, John Gilliatt (m. 1848) paid for Clayton and Bell to install stained glass in the little window at the east end of the south side.[26]

Scott's work in the Chapel has received much—justified—criticism. Whatever the intrinsic merits of the richly decorated and highly coloured marble and stone of his reredos and arcading, their high Victorian style clashed discordantly with the seventeenth-century interior. Even if a new east window was required, the decision to give it five lights rather than three has made it too large, and its style is at odds with the van Linge windows; and the new roof, with its large stone corbels, is also totally out of character. As Harvey Gem wrote:

> Of course it had been a mistake to let loose Gilbert Scott upon a Jacobean Chapel. Though excellent in his own line of strict Gothic, he was likely to damage a Jacobean Chapel, & he obliterated parts of it.[27]

Happier changes occurred in the liturgical life of the Chapel. There had been no music there at least since the Reformation, but in April 1863 the College agreed 'to introduce some amount of music in the services in the College chapel'. Canticles were to be sung on Sunday evening, and copies of the newly published *Hymns Ancient and Modern* acquired. Soon afterwards a harmonium was hired. In 1865 Goldwin Smith, no less, arranged to defray the costs of a new organ from his Fellowship stipend. It was designed by J. W. Walker & Sons, and had one keyboard only. The pipes were installed in the false window on the north side, hiding the painting of Lot's wife, and the keyboard installed at ground level, where the organist and organ blower took up four stalls. Although a good organ in itself, its position made it difficult to be heard properly. In the 1870s the College even employed an

---

[25] Oak stalls: UC:BU2/F1/7 fos. 48^v and 56^v (some of which were still there in the 1950s (*UCR* 1951/2, pp. 13–14)); Gem's account: UC:FA5/3/C2/1; appeal to Old Members: UC:GB4/A1/2 pp. 40 and 44, and UC:FA5/2/F1/1; dislike of seventeenth-century style: Howell 2000: 759.

[26] Scott's plans: UC:GB4/A1/2 p. 48; Plumptre's gift: UC:GB4/A1/2 p. 50; extension of Scott's work: UC:GB4/A1/2 p. 66; donation to Hubberholme: UC:GB4/A1/2 p. 67; Gillatt's gift: UC:GB4/A1/2 pp. 81 and 90.

[27] UC:FA5/3/C2/1.

organist and some boy choristers in the Chapel, although the latter were dispensed with after a few years.[28]

Plumptre's final architectural initiative reflected the increasing size of the College (see Graph 15.1). The house immediately to the east of Logic Lane, known as the 'Alfred's Head', was part of the property administered by the trustees of John Browne. In 1867 the College took over the lease on this house, annexing it for student accommodation, and by 1868 there were sixteen rooms available in what was now called University Hall. From October 1874, there was a new College official, the 'Dean of the Hall', who acted as a Dean in this Hall rather as the main Dean acted in the main College.[29]

Plumptre's College continued, like New College, Balliol, and Christ Church, to have an unusually large concentration of undergraduates from the major public schools. Plumptre's admission books show that, of the 50 (out of 84) undergraduates who came up in 1853–6 and the 60 (out of 85) in 1863–6 whose previous education is known, almost half came from the so-called 'Clarendon' Schools. The College remained popular: even in the 1860s, some undergraduates' families were putting their names down up to four years in advance of their coming up.[30]

This generation of undergraduates read a far wider range of subjects than its predecessors. From 1850 examinations had been established in natural science and a joint school in law and modern history, although until 1864, one could only get an honours degree if one sat exams in Literae Humaniores and then in mathematics and physics, natural science, or law and history. Also in 1850 a new intermediate exam, Honour Moderations ('Mods'), was introduced. In due course other undergraduate honours schools were created, such as theology in 1869, and separate schools for law and modern history in 1872. A similar widening of the syllabus also took place in the pass degree. University College had to react to these changes, establishing a lectureship in modern history in 1853. Unfortunately, it took time for the tutors—who still took complete responsibility for all College teaching—to match these new

---

[28] Hymnbooks: UC:GB4/A1/2 p. 48; harmonium: UC:BU2/F1/7 fo. 127^v; organ: UC:GB4/A1/2 pp. 73 and 79 and Paul 1954/5: 70–1; organist and choirboys: UC:GB4/A1/3 p. 94 (March 1873), and UC:BU2/F1/7 fos. 211^r, 219^r, 227^r, 235^r, 242^v, and 250^v (College accounts from 1873/4 to 1878/9); music in other colleges: Bury 1952: 60–1 (harmonium and choristers introduced at Corpus Christi, Cambridge, in 1856 and organ in 1861), Brooke 1996: 215–17 (sung services introduced at Gonville and Caius in the 1860s); Twigg 1987: 265 (choristers at Queens' in the 1870s); Green 1957: 228 (undergraduate requests at Lincoln to sing hymns in the 1860s refused); and Curthoys 2000: 147–8.

[29] Annexation of property: UC:GB4/A1/2 pp. 86 and 89; number of rooms: UC:BU3/F3/47 pp. 66–8; Dean of Hall: UC:GB3/A1/3 p. 123.

[30] Plumptre's notebooks: UC:J4/A1/2–3; the nine Clarendon Schools (Charterhouse, Eton, Harrow, Merchant Taylors', Rugby, St Paul's, Shrewsbury, Westminster, and Winchester) took their name from the Clarendon Commission of 1868 which investigated the state of the public schools, based on these nine; context: Honey and Curthoys 2000: 550.

demands. Alongside such paragons as William Bright or Charles Faulkner, there was also Thomas Shadforth (m. 1834; F. 1839–52; Tutor 1846–58), who, according to Augustus Hare:

has the character of being universally beloved and having no authority at all. The undergraduates knock at his door and walk in. He sits at a table in the middle, they on cane-chairs all round the room, and his lecture is a desultory conversation.... But he dawdles and twaddles so much over details, we have generally done very little before the hour ends, when he says, 'I will not detain you any longer.'[31]

The 1850s and 1860s also saw changes in undergraduate life outside work. Riding remained popular with those who could afford it: two undergraduates who came up in 1859, John Hill and John Horsfall, both kept photograph albums which show them and their friends keeping horses in Oxford and attending meetings of the South Oxfordshire Hunt (University College even held annual steeplechases in the early 1860s).[32] This was, however, a time when competitive sports, especially rowing, came into their own. There was one especially important innovation in rowing. In 1856 the London livery companies discontinued their annual river procession to mark the appointment of a Lord Mayor, each company travelling in its own grand barge. The companies began to sell their barges, and several colleges acquired them to moor by the river, where they provided a landing stage for boats, changing rooms on the ground floor, and—no less important—space on the roof from which supporters could watch the races. Some companies had already disposed of their barges, University College Boat Club being one of the first colleges to take an interest when it acquired the Merchant Taylors' barge in 1854 (Fig. 16.4). In 1873 it replaced this with the former Stationers' barge, but in 1878 it abandoned this barge too, and commissioned a brand new barge from John Oldrid Scott (Fig. 17.6). Queen's seems to have been the first college to commission a new barge, in 1872, so University College Boat Club was quick to follow a new trend.[33]

By the mid-1850s the Boat Club had become an important part of undergraduate life. Augustus Hare was unimpressed to find that his first visitor, on his arrival in College, was a member of the Club inviting him to row—an invitation Hare swiftly refused—but he could not ignore the fact that Eights Week had become a major part of the social calendar. One sign of the club's self-awareness is that it is the earliest known College society to keep records of its affairs, with extant photograph albums and captains' notebooks reaching back to the 1860s. The notebooks bring to life the undergraduates' own

---

[31] Examinations: Curthoys 1997b: 352–5 and Jenkyns and Murray 1997: 514; history lecturer (unnamed): UC:GB4/A1/2 p. 26; Shadforth: Hare 1896–1900: i. 415.

[32] Hill's and Horsfall's albums: UC:P4/P/1 and UC:P167/P1/1.

[33] The livery companies' barges: Palmer 1997, with 46–9, 126–7, and 150 about the Merchant Taylor's and Stationers' barges; University College's barges: Sherriff 2003: 7, 36–44, and 108, and *passim* on college boat clubs and their barges.

FIGURE 16.4 The University College Eight of 1862, seated in the bow of the former Merchant Taylors' Barge.

language of the 1860s and 1870s: in particular, colleges get nicknames, like 'Belial' or 'Quaggers', and, of course, for the first time, 'Univ.' itself.[34]

'Quaggers', first recorded in the early 1880s, is typical of a famous Oxford fad of the later nineteenth century for creating nicknames ending in '-er' (such as 'brekker', 'rugger', or, for wastepaper basket, 'wagger-pagger-bagger'). In the 1920s, the antiquarian Falconer Madan specifically credited University College as the source of this slang, claiming that it was introduced there in Michaelmas Term 1875 by a group of old boys from Rugby, and the 1933 Supplement to the *Oxford English Dictionary* followed his suggestion. Of the twenty-four people who came up to University College that term, at least five did come from Rugby, so that there were sufficient Rugbeians to import the slang and spread it, but the captain's notebook, in recording the College's celebrations on going Head of the River in Torpids in March 1872, having proclaimed ecstatically,

HEAD OF THE RIVER
for the 4th year in succession
HOOROO

[34] Invitation to row: Hare 1896–1900: i. 414 and 419; UC:O4/A1/1 is the notebook covering the years 1864–92.

WELL ROWED EVERYBODY
Splice the Mainbrace

went on to note that 'The Bursar Fogger was in great form'—'Fogger', of course, being Charles Faulkner (p. 371). This shows that some 'Univ.' men were using the new slang at least three years before Madan claimed, so that the matter needs further investigation.[35]

Oarsmen took their sport seriously. One undergraduate from Plumptre's last years, Charles Cree (m. 1868), kept a diary in 1871, which reveals him as an enthusiastic rower, taking to the water most days. He wrote of one outing on 25 January 1871:

After lunch went to the river, and rowed twice to Iffley. Good hard frost the water freezing on the blades of the oars. My hand blistered and a great tendency to become like a cherub, i.e. by losing the power of sitting.[36]

Cree was up during arguably the most successful period in the College's rowing history. Having gone Head of the River in both Torpids and Eights in 1869, University College remained Head in Torpids every year until 1873, and went Head in Eights in 1869–71, 1874–5, and 1877–8. Cree remembered the celebrations after Eights Week in 1871:

Univ. Head in *the EIGHTS*. Univ, though Balliol came near them were never in danger.... The Eight supped with Snell and the rest of us joined them after supper, and had a glorious evening. Singing and shouting as well as our voices would let us - Everything went off well no one being drunk.[37]

Other competitive sports came in during the 1860s and 1870s. In the 1860s, for example, the College was holding athletic competitions. University College appears to have been particularly sports-minded: the Oxford teams in the first Varsity matches in athletics (1864), rugby (1872), football (1874), and golf (1878) all included at least one member of University College. It has been suggested that this enthusiasm became self-perpetuating: as public schools took on young masters, who had been keen sportsmen at university, so they popularized competitive sports among their pupils, who in turn came up to university eager to continue the tradition. The rise of sports may have affected the College in other ways: dinner time was moved later to 6 p.m. in 1868 and 7 p.m. in 1882, a move reflected in other colleges—and a later dinner gave more time for sports in the afternoons. However, this growth of interest in sport happened without any signs of interest or support from the Master or Fellows.[38]

---

[35] The '-er' suffix: Madan 1925: 162–3, and the *Oxford English Dictionary*, on-line edition (accessed December 2007), under '-ER *suffix*⁶'; quotations taken from UC:O4/A1/1.
[36] Cree 1974: 14.
[37] Cree 1974: 31.
[38] Athletics: UC:P167/P1/1 fos. 44ᵛ–45ʳ; early Blues: Abrahams and Bruce-Kerr 1931: 2, 306, 330, and 358; growth in sports: Chandler 1988; changes in dinner times: UC:GB4/A1/2 p. 100

Undergraduates of a more intellectual bent organized their own amusements. In the early 1860s there was a University College Debating Society; records of its meetings from 1862 show that their members discussed such varied topics as: which side to support in the American Civil War (neither); the dangers of prize-fighting; the abolition of capital punishment (defeated); and a claim that the university 'gives too exclusive an encouragement to classical education' (defeated). Undergraduates of the 1860s also participated in amateur dramatics, performing mainly farces and melodramas, and assuming both male and female roles. University College's undergraduates were not immune: extant photographs depict productions featuring members of the College, including some in 'drag', either as old dragons or romantic leads (Fig. 16.5). These drama groups, however, were banned at the end of the decade, following suspicions (not, apparently, unjustified) regarding the potential for scandal in all-male productions.[39]

There was plenty of time for the Victorian undergraduate to enjoy himself. Although mornings tended to be devoted to work, it was customary to devote the afternoon to exercise. The athletic Charles Cree, of course, would go to the gym or go rowing, in all weathers. Even the comparatively unclubbable Augustus Hare celebrated his coming of age in 1855 with a convivial 'wine', while Charles Cree's diary is filled with tales of convivial evenings spent among friends.[40]

These changes in undergraduate life are easily observable; another change is rather more intangible. Until now, there have been few indications that the undergraduates of University College saw themselves as a clearly defined group. Undergraduates had come together to rebel against Nathan Wetherell's plans to increase their workload, or play jokes on George Rowley, but undergraduates of the 1860s appear more aware of themselves as a body which could decide and act for itself. It is as though the discipline required to think as one in team sports started to affect people in other areas of their lives. An early example of this self-awareness was a remarkable campaign in 1864 which substantially changed the conditions of employment of the College's servants.

Some changes to the servants' lot had already taken place—by the late 1850s there was a College Bedmakers' Fund, which provided for salaries for the College's scouts, to supplement tips from Fellows and undergraduates, and there were pension arrangements for servants who had given up work

and UC:GB4/A1/4 fo. 59ʳ; other colleges: Magrath 1921: ii. 189 (dinner time at Queen's moved to 6 p.m. in 1865 and to 7 p.m. in 1878) and Hopkins 2005: 250 (dinner time at Trinity moved to 6 p.m. in 1867); reason for change: Twigg 1987: 252–62.

[39] Debating Society: UC:O12/A1/1–2; drama: MCA MC:FA1/9/2P/1 fo. 61 no 2; acting elsewhere: Carpenter 1985: 12–14.

[40] Hopkins 2005: 246, gives a similar account of the daily routine at Trinity in 1867; 'wines': Hare 1896–1900: i. 485.

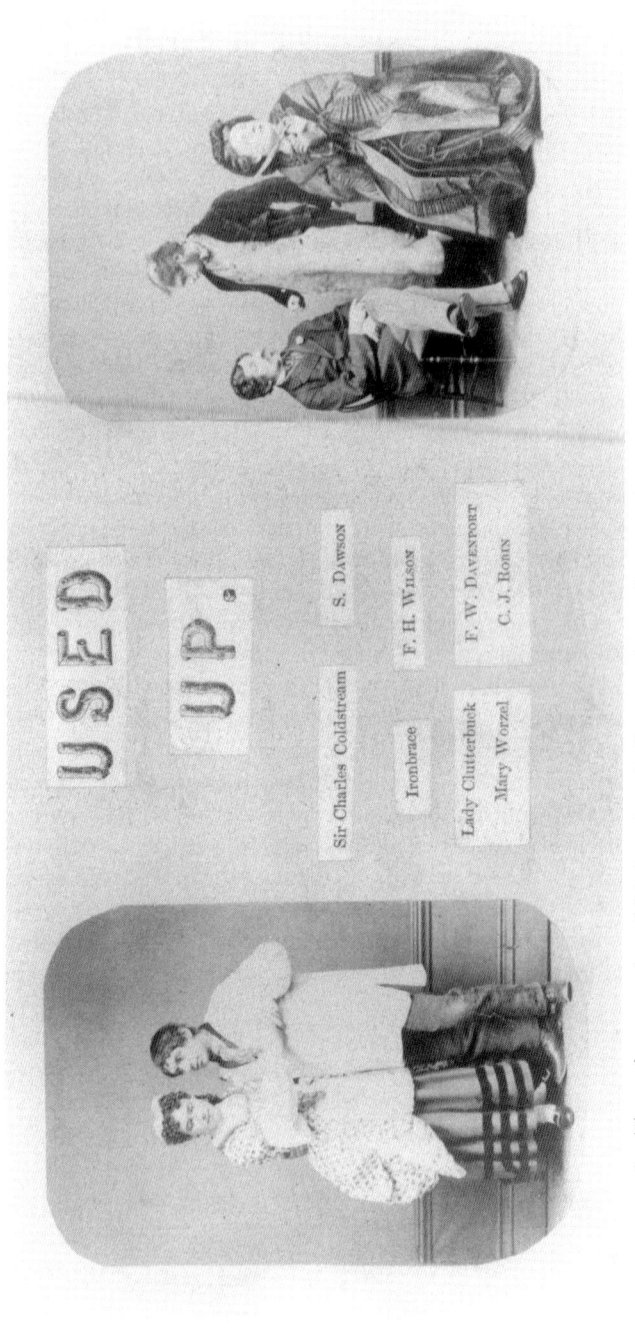

FIGURE 16.5 Two photographs of University College undergraduates taking part in a production of 'Used Up': A Comic Drama, by Charles James Mathews, in the late 1860s. The actors named are: Francis William Davenport, m. 1865, Stewart Dawson, m. 1866, Charles Robin, m. 1867, and Francis Wilson, m. 1866.

due to ill-health—but much of a servant's income still depended on perquisites and other unofficial sources of money. Such a system was open to abuse, and early in 1864, a meeting of exasperated College undergraduates appointed a Committee under the future Fellow of New College, Alfred Robinson, to examine the matter. On the Committee's advice, it was agreed unanimously to print a petition setting out their grievances, signed by Robinson and three others, and to present it to the Master and Fellows.[41]

The petition paints a damning picture of the College's servants (and of the undergraduates' view of them). It is suggested, drily, that 'when Scouts became unable or unwilling to perform their duties properly, they be dismissed'. Dinners in Hall come in for especial criticism—the food should be served with covers; the beer is bad and expensive; and the cheese 'seldom, if ever, good'—and particular wrath is directed against the Cook:

> The Cook has contrived to secure the universal disapprobation of the College. It is generally agreed, that his puddings and potatoes are bad, his vegetables scanty, and his coffee undrinkable.

The main problem in Hall, however, were the so-called 'remains'. It was customary that, after dinner, all left-over food—the 'remains'—could be taken away by the serving staff as a perquisite. This system was vulnerable to abuse: it was easy to produce far more food than was required, so that the remains would be agreeably large, while College members were charged for everything which was served. Furthermore, as the petition observed, the serving staff displayed an unwelcome eagerness to exercise their rights:

> When the Fellows have left the Hall, the scouts, with the kitchen servants, crowd round the open door: this is a very unpleasant and unseemly sight at any time, and still more so on Strangers' nights [nights when guests were admitted].

The petition had an effect: almost at once the Fellows ordered the Cook to improve his work or be replaced. After a year's deliberation, they issued new regulations: 'remains' were abolished—uneaten food was to be taken back to the kitchen, and the Cook had to pay the College for it—and the serving staff were given a proportionate increase in their wages. By 1867/8, the servants' wages are recorded in a more regular manner, and more servants are on the College's payroll. There was one other action which was thought an improvement: in November 1867, the College formally invited its servants to attend Sunday evening service, albeit only in the Antechapel.[42]

---

[41] Bedmakers' Fund: see, for example, UC:BU3/F3/27 pp. 23–4; pensions: UC:GB4/A1/2 p. 43; undergraduates' meeting: UC:O12/A1/2 (at the back of the book); the petition: UC:P41/N/1. By now, scouts were almost entirely male. At Cambridge, by contrast, the equivalent duties were divided between the 'gyp', usually male, and the 'bedmaker', usually female (Searby 1997: 597–8).

[42] The Fellows' deliberations: UC:GB4/A1/2 pp. 62–4 and 70–1; new servants' payroll: UC:BU1/F1/7 fo. 162ᵛ; servants in Chapel: UC:GB4/A1/2 p. 91. University College was not alone in its catering troubles: similar tales from the 1860s can be found at Green 1957: 282

FIGURE 16.6 H. Neville, scout of John Hill, m. 1859, from the latter's photograph album.

Not only did the reforms of the 1860s and 1870s change the financial circumstances of the College's servants, but they raised their profile within the College. College servants of the middle of the century, both in fact and fiction, enjoy an unhappy reputation as fleecers of the men whom they serve. This was not wholly fair—John Hill included pictures of his scout and the head porter in his photograph album (Fig. 16.6; the earliest known photos of servants from this College)—but by the end of the century a closer and more friendly relationship had certainly grown up, especially between the undergraduates and the scouts and porters.[43]

Undergraduate unity also worked in more subversive ways. On the morning of 23 March 1868, three Fellows, an undergraduate, and a porter had the outer doors of their rooms screwed up.[44] The Dean, Peter Medd, found himself in an episode worthy of a bedroom farce:

The Dean, hearing the noise made in the act of fixing the screws in the door which leads from the staircase (no. iv) into his bedroom reached the outer door of his lecture room (on staircase iii) in time to prevent its being fastened. Pursuing the person whom he found at work, he caught him in the quadrangle. After holding him for some time he let him go, without being able to recognise him, as it was quite dark.

(Lincoln), Bill and Mason 1970: 132–41 (Christ Church), and, more generally, Curthoys 2000: 145–6 and Searby 1997: 142–6.

[43] Hill's photograph album: UC:P4/P/1.
[44] This episode is told in UC:GB4/A1/2 pp. 95–7.

On the following day, Plumptre himself addressed the undergraduates, expressing his displeasure at the incident and his regret that no one had come forward. However, the undergraduates stood up to the Master, for they wrote to him and the Fellows, regretting what had happened, but explaining they were influenced 'by the disapproval felt by the College at a recent decision [unknown] of the common room'. The signatories disassociated themselves from the action, and wished to re-establish good relations between Fellows and undergraduates. The apology was accepted, but the situation left unresolved: the undergraduates were clearly not going to name any names, and the Fellows were in no position to extract them.

A few weeks later, two more breaches of discipline were reported.[45] Another Fellow had his room screwed up, but in addition, 'on several occasions lately Mr. Crawford's door has been broken, his furniture damaged, and his person attacked'. 'Mr Crawford' was John Crawford, a Gunsley Exhibitioner who had only come up that April. The screwing-up came to nothing: the College now threatened to order all undergraduates not reading for exams to leave Oxford, but, after an emergency meeting between about forty undergraduates and Goldwin Smith, acting as intermediary, in which the undergraduates admitted (or at least claimed) that they did not know who had committed this act, and expressed their disapproval both of the act, and the offenders' unwillingness to come forward, this order was rescinded. The Fellows, however, reacted very differently towards the bullying of John Crawford—one of the first such instances recorded in the College. Within a day of the incident being reported, four undergraduates were sent down, and five more rusticated. One wonders, too, whether the undergraduates were more willing to cooperate in these circumstances. Significantly, John Crawford had been to Maidstone Grammar School, but his tormentors included two Etonians, and one old boy each from Marlborough and Repton. Crawford himself remained in residence (in one of the cheapest rooms in College) for three years, but eventually took his BA in 1875 as a non-Collegiate student.

The attitude displayed by the Fellows in these cases is revealing. Goldwin Smith remembers a colleague observing to the undergraduates, quite possibly in relation to these two incidents, 'Boys will be boys, and if you play pranks on me or my colleagues you will be punished if we are so unlucky as to catch you; but we are not insulted. Your fellow-student, if you maltreat him, is insulted. We are the guardians of the honour and feelings of everybody under this roof, and we mean to fulfil our trust.'[46] In a few years' time, under a different regime, when one side had come to take a different view of such actions, but the other had not, this would lead to trouble.

[45] These episodes are told in UC:GB4/A1/2 pp. 98–9.
[46] Smith 1910: 77.

THE NEW BROOM: THE ARRIVAL OF GEORGE BRADLEY

Frederick Plumptre died in the Lodgings on 21 November 1870. *The Times* for 22 November 1870, recalling that his 'tall figure was familiar to all Oxonians for the last 50 years', described him as 'a man of great courtesy and kindness, very moderate in his religious opinions, and much and deservedly respected throughout his College and the whole University'. Generous to the end to the College he had known for almost sixty years, he endowed exhibitions and prizes to University College in his will. In some respects he had become a figure of the past, yet this kindly fossil had presented the new University Museum with two of its magnificent interior column shafts, and urged that its new keeper should receive a salary appropriate to a professor. Furthermore, shortly before his death, Plumptre had written a memorandum on the study of science at Oxford, recommending that 'some greater encouragement for the study of Natural Science should be given in the University by establishing a larger number of Scholarships or Exhibitions to be appropriated for Proficiency in this department'. Plumptre had proved himself a better Master—and reformer—than his stiff and old-fashioned ways might suggest. He held the Fellowship together through a time of great upheaval, attracting some first-rate Fellows along the way, and he had done much to reawaken the College from its slumber of the previous decades. A touching tribute was paid by John Watts far away in Dorset, who erected a window in his church at Tarrant Gunville in memory of Plumptre, 'a man generally beloved and deeply lamented by his friend J. W. Rector'.[47]

The election of Plumptre's successor proved as significant and divisive as that of Nathan Wetherell a century earlier. Once again there was a choice of futures for the College, between Peter Medd, the upholder of clerical tradition, and Arthur Stanley's pupil, George Granville Bradley. In 1846, while still a Fellow, Bradley had become an assistant Master at Rugby, and in 1858 he was appointed headmaster of Marlborough. He was a known progressive: in 1866, when the Regius Professorship of Ecclesiastical History was vacant, William Bright anxiously observed that 'the Liberals are again stirring for Bradley'.[48]

As in 1764, the election proved close. Four Fellows—all clergymen—voted for Medd (including Medd himself), and six—including the known liberals—for Bradley. As an obituary to Medd commented, he 'was too much wedded to the old traditions, while others, whose votes determined the matter, had no sympathy with his or any ecclesiastical tendencies'. Medd chose not to make life difficult for his successor; he had just been appointed to the living of

---

[47] Death: UC:GB3/A1/3 pp. 83; bequests: UC:BE38 (*passim*) and UC:GB3/A1/3 pp. 87–91 (although the final sums were less than had been expected); University Museum: Morrell 2005: 312 and 314; Natural Science: UC:MA40/C2/13.
[48] Bright on Bradley: Kidd 1903: 265 (also Bill and Mason 1970: 86).

FIGURE 16.7 George Granville Bradley, m. 1840, Fellow 1844–50, and Master 1870–81.

Barnes, which he was allowed to hold with his Fellowship, and, on the day after Bradley's election, he resigned as Dean and Tutor and moved to his parish.[49]

What, then, of the new Master, George Bradley (Fig. 16.7)? All agreed that he had been a signal success as a headmaster, making Marlborough one of the foremost schools in England.[50] As well as being an excellent teacher, he was a tough disciplinarian. One of his greatest weapons was his sarcasm; even admirers admitted 'his tongue was a whip which sometimes pained boys'. He sometimes used the grand gesture: on hearing that some Marlburians had been poaching on a nearby estate, Bradley strode into the dining hall, and demanded that the culprits should come before him within an hour, or else. The names were given up at once. He was also firm with this staff, forbidding them to smoke or wear light coats when on duty, so that, as one biographer wrote, 'he was both loved and feared by his Masters as by his boys'.[51] Bradley was evidently selected to shake things up: the liberals wanted someone more

---

[49] Votes cast: UC:GB3/A1/3 pp. 84–5; obituary quoted in Whale 1983: 269; living: UC:GB3/A1/3 p. 82; resignation of offices: UC:GB4/A1/3 p. 41.
[50] Bradley at Marlborough: How 1904: 226–69 and Hinde 1992: 63–75.
[51] How 1904: 243 (sarcasm); 249 (grand gesture); 252–3 (staff).

dynamic than Plumptre, and a reforming public school headmaster was thought just right.

Charles Cree, the keen rower, was unimpressed with his first encounter with the Master:

> Came in contact with Bradley the new Master for the first time. He appointed hours for a lecture in the 'Acts', and gave us a very 'mealy' speech expressing his hopes that we should not find too much of his old profession in him, and finishing up by saying that a little weakness of his was love of punctuality.... I hope and trust my first impressions may prove false as regards the worthy gentleman.[52]

It quickly became clear that Bradley had trouble distinguishing the treatment of undergraduates from the treatment of schoolboys. He first discovered this with regard to the keeping of dogs in the College. This had been a long-running battle—back in 1854, Plumptre had tried to ban them—but in March 1871 Bradley declared it illegal from the start of next term to keep dogs, putting up a notice to that effect. In response the notice was torn down, and that evening, according to Charles Cree, 'great howlings were heard in quad demonstrative of the indignation felt by certain members of the College'. Bradley then tried a Marlborough method on the undergraduates:

> After Hall Bradley made a long speech and a great fool of himself about the notice about dogs being torn down. His speech came to nothing in the end and only gave rise to a vast amount of noise in the evening.[53]

Bradley had to learn that headmasterly wrath did not work on undergraduates like Charles Cree. In March 1871, Cree missed one of Bradley's lectures due to a hangover. As he wrote, 'Master sent for me for cutting lecture but the concert unavoidably prevented my going to him.' On the following day, he did see the Master, and nonchalantly recorded: 'I let him talk without saying much as it seemed to give him satisfaction and certainly did not hurt me.'[54]

Regular absentees from Chapel were summoned and asked innocently whether 'the abstention was due to principle or mere indolence'. At other times, Bradley went for the jugular:

> [Bradley] one day sent for an undergraduate whose batells had been very high...and on the man appearing, Bradley apostrophised him thus: 'I only sent for you, sir, to tell you that you are the typical glutton of the college!'—a remark remembered with indignation to this day.[55]

---

[52] Cree 1974: 14 (entry for 24 January).
[53] Plumptre and dogs: UC:P167/P1/1 fos. 48ᵛ–49ʳ; Bradley's notice: UC:GB4/A1/2 p. 111; undergraduate reaction: Cree 1974: 24–5.
[54] Cree 1974: 23–4.
[55] Absentees: *Pall Mall Gazette*, 1 September 1881; gluttony: How 1904: 266; Bradley's headmasterly ways in general: Mallet 1932: 44.

Bradley was determined to improve the academic standing of the College. Leading from the front, he gave lectures himself on theology and Greek literature. He also reformed the College's lecture system. Although undergraduates had been able to attend lectures in other colleges (as with Stanley's lectures in the 1840s), this was entirely an unofficial arrangement. In 1871, however, University College made a formal agreement with Balliol and New College to make their lectures open to each other's undergraduates. A surviving register of lecture attendance in 1871–4 shows men from New College, Balliol, and University College attending lectures at all three colleges. By 1873 men from Trinity, Exeter, and Worcester were also joining the scheme.[56]

This was a significant reform: when college tutors had to teach everything, it took someone with the brilliance and application of a William Scott or Arthur Stanley to lift lectures from a dreary mediocrity. Now that students could attend lectures at different colleges, individual tutors could lecture on a narrower—and better prepared—range of subjects. In turn there would be less need for private coaching, when the student with intellectual ambitions could 'shop around' for the best lecturers.[57]

Undergraduates were kept up to the mark in other ways. In the late 1860s Edwin Lendon had been saved by Charles Faulkner from trouble in an end-of-term collection. His account suggests something akin to a reading of reports, but Charles Cree's account of his collections in March 1871 ('Then collections in History Eng. and French. Lunched with Senior. Afterwards collection in Roman Law') implies something more like an actual examination. A still more important aspect of the modern university is the weekly tutorial between don and one or two undergraduates; unfortunately, it is very hard to trace the origins of the modern tutorial, comparatively recent though it is. At University College, for example, it is not known whether there were tutorials before 1870, but there is evidence for their existence under Bradley.[58]

Bradley's methods clearly worked. In 1851–65, just over one-third of University College men were taking honours degrees, as compared with three-quarters of Balliol men. Matters had improved by 1866–70, when just over half of University College's undergraduates achieved this. Under Bradley, however, just over two-thirds of undergraduates coming up in 1871–5 achieved honours degrees, and just over three-quarters of those coming up in 1876–80 did so. This was well above the current Oxford average of half of all

[56] Lecture agreement: UC:GB4/A1/3 p. 61 and George 1906: 35–8; lecture register: UC:J7/A1/1 (among the Balliol undergraduates attending Bradley's lectures on Sophocles was the future Prime Minister H. H. Asquith).

[57] See further Engel 1983: 81–93.

[58] Collections: Cree 1974: 25 (although it is not known when collections started at University College, they were held at Christ Church in the eighteenth century, and at Trinity in the early nineteenth (Hopkins 2005: 208)); origins of tutorials: Curthoys 2000: 133–4; at University College: Brock 2000a: 51.

undergraduates taking honours degrees, and University College came to be regarded as a progressive college alongside Corpus, Balliol, and New.[59]

A glimpse of how University College saw itself early in Bradley's Mastership is afforded by a grand 'Millenary Dinner' held in the Hall on 12 June 1872 to mark the College's supposed one thousandth anniversary, and attended by such eminent Old Members and former Fellows as Arthur Stanley, Robert Lowe (currently Chancellor of the Exchequer), and Piers Claughton (now the retired Bishop of Colombo).[60] Like many grand Victorian dinners, it provided a pretext for immense speechifying, with some thirteen speeches recorded in the papers. There was some tongue in cheek about the anniversary: legend has it that the Professor of Modern History sent the College some burnt cakes for the occasion. Bradley himself admitted that:

> there might be an infinite divergence of opinion on the story which connected the College with King Alfred; some might think it a deliberate falsehood and others a pleasing legend; others an undoubted fact; but whatever might be their opinions on this interesting question, no one in dining there that day pledged himself to any one of those beliefs rather than to any other.

Indeed, King Alfred was being quietly dropped: by 1895, Goldwin Smith was sure that William of Durham was the true founder of the College.[61]

More serious matters were alluded to. In proposing the health of the Visitor, Bradley expressed gratitude that the Lord Chancellor as *de facto* Visitor had been 'most willing to further those schemes of improvement which the college had lately originated with a view to increased efficiency and the carrying out of liberal principles in its functions as an educating body'. When proposing 'The Church', Bradley faced up to the increasing secularization of Oxford:

> while acknowledging that the old connection between the Universities and the Church, which had made the position of a Fellowship almost synonymous with Holy Orders, was passing out of date, [he] drew attention to the benefits which the college had received from clerical benefactors, from William of Durham down to the late honoured Master. If in future times the severance between the clerical and a University life should still continue, religion need not suffer or feel itself banished from practical influence on college life.

In reply, Piers Claughton tactfully mentioned the unease felt in some quarters at these changes:

> the change referred to by the chairman had come so suddenly and forcibly that they must bear with the clergy if they showed signs of alarm. They had to stand outside, where before they were able to stand inside, but their assistance was still essential.

---

[59] Balliol: Prest 2000: 160; wider context: Curthoys 1997*b*: 360 and Harvie 2000: 93.
[60] What follows is drawn from a report of the event in the *Guardian* of 19 June 1872. UC:P167/P1/1 fos. 51ᵛ–52ʳ include some ephemera relating to the dinner.
[61] Smith 1895: 50.

Claughton's anxiety was justifiable. In 1871, all remaining religious restrictions on either coming to or taking degrees from Oxford and Cambridge had at last been abolished, so that not only non-Anglicans but even non-Christians could be admitted and become fellows. In October 1872 the College relaxed its rules on Chapel attendance. Although both Sunday services remained compulsory, unless undergraduates' parents asked otherwise, the weekday services now became optional, and undergraduates could instead present themselves for a roll call at 8 a.m.[62]

Sadly, there was one notable absentee from the Millenary Dinner. After Travers Twiss had married and resigned his Fellowship in 1863, his career had prospered, and he was knighted in 1867. Unfortunately, a blackmailer then spread dark rumours about Lady Twiss's sexual past, and the Twisses eventually sued for libel in March 1872. After a few days, Lady Twiss fled abroad, abandoning the case, an action which implied, rightly or wrongly, some truth in the allegations. For his wife's sake, Twiss resigned all his public offices, and spent the rest of his life in scholarly retirement, cutting links with old friends. Goldwin Smith sadly remembered how, some years later, when he saw Twiss in the Strand and crossed over to greet him, Twiss promptly disappeared into the crowd.[63] At the Millenary Dinner, held so soon after his wife's disgrace, Twiss could not even be named: Arthur Stanley had to make do with a graceful but oblique tribute to 'one who is not and could not be here today, but whom I cannot fail to recall with grateful remembrance'.

Twiss's legacy of reform, however, lived on, for also in 1872 the College revised its statutes once more. The new statutes contained two major changes. The first stated that a two-thirds majority of the Master and Fellows might now elect a Fellow who was married or otherwise ineligible, on condition that he either performed a College office, was a Professor in the university, or was 'a person of special eminence in literature, science or art'. For the first time, therefore, a Fellow of University College need not resign his post on marrying. One Fellow quickly took advantage of the new rule. Charles Septimus Medd, brother of Peter and Fellow since 1864, had married in 1871, and been granted the usual year's grace. In 1872 Medd successfully asked to have the new exemption concerning marriage applied to him, so that he retained his Fellowship until 1874, thus becoming the first married Fellow of University College.[64]

---

[62] UC:GB4/A1/2 p. 122. In 1879, only one Sunday service was made compulsory (UC:GB4/A1/3 p. 263).
[63] The case's sensational details were fully recorded in *The Times* for March 1872; Smith's encounter: Smith 1910: 87.
[64] Medd's change of mind: UC:GB3/A1/3 pp. 91 and 103. By way of comparison, at Queen's, permission to marry was granted just to a few senior Fellows in 1881, and Lincoln's celibacy rules were only lifted in 1898 (Hodgkin 1949: 186–7 and Green 1979: 525).

This innovation was controversial, even among reformers. From across the Atlantic, Goldwin Smith described the marriage of Fellows as 'a pity', but 'necessary to secure teachers permanently devoted to their calling, which the celibate Fellows and Tutors of former days could not be'. More pragmatically, George Bradley's daughter Margaret, who later married a Fellow and future President of Trinity, Henry Woods, thought that the lifting of the marriage restrictions greatly broadened and improved university society.[65]

The second innovation limited the tenure of Fellowships. Fellows now had to vacate their posts after eight years, but any period during which they had held a College office was not counted. A Fellow who held any College office for ten years could remain a Fellow 'for a period from the day of his election equal in all to twice the period of such service'; and had he been an officer for twenty, then he could hold his Fellowship for life. The day of the Fellow who took no part in College life, but merely drew his annual stipend, was over. Where once the distinction had been between resident and non-resident Fellows, there was now a contrast between the hard-working 'tutorial' Fellows, and the drone-like 'prize' ones. The 1872 statutes ensured that no future Fellow could be elected who could draw his stipend for life without lifting a finger to help the College.[66]

These reforms, which occurred elsewhere in Oxford, were not of course retrospectively applied. It was thus possible for Sydney Skeffington, elected in 1869, to hold no office and to live outside College after 1871, but remain a Fellow until his death in 1917. Skeffington, however, was a special case: from 1875 until his death he was regularly described as being 'incapacitated by illness'. The nature of his 'illness' is revealed in the 1881 census, where Skeffington appears in Herne Bay, Kent, as a 'Lunatic'. Skeffington's unhappy fate meant that for half a century one of the College's twelve Fellowships was effectively vacant.[67]

Meanwhile Bradley's College was run by an increasingly professionalized, specialized—and lay—Fellowship. Some posts were now advertised as being only for specialists in a given subject. The first case was in March 1881, when a team including no less a figure than Thomas Huxley was asked to examine Fellowship candidates 'in Biology and kindred subjects'.[68]

Several new Fellows came from Balliol. The 'export' of Balliol men was common to all of Oxford—over a quarter of the fellows elected throughout Oxford in 1860–78 had been Balliol undergraduates—but at University College the figure during this time was one-third.[69] Some combined scholarship

---

[65] Smith 1910: 76 and Woods 1941.   [66] See further Engel 1983: 156–201.
[67] Letter from P. G. Medd: UC:GB1 (uncatalogued papers). Skeffington appeared in the 1891 census still living as a lunatic in Kent.
[68] UC:GB3/A1/3 p. 183.
[69] Curthoys 2000: 131. A quarter of all Fellows of University College elected in 1856–1914 (not including Stowell Fellows) had been at Balliol.

with public service, like Charles Fyffe (F. 1870–92), who in the 1880s published *A History of Modern Europe*, a three-volume work covering the years 1792–1878, which proved a great popular and critical success, being reprinted as late as 1924, and even today reads well. However, Fyffe also sometimes worked as a journalist, taking leave from Oxford soon after his election as a Fellow in January 1870 to report for the *Daily News* on the Franco-Prussian War. He also entered politics as a Liberal, and might have become an MP, had it not been for his untimely death.[70]

Other Balliol imports were less scholarly, such as Arthur Dendy (Stowell Law Fellow 1868–73; F. 1873–1900), a keen hunter who, as Charles Cree found, often scrapped his lectures if hunting was to be had (even in the 1890s he still hunted two or three days a week, and regularly walked around College in his hunting clothes). Dendy, however, was generally regarded with affection: the philosopher Bernard Bosanquet (F. 1870–84) regularly took summer holidays with him in the Orkneys, and a much younger Fellow, Edgar Carritt, remembered that Dendy allowed no smoking in Common Room, 'a taste', he wrote, 'which perhaps had kept his keen sense of smell, for when he had an orange at dessert he would throw the peel in the coal fire to get that pleasure'.[71]

Bradley found it as hard to drop his Marlborough ways with the Fellows as the undergraduates. At least he realized the sensitivity of his position, admitting that, when elected, he was 'an entire stranger to almost every member of the Corporation'. Unfortunately, in 1873, Bradley found himself isolated against the Fellowship, thanks to a provision in the 1872 statutes which introduced the idea of a pension scheme for the Fellows. When the Fellowship consisted largely of clergymen, livings had acted as a kind of pension scheme, but, as the Fellowship became ever more secular, something had to be done for lay Fellows. The proposals were generous: for example, a Praelector of twenty years' standing would receive £200 a year, and one of fifteen £150. Investment from the proceeds of the sale of a College living would supply the funding. Some other reforms clipped the Master's wings: he would now have to retire at the age of 70; and, whereas the Master had previously appointed two of the three Tutors, all three were now to be chosen by the Governing Body.[72]

Almost as soon as the statutes had been drawn up, Bradley took alarm. As he explained in a letter of June 1873 to the Lord Chancellor, he feared that the scheme was unaffordable and open to abuse, imagining a young Praelector

---

[70] Fyffe: *ODNB* entry and Darwall-Smith 2001: 72–6 and 79–81.
[71] Dendy the hunter: Cree 1974: 23 and Moore 1954: 13; Dendy as companion: Bosanquet 1924: 29, and Carritt 1960: 40.
[72] Bradley on the Fellows: Bradley 1873: 21–2; the pension scheme in the 1872 statutes: UC:GB3/A1/3 pp. 113–17 (for another account of this incident, see Engel 1983: 70–4); Balliol and Merton were also instituting pension schemes at this time (Brock 2000a: 17–18).

doing twenty years' service, and then retiring in his forties to scrounge off the College for the rest of his life. He also feared that the statutes would place power in the hands of the Tutors, at the expense of the Master and the non-resident Fellows. Bradley admitted that he stood alone, and indeed a letter sent in November to the Lord Chancellor rebutting his claims was signed by all but two of the Fellows, one of whom was the incapacitated Skeffington. The following month, Bradley privately published two letters to the Lord Chancellor, setting out his arguments once again. The Lord Chancellor effectively ducked the decision: the proposals were rejected for the present, only because a new Royal Commission was in place.[73]

Bradley's solitary opposition would have made relations with his Fellows hard enough; but the hectoring and self-righteous tone of his printed letters would not improve matters:

Nor did I, my Lord, till I read the letter of the Fellows, ever hear, either in public or private, a whisper of the suggestion now made, 'that the College would hesitate to grant a Pension to a Tutor after twenty years' service, unless with a view to important and productive study.' ... But, my Lord, impressions may be false, recollections erroneous, conversations forgotten or misunderstood. Unrecorded debates have, I am aware, no authority.[74]

Writing to Charles Faulkner in January 1874, Bradley admitted that the affair had left its scars:

I ought to thank you again for the kind manner in which you speak of the discussion before [the Visitor]. It is difficult for me, seeing as I think the College ruined, to preserve peace of mind on the matter but at least I shall not willingly cause to any one else the pain which I have suffered myself.[75]

Oxford gossip was aware of the Master's troubles. One student magazine of 1874, in a skit on prominent Oxford personalities, had one 'G. G. B.—' introduce himself thus:

> I come from Rugby, and my name is Br*dl*y,
> I am a master: and regret it sadly.[76]

Nevertheless, Bradley somehow persuaded the Fellowship to elect to their number two men who were effectively his creatures. In October 1874, James Franck Bright (m. 1851), a housemaster at Marlborough under Bradley, was elected Fellow without any probationary period. He became Dean in January 1875, and Praelector in Modern History in March, so that within only a few weeks of his election he was a senior figure of authority. Bradley performed a

---

[73] Bradley in June 1873 and the Fellows' reply: UC:GB1 (uncatalogued papers); his later letters: Bradley 1873.
[74] Bradley 1873: 6–7.
[75] UC:GB1 (uncatalogued papers).
[76] Anon. 1874: 60.

similar trick in June 1876, when Samuel Butcher, Senior Classic at Cambridge in 1873, who had had to resign a Fellowship at Trinity when he married, was elected Fellow without examination, and made Praelector, first of Philosophy, and then of Latin. Butcher, the first Fellow of University College to be elected with a wife still alive (Bright was a widower with four daughters), was a former pupil of Bradley's at Marlborough, and Bradley clearly wanted him to strengthen the College's classics teaching.[77]

Fortunately Bradley's protégés proved both academically successful and personally popular. One of Samuel Butcher's pupils, Frederick Conybeare (m. 1876; F. 1880–7), while remembering Butcher's 'beautiful and accomplished bride', recalled his lectures on Demosthenes to a packed Hall, and the way that 'in each lecture nearly a few graphic and vivid remarks and characterisations would bring home to our minds the social and political forces at work in the decadence of Greece and Athens'. In 1879 Butcher became known to a wider audience when he collaborated with Andrew Lang in an immensely successful translation of the *Odyssey*. Conybeare also remembered that 'a fund of kindly Irish humour in Butcher, which would often shew itself in quizzing Dendy. There was nothing the latter more enjoyed, especially when Mrs. Butcher, who had the same sort of humour, took part in it and assisted her husband.'[78]

James Bright was a less obviously brilliant man than Butcher, but a no less important addition. He was the first Fellow of University College to have taken the examinations in Jurisprudence and Modern History, and was, like Bradley, a theological liberal. In a sermon preached in 1858/9, he declared that 'modern criticism has taught us, and rightly, that the Bible must not be considered as a united whole, but as a series of books by different hands, written under different circumstances and in different states of feeling and knowledge.'[79] As for his work as Fellow and teacher, the *Pall Mall Gazette* of 28 November 1881 called Bright 'the most popular member of the body, and one who as dean of the College has been in the closest and most friendly relations with the undergraduates'. In a rather more feline manner, the paper continued 'He is the author of the fullest and most complete school History of England—a work which, without any attraction of style, has gradually won its way by careful accuracy and learning.'

Bradley's College showed its enlightenment in unexpected ways. In 1878 Bradley chaired a meeting at which it was agreed to establish an Association for Promoting the Higher Education of Women, and which would lead to the creation of Oxford's first women's colleges. A year earlier, in November

---

[77] Bright (no relation of William Bright): UC:GB3/A1/3 pp. 122–4, How 1904: 233 and 239, and Hinde 1992: 70; Butcher: UC:GB3/A1/3 pp. 127–8.
[78] Information taken from an address given by Reginald Macan in January 1911 on Butcher's death, which quotes Conybeare's reminiscences (UC:MA43/MS4/10).
[79] UC:MA42/MS1/1.

1877, a young BA called Christian Cole was permitted to migrate to University College. Cole, a native of Sierra Leone, was apparently the first black African to take an Oxford degree. In spite of his poverty (he had been a non-Collegiate student, in order to save money), he had the determination to obtain a Fourth in Greats and to train as a barrister, and the courage to cope with being almost the only black man in Oxford. This gesture was a simple one, but important to Cole, who now could—and did—proudly call himself a BA of University College. On the other hand, Bradley had no interest in those unable to match his academic standards. One of the most famous of his rejects was Cecil Rhodes, who could only study at Oxford intermittently, and for a pass degree at that. Rhodes went to Oriel instead.[80]

Bradley's efforts did not pass unnoticed. In 1874, Benjamin Jowett observed that the best Oxford Colleges were now Balliol, New College, University College, Trinity, and Lincoln. Another sign of approval came from the eminent men who chose to send their sons to University College. In 1872, the Prime Minister himself, W. E. Gladstone, sent his fourth son, Herbert, not to his own college of Christ Church, but to University College, and in 1878 Lord Selborne, Goldwin Smith's old friend and Gladstone's Lord Chancellor in 1872–4 and 1880–5, did likewise. The presence of Liberal politicians' sons should not surprise, but the Conservative Sir Stafford Northcote, Disraeli's Chancellor of the Exchequer, also sent a son up in 1882, and, more significantly, the Chancellor of Oxford and future Prime Minister, the Marquess of Salisbury, sent four of his five sons to University College, beginning with James, Viscount Cranborne, in 1880. In Salisbury's case, fears of the rowdiness of Christ Church (his old college, like Gladstone's) combined with suspicions about the supposed unorthodoxy of a Student there, Reginald Macan, whom we shall meet again. These young men were expected to work: Herbert Gladstone was advised to study seven hours a day by his father; Lord Selborne was delighted when his son won a First in modern history; and two of Lord Salisbury's sons achieved Firsts. Despite the political differences between their fathers, a friendship grew up between Selborne and Salisbury's sons, which deepened when Selborne's son William Palmer married Lady Maud Cecil, Salisbury's daughter, in 1883.[81]

The College's growth under Bradley (Graph 15.1) put increasing pressure on space. By the mid-1870s, there were said to be 110 resident undergraduates,

---

[80] Bradley and women's education: Adams 1996: 10–11 and Howarth 2000a: 247; Christian Cole (who advertised his new status in Cole 1883): UC:GB4/A1/3 p. 211, as well as Symonds 1986: 270 and Fyfe 1993: 400 (unfortunately, Cole died young in 1885); Rhodes: see, for example, Clark 1953: 1.

[81] Jowett on University College: Tuckwell 1900: 214; Herbert Gladstone (who took an interest in Christian Cole and apparently drew him to Bradley's notice): Mallet 1932: 37–8, 41, and 65–6; Selborne: Selborne 1898: i. 420, and ii. 38 and 89; Northcote: Mallet 1932: 40; Salisbury: Rose 1975: 63.

of whom only 64 could live in the College. In 1876 the architects George Bodley and Thomas Garner designed an extension to the kitchen block which was not adopted. In the following year, however, the Lord Chancellor permitted the College to spend £10,000 converting the existing Master's Lodgings in Radcliffe Quadrangle into undergraduate accommodation, and building a new Lodgings on part of the Master's Garden.[82] Bodley and Garner were invited back, and on 31 January 1877, Bodley wrote:

> I shall be glad to design the proposed new Lodge for the Master, University College. The site is a good one.....The style of the building should, I think, be that of the later part of the sixteenth century, & the material stone.[83]

Bodley and Garner had a better contextual sense than Gilbert Scott: their fine homage to the Tudor Renaissance, rightly praised for its 'refinement and discipline', is a more harmonious addition to the College than Scott's Library. There may have been more to this choice. In 1873, Charles Faulkner and Charles Fyffe had successfully opposed a High Gothic design for the proposed Examination Schools, and it has been suggested that, by the late 1870s, the Gothic style in Oxford tended to be associated with conservatism and ecclesiasticism, and a more eclectic Renaissance style with reform. A reformer like Bradley would not have minded a design with such connotations.[84]

Unfortunately, the building of the Lodgings proved an unhappy affair. Faulkner's decision, rather unusually, to hire a clerk of works to manage it, was unwise: a clerk of works had to engage all the workers and find the materials, whereas a firm of builders already had a team of professionals, and a store of material purchased bought in bulk at a discount. Faulkner found the costs of the project rising inexorably: a building which in May 1877 Bodley had thought would cost £7,800 eventually came to £10,500. It is no wonder that, in October 1879, he scribbled on a letter from Bodley that 'from a *money* point of view the matter was frightful'.[85]

Meanwhile, during 1879 and 1880, the former Master's Lodgings was converted into sets of rooms for undergraduates. A new doorway was inserted into the middle of the east range of Radcliffe Quadrangle and Staircase XII was created, and three outer doorways were blocked up. Some rooms hint at their former use—the former dining room retains its fine ceiling—but the former library was split in half. Charles Faulkner kept

---

[82] Size of College: UC:GB3/A1/3 pp. 130–3; Bodley and Garner's 1876 design: UC:FA3/3/Y1/1–4; approval for new Lodgings: UC:GB3/A1/3 pp. 130–3.
[83] UC:FA9/1/C1/2 no. 2.
[84] Bodley's design: Howell 2000: 750; style wars: Whyte 2001: 97–103.
[85] Building costs: UC:FA9/1/F2/1 (the clerk's daily account book), UC:FA9/MS1/6, and Faulkner's correspondence at UC:FA9/1/C1/2, which, as Howell 2000: 750 observed, 'makes the heart bleed for him'.

detailed notes on the conversion which record which curtains, carpets, and wallpaper were ordered, including wallpaper from Morris & Co., some of which was designed by Faulkner's sister, Kate. His tastes in decoration were not universally shared, as his pupil Edwin Lendon remembered:

> It was part of C. J. Faulkner's duties, as Bursar, to re-paper the men's rooms when they were shabby or dirty, and I remember his complaining that the young Philistines used to take off Morris's lovely paper-hangings.[86]

Faulkner's greatest role in the mid-century College, however, was to oversee its finances, for he served variously as Vice-Bursar in 1864–6, Bursar in 1866–1876, and Senior Bursar in 1876–1882. Already by the 1840s, the post of Bursar was held by fewer Fellows, sometimes for three or four years at a stretch, but Faulkner was the first Fellow to be Bursar for so long. The names of Faulkner's offices are also significant: in 1843, for the first time, two Bursars were appointed, although this innovation was only intermittent until 1926.[87]

One of the most important changes overseen by Faulkner was the conversion into rack rents of the College's remaining beneficial leases, a system which finally ended in 1875/6 when it was decided to raise a loan in lieu of receiving an entry fine on the properties in St Giles. Another change resulted from the Universities and College Estates Acts of 1858 and 1860. The first Act permitted colleges and universities to grant leases of lands or houses for a maximum of twenty-one years, but also to grant building leases for up to ninety-nine years. The colleges could even sell property, but the money had to be paid to the Board of Agriculture, to be laid out on purchasing other properties, making investments, or on capital projects for college buildings or estates. The 1860 Act permitted colleges to raise loans as compensation for the lack of entry fines. This solved a real problem: when a college moved to rack rents, there was an awkward interim period when its cash flow suffered from the lack of entry fines, before the gains from increased annual rents had yet to cut in—but, because under rack rents it was the college which now paid for the upkeep of its estates, there were suddenly unprecedented levels of expenditure. At University College, although the move to rack rents did indeed increase the College's income—it almost doubled in the 1870s (Graph 15.2)—the College had to spend more money on its property. In 1869/70, for example, the rent from one Welsh property rose from £49 to £442, but three-quarters of the total increase in the income from all the Welsh properties that year was ploughed straight back into repairs upon them.

---

[86] Papers concerning the reconstruction: UC:FA6/1 *passim*; the new doorway: UC:FA6/1/C1/3; wallpaper, UC:FA6/1/MS1/6; Lendon: Anon. 1930/1: 21.

[87] Dunbabin 1997: 419–20 suggests that most colleges were appointing Bursars for long terms by the 1850s.

Fortunately, more money came in from other sources—dues from College expenses trebled in 1867/8—and income was also recorded more efficiently. For some years there had been a separately managed tuition fund, into which undergraduates paid money for their teaching, which in 1879/80 was formally included in the accounts.[88]

Fellows' and Masters' stipends from the 1850s to the 1870s changed little, but the stipends for College officers did start to rise. In particular, the stipends of praelectors rose from £258 15s. 4d. to £368 5s. 4d. in 1873/4, and again to £737 13s. 4d. in 1876/7. George Bradley played the College's finances very well. By taking on a College lectureship and accepting payments from undergraduates from other colleges attending his lectures, he increased his salary to an average of over £1,000 a year—not including his supplement from the Linton Fund.[89]

As Bursar, Faulkner managed the College's estates, and he recorded his work in a series of diaries, which bring into new and lively relief the relations between the College and its tenants. The diaries certainly show the busy life of a Victorian Bursar. Faulkner visited most College properties at least once a year: in 1874, for example, he visited Hailey (Oxon.) in March, Handley Park (Northants.) in April, Marks Hall (Essex) and Edgiock (Worcs.) in May, Wales in July, the College's Yorkshire properties in Pontefract, Linton, and Arncliffe in August and September, and Handley Park again in October.[90]

Faulkner took detailed notes of what he found, and in the privacy of his diaries passed waspish comments on the College's tenants and of other people with whom he had dealings: 'drunk and quite unmanageable...a drunken brute' (Mr Stewart, tenant of a house in York); 'A conceited young ass' (Mr Coleman, town clerk of Pontefract).[91] There were tales of petty crime, as when in 1881 Faulkner visited Mrs Roberts, a tenant in Wales, and her family:

The elder son is a slouching, sulky, idle young vagabond, and the younger though not so bad follows his example. Jones of Park described their house as the haunt of a set of poachers.[92]

---

[88] The end of beneficial leases: UC:EB2/F/2 and UC:BU2/F1/7 fo. 230^r; the 1858 and 1860 Acts: Shadwell 1898: 19–30, Howard 1935: 189–91, and Dunbabin 1997: 386; the Welsh estates: UC:BU2/F1/7 fos. 175^r and 181^r (Dunbabin 1997: 381, suggests that colleges on average increased their gross external receipts by 25 per cent in 1850–71); College dues: UC:BU2/F1/7 fo. 150^v; tuition fund: UC:BU2/F1/67 fos. 257^v and 263^v.

[89] Fellows' stipends: UC:BU2/F1/7 fos. 209^v–210^r and 233^v; Bradley: see, for example, UC:BU3/F3/52 pp. 91–2 and UC:BU3/F3/57, pp. 79–80. In comparison, the Rector of Lincoln College in the 1870s earned £735 12s. 6d., and the Fellows' stipends ranged from £424 17s. 10d. to £377 (Green 1979: 573).

[90] Faulkner's diaries: UC:EB4/J1/1–6. Thanks to the railways, college Bursars were generally more mobile now: see Dunbabin 1997: 419–20.

[91] UC:EB4/J1/3 fo. 29^r (Stewart); UC:EB4/J1/3 fo. 60^r (Coleman).

[92] UC:EB4/J1/6 fo. 138^r.

He encountered domestic tragedies, as with the hapless Mr Marton, tenant of Flamstead in 1877:

> Marton was said to be insane in consequence of the infidelity of his wife who had gone off with some other man. He is now about 75 years old, and married his wife (a second or third) some 7 or 8 years ago she being then about 20 years old.[93]

Faulkner also found himself reaping the consequences of leaving the College's tenants to maintain their properties, as when in January 1877, he discovered the state of the Trinities in Pontefract:

> Many of these houses in the Trinities are horrible dens. It is not that they are unsubstantially built, but the miserable arrangements and total lack of proper offices drive the unfortunate occupants to live in a filthy way.[94]

Any discussion of the College's finances at this time cannot ignore the fact that, once again, Parliament was intervening in Oxford and Cambridge's affairs. In 1872 the Cleveland Commission was instituted with the aim of inquiring into the property and income of both universities and their colleges. A few years later, the Selborne Commission of 1877 (chaired by Lord Selborne, soon to send his son to University College) was set up as a statutory commission, intended to give new statutes to all the colleges at both universities. University College was not represented on the Cleveland Commission, but in October 1880, G. G. Bradley was co-opted onto the Selborne Commission.[95]

The two Commissions wrought changes in the colleges as drastic as those of the 1850s. The individual and idiosyncratic accounting systems adopted by the colleges, some of which, like University College's, were traceable in style back to the fourteenth century, were all abolished, and from 1 January 1883 all colleges had to adopt a similar accounting method, abstracts of which were printed. There was another financial novelty, brought in by the Selborne Commission: colleges now had to pay contributions for university purposes. These were levied in line with a college's income, so that University College was stung far less hard than wealthy Magdalen.[96]

However, it was the new statutes of University College, which after much difficult negotiation were drawn up in June 1881 and approved by the Privy Council the following May, which brought the greatest changes.[97] There was

---

[93] UC:EB4/J1/4 fo. 48ʳ. Eventually Marton was removed to an asylum (UC:EB4/J1/5 fo. 21).

[94] UC:EB4/J1/3 fo. 33ʳ. In fairness, Faulkner spent much of 1877 and 1878 arranging for several College houses in Pontefract to be rebuilt.

[95] The Cleveland Commission: Engel 1983: 93–105, Ward 1965: 292–6 and Harvie 2000: 67–73; the Selborne Commission: Ward 1965: 300–11, Harvie 2000: 79–90, and (for a Cambridge perspective) Brooke 1993: 82–9; Bradley on the Selborne Commission: UC:GB4/A1/4 fo. 9ʳ, and Harvie 2000: 86.

[96] Harvie 2000: 86–7.

[97] The College's tortuous negotiations in 1878–81 with the Commissioners are traced in UC:GB3/A1/3 pp. 137–63 and 166–73.

now no stipulation about the Master having to be in holy orders; indeed, only one Fellow had to be a priest, to act as Chaplain. At last a pension scheme for Fellows was introduced, and the rules about their tenure were refined: Fellows had to resign after seven years except for those acting as Praelector or Tutor. Fellows resident in Oxford might receive an extension of two years, and Fellows 'engaged in some definite literary or scientific work or work of art or research' one of seven years. The rules on marriage were simplified: Fellows who married had to resign, but could be re-elected. Many of these changes, especially those concerning the so-called 'prize' Fellowships of seven years' duration, were now common to most other colleges in Oxford and Cambridge, imposing some kind of homogeneity on both universities.[98] The major mid-Victorian reforms were now complete, and University College was, like its fellow-institutions, transformed.

BRADLEY UNRAVELLED: FELLOWS VERSUS UNDERGRADUATES

George Bradley had ceased to be Master when the new statutes were approved. He had changed much in the College for the better, taking its academic standards to unheard-of heights, and attracting sons of great men to an extent that not even Nathan Wetherell had achieved—but at a cost. In Plumptre's last days, undergraduates had shown themselves capable of standing up to the Fellows, not always in the most constructive of ways: Bradley's College never quite solved this problem. It was not only due to Bradley's continuing to play the headmaster; at a time when University College's sporting reputation excelled, especially on the river, he took no interest in sports at all—he once reproved his listeners in a lecture for paying too much attention to athletics, proudly declaring that he had never taken any exercise in his life.[99] He was not alone: none of the other Fellows appear to have taken much interest in undergraduate activities; even Arthur Dendy does not seem to have hunted with undergraduates.

There were some notable innovations in undergraduate life. A request from the undergraduates in 1872 to mark the 'commemoration of the mythical foundation of the college by King Alfred in 872' with a ball in the College was turned down, but another request in June 1874 was granted, and in 1875 it was agreed to hold College balls every three years. There was also a University College Essay Society in existence at least by 1879, and Charles Cree knew of a Shakespeare Reading Society devoted to play-reading. This should not be confused with the Shakespeare Club (or Society), whose origins go back at least to 1876. 'The Shaker', its membership limited just to twelve, became the

---

[98] For changes in other colleges, see, for example, Bury 1952: 89–90, Brooke 1996: 234, and Hodgkin 1949: 186–7.
[99] Sladen 1915: 128.

College's most prestigious dining club—although it never developed the arcana of dining societies in other colleges, such as the Myrmidons at Merton or the Phoenix at Brasenose, which also had distinctive uniforms—and very pointedly read no Shakespeare at all.[100]

Unfortunately the problem of undergraduate indiscipline remained. One Magdalen undergraduate, Lewin Cholmeley, recorded in his diary for 7 November 1873 some gossip passed on by John Boustead (m. 1872): 'they had had', Boustead told Cholmey, 'a splendid row in Univ on the 5: blown [*sic*] the Master's door, hustled their dons, &c, two men were sent down for a term.' In March 1874, some undergraduates broke the windows of two Fellows' rooms by throwing coal and soda water bottles through them. University College was not alone: at Christ Church in 1870, some statues were hauled out of the library, and placed in a bonfire by a group of drunken undergraduates, and at Wadham in 1879 the Dean's door was 'jammed', and eight men were rusticated. It was, however, at University College that a major confrontation brought this problem to national attention.[101]

At a dinner party on the night of 11 May 1880, it was planned to screw up (not for the first time) the door of one of the Fellows, Albert Chavasse.[102] Chavasse was out, and it was claimed that he needed a ladder to enter his rooms. The chief perpetrator, Samuel Sandbach (m. 1876), left early next morning to join a yeomanry camp in Wales, 'never thinking,' wrote a contemporary, George Stapylton Barnes (m. 1876), 'that any special notice would be taken of the screwing up of Chavasse's door'. Unfortunately it was. On the next morning, the rest of the College was summoned to the Hall, to be met by the Master, the Dean (Bright), and other Fellows, including Chavasse, Dendy, and Faulkner. As Barnes remembered it:

The Master began his speech with the words,—'Gentlemen, if I may still call you by that name', went on to tell us that the gravity of our offence was greatly increased by the fact that Chavasse was Senior Proctor, and ended his speech by reading a Notice which was afterwards put up on the Board, and which ran as follows,—'The College is sent down, and members must leave by 4 o'clock today. Any gentleman who likes to give in his name as having had nothing to do with the disgraceful affair of last night may stay up'.

---

[100] College Balls: UC:GB4/A1/3 pp. 79, 129, and 152 (Cambridge's first May Ball was held at Trinity in 1866, but few colleges followed suit until the 1880s (Hyam in Cunich and others 1994: 201)); Debating Society: UC:O12/A1/2 (other colleges' debating societies: Twigg 1987: 242–5 and Curthoys 2000: 149–50); Essay Society: UC:P116/P1/1; Shakespeare Reading Society: Cree 1974: 38–9 and 41; the Shakespeare Club's first photograph album (UC:O15/P1/1) begins in 1876.

[101] Cholmeley: MCA MC:P234/J1/1 p. 109 (the incident is also mentioned in UC:GB3/A1/3 p. 118); the 1874 incident: UC:GB4/A1/3 pp. 120 and 125; Christ Church: Hiscock 1946: 97–101 and Mason 2000: 221–2; Wadham: Davies in Davies and Garnett 1994: 46–7 (see also Curthoys 2000: 140).

[102] The best primary source for what follows is a memoir written by George Stapylton Barnes in UC:P45/MS/1. The best modern account is Mitchell 1996.

Barnes continued:

The Master's speech was an absolute bomb-shell to all of us. I do not think that it occurred to anybody that the screwing up was anything more than a practical joke, and the idea of insulting a high Dignitary of the University, I feel sure, never entered into the mind of anyone.

After a deputation was sent to the Master, who refused to change his mind, Barnes called on Chavasse, who asked why he had been screwed up. Put on the spot, Barnes

> blurted out that the general view was that we had a sort of vested right to screw up his oak, and that there was no ill-feeling involved. Chavasse was immensely tickled at the idea of a vested right, and for some time laughed heartily about it. He bore no resentment whatever, and told me that he alone had voted against sending the College down, the voting being otherwise unanimous.

None of the undergraduates wished to reveal Sandbach as the culprit, nor did they wish, by exculpating themselves, to implicate others. As a result, to universal amazement, some forty undergraduates left Oxford forthwith, with a stern letter from Bradley for their parents.[103] There was amusement at University College's expense: 'Rooms to let' signs were placed on the College walls, and local cartoonists enjoyed depicting the affair (Fig. 16.8). Barnes urgently contacted Sandbach in Wales asking him to confess. Sandbach admitted his role to the Master, and the College reconvened after a week's unexpected holiday.

This extraordinary incident raised many questions. First of all, it revealed the problems attached to the undergraduate code of honour. Previously, the College authorities had relied on undergraduates to confess their misdemeanours. In 1880, however, the offender was out of Oxford, and those left behind would not sneak on him. It was only when Sandbach was at last contacted, and immediately confessed, that matters could be resolved. It also shed light on the unhappy relations between Fellows and undergraduates. A letter printed in *The Times* of 20 May 1880 in the aftermath of the affair drew attention to the disrespect frequently shown by undergraduates towards Tutors who were felt to be a little different.[104] Some undergraduates, valuing gentlemanly ways above intellectual achievement, found some Fellows—like the Brummie Charles Faulkner—hard to respect. Finally, it raised questions about Bradley's style of running University College.

Within University College itself, noisy parties did not stop,[105] but there are no records of later undergraduates emulating Samuel Sandbach's activities

---

[103] UC:P45/MS/2.
[104] Quoted in Mitchell 1996: 80–1.
[105] One such in May 1881 resulted in 'a great uproar', and the rustication of the host (UC:GB4/A1/4 fo. 38ʳ).

FIGURE 16.8 'Tale of a Screw': a contemporary cartoon telling the tale of the sending down of University College in 1880 (the date of 1878 was added in error). Albert Chavasse is seen climbing into his rooms in the middle of the picture, James Bright is in the top right-hand corner, and a contrite Master Bradley in the bottom right-hand corner.

with a screwdriver. They had clearly seen the wisdom of ceding certain 'vested rights'. On the other hand, the College's reputation suffered. Whereas thirty-five men had come up in 1880, only nineteen did so in 1881, and indeed overall matriculation numbers fell slightly during the next decade.[106]

It was perhaps as well that something changed the situation. On 18 July 1881, Arthur Stanley died, and a month later George Bradley was named as his successor as Dean of Westminster.[107] A letter of 29 August 1881 from Charles Fyffe to Charles Faulkner shows how some Fellows had come to regard their Master:

> You were right about Westminster. I thought, when nothing appeared in confirmation of your conjecture about the little man's visit to London, that your imagination had carried him away, like the Angel and the prophet Habukkuk.[108]

Although it was not until late October that Bradley formally announced his intention to resign as Master,[109] the Fellows were soon discussing a successor. In August, Albert Chavasse recommended Goldwin Smith to Charles Faulkner:

> I think he is the man, and that we might carry him ... His connection with the former Commission would stand us now in stead before the Privy Council & in Parliament ... If we could offer Goldwin Smith a unanimous election, he would probably *sacrifice himself for a time at all events* & 'come over & help us'.... The time is a crisis in the history of the College & of the University.[110]

Goldwin Smith could not be persuaded, and the College approached the zoologist Thomas Huxley. This would have been a remarkable choice. Not only was Huxley, like Smith, a layman, but he was also a prominent supporter of the theories of Charles Darwin, and an agnostic. This offer shows how far University College had travelled since the 1850s. Huxley, however, refused. As he explained to his son, he would have had to take a cut in salary, and 'I do not think I am cut out for a Don, nor your mother for a Donness.' Eventually the College chose one of their own. On 26 November 1881, James Franck Bright was elected.[111]

Contemporary observers were divided about Bradley's legacy. *The Times* observed:

> It is no secret that he found the college in rather a disorganised condition, and that he was disposed at first to be a little too radical and peremptory in his changes. The result

---

[106] 145 men matriculated from University College in 1876–80, but the totals for 1881–5 and 1886–90 were 139 and 130.
[107] *Times*, 27 August 1881.
[108] UC:GB1: uncatalogued papers.
[109] UC:GB3/A1/3 p. 185.
[110] UC:GB1: uncatalogued papers.
[111] Huxley: Huxley 1900: ii. 31–2; Bright: UC:GB3/A1/3 p. 185.

has been that at the present time, after Balliol which has long suffered no equal or second in academical distinctions, University ranks with Corpus and New College in the intellectual race.[112]

An unknown newspaper was much less charitable:

> It may be doubted whether he [Bradley] was ever really a success, at University College. His ways were that of a schoolmaster,... and his manner towards his subordinates reminded them unpleasantly of the time when his monthly visitations used to be a terror to his under-masters at Marlborough. He was, too, very unfortunate in his disciplinary assistants; then, as now, University College being the worst-governed and worst-ordered college in Oxford.... The last occurrrence [sic] which resulted in the whole college being sent down, did a great deal of harm to both dons and Master, although the act of banishment was due more to the impatient arbitrariness of the Fellows than the hesitating government at their head.[113]

It is striking that, of the various Oxford colleges in the second half of the nineteenth century who elected public school headmasters as their head, several, in particular Christ Church, Trinity, and Jesus, had found the experience as uncomfortable as University College.[114]

Bradley himself, in an address given in the Chapel in October 1881 on the death of Arthur Stanley, drew some pointed contrasts with the College of the 1840s.[115] On relations between undergraduates and tutors, Bradley thought that those of the 1840s were 'not close, but pleasant and friendly', but never remembered 'any feeling of hostility, still less of any expression given to it, on the part of the men towards their tutors' (unlike the previous year). He also could not resist one last piece of headmasterly finger-wagging:

> I may be quite wrong, but it seems to me that we were in some ways, superficial enough, no doubt, older for our years than you are. Was it that amusements and games were far less organized? the number of public schools far less? we were less gregarious I think; some feature of our boyhood, if I may say so, ended sooner... the noisy and boisterous, the mere schoolboy element was less present or less felt than in later times.

Bradley had achieved much, but undone much too. Having effectively made his College a laughing-stock, he needed to move on.

---

[112] *Times*, 27 August 1881.
[113] Pasted into UC:P167/P1/1 fos. 42ᵛ–43ʳ.
[114] Christ Church: Dean Liddell's *ODNB* entry: Trinity: Hopkins 2005: 254–87 (on John Percival, Headmaster of Clifton); Baker 1971: 71–6 (Hugh Harper, Headmaster of Sherborne); see too Curthoys 2000: 128–9.
[115] Bayley 1963: 186.

17
The 'D.O.C.': 1881–1914

Many Edwardian dinner menus from University College include a long list of toasts, the last of which was almost always to the 'D.O.C.'—the 'Dear Old College', an affectionate nickname which survived well into the twentieth century. It sums up the atmosphere of a College which, between George Bradley's move to Westminster and the outbreak of the First World War, exchanged the institutional upheavals of the previous decades for a less hectic and perhaps happier time, but at the expense of its academic advances.

JAMES FRANCK BRIGHT AND THE HEALING OF WOUNDS

The new Master, James Franck Bright (Fig. 17.1), did not take up his office under the best of auspices. He was only a second-best candidate after Thomas Huxley, and some might wonder about the wisdom of replacing Bradley with another former schoolmaster. Bright, however, confounded expectations, and his long Mastership both consolidated many of Bradley's reforms, and healed the wounds of the 1870s.

Fred Bickerton, employed as a College servant in 1897, remembered Bright as 'an imposing man, with a large beard, [who] always walked with a scholarly stoop, one hand behind his back, the other grasping a walking-stick.' Edgar Carritt (F. 1898–1945) admired Bright for taking time to talk to younger Fellows: 'I have seldom met', he wrote, 'so old a man who could talk and argue with juniors so easily, quite concealing the superiority which was his.' Undergraduates, however, found the Master (nicknamed, inevitably, 'the Mugger') rather shy, and his dinner-parties daunting occasions. Fortunately, his Sunday tea parties, hosted by his daughters (nicknamed logically, if ungallantly, 'the Muglets'), were more relaxed affairs.[1]

Bright, a widower with four daughters, may have had ulterior motives in organizing tea parties. William Carr (m. 1882), scholar enough to get a Second in history, but also heir to a substantial fortune, was permitted to meet the Master's daughters, and an understanding grew between him and Margaret Bright, to the point where he asked for her hand in marriage. Carr's

[1] Bickerton 1953: 130–1; Carritt 1960: 39; Moore 1954: 14–15.

FIGURE 17.1 James Franck Bright, m. 1851, Fellow 1874–81, and Master 1881–1906, by Sir George Reid.

father, on hearing the news, was mortified that his son had thus abused the Master's hospitality, but Carr's granddaughter suspected that the Master would have been delighted with such an eligible son-in-law, and might even have assisted the match himself.[2] Carr was indeed an excellent addition to the family: financially independent, he lived on his estate in Norfolk, where he wrote several articles for the *Dictionary of National Biography*, and, in 1902, the second history of University College.

Bright was as liberal in his theology and politics as Bradley; Vernon Storr (F. 1895–9 and 1905–13) claimed that he was briefly suspended from preaching in the diocese of Oxford on account of his broad theological views. One observer called him 'a Churchman of a type never quite extinct in Oxford to whom whatever discoveries and new thoughts the course of the world might bring were heartily welcome, and could cast no shadow either of doubt or of depreciation upon the central thought which was the staple of their creed,' and Bright's extant sermons show that neither his personal devotion nor his seriousness of purpose could be questioned.[3] Preaching in the College Chapel on Whitsunday 1886, he warned his congregation:

[2] Athill 2002: 68–70.
[3] Storr: UC:R2/MS1/7; Bright's religion: Charnwood 1930: 12; Bright's sermons are preserved as UC:MA42/MS1/1–31.

The temptations of youth are very absorbing & multiform, the consciousness of stirring life within you, the hot blood of youth makes passion so easy & natural that its indulgence seems rather a trivial & venial error than a crime.... Or perhaps, the worst danger of all, the simple enjoyment of living is so great that effort and energy disappear from your livings, & mere vacuity & frivolous idleness fritter away the high gifts of body and intellect the improvement of which is the real object of your life.[4]

Bright revealed his liberalism in two symbolic gestures. In 1882, barely three years after the foundation of the first women's colleges in Oxford, he became one of the first dons to admit women to his lectures. Of course, the women who attended Bright's lectures in the Hall were chaperoned, and sat apart from the men, but the act was a significant one: in Bright's opinion, women had as much right as men to study history.[5]

His second gesture was a daring appointment. Reginald Macan, a Scholar at University College in 1868–73, had been elected a Student of Christ Church. In 1877 he published *The Resurrection of Jesus Christ*, which was thought to be dangerously unorthodox. In June 1882, Macan had to be re-elected following his marriage, in accordance with the new statutes given to the colleges. A routine re-election was transformed when the aged Dr Pusey, rising one last time to defend his vision of church and the university, and the other canons (including William Bright) defeated the motion to re-elect the heretic. Fortunately, Macan's old College and its Master were on hand to assist, for almost at once Macan was given teaching responsibilities both at University College and at Brasenose. Then, in January 1884, Bright personally invited Macan to become Tutor and Praelector in Ancient History at University College, and when in November 1884 a Fellowship became vacant, Macan was elected.[6]

Some members of the Governing Body left Bright far behind in their political views. In 1882, Charles Faulkner stepped down as Bursar, to devote himself to politics. Faulkner had always been a liberal, but by the early 1880s, he was following his friend William Morris down the road to socialism. In November 1883 he arranged for Morris to give a lecture titled 'Art and Democracy' in the College Hall at a meeting attended by John Ruskin. Morris caused a sensation (and disturbed Bright) by making his first major public avowal of socialism, and appealing to his listeners to join in his campaign. In 1885

---

[4] UC:MA42/MS1/27.
[5] Bright's lectures: UC:GB4/A1/4 fo. 73ʳ (also Adams 1996: 33–4 and Howarth 2000a: 248). Bright nevertheless had mixed feelings about women's education. In a lecture titled 'The condition and prospects of the Female Sex' (UC:MA42/MS2/2), while regretting that 'woman's intellect...has hitherto been most unwarrantably neglected', he did not want women to study science, anxious that a 'familiarity with hard facts' would 'blunt the finer feelings' of 'the purveyor of more faithful if less logical beliefs'.
[6] Mason 2000: 222–3. Macan's diary (UC:MA43/J1/1) gives his own account of the affair, and its aftermath, including the invitation from Bright.

Faulkner created an Oxford Socialist League, and the *Oxford Magazine* of 1885 caricatured him as 'an alehouse anarchist'. Tragically, Faulkner fell victim to an incapacitating stroke in 1888, and remained an invalid until his death in 1892.[7]

Another eminent socialist was A. J. Carlyle (Fig. 17.5). Although Carlyle was only a Fellow in 1893–5, after which he became vicar of St Martin's and All Saints, Oxford, he remained a College Tutor and Chaplain, and exercised an important influence. Clement Attlee (m. 1901), who only turned to socialism after going down, remembered Carlyle as one of the few men in Oxford who kept the flame of socialism burning. Indeed, Carlyle took an interest unusual among Oxford dons in city politics, especially in support of working men. He hosted Sunday afternoon teas, remembered for their pleasant informality—and, rather daringly, for including students from the women's colleges. Some, however, remembered Carlyle for his 'whimsical' appearance and speech, and his 'delightfully unconventional' sermons.[8]

Several undergraduates, both socialists and paternalistic Tories, felt it their duty to do something for the poor: many public schools and colleges created missions in the East End. These tended not to be organized by the college or school itself, but by old boys coming together through memories of past comradeship. Such was the case with the Devas Institute and University College. Jocelyn Devas (m. 1878) set up University College House in Battersea above a coffee shop in 1884, aiming to provide local boys with some education or the chance to learn a trade. After Devas's tragic death in a climbing accident two years later, his father, Thomas, endowed a Devas Institute to further his aims. The College appointed members to the Committee of Management, and the College's links with the Institute continue to the present day.[9]

It will have been observed that Macan was appointed to a teaching post before he was elected a Fellow. This reflected a change in the College's teaching staff. As undergraduates studied an ever wider range of subjects, so a small Fellowship like University College's could not provide a complete set of specialist tutors, and non-Fellows were needed. A new category of College members grew up in a between-stairs world: granted membership of the Senior Common Room, they were not Fellows, took no part in College decisions, and received no Fellows' perquisites, but nevertheless played an important role in the teaching of undergraduates. Such SCR members first appear in College accounts in 1881/2. One of the most interesting of this new

---

[7] Faulkner's politics: Pinkney 2007: 82–91 and 106–14; Morris's lecture: Morris 1984: 57–85 (text) and Pinkney 2007: 47–70: reactions to Faulkner: Day 1997: 469.

[8] Socialism: Attlee 1954: 15; city politics: Day 1997: 467–8; tea parties: Moore 1954: 15; sermons: McFadyean 1964: 33.

[9] The Devas Institute: Gee and Wild 1979; similar college missions: Ockwell and Pollins 2000: 670–3.

class of College member was Ernest de Sélincourt (m. 1890), who, having studied classics, was drawn into the new honours school of English. In 1895, de Sélincourt (Fig. 17.5) was appointed a lecturer in English by the College—the first English lecturer appointed by any college—and he seems to have handled most of the English teaching throughout Oxford over the next decade.[10]

One of the best remembered non-Fellows was Arthur Johnson, Chaplain of All Souls, and senior history tutor at University College. Like Arthur Dendy, 'The Johnner' was an enthusiastic huntsman, who sometimes took tutorials clad in his muddy hunting-kit, and even consuming tea and toast while essays were read to him. For some undergraduates, Johnson would have had a far greater impact on their lives than many of the Fellows of the College, although his teaching seems to have been somewhat rough and ready: Clement Attlee, one of his pupils, once admitted that he thought that he might have got a First had he been better taught, and Edgar Carritt heard how, having 'once reduced a Univ. pupil to tears', Johnson 'put his arm round the man and said "Don't be a fool. I'm paid to talk to you like that." '[11]

Another change in the Fellowship occurred in 1901, when William Sollas, Professor of Geology, was elected a Fellow. Other colleges, such as Magdalen and Corpus, had been obliged to attach some of their fellowships—and their income—to university professorships, but Sollas was the first such professor at University College, and in 1912 the College's statutes were emended to attach one Fellowship permanently to the Geology Professorship.[12]

Two clouds hung over Bright's early Mastership. The first was the sending-down of 1880, an incident which popular memory magnified and kept on misdating. Henry Goudge (m. 1885) claimed that the College was 'three-parts empty' on account of 'the mishandling of a "rag" ', and William Bateson (Fig. 19.1), who started working as a servant aged 14 in 1887, claimed 'I came the year after the sending-down of the College [sic]. That was a very bad time for the College. Half the rooms were empty the following year, for so many of the men wouldn't come back.' There was some basis in fact for these memories, for admissions did fall slightly in the early 1880s (Graph 15.1).[13]

The second problem faced by Bright was one of the worst peacetime financial crises which Oxford and Cambridge have ever faced, namely a nationwide agricultural depression caused when corn prices, especially in the south and east of England, collapsed. Matters were made only worse by a

---

[10] College accounts of 1881/2: UC:BU3/F3/60; de Sélincourt: UC:GB3/A1/3 p. 309, Bayley 2006: 115, Palmer 2000: 405, and (for his teaching elsewhere) Hopkins 2005: 201.

[11] Johnson: Rushbrook Williams 1975: 24, Woods 1941: 276–7, Hopkinson 1958: 177, *UCR* Vol. V no. 3 (1968), 160 (Attlee), and Carritt 1958: 191. Johnson's wife Bertha was a prominent supporter of women's education in Oxford (*ODNB* entry).

[12] UC:GB3/A1/3 p. 383.

[13] Goudge: Goudge 1940: 14–15; Bateson: Bayley 1954*b*: 33.

series of bad harvests. Already in 1879/80 the Fellows had had to accept a reduced dividend 'in view of the heavy remissions of rent to be made to tenants in consequence of the bad seasons'. Charles Faulkner encountered tales of woe on his travels: in January 1881, he was told at Pontefact of 'the great depreciation of property' over the last two years, and when the College's agent went to Wales in May, he brought back news of a countryside *denuded of sheep*. The problems of Marks Hall proved worst of all. When Faulkner visited in September 1881, Joshua Gooday, the tenant, 'complained bitterly of a *very fine crop* which he would have had having been utterly spoilt by the 3 weeks rain at the end of August. It is too true.' In December 1881, Gooday became bankrupt. Not only did Faulkner have to eject a creditor from the property, but he had trouble finding anyone to take up the tenancy, even at a third of the original rent.[14]

The College's accounts reveal its difficulties (Graph 15.2). Those for 1880/1 claim that the rents from properties outside Oxford rose from £7,220 5s. to £7,848 18s. 7d., but there was also a large increase in estates expenses from £3,401 6s. 8d. to £4,355 17s. 8d. Much of this came from remissions of rent, which amounted to £1,142 18s. 11d.—almost 15 per cent of the College's expected rental for the year. In 1881/2, rents from non-Oxford properties fell back to £7,056 19s. 1d., and the Fellows agreed not to receive their dividends in full until there was some reduction in their rent arrears, which currently amounted to about £3,000. Furthermore the College had to repay the equivalent of one and a half times its gross income from estates, which it had borrowed to improve them. It has been calculated that the income from University College's estates in 1890 was barely half those in 1871—although, in fairness, prices fell sharply in the late 1880s, so that the actual fall in University College's income was not quite as great as it might appear.[15]

Cutbacks were made: in 1884 the College ceased to make grants from the Linton Fund to the incumbents of College livings, and in 1887 the Master and Fellows agreed to reduce their stipends and keep the next vacant Fellowship unfilled. Worse followed when, in 1890, the College was ordered by the Charity Commissioners to increase its payments to the Freeston Charities, and froze a second Fellowship to help pay for this. The Bursars' Books show that, whereas in the 1870s a resident Fellow with a College office received at least £600 or £700, in 1883 most of them received less than £500. Only in the later 1890s did

---

[14] General context of this depression: Dunbabin 1997: 401–9, and Engel 1983: 202–7; reduced dividend: UC:BU2/F1/7 fo. 264[r]; Pontefract: UC:EB4/J1/6 fos. 80[r] and 83[r] (matters there worsened in autumn 1881 when the College's agent disappeared, taking its rent money with him—UC:EB4/J1/6 fos. 110[r]–111[r]); Wales: UC:EB4/J1/6 fo. 95[r]; Essex: UC:EB4/J1/6 fos. 94[r], 116[r], 119[r], and 153[r] (and also UC:E3/C1/33–48).

[15] College accounts in 1880/1: UC:BU2/F1/7 fos. 265[v] and 270–3; in 1881/2: UC:BU2/F1/7 fos. 276[v]–277[r] and 285[r]; figures for College loans (fairly typical of other colleges) from Dunbabin 1997: 388–9; decline in income: tables in Jones 1997; fall in prices: Phelps Brown and Hopkins 1956.

Fellows' stipends return to the levels of twenty years earlier. When colleges like University College had to suspend their Fellowships, it was more sensible to suspend 'prize' Fellowships, and keep open tutorial ones. It was not until the later 1890s University College's disposable income rose again, mainly thanks to an increase in its internal income, especially undergraduate fees.[16]

The College's sufferings were not unique. Net income throughout the colleges fell by at least 15 per cent during the 1880s and early 1890s, and the loans eagerly taken out during the good times became harder to repay. However, University College was especially unfortunate, because it depended heavily upon its agricultural estates. Colleges with a significantly higher proportion of non-agricultural properties, like Merton and Magdalen (and, indeed, who had been slower to move to rack rents), weathered the storm rather better.[17]

In such circumstances, it was unfortunate that two domestic tragedies afflicted the College in the early 1890s, both rather more worthy of a sensational novel than a college history. The first arose out of Bright's search for sons-in-law.[18] In 1884, John Haines, a Balliol graduate, was elected a Fellow of University College. Soon appointed Praelector in Latin and Junior Dean, he became a Tutor in 1889. His prospects were good, and in 1890 he became engaged to Emily Bright. Once more, it seemed, the Master had made a suitable match. Unfortunately, on 6 November 1890, a woman named Catherine Riordan visited the College, claiming that she had had an understanding with John Haines before his engagement, and demanding revenge. Having tried unsuccessfully to see Haines, she then called on the Lodgings and spoke to the Master. Almost at once, she made a second visit to the Lodgings, only this time she drew a pistol, and shot the Master in the abdomen—fortunately not fatally (A. S. L. Farquharson, a future Fellow, claimed years later that Bright told him with his stammer 'F-f-fortunately, F-f-farkie, she only hit me in p-p-profile'). During Riordan's trial, it became clear that Haines's relationship with her was, if not improper, then certainly susceptible of such an interpretation, and, although she was sentenced to six years' imprisonment, she won much public sympathy. Haines's career was destroyed: his engagement was broken off, and he resigned his Fellowship on 8 November 1890.[19]

---

[16] Stipend supplements cut: UC:GB4/A1/4 fo. 145ʳ; reduced stipends and first frozen Fellowship: UC:GB3/A1/3 pp. 258–67; second freezing: UC:GB3/A1/3 pp. 281–3; decline in prize Fellowships: Engel 1983: 258–9; internal income: Dunbabin 1997: 403–4 and 414.

[17] Engel 1983: 202–7; other colleges who suffered: Austen Leigh 1899: 292 (King's), Howard 1935: 226–32 (St John's, Cambridge), Hyam in Cunich and others 1994: 216 (Magdalene, Cambridge), Green 1957: 292–4 (Lincoln), and Davies in Davies and Garnett 1994: 46 (Wadham).

[18] This tale is told more fully in Mitchell 1995, with extra information at UC:P39/C/1.

[19] Haines's resignation: UC:GB3/A1/3 p. 284; Bright's reaction: Bayley 2002: 93. Emily Bright later married John Arthur Gibbs, a second cousin (UC:P39/C/1), and Haines became a private tutor, and received the OBE for war work (Elliott 1934: 118).

Only a few months after Bright was shot, tragedy struck Charles Fyffe. In 1882 Fyffe had succeeded Charles Faulkner as Senior Bursar, under the title of Estates Bursar, and done his best to manage the College's finances during difficult times. He had married, and might have been elected to Parliament. However, in April 1891, Fyffe was arrested on a charge of committing an indecent act with another man in a railway carriage, and shortly afterwards cut his throat in a suicide attempt. In fact the case was thrown out in July 1891: whatever occurred in the carriage, the fact that Fyffe and his accuser had travelled past several stations before any charge was laid raised the strong possibility that he had merely been a victim of blackmail. Sadly, Fyffe never recovered, lingering until death intervened mercifully the following February.[20]

Fyffe had been a non-resident Fellow for several years, and his sad end could be hushed up; but the shooting of the Master in his Lodgings could not. Nigel Playfair (m. 1892), later a theatrical impresario, recollected that University College was suffering 'from the effect of two eclipses', the sending down of 1880, which Playfair thought had happened only recently, and the shooting of the Master. Indeed, whereas twenty-nine men had come up to University College in 1890, only nineteen did so in 1891.[21]

One observer thought that the College's undergraduate intake was also affected by its financial troubles. A memorandum prepared in 1894 for the Catholic Church about the universities noted that, although many more Oxford undergraduates now read for honours than, say, thirty years earlier, 'some colleges, like University College and Wadham, are too poor to insist upon it as much as they would like'.[22] This comment is supported by the evidence: in the 1880s, as in the later 1870s, roughly three-quarters of University College's undergraduates were awarded honours degrees, but the proportion fell in 1891–5 to just over 60 per cent.

There were, however, some encouraging trends in the College's admissions in the later nineteenth century. Matriculation numbers recovered from the scandal of the Master's shooting, doubling in 1891–1911, so that the College became for the first time one of the larger Oxford colleges (Graph 15.1). The Marquess of Salisbury continued sending his sons to University College, even after the arrival of Reginald Macan. Furthermore, the proportion of undergraduates reading honours degrees rose in 1896–1905 to between 70 and 75 per cent.[23]

Many contemporaries thought that Bright received valuable assistance in the revival in the College's fortunes from Hubert Burge (m. 1882; F. 1890–

---

[20] See further Darwall-Smith 2001.
[21] Playfair 1930: 72–3. University College was not alone in this: Christ Church suffered a fall in numbers in the 1890s after similar scandals (Curthoys 2000: 124–5).
[22] Reprinted in Drumm 1991: 148.
[23] Size of College: Curthoys 2000: 123.

1900)—who in 1898 became another son-in-law of the Master. For Arthur Moore (m. 1896) University College in his day was 'in the spring of its renaissance under Hubert Burge'. Arthur Hopkinson (m. 1893) called Burge 'a great and holy man', who 'had the royal gift of remembering names and faces, and was never too busy to show kindness to the insignificant'. Among the servants William Bateson claimed that 'it was Dr. Burge I think chiefly who pulled the College up again'.[24]

Burge was a somewhat unusual Fellow, both for taking orders when few Fellows now did so and for acting as a conduit between the Senior and Junior Common Rooms in a way which—rather to its cost—had not been seen in the College for many years, and which would set an example to later generations. It was said that he tried to get to know every undergraduate in College, and was often seen standing at the foot of his staircase conversing with a group of them. A 'muscular Christian' of the best sort, he also participated in undergraduates' leisure activities, playing golf with them, and as a good cricketer, able to sympathize with their enthusiasms—and win their respect. Unfortunately, he did not stay at University College long, turning to a teaching career, which culminated in his becoming Headmaster of Winchester.[25]

Another Fellow who involved himself in undergraduate life was Arthur Spencer Loat Farquharson (Fig. 17.5; m.1890; F. 1899–1942), universally known as 'Farky' (also 'Farquhie') or 'The Fark'. For four decades he was a great College 'character', remembered for his eccentricities, and his conversation, which Edgar Carritt once described to C. S. Lewis (m. 1917) as being 'very good', but 'always within an inch of being mere silliness'.[26] He was remembered too as a sporting enthusiast: Laurence Rushbrook Williams (m. 1909) described 'the Fark' as:

A keen Territorial, a notable cricketer, well-beloved in College for his leniency to the academic shortcomings of rowing, rugger, soccer, cricket and hockey Blues of whom he was, like all of us, so proud. In later years...when I brought up for a weekend at Oxford one of his most cherished idols, the great 'Ranji' [the great cricketer Ranjitsinhji]...I gave a dinner party at which Ranji sat next to Farquharson who was almost tongue-tied with delight.[27]

Farquharson was a Volunteer and Territorial Officer before 1914, and in later life he liked to be known as *Colonel* Farquharson.

Farquharson's heartiness, however, was not quite what it seemed. His undergraduate contemporaries had thought him something of an aesthete,

---

[24] Moore 1954: 1; Hopkinson 1958: 177; Bayley: 1954*b*: 33 (on Bateson); see too Charnwood 1930: 14.
[25] Knowing undergraduates: Moore 1954: 13–14; golf: Scott 1971: 29; cricket: Jones 2000: 527.
[26] Lewis 1991: 293. Lewis himself (Lewis 1991: 43) found Farquharson 'oily'.
[27] Rushbrook Williams 1975: 24–5.

but he learned to suppress this. He once admitted that, as a Freshman in 1890, when he was enthusing over some fine elms in the University Parks with one of Bright's daughters, the Master stammered in rebuke, 'Farquharson, don't become a foolish aesthete.' And so indeed he did not.[28]

Farquharson was also a scholar of some worth, though almost in secret. In the 1920s and 1930s he provided valuable assistance to a major revision of Liddell and Scott's Greek Lexicon, and he devoted his life to a highly regarded edition, translation, and commentary of the *Meditations* of Marcus Aurelius. Yet this side of him remained largely hidden: Old Members who remember 'Farky' as the College eccentric express astonishment when informed of his scholarly work. It took a percipient observer like Eric Dodds (m. 1912), a future Regius Professor of Greek, to understand both sides of the man:

I recall a tutorial at which he illustrated Aristotle's mistaken view of how a horse trots by getting down on all fours and trotting round the room in that posture.... But Farky was something more than a subject for anecdotes. Many years later, when in his old age I came to know him better, I discovered in him a serious solitary man, earnestly endeavouring to live the life of a good Stoic as taught by his beloved exemplar, the Emperor Marcus Aurelius.[29]

'The Fark' stands as a telling example of a type of Oxford don of the early twentieth century, taking immense pains to bury a sensitive and intelligent mind beneath a self-consciously hearty exterior.

The other major classicist in the College was Arthur Blackbourne Poynton, an undergraduate of Balliol, and then Fellow of Hertford College, who was elected a Fellow in 1894, and taught Greek and Latin language and literature. 'The Poynt' largely confined himself to what E. R. Dodds described as 'the transmission of the most exact possible knowledge of two ancient languages'. Nevertheless, C. S. Lewis admired him as a tutor, and enjoyed his sense of humour. He also became sole Bursar in 1900 (laying aside the domestic aspects of his post in 1926, since when the College has always had two Bursars, an Estates and a Domestic). Edmund Bowen (F. 1922–65) recalled how he 'ruled as Estates Bursar in an easy, autocratic way', producing incomprehensible annual reports, lightened by news of bonuses for the Fellows. Tenants remembered his visits to their estates, his painstaking checks of what repairs were needed, his love of cricket, and his slightly formal speech (eating a bitter rhubarb pie, he observed 'It resists the sugar'). Bowen also recalled that Poynton oversaw the Fellows' Garden, and, as a whim, grew poisonous plants there. He was also a successful Public Orator in 1925–32, even giving a lecture in Greek in 1928. Once, when

---

[28] Aestheticism: Moore 1954: 4; rebuke: Farquharson 1934: 11.
[29] Dodds 1977: 44.

warning undergraduates about a thief entering people's rooms, he put up a notice in Latin verse.[30]

As University College's reputation rose, so it became once again socially exclusive, surpassed only by Balliol, Christ Church, and Magdalen. Little is known of undergraduates' schooling during the 1880s and early 1890s, but in 1896 the College began to print tutorial lists of junior members, giving their subjects and schools. These show that, of the 162 undergraduates who came up in 1894–7, almost sixty came from the 'Clarendon' Schools (p. 377), and two-thirds of these from Eton, Winchester, Harrow, and Rugby alone. Six men came from Radley and ten from Wellington, while just five undergraduates came from grammar schools—and these were Maidstone, Rochester, and Wakefield, with their College Scholarships. One of the few who came from a comparatively humble background was Gordon Hewart (m. 1887), a draper's son from Bury, who attended Manchester Grammar School. Hewart, sensitive to his background, feared that his Lancashire accent was a handicap, and altered it accordingly. Hewart possessed ambition, application, and luck, for he became Lord Chief Justice of England.[31]

An important change in the College's membership occurred in 1903, when Cecil Rhodes's endowment of Scholarships enabled students from the USA, Canada, Australia, New Zealand, South Africa, Rhodesia, and Germany to study at Oxford. University College willingly engaged with this novelty: the first Rhodes Scholars came up to Oxford in October 1903, and the first at University College arrived the following year, from Germany and the USA, with the first Canadians and Rhodesians following in 1905.[32] Rhodes Scholars increased the proportion of non-British junior members, and stimulated the internationalization of the College and the university which has continued ever since. In 1909 the College was one of the first to elect a former Rhodes Scholar as Fellow, when the Australian John Behan became the new Stowell Law Fellow. Behan was a phenomenon: in his second year, he sat both the BA in Jurisprudence and the BCL. Two papers were scheduled for the same time; so having finished one paper in half the time allowed, he ran to the other examination room to sit the second paper in the time remaining. He was awarded a First in both examinations.[33]

As the College's membership grew and changed, so its buildings were altered. Electric lighting was installed in 1893 in almost every part of the

---

[30] Poynton's teaching: Dodds 1977: 26–7 (Todd 2004 explores further Dodds's relations with Poynton) and Lewis 2000: 430–2 and 444; Bowen: UC:P22/MS/1; tenant's perspective: interview with Henry Ritchie, former tenant of Marks Hall, 17 July 2006; Greek lecture: *UCR* 1927/8 p. 2; notice: Logan 1974: 369.

[31] Social exclusivity: Honey and Curthoys 2000: 551, and Curthoys 1997c: 509; Tutorial lists from 1896: UC:J7/A1/2; Hewart at Oxford: Jackson 1959: 11–12 and 18–20 (his change of accent was not uncommon: Honey and Curthoys 2000: 548).

[32] Darwall-Smith 2003: 74–5 gives more details about the College's first Rhodes Scholars.

[33] Behan: Poynter in Kenny 2001: 324–5.

College, and in 1896 a basement in Radcliffe Quadrangle was converted into the College's first fitted bathroom (and, according to some, in any college). Originally, it had only three or four baths, and was open from 3 to 7 p.m. only—undoubtedly to benefit muddy sports players.[34]

The College also expanded its central site. On the east side, in 1885/6 Magdalen College sold to University College 86–7 High Street and 9–12 Merton Street, with the land between, in return for Drawda Hall; and in 1899 University College purchased 85 High Street from Queen's College, so that it now owned all the land between Radcliffe Quadrangle and the Examination Schools. Although the properties were leased as whole houses—during the later nineteenth century, 83 and 84 High Street were leased to Frank Cooper, famed for his Oxford Marmalade—the College could now expand eastwards if it so wished. Meanwhile, to the west, the College had shown interest in purchasing 90 High Street from Christ Church as early as 1873, although only in 1905 was a sale agreed for £8,000. It was decided to convert the greater part of this house—already rated by some 'the outstanding digs in Oxford'—into student accommodation at once, and the first occupants moved in two years later.[35]

The first new building of Bright's Mastership, however, was intended for a Fellow. In the 1880s, several colleges, concerned at the consequences of married Fellows moving out, built houses on their central sites where such Fellows could live with their families. University College built such a house in 1887 near the Library. Henry Wilkinson Moore, its architect, was the nephew of William Wilkinson, who built the Randolph Hotel, and both men played leading roles in the development by St John's College of its North Oxford estate. Reginald Macan, who was offered first refusal on the house, may have influenced Moore's appointment, because his house in St Margaret's Road was designed by Wilkinson and Moore. The new Tutor's House (now known as Kybald House) brought a little breath of North Oxford into the College, especially when viewed from the grand Kybald Street entrance rather than the poky servants' entrance (its only access from the College). The evident success of this project resulted in Moore's becoming University College's favoured architect for the next two decades.[36]

---

[34] Electricity: UC:GB4/A1/5 fo. 286^r and UC:BU3/F3/72 fos. 78^v–81^r; bathrooms: UC:GB4/A1/6 fos. 84^r and 92–3, and Hopkinson 1958: 176–7.

[35] 86–7 High Street: UC:EB1/A/6 pp. 266–7; 85 High Street: UC:E/B8/C/1; leases to members of the Cooper family: UC:EB1/A/5 p. 498, UC:EB1/A/6 pp. 73–4 and 349–50, and UC:EB1/A/7 pp. 1–3; 90 High Street: UC:GB4/A1/2 p. 135 (discussions of 1873), UC:GB4/A1/6 fo. 291^r (purchase), UC:GB4/A1/7 fos. 12^r and 40^r (function), and Mackenzie 1964: 148 (quality of accommodation).

[36] The context: Curthoys 2000: 140–1; discussions on Kybald House: UC:GB4/A1/4 fos. 227–9 and UC:GB3/A1/3 pp. 254–7; plans of the same: UC:FA10/1/Y1/1; houses designed by Wilkinson and Moore: Hinchliffe 1992: 216–43 (Macan's house is on p. 236).

Moore, however, was not involved in the College's next architectural project, a memorial to Percy Shelley.[37] As with the statues of the Scott brothers in the Library, University College found itself providing a home for an unwanted sculpture. Jane Shelley, the poet's daughter-in-law, who devoted her life to the purifying—if not bowdlerizing—of Shelley's image, had commissioned a piece from the sculptor Edward Onslow Ford for Shelley's grave in the Protestant cemetery at Rome. Unfortunately, it proved too big for the site, and in September 1891 Lady Shelley wrote to her friend Benjamin Jowett about the problem. Bright, as it happened, was well known to Jowett, having been a History Tutor at Balliol in 1872–81, and an Honorary Fellow there since 1877. Whether or not Jowett applied any pressure on Bright, University College did agree to accept Ford's monument in November, although they could not afford to house it.[38] Lady Shelley now wrote to the College, on 1 December 1891, formally offering them 'a beautiful work in marble and bronze'. She only required that it be appropriately housed, and offered £500 towards this, adding optimistically 'the remainder of the sum may, it is hoped, be raised by the poet's admirers'. She concluded ingenuously:

The place was one in which he must have passed many happy hours, and the circumstances under which he left the College are hardly worth considering now.[39]

Basil Champneys, who had just built the Indian Institute and Mansfield College, and would work at New College and Oriel, was commissioned to design an enclosure for the memorial. Unfortunately, Champneys was caught between the College's unwillingness to spend much money on a not wholly welcome gift, and the need to satisfy Onslow Ford and Lady Shelley. Successive designs were rejected by the College, with still more requests to reduce costs, but Champneys' final design seems to have pleased everyone. The statue was placed under a dome, which contained a window to light it, and the enclosure fitted into a rectangular box, with a passageway to the south. It was situated on the site of Deep Hall, which had been left vacant since its demolition.[40]

The Memorial was opened on 14 June 1893. Lady Shelley, Onslow Ford, and Champneys were joined by several Oxford worthies, including Benjamin Jowett. Forty years later Ernest de Sélincourt, chosen to represent the Junior Members, could still remember seeing Lady Shelley walking about on

---

[37] The history of the Memorial's construction is discussed in Darwall-Smith 2000a.
[38] Bright at Balliol: Elliott 1934: 74; Lady Shelley writing to Jowett: BCL Jowett Papers II C1/151 and 153; University College accepts the memorial: UC:GB4/A1/5 fo. 205r.
[39] UC:FA11/2/C1/1 no. 1; Shelley's 'many happy hours' are discussed in Chapter 15.
[40] In 1866, the architect Charles Buckeridge designed two buildings for this site (UC:FA11/1/Y1/1–5), one of which copied the façade of the Main Quadrangle, ogee gables and all, and another in a more typically Victorian Gothic style, but these came to nothing.

FIGURE 17.2 The Shelley Memorial, by Edward Onslow Ford.

Jowett's arm. Lady Shelley's and Bright's speeches were recorded in some detail in press reports of the event.[41] Lady Shelley thanked the College and the sculptor for 'enabling her to fulfil one of the dearest wishes of her heart', while Bright chivalrously spoke of the gift receiving 'fresh charms from the tender way in which she had delivered it over to them'. He was, however, unsure what to make of the statue itself. According to *Jackson's Oxford Journal*:

> He did not suppose it laid with him to praise that work of art which he should naturally wish to do. They could all of them see it was a thing which any giver might be proud to give, and any receiver might be proud to receive... But he could not help thanking Lady Shelley more especially for giving them this, because it was not often that a College in Oxford had a piece of art given to it at all belonging to this generation.

Indeed Edward Onslow Ford's masterpiece (Fig. 17.2) continues to fascinate and to disturb.[42] Ford was a prominent member of the so-called 'New Sculpture' (best known today through Alfred Gilbert's statue of Eros in Piccadilly Circus), which in the early 1890s represented the height of modernity. The memorial's lush exploitation of different marbles and metals—originally enhanced by the presence of a gilt-bronze laurel wreath on

---

[41] De Sélincourt: UC:FA11/3/C1/7 item 14. The inauguration was reported in The *Times* of 15 June, and in *Jackson's Oxford Journal* of 18 June.
[42] Getsy 2004: 119–41 provides an important analysis of the sculpture.

Shelley's brow—is coupled with the uncomfortable realization that one is being invited to linger over the beauty of a drowned corpse washed ashore. Furthermore, Ford's interest in androgyny led him to give Shelley's body some strangely feminine aspects, such as the shape of the hips. University College has maintained an uneasy relationship with the Memorial. Generations of undergraduates have played pranks on it (worthy of its subject, perhaps), and there have been discussions about moving it elsewhere, but the sculpture remains in the enclosure specially designed for it, and, after restoration work in the 1980s and in 2002/3, with its original colour scheme.

In the later 1890s, University College reviewed its undergraduate accommodation. University Hall was inconveniently cut off from the rest of the College, and in 1894 the College considered erecting a bridge to it over Logic Lane. It also did not provide enough accommodation: in 1895–6, ten new rooms were built behind it. However, the Hall's central problem was its poor condition, and the College eventually decided in October 1901 to demolish it, and commission a replacement from Moore. The new building, named Durham Buildings, was built at a cost of about £8,000, and first occupied in 1903. One part of University Hall escaped destruction: one of its rooms contained some remarkable sixteenth-century panelling, filled with lively carvings of moralizing scenes. These were too good to lose, and were re-erected in the Summer Common Room. Meanwhile, the building work revived the question of a bridge over Logic Lane. Unfortunately, the College found itself in dispute with Oxford City Council about the freehold of the lane, and its right to erect a bridge over it. After a two-year court case, the College won, and a bridge linking Durham Buildings and Radcliffe Quadrangle was built in 1905.[43]

Bright's last architectural project was to remove the Hall's 'Gothick' ceiling and panelling. Keene's work, once so daring and unusual, had long fallen from favour, and the continuing expansion of the College, which made the Hall too small, provided a pretext for its removal. In October 1898, therefore, a committee was formed to consider plans for the improvement of the Hall. Henry Wilkinson Moore discovered that enough of the original roof remained above Keene's ceiling to make a restoration possible; and in 1903–4 he removed Keene's additions, restored the old roof, and enlarged the Hall. The Hall was given new panelling (part of which covered up Keene's fireplace, leaving only a little roundel of King Alfred visible) and new

---

[43] Bridge: UC:GB4/A1/6 fos. 32^r and 51^r; new rooms: UC:GB4/A1/6 fos. 56–7 and 65, and UC:GB4/A1/6 fo. 96^r; debates on the building: UC:GB4/A1/6 fos. 189^r, 203^r, 207^r, 213^r, and 239^r; name: UC:GB3/A1/3 p. 340; costs taken from UC:BU3/F3/80–82; first occupants: UC:BU3/F3/82 p. 74; removal of carvings (discussed in detail in Bayley 1958–60): UC:GB4/A1/6 fo. 213^r (the fate of the panelling installed in the Summer Common Room in the 1840s (p. 353) is unknown); the College minutes for 1902–5 (in UC:GB3/A1/3) record the dispute with the City Council for the proposed bridge in detail.

windows—the new west window being a gift from Bright himself—and was formally reopened with a Gaudy in June 1905. Although the dismantling of Keene's work deprived later ages of an important early Gothic Revival interior, it would be churlish not to be grateful to Moore for revealing the splendid 1650s roof, and for his sensitive additions.[44]

Some of Keene's work nevertheless survives. In May 1865, the rooms on the ground floor of Staircase I had been appropriated to the use of the Senior Common Room, but at the time the Fellows only exploited this to make a passageway to the Hall, leaving the rest of the space for use as a lecture room for the Dean and a bedroom for non-resident Fellows. In 1904, however, the passageway and bedroom were removed, and the new space converted into a library to house a collection of books on American history assembled by Ernest Payne (F. 1872–1904), which were donated by his widow to the College, and some of Keene's panelling from the Hall was hung on the walls of the new Payne Library.[45]

The 1905 Gaudy was the last major event of James Bright's Mastership, for he resigned in February 1906.[46] He retired to live near William and Margaret Carr in Norfolk, and died in 1920. Bright resembles Thomas Cockman in some respects: neither man was particularly charismatic or dynamic, but, both possessed of a quiet integrity, they calmed the College down after difficult times. If University College was a more harmonious place in 1906 than it was in 1881, Bright deserves much of the credit.

REGINALD MACAN

The new Master, elected in March 1906, was the heretic of Christ Church, Reginald Macan (Fig. 17.3).[47] The Macan of 1906, however, had changed from the Macan of the 1870s: he had long since turned to the study of ancient history, and of Herodotus in particular, and was unusual among British scholars of his generation in attempting to apply archaeological discoveries to the study of ancient history. A native of Dublin, Macan preserved his Irish accent at least until the 1890s.[48]

He had been something of a liberal. As a young man he had been in Germany to learn the latest scholarship there, and along with another

---

[44] Committee: UC:GB4/A1/6 fo. 144ʳ; Moore's report: UC:FA4/2/Y1/1; fund-raising: UC:GB4/A1/6 fos. 222ʳ and 233ʳ, and UC:FA4/2/MS1/1; progress of work: UC:GB3/A1/3 pp. 341, 347, and 354.

[45] Conversion of the room in 1865: UC:GB4/A1/2 pp. 72–3; donation of Payne's books: *UCR* 1904/5. Although the reuse of Keene's work is nowhere documented explicitly, a comparison of the panelling currently in the Payne Room with that seen in photographs of the Hall before 1904 makes its provenance clear.

[46] UC:GB3/A1/3 p. 357.

[47] UD:GB3/A1/3 p. 358–9.

[48] Macan's research, and his accent: Moore 1954: 16.

FIGURE 17.3 Reginald Macan, m. 1868, Fellow 1884–1906, and Master 1906–23, by Maurice Greiffenhagen.

classicist, Lewis Farnell, Fellow and later Rector of Exeter, he set up a club in 1889, whose aim, as Farnell recalled:

was mainly to maintain and develop the character of the University as a home of learning and science and this purpose to place the interests of the University as a whole above those of the separate colleges: to strengthen the influence of the professoriate and to diffuse the ideal of research throughout the college teaching-staffs: to encourage new subjects of study, but to keep the examination system within bounds and to exorcise the examination spirit.[49]

As Macan grew older, so he took himself more seriously. Alexander Lindsay (m. 1898), future Master of Balliol, thought Macan 'fussy', and Edgar Carritt remembers Macan's being brought down to earth by Frederick Conybeare (F. 1880–7):

Macan, then senior Fellow, offering him the last of a great vintage port, asked: 'Do know what you are drinking?' We all knew what answer he had prepared for his rhetorical question: 'Potable gold'. But Conybeare, tasting it, replied: 'Corked'. It was.[50]

Macan was the first lay Master since Antony Gate over 300 years earlier. Both in college and public school, lay heads were still the exception, and Macan felt

[49] Farnell 1934: 270–1 (see too Howarth 2000b: 627–9).
[50] Scott 1971: 30 (Lindsay) and Carritt 1960: 42.

this acutely.⁵¹ In particular, he wished to play his part in the religious life of the College. A month after his election, Macan gave an address in the College Chapel, in which he said:

> For a mere layman at any time to speak in an expressly religious sense may seem to be taking much—perhaps too much—upon him. . . . [But] It has been usual for the Master of the College to speak in this place. . . . As the first Lay Head of this House I have had to face the question—whether I should keep silence in this place, where I have undoubtedly the right to speak. That right seems to me to carry with it a duty—and the duty seems to me a privilege—perhaps the highest attaching to my office.⁵²

Macan gave at least one Chapel address a year, usually early in Michaelmas Term, regularly setting out his vision of the College, as in this passage from an address given on 14 October 1906:

> Our best tradition is to have been a United Society: a Society free from divisions, sets, jealousies; a Society in which all work and play together, so far as may be, harmoniously, for the common good, including the good reputation of the College. Let us hold fast by that tradition! A College with such a tradition makes other good things natural, for its members—it makes vice, in every form, look uglier and more unwholesome—it makes a clean, healthy, high-spirited, joyous, athletic and intellectual life easier.⁵³

Those who shared Macan's visions admired him. Edmund Bowen remembered Macan as 'an impressive but genial presider over college meetings', which 'were conducted with Victorian formality and with great respect for the Master's views'. He also recalled that Macan 'used to lead Chapel singing with his powerful bass voice'.⁵⁴ Fred Bickerton admired Macan greatly:

> He was a strict disciplinarian, but he never exerted authority for his own sake. He was tactful and had great personal charm . . . I remember him very well indeed, a burly thickset figure. On occasion he could unbend, too. I was once at a College Servants' Party, at which the Master was invited to sing. We waited with baited breath to see what would happen. But the Master smiled and very graciously accepted the invitation. He sang 'Off to Philadelphia in the morning'.⁵⁵

Some undergraduates were less impressed with the 'Mugger' (Macan inherited Bright's nickname). Andrew McFadyean (m. 1905), later a politician, remembered Macan's ponderous lectures and his pretty daughters, and C. S. Lewis was surprised in 1922 to be told about Macan's heretical past.⁵⁶ Eric Dodds

---

⁵¹ Public schools: Witheridge 2005: 99–105. James Bright supported the appointment of Frank Fletcher to Marlborough in 1903 as the first lay head of a major public school.
⁵² UC:MA43/MS4/1.
⁵³ UC:MA43/MS4/2.
⁵⁴ UC:P22/MS/1.
⁵⁵ Bickerton 1953: 131–2.
⁵⁶ McFadyean 1964: 32 and Lewis 1991: 31.

actively disliked Macan. When he asked the Master to be exempted from reading lessons in Chapel, because he did not believe in Christianity,

> The request was ill received. Was I, he inquired, a Buddhist, a Muhammedan, or a Jew? 'No,' I replied rather crossly, 'I am an atheist.' He made that noise, indicative of contemptuous displeasure, which used to be represented by the word 'Pshaw!' I got my exemption, but I got a black mark with it, despite the fact that Macan himself was said to have been deprived in his youth of an appointment at Christ Church by reason of doubts about his orthodoxy.[57]

Relations between Macan and Dodds would have been difficult anyway, for, although Dodds was also Irish, he inclined towards the Nationalist side, and Macan to the Unionist.

A more serious charge against Macan is that academic standards fell during his Mastership. University College certainly remained an exclusive place: the 169 undergraduates who came up in 1904–7 included barely half a dozen grammar school students, but there were 74 from the 'Clarendon' schools, including 16 Etonians, 20 Wykhamists, 14 Rugbeians, and 10 each from Charterhouse (Macan's old school) and Harrow, while 18 came from Marlborough, and out of 93 undergraduates who came up in 1912–13, no fewer than 41 came from the Clarendon Schools, with 24 from Eton, Harrow, and Winchester, and 11 from Charterhouse. This exclusivity came at a cost: fewer than two-thirds of the undergraduates who came up in 1906–10 achieved honours degrees, at a time when four-fifths of undergraduates throughout Oxford were obtaining them. Standards were still set—Laurence Rushbrook Williams sat six three-hour papers in three days to be admitted—but the College was no longer George Bradley's academic powerhouse.[58]

THE 'HEARTY' COLLEGE: UNDERGRADUATE LIFE BEFORE 1914

It is therefore time to examine undergraduate life under Bright and Macan, and study further the results of University College turning itself into a smart, but unintellectual, College. The daily routine remained leisurely. Breakfast was the major social event of the day; mornings were spent in work, afternoons in recreation. Scientists, though, were restricted by laboratory hours: A. D. Gardner (m. 1903; F. 1927–48), universally known as 'Duncs', a lawyer who switched to medicine, remembered that scientists 'were considered rather poor fish by the Greats men and lawyers'.[59]

Compulsory Chapel was limited to at least once on Sundays (on weekday mornings, one could either attend Chapel or sign one's name in the Porter's

---

[57] Dodds 1977: 44–5.
[58] Honours degrees: Brock 2000b: 788–9 and Curthoys 1997b: 360; exams in 1909: Rushbrook Williams 1975: 22.
[59] Breakfast: Moore 1954: 5; scientists: Gardner 1975: 69.

FIGURE 17.4 Interior of room (Staircase X:1) occupied by Richard Slater, m. 1898, in 1901.

Lodge), and other services grew less popular. The Chapel was usually no more than one-quarter to one-third full for morning services, and the evening services were usually attended only by the Chaplain and the Scholar who had to read the lessons that week. There were attempts to improve the music: in 1901–5 John Varley Roberts, the organist of Magdalen College, acted as a 'Precentor', in order 'to undertake the training of the undergraduate voices'.[60]

Inventories from the early 1910s shed light on how undergraduates furnished their rooms (Fig. 17.4). There was considerable variation: James Allan (m. 1912), although from Charterhouse, had a poorly furnished room valued at £32, while Christopher Tinne, the great sportsman of the day (see below), had a large set in Staircase VI valued at £60. While Allen had some carpets and rugs, a dining table, some window cushions, curtains, blinds, and two chairs with tapestry covers, Tinne had all these, but also six chairs, a settee with a tapestry cover, and curtains.[61]

[60] Rules: UC:J8/N1/6; Moore 1954: 7–8, and 'A. A. L. P.' (Alfred Parsons (m. 1901)) in *UCR* Vol. IV no. 1 (1961), 50; falling attendances elsewhere: Hinchliff 2000: 106–7; Roberts as Precentor: UC:GB4/A1/6 fos. 139^r, 215^r, and 295^r.
[61] Inventories: UC:FA1/3/MS4/1–42; Allen: UC:FA1/3/MS4/33; Tinne UC:FA1/3/MS4/12.

During his undergraduate years at University College, Andrew McFadyean kept an account book, recording all his expenditure, down to tips for servants, cab fares, and haircuts.[62] There were clothes to buy, including a smoking jacket, a surplice for Chapel, and sports kit (he played football and tennis); but McFadyean also bought groceries such as cocoa, biscuits, apples, and candles, although he did not purchase wine, sherry, or port. He also bought much crockery, presumably for entertaining, and even hired a piano. McFadyean purchased many books—he got a First in classics—but he took time off to go to the theatre or the opera. He also subscribed to charities such as the Oxford Mission in the East End or Toynbee Hall. However, one regular item, namely chilblain lotion, reminds us that College life, especially in winter, was not quite as comfortable as one might imagine.

Undergraduate social life was transformed by the creation of a Junior Common Room. Since the 1860s, there had been informal groupings of undergraduates confident enough to meet the Fellowship as a body, as on the occasion of the catering petition of 1864, but no room was allocated for general undergraduate use. This changed in the 1880s and 1890s: Farquharson, coming up in 1890, was under the impression that the 'Common Room' had been merely a social group within the College, but had only just opened up to all its undergraduates. University College had been rather slow off the mark, for other colleges had had official Junior Common Rooms since the 1860s. In March 1889, a room in Staircase X was offered as a Junior Common Room, but the first room so identified was on the first floor of Staircase V, in 1892. In Michaelmas Term 1893 the JCR moved to the first floor of Staircase II, where it has remained ever since, later incorporating the adjoining room in Staircase I. The first known President of the JCR, elected for 1894/5, was Gerald Mordaunt, a Cricket Blue continuously throughout 1893–6. By the late 1890s Sunday JCR meetings after Formal Hall had become a popular venue for meetings and debates. It was customary for motions to be introduced by visiting Old Members, the combative Tory MP Lord Hugh Cecil (m. 1887) being a regular and popular speaker.[63]

By the early twentieth century, the College had four main undergraduate societies, according to 'Duncs' Gardner. The first of them was the exclusive Shakespeare Club ('the Shaker'). Next came the Martlets (Fig. 17.5), founded in 1892, which like the 'Shaker' has survived intermittently to the present; Gardner remembered it as 'a serious literary club', attended mostly by Scholars and younger Fellows, and its members were given a list of literary subjects to prepare, preferably around a single period or genre.

---

[62] UC:P28/F/1.
[63] Opening up of Common Room: Farquharson 1934: 9; JCR's elsewhere: Curthoys 2000: 150–1; offer of a room: UC:GB4/A1/5 fos. 82ʳ and 91ʳ; the first rooms: UC:BU3/F3/71 fo. 35ʳ and UC:BU3/F3/72 fo. 34ᵛ; guest speakers: Moore 1954: 9.

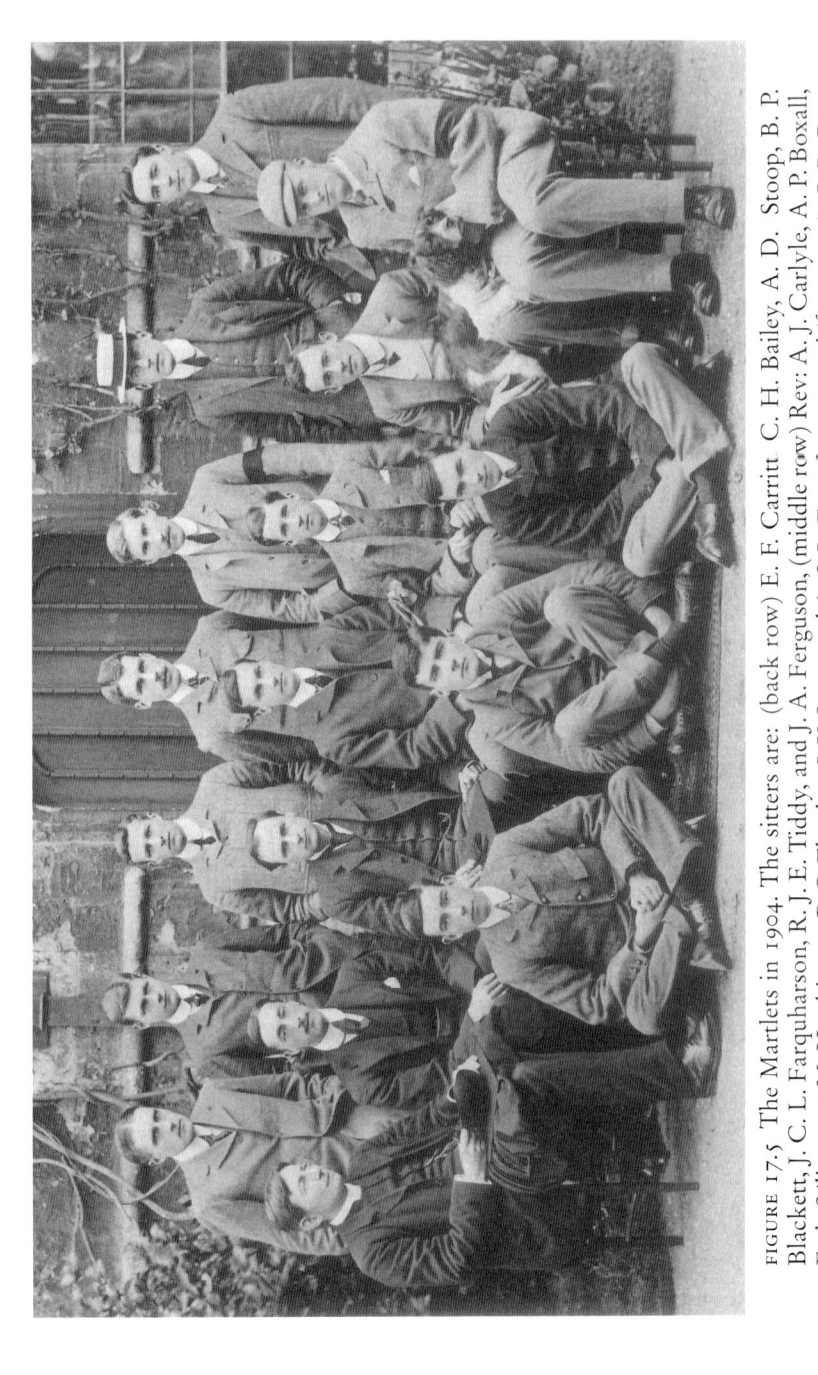

FIGURE 17.5 The Martlets in 1904. The sitters are: (back row) E. F. Carritt, C. H. Bailey, A. D. Stoop, B. P. Blackett, J. C. L. Farquharson, R. J. E. Tiddy, and J. A. Ferguson, (middle row) Rev: A. J. Carlyle, A. P. Boxall, E. de Sélincourt, M. Hopkinson, P. C. Fletcher, J. Y. Scott, and A. S. L. Farquharson, and (front row), G. R. Day, A. Fox, and C. R. Attlee.

A third society, the Durham Society (the 'Durrer'), read more modern plays, and indeed the Society's minute book (which starts in 1891) shows the society reading works by Lytton, Byron, Shelley, Sheridan, and even Ibsen (*The Master Builder*). Farquharson was an undergraduate member of the society, and some Fellows joined in: it must have been a rather incongruous occasion in April 1893, when Albert Chavasse (the same Chavasse screwed up in 1880) read the part of Cleopatra. Finally, there were the Churchwardens (the 'Chuggerwuggers'), who 'smoked long clay pipes, drank coffee, and enjoyed the solemnly ribald reading of the works of Shakespeare'. Some of these societies' meetings were attended by both Fellows and undergraduates—a sign of more harmonious relations between the Common Rooms.[64]

Musical life in the College was fairly informal, centring on so-called 'Smoking Concerts', which comprised a mixture of orchestral items, songs, instrumental pieces, and recitations, performed mainly by members of the College and occasionally some Old Members such as Nigel Playfair, now engaged on a theatrical career, who in 1901 delivered a recitation and sang some songs. In a concert of 1905, a recitation was given by a current undergraduate, Cecil William Mercer, later well known for the thrillers which he wrote under his pseudonym of Dornford Yates.[65]

By now there was also a flourishing world of university clubs and societies outside the College. Student drama had revived at Oxford in 1885 with the creation of the Oxford University Dramatic Society (OUDS), soon joined by members of University College. A memorable production of *Alice in Wonderland* in Worcester Gardens in 1895—said to be the first OUDS open-air show—included both Nigel Playfair and Paul Rubens (m. 1893), later a well-known composer of musicals. There was also the world of the student journal: several members of University College, including Desmond Coke (m. 1899), a future minor man of letters, collaborated with a Magdalen undergraduate, Compton Mackenzie, future author of *Whisky Galore*, in creating a literary magazine, *The Oxford Point of View*, in 1902.[66]

Despite these artistic efforts, Oxbridge life before 1914 was dominated by the enthusiasm for sport. Sporting success enhanced a college's reputation, and University College's reputation stood high: it went Head of the River in Eights Week in 1902 and 1914 and in Torpids in 1905–6, the Rugby team won the Inter-Collegiate Cup in 1914, and 'Univ.' men appeared in the Blues teams in many sports. Even non-athletic undergraduates like Clement Attlee were proud of their College's sporting reputation, which may have been a

---

[64] The clubs: Gardner 1975: 72; the Martlets: Anon. 1950 (a Martlets termcard from 1903/4 (UC:P32/X1/3) shows its members all given subjects: Farquharson was listed under 'The English Romantic School', Clement Attlee under 'Blake', and so on); Durham Club: UC:O16/A1/1; Churchwardens: UC:P10/P/1; other examples of this range of societies: Green 1979: 564 (for Lincoln).

[65] Programmes for smoking concerts: UC:O9/X1/1–3, UC:P32/X1/1 (where Playfair appeared), and UC:P79/X1/1; smoking concerts elsewhere: Twigg 1987: 248.

[66] OUDS: Carpenter 1985: 50; student journalism: Mackenzie 1964: 90 and 98–9.

draw for Rhodes Scholars. Eights Week was a major social event, with the roof of the College barge crowded with cheering families and friends (Fig. 17.6), and sporting successes were regularly celebrated with grand dinners in the Hall.[67]

The range of sports had broadened, as College teams now competed in rowing, cricket, football, golf, hockey, rugby, tennis, and athletics. In the 1890s the 'Amalgamated Clubs' were created, which managed the finances of the cricket, rowing, football, rugby, and athletics teams by raising a levy on undergraduates' batells. The College also improved its sporting facilities. Undergraduates had previously used Cowley and the University Parks, but in autumn 1910 the Fellows, inspired by A. S. L. Farquharson, set aside part of the Eastwick Farm estate off the Abingdon Road for a sports field. A cricket pavilion was built, designed by Clough Williams Ellis, and it and the new sports ground were opened on 23 May 1914. Shortly afterwards, in July 1914, the field was formally leased to Farquharson as Treasurer of the University College Undergraduates' Funds Committee.[68]

The *beau ideal* of the Edwardian College was Christopher Tinne, an Etonian who came up in 1910 and served as JCR President in 1912/13. A contemporary remembered him as 'the most perfect type of an Englishman', praising him for his athletic and scholarly skills, but also noting that 'he was kind and sympathetic to everyone and always ready to help those who were less gifted than himself'. Tinne notionally read chemistry, in which he got a Third in 1914, but for his contemporaries Tinne was the great sportsman. He rowed in the Oxford Eight in 1911 and 1912, but when he was not selected in 1913 (on account of intrigues involving the Magdalen College Boat Club, according to his family), he devoted himself to College sports, and ensured that University College went Head of the River in 1914. Tinne was also capable of ingenious practical jokes. One such involved sending Farquharson, then Dean, an anonymous note warning him to 'sport his oak' (i.e. keep the outer door of his rooms closed) all day against any pranksters. Tinne then dressed up as a woman of doubtful character, entered the College, went to 'Farky's' staircase, but promptly changed out of his costume in the rooms of a friend who lived just below. The Porter and Master, observing the locked door of the Dean, and the disappearance of the 'lady' up his staircase, were not readily persuaded by his pained expressions of innocence.[69]

---

[67] Attitudes to sport: Attlee 1954: 14, Gardner 1975: 66 and McFadyean 1964: 31; Rhodes Scholars: Rushbrook Williams 1975: 23.

[68] General context: Farquharson 1934: 9–13; move to Abingdon Road: UC:GB4/A1/7 fos. 121–3 and UC:E/H1/3D/1; the pavilion: UC:E/H1/Y2/1 and UC:E/H1/C4/1–3; opening of the same: *UCR* 1913/14, p. 2; other college pavilions: Howell 2000: 756.

[69] Tinne's character: obituary in *UCR* Vol. VI no. 1 (1971), 90–1; family tradition: interview with his son, Michael Tinne (m. 1949), 15 May 1999; his practical joke: *UCR* Vol. XII no. 1 (1997), 82–3.

FIGURE 17.6. The last day of Eights Week 1902: the 'Univ.' Eight, Head of the River, rows back to the College Barge to a suitably ecstatic reception.

FIGURE 17.7 The convivial College: photograph taken at the end of the coming-of-age dinner party of Herbert Adams, m. 1898, in 1900. The subjects are: (back row from left): R. A. Williams, H. R. Vickers, L. Burra, and F. P. Clarke, and (front row from left), H. F. Terry, H. W. Goldberg, J. E. Crabbie, F. O. J. Huntley, Adams, G. L. Tottenham, E. N. Bell, and Richard Slater, whose room is seen in Fig. 17.4.

This was indeed a time for 'japes' and high spirits: Fred Bickerton remembered a barrel organ being carried into Radcliffe Quadrangle and played to great effect in the early hours, while Robert Mendl (m. 1911), a keen musician, woke up to find that his piano had been abstracted from his rooms, and moved to the college lavatories. He accepted it in good humour, playing Chopin's Funeral March in his piano's temporary home, before having it shipped back. Comings of age were marked by special—and well-lubricated—dinners (Fig. 17.7), and bonfires lit in the quadrangle for special occasions. Inhibitions disappeared in this heady atmosphere: Gordon Hewart, the shy draper's son, was standing by a bonfire in his first term, when some colleagues discussed what it felt like to be burnt at the stake. Hewart commented that the only way was to jump into the bonfire—which he promptly did, fortunately emerging safely on the other side.[70]

Many former undergraduates looked back on this period as a particularly happy one. For 'Duncs' Gardner, 'Univ. was an undergraduate's paradise', while Laurence Rushbrook Williams thought that 'Univ. was a particularly friendly college; we all seemed to know each other, regardless of background, wealth (or lack of it), and academic or athletic ability.'[71] Arthur Moore claimed:

> We do not seem to have produced scholars of distinction just then, or lawyers, but prided ourselves on attracting men of general ability and varied interests which I still think is the best aim of a College.... We were not noisy (like the House and Brasenose just then) for though there were the annual Freshers' and Seniors' 'Wines' and the inevitable bonfires and good-humoured ragging, there was never any serious trouble.[72]

Moore, who had attended what he considered a minor public school, also thought that the College was notable for its lack of cliques, which he felt owed much to Hubert Burge. Clement Attlee agreed, observing that 'there was no division between athletes and scholars'.[73]

These are the recollections of nostalgic old men, but they are corroborated by contemporaries. In 1912, a German student at University College, Alexander Grunelius (m. 1910), and a friend of his at Trinity published anonymously a guide to Oxford for German students, which included a description of the colleges. Here is their entry for University College:

> University (Master) is one of the oldest and best Colleges, whose origin is traced back to a foundation of Alfred the Great. It does not offer much for intellectual stimulation. Instead the College distinguishes itself through friendliness and fine sporting achievements. The Master (Dr Macan) has a great understanding of Germany, where he had studied in his youth.[74]

The official voice of the College was not so very different from that of the undergraduates: in 1912 its annual newsletter, the *University College Record*, having reported on major academic distinctions that year, commented 'These distinctions were not gained at the expense of slackness or inefficiency on the

---

[70] Bickerton 1953: 43; Mendl 1971: 51–2; Hewart: Jackson 1959: 20–1; japes elsewhere: Brock 2000b: 790–5, Farnell 1934: 136–8, and Hopkins 2005: 319–26 and 343.
[71] Gardner 1975: 64–5; Rushbrook Williams 1975: 25.
[72] Moore 1954: 31–2.
[73] Moore 1954: 30; Attlee 1954: 14.
[74] Von Bernstorff and Grunelius 1912: 45–6. The original German reads: *University (Master) ist eines der ältesten und besten Colleges, dessen Ursprung auf einer Gründung Alfreds des Großen zurückgeführt wird. An geistigen Anregungen biete es nicht viel. Dafür zeichnet sich das College aber durch Kameradschaftlichkeit und schöne sportliche Leistungen aus. Der Master (Dr. Macan) hat großes Verständnis für Deutschland, wo er in siener Jugend studiert hat.* My thanks to Richard Sheppard for showing me this work.

river or in the fields.' Even if written partly in jest, such words show how sport was valued at the expense of academic work.

Not all enjoyed this hearty world. One nonconformist, Eric Dodds, felt acutely aware of a gulf between commoners and the Scholars, recalling that the College's sporting reputation 'attracted as commoners mainly athletes from the public schools, young men of means and muscle who came up with the simple aim of rowing or playing rugby and having a good time'. They and the scholars lived in different worlds, although Dodds wondered whether the 'hearties' thought that 'in our eccentric way we did after all do the college some credit'. Dodds's socializing centred on a more intellectual world, tempered by the occasional smoking of cannabis resin.[75]

There were also more social divisions than some Old Members cared to recall. 'Dunce' Gardner suspected that James Bright refused to admit anyone whom he could not introduce to his daughters, and observed that, apart from 'an Indian princeling, handsome and charming', there were no other non-white undergraduates when he was up. In 1894–1904, indeed, there are barely half a dozen undergraduates who can definitely be identified as non-white. One fears that a Christian Cole would not have been welcomed.[76]

Macan's friend Lewis Farnell thought that 'the games-cult, giving an almost religious value to play, has deadened much of our sense of humour, and destroyed much of the joy naturally attaching to the game'. He also feared for the influence of the public schools:

The public-school temper tends to demand uniformity and to be intolerant of aberration from the norm. And hence could arise persecutions of the eccentric members who would not conform, and this persecution might vary from harmless chaff or merry 'ragging' to something much graver.[77]

Farnell's anxieties were no fantasy. Fred Bickerton recalls the fate of one such character at University College about the time of the Boer War, whom he left unnamed.[78] Bickerton remembered him as 'extremely unpopular', because he took no part in College life, not because he could not afford it, but because he did not want to. 'In those days', Bickerton explained, 'the Colleges kept far more to themselves than they do now, and such conduct as this was regarded as insulting.' It was therefore decided to punish him. Bickerton recalled what happened next:

I was on duty in the Lodge that night. It was quiet, and one of the College servants had stopped for a few minutes to gossip with me. Then, suddenly, there was a terrific hullabaloo—a fearsome scream—and into the Lodge there rushed an appalling

---

[75] Dodds 1977: 29–31 and 33.
[76] Gardner 1975: 66–7 and Darwall-Smith 2003: 69–73.
[77] Farnell 1934: 141 and 143.
[78] Bickerton 1953: 34–5. Neither the date of these events, nor the identity of the undergraduate, can be identified.

apparition, naked and black from head to foot, with fluffy feathers stuck all over the glistening tar. He looked like a chicken in a nightmare. He was gibbering with terror, shaking and shivering all over, and in hysterics.... His rooms were in utter chaos. The raggers had overturned his pianola... His pictures and furniture had been thrown out into the quadrangle. The drawers had been pulled out of the dressing table and the contents scattered all over the floor. I noticed powder-puffs among the wreckage!

The Governing Body could do nothing: no undergraduate confessed or passed on information. All that could be done for the unfortunate undergraduate was to help him move out into lodgings. It is hard to say which is more chilling, the event, or Bickerton's attitude. Either way, it reveals a College taking a terrible revenge against someone unwilling to conform socially (or, as Bickerton hints, sexually).

A more complicated tale involved Oskar Rosenberger (m. 1911), a Rhodes Scholar from Frankfurt, who lived a quiet life within College. Some other German Rhodes Scholars, of very different character, deciding to teach Rosenberger a lesson, entered the College and turned his rooms upside down. However, news of the plan had been leaked, and the men of University College felt that outside attacks on one of their own were intolerable. When, therefore, the visitors had done their work, they found a phalanx of heavily-built 'Univ.' men asking them, politely but firmly, to put Rosenberger's room to rights before they could leave. Rosenberger evidently reflected that his rescue did not necessarily leave him safe from members of his own College, for he knew the merits of a tactful gesture. He gave an especially generous contribution towards the College's new playing field.[79]

Some nonconformists survived and even prospered by sheer force of character. One such was the musical Paul Rubens. His friend Nigel Playfair once heard a Blue confess that he would rather be Paul Rubens than himself, yet, as Playfair said,

Paul Rubens was a German Jew by origin, was no athlete and a quiet and most unassuming nature, and in spite of his humour had a somewhat sad and depressed outlook on life. But he had a certain charm, quite apart from his musical gifts, which was irresistible in any society.[80]

Arthur Moore remembered how at Smoking Concerts Rubens

always turned up to give an amusing self-accompanied song-recital in that difficult half hour after the interval when he alone could keep an exhilarated and refreshed audience in good humour and within bounds.[81]

Perhaps the most extraordinary College undergraduate during this period matriculated in 1909 under the alias of Count Felix Elston. This was Prince

---

[79] Anonymous reminiscence in *UCR* Vol. V no. 2 (1967), 124–5. Bickerton 1953: 52 claimed that Rosenberger had uttered pro-British sentiments.
[80] Playfair 1930: 84 (also Rubens's *ODNB* entry).
[81] Moore 1954: 32.

FIGURE 17.8 Detail from a College group photograph of 1911. Prince Felix Yusupov, m. 1909, is seated on the ground in the front row, fourth from the left.

Felix Yusupov (Fig. 17.8), member of one of the wealthiest families in Russia, and the future assassin of Rasputin. He had been sent to Oxford to sort himself out, and the Tsarina herself asked the Bishop of London to find appropriate friends at the College. One of them was Eric Hamilton, a future Bishop. Despite being thrown together in this way, Yusupov and Hamilton became great friends, with Hamilton being invited to spend the Long Vacation of 1910 with Yusupov in St Petersburg, Moscow, and on some of the family estates. Yusupov was unlike any other undergraduate: he had far more money, and more exotic tastes. Edgar Carritt, who taught Yusupov, when invited to lunch in his lodgings, encountered a pet bear-cub under his host's table. Yusupov himself enjoyed Oxford. His rooms in Staircase VI, facing on to the High Street, became a popular social centre, and he helped undergraduates climb into his rooms after the doors were locked. His only complaint was the coldness of his College rooms in winter.[82]

---

[82] Hamilton: UC:P25/MS/2; Carritt 1960: 61; Yusupov (the usual modern transliteration): Youssoupoff 1953: 138 and 142–3. Lewis 1991: 40 and 450 mention anecdotes recounted about Yusupov by his tutors.

Many undergraduates retained close links with their 'D.O.C.' after they left, links nurtured by the creation of a newsletter, the *University College Record*, in 1900. One well-documented example of this relationship is provided by Clement Attlee (Fig. 17.5), the only undergraduate of the College to have become Prime Minister of the United Kingdom. Attlee's Oxford career was modestly successful: an intellectual rather than a hearty, he joined the Martlets and the Churchwardens, and just missed a First. He did not even show much interest in politics: this only came after he had left Oxford, and worked in the East End mission of his old school, Haileybury. People did not notice Attlee much; 'Duncs' Gardner, for example, remembered him as 'a friendly, gentlemanly, undistinguished quiet man of the standard Public School type'. Fifty years later Attlee himself wrote that 'I spent...three exceedingly happy years at Oxford....I played all games but without distinction, amused myself on the river, especially on the upper river, in sailing boats, and savoured to the full all the joys of Oxford,' and that 'I left Oxford with an abiding love of the City and the University and especially for my own College.'[83]

Attlee was not just being polite: he once admitted that, during the First World War, he would calm his nerves when under shell-fire by taking an imaginary walk through Oxford. Even in 1947, when Prime Minister, he attended an Old Members' dinner, and 'in a charming speech he expressed his devotion to the College and his good wishes for it'. Fred Bickerton proudly recorded that Attlee always asked after him when visiting Oxford, and quoted the letter which Attlee wrote to him on his retirement. The College Boat Club of 1949 sent the Prime Minister a copy of the Eights Week Programme, and Attlee made sure that they were thanked. In retirement, he attended College feasts well into his eighties. Attlee's eminence makes it easy to trace his relationship with University College, but he was not unusual.[84]

The relationship between Attlee and Bickerton leads us to consider again the role of the College servants, whose condition was regularized in the later nineteenth century. There were little gestures, like Christmas or New Year parties, and more seriously, a servants' pension scheme began in 1893. The servants developed their own identity, creating a parallel world to match that of the undergraduates. There was a College servants' rowing team, and by 1901, at least, there was a University College Servants' cricket club, which played servants' teams from other colleges, local village sides, and, regularly, undergraduates from University College itself.[85]

---

[83] Gardner 1975: 162; Attlee 1954: 14 and 16.
[84] Calm under fire: Brock 2000c: 873; speech of 1947: *UCR* 1948, p. 4; Attlee and Fred: Bickerton 1953: 20; Attlee and the Boat Club: UC:O4/C1/1.
[85] Parties: UC:GB4/A1/6 fo. 48^r and UC:P143/X1/1; pensions: UC:GB3/A1/3 p. 296; cricket: UC:O24/MS1/1.

Servants agreed that a post in a College was much to be desired—Fred Bickerton, who worked at the College in 1897–1950, and was Head Porter for two-thirds of that time, was especially eager to find work in a College—but the recruitment process was stiff: William Bateson, appointed in 1887, was interviewed by the Master himself, and asked all about his family background.[86] Many began on the bottom rung, as under-scouts. Despite the changes of the 1860s, under-scouts' wages were still small, and they depended on extras. Reminiscing with a young undergraduate, David Strawbridge (m. 1939), Bateson recalled that, when appointed, he was informed that his salary would be a certain sum, 'plus perquisites'. 'Well now, sir,' said Bateson, 'it was an invitation to daylight robbery.' He claimed that perquisites worked thus: when the student wanted coal, the scout would order a certain amount (and charge the student for this), but creamed off a portion of this for himself. Bateson also claimed that, before 1914, when 'a gentleman' went down, he often left the contents of his wardrobe to his scout to sell on. The employment was irregular too: Bickerton remembered that many servants were laid off during the vacations, and usually took temporary jobs in seaside hotels.[87]

Scouts had long working hours: Bickerton was in College by 6 a.m. to tidy rooms up. Undergraduates were woken at 6.45. During the mornings, he served breakfast and then lunch in his men's rooms. He was then off duty from 2 p.m. until 5 p.m. He then returned to clear tea-things and serve dinner in the Hall. He usually stopped work at 9 p.m. Bickerton, however, did not begrudge his long hours:

You may imagine I did not have very much time to myself. I look back with pleasure on it all, though. I served some fine young people, and I helped to make their years in Oxford pleasant for them.[88]

One may understand Bickerton's comments more easily if one compares his lot with that of others of his class at this time, such as factory workers or miners. Nevertheless, Bickerton had ambitions for his family. Of his two sons, one became a major with the Royal Artillery, and the other an Anglican priest.[89] Servants like Bickerton and Bateson enjoyed a very different relationship with other members of the College from their predecessors. They inspired affection among the undergraduates—sometimes more successfully than some Fellows—and the latest news of 'Fred' became as important to Old Members as any other piece of College information.

---

[86] Bickerton 1953: 4–5; Bayley 1954b: 33.
[87] Interview with David Strawbridge, 14 April 1999; Bickerton 1953: 5. This migratory life remained common practice for College servants until at least the 1950s.
[88] Bickerton 1953: 5–9.
[89] Ibid. 19.

AN ERA ENDS

Readers of a chapter which ends in 1914 know too well what is to come. It is indeed easy to find poignant aspects in Trinity Term 1914: what the *University College Record* for 1913/14 described as 'an *annus mirabilis* for the College' in sports, during which the Rugby Team (five of whose members were Blues) won Cuppers and the 'D.O.C.' went Head of the River, was crowned by the opening of the new sports ground and pavilion. There were even some good academic results: Eric Dodds got a brilliant First in Mods, and a New Brunswicker Rhodes Scholar, John McNair (m. 1911), obtained the highest honours in his BCL examination. In July, a dinner was planned to celebrate the two hundredth anniversary of the death of John Radcliffe. Other activities ring sadly hollow: Alexander Grunelius had created in May 1911 a 'Hanover Club' to foster good relations between Britons and Germans at Oxford, and Robert Lorenz (m. 1910), was specially commended in his Finals in Trinity Term 1914 for his proficiency in the colloquial use of German. The Officers' Training Corps was popular, undoubtedly nurtured by that keen Territorial man, A. S. L. Farquharson, and in 1912/13 it included two officers and sixty-three cadets from University College.[90]

A small tablet in the Chapel, however, should have given these cadets pause for thought. Just over a decade earlier, Britain was engaged in the Boer War, and Oxford undergraduates were permitted, for the first time since the 1640s, to interrupt their studies and join up. Thus in January 1900 three undergraduates of University College were 'allowed one year's further study in their honours school, in consideration of serving with the troops in South Africa'. One of them, Charles Toller (m. 1897), died of wounds in June 1900, the College's first undergraduate to die on active service since the Civil War.[91] Undergraduates followed the war with keen interest (Fred Bickerton remembered the celebrations for the victories at Mafeking and Ladysmith), and the College marked the deaths of Toller and three other Old Members who fell in the war in a new way. Public schools had been erecting war memorials for some time—Eton and Harrow had created memorials for old boys who had fallen in the Crimea and in later conflicts—but now, at the request of some Old Members, a memorial tablet was erected in the Chapel in 1904.[92] Other colleges reacted similarly. The Boer War memorial tablet was the first of its kind in University College; but within half a century it would have two companions in grief.

---

[90] Athletic and academic results: *UCR* 1913/14, pp. 1–2; Radcliffe celebration: UC:GB4/A1/7 fo. 238ʳ; Hanover Club: Weber 2008: 65–80; Officer Training Corps: *UCR* 1912/13, p. 2.

[91] Army leave: UC:GB3/A1/3 p. 324; Toller's death: memorial in Chapel. There is a second memorial to a fifth Boer War casualty, Cecil Boyle (m. 1872). See also Miller 2008: 13.

[92] Bonfires: Bickerton 1953: 14; war memorial: UC:GB4/A1/6 fo. 259ʳ and UC:GB3/A1/3 pp. 345–6; Eton and Harrow's memorials: Card 2001: 167 and Tyerman 2000: 256.

18

Preserving Continuity: 1914–1945

THE FIRST WORLD WAR: 1914–1918[1]

War with Germany broke out during the Long Vacation of 1914—Eric Dodds, then travelling in Germany and Austria, got out just in time to avoid internment—and its effects were quickly felt in the College. The very first month of the war saw two Old Members, Mordaunt Clarke (m. 1904) and William Coghlan (m. 1909), killed in action, and Michaelmas Term 1914 opened with just 45 undergraduates resident, 23 of them freshmen, in the College (a year earlier the figures had been 150 and 46). Many men given a place that term had deferred their entry. One of them, Charles Hamilton Sorley, killed at Loos at October 1915, was a promising poet, whose bleakly honest work prefigures Siegfried Sassoon and Wilfred Owen. Eric Dodds, an Irishman, was exempted from military service by reason of his nationality, but did not wish to join up for political reasons. Others, like Robert Mendl, yielded to family persuasion to sit their Finals. Ever fewer undergraduates came up as the war progressed (Graph 18.1), and by 1916 there were only eight men in residence, most of whom were exempt from conscription on grounds of health or nationality. The Martlets ceased to meet after June 1915, and in 1917–18 there was no JCR President.[2]

Many Fellows were absent on active service. Farquharson worked in the censorship department of the War Office, being made a lieutenant-colonel and a CBE, while the chemist Robert Bourdillon (F. 1913–23) joined the Royal Flying Corps. More or less the only Fellows left were the Master, Poynton, and John Behan, the Australian Stowell Law Fellow. In May 1915, University College, like other colleges, passed emergency statutes which suspended regulations on Fellows' residence, and permitted vacant Fellowships or Scholarships to remain unfilled.[3]

---

[1] Overviews of the war as seen from Oxford: Screaton 1984 and Winter 1994.
[2] Dodds 1977: 36–9; Wilson 1985 (Sorley); Mendl 1971: 78–9; College numbers: UC:J7/A1/2 and *UCR* 1914/15–1915/16; Martlets: Bodl. MS Top. Oxon. d. 95/3.
[3] Farquharson: UC:GB3/A1/4 fo. 32^v and Bickerton 1953: 53; Bourdillon: *UCR* Vol. VI no. 1 (1971), 16–18; Fellows left behind: *UCR* 1915/16; emergency statutes: UC:GB3/A1/4 fos. 11–15 (another college's statutes: Hopkins 2005: 349).

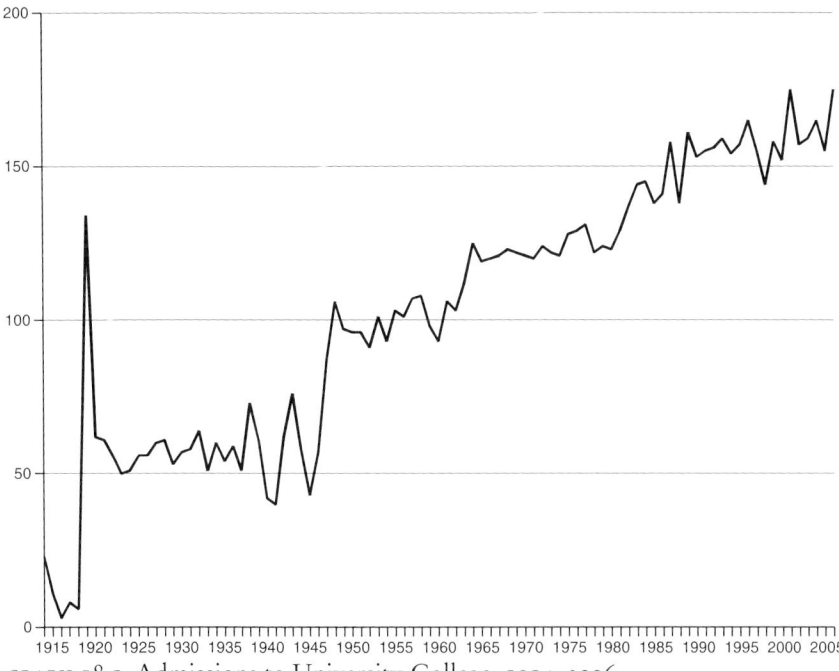

GRAPH 18.1 Admissions to University College, 1914–2006.

Parts of the College were requisitioned: 90 High Street became a Recruiting Depot, and Durham Buildings an extension of the 3rd Southern General Hospital; the Hall was used for the patients' meals, while undergraduates dined in a lecture room and Fellows in their common room. In March 1917 the Radcliffe Quadrangle and the eastern range of the Main Quadrangle were requisitioned by the hospital, and the recruiting authorities expanded into New Buildings soon after, leaving the remaining Fellows and undergraduates squeezed into two or three staircases in the Main Quadrangle.[4]

One wartime undergraduate was C. S. Lewis (m. 1917; Fig. 18.1), an Irishman who did choose to join up, and was allowed to start his course before his formal training. He found barely a dozen undergraduates in residence, and his room still fitted with its previous occupant's furniture. The deserted College intrigued him. One July evening, he explored it, looking into staircases where no one ever entered, and walking through passages with locked rooms, until he discovered an open door leading to a dark and

---

[4] Requisition of buildings: UC:GB4/A1/7 fos. 282ʳ and 298ʳ, UC:GB4/A1/8 fos. 20ʳ and 28ʳ, and *UCR* 1916/17; College dinners: UC:GB4/A1/7 fo. 281ʳ and UC:GB4/A1/8 fo. 29ʳ. Almost all the colleges were requisitioned for similar purposes (Winter 1994: 10–11).

FIGURE 18.1 The depopulated College: group photograph of College members in 1917. C. S. Lewis is standing in the back row on the right.

dusty room with its owner's furniture, photos, and books all left untouched. Lewis was entranced by the 'strange poetry of the thing'.[5]

Almost every month of the war, even November 1918, brought news of fresh deaths to the College. The cruellest year was 1916, with over fifty deaths recorded, and July 1916 the cruellest month: at least eighteen men died then, six of them on the first day of the Somme. On the university's roll of honour 714 members of the College were recorded as having joined up, and the College's War Memorial bears 173 names (including 23 men accepted for matriculation). In fact 178 men are thought to have fallen, including one German, Rolf Wilhelm von Seldeneck (m. 1911), killed on the eastern front, and omitted from the memorial. In other words, almost a quarter of the members of University College who joined up perished: indeed, a quarter of all the undergraduates who matriculated in 1912 and 1913 did not return. Among Oxford colleges, only Corpus Christi lost a greater proportion of its members. The average loss throughout the country was about one-tenth, and the higher fatalities are reasonably ascribed to the fact that most Oxbridge

[5] Lewis 2000: 295–9 and 324. Lewis joined up in September 1917.

men served as junior officers, a class which suffered disproportionately heavy losses.[6]

One can comprehend a little better the magnitude of this loss, and its impact on the living, by re-examining two pre-war photographs. Of the guests celebrating Herbert Adams's coming-of-age dinner (Fig. 17.7), two, Walter Goldberg and Edward Bell, were killed, and of the 1904 Martlets (Fig. 17.5), two undergraduates, James Farquharson—A. S. L. Farquharson's brother—and James Scott, and one Fellow, Reginald Tiddy, fell. The dead also included a second Fellow, Arthur Sidgwick, and Reginald Macan's only surviving son. Even survivors were not unscathed: C. S. Lewis was badly injured in April 1918, but eventually resumed his academic career. Christopher Tinne, the great sportsman of the 1910s, was badly gassed in Belgium, and unable to find employment for the next decade. Fortunately, in 1930 he was invited to become the Bursar of the newly founded St Peter's Hall, a post he held until his retirement in 1956.[7]

The war brought other problems. As in the 1640s, though for different reasons, the College's income fell. In 1913 University College had received £8,196 16s. 3d. from estates, £1,003 5s. 2d. from investments, £8,755 6s. 1d. from internal sources, and £2,268 8s. 8d. from trust funds. During the war, while the income from estates, investments, and trust funds remained reasonably steady, the College's revenue from internal sources collapsed, falling to £925 13s. 11d. in 1918.[8]

There were occasional embarrassments within the College. In April 1915, a letter by an Honorary Fellow, Frederick Conybeare, appeared in a New York newspaper, the *Vital Issue*, criticizing the British government's war policy, and accusing the Foreign Secretary, Sir Edward Grey, of lying. A chastened Conybeare publicly withdrew his remarks, and the matter was closed. Another problem was caused by Eric Dodds, who, having refused to join up, spent much of 1915 working in hospitals in Serbia with another Irishman, Theobald Butler (m. 1913). On returning to Oxford, Dodds openly declared his support for the Easter Rising of 1916. For the Unionist (and recently bereaved) Macan, such support for what he deemed traitors was intolerable, and Dodds was forbidden to sit Finals for a year.[9]

---

[6] Miller 2008: 18–81 provides a biographical register of the College's war dead (see too Winter 1994: 19–21 and Screaton 1984: 346–7). Losses in other colleges: Jones 2005: 247 (Balliol), Green 1979: 528 (Lincoln), Hopkins 2005: 356 (Trinity, Oxford), and Wilkinson 1980: 68 (King's).

[7] Tinne: *UCR* Vol. III no. 1 (1956), 58 and Vol. VI no. 1 (1971), 90–1, and interview with his son, Michael Tinne (m. 1949), 15 May 1999.

[8] Figures taken from the printed accounts submitted to the university. Winter 1994: 11–12 shows that other colleges suffered similarly.

[9] Conybeare: UC:S20/MS1/1–2, UC:GB4/A1/7 fo. 269ʳ and *Times* 2 July 1915; Dodds 1977: 45–52. Lewis 1991: 51 remembered Dodds as 'the drunken Sinn Féiner'.

STARTING UP AGAIN: 1919–1923

The Armistice was declared halfway through Michaelmas Term 1918, and it was only in January 1919 that the College began to fill up, as forty undergraduates took up residence. It took time to refurbish the College's requisitioned buildings, but other aspects of College life quickly revived. Macan's wife Mildred noted in her diary for 19 January 1919: 'Chapel as of old at 8.30. Much larger congregation. Mr. [Edgar] Carritt came in to breakfast, whom it seemed like old times to see again.'[10]

Few freshmen of 1913 and 1914 chose to return, but there was now a whole generation of men previously deprived of a university education, and in 1919 University College accepted 134 freshmen—a total not exceeded until 1982 (Graph 18.1). They were, inevitably, older than usual: more than half the freshmen of 1919, and even one-third of those of 1920, were aged 20 or over. To clear this backlog, special two-year courses were offered, as alternatives to the traditional honours degrees.[11]

College traditions were rekindled by the dons and the few pre-war undergraduates, such as the JCR President in 1919/20, Digby Lawson (m. 1913), who had spent four years in a German prison camp. When the Martlets held their first post-war meeting on 29 January 1919, Lawson and A. J. Carlyle came to explain the history and aims of the society to a new generation. Among the undergraduates, James Macphail (m. 1919) remembered the 'general euphoria in Oxford and a feeling that we should have a good time'. Buel Trowbridge, an American Rhodes Scholar (m. 1920), observed that, although many of his British friends had served in the war, only once did he ever hear them discuss their experiences, and undergraduates too young to have fought, like Harold Mitchell (m. 1919), had difficulty relating to former soldiers.[12]

These wartime memories required some public laying to rest. As early as 1917 the College had discussed a possible memorial, and on 2 November 1921, after an appeal to Old Members, a War Memorial was dedicated in the Antechapel by Hubert Burge, now Bishop of Oxford. The appeal also secured an endowment for War Memorial Medical Scholarships for medical students. There were unexpected souvenirs: in December 1919, like other colleges, University College received as a war trophy a German heavy gun and carriage, which was put on the cricket field.[13]

---

[10] Undergraduates return: UC:BU3/F3/93; buildings recovered: UC:GB4/A1/8 fos. 72ʳ and 83ʳ; Mrs Macan's diary: UC:MA43/J1/6.

[11] Information in this paragraph from UC:BU3/F3/93 and UC:J7/A1/2; large numbers of freshmen elsewhere: Jones 2005: 258 (Balliol) and Hopkins 2005: 356 (Trinity).

[12] Lawson: Macphail 1980: 48; the Martlets: Bodl. MS Top. Oxon. d. 95/3 p. 61; Macphail 1980: 41; Trowbridge 1976: 27; Mitchell 1974: 27–8 (see also Winter 1994: 23–4 on the gap between combatant and non-combatant undergraduates).

[13] War Memorial: *UCR* 1916/17 and 1921, p. 4; German gun: UC:GB4/A1/8 fos. 110ʳ, 113ʳ, and 116ʳ (its later fate is unknown); other colleges: Jones 2005: 258 (Balliol) and Green 1979: 537 (Lincoln).

Undergraduates still had to obey many pre-war regulations, but Fred Bickerton thought the former soldiers were 'very steady in their conduct'; it was the undergraduates who had come straight up from school who were rather more unruly. Some old ways returned: breakfast parties once again became the most popular form of hospitality.[14]

The greatest symbol of continuity was Reginald Macan himself. For C. S. Lewis, he was 'a clean shaven, white haired, jolly old man'; Reginald Rathbone (m. 1914) recalled 'that delightfully courtly, spic and span Macan'. Buel Trowbridge, however, found Macan rather forbidding, until they discovered a mutual enjoyment of golf. Unfortunately, Trowbridge also observed that Macan discouraged applicants from ethnic minorities from being admitted, and encountered instances of casual racism. Once, when watching a rugger match, he was talking to some Indian friends, only to see some College contemporaries sniggering at him. When he asked what the joke was, one of them asked, to his horrified surprise, 'Who are your nigger friends, Trowbridge?'[15]

Yet there were changes, be they simple, such as the new craze for mid-morning coffee breaks, or significant, such as the abolition of compulsory Greek as an entrance requirement in 1920. The *University College Record* for 1919/20 contrasted the present size of the College, with about 200 resident members, with the 1860s, when five teaching Fellows met all the College's educational requirements. It also lamented the increased demands made by the university or the government, a cry repeated throughout the century.[16]

Meanwhile, the College put its finances in order. Its internal revenue returned to pre-war levels, but A. B. Poynton reported to a College meeting on 28 October 1919 that, although the authorities had given £495 towards reconstructing the College, the total cost would be nearer £1,200.[17] The College needed assets which yielded more income, and in 1919–23 Poynton sold off many unprofitable estates, mainly to their existing tenants. All the lands in Wales were sold, as were the Freeston lands in and around Pontefract; land in Flamstead, Hailey, and Edgiock went, as did Friars Mead in Oxford and the Blandford Arms in Woodstock. By 1923 the College had realized over £80,000 this way.[18]

The proceeds, which still had to be passed to the Ministry of Agriculture, were invested. In 1919, the College received £8,026 15s. 4d. from estates and £1,344 16s. 3d. from investments—much the same proportion as before 1914. In 1921, however, the College received £7,650 9s. 10d. from land, and £3,770 7s. 7d. from investments, and in 1923 the respective figures were £7,789 9s.

---

[14] Returning to normal: Macphail 1980: 44–5 and 47, Bickerton 1953: 60, and UC:P34/MS1/1.
[15] Lewis 2000: 267; Rathbone: *UCR* Vol. VIII no. 5 (1984), 322; Trowbridge 1976: 14–15 and 71.
[16] Coffee: Bickerton 1953: 61; Greek: Currie 1994: 111.
[17] UC:GB4/A1/8 fos. 102–3.
[18] Copies of these conveyances are in UC:EB1/A/7.

6d. and £4,329 6s. 9d. At the same time, the College's internal revenues rose from £14,565 17s. 9d. in 1921 to £16,066 1s. 8d. in 1923. These proportions remained largely unchanged during the 1920s and 1930s (even during the Depression), apart from a rise in internal income. Other colleges also sold off unwanted property, mainly agricultural, after 1919.[19]

After the emergency statutes were repealed in March 1920, the vacant Fellowships were quickly filled.[20] Among the new Fellows was Edmund 'Ted' Bowen, elected a lecturer in chemistry in 1921, and a Fellow in 1922. A Balliol man, he worked from the Balliol and Trinity Laboratory (the Physical Chemistry Laboratory was not opened until 1940). Conditions were primitive: University College men occupied some old bathrooms in Trinity, and one pupil remembered setting up a piece of apparatus using a biscuit tin, a brass tube, and a photo-sensitive cell. Although Bowen was not the first scientist to be elected a Fellow, he stayed much longer than any of his predecessors, only retiring in 1965, and became a popular figure in College life. His interests were wide-ranging (a species of ammonite was named after him), but his major area of research was light, on which he published a major study, *The Chemical Aspects of Light* (1942), and he became an FRS. Pupils accustomed to more help with their studies found that Bowen preferred them to arrive armed with questions to which he could then offer helpful answers, but those who could keep up found his tutorials a stimulating experience.[21]

The post-war university was dominated by a new Royal Commission into Oxford and Cambridge, created in 1919, with the Oxford section chaired by Herbert Asquith, the former Prime Minister.[22] A Report was issued in 1922, and new statutes prepared for each college. The Oxford and Cambridge groups came to significantly different conclusions on the roles of the colleges and the university. Cambridge chose to bring them closer together by increasing the number of university teachers, reducing the amount of tutorial work for each academic, and obliging colleges to reserve a number of fellowships for teaching officers of the university. Cambridge therefore came to see its university teaching staff as a class of people who needed a college place. Oxford, however, gave greater weight to the colleges, and decided that every university professor would have a place in a college, and every tutor appointed by a college would receive an appointment as a university lecturer.

---

[19] Statistics taken from the College's official printed accounts; other colleges: Green 1979: 534 (Lincoln), Wilkinson 1980: 83–6 (King's), Howard 1935: 236–7 (St John's Cambridge), and Bendall and others 1999: 469 (Emmanuel).

[20] UC:GB4/A1/8 fo. 123ʳ. The Stowell Law Fellowship was now made a permanent Fellowship (UC:GB4/A1/8 fo. 143ʳ).

[21] Bowen's career: *UCR* Vol. V no. 5 (1965), 308–10; his laboratory: UC:R2/MS1/9, Hopkins 2005: 378, and interview with James Reddyhoff (m. 1937), 27 September 2003; his teaching: UC:P5/MS/1, UC:P34/MS1/1, and interview with James Reddyhoff (as above).

[22] The Asquith Commission: Prest 1994 and Mallet 1924–7: iii. 489–94, and (for its work in Cambridge) Brooke 1993: 341–69.

The statutes issued in 1926 to University College, like those of other colleges, reflected these changes. There would be no more 'prize' Fellows. Instead, Fellows were divided into two kinds, Stipendiary and Non-Stipendiary. Stipendiary Fellows comprised persons holding any college post, university lecturers, inter-collegiate lecturers, 'persons of exceptional distinction' who are to be Senior Research Fellows, and (a new concept) Junior Research Fellows. Official Stipendiary Fellows could hold their posts for up to seven years, with the option of re-election, but Senior Research Fellows and Junior Research Fellows had non-renewable terms of five and three years respectively. Non-Stipendiary Fellows were university professors (see p. 466 below) or Emeritus Fellows.

Finally, the College could also elect Special Supernumerary Fellows who needed no College stipend, but whose services it 'may deem to be of advantage to the College'. University College's first Special Supernumerary Fellow, elected in 1927, was A. D. 'Duncs' Gardner. In 1914 Gardner became a Radcliffe Travelling Fellow, and returned to Oxford in 1915 to work in the Standards Laboratory of the School of Pathology. He became Professor of Bacteriology in 1936, and later assisted Howard Florey and Ernest Chain in their research into penicillin. As a Fellow of his old College, he was assigned no official duties, but he involved himself fully in the social life of the Senior Common Room.[23]

THE MASTERSHIP OF SIR MICHAEL SADLER: 1923–1934

The new statutes were introduced under a new Master. In October 1922 Reginald Macan announced his intention to retire on 1 April 1923, when he would be 75 years old. He had returned the College to normal, and his retirement was well earned. Choosing his successor proved difficult, as two senior Fellows, A. B. Poynton and A. S. L. Farquharson, both sought the post.[24] Not only might the College face a damaging split by choosing one man over the other, but, for all their loyalty to the College, Poynton and Farquharson were slightly insular—if not eccentric—figures. Some, led by the medical Fellow, Ernest Ainley Walker, looked elsewhere. Their first choice, Hubert Burge, was interested, but the Archbishop of Canterbury forbade him to resign his see of Oxford. The second choice was the first outsider since Arthur Charlett, Sir Michael Sadler, the Vice-Chancellor of Leeds, and, like Charlett, a graduate of Trinity College. Sadler was elected

---

[23] Gardner 1975: 134–5 (election) and 203–18 (penicillin); UC:GB4/A1/9 fos. 110–11 and 114ʳ.
[24] Macan's retirement: UC:GB4/A1/8 fo. 231ʳ. The 1923 election is described by Edmund Bowen (UC:P22/MS/1) and John Wild (Wild 1988: 47–8). Even undergraduates heard that the Fellows were having trouble finding a successor (Lewis 1991: 222).

Master on 26 April 1923, nine Fellows voting for him, and two (Poynton and Farquharson) for Farquharson.[25]

If the College had sought a Master with interests beyond Oxford, then they chose well. Having worked on the Board of Education, been a Professor at Manchester University, and led a Commission at Calcutta University, Sadler had become one of the foremost educationalists of his age. Few previous Masters had enjoyed such a wide-ranging life, and Sadler represents a type which would become common in the twentieth century, someone for whom a college headship is the culmination of an eminent career. He was also an enthusiastic collector of modern art, being among the first British connoisseurs to purchase works by Cezanne, Van Gogh, and Kandinsky, and he filled the Master's Lodgings with his collection. In 1923 he wrote an introduction for the catalogue to Van Gogh's first one-man show in England, even purchasing two Van Gogh paintings and three drawings.[26] He also collected African and Polynesian art.

Sadler was undoubtedly a breath of fresh air. He transformed the *University College Record* from a tiny pamphlet into a full-length magazine. In 1924 he concealed George Gilbert Scott's unfortunate reredos in the Chapel by restoring the original panelling, and hanging curtains to either side, partly at his own expense. Characteristically, Sadler did not destroy Scott's work, in case a later age might find it more sympathetic. In 1931, he covered up the outer lights of the east window, reducing it to the scale of Henry Gyles's window. Apparently Sadler did this himself, and was caught in the act, balancing on the ledge above the altar. He also oversaw work on the Shelley Memorial. The wreath on Shelley's brow was removed after one student prank too many, and, in 1933/4 Sadler paid to have the enclosure redecorated and the grilles around it altered for improved visibility.[27]

Unfortunately, there was next to no architectural activity during Sadler's Mastership. A. S. G. Butler, an architect friend of Sadler's son, designed an ambitious development for the area between 83–7 High Street and Logic Lane, and a brand new enclosure for the Shelley Memorial, both of which came to nothing. The only new building in the College was a squash court erected in 1925/6 to the south of Bostar Hall, donated by James Terry, the father of an undergraduate.[28]

---

[25] Sadler's election: UC:GB4/A1/8 fo. 254ʳ and UC:GB3/A1/4 fos. 58–60. The main studies of his life and work remain Sadleir 1949 and Grier 1952.

[26] Bailey 2006: 24–5.

[27] Sadler in the Chapel: *UCR* 1924, p. 1, UC:GB4/A1/8 fo. 297ʳ and UC:GB4/A1/9 fos. 5ʳ, 7ʳ, and 13ʳ, *UCR* 1930/1, pp. 5–6 and UC:GB3/A1/4 fo. 190; caught in the act: Redcliffe-Maud 1973: 252; the Shelley Memorial: Darwall-Smith 2000*a*: 80–2 (the wreath is now in the College archives).

[28] Butler's proposals for 83–7 High Street: UC:FA18/2/Y1/1–3, and Acc. 307; the Shelley Memorial: UC:FA11/3/Y1/4; squash court: UC:MA44/8/C1/1–2 and *UCR* 1925/6 p. 5.

Sadler had many outside interests. He was involved in the first planning stages of the New Bodleian Library; he joined the Oxford Preservation Trust; he created a luncheon club for dons and city men, and was made a Freeman of the City; and there were always one-off speaking engagements which the Master felt unable to refuse. In November 1934 he even endured a visit from Joachim von Ribbentrop, sent by Hitler to sound out British opinion. Sadler, well aware of Nazi persecution of the Jews, found the experience uncomfortable, claiming later he only received him at the request of an unnamed Old Member and friend of Ribbentrop.[29]

Soon after Sadler's election, the College took a momentous decision about its teaching. By the 1920s, new arts subjects were coming to the fore. For C. S. Lewis, fresh from a First in classics in 1922, and seeking an academic career, English was the rising subject, and he took a second First in that in 1923. However, a school of Politics, Philosophy, and Economics had been created in 1920. A small Fellowship had to choose carefully what to support, and University College's choice was aided by a benefaction. In 1894, an Old Member, Robert Mynors (m. 1835), had left the College money to endow a Fellowship 'for the study and teaching of Social Science to be held on such terms as they shall see fit'. Due to certain life interests, the bequest only arrived in 1920, and the College agreed in April 1924 to use it to create a Fellowship in Economics and Politics, whose stipend could be enlarged thanks to an agreement with the university that it be held jointly with a Readership in Economics or Politics. Sadler's support is generally agreed to have been crucial for this initiative. There was one sad consequence: although C. S. Lewis's two Firsts had shown that he was Fellowship material, and he wanted to stay in a College he greatly liked, the arrival of PPE left no room for an English scholar. After spending 1924/5 teaching philosophy while Carritt was in America and seeking a post somewhere in Oxford, Lewis was eventually elected to an English Fellowship at Magdalen, and University College lost one of its brightest talents.[30]

On the other hand, when in May 1925 the first Mynors Fellow, G. D. H. Cole (who had applied through Sadler's encouragement) was elected, the College possessed a complete set of PPE Tutors: the philosophy was taught by Farquharson and Carritt, the politics by A. J. Carlyle, and the economics by Cole. The support for PPE went further: John Maud, the College's first Junior Research Fellow, was elected in 1929 to study politics. Cole himself cut an unusual figure. Whereas most Fellows were still elected fairly soon

---

[29] Luncheon club: UC:P22/MS/1; Freeman: Redcliffe-Maud 1973: 253; Ribbentrop: Sadleir 1949: 369–72.
[30] Lewis 2000: 591; creation of PPE: Currie 1994: 111–16; Mynors Fellowship: UC:GB4/A1/8 fo. 143ʳ, UC:GB4/A1/9 fo. 33ʳ and *UCR* 1922 and 1924, p. 2; Sadler's interest: Grier 1952: 250; Lewis's move to Magdalen: Redcliffe-Maud 1981: 20–2, Lewis 2000: 614, 621, and 640, and Bayley 2006: 116. His search for a Fellowship is evident from Lewis 1991.

after sitting Finals, he was in his mid-thirties and already well known as a political theorist for the socialist movement and the Labour party—and also for the detective novels which he wrote with his wife Margaret, herself a significant political theorist. Cole made no secret of his beliefs, which could be disconcerting. When John Wild (F. 1933–45) first sat next to him at dinner after his election as Chaplain, Cole, an atheist who never entered Hall until Grace was over, abruptly said to him 'I hope you realise that you were only elected here over my dead body, as I consider that you are entirely unnecessary.' After this unpromising start, Wild came to realize that Cole had only spoken thus to make his position clear, and they came to get on well.[31]

Cole was a charismatic tutor. One pupil, Harold Marks (m. 1932), thought him 'absolutely incredible', and admired his stamina in giving him a tutorial at 10.30 p.m. Cole also created an informal undergraduate discussion club, known as the 'Cole Group'. Like a modern seminar, it met weekly, and attracted members from all over the university. The Cole Group was a stimulating experience, and many of its members pursued careers in (usually left-wing) politics—although, as John Maud noted, Cole observed complete political neutrality towards his pupils.[32]

Cole's political views left him isolated during the General Strike of May 1926. As talks between the government and the trade unions broke down, so the university permitted undergraduates to enrol to carry out public work. In response, University College nearly emptied of its members, both junior and senior: the Law Fellow, C. K. Allen, to his wife's amusement (but also her approval), fulfilled a lifetime's ambition by becoming a guard on an underground train. Just before he left, Allen met C. S. Lewis, who 'got from him a whiff of solid Univ. Toryism—sarcastic, frightened, worldly-wisdom.' Some undergraduates worked in the docks, and others, like the American P. S. Havens (m. 1925)—eager, as he said, to extinguish a fire in a house where he was a guest—drove trams, in his case in Hull. After a slightly hostile initial reception, Havens found that the atmosphere improved: people concluded that using a tram driven by an undergraduate was not strike-breaking. Undergraduate high spirits soon seeped out. Havens decorated his tram with ribbons of the 'Univ.' colours of blue and gold, and other trams were soon decked out in the colours of different colleges. Trams were named after their drivers' colleges, and some drivers tried to 'bump' trams in front of them in mimicry of Eights Week. Havens portrays his time in Hull as a

---

[31] Cole's standard biography remains Cole 1971; his election: UC:GB4/A1/9 fos. 49–50 (he was elected first as a Reader, his subsequent election as Fellow being a formality); Sadler's encouragement: Cole 1971: 140; his detective fiction: Mitchell 2005; Cole and Wild: Wild 1988: 42.

[32] Interview with Harold Marks 1 July 2003; Cole's seminars: Cole 1971: 156–8 and 206, M. B. Brown in Harrison 1994a: 123, Harrison 1994c: 396–7, and Redcliffe-Maud 1981: 29.

good-natured romp; what the locals made of their visitors is harder to determine.[33]

Back in Oxford, Cole supported striking printers at the University Press, and a speech he gave in St Giles caused some resentment in College, especially from Poynton. Sadler himself disapproved of such open support, but Cole recalled that when a deputation of Fellows demanded that he be deprived of his Fellowship for his behaviour, the Master refused.[34]

This generosity of spirit was typical of Sadler. Some Fellows, however, especially Poynton, never fully reconciled themselves to his election. Poynton once discussed his defeat with John Wild 'in a voice shaking with pent-up emotion', and a pupil, Richard Ratcliff (m. 1928), remembered how, when entertaining Ratcliff to lunch, Poynton saw Sadler walking by and 'danced across to the window, exclaiming "There goes the Master of University College".' Margaret Cole claimed that Poynton refused to climb the stairs in the Master's Lodgings until 'a peculiar piece of Easter Island sculpture' was removed from the niche halfway up. John Maud noticed that some Fellows were unhappy at Sadler's election, and even he was sometimes exasperated when Sadler, 'so far from ever stifling debate... would invite notorious ditherers to express themselves just as a long-delayed conclusion seemed in sight'. Nevertheless, both Maud and Wild admired him, and the historian Kenneth Leys (F. 1908–42) told Wild that Sadler's election was the best thing the College ever did.[35]

Among undergraduates, the poet Stephen Spender (m. 1927) thought that Sadler's 'interest in education seemed to stop or be arrested when it came to governing his own College,' and David Renton (m. 1927) similarly believed that, on account of his many outside distractions, Sadler was not interested in the College, its dons, or its undergraduates, while Harold Marks remembered Sadler as rather a withdrawn figure in the Lodgings. In fairness to Sadler, some distractions were not of his making. He was badly ill in 1927 and 1929, and in 1931 his wife died, all of which would inevitably have left him less visible in the College.[36]

Those whose interests coincided with Sadler's had happier memories. Justin Evans (m. 1926), a member of the Martlets, was thrilled when in May 1928 the Master gave them dinner in the Senior Common Room with T. S. Eliot as his guest. Both John Wild and Frederick Yarnold (m. 1930)

---

[33] University orders: UC:GB4/A1/9 fos. 83–4; C. K. Allen: Allen 1960: 25 and Lewis 1991: 389; dock working: UC:P14/C/2; tram driving: Havens 1979. Undergraduates elsewhere behaved similarly: Hopkins 2005: 380–1 (Trinity, Oxford), Twigg 1987: 344–5 (Queens'), and Wilkinson 1980: 77 (King's).

[34] Printers: UC:BG4/A1/9 fos. 84^r and 86^r; speech: UC:MA44/2/J1/1 (see too Cole 1971: 154–6); Sadler and Cole: UC:P14/C/2, and letter from Edmund Seyd (m. 1928), 10 August 2002.

[35] Poynton: Wild 1988: 47–8, UC:R2/MS1/5 (Ratcliff), and Cole 1971: 140; other views: Redcliffe-Maud 1973: 250–3 and Wild 1988: 43. Edgar Carritt also admired Sadler (Carritt 1960: 58).

[36] Spender 1951: 38; Renton 2006: 31, and interviews with Lord Renton, 4 October 2002, and Harold Marks, 1 July 2003; Sadler's illnesses: UC:GB4/A1/9 fos. 122^r, 189^r, and 194^r.

remembered Sadler's pleasure in showing off his latest acquisitions, and when John Maud married, Sadler lent him a painting. Tours of his collection brought out Sadler's mischievous side: John Wild noted that he would show especially daring pieces to the likes of Poynton to see their reactions, and Edward Edmonds (m. 1934) when dining in the Lodgings, found himself and his companions being asked to comment on the Master's surrealist paintings. After letting them flounder for a while, Sadler 'beamingly' admitted that he had hung them upside down as a test.[37]

Sadler retired on 31 December 1934. When informed of a plan to commission his portrait, he said that he would prefer a group portrait of himself and the Fellows. The resulting conversation piece by F. H. S. Shepherd (Plate 15, nicknamed, according to Edmund Bowen, 'Michael and all angels') was hung in the Senior Common Room, but in 1937 his second wife presented a bust of him, which lives in the Hall. Sadler retired to Headington, working on an unfinished biography of Obadiah Walker until his death. In the end perhaps Sadler and the College never quite related to one another. As John Maud put it, Sadler 'was too shrewd not to detect the undercurrent of our indifference to great modern art', and so, unlike at Leeds University, whose Art Collection was started up with a donation from Sadler, University College never received anything from his art collection.[38]

ARTHUR POYNTON AND SIR WILLIAM BEVERIDGE

Because he was elected before the 1926 Statutes, Sadler could have remained Master until 1936, but resigned early, partly, John Maud suspected, 'to give the Fellows another chance of electing someone disappointed by his own election'. He was right: Arthur Poynton (Fig. 18.2) and A. S. L. Farquharson were once again the main candidates. The Fellows did not want Farquharson, largely because his wife was a reclusive invalid, but Poynton appeared reluctant to put his name forward. Eventually, upon tactful enquiry, it became clear, as John Wild remembered, 'that Poynton wanted it [the Mastership] more than anything else'. Poynton was therefore elected Master on 22 February 1935. His election was clearly a consolation prize, not least as he would have to retire after only two years, and some felt that this gesture was not necessarily prudent. Robert Hilton (m. 1933) thought that, under Poyn-

---

[37] Justin Evans: UC:P9/J/1, pp. 100–1; the collections: Wild 1988: 46, interview with Frederick Yarnold, 11 January 2000, and Redcliffe-Maud 1973: 252; Sadler's humour: Wild loc. cit. and UC:P13/C/1.

[38] The conversation piece: UC:P22/MS/1 and Gardner 1975: 150–1 (Shepherd had already painted at Sadler's behest a conversation piece of the four sons of the Marquess of Salisbury who were Old Members (UC:GB4/A1/9 fos. 158ʳ and 175ʳ)); the bust: *UCR* 1937, p. 9; the art collection: Redcliffe-Maud 1973: 253.

FIGURE 18.2 Arthur Poynton, Fellow 1894–1935 and Master 1935–7, by William Rothenstein.

ton, 'dear though he was', 'it seem[ed] the College lacked a head, wanted features'.[39]

Poynton's Mastership was dominated by two significant rebuilding works. The first was in 1935, when the upper floors of 83 and 84 High Street were converted into ten sets of undergraduate rooms. The second was the refitting of the Library. Gilbert Scott's Library, like his work in the Chapel, had fallen from favour. As early as 1932, the Fellows had discussed its alteration, and in 1937 it was called 'a byword as a building which provided the minimum of seating for its cubic capacity and excluded the maximum of light'. The refitting was designed by A. S. G. Butler: a new floor was inserted; the coloured glass windows were replaced with plain glass ones; the pine roof, once stained a dark colour, was painted white; and the statues of Lord Eldon and Lord Stowell were moved to the front entrance, where they would spend the next half-century glowering in the gloom at all who entered there. The new room was called the Poynton Reading Room, after an Old Member,

---

[39] Poynton's election: Redcliffe-Maud 1973: 253, Wild 1988: 47–8, and UC:GB4/A1/10 fo. 132ʳ: Mrs Farquharson: C. S. Lewis once referred to 'a wife one never meets' (Lewis 2000: 874); Hilton: Grier 1952: 247.

FIGURE 18.3 Lord Beveridge, Master 1937–45, being presented with his portrait by Allan Gwynne-Jones in 1959. From left to right: Arthur Goodhart, Master 1951–63, Lady Beveridge, Lord Beveridge, Peter Bayley, and Freddie Wells.

John Burn (m. 1883), who had paid for most of the refurbishment, insisted on this choice of name.[40]

When the refurbished Library was opened in autumn 1937, Poynton had retired. Edmund Bowen recalled that the College sought in his successor 'an old Univ. man with a distinguished record'. John Maud claimed that the Professor of Jurisprudence, the American Arthur Goodhart, of whom more later, refused an invitation to stand. Instead the College, partly guided by G. D. H. Cole, looked to the Director of the London School of Economics, Sir William Beveridge (Fig. 18.3).[41] Beveridge, a Stowell Law Fellow in 1902–9, had discovered soon after his election that he had no taste for the law, but the College allowed him to devote himself instead to the study of social issues, whilst retaining his Fellowship, and won Beveridge's lifelong gratitude. Beveridge published an important study of unemployment in 1909, and played a leading role in the creation of Labour Exchanges. After his Fellow-

---

[40] 83–4 High Street: *UCR* 1935, p. 9 and UC:GB4/A1/10 fos. 116^r, 119^r, 124^r, and 126^r; the Library: UC:GB4/A1/10 fo. 25^r, *UCR* 1937, pp. 8–9, UC:FA8/2/Y1/1–3 and Acc. 307/69, and Park 1992: 55–7; John Burn: Wild 1988: 50–1.

[41] Bowen: UC:P22/MS/1; Goodhart: *UCR* Vol. VII no. 5 (1979), 226. G. D. H. Cole's role in Beveridge's election: Cole 1971: 227–8. The major biography of Beveridge is Harris 1997.

ship expired, Beveridge spent ten years in the civil service, working in the Ministries of Labour, Munitions, and Food, for which he received a knighthood, and in 1919, he became Director of the LSE. This was a brilliant period in the School's history, when it was effectively transformed into a modern research university. Beveridge himself claimed that he was approached unexpectedly in February 1937 to submit himself for election as Master. After he had met the Fellows, all sides were satisfied, and Beveridge was formally pre-elected Master on 22 April 1937, taking up his office in October.[42]

At first Master and College liked each other. Beveridge's last years at the LSE had been disputatious and unhappy: although capable of charm and acts of kindness, he never suffered fools gladly, and could be a difficult colleague. At Oxford, however, he enjoyed the company of the Fellows and above all the undergraduates, who brought out the best in him. Beveridge, a bachelor, had his cousin's daughter, Elspeth Mair, as his housekeeper, and they regularly held parties for the undergraduates, with the Master a genial and generous host.[43]

Edmund Bowen found Beveridge 'an impatient man of insatiable energy, well aware of his abilities'. Soon after his arrival in Oxford, he instituted a major change among the College's servants. Soon after his election, Beveridge asked John Wild to investigate claims that College accommodation was particularly expensive. In February 1938 a Committee on Undergraduate Costs reported that University College was seriously overmanned and was one of the most expensive colleges in Oxford. On recommendations from Beveridge himself, half the rooms in College were supplied with electric heaters, rather than coal fires, and all of them with power points. Breakfast was now served only in Hall, and roll-call abolished (lunch was still supplied to rooms). The absence of coal fires meant that scouts no longer needed under-scouts, and so, as the *University College Record* rather too blithely observed, 'The under-scouts, for whom there was no prospect of promotion in College, have left, and all have found other posts.' On the other hand undergraduate costs were indeed reduced.[44]

Beveridge also urged the College to take in what 'Duncs' Gardner recalled him calling 'his brilliant young assistant'. This was a graduate of Jesus

---

[42] Beveridge's Fellowship: Beveridge 1953: 10, 19, and 29; Beveridge at the LSE: Dahrendorf 1995: 137–329; his election (described in Redcliffe-Maud 1981: 11–12 as 'a blind date'): Beveridge 1953: 250 and 257, and UC:GB4/A1/10 fo. 231ʳ. Mastership elections had previously been held after the Master had died or resigned. Beveridge was the first Master to be 'pre-elected'—i.e. chosen before the sitting Master retired.

[43] Beveridge settling in: Harris 1997: 296–301 and 350–1, Beveridge 1953: 264, and UC:R2/MS1/10.

[44] Bowen: UC:P22/MS/1; report on College employment: UC:GB4/A1/10 fo. 262ʳ; reforms: *UCR* 1938, pp. 11–12 and UC:GB4/A1/10 fo. 264ʳ.

College called Harold Wilson, who had just won a First in PPE in 1937, and who in May 1938 was elected a Junior Research Fellow in economics.[45]

A year after he arrived at University College, Beveridge's relationship with it changed, when Elspeth's mother Jessy (later Janet) Mair became his housekeeper in the Lodgings. Mrs Mair had been Secretary of the LSE, and been Beveridge's close companion both professionally and personally. Unfortunately, she could be overbearing, possessive towards Beveridge, and vindictive to those who displeased her, and the nature of her relationship with Beveridge aroused gossip. Many believed that Beveridge's difficulties at the LSE were caused in part by the dislike aroused by Mrs Mair, and her reputation preceded her to Oxford. Gardner claimed that, on Beveridge's election, the Fellows privately stipulated that he should not bring Mrs Mair to Oxford, 'partly because it would hardly be proper, and partly because her masterful ways might well conflict with the sturdy independence of the Dons'. The Fellows' fears were justified. Although she could be hospitable—Harold Wilson's wife, Mary, remembered her presiding over an enjoyable Scottish dancing party in the Lodgings—she was generally unpopular, especially with College servants, whom she bullied and tried to manage.[46]

'THE PUB ON THE HIGH'

For many Oxonians in the 1920s and 1930s, University College was simply 'The Pub on the High'. J. G. S. Macphail even claimed that the nickname was created in 1919. As he saw it, undergraduates of University College were not particularly prone to drinking, 'but their position was more exposed than most of them to the public view'.[47]

The College could indeed live up to its nickname, when post-war undergraduates let off steam as exuberantly—if not alarmingly—as their predecessors. The American Buel Trowbridge recalled a Bump Supper from the early 1920s at which, after the Master and Fellows withdrew, the undergraduates stood on the tables, linked arms, and ceremoniously stamped on every plate or glass they could. A dance band played in the Hall, as more plates and glasses were smashed, and a bonfire was lit in the quadrangle, fuelled by floorboards from the showers and lavatory seats. A Fellow explained to a bewildered Trowbridge that such behaviour was tolerated, so long as it was within the College's walls, and everyone paid for the damage. He also observed that it gave the undergraduates a chance to have some fun after their experiences in Flanders.[48] Harold Brodribb (m. 1928), however, who

---

[45] Gardner 1975: 169; Beveridge 1953: 260 and UC:GB4/A1/10 fos. 274ʳ and 276ʳ.
[46] Beveridge and Mrs Mair: Harris 1997: 6–42 and Dahrendorf 1995: 150–9; Mrs Mair in Oxford: Gardner 1975: 154, Mary Wilson in *UCR* Vol. XI no. 3 (1995), 19, and UC:P22/MS/1.
[47] Macphail 1980: 50. He also observed that alcohol was one way of expressing one's freedom after the war.
[48] Trowbridge 1976: 37–9.

lived on the ground floor of the Main Quadrangle, was always apprehensive when any major celebrations took place outside them. Fellows occasionally joined in the fun. Thomas Peacocke (m. 1927) recalled this aftermath of a Bump Supper:

> I can remember Dr. [*sic*] Farquharson...sitting on a jerry [chamber pot] with an umbrella in his hand and scraping the jerry up and down on the flag stones saying 'Well rowed, Univ, well rowed'. D. L. Keir [the Dean] was seen walking about with a rear seat around his neck and saying to some young man armed with a roll of lavatory paper 'You must not take that. The porter wants that.'[49]

One drinking custom, common to many colleges at least until the late 1970s, was 'sconcing'. People who entered Hall late or inappropriately dressed, mentioned a lady's name, discussed their work or the portraits on the walls, or otherwise committed a *faux pas* over dinner, could be 'sconced'. The victim was given a tankard containing two and a half pints of beer. He could either pay for it, and distribute it among the people sitting at his table, or he could drink it all in one go in 25 seconds, with the butler holding a stopwatch alongside him. If he succeeded in this, the 'sconcer' had to pay for the drink.[50]

Interwar Oxford is traditionally seen as a battleground between the aesthetes and the hearties, and University College was no exception. T. C. Fraser (m. 1928) recalled an episode when some 'aesthetic' rooms were wrecked, but the President and Secretary of the Junior Common Room 'repudiated and held personally responsible' the culprits. Douglas Logan (m. 1928), thought University a 'hearty' College. He had heard about aesthetes being bullied by ex-service students a few years earlier, but found the College 'fairly tolerant' by his time.[51]

Perhaps University College's two most notable aesthetes were Stephen Spender and Edward Tangye Lean (m. 1929), who later worked for the BBC. In his autobiography Spender brutally observed that the hearties 'lacked conviction and that there was a certain hysteria about their athleticism'. He also thought that the Scholars became 'coarse and drunken, as though they would not admit the fineness of their sensibilities'. Spender took a certain pleasure in provoking reactions. He hung reproductions of modern paintings in his rooms, wore a red tie, and sat on a cushion in a quadrangle reading poetry. When a party entered his rooms to break them up, he nonchalantly sat back reading Blake until they grew bored and gave up. In the end, Spender found friendship in W. H. Auden at Christ Church, and looked outside Oxford, spending vacations in Germany, and getting his first poems pub-

---

[49] Brodribb: UC:P12/C/1; Peacocke: UC:P34/MS1/1.
[50] The origins of sconcing are unknown, but it was in existence by the 1920s or 1930s. Accounts of its workings are given in Bamford 1959: 46–7 and Bickerton 1953: 107–8.
[51] Fraser: *UCR* Vol. VII no. 2 (1976), 93; Logan 1974: 368–9.

lished. Contemporaries remembered Spender as pleasant, if rather immature: John Yeldham (m. 1927) thought his red tie a 'demonstration of defiance', but John Maud observed that Spender had friends among the rowers.[52]

Edward Tangye Lean had a rougher ride. In the *Oxford Mail* of 10 November 1932, he claimed that he had got off to a bad start because on his first night he refused to join the boat club. His pictures were smashed and his books covered in marmalade. Only his fencing skills kept people at bay.[53] In 1932, he published a novel, *Storm in Oxford*, which attacked the athletics cult, and he was thrown in the Cherwell by some hearties. Michael Sadler was unsympathetic; although he suspected that some of Lean's assailants came from the College, he called the attack 'silly', and thought that Lean had been provocative, with 'a little of Shelley's notoriety'. He also heard rumours that the ducking had been arranged by some of Lean's friends.[54]

Most undergraduates, however, were neither particularly hearty nor particularly aesthetic. Justin Evans, a serious-minded Welshman from Liverpool, played games a little, but also attended concerts, plays, and the Oxford Union. He joined the Martlets, and sang in the Oxford Bach Choir. Evans did not always approve of his contemporaries: as he put it, 'avoiding men without intellect or with inebriate or pornographic tastes' restricted his social life. Desmond Cooper (m. 1932) likewise led a life involving some sports, concerts, the theatre, and the cinema, or just sitting in friends' rooms listening to gramophone records. He was aware of a slightly noisy set which 'used to go shouting & singing & belching around the place at night', but they were in the minority.[55]

Nevertheless the dominant interest of most ordinary members of University College was sport. Foreign students like Buel Trowbridge who found it difficult to adjust to English reserve discovered that taking up a sport—in Trowbridge's case, rugby—broke down barriers. Indeed Trowbridge and another rugby-playing Rhodes Scholar, the New Zealander Malcolm 'Mac' Cooper (m. 1935), achieved such social success that they were elected JCR Presidents in 1922/3 and 1936/7 respectively (Fig. 18.4). College teams won Hockey Cuppers in 1930–1 and 1932 and Rugby Cuppers in 1931 and 1935–7, while the First Eight went Head of the River in Torpids in 1926, and was runner-up in Torpids in 1925 and 1929 and Eights Week in 1930 and 1931. At a less serious level, there was a particular fondness for informal cricket. In the early 1920s the 'Univ. Uniques' played the 'Trinity Trifflers' once a year, but in fancy dress, and after a well-lubricated lunch. A more durable club was the

---

[52] Spender 1951: 33–4, 38, and 49–62; reactions to Spender: Renton 2006: 32; UC:P38/C/1 (Yeldham), and Redcliffe-Maud 1981: 26.

[53] Lean's fencing skills against the 'rugger buggers' was remembered by others (letter from Edmund Seyd, 10 August 2002).

[54] Bodl. MS Eng. Misc. c. 544 fos. 156^r and 160^r.

[55] Evans's diary: UC:P9/J/1 (the comments on his contemporaries are on p. 48); Cooper's reminiscences: UC:P34/MS3/1 (p. 51 mentions the noisy set).

FIGURE 18.4 The College Rugby XV of 1921/2 Buel Trowbridge, m. 1920, is seated on the sofa on the second row from top, on the right-hand end.

'Utopers', apparently founded in the late 1920s. The Utopers played against teams from local villages, and membership was open to anyone: early members recalled that at Utopers' games the blue and the tyro could meet on equal terms.[56]

Some College sportsmen became legendary: 'Mac' Cooper picked up three rugby Blues and played for Scotland; Cyril Tolley (m. 1919) was arguably the greatest amateur golfer of his generation; but most remarkable of all was Christopher Charles Mackintosh (m. 1922), who in 1924 played rugby for Scotland, won a downhill ski race in France, represented Britain in the long jump at the Paris Olympics, and then Oxford in another downhill skiing race against Cambridge.[57]

---

[56] Attitudes to sport: letters from Donald Hanson (m. 1927), 29 May 2002 and Edmund Seyd, 10 August 2002; Trowbridge 1976: 19–21 and 23–7; Univ. Uniques: Trowbridge 1976: 36–7; the Utopers: *UCR* Vol. IX no. 1 (1985), 24–5, *UCR* Vol. IX no. 2 (1986), 28–9, UC:P32/MS/1, and Renton 2006: 32–3.
[57] Cooper: Craven 2000: 44–51; Tolley: *ODNB* entry; Mackintosh's obituary in *Times* 2 February 1974, and *UCR* 1924.

There were also College societies of a more intellectual and artistic bent.[58] After its revival in 1919, with C. S. Lewis as its Secretary, the Martlets offered the same pre-war mixture of papers from undergraduate and senior members. In June 1926 G. D. H. Cole read a paper on detective fiction; current undergraduates like Stephen Spender, and eminent former members like Ernest de Sélincourt and C. S. Lewis read papers, as did such outside guests as Ronald Knox and Cecil Day Lewis.[59]

The most important new cultural initiative was the University College Musical Society, created by John Maud and his fiancée Jean Hamilton, a talented concert pianist. Maud, aware of concern among some Fellows that such a society might not flourish, diplomatically won the support of the captains of boats and the rugby team for his venture. The first concert was held on 1 June 1930 in the lecture room in 90 High Street, where Hamilton accompanied the tenor Steuart Wilson. The Society offered recitals by professional musicians, informal concerts given by Fellows and undergraduates, and 'gramophone recitals', when members would listen to music in someone's room. In 1934, it began a choir, first called a 'Singing Club', which in June that year tackled Elgar's *The Music Makers*. An important figure in the society was John Webster (m. 1934), who became organist of St Mary the Virgin in 1938 but retained lifelong links with College music. He conducted the society's choir, and encouraged new repertoire, including Fauré's *Requiem*, of which the choir gave the first Oxford performance in February 1940.[60]

Certain subjects attracted their own societies. A Robert Boyle Society was founded in 1931 for College scientists; the Eldon Society, for lawyers, is recorded as existing in 1930; and a Cecil Club discussed politics and modern history. There were also many ephemeral societies, one of which attained an accidental immortality. In the early 1930s, Edward Tangye Lean founded a literary society at which junior and senior members could read their unpublished compositions. Among its senior members were C. S. Lewis, Tangye Lean's tutor, and J. R. R. Tolkien, then Professor of Anglo-Saxon. When some of Lewis's friends, including Tolkien, later met at Magdalen and read out their compositions, Lewis gave this group the name Tangye Lean had created for his society—'The Inklings'.[61]

---

[58] For an example of this development elsewhere, see Hodgkin 1949: 206–7.

[59] Bodl. MS Top. Oxon. d. 95/3 fos. 62[r] (Lewis as Secretary), d. 95/4 fols. 47[r] (Cole), 97[r] (Spender), and 105[r] (de Sélincourt), and d. 95/5 pp. 28 (Knox), 48 (C. Day Lewis) and 99 (C. S. Lewis). Lewis 1991 includes several detailed accounts of Martlets meetings. The Churchwardens and the Durham Society were apparently not refounded.

[60] The foundation of the Music Society: *UCR* 1929/30 p. 9, UC:GB4/A1/9 fo. 250[r], Redcliffe-Maud 1978: 188–91, and UC:O8/A1/1; sporting support: Redcliffe-Maud 1981: 108–9; John Webster: Walker 1974; Fauré: UC:O8/A1/1 pp. 129–31.

[61] Robert Boyle Society: UC:O11/A1/1; Eldon Society: Renton 2006: 29; the first 'Inklings' (no records of which are known to survive): Carpenter 1981: 387–8.

As for the population of the College as a whole, an examination of undergraduates who came up in 1922–5 and 1932–5 sheds some light on their social composition and education.[62] In both periods, roughly two-thirds of all undergraduates had attended public school, although the proportion from the elite 'Clarendon' group (p. 377) varied, from a quarter of all undergraduates in 1923 to almost half in 1924, and then in 1932–5 to only between a quarter and a fifth of the full total. Each year also saw at least half a dozen men, mainly Rhodes Scholars, who had been educated abroad. In 1923 just three men (out of forty-six) had been to a grammar school, but by 1932–5 they formed one-fifth of all freshmen. This change has been attributed to Sir Michael Sadler—John Burton (m. 1931) once heard his scout complain that Sadler admitted too many grammar school boys, but he was merely bringing University College more in line with other colleges: one-fifth of all Oxford undergraduates in 1920–39 had attended one of the Clarendon Schools, so University had been especially biased in the early 1920s.[63]

The fathers of University College's undergraduates were slightly more middle class than those at some other colleges.[64] In 1922–5 they divided half-and-half between the traditional professions (army, teaching, medicine, the law, and the civil service) and business, manufacturing, or banking, but in 1932–5 there were slightly more fathers from the latter category. Some grammar school boys came from significantly lower classes, such as the son of a commercial traveller in 1924 or a miner's son in 1925 (the latter coming from Normanton Grammar School). In the 1930s there were a few more sons of miners, mason's labourers, quarry labourers, or postmen, but they remained a small minority.

Without special funding, people of modest means could not afford an Oxford education. C. S. Lewis was able to obtain two undergraduate degrees, and then stay in Oxford for two years more before his election to Magdalen only thanks to his father's assistance. In December 1933, a survey of University College's undergraduates revealed that two-thirds of them did not need financial assistance; of the rest, half could only study at Oxford thanks to aid from public funds, and the other half thanks to school exhibitions or similar endowments. A few, like Justin Evans, were lucky enough to find a local benefactor. The Freeston and Gunsley Scholarships undoubtedly provided assistance, but there were now other sources, such as Miners' Welfare Scholarships. Although Stephen Spender observed that the grants awarded to one of his friends were so small that he 'lived a kind of slum life in his college', nevertheless they enabled undergraduates from poor backgrounds to study in Oxford. One such was Samuel Hughes (m. 1932), whose father, a miner, had

---

[62] Information derived from matriculation forms for 1922–5 and 1932–5 (UC:J10/A1/1–3).
[63] Sadler: UC:P34/MS7/1 p. 2 (also Grier 1952: 249); grammar school boys in Oxford: Greenstein 1994: 47.
[64] Greenstein 1994: 56.

been killed in an accident while Hughes was at school. Continuing his education despite family hardship, Hughes won both a Freeston Scholarship and a Miners' Welfare Scholarship.[65]

Memories differ as to how different social groups co-existed. John Linton (m. 1929) and David Hopkinson (m. 1932) both noticed a marked distinction between the public school and grammar school boys; Frank Hawking (m. 1923), coming from a minor public school, found himself more at ease with men from grammar schools than the 'rich sporting set', whereas David Renton found the College easy to fit into socially, with no cliques as such.[66]

There were certainly few political conflicts. Apart from G. D. H. Cole, the College was generally right wing or indifferent: Harold Mitchell, a future MP and Vice-Chairman of the Conservative Party, was amused by the fact that radical Balliol produced Harold Macmillan and Edward Heath, whereas University College nurtured Clement Attlee and Harold Wilson. Desmond Cooper remembered the JCR mainly as a social club: in February 1934, it refused to send a representative to an Undergraduates' Council which was regarded as too left wing. Harold Marks was one of his few socialist contemporaries, and Cooper had 'a superb argument' with him about George V's Jubilee in 1935.[67]

There were changes in the College's religious life. After the layman Macan became Master in 1906, A. J. Carlyle acted as Chaplain, and then in 1912 Cuthbert Parker became the first Fellow specifically elected as Chaplain to the College. Meanwhile, weekday services became ever less popular. Buel Trowbridge, who was studying theology when JCR President, was encouraged by the Master to attend morning services to set an example; he found only about ten older students and a few freshmen joining him.[68]

Perhaps the best known religious movement of the 1920s and 1930 was the so-called Oxford Group, or 'Buchmanites', named after the American preacher Frank Buchman, who first visited Oxford in 1921. Many undergraduates (and some Fellows, like John Maud) were inspired by Buchman's programme of meditation in so-called 'quiet times', public confessions of sins, and his philosophy of a total surrender to God. The Group was controversial: several found its methods manipulative, and disliked the cult surrounding Buchman himself. Buel Trowbridge embraced the Group in his second year, but became disturbed by Buchman's philosophy of total surrender, which, he feared, helped cause his failure in his Finals exams. Trowbridge, who himself

---

[65] Undergraduate finances: UC:GB4/A1/10 fo. 95ʳ; Justin Evans: UC:P9/J/1 passim; Spender 1951: 36; Hughes (who became a headmaster and received the CBE for his services to education): UCR Vol. XIV no. 2 (2006), 153–4.

[66] Linton: UC:P34/MS5/1 p. 2; Hopkinson: UC:P34/MS9/1 p. 2; Hawking: UC:P11/MS/1; Renton: interview of 4 October 2002.

[67] Mitchell 1974: 78; Cooper: UC:P34/MS1/1 pp. 24, 58, and 120.

[68] A Chaplain Fellow: UC:GB4/A1/9 fo. 286–7 and 299–300; UC:GB4/A1/10 fos. 42ʳ and 64ʳ; Trowbridge 1976: 62.

later taught theology, happily acknowledged that it was his less fundamentalist and more enlightened teachers, including the Chaplain Cyril Emmet (F. 1920–3), who influenced him most.[69]

Little attention has so far been paid to academic life in the College. Whatever its other qualities, University College was not as fiercely academic as it had been in the 1870s. Although there were now start-of-term collections, in the sense of informal examinations, they were not taken seriously: C. S. Lewis described some philosophy collections from April 1922, during which people 'talked and ragged and talked', and asked for help in answering questions. One German Rhodes Scholar, Adolf Schlepegrell (m. 1931), claimed that although Oxford men received an excellent general education, they worked less hard than their German equivalents. Nevertheless, one observer thought that University College had 'a reputation for scholarship in 1919 in a quiet way, unlike Balliol'. In 1926, Justin Evans sat a day-long set of entrance exams, including a general paper, Greek and Latin unseens, a Latin Prose, and was interviewed by the Master, Senior Tutor, Dean, and another Fellow. On the other hand, it was claimed that one could get a Third in PPE simply by reading *The Times* every day. In fairness, there was little incentive for those uninterested in an academic career to obtain a good degree: employers did not usually ask Oxford men for their degree class.[70]

As for what subjects were studied, a re-examination of the undergraduates of 1922–5 and 1932–5 shows that the most popular subjects in the 1920s were law and modern history, followed by classics. PPE had just four or five finalists each year, and English between one and five. Medicine was the most popular science, perhaps thanks to the presence of Ernest Ainley Walker (F. 1903–38; apparently the first Tutorial Fellow in medicine in any college)—but, despite the appointment of Edmund Bowen, only a few men read chemistry. In 1932–5, law and modern history remained the most popular subjects, but PPE had taken over in third place. Other arts subjects, like English, modern languages, and theology, were also a little more popular. Medicine was still the most popular science, with chemistry, physics, and engineering still little studied. Indeed the non-medical sciences remained poor relations of the arts in the 1920s and 1930s, most colleges still having no more than one or two scientists among their Fellowship; this made the presence of Walker, Bowen, and Gardner at University College striking.[71]

---

[69] The Oxford Group in general: Turner 1994: 301–2; the Oxford Group at University College: Evans 1981, UC:P7/C/1, UC:P12/C/1, and UC:P34/MS5/1 pp. 6–7, and Trowbridge 1976: 46–50 and 69.

[70] Lewis 1991: 25–6; Schlepegrell 1934 (his later career, which involved escaping the Nazi regime first to Britain and then to Canada is outlined in *UCR* Vol. XVI no. 1 (2005), 124–6); academic standards: Macphail 1980: 50; Evans's exam: UC:P9/J/1 p. 14; PPE: Parsons 2003: 90; jobs: UC:P34/MS5/1 p. 2 and UC:P34/MS6/1 p. 4.

[71] Information derived from the Tutorial Lists in UC:J7/A1/2 for 1922–5 and 1932–5 and the Finals Results for 1925–8 and 1935–8; science subjects: Morrell 1994: 140–2.

The 1920s saw the first modern postgraduate students, especially after the D.Phil. was introduced at Oxford in 1917 and the Ph.D. at Cambridge in 1920, mainly, it was claimed, in response to American demands. However, of the 200 or so men who came up in 1922–5, barely half a dozen took a postgraduate degree, and the proportion was little changed in 1932–5. When C. S. Lewis told his father in 1924 that 'the D.Phil. would add very little to my Firsts in the way of qualification', he spoke for many. No Fellow of University College elected before 1939 had a D.Phil.[72]

Postgraduates did not fit in easily. David Hopkinson thought that they were regarded as figures of fun; Colin Cooke (m. 1934), a graduate of Manchester University, who was admitted to University College on a two-year Leverhulme Research Fellowship, was treated administratively as a first-year undergraduate despite being 31 years old, because his Manchester degree was not recognized at Oxford, and required permission to live outside College with his family. When in his second year Cooke gave lectures in social sciences, he was made a member of the Senior Common Room. Sir Michael Sadler, who had invited him to Oxford, and the American Arthur Goodhart were sympathetic to Cooke, but Poynton and Farquharson looked askance on someone who lacked an Oxford degree. Another postgraduate who defied the usual categories was the rugby-playing Rhodes Scholar 'Mac' Cooper, whose undergraduate degree was from an agricultural college. No one was quite sure what he should read at Oxford, until eventually he was accepted for a D.Phil. studying the dairy industry.[73]

This leaves the Fellows of University College, whose numbers were swelled both by the Mynors Fellowship, held by G. D. H. Cole, and a bequest from Sir Ernest Wallis Budge, the Egyptologist, who in 1934 bequeathed half his estate to the College 'for the encouragement of the study of Egyptology'. It was decided to create a Junior Research Fellowship in Egyptology, and the first Lady Wallis Budge Fellow, Alec Dakin, was elected in the summer of 1936. Since then, the Fellowship has changed in nature several times, but it has given several important Egyptologists significant starts in their careers.[74]

The Fellows of the early twentieth century were under no pressure to publish. It is therefore hard, for example, to judge Poynton's scholarship on the basis of his few publications. Some Fellows even thought it bad form to reveal their academic skills, above all Farquharson, who seemed in the 1920s or 1930s slightly buffoonish: C. S. Lewis observed 'It is an old subject of

---

[72] The D.Phil. and Ph.D.: Harrison 1994*b*: 89, Currie 1994: 124–5, Wilkinson 1980: 83 and Darwin 1994: 616; Lewis 2000: 624 (and Lewis 1991: 296).

[73] Hopkinson: UC:P34/MS9/1 p. 2; Cooke: UC:P188/C1/1 and interview, 6 April 2001; Cooper: Craven 2000: 39–41 (Cooper later became an important figure in agricultural theory).

[74] The Wallis Budge Fellowship: UC:GB4/A1/10 fos. 124^r, 130^r, 163^r, 185^r, and 197–8 (Budge, a Cambridge man, had incorporated from University College in 1898).

FIGURE 18.5 Edgar Carritt giving a tutorial in 1938.

controversy just how mad the Fark is', and people smiled at his military titles. Yet in addition to all his scholarly work, Farquharson served on the Hebdomadal Council for fourteen years, and was a delegate of OUP. The undergraduate once gruffly teased by James Bright as an aesthete had succeeded almost too well in hiding his true abilities.[75]

The philosopher Edgar Carritt (Fig. 18.5), however, was recognized for his books on aesthetics, and remembered by former pupils as 'clear and incisive, with a dry humour and no patience for rhetoric of verbiage, but stimulating in the cogency and economy of his style'. The ancient historian George Hope Stevenson (whose refined Scottish accent could be mimicked decades later) produced a well-regarded book, *Roman Provincial Administration*, although pupils thought his teaching rather exam orientated, and a Fellow of Corpus Christi College cruelly dismissed him as 'that parboiled old poop'. Several Fellows achieved greater success as administrators. C. K. Allen was a good law tutor, and even became Professor of Jurisprudence, but his career culminated in his appointment as Warden of Rhodes House in 1930. Two popular Deans of the 1920s and 1930s, David Lindsay Keir and John Maud, both won promotion in 1939 when Keir became Vice-Chancellor of Queen's University, Belfast, and Maud Master of Birkbeck College, London.[76]

---

[75] Lewis 2000: 874–5; Farquharson's offices: Harrison 1994d: 686 and *UCR* 1937, p. 4.
[76] Carritt: *UCR* Vol. IV no 4 (1964), 239 (and frequent admiring references in Lewis 1991); Stevenson: Currie 1994: 135, UC:R2/MS1/5, interview with Frederick Yarnold, 11 January 2000, and J. Peck in Harrison 1994a: 90. Keir returned to Oxford in 1949 as Master of Balliol—an unhappy appointment (Jones 2005: 290–2)—while Maud embarked on a successful career in the civil service before returning to University College in 1964.

Perhaps the most remarkable academic attached to the College was A. J. Carlyle, who continued to exercise his polymathic magic, acting as Chaplain and Lecturer in Politics and Economics, teaching English at Lincoln College, and acquiring a reputation as an authority on medieval political history. Writing to Carlyle's daughters after his death, C. S. Lewis declared that he had 'no single memory of him that is not good and happy all through'.[77]

The decision to attach professorships to colleges affected University College. It already possessed the Professorship in Geology, but in 1926 the Corpus Professorship of Jurisprudence (along with its current holder, Walter Ashburner) was attached to a College Fellowship. On Ashburner's retirement, C. K. Allen briefly held the post, before being replaced by Arthur Lehman Goodhart, a Fellow of Corpus Christi, Cambridge. Goodhart, the first American Fellow of University College, brought significant scholarly credentials: in particular, he edited a major law journal, the *Law Quarterly Review* from 1925 to 1975.[78]

The Senior Common Room was a friendly place. There were some differences—'Duncs' Gardner suspected that some arts Fellows, fearing the march of science, had opposed his election, and there were political differences (Carritt, Leys, and, of course, Cole leaned to the left, and Farquharson, Ainley Walker, Goodhart, and Stevenson to the right). Nevertheless, the Fellows could agree to differ, and John Maud praised Gardner for his 'sweetness of character that set the tone and helped preserve an unprecarious peace'. At Magdalen, C. S. Lewis missed his old College, telling his father that he would 'never find a common room that I did not like better', and after dining at University College in 1926, he observed that he had forgotten 'how good Univ. conversation was'.[79]

College life still required some Fellows to live in, and Fellows still had to seek the College's permission to marry. On his election in 1929 John Maud undertook not to marry for three years, and was only permitted to do so earlier because he could live in Kybald Street. Nevertheless, as Dean, he saw little of his wife and young family during term time. He could at least live with them: when C. K. Allen was elected Dean in 1924, he was expected to live in College during the term. His wife Dorothy was philosophical: 'If I had not had so many friends and interests', she remarked, 'I should have found our flat rather a lonely and creepy place.' Some wives involved themselves in College life: the wives of John Maud and Edmund Bowen helped decorate and furnish 83/4 High Street during their conversion into undergraduate rooms.[80]

---

[77] Teaching activities: *UCR* 1929/30, pp. 11–12, Green 1979: 331 and Carritt 1960: 55; Lewis on Carlyle: Lewis 2004: 578.

[78] The Law Professorship: UC:GB4/A1/9 fo. 76ʳ; Ashburner: Carritt 1960: 42.

[79] Gardner's election: Gardner 1975: 134; politics: *UCR* Vol. VII no. 4 (1978), 165 (cf. Wild 1988: 44); Lewis 2000: 648 and Lewis 1991: 398.

[80] Redcliffe-Maud 1991: 49 and 27; Allen 1960: 24; help from Mrs Maud and Mrs Bowen: UC:GB4/A1/10 fo. 152ʳ.

FIGURE 18.6 The University College Servants Rowing Club in 1937, winners of the Challenge Fours. The sitters are (back row) D. Primer and H. V. Quelch (coach from Christ Church), (middle row) W. Buckingham, N. King, and N. Dix, and in the front R. Smith.

Other wives pursued academic careers of their own—both Kenneth Leys's wives, Margaret and Agnes, were historians, the one at Royal Holloway and then Somerville, the other at St Hilda's—but Margaret Cole, who was not attached to a women's college, found herself effectively shut out of intellectual life. She felt such frustration at this isolation that the Coles eventually returned to London, with her husband living in College during the week.[81]

College servants of the interwar years, on the other hand, were deeply involved in College life. There existed a parallel universe of servants' intercollegiate sporting tournaments, especially in rowing (Fig. 18.6) and cricket, with regular Oxford–Cambridge matches. Although Lord Nuffield's Cowley works offered an important alternative source of employment, College posts were still considered desirable, and even the most menial ones, such as that of under-scout, were keenly competed for. Many servants appointed in the 1920s and 1930s remained in the College for the rest of their working lives.[82]

---

[81] Margaret Leys: Rayner 1993: 30–1 and Adams 1996: 76; Agnes Leys: Rayner 1993: 64–5; Margaret Cole: Cole 1971: 145.

[82] Contemporary issues of *UCR* regularly report on servants' activities; other information taken from interviews with Norman Dix, 25 March 1997 and 4 September 2001 (Dix's father had worked for the College); servants' sports: Wenden 1994: 528–9.

There remained a certain sense of deference on one side and of obligation on the other. Norman Dix, employed by the College in 1931, disliked later being called a member of staff, deeming 'servant' a complimentary term. In turn, the College was an understanding employer, paying sick servants part of their wages when this was not mandatory, and among undergraduates, as David Hopkinson recalled, 'to be careless in the way one treated college servants' was thought bad form.[83]

The two most senior servants in the College were the Head Porter, Fred Bickerton (Fig. 19.1), and Frank Collett, College Butler in 1932–57. Bickerton not unreasonably saw himself as the senior servant of the College, and as a buffer between the undergraduates and the Governing Body. However, Douglas Millin, who joined the Lodge in 1947 observed with customary bluntness that Fred 'was alright, a bit of a snob, a dead loss'. Others remembered the Porter's Lodge as a sanctum, into which only the JCR President and other distinguished undergraduates could be admitted, and where much informal College business was transacted. On the other hand, Collett, employed by the College since 1907, was widely respected—and liked—as a man of considerable intellect and ability, and ended up largely running the College's domestic affairs. John Maud was one of many Fellows grateful for his advice, and Peter Strawson (F. 1948–68) thought that, had Collett been granted a better education, he could have had a successful career in the civil service. This example reminds us how much colleges once relied on intelligent men from poor backgrounds with few alternative prospects.[84]

Sir Michael Sadler created a new class of servant when he employed Rosamund Elliott as the College's first female secretary. The first College secretaries worked jointly for the Master, the Senior Tutor, and Dean. One of them, Mary Zvegintzov, a Russian emigrée, married the Law Fellow Richard Holdsworth in 1940, and in her widowhood transformed herself into an academic, becoming Principal of St Mary's College, Durham. Her successor, Lucia Turin, another Russian emigrée, had worked with Beveridge at the LSE.[85]

Nevertheless, in spite of these changes, and such dynamic Masters as Sir Michael Sadler and Sir William Beveridge, the undergraduate of 1913 would have found the College of 1938 recognizable in many respects, whereas he would have found the College of the 1950s totally different. In spite of some significant Fellows, University College was not at the academic forefront of the university. Yet that nickname of 'The Pub on the High' should not be dismissed as an embarrassment. If pubs are not always places of intellectual

---

[83] Dix: *UCR* Vol. XIV no. 1 (2005), 41; Hopkinson: UC:P34/MS9/1 p. 3.
[84] Bickerton seen by himself and others: Bickerton 1953: 103, and UC:P34/MS9/1 p. 2; Millin on Bickerton: Park 1989: 49; Collett: *UCR* Vol. III no. 3 (1958), 153–4, Redcliffe-Maud 1981: 25–6, and interview with Sir Peter Strawson, 8 October 2002.
[85] Rosamund Elliott: *UCR* Vol. VIII no. 5 (1984), 234; Mary Holdsworth *UCR* Vol. VII no. 5 (1979), 235; Lucia Turin: *UCR* Vol. VI no. 3 (1973), 303–4. Balliol employed its first College Secretary in 1924 (Jones 2005: 275).

stimulation, yet they can be friendly, and for many people, be they Fellow, undergraduate, or servant, University College was just that.

THE COLLEGE AND THE SECOND WORLD WAR: 1939–1945[86]

Far-sighted members of the College had feared war long before 1939: the editor of the *University College Record* of 1938 wondered whether College would assemble that Michaelmas Term. When war did come, the College did not empty as it had in 1914. Undergraduates in reserved occupations, such as chemists and medical students, were allowed to remain; also the government did not call up men under the age of 20, and permitted Finalists to complete their course. The College took time to adjust to the new conditions. David Strawbridge, coming up in 1939 from a Dorset grammar school to read chemistry, was disconcerted to be asked to bring a full dinner service for six, and then relieved to be told subsequently that, because of hostilities, all meals would be taken in Hall, and that he need only bring a teapot and a couple of cups and plates.[87]

The College retained its own site, and took in members from colleges requisitioned for government purposes, such as Merton from 1939 to 1941 and Keble from 1940 to 1945. University College and Merton even operated joint sports teams. Another University–Merton collaboration was of a more novel kind. Peter Bayley (m. 1940) had created a play-reading society on coming up; that summer, Merton Floats, Merton's drama society, wished to perform *The Comedy of Errors*, but lacked enough men. To make good the deficiency, Bayley created the Univ. Players.[88]

The early months of the war proved frustrating. Gus Green (m. 1938) volunteered for the Fleet Air Arm, but found himself stuck in Oxford awaiting his call-up, his boredom only alleviated by tutorials with C. S. Lewis. Preparations for war, however, did not cease. The Chapel windows were taken down, and blackout regulations enforced. The most time-consuming war work for undergraduates was fire-watching. Every night, they took turns sitting on its roofs looking out for passing aeroplanes, some sitting in boredom, others enjoying plane-spotting. They even shared these duties during the vacation, with the College paying their board and lodging.[89]

---

[86] Other accounts of Oxford and University College respectively during the war can be found in Addison 1994 and Darwall-Smith 2005c.
[87] Forebodings: *UCR* 1938, p. 3; exemptions from service: *UCR* 1939, pp. 7–9; crockery: UC:P214/MS1/20 (Hopkins 2005: 387 reports similar modifications at Trinity).
[88] Merton: *UCR* 1939, p. 7, UC:GB4/A1/11 fos. 27^r, and 31^r, and Martin and Highfield 1997: 340–1; Keble: Wild 1971: 48; Univ. Players: Bayley 2000; Merton Floats: Martin and Highfield 1997: 339.
[89] Green 1995: 15–16: ARP activities: Wild 1972 (it was later calculated (*UCR* 1946, p. 5) that some undergraduates at least were in residence every day between January 1941 and 2 December 1944).

The College lost several Fellows to the war effort. Richard Holdsworth, a popular young Law Fellow who had combined a rowing Blue with a First in Jurisprudence, joined the RAF, while Harold Wilson was seconded to Whitehall. A. F. 'Freddie' Wells, the Classics Fellow, worked for Naval Intelligence, eventually becoming Editor-in-Chief of the Inter-Services Topographical Division, overseeing the collation of information about places of interest to the Allied Forces. Nevertheless, fewer Fellows were called up for service than in the First World War—one of those left behind, James Douglas, the Geology Professor, commanded the Oxford City Home Guard—not least because several, including Farquharson, Stevenson, Carritt, and Leys, had been elected before 1914. Some, like Carritt, delayed their retirement until peacetime. Some pupils felt that this affected the quality of their teaching: one undergraduate remembered that his elderly tutors gave him 'essay subjects week by week in a haphazard way unrelated to any syllabus'.[90]

The two 'young' Fellows left in College were Kenneth Wheare (F. 1939–44) and John Wild, exempted from service respectively as an Australian and on health grounds. Wheare served as Dean from 1942, and Wild, while serving as Chaplain, was also Domestic Bursar in 1938–45, Dean in 1940–2, and then Vice- and Pro-Master in 1942–5. Another Fellow exempted from war service was the American Arthur Goodhart, who broadcast regularly on British and American radio and advised several government departments, and was awarded an honorary KBE in 1948. In Oxford he created a series of short courses, so that soldiers on leave could spend a few days in an Oxford College, enjoying a blend of lectures and entertainments. Balliol College was set aside for this function. Giles Alington, a young graduate of Trinity and, like Wild, a non-combatant on health grounds, was appointed coordinator of the courses.[91]

As the war worsened, so the College suffered a bewildering and tragic event.[92] Around lunchtime on 17 May 1940, some undergraduates walking out from Hall into the Main Quadrangle were shot at by the undergraduate occupant of a top-floor room directly opposite. One, Charles Moffatt, was killed, and two more wounded, and a servant coming to their aid was struck on his shoe. One of the wounded, Denis Melrose (m. 1939), later a pioneering heart surgeon, remembered seeing his friend Moffatt fall, and thought he was 'playing dead', but when Melrose tried to lift him, he was hit himself in the chest, saved from death only by the bullet ricocheting off the fountain pen in his jacket pocket. John Wild emerged from the Senior Common Room through Staircase II—directly in the firing line—to see what was happening,

---

[90] Wells: McLachlan 1968: chapters 13 and 14; Douglas: Roche 1994: 251; poor teaching: UC:P34/MS8/1.
[91] Goodhart's courses: Allen 1960: 128–30, Addison 1994: 178, and Jones 2005: 281–3.
[92] This account is based on reports from eyewitnesses, information from Denis Melrose's family, and a collection of contemporary newscuttings (UC:P24/N/1).

and found the undergraduate ready to give himself up. Every contemporary witness praised Wild's bravery that day. It became clear that the killer was suffering from schizophrenia, and had taken a paranoid dislike to his victims. Some claimed that he believed that one of his victims played loud music and entertained girls in his rooms nearby especially to annoy him, but Norman Dix also remembered breaking up at breakfast that day an argument about conscientious objectors, with the killer defending them against Melrose and his friends.[93] He was a crack shot, and had then borrowed a rifle and ammunition from another undergraduate, and lain in wait for his disputants that lunchtime. He was tried in July 1940, and found guilty but insane.

Although Oxford was never bombed, the war's effects were felt. In September 1940, the College briefly accommodated evacuees from Ashford, Kent, in Radcliffe Quadrangle; amused observers observed clothes lines hanging there, children playing in the Main Quadrangle, and the Junior Common Room turned into a nursery. In September 1941 some evacuees from Bristol were also briefly put up in the College. Another refugee was Margaret Cole, allowed to stay in her husband's rooms to escape the Blitz. She was amused at the eyebrows raised, even at 'a wife of over twenty years' standing, being allowed to spend nights in the sacred precincts', and she suspected that Mrs Mair had helped arrange this.[94]

Rationing gradually affected College life. From January 1941 members received two-course dinners, rather than three. One undergraduate remembered lunch becoming 'something of a disgrace—frequently no more than a bowl of soup or (not "and") a black pudding, supplemented by bread (unrationed) and one's own butter, cheese, etc. as required.' Another notorious dish was a soup which tasted of little else but pepper. By 1944, regular dishes included rabbit stew, plenty of fish, and spam fritters and chips.[95]

From 1942 the university introduced six-month short courses for service cadets. Army cadets were restricted to science courses, but navy and air cadets could study other subjects. The status of these forces students was slightly uncertain: one thought that 'though *in* College, we were not quite *of* it'. Nevertheless, they signed the Admissions Register, and participated in College life. They combined their academic work with daily training exercises.[96]

The training exercises were no formality: the Second World War Memorial in the College Chapel bears eighty-nine names. Unlike in the First World War, the full total of College members on active service is not known, but it is enough to know that one-eighth of those who matriculated in 1937 and 1938 were killed. Among the fallen was one Fellow, Richard Holdsworth, killed in

---

[93] Theories: UC:P34/MS12/1; and interview with Norman Dix, 25 March 1997.
[94] Evacuees: Wild 1971: 49; Cole 1971: 233.
[95] Tales of food: UC:P214/MS1/16 and 19–20.
[96] Army cadets: Addison 1994: 175–6; reminiscences from University College: UC:P214/MS1/8 and 18–19, UC:P34/MS11/1, and Rudd 1990: 21–4.

a flying accident in 1942. Sorrow for the dead mingled with anxiety for the captured: John Wild had a brother, and Fred Bickerton a son, who were both prisoners of war under the Japanese. Both survived, but Wild's brother was killed in a plane crash soon after.[97]

Others did not survive the war. Reginald Macan died in 1941, Sir Michael Sadler in 1943, and Arthur Poynton in 1944, two days after being knocked down by a car in High Street. Another loss was 'Farkie', whose Fellowship expired at the end of Hilary Term 1942. He was granted a place and a vote at College meetings for the rest of the war; but it was as if his life ended with his Fellowship. As Registrar, he began to write the minutes of the College meeting of 13 June 1942 in a noticeably feebler hand than usual, but laid down his pen after a few lines. On 5 August he died suddenly, leaving his commentary on Marcus Aurelius almost ready for publication.[98]

Meanwhile, the current Master began the war in a mood of frustration. Having spent the First World War in Whitehall, Beveridge wanted to be there again, but there were suspicions over his temperament. Eventually, in the summer of 1940, he was made Chairman of the Manpower Requirements Committee of the Production Council, and in December that year he became Under-Secretary in the Ministry of Labour. In June 1941 he was moved on again, to become Chairman of the Social Insurance Committee. In his new role, Beveridge was asked to submit a report to the government. The astonishing result, the Beveridge Report, laid down guidelines for a post-war settlement providing for a national health service, family allowances, and the goal of full employment, policies which, as partly implemented by Clement Attlee's government after 1945, created the modern welfare state. No document produced by a Master of University College can have had such significance. When published in December 1942, its message of an optimistic post-war future was just what many people wanted to hear. Even before the report was published, Beveridge himself had appeared regularly in the media, and became a national figure for the first time in his life.[99]

Undergraduates at University College enjoyed the reflected glory brought by the Beveridge Report. This glory, however, came at a cost, because Beveridge was less and less involved in daily College business. He first commuted into London daily, finding time to greet early-rising undergraduates; but as the war drew on, so he was regularly resident in London during the week, returning to Oxford only at weekends. College meetings were moved to Saturday mornings, and the post of Vice-Master, held first by Farquharson and then by Wild, took on an increasing significance. Some Fellows took rather a detached view of

---

[97] Holdsworth: Redcliffe-Maud 1978: 191; prisoners: Parsons 2003: 162–3 and Bickerton 1953: 96. Miller 2008: 89–114 lists the College's war dead.

[98] At College meetings: UC:GB4/A1/11 fo. 125ʳ; last entry in Register: UC:GB3/A1/5 p. 107. Farquharson's commentary was published in 1944, and the translation it included was recently reissued separately in the Oxford World's Classics series.

[99] Beveridge's wartime work, especially his Report, is described in Beveridge 1953: 268–9 and 296–333 and Harris 1997: 353–423.

Beveridge's outside interests. He was not amused when Kenneth Wheare once asked him, 'Well, Master, how's Mein Pamph going?'[100]

In the same month as the publication of the Report, Mrs Mair, recently widowed, married the Master. The war years had not improved her reputation; staff continued to find her bossy, and she was not liked by undergraduates. Fellows looked upon the marriage somewhat askance, and the undergraduates celebrated the event in their own way: on the day when the Beveridges returned to College after their marriage, a group of them serenaded the happy couple from the Master's Garden with the music-hall song 'The Old Gray Mare, she ain't what she used to be'. Their audience waved benignly at the singers, apparently unaware of the words.[101]

As the war drew to a close, its Fellows returned. Harold Wilson was elected to a full Fellowship in March 1944, and appointed Domestic Bursar. That autumn, however, he decided to stand for Parliament at the next General Election, and, as had been agreed, resigned his Fellowship on winning his seat; and so University College gave the Labour party a second future Prime Minister.[102]

Political ambition also led to the loss of the Master. Relations between Beveridge and several Fellows had deteriorated: as early as November 1940, Farquharson had expressed his unease to John and Jean Maud at the Master's absences, and observed that the College was getting 'restive'. Even in the 1950s, Peter Bayley, who as an undergraduate had liked Beveridge, found that his proposal to commission a portrait of him aroused strong opposition. 'He was a disaster for the College,' said one Fellow, and Gardner described him as 'the likeable, dislikeable, admirable, ridiculous historical Beveridge'. John Wild tactfully observed that 'Coming from London, the Master never fully grasped the traditional convention of relations between the Head of a College and its Governing Body.'[103]

The final straw came when Beveridge stood as the Liberal candidate in a by-election at Berwick-on-Tweed in October 1944 (Harold Wilson, at least, had agreed to wait until a General Election). Several Fellows thought that enough was enough, and that Beveridge's duties as an MP would be incompatible with the Mastership. C. K. Allen was persuaded to speak to the Master, urging him to lay aside his College duties. Allen succeeded: the College minutes of 19 September 1944 record both the Master's decision to stand for Parliament, and an agreement that he would resign as Master when

---

[100] Reactions: Rudd 1990: 39–43; Beveridge's absences: UC:R2/MS1/10, and Beveridge 1953: 312–13 (the Vice-Mastership was by statute only a temporary post, so that in 1943 a special statute had to make Wild 'Pro-Master'); Wheare: UC:P22/MS/1 (others attribute the remark to Farquharson).

[101] Beveridge's marriage: Harris 1997: 424–5; Fellows: UC:P210/MS1/1; the serenade: UC:P22/MS/1 and Gardner 1975: 159.

[102] UC:GB4/A1/12 fos. 22ʳ and 25ʳ.

[103] Farquharson: Redcliffe-Maud 1991: 124; Beveridge's portrait Bayley 1993: 54; Wild: UC:R2/MS1/10.

a successor was appointed. Beveridge himself claimed that eight Fellows had protested to him that his Parliamentary duties would be incompatible with those as a Master, and although he wished the question to be left in abeyance until a General Election, he agreed to resign.[104]

On 18 January 1945, John Wild was pre-elected Master from 5 April, and on 11 March Beveridge delivered a farewell address to the College, in which he observed that 'What I planned to do in my life has again and again been prevented by events beyond my control: yet on each occasion I found something else worth doing.'[105] Another event beyond Beveridge's control was yet to come, for he lost his seat in the General Election of July 1945. Consolation came in the form of ennoblement as Baron Beveridge of Tuggal, and his appointment as leader of the Liberals in the House of Lords.[106]

Beveridge had left the College before VE Day was celebrated. That night, a bonfire was set up in the High Street opposite Queen's College. Effigies of Hitler and Mussolini were burned, and rumour had it that some furniture from University College helped kindle the blaze. The end of the Second World War would have a much greater impact on the College than the end of the First. It was not only that there was a new Master in place, and that a generation of newly elected young Fellows would transform the Senior Common Room. After that good College man, Clement Attlee, became Prime Minister, the relationship between the College, the university, and central government would change radically, and managing that change would be the great challenge for the post-war College.

---

[104] Beveridge's election: Harris 1997: 444–8; resignation as Master: UC:GB4/A1/12 fo. 24ʳ, UC:P22/MS/1, Gardner 1975: 155–6, and Beveridge 1953: 339–41 (Beveridge says that Arthur Goodhart and G. D. H. Cole were not among the eight).
[105] Wild's election: UC:GB4/A1/12 fo. 37ʳ. A copy of Beveridge's address is at UC:P251/X1/3.
[106] Harris 1997: 449–53. Beveridge spent his last years living in a flat owned by the College at 104 Woodstock Road.

19

The College Renewed: 1945–1979

JOHN WILD AND GILES ALINGTON

John Wild (Fig. 19.1) was a rather unexpected college head. The only clerical Master elected in the twentieth century, he was not an eminent academic, nor had he achieved fame elsewhere, but his devoted—and efficient—service to the College during the war made him the obvious candidate for the Mastership at the time. William Beveridge understood his successor well: in November 1940 he called him 'a quite admirable character whom I respect more than any other Fellow of the College', while admitting that 'his mind is not of the first-class order'.[1]

Wild and his young wife Margaret had a harder task than the Macans in 1919, for all the horrors of the First World War, and the effective closing down of the College. In 1945 the Lodgings were sparsely furnished, and Margaret Wild found herself wrestling with the difficulties of obtaining food, household utensils, and furniture, while being expected to participate in the gracious pre-war rounds of formal visiting.[2]

The College's fabric had suffered from wartime neglect. Even in the early 1950s, it was a dowdy place, with everything painted 'Bursar's brown', cream, or dark green. In 1960 the Hall was remembered as having been 'a deep depressing khaki', with many disused picture hooks still in place. The floorboards had rotted away in some rooms, and, with so much post-war reconstruction needed, there were strict controls on building activity until 1951. Overseas students like Bob Hawke (m. 1953), future Prime Minister of Australia, were taken aback at their cold dilapidated rooms, or at having to cross a quadrangle to have a bath. The two-bar electric fires introduced by Beveridge did not warm rooms effectively, and the power cuts of the cold winter of 1947 made conditions worse. It was small consolation that other colleges were in a similar predicament.[3]

---

[1] Uncatalogued file 'Correspondence with and about Fellows Oct. 1940–Oct. 1944'.
[2] Wild 1999. Some claimed that Lady Beveridge had removed more than she should on moving out.
[3] State of the College: *UCR* Vol. III no. 2 (1957), 91, and (on the Hall) *UCR* Vol. III no. 5 (1960), 301; overseas students: Hawke 1994: 23. Bamford 1959: 37; other colleges: Kay 1994 and Tyack

FIGURE 19.1 John Wild, Fellow 1933–45 and Master 1945–51, with several former College servants, taken in May 1949. William Bateson stands at the right end of the back row, with Fred Bickerton to his left.

As in 1919, the College filled up with a mixture of demobbed ex-servicemen and ex-schoolboys.[4] Again, few undergraduates who had matriculated before the war returned, but, unlike in 1919, there were several men who had either started their degree during the war or done a cadet course. All were invited to return, and roughly one-third did so. Of the remainder, some had decided on a non-university career—like Warren Misell (m. 1944), later a famous actor under his stage name of Warren Mitchell—and others opted for an undergraduate degree elsewhere, like the architect Philip Dowson (m. 1943). Processing those who did return took time: the last pre-1945 undergraduates did not arrive until October 1949.

By 1947/8, there were 260 junior members as against a pre-war average of about 150, and the number of matriculands continued to rise (Graph 18.1). Many junior members had to live out, and the lucky ones who lived in found their rooms filled with the coats, briefcases, and shopping bags of friends who lived out and needed somewhere in College to leave their things.[5]

1998: 304–29, Thompson in Davies and Garnett 1994: 76–7 (Wadham) and J. Griffin in Harrison 1994a: 253 (Corpus Christi), Hopkins 2005: 408 (Trinity), and Tyack 2005: 19 (St John's).

[4] Information from the Tutorial Lists for 1945–9 (each year contained roughly half a dozen undergraduates reading chemistry and medicine, who were exempt from active service); mixture of ages: UC:P214/MS1/5 and (from elsewhere) Davidson in Harrison 1994a: 215.

[5] Size of College: *UCR* 1948, pp. 6–7; rooms therein: UC:P34/MS8/1; similar experiences from elsewhere: Gott in Harrison 1994a: 269–70.

THE COLLEGE RENEWED: 1945–1979   477

The College had to respond to this influx. In 1946, the upper floors of 85 High Street were converted for student use, as were those in Bostar Hall in 1949, so that the College now extended continuously from 83 to 90 High Street; 18 Merton Street also became a College annexe, and some existing sets were split into bedsits. To accommodate the enlarged number of Fellows and lecturers, the Payne Lecture Room was incorporated into the Senior Common Room in 1949.[6]

The architect who oversaw this reconstruction was Frederick Jelley, who had worked with Beveridge at the LSE, and a jesting semi-official term—'Jelleyfication'—was coined to describe his multifaceted activities. 'Jelleyfication' went beyond the creation of new rooms. As building materials became more accessible, so more extensive work could be carried out: in 1952–6 washbasins were installed in rooms and bedsits, and bathrooms and lavatories in almost every staircase. No longer would resident members face the difficult midnight decision between using a chamber pot and a nocturnal trip to 'South Side'.[7]

The Chapel also saw changes. In 1952, its Victorian stall fronts were removed, so that its original internal proportions were restored to happy effect, and its organ was rebuilt in 1955. This latter project was funded partly by a bequest from George Stevenson, and mostly from the War Memorial Fund. John Webster drew up the specifications, and the firm of J. W. Walker carried out the work. Although much of the original organ was retained, its pipes were moved to the west wall of the Antechapel, into an oak case designed by Sir Albert Richardson, and the keyboard and pedal-board were installed in the pipes' former home.[8]

By now the College's stonework was as badly weathered as anywhere in Oxford. The university and some colleges launched a Historic Buildings Appeal in 1957, and, although University College was a beneficiary, more money was needed from Old Members. Most existing stone was replaced with Clipsham stone, now Oxford's stone of choice, but Griffith's façade of the Hall and Chapel was in such a sorry state that it needed complete replacement. Steven Dykes Bower prepared two designs, one in a Gothic style, the other slightly more baroque. The Gothic design was preferred, but was never fully executed: Dykes Bower proposed to adorn his façade with four tall pinnacles, which the College did not erect on grounds of cost. Even though this final task was not quite completed, nevertheless the College had

---

[6] Conversion of 85 High Street, Bostar Hall and 18 Merton Street: *UCR* 1948/9, pp. 5–6, UC:GB4/A1/12 fo. 92^r, UC:GB4/A1/13, fos. 101–2, 108^r, and 121^r, and UC:BU3/F3/115 and 118; Payne Lecture Room: UC:GB4/A1/14 fo. 10^r.

[7] Jelley: Beveridge 1953: 172–3; 'Jelleyfication': *UCR* 1952/3, p. 12, *UCR* 1954/5, pp. 64–9, and *UCR* Vol. III no. 1 (1956), 26.

[8] Stall fronts: *UCR* 1951/2, pp. 13–14; organ: Paul 1954/5.

been transformed. The buildings which had been black and peeling took on a new and clean appearance, which has largely survived to the present day.[9]

The returning veterans had more to deal with than poor accommodation. Men who had fought in Normandy, on the Atlantic, and in the Far East were now forbidden to enter pubs, and had to observe the rules about locking in; but most accepted the rules—or found ways of circumventing them. An especial problem was food. Rationing continued until the 1950s, and civilians received smaller rations than servicemen. Ex-servicemen were furious at the apparent disappearance of their food, until the Master laid out one week's civilian rations before an astonished audience. They did, however, enjoy one great benefit: the 1944 Education Act created publicly funded scholarships for ex-servicemen.[10]

College societies were soon revived. The Univ. Players was re-founded in earnest, and its first production, *Measure for Measure*, was staged in May 1946. The Martlets were briefly replaced by a so-called 'Shelley Society', before being restored under their own name in Michaelmas Term 1950, when Edgar Carritt was invited to transmit the society's traditions. The Music Society was still supported by John Webster, who remained College organist and conductor of the Society's choir. There were sadder echoes of 1919: a new War Memorial designed by Walter Godfrey and paid for by Old Members was installed in the Antechapel and dedicated on Michaelmas Day 1949 by Prince Yusupov's old friend Eric Hamilton, now Dean of Windsor.[11]

The post-war years were not completely bleak. The College could take pleasure in its first Prime Minister when Clement Attlee won the General Election of July 1945. High office did not alter Attlee's affection towards his College, and in December 1945 he dined with the Fellows in the Senior Common Room. In May 1948 the heir presumptive, Princess Elizabeth, visiting Oxford to receive a DCL, was treated to a specially composed masque, *The Masque of Hope*, performed by members of OUDS in Radcliffe Quadrangle. Perhaps the happiest post-war events occurred in 1949, when the College celebrated the 700th anniversary of William of Durham's benefaction with a grand luncheon attended by the Lord Chancellor and the Chancellor of the university, a Garden Party, and a Centenary Ball graced by the presence of Mr and Mrs Attlee.[12]

---

[9] Funding: *UCR* Vol. III no. 2 (1957), 87–8 and *UCR* Vol. III no. 3 (1958), 166–7; stone: *UCR* Vol. III no. 2 (1957), 119; Dykes Bower: *UCR* Vol. III no. 2 (1957), 110–14 and *UCR* Vol. III no. 3 (1958), 168–9.

[10] Food: Wild 1999: 92–6, and interview with Norman Dix, 25 March 1997; funding: Soares 1999: 56–7.

[11] Univ. Players: Bayley 2000 and *UCR* Vol. XIII no. 1 (2001), 88–90; the Shelley Society and the Martlets: *UCR* 1948, p. 8, and *UCR* 1949/50, p. 18; War Memorial: *UCR* 1948/9, p. 20–1. So large was the War Memorial Fund that the College proposed to spend the balance on a new dining room, designed by Godfrey, on the site of the Shelley Memorial and move the statue elsewhere. This plan came to nothing (see Darwall-Smith 2000a: 83–7).

[12] Attlee: *UCR* 1946, p. 4; the masque: *UCR* 1948, pp. 4–5, Coghill 1948: and Carpenter 1985: 160; 700th anniversary: *UCR* 1948/9, pp. 3–4.

The Fellowship changed considerably after 1945. Several Fellows had retired, and some younger ones were moving on, such as Harold Wilson, now starting a life as an MP. As a result, only three Tutorial Fellows from 1939 (Bowen, Wells, and Cox) were still there ten years later. The new intake included the College's first English Fellow. Two decades earlier, it had lost C. S. Lewis to Magdalen, but now University College retained another ex-serviceman Old Member who had read English, Peter Bayley, electing him a Junior Research Fellow in 1947 and a Tutorial Fellow in 1949. In the latter year, George Stevenson was replaced as Fellow in Ancient History by George Cawkwell, a former Rhodes Scholar from New Zealand. A pupil from Corpus Christi College praised Cawkwell as being the only tutor he ever encountered for whom he felt a duty to work hard. Cawkwell, he said, 'matched trenchant writing and provocative teaching with a heavy administrative workload; he accepted no nonsense from anybody.'[13]

Among the most distinguished of this younger generation were the philosophers George Paul (F. 1945–62) and Peter Strawson (F. 1948–68). Paul, a scholar of Wittgenstein, also served as a well-regarded Domestic Bursar and Garden Master, and his premature death in a boating accident in 1962 was a loss to his subject and the College. Peter Strawson, however, would become one of the most eminent philosophers of his generation, making his name in 1950 with a devastating critique of Bertrand Russell's theory of descriptions, and building on it with a succession of important books. Strawson also took on a large teaching burden—regularly teaching for fifteen or sixteen hours a week, and sometimes twenty-two hours—leaving affectionate and awed memories among his pupils, and served as Domestic Bursar in 1950–5.[14]

The dominant Fellow in the post-war College, however, never aspired to these academic heights. This was Giles Alington (Fig. 19.2). As with Wild, ill health (in Alington's case kidney trouble) prevented him from joining up, and instead he ran Arthur Goodhart's short courses at Balliol, and was elected a History Fellow at University College in June 1944. Alington came from an intellectual and social elite. His father Cyril was successively Headmaster of Eton and Dean of Durham, and one of his sisters married the Foreign Secretary and Prime Minister Alec Douglas-Home.[15]

---

[13] Bayley: Bayley 2006: 117–20; Cawkwell: Wilsdon in Harrison 1994*a*: 410.
[14] Paul: UC:P34/MS8/1, interview with Norman Dix, 25 March 1997, and *UCR* Vol. IV no. 2 (1962), 73–5; Strawson: *UCR* Vol. XIV no. 2 (2006), 27–33, and interviews with him, 5 February and 8 October 2002.
[15] Health: Hayter 1996: 45 and 50–2; family and career: *UCR* Vol. III no. 1 (1956), 3–8, and Hayter 1996 *passim*; Cyril Alington's time at Eton: Card 1994: 145–59; relations: in 1963–4 the Prime Minister (Douglas-Home) was Alington's brother-in-law, and the Leader of the Opposition (Wilson) an old friend and colleague.

FIGURE 19.2 Giles Alington, Fellow 1944–56.

Alington only achieved a Third in his Finals (his poor health exacerbating matters) but he had other talents. The Headmaster of Charterhouse, Robert Birley, who had taught him at Eton, wrote Beveridge a remarkable reference:

I should say that if you want someone who will raise the standard of History Scholarship in the College he is hardly the man. But if you want someone who will do well with the general run of undergraduates, and will have some pastoral feeling towards his pupils, he would be first rate. I can imagine him—in due course—making a very good dean, for instance. And I believe every college needs some men of that kind.[16]

In 1945 Alington was indeed appointed Dean, a post which he combined with the Senior Tutorship from 1948 until his death. His position might have been difficult. Not only had he not served in the armed forces, but he was not much older than many returning servicemen. Nevertheless he won people over. He adopted a carefully honed image, always sporting a pipe, preferably a long 'churchwarden' specimen, and cultivated a dry sense of humour. People collected Alingtonian *bons mots*: when at Balliol, he began a talk to some Americans, 'Gentlemen, you may be interested to know that I like

[16] Acc. 464 (file on G. Alington).

Americans', adding, when the applause had died down, 'I am paid to do so.' He enjoyed writing self-consciously orotund letters, as when he wrote to an English Finalist after a particularly successful year that the English class lists were 'the sort of notice one rather hopes one may forget to take down'.[17]

Indeed Alington's greatest talents lay in his administrative and pastoral, rather than his academic, abilities. Holding two senior offices simultaneously, Alington wielded considerable power, playing a central role as Senior Tutor in admissions. As a tutor, he was a good encourager: a pupil, suffering from severe pre-Finals nerves, was taken to the Fellows' Garden, given a beer, and talked through some specimen questions. At the same time those undergraduates who were sick or in need of help could always rely on the Dean's active goodwill. For example, when Abdul Hafiz Kardar (m. 1946), who later captained the Pakistan cricket team on its first English tour in 1953, had been operated on for appendicitis, Alington took him to convalesce with his family in Durham.[18]

Some thought that he was a little too indulgent towards Etonians, but, like his mother, who had involved herself in the welfare of unemployed Durham miners in the 1930s, he was no snob. In the late 1940s, he and the College Secretary, Gwynne Ovenstone, attended the wedding of an Old Member in London, at which another Old Member had been best man. On the way back, Alington observed that the bridegroom had been an Etonian and the best man the son of a miner. That, he observed, was what University College was all about. Others might have commented that Alington himself was what the College was all about. He remained a beloved figure in their memories, and some, including Harold and Mary Wilson, even named their sons Giles after him.[19]

Outsiders were less impressed. In April 1945, Isaiah Berlin wrote of 'the moronic Alington and the scarcely more impressive Wilde [sic] at Univ.', and Hugh Trevor-Roper was entertainingly dismissive: observing to Bernard Berenson that the Mastership election at University College in 1951 was—unusually for Oxford—'almost secret in fact', he continued:

This was partly, of course, because no one is much interested in what goes on in University College, so the usual system of espionage has never been developed. The college is a sort of Oxford Tibet, with primitive inhabitants, strange superstitions, and few economic attractions for colonising powers. Consequently the election was enveloped in that secrecy which customarily shrouds (it is said) the election in Lhasa of a Dalai Lama.[20]

[17] Americans: *UCR* Vol. III no. 1 (1956), 5; English results: Bayley 2006: 117.
[18] Conversation with Leslie Stell (m. 1951), 27 September 2003, and Kardar 1987: 62.
[19] Alington's mother: Hayter 1996: 20; wedding: conversation with Gwynne Ovenstone, 9 July 2002; children: conversation with Lady Wilson, 21 March 2002.
[20] Berlin 2004: 542; Trevor-Roper: Davenport-Hines 2006: 66 (although the fact that University College had elected David Cox a Fellow in preference to Trevor-Roper may have affected his view of the place).

On the other hand, in 1951, when St Catherine's Society (later St Catherine's College) was seeking a new head, Alington was seriously considered.[21]

Moreover, although Alington was no academic, colleagues respected his administrative ability, and Douglas Millin, Fred Bickerton's successor as Head Porter, thought him 'too clever for half of them [the Fellows]'. Alington might well have thrived in the modern world of the professional Senior Tutor. Undergraduates also knew that his laid-back persona concealed considerable firmness, leavened by a certain puckish humour. One undergraduate, who had been holding onto a book loaned by Alington for a little too long, received a note from him asking for its return, 'or I will do something which will greatly surprise you'. The book was returned instantly.[22]

Meanwhile, there were some significant new members of College staff, including a new Head Porter and new College Secretary. Indeed, because Douglas Millin (Fig. 20.3) and Gwynne Ovenstone (Fig. 19.3) were much better known—always as Douglas and Gwynne—to many generations of junior members than most Fellows, they assumed almost paternal and maternal capacities. Douglas Millin came to the College as a Porter in 1947 having been a sergeant-major in the Royal Artillery, and three years later succeeded Fred Bickerton as Head Porter, a post he held until 1983.[23] Those who knew both men generally thought Douglas the more impressive—and more intelligent—figure.

Douglas retained his sergeant-major's demeanour—and vocabulary—which was to his advantage in dealing with those students who had been of officer class during their national service. He created a persona as famous as that of Giles Alington, and his own gruff one-liners were collected no less eagerly. His first words to a group of Rhodes Scholars arriving at the College in the early 1970s was 'Revolting Colonials, that's what you'd be.' He also claimed to be unimpressed by having 'f—ing schoolboys' coming up to College rather than men who had been through war or national service. Douglas likewise appeared to be totally unimpressed by Old Members who achieved greatness. General Bernard Rogers (m. 1947), on ringing Douglas at the time when he was Army Chief of Staff at NATO, received the reply 'Oh, this is God's bloody gift to the defence of the Western Hemisphere, is it?'[24]

People quickly discovered the shrewdness behind the gruff façade. For all that Douglas loved to tease Rhodes Scholars, yet in the 1950s, when they

---

[21] Davies and Davies 1997: 9.
[22] Millin: Park 1989: 52; returning a book: conversation with Colin Bayne-Jardine (m. 1953), 4 December 2004.
[23] Appointment and retirement: *UCR* 1949/50, pp. 4–5, *UCR* Vol. VIII no. 4 (1983), 247–8, and *UCR* Vol. VIII no. 5 (1984), 320–2. Park 1989 is an interview with Millin.
[24] Dealing with students: Park 1989: 49–50; Rhodes Scholars: Zoeller 2006: 1; attitudes to national service: York 1991: 70; General Rogers: Zoeller 2006: 7.

FIGURE 19.3 Gwynne Ovenstone, College Secretary 1947–87.

could not easily go home during vacations, he and his wife would take some of them in as lodgers. His relationship with one Scholar, Bill Clinton (m. 1968), is typical. When he first met Clinton and his group of Rhodes Scholars, Douglas, seeing among them Robert Reich (m. 1968), who was less than five foot tall, observed that 'he'd been told he was getting four Yanks, but they'd sent him only three and a half.' Years later, when Clinton revisited Oxford, having been elected Governor of Arkansas, Douglas called out 'Clinton, I hear you've just been elected king of some place with three men and a dog.' Yet it was Douglas whom Clinton came to like almost more than anyone else he knew in the College. When in 1992 Clinton was elected President of the United States—the first Oxford student to achieve this honour—and contemporaries tried to remember what he was like at Oxford with them, some realized that he was the American often seen in the Lodge drinking coffee with Douglas. Many were the problems which Douglas discreetly sorted out, and a later Master, John Maud, described him as 'one of the two people who did most to teach me my job as Master'.[25]

---

[25] Clinton and Douglas: Clinton 2004: 137–8 and conversation with Alastair Lack, 8 March 2002 (Robert Reich served as Secretary of Labor under Clinton in 1993–7); Redcliffe-Maud 1981: 113.

Maud's other 'teacher' was Gwynne Ovenstone, appointed Assistant College Secretary in 1947, and College Secretary in 1950. Maud likened her to the perfect Permanent Secretary, 'discreet, wise, entertaining, incorruptible'. There had been previous College Secretaries, but none stayed so long (Gwynne retired in 1987), and none left quite such an impact. Nothing escaped the notice of the College Office in Staircase XII, and the wise Master or College officer relied on her encyclopaedic knowledge of the College and every single member.[26] Just like Douglas, Gwynne attracted tales of her own. It was said that she admitted three students in error, but one got a First, another a Second, and the third a Hockey Blue. She would assign rooms to freshers with surnames that matched, or to unrelated people of the same name. Toy magnetic ladybirds were kept for a while on her filing cabinets, each one representing a Fellow. The nearer the floor the ladybird was, the lower their reputation in the College Office (at least one ladybird descended to the basement). When Gwynne received an MBE in the New Year Honours List of 2000, many generations of College members felt that she had received no more than her due.[27]

Many appointments of Fellows and members of staff made during Wild's Mastership affected College life for several decades, but Wild would not see this. The Mastership came to be something of a burden to him: he fell seriously ill in 1948 and 1950, and suffered several close family bereavements. He did not always find it easy to deal with the new Fellows: at Governing Body meetings, Giles Alington did not always quite conceal his impatience with the Master's careful, slightly diffident, chairmanship. At a time when other colleges were electing heads who had achieved eminence in academic or public life, the less flamboyant qualities of loyalty and hard work which had made Wild an obvious candidate in 1945 were harder to appreciate.

Something unexpected resolved the situation. By December 1950 it was known that Cyril Alington, Giles's father, planned to retire as Dean of Durham. John Wild was soon mentioned as a possible successor, even by Cyril Alington himself, who condescendingly observed (perhaps based on his son's information?), 'he's not distinguished as Head of a College, but might, it is thought, make a good Dean. He's a very nice chap, and has a nice wife.' On 14 March 1951, Clement Attlee was offered a choice of two names for the post, John Wild and Leonard Hodgson, the Regius Professor of Divinity of Oxford. Attlee made up his mind that same day, scribbling 'I incline to Wild. CRA'. The appointment was made public next month, and John Wild resigned the Mastership in October.[28]

---

[26] Redcliffe-Maud 1981: 113, *UCR* Vol. IX no. 3 (1987), 13–17 and Snow 1991: 113–14.
[27] Gwynne was not the only member of staff to be thus honoured. Bob Morris, who joined the College in 1950 and became Head Scout, was awarded an MBE in the Queen's Birthday Honours List of 1999 (*UCR* Vol. XII no. 3 (1999), 86).
[28] Attlee's correspondence file about Wild's appointment to Durham: TNA PREM/5/285.

The move benefited all parties—Wild was promoted to a senior post in the church, and the College could seek a new Master—and recalled the dealings of Lord North and Nathan Wetherell in the 1770s (how Wetherell would have envied Wild's grander Deanery). In his twenty-two years at Durham, however, Wild showed himself a worthier Dean than the largely non-resident Wetherell. Whereas the west front of Hereford cathedral had fallen down during Wetherell's Deanship, Wild, the former Domestic Bursar, examined the fabric of his cathedral himself, and even introduced competitive tendering. His kindly nature also made him popular among his staff and congregation. Clement Attlee, who regularly visited the Wilds in their new home, would have seen for himself the wisdom of choosing a good 'Univ.' man.[29]

THE GREAT BENEFACTOR: ARTHUR GOODHART

Arthur Goodhart (Fig. 19.4), Professor of Jurisprudence and Fellow of University College since 1931, was elected Master in October 1951, the only other major candidate being Kenneth Wheare. Goodhart was hardly an unknown quantity. As seen in the previous chapter, his scholarship was respected, his war work had won him a KBE, and he had been considered for the Mastership in 1937. Goodhart, however, was also the first American and the first Jew to be elected Head of an Oxford or Cambridge college—and, furthermore, he came from a very wealthy family.[30]

Goodhart proved a happy choice. Undergraduates warmed to the kindly eyes behind the pince-nez, and Fellows respected his sound good sense. When he wrote to a young lawyer formally offering him a lectureship in the College, he added a postscript warmly welcoming him 'so that we can talk law'. The lecturer could hardly believe that the great editor of the *Law Quarterly Review* could be so friendly when offering such a junior academic appointment.[31] Goodhart was supported by his English wife Cecily. The Goodharts made a superb team in College life, in spite of Cecily's shyness (she could sometimes daunt undergraduates by taking them by the arm at receptions and introducing them to high-powered guests). Even those who felt the Master slightly remote from their own lives could still respect him and have great affection for him and of his wife. The Goodharts had a house in Boars Hill, and many parties were held there for Fellows, staff, and students alike. Cecily Goodhart helped in other ways, such as briefing her husband over breakfast about the College meeting to be held later that day.[32]

---

[29] Attlee's visits: conversation with Margaret Wild, 21 March 2003.
[30] Election: UC:GB4/A1/14, fo. 82ʳ; Wheare: interview with Sir Peter Strawson, 8 October 2002; Goodhart's career: *UCR* Vol. VII no. 5 (1979), 221–9.
[31] Letter: UC:P200/MS1/1, and interview with Sir Guenter Treitel (Fellow of Magdalen from 1954 and Vinerian Professor of English Law from 1979), 13 September 2002.
[32] Conversations with Derek Wood, 3 October 2003, and Norman Dix, 25 March 1997. A tribute to Cecily Goodhart is given in Redcliffe-Maud 1991: 259–62.

FIGURE 19.4 Arthur Goodhart, Fellow 1931–51 and Master 1951–63, and Cecily Goodhart, to the left, and John Maud, Fellow 1929–39 and Master 1963–76, with Jean Maud, to the right.

Some felt that Goodhart could be too cautious for his own good. Although he responded quickly to initiatives brought to him, he was reluctant to put something forward himself. Herbert Hart, Goodhart's successor as Professor, thought his editorial policy in the *Law Quarterly Review* too deferential to judicial opinion, and his scholarship insufficiently philosophical—although Hart, a former philosopher, inevitably approached jurisprudence from a totally different direction from a lawyer like Goodhart. Hart, though, warmed to Goodhart personally, and Goodhart respected Hart's ability.[33]

It is difficult, however, to assess Goodhart's qualities whilst ignoring his considerable wealth—and generosity. He refused to accept his stipend as Master, putting it into a separate College fund,[34] and he also persuaded his family to support his College, especially his sister Helen and her husband Frank Altschul, Vice-President of the United States Council on Foreign Relations and Vice-Chairman of the United States National Planning Association.

[33] Lacey 2004: 157–8, 171, and 263.
[34] UC:GB4/A1/14 fo. 110ʳ.

Goodhart showed his generosity most especially in buildings. At a time when the College's resources were taken up with essential rebuilding work, Goodhart and his family supported new projects which would otherwise have been completely impossible. His first gift was a new dining room, following the final shelving of the proposal to replace the Shelley Memorial with one. In 1953 it was agreed to create it in the site of the old library, taking over four of the undergraduate sets created in the 1860s. Jelley oversaw the early planning, which included the creation of a new staircase from the kitchen, but the room's rich wooden decoration was designed by Sir Albert Richardson, who had worked on the Chapel organ.[35]

The new room should have been named in Goodhart's honour, but events decreed otherwise. In 1956, only in his early forties, Giles Alington died of cancer. Goodhart stood by his deathbed in tears, saying 'I hoped you would be Master'; Clement Attlee attended his funeral; and letters to Alington's mother from 'his' undergraduates convey the feelings of a generation bereaved:

He was the only person I've ever known who would always understand, no matter what one said or did.
No one could be kinder and no one could be better company.
I am nearly desolate—he was always so friendly and kind, so honest in his dealings and so very fair.[36]

Robert Birley recalled his reference of a dozen years ago:

Well, he did all I expected and *far more*. All kinds of people, Head Masters—and some of them Head Masters of small, quite obscure schools—Chief Education Officers and others, have told me that they thought him unique in the way that he looked after his undergraduates, knew them and helped them.[37]

Alington's premature death won him an almost legendary reputation among those who knew and loved him, but a half a century later one can re-examine that reputation more dispassionately. Some colleagues, like David Cox, feared that he held too many major College offices at once, and Wild's successor as Chaplain, Tom Parker, later remarked to a younger Fellow that he thought Alington stupid. Yet he still poses important questions for his successors. Someone with a Third would never be considered for a Fellowship today, but Robert Birley's observation that every College needs someone like Alington cannot be lightly dismissed. Since the time of Hubert Burge, University College has generally benefited from the presence of at

---

[35] Discussed in UC:GB4/A1/14 fos. 122[r] and 12[r] and UC:GB4/A1/15 fos. 7[r], 10[r], and in *UCR* 1952/3, pp. 11–12, *UCR* 1954/5, pp. 65–6, and *UCR* Vol. III no. 1 (1956), 34–40.
[36] Goodhart: Hayter 1996: 113–14; Attlee: *UCR* Vol. III no. 1 (1956), 8; reactions: Alington 1957: 64–6.
[37] Alington 1957: 67.

FIGURE 19.5 The Alington Room shortly after completion looking towards the north end.

least one Fellow who provides a crucial link with junior members. It was entirely appropriate that, shortly after his death, the new dining room was named the Alington Room in his memory (Fig. 19.5).[38]

The Alington Room was a prelude to still greater gifts. The College was taking an interest in Parsons' Almshouse, a building next to Kybald House; in 1957 the Altschuls offered to purchase it. This proved a complex business, not least because the occupants of the Almshouse needed accommodation elsewhere. In the end, the Altschuls also paid (at a cost of over £10,000) for a new almshouse in St Clements. The College took possession of the house in August 1959, and the first students took up rooms there in October.[39]

Building the new almshouse had proved a protracted business, but this produced an unexpected result. When planning permission for it was turned down (it was eventually granted), the Estates Bursar, Maurice Shock, tried to cheer the Master by suggesting a development elsewhere in the College. The area between the Master's Lodgings and the Examination Schools was a mess,

[38] Cox: interview with Sir Peter Strawson, 8 October 2002; naming the room: UC:GB4/A1/15 fo. 51ʳ.
[39] UC:GB4/A1/15 fos. 76ʳ and 85ʳ, and *UCR* Vol. III no. 4 (1959), 235–6. Cost of new almshouse: UC:GB4/A1/15 fos. 94ʳ and 97ʳ.

containing a cottage, some garages, and a rickety furniture store. Master and Bursar clambered to the top of the furniture store, and the latter suggested that something could be done with it. Goodhart's imagination was fired, and when in April 1958 the almshouse plans were deadlocked, discussions arose as to how to develop the Logic Lane site into a new quadrangle with accommodation, parking facilities, and a new squash court (because the existing one would have to go). A portion of Durham Buildings would also need to be demolished to create space.[40]

Stirrat Johnson-Marshall, of the firm of Robert Matthew and Johnson-Marshall, won the commission for the new building, which would form two sides of a quadrangle. On the east side was an accommodation block of five floors, with a penthouse on top, and a squash court in the basement, and on the south was a two-storey building with a seminar room on the first floor, topped by a somewhat whimsical weather-vane. The architects first proposed that the building should be fronted with Westmorland stone, but fortunately Laurence Wager, the Geology Professor, queried the durability of this medium, and the building was instead fronted in brick.[41]

Goodhart had insisted from the first that he would find the money for the new building, and even in 1960, before work had started, the College insisted that it bear his name. The Goodhart Building and Seminar Room (Fig. 19.6) eventually cost just over £220,000, of which over £190,000 was raised or given by Goodhart himself. They were opened on 18 May 1962 by the American Ambassador, David Bruce. The finished buildings are perhaps not outstanding, but the block-like nature of the accommodation building is softened with oriel windows, a ground-floor cloister, and a zigzag roof. Nikolaus Pevsner called the Goodhart Building 'restless with its ever-changing fenestration', and thought the seminar room with its spire 'much more successful'.[42]

The Altschuls did not lag behind. Apart from helping finance the Goodhart Building, they completed the redevelopment of the almshouses, when in 1963 a barn to the north of them was converted into four studio rooms by the firm of Booth, Ledeboer, and Pinckheard. The new complex was opened on 2 July 1964 by Viscount Soulbury, Honorary Fellow of the College, and was named Helen's Court in honour of Helen Altschul.[43]

---

[40] Conversations with Sir Maurice Shock, 16 March 2001 and 4 October 2002, and UC:GB4/A1/15 fo. 85ʳ and Acc. 697. Also *UCR* Vol. III no. 5 (1960), 304–8.

[41] UC:GB4/A1/15 fo. 106ʳ. Johnson-Marshall also designed the Junior and Senior Combination Rooms at Selwyn College, Cambridge (Brock and Cooper 1994: 250–2).

[42] Funding and naming: UC:GB4/A1/15 fo. 124ʳ, and Acc. 275 (file inscribed 'A. L. Goodhart Fund and Alington Room 1952–1964'); opening: *UCR* Vol. IV no. 2 (1962), 79–81; assessments: Sherwood and Pevsner: 1974: 213 and Kay 1994: 510. It was intended that the whole complex be called 'Goodhart Quad', but this name never stuck, and its two parts are known as the Goodhart Building (or just 'Goodhart') and the Goodhart Seminar Room.

[43] Other gifts: UC:GB4/A1/16 fos. 1ʳ, 21ʳ, and 41ʳ; the conversion: *UCR* Vol. IV no. 3 (1963), 168–9; the opening: *UCR* Vol. IV no. 5 (1965), 303–4.

FIGURE 19.6 Photograph of the Goodhart Building, as seen from the colonnade under the Goodhart Seminar Room.

The Fellows made clear their own opinion of Goodhart when in 1961, just before he was due to retire, they extended his term of office by two more years. On his retirement, the Goodharts received one special tribute. On 17 May 1963, a farewell dinner was given in their honour in the Hall, and Cecily Goodhart became the first woman since Hester Thrale to dine there. To the end Goodhart retained his good nature. In retirement he and Cecily occupied the penthouse at the top of 'his' building, from where they never intervened in College affairs, remaining familiar figures, living amidst chaotic domesticity, until Goodhart's death in 1978.[44]

Goodhart left a large mark on the College. Michael Sadler and William Beveridge may have had more glittering careers, and there have been other successful husband and wife teams, but Goodhart stands apart, largely on account of his generosity. On his retirement, it was estimated that he had

[44] Extension of office: UC:GB4/A1/16 fo. 3ʳ; dining in Hall: *UCR* Vol. IV no. 3 (1963), 179.

given the College almost one million dollars, a sum not far off five or six million pounds in current terms, and he and the Altschuls would give more before they died.[45] The difficulties of comparing donations made in different times mean that it is not really possible or meaningful to say who was the greatest single benefactor to University College, but the three strongest contenders for the title are Sir Simon Bennet, John Radcliffe, and Arthur Goodhart.

THE POST-WAR COLLEGE

The war cast a long shadow over the College. Almost all the Fellows elected in 1944/5 and for some years afterwards had had their careers interrupted by it, so that there was much catching up to do when they returned to civilian life. Nevertheless certain pre-war attitudes persisted. It was intimated to one young married Fellow with a family that the College had hoped to elect a bachelor. Just like C. K. Allen two decades earlier, therefore, the Fellow agreed to spend several terms in College, while his wife and young family lived elsewhere in Oxford. As late as the 1970s, it was expected that a married Fellow acting as Junior Dean should be in College during Saturday evenings in term time.[46]

The small size of the Fellowship created a certain friendly informality, especially in comparison with larger colleges. Guenter Treitel, who knew University College as a lecturer and Magdalen as a Fellow in the 1950s, found University more like a large family, to the point that over lunch people commonly talked about domestic concerns, whereas home life was hardly ever discussed at Magdalen.[47]

To a degree the tone was set by the classicist Freddie Wells and the historian David Cox, who after Giles Alington's death served respectively as Dean and Senior Tutor. Wells was a quieter figure than Alington, much liked by Fellows, junior members, and servants alike for his sweetness of temper, but, like Cox, respected for his firmness. Cox and Wells were typical of their generation in that neither produced much in print: Cox devoted himself to exploring the College's archives, occasionally revealing the fruits of his work the *University College Record*, while Wells was held up to a younger generation as an example of someone whose scholarship could not be measured in terms of publications. His only memorials are his fair versions of Latin proses, much admired by his successors.[48] Perhaps the experiences of the Second World War had left such men with the feeling that there were things more important than going into print; but there was also a belief that teaching came first. Arguably Cox, Wells, and others of their generation did

---

[45] *UCR* Vol. IV no. 3 (1963), 166.
[46] Conversations with Pat Cawkwell, 7 February 1999, and Christopher Pelling (Junior Dean 1974–6), 9 September 2003.
[47] Interview with Sir Guenter Treitel, 13 September 2002.
[48] Interview with Christopher Pelling, 2 December 2003.

'produce' something, namely the pupils whose lives they had touched to their benefit.

Nevertheless the Fellowship did become more self-consciously 'academic'. The first Fellow of the College to obtain a D.Phil. was John Barns, the Lady Wallis Budge Fellow in Egyptology, in November 1945, and by 1967 more than half the Fellowship had doctorates of some kind.[49] The Fellows also tried to streamline College business by creating in 1947 a General Purposes Committee, which discussed matters submitted to the College in advance of a College meeting.[50] The Governing Body was also refreshed by such arrivals as the new chaplain, Tom Parker, and the new Professor of Jurisprudence, Herbert Hart, both elected in 1952.

Although Tom Parker was elected as Chaplain, he also taught history, and became remembered as much for his short stature, large girth, and wide-brimmed hats as for his saintliness and extraordinary learning. Even Douglas Millin said of Parker he had 'never met a more saintly bloke'.[51] He professed certain radical opinions, including a fervent dislike of bishops, but religion—and High Church Anglicanism—remained central. Parker had refused to become chaplain of Lincoln College because he would be expected to offer communion to non-Anglicans.[52]

Herbert Hart's election as Professor was somewhat unexpected, because although he had trained as a barrister he had been a philosophy Fellow at New College. Hart brought a philosophical approach to law which transformed the study of the subject. Like Goodhart before him, he became a well-established figure in the Common Room. In 1978, after he had retired as Principal of Brasenose College, Lord Goodman, then Master, paid for Hart to have rooms there, which he retained until his death, remaining a benign presence in College, like Sir Peter Strawson two decades later.[53]

Hart's involvement in College life was, like Goodhart's, notable because, as a professorial Fellow he had no tutorial or College duties. Professorial Fellows have always been faced with the question of how much to participate in College life: Homer Dubs, the College's first Professor in Chinese, certainly enjoyed SCR life, importing there a certain waggish eccentricity, but for Laurence 'Bill' Wager, Professor of Geology in 1950–65, lunching and dining in College was, according to his daughter, 'necessary... but not much welcomed by him'.[54] Significantly, David Hawkins's affectionate 'group

---

[49] Information from lists of Fellows in *UCR*. Barns was originally a Junior Research Fellow, with no place or vote at College meetings, but became a full Fellow in 1948.
[50] UC:GB4/A1/13 fo. 34^r.
[51] Park 1989: 51.
[52] Green 1979: 540.
[53] See now Lacey 2004, especially 149–50 and 323–4.
[54] Hargreaves 1991: 100.

THE COLLEGE RENEWED: 1945–1979

caricature' from 1962 of the Fellows and their benign *paterfamilias*, Arthur Goodhart (Fig. 19.7), includes Herbert Hart, but not Laurence Wager.

Consideration of the post-war undergraduates must start with their age. Even after the war ended, potential undergraduates until 1957 had to undergo two years' national service. The late 1940s and 1950s therefore saw the oldest freshmen in the College's history. In 1947 their average age was 25; in 1950 it was 21; in 1955 and 1957, it was just over 20. Finally in 1960, after national service had ended, it fell to 19. Young men change greatly in two years, and the presence of so many older freshmen undoubtedly affected the College's atmosphere in the 1950s. Contemporaries could detect a difference between those who had been away and those, like chemists and medical students, who had not. It was felt that the Fellows of University College were particularly understanding towards ex-national servicemen.[55]

Admissions procedures changed. In the late 1940s, it was still customary that, while admissions of Scholars and Exhibitioners were handled by subject tutors only, the Master attended all the interviews for commoners, assisted by the Senior Tutor (Giles Alington for several years) and subject tutors. The Master therefore had considerable influence over admissions, and although he never had an official right to nominate candidates, as, say, at Magdalen, there was an unofficial convention even in the late 1960s that he could fill any places left over at the end of the admissions process. There was another screening process: waiting candidates sat with Gwynne Ovenstone, and her opinion was regularly sought. As the administrative burden of admissions grew, so David Cox, the Senior Tutor, needed help; in 1959 the College created an Admissions Committee, and in 1962 Peter Bayley became the College's first Tutor for Admissions.[56]

Perhaps the greatest change among junior members—as elsewhere in Oxford—was the growth of postgraduate research. Before the war, there were negligible numbers of postgraduate students, but already in 1949, one-sixth of all junior members studied for further degrees, and the *University College Record* of 1948/9 noted 'an enormous increase in the number of men reading for Research Degrees'. During the 1950s postgraduates came to make up between one-fifth and one-sixth of junior members, and in the 1960s and early 1970s this rose to almost one-quarter.[57]

From the first, at least one-third, sometimes more, of the College's postgraduates came from abroad (almost half the College's postgraduates in 1955 had done their first degree abroad). The USA and Canada sent the highest

---

[55] Information on ages from the College's Admission Registers; effects of national service: conversation with John Duncan (m. 1954), and Ingrams 2005: 11–12.

[56] Conversation with Gwynne Ovenstone, 20 May 2002; Admissions Committee: UC:GB4/A1/15 fo. 94ʳ; Tutor for Admissions: UC:GB4/A1/16 fo. 30ʳ.

[57] *UCR* 1948, p. 7. Data on postgraduates is taken from a sample of Tutorial Lists from 1949–50, 1955–6, 1961–2, 1967–8, and 1973–4.

FIGURE 19.7 Caricature by David Hawkins (m. 1958) of the Master and Fellows of University College, commissioned for the 1962 *University College Record*. They are: (back row) Tony Firth and Tony Guest; (middle row) Edmund Bowen, Arthur Goodhart, Carleton Allen, and David Cox; and (front row) Herbert Hart, Peter Strawson, Peter Bayley, Freddie Wells, Tom Parker, and George Cawkwell.

proportion of students, followed by Australasia, but there were students from other African states beyond South Africa and Rhodesia, and also the Caribbean, mostly from current or former British colonies. The then Warden of Rhodes House, Edgar 'Bill' Williams, took an interest in the College, and regularly encouraged Rhodes Scholars to apply there. Of the British students, by the 1960s and early 1970s between one-third and one-half of all postgraduates had done their first degree at University College.[58]

In 1945 postgraduates remained members of the Junior Common Room, but this was unsatisfactory, not least because postgraduates were more likely to live out and remain in Oxford during vacations. In 1960, therefore, the Governing Body set aside Staircase VI Room 2 as a separate postgraduate common room. A donation from James Weir, of whom more below, paid for the furnishing of what became known as the Weir Common Room, and the graduate common room became known, almost interchangeably, as either the MCR or WCR. The College quickly accepted the special needs of postgraduates and created the post of Tutor for Graduate Admissions in 1965.[59]

Undergraduates and postgraduates alike needed recreation, and the College continued to attract sportsmen after the war. The cricketer Hafiz Kardar chose University College because it had a reputation for being a College of sportsmen from the Commonwealth and the Dominions. Another international cricketer, this time for South Africa, was Clive van Ryneveld (m. 1947), while Bob Hawke proved a good batsman at College level. A different kind of sporting success came in 1953 when D. A. Yanofsky (m. 1951) won the British Chess Championships—and achieved a First in his BCL. Sport continued to be a good means of making friends, as discovered by the cosmologist Stephen Hawking (m. 1959) when he took up coxing.[60]

There were non-sporting societies: by 1951 the Eldon Society for the lawyers could attract Lord Goddard, the Lord Chief Justice, as an after-dinner speaker; and from 1957, there was a new Boyle Society, this time intended only for physicists. There was also the Univ. Players. For female parts, the Players regularly looked to the Oxford Playhouse; thus the future Dame Maggie Smith, fresh from school and attending a training scheme at the Playhouse, participated in the Players' production of Andreyev's *He Who Gets Slapped* in 1953. One of the Players' greatest early triumphs was *The Miracles*, an adaptation of medieval religious plays

---

[58] Rhodes Scholars: information from Hartmut Pogge von Strandmann, July 2007. Several of the 8% of undergraduates who came from outside the United Kingdom were Rhodes Scholars who, despite already having degrees, were advised to experience Oxford's tutorial system by taking a second undergraduate course. This became less common after taught postgraduate courses were introduced in the 1960s and 1970s.

[59] Creation of MCR: UC:GB4/A1/15 fos. 109^r, 118^r, and 127^r; Weir's gift: *UCR* Vol. III no. 5 (1960), 312; admissions: UC:GB4/A1/17 fo. 8^r.

[60] Kardar 1987: 76; Hawke: *UCR* 1952/3, p. 39; Yanofsky: *UCR* 1952/3, p. 5; Hawking: White and Gribbin 1992: 49–52.

prepared by Gordon Honeycombe (m. 1957; later an ITN newsreader), while recovering from tuberculosis, and William Tydeman, and directed and produced in 1960 by John Duncan (m. 1958) and Honeycombe. There was a cast of over eighty, and the *University College Record* (edited by the Players' founder) acclaimed the production as 'a great triumph, histrionic, artistic, administrative and financial'. Such was the College's reputation that the future star of *Cabaret* and *Logan's Run*, Michael York (m. 1961), happily admitted that he applied there because it was known as an actors' College.[61]

Some aspects of pre-war undergraduate life survived. Undergraduates regularly had their trunks brought up by train, and when living outside College still lived in digs with landladies, many of whom were associated with particular colleges. Thus a Miss Spiller at 32 Iffley Road usually put up men only from University College, and had photographs of her 'young men' hanging on her walls. Even in the early 1950s it was still customary for a servant to knock on the bottom of the staircases with a heavy mallet to wake undergraduates up, a practice known as 'knocking up'. Bob Morris, first employed by the College in 1950, claimed that the custom ended after people complained about his whistling while doing his hammering, but the authorities were also mindful of the damage done to the stairs by the mallet. The tradition that mornings were given over to lectures and tutorials and afternoons for sports practice still continued. There might be tutorials in the evening, followed by a drink in the beer cellar before Hall. Coffee and port were served in the Junior Common Room afterwards. A South African Rhodes Scholar, Brian Bamford (m. 1951), was struck by people's conservatism in dress. In the summer months, he observed, 'the duffle-coats disappear, only to reveal baggy trousers and faded sports coats'. He observed his male contemporaries only allowing themselves any licence for flamboyance in their waistcoats. The practice of sconcing remained (p. 457)—Bob Hawke downed his sconce in eleven seconds, a world record—but one of the reasons for which one could be sconced became obsolete when, in October 1958, the College grace no longer had to be recited from memory.[62]

Rationing at last ceased in the mid-1950s, and colour returned to College food, sometimes alarmingly so. A regular dish was the 'University Charlotte', a moulded jelly of the College coat of arms. The cross was made from bananas, and blue put behind the jelly to reflect the colour. It was a time-consuming dish,

---

[61] Boyle Society: *UCR* Vol. III no. 3 (1958), 170; Maggie Smith: UC:P86/C1/1; *The Miracles*: UC:P105/MS1/2, *UCR* Vol. III no. 5 (1960), 318, and Carpenter 1985: 160 (who quoted one observer that it 'far outshone any other university production I have seen anywhere at any time'); the actors' College: York 1991: 63. Bayley 2000 lists the Players' productions from 1940 to 1970.

[62] Trains: conversation with Gerald Nix and Bob Morris, 3 September 2001; Miss Spiller: conversation with Colin Bayne-Jardine (m. 1953), 4 December 2004; knocking up: Morris 1990: 54; Bamford 1959: 38 and 42–7 (daily round) and 109–10 (clothes); Hawke 1994: 28; grace: UC:GB4/A1/15 fo. 86ʳ.

requiring a special mould. At a less elevated level, in May 1958 a cafeteria system was introduced for lunches on an experimental basis.[63]

One perspective on College life of the early 1950s exists in the correspondence of the Nobel Prizewinning writer V. S. Naipaul (m. 1950). Coming from Trinidad, Naipaul had an especially dislocating experience, although he was inevitably struck by Giles Alington. He reported that Alington's homily to the freshmen included the observation that everything is not to be found in books, but that it is folly to think that nothing can be found in books, and two years later, when Naipaul held a drinks party, he was amused to report that Alington dropped by to see how it was going, and stayed for over an hour. The letters show his tutor, Peter Bayley, encouraging him in his writing, and indeed Naipaul was deeply involved in student journalism, writing for *Isis* for a time. There is a feeling, however, from the letters that Naipaul did not find it easy to adjust to English ways, and he observed the College as something of an outsider.[64]

The College's relationship with women altered in the 1950s, as rules about the admission of women visitors were also relaxed. In December 1956, after the end of term, a dinner was held in the Senior Common Room to which Fellows could invite women guests; this proved a success, and under the name of the St Lucy Dinner became an annual event for several years. Furthermore, at least from 1942 services of blessing for civil marriages could be performed in the College Chapel, and from 1946 it was possible to celebrate actual marriages there, after the appropriate licence had been obtained. The Chapel has since become a popular wedding venue for Fellows, junior members, and staff alike.[65]

One of the most significant changes in undergraduate life was financial rather than social. Since 1944 the numbers of students eligible for government funding had grown greatly, especially for ex-servicemen, as the government sought to encourage people to go to university and even to stay on for postgraduate work. In 1962 an Act of Parliament decreed that local education authorities should offer a grant to any student who secured a university place. Many people for whom an Oxford education would have been an impossibility could now attain it. It may well have helped that in 1960 Latin was no longer made compulsory for candidates wishing to study science at Oxford, and in 1962 the university's admissions policy was overhauled. University College in particular tried hard to attract people who would not otherwise

---

[63] University Charlotte: conversation with Ken Tucker, 14 March 2006; Cafeteria: Acc. 437 (file marked 'Meals').
[64] Naipaul: Naipaul 1999: 27 and 195 (Alington), and 149 (writing). Naipaul's younger brother, Shiva, who also became a writer, came up to University College in 1964.
[65] Women visitors: UC:GB4/A1/15 fo. 81r; St Lucy Dinner: *UCR* Vol. III no. 5 (1960), 299–300 (St Lucy's day is 13 December); weddings: UC:C1/R1/1–2 and UC:GB4/A1/13 fo. 4r.

have thought of applying: in 1964, for example, the College joined Merton in a special initiative to encourage applicants from the West Riding of Yorkshire.[66]

In academic terms, undergraduates from University College certainly won Firsts or good Seconds. In 1956 the College achieved ten Firsts in Finals, a total exceeded only by Balliol, and in 1959 and 1960 10 per cent of its Finalists were awarded Firsts, a percentage which placed it between seventh and ninth among colleges. However, the College's Finalists in 1960 included not only 9 Firsts and 49 Seconds, but also 30 Thirds and 7 Fourths. Attempts were made to improve academic facilities, as when a separate Law Library was created in 1949/50 in Durham Buildings. The system for assessing students was regularly reviewed; Alington tightened up the regulations of end-of-term collections in 1947, and in 1964 the College decided that all undergraduates should sit at least one collection paper at the start of each term.[67]

As for the College's financial health, thanks to the continuing presence of undergraduates during the war, the College was in a better state in 1945 than it had been in 1918/19. Indeed, the College's finances were healthy enough to earn it an unwelcome privilege. Since the 1880s, wealthier colleges had made payments into a central university fund, each according to their means; in 1948, University joined this group of paying colleges (although its contribution of £240 was the smallest of the eleven—Magdalen had to pay £3,534).[68]

The arrival of peace offered opportunities for reassessment of the College's finances, especially once George Stevenson retired as Estates Bursar in 1949. His successor, Norman Marsh, found that the College's overdraft that year had fallen from £21,000 to £9,000, in spite of heavy expenditure on College fabric. However, the College's estate management had slipped somewhat: there were tales that tenants in remote properties were no longer aware that the College, and not their estate manager, was their landlord. In 1954 Marsh noted that internal expenditure had more than doubled between 1944 and 1953, but, although external income had risen well, internal income had not risen proportionately. The College also benefited from investing more in flats and shops, which were cheaper to manage, than in farms, such as Marks Hall, which was sold in 1953 after 450 years of ownership by the College. Colleges were exploring other ways of investing money: in the 1950s they were permitted to invest in equities, and in 1964 the 1925 Universities and Colleges Estates Act was amended to give them more freedom to manage their finances.[69]

---

[66] Student grants: Greenstein 1994: 46–50; the national context: Anderson 2006: 131–45; Latin: Harris 1994: 225; admissions policy: Thomas 1994: 194; West Riding scheme: UC:GB4/A1/16 fo. 78r.

[67] Exam results taken from relevant editions of *UCR*; Law Library: *UCR* 1949/50, p. 6; collections: UC:GB4/A1/13 fo. 26r, UC:GB4/A1/15 fo. 137r, and UC:GB4/A1/16 fo. 73r.

[68] UC:GB4/A1/14 fo. 47r. It is interesting to observe in this context that whereas University's post-war financial position improved, that of Magdalen declined (Hegarty in Brockliss (forthcoming)).

[69] Overdraft: UC:GB4/A1/14 fo. 14r; tenants: interview with Norman Dix, 25 March 1997; investments: UC:GB4/A1/15 fo. 22r; sale of Marks Hall: *UCR* 1953/4, p. 10; equities: Dunbabin

There was, however, one change far more important than these. After the Asquith Commission, the government had begun to make grants to the universities of Oxford and Cambridge, but for university purposes only. For the time being, colleges had to depend on their own resources. Arguably government funding only affected colleges in the case of undergraduates who received scholarships from their local authorities. In 1949, however, the University Grants Committee (UGC) proposed to contribute towards the salaries of college tutors by making arts tutors Common University Fund (CUF) lecturers, so that their salaries would be paid for partly by the colleges themselves, and partly from a central university fund. Fifty such lecturers were created in the first instance, and the scheme was initially considered a great success. In November 1950 Peter Bayley and George Cawkwell became the first CUF lecturers at University College.[70]

The College still received private benefactions. Apart from Arthur Goodhart and his family, the most significant gifts in the 1950s and 1960s were the Weir and Salvesen Fellowships. James Weir was not himself a member of the College, but his son Colin had come up in 1949, and died young in 1954; in that year, Weir endowed a Politics Fellowship (the Colin Weir Fellowship), and later endowed other Fellowships and Junior Research Fellowships. Ten years later, Harold Salvesen (m. 1921) endowed a Harold Salvesen Junior Fellowship.[71]

This survey of College life from this period ends with what increasingly became known as the College staff, as the term 'servant' fell from favour after the war. Furthermore, as Norman Dix noticed, fewer men now wished to become scouts or waiters, this being thought too demeaning, and these posts were increasingly taken by women. Thanks to the Cowley works, Oxford now had other types of employment with more regular hours for its inhabitants. Some remarkable 'old stagers' remained. In 1963, for example, George Heath retired aged almost 80 after sixty-one years of service to the College, and Mrs Cooke retired—not wholly willingly—in 1986 at the age of 90 after forty-five years' service as a scout in Kybald House. Other staff members appointed after 1950 remained for many years, such as Gerald Nix, who retired from the Works Department in 2001 after forty-eight years, and Ken Tucker, who began in the kitchen in 1960 and retired as Head Chef in 2006.[72]

1994: 670–1; other colleges' finances: Dunbabin 1994 *passim*; Adams 1996: 262 (Somerville), Brooke 1996: 272–3 (Caius), Hegarty in Brockliss (forthcoming) (Magdalen), and Bendall and others 1999: 468–74 (Emmanuel) and (on the 1964 act) 460–3.

[70] Funding for colleges: Dunbabin 1994: 650–6, Thomas 1994: 190, Soares 1999: 22–3, and Tapper and Palfreyman 2000: 47–9; the first CUF's: UC:GB4/A1/14 fo. 60^r.

[71] Weir's gifts: UC:GB4/A1/15 fos. 26–7 and 94^r, and *UCR* 1952/3, pp. 3 and 8, *UCR* Vol. III no. 1 (1956), 24, and *UCR* Vol. III no. 2 (1957), 95–6; Salvesen: *UCR* Vol. IV no. 4 (1964), 235.

[72] Recruitment: interview with Norman Dix, 4 September 2001 (other colleges were in a similar predicament: Hopkins 2005: 427–8 and Thomas 1994: 207–8); Heath: *UCR* Vol. IV no. 3 (1963), 180, Cooke: *UCR* Vol. IX no. 2 (1986), 27; examples of similar loyalty at another college: Hopkins 2005: 424–7.

Staff numbers did increase: in 1962 there were just under fifty servants, and in 1974 there were over sixty. This pattern was repeated in other colleges, the greatest increases being among clerical staff. The demands made of staff rose, too, in return for greater job security. No longer were they laid off over the summer; they had to look after the ever-increasing number of conferences. By 1974, the then Domestic Bursar, David Burgess, observed that 'for the administration of the College, the distinction between term time and vacation has become almost non-existent'. There were some losses: the Servants' Rowing Club had largely ceased to exist by the 1960s, although servants' cricket and football clubs lasted slightly longer.[73]

The administration of the College's staff had to change. No longer could one rely on a Fellow simply to take up the reins of the Domestic Bursarship. After 1950, the College briefly divided the Domestic Bursar's duties into three parts, each one managed by a different Fellow, and, after an experiment in 1963–4 when an Old Member, Michael Maude (m. 1935), was appointed as a part time professional Domestic Bursar, it was decided to employ a full-time professional. They chose Vice-Admiral Sir Peter Gretton, who, having served as a convey escort commander in the Battle of the Atlantic, had remained in the navy until he retired on grounds of ill-health in 1963. Gretton took up his new post in 1965, the first full-time professional Domestic Bursar in University College, although not in Oxford. People did not always respond well to him—when he unwisely asked Douglas Millin what his duties entailed, an irritated Douglas replied 'my jobs stretch from cutting a bloke down who's hung his bloody self to finding a safety pin for a lady's elastic knickers that's fallen down'—but Gretton himself was unimpressed by the filthy kitchens and drinking problems among some staff members, and attempted a more professional approach to the domestic administration of the College. He resigned the Domestic Bursarship in 1970 on health grounds, and the post returned to the Fellowship for a decade and a half. Gretton left some advice for his successors: 'You can either be a good Domestic Bursar or a popular one but not both.'[74]

JOHN MAUD, ARNOLD GOODMAN, AND THE CHANGES OF THE 1960S

The College chose as Arthur Goodhart's successor Sir John Maud (Fig. 19.4), another pre-war Fellow, but one who had entered public life, and pre-elected

---

[73] Staff numbers: *UCR* Vol. IV no. 2 (1962), 94–5 and *UCR* Vol. VI no. 4 (1974), 359 (at Merton there were 40 staff in 1901 and 83 in 1983: Martin and Highfield 1997: 352); extra hours: *UCR* Vol. VI no. 4 (1974), 358; staff sports: Sherriff 2003: 25–6, and conversations with Gerald Nix, 3 September 2001, and Ken Tucker, 14 March 2006.

[74] Three Bursars: UC:GB4/A1/14 fo. 32ʳ; Michael Maude: UC:GB4/A1/16 fos. 43ʳ and 55ʳ, and *UCR* Vol. IV no. 3 (1963), 147 and *UCR* Vol. IV no. 4 (1964), 261; Gretton's career *ODNB* entry; Gretton's appointment: *UCR* Vol. IV no. 5 (1965), 317–18 (Wadham had appointed a professional Domestic Bursar in 1958: Thompson in Davies and Garnett 1994: 83); dealing with staff: interview with Norman Dix, 25 March 1997, and Park 1989: 50; Gretton's memoirs: UC:P6/MS/1; Gretton's advice: *UCR* Vol. VIII no. 3 (1982), 168.

him in February 1963.[75] Since leaving University College in 1939, Maud had joined the civil service, serving as Permanent Secretary at the Ministry of Education and the Ministry of Fuel and Power. In 1956 he had been elected an Honorary Fellow of the College. Since 1958 he had been High Commissioner and then Ambassador in South Africa—and an unhappy observer of the rise of the apartheid regime. It was there that Maud received a letter from Freddie Wells asking if he would be interested in becoming Master.[76]

Some Fellows felt that the new Master took time to readjust to College life, where he could not always get his own way in meetings. He retained an interest in public life, accepting in 1966 the Chairmanship of a Royal Commission on the Local Government of England, which redefined English county boundaries in a way not seen in almost a millennium. Maud eventually understood his situation well. When talking to his successor about the role of Master, he said that the Governing Body 'cannot be bullied or coerced, but it can be cajoled. In short,... the Master has influence but no power.'[77]

Maurice Bowra is supposed to have observed wickedly that, with John Maud, one had to take the smooth with the smooth, but none could deny the charm of the new Master and his wife. The Mauds took an active interest in all parts of College life, but they were especial supporters of the Musical Society which they had founded three decades earlier; one of their greatest coups was to engage Benjamin Britten and Peter Pears to give a concert in the Town Hall in April 1967.[78] They also made a point of getting to know all the freshmen quickly, carefully scrutinizing the Freshers' photo each year.

Just as the new Master took up his post, the Robbins Report into higher education appeared, making several criticisms of Oxford and Cambridge and urging greater accessibility to higher education. Oxford instigated a commission of its own, chaired by Lord Franks, which investigated every aspect of collegiate and university life, and which included among its members Maurice Shock, the Politics Fellow and Estates Bursar of University College. Although the Franks Commission's report, published in 1966, recommended changes in the appointment of a Vice-Chancellor, a strengthening of the

---

[75] UC:GB4/A1/16 fo. 48ʳ. Herbert Hart and Richard Southern were also considered (UC:S25/MS1/1). It has been observed that Shepherd's conversation piece of 1934 (Plate 15) prophetically posed three future Masters (Wild, Goodhart, and Maud) together.

[76] Redcliffe-Maud 1991: 265. On Maud's life, see Redcliffe-Maud 1981. When Maud was elected Master, he was still Sir John Maud and his wife Lady Maud. On becoming a life peer in 1967, Maud took the title Lord Redcliffe-Maud, and his wife became Lady Redcliffe-Maud. They are generally referred to here under their family name, but the change in status should be remembered throughout.

[77] Master and Fellows: interview with Sir Peter Strawson, 8 October 2002; the Royal Commission: *UCR* Vol. V no. 1 (1966), 17; advice to successor: Goodman 1993: 424.

[78] Redcliffe-Maud 1981: 115; Britten's concert: *UCR* Vol. V no. 2 (1967), 93–4 and 107 (Britten and Pears were personal friends of the Mauds, and Britten's *Young Person's Guide to the Orchestra* is dedicated to their children).

powers of the Hebdomadal Council, and the creation of a Conference of Colleges, it also upheld the collegiate traditions of the university.[79]

One of the criticisms made of Oxford at this time was its lack of support for science. Although somewhat exaggerated, the point remained that more undergraduates selected arts subjects than science ones. However, during the early 1960s University College invested heavily in the sciences, starting with its Fellowship. As the government's financial support for academic posts grew, so the Fellowship doubled from fifteen to thirty between 1954 and 1964. Many of these new Fellows were scientists. In 1955 Robert Berman joined the medic Dan Cunningham and the chemist Edmund Bowen as the College's first physics Fellows, and in 1959 University became only the second Oxford college to appoint a Tutorial Fellow in engineering when it elected Denis Campbell. Three years later Gordon Screaton was elected the first mathematics Fellow since Charles Faulkner a century earlier, and in 1963 John Albery became the College's second Fellow in chemistry. In 1964–89 the proportion of Fellows and lecturers teaching science and technology at the College rose from 32 to 45 per cent. Only two colleges (Brasenose and St Catherine's) achieved this proportion; only one (St Edmund Hall) exceeded it.[80]

As for subjects now read by undergraduates, history, law, and PPE, just as in the 1930s, remained three of the four most popular subjects after 1945. However the identity of the fourth subject changed. In the late 1940s and 1950s it was modern languages, although the College lacked a Fellow in that subject until John Fennell in 1964. In the early 1960s it was classics once again. The College then decided to increase the number of its chemists: five chemists were admitted in 1963, as had been usual, but the figure doubled in 1964. As a result, chemistry became fully established as the College's fourth major subject.[81]

Other sciences blossomed in the College. In the late 1940s and 1950s, between a fifth and a quarter of the College's undergraduates were reading a science subject; in the 1960s, this proportion climbed to a third, and by the early 1970s to around 45 per cent. Meanwhile, elsewhere only about one-fifth of all finalists in 1960 were scientists, when Oxford had the largest undergraduate schools in physics and chemistry in the country. It was not until the mid-1980s that the university's arts–science ratio had fallen even to 60:40, still some way behind University College.[82]

---

[79] See in general Halsey 1994b and Anderson 2006: 147–54. There had been a similar commission at Cambridge a few years earlier (Leedham-Green 1996: 204–5).

[80] Size of Fellowship: *UCR* Vol. IV no. 5 (1965), 312; scientists: Soares 1999: 118. Trinity's Fellowship expanded from 14 to 24 in 1949–69 and Merton's Tutorial Fellowship from 8 to 24 in 1951–86 (Hopkins 2005: 414, and Martin and Highfield 1997: 344).

[81] These figures are taken from Tutorial Lists for 1949–50, 1955–6, 1961–2, 1967–8, and 1973–4. In the 1960s the College began to concentrate only on subjects where it had Fellows. Since John Fennell and his successors were Russian specialists, from then on only Modern Linguists who studied Russian were accepted.

[82] Finalists: Greenstein 1994: 60; undergraduate numbers: Roche 1994: 255.

University College also played its part in resolving a problem which had arisen after the war: that of the 'non-dons'—scientists who now worked in the central laboratories and faculties and who lacked a college affiliation. Several 'non-dons', who had developed connections with University College, were accordingly elected Supernumerary Fellows. Thus the geologist Kenneth Sandford (an Old Member of the College) and the geographer Robert Beckinsale, both elected Supernumerary Fellows in 1965, were already College lecturers. Brian Loughman the plant scientist and David Bell the geologist were likewise elected to Fellowships from university posts in 1970, having also been College lecturers. Many of these new Fellows enjoyed their double life between faculty and College, and involved themselves fully in the affairs of their College; Bell and Loughman, for example, served long terms as Dean and Dean of Graduates respectively.[83]

The growth in science was not the only change of the 1960s. Maud was struck by the greatly enlarged College to which he returned. Indeed the College continued to grow in the 1960s, reflecting trends throughout British universities (Graph 18.1).[84] Above all, however, the late 1960s and 1970s are remembered as a period of great social upheaval in Britain, when the stereotypical student was a flag-waving political activist. In fact active discontent within Oxford tended to be directed, not towards colleges, but towards central university organizations. Some colleges were more politically engaged than others, notably Balliol, but the worst unrest which University College experienced was indirect, when the Examination Schools suffered a sit-in in November 1973. There was an awkward moment when, after the authorities turned off the electricity supplies there, extension leads were sent out from the Goodhart Building. The Governing Body was asked to stop this, but decided not to, observing both that the protest would fizzle out (which it did), and that they did not wish to put the College in the firing line.[85]

On the whole Oxford was calmer than other universities in the United Kingdom, let alone those in the USA, Germany, or France. Tony Firth, Giles Alington's protégé and successor as History Fellow, wrote a piece for the *University College Record* about his experiences as Junior Proctor in 1969/70. Firth was phlegmatic: in spite of all the student activity he encountered that year, including a long sit-in at the Clarendon Building, he thought that Oxford remained fairly quiet, observing that there were barely 'three or four from each College', who, 'without being either wicked or stupid, though

---

[83] The 'non-dons': Roche 1994: 284–6, Soares 1999: 121–34 and (for similar problems in Cambridge) Leedham-Green 1996: 202–3; Sandford and Beckinsale: *UCR* Vol. IV no. 5 (1965), 312–13.

[84] Redcliffe-Maud 1981: 97, Thomas 1994: 190, and Halsey 1994a: 577–84.

[85] Overall context: Thomas 1994: 205; Balliol and other examples of student confrontation which to a degree passed University College by: Jones 2005: 303–6, Adams 1996: 288–91, Twigg 1987: 406–33, and Bendall and others 1999: 558–60; Examination Schools: Brock 1994: 745, and conversation with David Burgess, 1 June 2002.

being quite clearly intolerant and naive, are...faithfully devoted to revolutionary causes.' Firth and the authorities did not overreact: only one student was sent down, and a few others fined.[86]

More significant rebellions occurred more quietly—literally so, when scouts complained in December 1968 that undergraduates were getting up much later—or more subtly, such as the increasing fashion for junior members to refer to themselves simply as 'students'. Gowns ceased to be worn regularly, and tweed jackets gave way to jeans and longer hair. Even the regulations about women not staying overnight could be ignored, depending on one's scout. Students nevertheless sometimes showed surprising conservatism. After Cecily Goodhart dined on High Table, the Fellows agreed that women could be invited to dinner in Michaelmas Term 1965. The students were unimpressed, and some remember the first women guests even being hissed.[87]

The greatest disputes within colleges arose over how much representation should be allowed to students, which resulted in Herbert Hart writing a report in 1967 into the relations between senior and junior members of the university. The response at University College was to create a joint SCR/WCR Committee, whose first recorded meeting took in November 1968, and a similar SCR/JCR Committee. In 1970 arrangements were made for JCR and WCR committee members to attend those parts of meetings of College Committees—and even the Governing Body—which were of special relevance and in 1981 a single Joint Consultative Committee was created, whose membership included representatives from all three common rooms.[88]

Attitudes to sport changed. One observer said of this period that 'When we arrived in Oxford, anybody who was anybody rowed and never wore jeans. When we left, anybody who was anybody never rowed and did wear jeans.' A truer comment would be that sport had yielded its position of despotic sway over college life at the start of the twentieth century, and became once again one recreational activity among many.[89]

Rowing still reigned supreme among the sports, but now from a different home: since the 1940s many colleges had exchanged their barges for boathouses. Beautiful as the barges were, they were expensive to maintain, and had no space for boats. University College retained its barge until the OUBC's lease on the boathouse built in the 1880s on part of Eastwick Farm expired in 1964. The College decided to take over the boathouse, selling

---

[86] Firth 1970.

[87] Staying in bed: UC:GB4/A1/17 fo. 87r; nomenclature: Thomas 1994: 204–5; also on gowns in the 1960s: Jones 2005: 307, and Green 1979: 585; women guests: UC:GB4/A1/16 fos. 92–3 and UC:GB4/A1/17 fo. 7r.

[88] The Hart Committee: Lacey 2004: 284–9 and Harrison 1994d: 706; joint committees: UC:GB4/A1/17 fo. 89r. UC:GB4/A1/18 fos. 18r and 20v, and Acc. 610. The voting age was reduced to 18 in 1969, thus enfranchising almost all Oxford's undergraduates at a stroke.

[89] Rowing: quoted in White and Gribbin 1992: 46. Sport likewise became less overwhelmingly important at Balliol in the 1950s and 1960s (Jones 2005: 286). See too Brooke 1993: 516.

the barge in 1965. The boathouse was in poor condition, but it became a new centre for College rowing, and the College could lease out space to other colleges lacking boathouses. The barge was sold to a local builder, and, after various vicissitudes, was sensitively restored in the 1990s.[90]

The Master and Lady Maud did not always find it easy to accept the changes among the junior members, be it a little graciousness lost, such as people not replying to invitations, or the JCR's motion to install a contraceptive machine in 1971; and divorced members of the College were not made welcome in the Lodgings. The Mauds, however, enjoyed one innovation. John Albery combined his chemistry research with a flair for sketchwriting, and he and a young history Fellow, Leslie Mitchell, instituted the first College revue in 1972, inevitably titled *Come into the Garden, Maud*. Following its success the revue became an annual event. Both the Master and Lady Maud tolerated the jests at their expense, and occasionally participated themselves, most notably when in 1976, just before their retirement, they ended the show *In Memaudiam* with a memorable rendition of 'My Old Man said follow the Van'.[91]

There were developments in the Governing Body. In University College, as elsewhere in Oxford, fewer Fellows lived in, and lunch took over from dinner as the main meal of the day when Fellows could be sure of meeting their colleagues. Some observers feared that, after the 1960s, undergraduates were rather less willing than their predecessors to 'cultivate the family atmosphere and the friendships with the dons'. Nevertheless for almost all of the pre-war years there were always at least one or two Fellows of University College who continued the honourable tradition of Giles Alington in acting as a conduit between SCR, JCR, and now MCR, from Freddie Wells and Tony Firth in the 1950s and 1960s, to Leslie Mitchell and Bill Sykes in more recent years.[92]

It was, however, the academic reputation of the College which underwent the greatest changes. There had been a change in mood with the young Fellows of the late 1940s, but twenty years later, with a fresh generation of Fellows, the College moved in a more self-consciously academic direction. Of course the College in the intervening decades had not been a particularly un- or even anti-intellectual place, and had not been so very socially exclusive: in 1961–5 the proportion of pupils from independent schools coming up

---

[90] Sale of the barge: *UCR* Vol. V no. 2 (1967), 119–20, and interviews with Norman Dix, 25 March 1997 and 4 September 2001; later history and restoration: Sherriff 2003: 40–4 (the barge is currently owned by Sherriff's husband). Sherriff's book provides a good overview of the replacement of barges by boathouses.

[91] Contraceptive machine: UC:GB4/A1/18 fos. 59–60; Balliol also got a machine at this time: Jones 2005: 306; College revues: *UCR* Vol. VI no. 2 (1972), 174–6, *UCR* Vol. VI no. 3 (1973), 270–2, and *UCR* Vol. VII no. 2 (1976), 81.

[92] Lunch: Thomas 1994: 197–8 and Redcliffe-Maud 1991: 106; relations with students: quotation from Hyam in Cunich and others 1994: 270–1. See too Thomas 1994: 200–1.

to University College dropped from 50.4 to 36 per cent, the others going to direct-grant or state schools (only seven other colleges had a smaller proportion of public-school boys by 1965). Nevertheless the College also produced rather a lot of Thirds and (until their abolition in 1967) Fourths. There was an almost Alingtonian tolerance of men who, while not very strong academically, could contribute to the College in other ways. When a table was created in 1963 to grade Oxford colleges by their Finals results, called the Norrington Table after the President of Trinity College who had created it, University College fluctuated between 7th and 23rd in its first few years.[93]

An important moment in the change in College culture was the appointment of John Albery as Tutor for Admissions in 1968.[94] Albery, like other recently elected Fellows, such as his fellow chemist Tony Orchard and the historian Leslie Mitchell, wished to nurture a more academic atmosphere. They were surprised by some attitudes even in the SCR. A Fellow in one arts subject who was publishing his first book was asked by a senior colleague in the same discipline whether he was not being a bit pushy.

Albery and his colleagues brought a different approach to the business of attracting applicants. After the example of the West Riding scheme, they encouraged state schools with no previous Oxbridge connections to invite their pupils to apply to University College. Some special schemes were set up, such as one to encourage more Scottish applicants. The new English Fellow, the Scotsman Roy Park (F. 1972–96), played a major role in this 'Scottish scheme'; at one point the College recruited three times more Scottish students than the Oxford average. Such techniques became common enough three decades later, but in the early 1970s they were still novel. Furthermore, as a university education became financially viable for a greater number of people, so the numbers applying to Oxford grew significantly, and it was easier to cream off the best. Nevertheless, a college has to make its own luck, and this University College did.[95]

More was demanded of those new undergraduates. During the 1970s they were increasingly set work in the vacation, and in the 1970s and 1980s tutors began regularly to issue reading lists, rather than give out oral suggestions. It was possible for an informal meeting of Tutorial Fellows, in November 1971, to express concern 'That the intellectual level of College life was not as high as it might be, or as it has been, and perhaps still is in some other colleges.'[96]

---

[93] Information about Finals results is taken from successive issues of *UCR*; information on schools: Soares 1999: 88. This change in mood was not unique to University College, but it elsewhere occurred at different times (Thomas 1994: 193–7): Trinity achieved just one First in Finals in 1970, and even in 1972 achieved just six (Hopkins 2005: 430).

[94] *UCR* Vol. VII no. 4 (1978), 165–7.

[95] The Scottish scheme: UC:GB4/A1/18 fo. 78[r] and *UCR* Vol. XI no. 4 (1996), 15; increase in applicants: Soares 1999: 208–10. These approaches paid off. In October 1971, there was a significantly greater percentage of students from state schools (UC:GB4/A1/18 fo. 58[r]).

[96] Collections: UC:GB4/A1/18 fos. 31[r] and 60[r] and UC:GB4/A1/19, fo. 2[r]; reading lists: interview with Christopher Pelling, 9 September 2003.

These changes had an effect. In 1972, for the first time, the number of Firsts in Finals matched with the number of Thirds, and since 1974 the College has always produced more Firsts than Thirds. In 1975, when it first achieved more than twenty Firsts, University College came top of the Norrington Table, a position it held four times in 1975–82. There can be a certain queasiness about using a blunt instrument like the Norrington Table to judge the health of a college, and it is true that the number of Thirds has declined throughout Oxford, but something had happened to the culture of College to give it an academic reputation not enjoyed since the 1870s. One Fellow, an undergraduate at another college in the mid-1960s and then a JRF outside Oxford, observed that, on his return to Oxford in the early 1970s, he found that the College had become significantly more eminent than it had been in his undergraduate days. A particularly pleasing sign of the change was that University College won the TV quiz show *University Challenge* in 1972 and 1976.[97]

After 1973 University College was at last able to offer College accommodation to its undergraduates throughout their time there, with the construction of an annexe in north Oxford. Such annexes are common enough places today, but they were still new three decades ago. Even with the Goodhart Building and the rooms in 85–7 High Street, the College's central site could not accommodate undergraduates for more than two years. To accommodate the rest, it had been agreed by 1966 to seek a site outside the College, and in June 1967 one was selected in north Oxford, covering 25 Staverton Road, and 100a, 102, and 104 Woodstock Road. Four blocks were planned, two for undergraduates and two for married graduates, and 102 Woodstock Road would be demolished to make way for them. In the meantime, the existing buildings on the site were set aside for student use in 1968, and additional accommodation was provided in St Giles, in the recently enlarged Old Parsonage.[98]

The architect selected was Sir Philip Dowson of Arup Associates, who had come up to University College in 1943 as a naval cadet. Although he later went to Clare College, Cambridge, Dowson retained a link with his first College as Freddie Wells's brother-in-law. In the 1950s he became an architect, and in 1958 had even been a runner-up for the Goodhart Building project. Since then his career had blossomed: in Oxford alone he designed the Vaughan and Fry block for Somerville College and the Sir Thomas White Building for St John's, and he would later build the Forbes-Mellon Library for his 'other' college, Clare.[99]

---

[97] *UCR* Vol. VI no. 2 (1972), 135 and *UCR* Vol. VII no. 2 (1976), 62.
[98] Finding a site: UC:GB4/A1/17 fos. 24ʳ and 56ʳ and *UCR* Vol. V no. 2 (1967), 123; moving into it: *UCR* Vol. V no. 3 (1968), 199 (in order to purchase the site, the College had to sell its properties to the north of the Old Parsonage); temporary accommodation: UC:GB4/A1/17 fo. 66ʳ and UC:GB4/A1/19 fo. 4ʳ.
[99] Goodhart Building: Acc. 697; Dowson's work elsewhere: Tyack 2005: 43–79, Adams 1996: 273–5, Tyack 1998: 317–20, and Shaw-Miller 2001: 199–200.

For his old College Dowson was asked to design something not too grand, and to arrange rooms in groups so that friends could live together. He created floors at half levels, so that people would feel closer to every level, with no sense of stratification. Some details took time to evolve, especially the question of catering. It was first assumed that undergraduates would wish to eat in College, and the earliest proposals for the undergraduate blocks made no provision for kitchens. It was eventually agreed to insert pantries on each floor for snacks: even male undergraduates might prefer to cook rather than cycle into College, especially on a wet winter's evening.[100]

The College could not afford such a large capital project itself, and so in October 1969 it launched an appeal to Old Members for £400,000. Techniques had changed since the last great building appeal from the 1660s: a brochure was prepared, and John Maud even travelled abroad to solicit support from overseas Old Members. By the end of 1970, well over two-thirds of the money had been raised from nearly 1,300 individuals, including the ever-generous Goodhart family. The final stages of the appeal were slower going, but the target sum was at last exceeded in 1974. Planning permission for the project was granted in October 1970, and work started a month later. The buildings' location inspired a nickname 'Stavertonia', which, in spite of some official disapproval, stuck, and in turn yielded the abbreviation 'Stavvers'.[101]

Stavertonia was not the only building project of the late 1960s. In 1968 a building was proposed which would at last provide a decent room for the WCR, accommodation for the Works Department, and extra space for the kitchens. The site selected lay to the south of the Library, and an old cottage was demolished to make way for it. Working in a confined space, John Fryman of the Architects Design Partnership created a graduate common room on the first floor with a works department and kitchen space below, an ensemble which Nikolaus Pevsner thought 'a cute little brick building'. Taking its name from Sir Harold Mitchell (m. 1919), who had generously paid for its construction, the Mitchell Building (Plate 16) was opened in June 1971.[102]

The College employed Fryman for a second piece of space-filling. Since 1968, the College had been planning to tidy up the space between 83–5 High Street and the Goodhart Building. In the early 1970s, Arthur Goodhart gave money for Fryman to create a little courtyard there. Opened in 1974, it was named Cecily's Court, after Cecily Goodhart, and joined Goodhart Building

---

[100] Interviews with Sir Philip Dowson, 3 April 2007, and George Cawkwell, 20 March 2001; also UC:FA17/C1/1–2.

[101] Appeal brochure: UC:CA7/N1/1; Maud's travels: *UCR* Vol. V no. 5 (1970), 297–8; donors to the Appeal: Acc. 464; chronology of construction work from UC:GB4/A1/18 fo. 35^r and UC:GB4/A1/19 fo. 7^r; name of building: interview with John Allen, 27 March 2007.

[102] Fryman: UC:GB4/A1/17 fos. 71^r and 82^r; Sherwood and Pevsner 1974: 212; opening: *UCR* Vol. VI no. 1 (1971), 24–5.

and Helen's Court as a third place to commemorate the generosity of Arthur Goodhart and his family.[103]

Unfortunately the building of Stavertonia proved a more protracted and troublesome process, for the 1970s was a time of great inflation. The costs of the project rose sharply, and the firm of contractors employed by the College went bankrupt in December 1971. The College had to step in to manage the project itself, taking on most of the workmen already in place. The then Chaplain Fellow, David Burgess (F. 1969–78), was currently Domestic Bursar, and it fell to him, and the Estates Bursar, Maurice Shock, to oversee the project through to the end.

Stavertonia was ready for its first occupants in the autumn of 1973. In honour of four great benefactors of the past, the graduate blocks were named Percy and Skirlaw, and the undergraduate ones Bennet and Greenwood.[104] In November 1973, *Martlet Pie*, a College undergraduate magazine, had its own mischievous take on the new annexe, providing a list of 'Stavertonian' phrases, with English translations, such as:

Aagh! (There are no locks on the shower doors)
Isn't the lighting seductive (The damn bulb has gone again)
Communal cooking is cosy (The kitchen is too small)
After you (The stairs are rather narrow)

In fact the annexe (Plate 17) provided accommodation well worthy of comparison with other modern college buildings. The College could at last offer all its undergraduates accommodation—but at a price. As the *University College Record* for 1974 ruefully commented, 'What should have cost £400,000 has in fact cost more than twice that amount. That loss will have to be met.'[105] The loss was exacerbated by a collapse in the stock market, and several College properties had to be sold.

Other colleges encountered similar difficulties. The final costs of Dowson's Sir Thomas White Building for St John's College, for example, grew so considerably that the original proposals were scaled down, and the main contractors received financial assistance to escape bankruptcy. Wealthy Magdalen College failed to maintain its momentum after 1945, and, having borrowed extensively to build the Waynflete Building in the 1960s, ran into financial trouble when major repairs on its tower were urgently needed in the mid-1970s.[106]

There was one piece of good fortune. In 1971 the National Westminster Bank intimated its willingness to sell 91 High Street; the College eagerly seized this opportunity to expand its central site, and agreed a purchase. It

---

[103] Cecily's Court: *UCR* Vol. VI no. 4 (1974), 336–7.
[104] UC:GB4/A1/19, fos. 1ʳ and 14ʳ, and *UCR* Vol. VI no. 3 (1973), 203–4.
[105] *UCR* Vol. VI no. 4 (1974), 360–4.
[106] St John's: Tyack 2005: 59–60 and 63–5; Magdalen: Hegarty and Brockliss in Brockliss (forthcoming).

was no easy matter to find the money, but the Bank lent the College the purchase price, allowing it to buy the property, and pay for it later.[107]

In 1976, shortly after the purchase of 91 High Street, John Maud retired as Master. His successor, like Sir Michael Sadler, had no previous College connections. To describe Arnold Goodman, who had been ennobled in 1965, as a solicitor was partly true, but it concealed a multifaceted life.[108] A Director of the Royal Opera House and of Sadler's Wells, and Chairman of the Arts Council in 1965–72, he also helped create the Open University. Furthermore he was well connected with many powerful figures in politics, notably Harold Wilson. Goodman himself claimed that he was first approached in the summer of 1974 through Michael Yudkin, the Biochemistry Fellow, for whose family Goodman had worked as a solicitor. After a dinner in College and a formal deputation, he agreed to accept. That deputation comprised David Cox and three other Fellows. It is said that they went to London to make the formal offer of the Mastership, having planned carefully what to say, but when Goodman met them, he said 'Gentlemen, I know why you are here, and the answer is yes.'[109] He was pre-elected Master in April 1976 and took up office that October.

Arnold Goodman had a very different style from his predecessors. He wished to continue his London work, and the College accepted their most non-resident Master since William Beveridge. Once again the post of Vice-Master had to be revived and made effectively permanent, to be held at first by David Cox and then George Cawkwell. In general, Goodman concluded that his policy as Master was to let people get on with their business uninterrupted, and only to intervene where his help was needed. Careful management of his diary meant that he was usually present to chair committee meetings. Thus he kept out of College politics, preferring to act as an umpire. This extended to his taking no part in the admissions procedure. His apparent lack of interest in fine details, however, did not always go down well: it was unwise, for example, to keep on thinking that the College Secretary was called 'Miss Cunningham'.[110]

Goodman himself thought that his dealings with students were 'close enough for me to regard my Mastership as a reasonably successful one'.[111] Students themselves, however, remember more clearly a vast and distant, if reasonably benign, figure, their daunting one-to-one conversations with him during their first term, and the no less daunting lunches in the Lodgings during their first year. On the other hand, there are many tales of how, when a student

---

[107] UC:GB4/A1/18 fo. 55[r] and UC:GB4/A1/19, fo. 5[r]. The loan was paid off by 1975.
[108] Goodman's life is described in Goodman 1993 and Brivati 1999.
[109] Goodman 1993: 419–21 *versus UCR* Vol. XI no. 3 (1995), 16 (and Brivati 1999: 263).
[110] Non-residence: Goodman 1993: 421; avoidance of politics: *UCR* Vol. XI no. 3 (1995), 17–18; admissions: conversation with Gwynne Ovenstone, 20 May 2002.
[111] Goodman 1993: 428.

needed financial or legal assistance, the Master was at hand to help. One such tale involved a student, who, in the third week of term, was still awaiting his grant cheque. When the Dean expressed concern at this, Goodman promptly rang up the Secretary of State for Education, in the Dean's presence, to tell her directly about the problem. That very afternoon a courier from the relevant local education authority turned up at College bearing the cheque.

The Master showed his generosity in other ways. He had a box at Covent Garden, and regularly invited a Fellow to select some students to have a free evening at the opera. He arranged for musicians such as Moura Lympany and Yehudi Menuhin to give free concerts in the College, and for the violinist Gidon Kremer and the cellist Karine Georgian to make their British debuts at University College. Through his agency Steinway grand pianos were provided both for the Hall and the Master's Lodgings. The Lodgings, although not as busy as they had been under the Mauds and Goodharts, were hardly quiet. The Master readily allowed the Musical Society to hold evenings there in his absence, and Fellows met the Master's eminent guests, often with a close female friend acting as hostess, like Jennie Lee, the former Minister for the Arts, or Anne Fleming, Ian Fleming's widow. He also helped the College purchase a remarkable portrait of himself by Graham Sutherland (Fig. 19.8). Utterly unsparing in depicting Goodman's appearance, Sutherland nevertheless conveyed his strength of character, and it stands out among the gentler portraits in the Hall.[112]

Many of those who held major College offices under Goodman found him an excellent colleague and a great support, possessed of a good sense of humour. Some talked of his reassuring 'grandfatherly' presence in the College. Tony Orchard, who served as Dean at the start and end of Goodman's Mastership, sometimes gained insights into Goodman's other lives, as when he once called on the Lodgings, to find him in conversation with James Callaghan. Having observed 'I don't need to introduce you to the Prime Minister, do I?', Goodman suggested that he call back later. Goodman undoubtedly had a well-organized mind, in which he could compartmentalize his different activities, but some have asked how fortunate or otherwise University College was to be just one compartment among several. Nevertheless, the Fellowship showed their high opinion of Goodman by voting, as they had done for Arthur Goodhart, to extend his Mastership by two years until 1986. In return, Goodman praised his former colleagues ('I do not know a harder-working body than the Fellows of an Oxford college'), and bought a retirement home in Headington.[113]

What is beyond dispute is that Goodman, aided by the Estates Bursar, Gordon Screaton, repaired the College's finances. Looking back to 1976,

---

[112] Debut concerts: *UCR* Vol. VII no. 4 (1978), 197–8 and *UCR* Vol. VIII no. 2 (1981), 102; pianos: *UCR* Vol. VII no. 5 (1979), 220.
[113] Conversation with Tony Orchard, 22 October 2002 (and Gordon Screaton's tribute in *UCR* Vol. XI no. 3 (1996), 16–18); Goodman on the Fellows: Goodman 1993: 433.

512   THE COLLEGE RENEWED: 1945–1979

FIGURE 19.8 Lord Goodman, Master 1976–86, by Graham Sutherland.

Screaton observed that 'the College was struggling to finish financing Stavertonia against a background of a collapsing stock and property market'. Goodman himself claimed to have made it clear that he would not regard it as part of his duties to raise money for the College, but if this was really true, he soon changed his mind. Goodman himself was not especially wealthy, but he had friends who were. In 1978, the Beaverbrook Foundation gave £10,000 a year for ten years to fund a Fellowship in English. Soon afterwards Lord Rayne and his foundation gave the College almost £500,000 for various purposes, including a Physics Fellowship. Goodman also raised loans on reasonable terms. On Goodman's retirement, it was observed that he had helped endow new Fellowships in Physiology, English, Physics, Plant Science, and Jurisprudence, and that much of the College had been rebuilt and refurbished. The restoration of the College's finances was arguably Goodman's greatest service to the College.[114]

---

[114] Finances in 1976: *UCR* Vol. XI no. 3 (1995), 16; College buildings: *UCR* Vol. IX no. 2 (1986), 6; Goodman on fund-raising: Goodman 1993: 435; help from the 'Friends of Arnold': Brivati 1999: 264–5.

A different service which Goodman performed, but one of arguably even greater significance for the College, was to oversee the admission of women. New College had discussed this as early as 1962, and it has been claimed that at the same time some Fellows of University College, including Peter Bayley, Freddie Wells, Herbert Hart, and George Paul, informally raised the matter here. The first time, however, that the subject was formally discussed was in November 1968, when the General Purposes Committee received a letter from the JCR asking the Governing Body to take steps to admit women. Their resolution was referred to an informal meeting of the Fellows, and the matter went no further. Another effort was made by the Philosophy Fellow, John Mackie, in 1970. John Maud, however, always opposed the idea. One argument regularly employed was that to discuss going mixed at the time of the appeal for Stavertonia would anger many Old Members and make them reluctant to contribute.[115]

Nevertheless, there was a mood for change. Several public schools were admitting girls at sixth-form level, with Marlborough setting an example in 1966. In 1972 three Cambridge colleges, Clare, Churchill, and King's, went mixed, and many in Oxford wished to follow. A compromise was reached: in 1972 it was agreed that five colleges—Brasenose, Hertford, Jesus, St Catherine's, and Wadham—should admit women in 1974, and that matters be reviewed in 1977. Meanwhile Balliol showed its sympathies by electing its first woman Fellow in 1973.[116]

University College also tested the waters. Many teacher training students in the university were unattached to any college, and it was decided to alter this. Among them were forty women who sought associate membership of men's colleges. In October 1972 six of these women were given associate membership of the Weir Common Room. This granted them access to the WCR itself, but they could only dine in Hall as guests of WCR members. Nevertheless, this was the first time that women students had been given some recognition in the College.[117]

In 1976, when Arnold Goodman became Master, the five-year moratorium was due to expire. Goodman himself approved of the College going mixed, and he thought that most Fellows did so. It was slyly observed that many Fellows were married, and capable of sharing bathrooms with the opposite sex. As regards the Old Members, several who had daughters had already intimated that they would be pleased to send them to the College. Another

---

[115] See further Mitchell 2004; JCR letter: UC:GB4/A1/17 fos. 87–8; opposition: Redcliffe-Maud 1981: 101–2. Sir Peter Strawson (interview, 8 October 2002) remembered the question being raised before he left the College in 1968.
[116] Marlborough: Hinde 1992: 203–7 and 215; Balliol: Jones 2005: 308–13.
[117] Acc. 678 (File on 'Middle Common Room'), and conversations with Brian Loughman, 18 December 2006 and 27 February 2007.

argument which carried weight was that the College's academic standards could suffer if it excluded women.[118]

The College moved swiftly. On 17 March 1977 the Governing Body agreed by a majority of 20 to 4 'to amend its Statutes to include a paragraph "The masculine shall include the feminine" ', and by a majority of 20 to 2 to admit women at all levels as soon as possible.

The university had other ideas. Other colleges wanted to go mixed, but the women's colleges feared for their future when women could apply anywhere within the university. In 1977, therefore, it was agreed that those colleges which wished to go mixed would do so gradually, starting with five—chosen by ballot—in 1979 and more following in later years. Tony Stokes, University College's Admissions Tutor and Fellow in Russian, and some of his colleagues from other colleges protested, and at a difficult meeting in June 1977 the university authorities tried to bind all parties to this transition. Stokes and the representative for Pembroke, declaring that their colleges had formally agreed to admit women in October 1979, remained opposed, despite talk of sanctions against the two 'rogue elephants'. The ballot was held that September, and, while Pembroke won a place for 1979, University did not. Stokes helped the College hold its nerve, and in October 1977 University College declared that it would still admit women in 1979, threatening to withdraw from all admissions agreements.[119]

Stokes and the College won: the university's ballot scheme collapsed, and all the men's colleges (except Christ Church and Oriel) and two women's colleges (St Anne's and Lady Margaret Hall) went mixed in Michaelmas Term 1979. It is worth emphasizing the magnitude of this change. In September 1974, there were no mixed undergraduate colleges; by October 1985, there were no all-male colleges, and just two all-female ones. The Fellows of University College had played no small part in the speed of these events.[120]

Reflecting on this, Stokes wrote in the *University College Record* of 1977 'we were not prompted by any feeling of dissatisfaction with our present condition,... but partly at least by the recognition that the one option that was not open to us was to remain as we are.' He also observed that 'reports filtering through from the outside world suggest that Old Members are known to have daughters as well as sons, and that they are equally concerned about the education of both'.[121]

Meanwhile the College prepared for the admission of women. Plans to create women-only staircases were scrapped, but it was agreed that the first

---

[118] Goodman 1993: 424, and interview with Brian Loughman, 8 December 2006.
[119] See further Mitchell 2004: 70–2.
[120] Brock 1994: 746–9. The same effects were seen at Cambridge during this time (Brooke 1993: 532–3).
[121] Stokes 1977.

women should not be given rooms in staircases with unsuitable lavatories or bathrooms, and that the showers and bathrooms in Staircase XI should have partitions and doors fitted. It was also agreed to install a women's lavatory and changing room in the College's pavilion. The main concern at several colleges was the installation of full-length mirrors.[122]

On the whole, the process of going mixed went through without any of the unhappiness felt in some other colleges. It was mainly long-standing members of staff like Gwynne Ovenstone, Douglas Millin, and Norman Dix who were most concerned about the change.[123] In 1978, the way was prepared by the election of University College's first woman Fellow, the medieval English scholar Helen Cooper. As Michaelmas Term 1979 approached, the College waited to see what would happen.

---

[122] See, for example, Jones 2005: 308–13 and Shaw-Miller 2001: 221.

[123] Park 1989: 55. Gwynne invented a female candidate for a Junior Research Fellowship whose subject of research was suitably 'feminist'. Only when her candidate was shortlisted did she cheerfully own up (*UCR* Vol. IX no. 3 (1987), 15–16).

20

Epilogue: 1979–2007

The two previous historians of University College treated the events of their own time rather differently. Whereas William Smith exposed the disputes of the 1720s, to general annoyance, William Carr stopped his narrative in 1870, thirty years before his book was published—but since that period included the sending down of the undergraduates, the suicide of an Estates Bursar, and the shooting of a Master, Carr's discretion is understandable. A middle way between Smith's candour and Carr's silence seems best, at the very least because it is too early to know what events or themes of the last three decades will prove most significant. It will fall to the College's next historian to examine this period more fully.[1]

No future historian, however, could deny the significance of the arrival of the College's first women students in October 1979. The first arrivals were three postgraduate students, with twenty-eight undergraduates coming a few days later. Perhaps the most striking aspect about the process was how smoothly it went. The first women in all three common rooms felt welcome, and the fears of alienating Old Members proved illusory: a very few were upset, but the overwhelming majority accepted the situation approvingly or just indifferently. Douglas Millin looked at one of the first women and observed 'Well, I suppose we've got to get used to having the likes of you around here.' Later that term he made a bet with a Fellow that there would be fewer women in College at midnight on a given Saturday than there were in 1978. In the boathouse Norman Dix observed somewhat suspiciously the first women who expressed an interest in rowing, but he refused to retreat from a challenge, and the College's first women rowers quickly found Dix just as supportive as he had been towards their male colleagues. Gwynne Ovenstone, observing that six of the first women were daughters of Old Members, took pleasure in assigning them the rooms once occupied by their fathers. She also appreciated the improvement in the personal hygiene of

---

[1] Some ground has already been covered in Snow 1991: 87–154, much of which is based on his observation of University College. My policy here has been to attempt to discuss in any detail only those people who are no longer Fellows or currently employed by the College in any capacity.

male students. The short undergraduate memory also eased the transition. By 1982, when all four undergraduate years were mixed, it was hard for that year's freshers to imagine the College had ever been all male.[2]

In that first year, the first 'Ladies VIII' (it was not called a 'Women's VIII' until the *University College Record* of 1985) took to the water, Fiona Barling became the College's first woman to win a Blue (in Hockey), and several women appeared in the College revue. In the next year, the first women members of the JCR Committee were elected. The first woman President of the JCR, Emma Haygarth, was elected in 1983. Most of those who voted for her thought of her merely as the best person for the post, and it was only afterwards that the historic nature of the vote became apparent. A new office of Counsellor for Women was created, and in 1978, in readiness for the arrival of women, a mixed Chapel choir was set up. Supported by the new Chaplain, Bill Sykes, and supplemented at first by women from St Hilda's, the choir soon became an important part of the religious and musical life of the College. There was one other happy result of going mixed: there have now been several weddings between College members.[3]

Most other former men's colleges enjoyed similar experiences. Women's colleges, however, saw their worst fears realized: now that women students could apply to almost two dozen colleges, and most of them preferred a mixed environment, the number of applications to the women's colleges fell. Men remained in the majority in University College, but that majority has fallen. In 1979, 31 out of 123 freshers were women, almost exactly a quarter of the whole intake; by the 1990s, women made up roughly a third of each year's intake, and in 2003, it was 44 per cent. Among the Fellows progress was slower. The College had its first woman JRF in 1984, and in 1988–90 three women were elected either as term Fellows or Senior Research Fellows, but it was not until the early 1990s that the College elected its first permanent women Fellows after Cooper.[4]

Lord Goodman retired as Master in 1986. His successor, Kingman Brewster (Fig. 20.1), also had no previous links with the College, and was proposed by the Professor of Jurisprudence, Ronald Dworkin (F. 1969–98). University College's second American Master had been a very successful

---

[2] Attitudes of women: interview with Helen Cooper, 7 September 2004, and accounts in Mitchell 2004: 72–5; Douglas Millin: Mitchell 2004: 73 and 75 (no one knows if he won the bet); Norman Dix: *UCR* Vol. XIV no. 1 (2005), 40; Gwynne Ovenstone: *UCR* Vol. VII no. 5 (1979), 236 and *UCR* Vol. IX no. 3 (1987), 17.

[3] Rowing, Blue, and revue: *UCR* Vol. VIII no. 1 (1980), 23, 30, and 52; JCR Committee: *UCR* Vol. VIII no. 2 (1981), 98; JCR President: *UCR* Vol. VIII no. 5 (1984), 326; Chapel choir: *UCR* Vol. VIII no. 1 (1980), 17.

[4] Elsewhere, Trinity College's first female intake comprised just 17 undergraduates and 6 postgraduates and only elected a woman Fellow in 1984 (Hopkins 2005: 436–8 and 441); Adams 1996: 276–80 described the consequences of mixed colleges as 'catastrophic' for Somerville; Wadham, although it went mixed in 1974, did not elect a woman Fellow until 1979 (Thompson in Davies and Garnett 1994: 88).

FIGURE 20.1 Kingman Brewster, Master 1986–8.

President of Yale in 1963–77, introducing much-needed reforms and holding the university together at a time when many American campuses endured troubles far beyond the imaginings of Oxford (and also serving as the model for 'President King', a character in the *Doonesbury* cartoon strip by Garry Trudeau). He had then served as the US Ambassador to London in 1977–81. Unfortunately, in the interval between his election and his arrival in the College, Brewster suffered a serious stroke. In spite of his determination to fight back and do his duty as Master, he remained in poor health throughout his Mastership, and died in November 1988, after only two years in office.[5] The one occurrence of note during Brewster's brief Mastership was a major appeal to its Old Members, which will be discussed later.

Brewster's successor was John Albery (Fig. 20.2), who had left University College for a Professorship at Imperial College, London, in 1978, and who now returned in January 1989 as the first Master to be a Fellow of the Royal

---

[5] Kabaservice 2004 is the major biography of Brewster; 'President King': Kabaservice 2004: 340.

FIGURE 20.2 John Albery, Fellow 1963–78 and Master 1989–97, by Daphne Todd.

FIGURE 20.3 Bill Clinton m. 1968, President of the United States 1993–2001, with Douglas Millin, Head Porter of University College 1950–83, on the former's visit to Oxford in 1994.

Society. Soon after his election, the College went Head of the River in Eights Week in 1990 for the first time since 1914, and maintained this position the following year. In June 1994 Albery headed a College which welcomed President Bill Clinton on his return to Oxford to receive an honorary DCL. The only specification made by the President regarding his visit was that he should have a private conversation with Douglas Millin. His wish was granted, and the great and the good had to wait while the most powerful man in the world spent time alone with the retired Head Porter of University College (Fig. 20.3).[6]

John Albery resigned as Master in 1997, and the College looked to the Civil Service and an Old Member, Sir Robin Butler (m. 1957; Plate 18). Butler had achieved the impressive combination of a First in classics and a Rugby Blue, he had been JCR President in 1959/60, and had taken part in the famous Univ. Players production of *The Miracles* (p. 495)—as indeed, had his future wife Jill. His civil service career had culminated in his service as Cabinet

[6] *UCR* Vol. XI no. 2 (1994), 24–33.

Secretary to three Prime Ministers (Margaret Thatcher, John Major, and Tony Blair), and he had been an Honorary Fellow of the College since 1989. The new Master took office in January 1998, just after his retirement from the Cabinet Office, and his ennoblement as Lord Butler of Brockwell.[7] Like John Maud, Butler was called back to public service, sitting on the Royal Commission on the Reform of the House of Lords in 1999, and chairing a Review of Intelligence on Weapons of Mass Destruction in 2004 following the invasion of Iraq the previous year.

The Butlers arrived to oversee the College's celebrations for the 750th anniversary of William of Durham's benefaction in 1999. There were reunions and parties for Old Members in Oxford and elsewhere (including Washington, DC); a special concert was given by members of the College in London; a series of lectures were given on the theme *Builders of the Millennium*, two given by the eminent Old Members Stephen Hawking and Sir V. S. Naipaul, and others by such figures as Tony Blair and Rupert Murdoch. The highlight of the year, however, was a visit on 21 May from the College's Visitor and its senior Honorary Fellow, the Queen and the Duke of Edinburgh—the first visit by a reigning monarch since James II (Fig. 20.4). The year was only marred by one unfortunate event, when in September the boathouse burned down in mysterious circumstances. After much delay, caused by the fact that it had been a listed building, a dramatic new boathouse was finally opened in 2007, designed by Belsize Architects.[8]

The new boathouse was the first new building erected by the College since Stavertonia, but much necessary modernization had been taking place, including the renovation of 90 and 91 High Street in the 1980s. There were responses to changing needs, as when the Porter's Lodge and the students' pigeonholes changed places in 1986 or a set of rooms in Radcliffe Quadrangle was converted for the use of a disabled undergraduate in 1990. More accommodation was found nearby. Not only did the College acquire 2, 4, and 5 Magpie Lane in 1989, and turn them into student accommodation, but many of its houses in Merton Street were converted to serve the same purpose. Attempts were made to restore two Victorian works of art to their original condition. The black coverings installed by Sir Michael Sadler around the east window of the Chapel were taken down in 1980, and Champneys' enclosure for the Shelley Memorial

---

[7] In 2003 Lord Butler became the first Head of an Oxford college to be appointed a Knight of the Garter, and the seventh member of University College. The others are John Tiptoft, Earl of Worcester (resident in the College 1440–3; appointed c.1461); Francis Rawdon, first Marquess of Hastings (m. 1771; appointed 1812); William, second Earl of Selborne (m. 1878; appointed 1909); James, fourth Marquess of Salisbury (m. 1880; appointed 1917); Clement Attlee (m. 1901; appointed 1956); and Harold Wilson (JRF and Fellow 1938–45; appointed 1976).
[8] The events of 1999 are recorded in *UCR* Vol. XII no. 3 (1999), 2–4 and 19–22 and *UCR* Vol. XII no. 4 (2000), 2–3; the new boathouse: *UCR* Vol. XIV no. 3 (2007), 105–6.

FIGURE 20.4 Queen Elizabeth II, Visitor of the College, in Radcliffe Quadrangle on 21 May 1999, accompained by Lord Butler of Brockwell, Master from 1998. Behind them is the Duke of Edinburgh, Honorary Fellow, with Gordon Screaton, Fellow 1962–2001.

underwent a major redecoration a few years later to reveal its original colour scheme.[9]

The Library probably went through more changes than anywhere else. Not only was it in 1987/8 one of the first College libraries to have an automated catalogue, but its interior was radically rebuilt. The ground floor, as created in 1937, was dark and cramped, and in 1967 all its science books had been moved to the basement of the Master's Lodgings. In the early 1990s the ground floor was converted into a light and airy Science Reading Room and stack, and the Librarian's office moved to the main entrance, while the statues of Lords Eldon and Stowell returned to the west end of the first

---

[9] Disabled access: *UCR* Vol. X no. 2 (1990), 23; Magpie Lane: *UCR* Vol. X no. 2 (1990), 24 and 46; Merton Street: *UCR* Vol. XIV no. 2 (2006), 122–3; Shelley: UC:FA11/4 (*passim*). In the autumn of 2007 work began on an extension to the kitchen and buttery, which will be the first new building on the College's central site since the Mitchell Building.

floor, in more or less exactly the same position (albeit several feet higher) that they had been placed in in 1861.[10]

Funding played a central role in College life in the 1980s and 1990s.[11] Even in the late 1970s the generous levels of governing funding of the universities were becoming more difficult to maintain, and, under the new government of Margaret Thatcher, it became clear that the value of government funding of higher education would be reduced. Whether or not this policy should be seen as an acceptance of the impossibility of funding higher education on the same scale as before, Oxford had to retrench, especially after 1981, when cuts in grants to the universities were imposed by the University Grants Committee (UGC). The greatest impact on the colleges was that they could no longer assume that vacant Fellowships would be filled. For example, when the philosopher John Mackie died in 1981, his CUF post was abolished, notwithstanding the College's great reputation in philosophy, which Mackie had helped nurture. A similar case was that of George Cawkwell, who through his scholarship and teaching had transformed the study of Greek History in the fourth century BC. Nevertheless it was clear even before he retired in 1987 that the university would not fund a successor, and so after 1987 the College's ancient historians had to be taught by a fellow of another college.

Students received less government aid than before. Between 1979 and 1986 the value of the student grant fell by 20 per cent, and in 1990 student loans were introduced. In 1998 tuition fees of £1,000 a year were introduced and maintenance grants abolished altogether. From 2006, universities could, if they wished, charge top-up fees of up to £3,000. At one point Robin Butler found himself intervening in his capacity as a member of the House of Lords, when in 2000 he persuaded the government to change its policy regarding student support, so that students would not be penalized by losing other grants if they had bursaries of more than £1,865. Students at the start of the new century would always start their post-university life several thousand pounds in debt, and the period from the late 1940s to the late 1980s may yet come to stand out as a unique time when university students received more state funding than at any other time before or since.[12] In the last decade, furthermore, the government's traditional practice of paying fees directly to colleges has ceased, giving it to the central university to distribute, thus giving the university more power over the colleges.

---

[10] Automation: *UCR* Vol. IX no. 4 (1988), 57; Science Library: UC:GB4/A1/17 fo. 63[r]; new ground floor: Park 1992.

[11] These matters are discussed more fully in Anderson 2006: 163–70, Brock 1994: 764–8, Soares 1999: 218–29 and 234–63, and, with regard to Cambridge, in Brooke 1993: 540–5, 553–5, and 561–6.

[12] Student grants: Adams 1996: 303; Lord Butler and bursaries: *UCR* Vol. XIII no. 1 (2001), 33; student loans and fees: Anderson 2006: 175–82.

Under these circumstances the College had to reconsider its attitudes towards fund-raising. American universities had a long tradition of nurturing their alumni, and instilling a culture of gift-giving, and Oxford now had to learn those ways. Arnold Goodman had advised against appealing to Old Members, claiming that University College had not had 'a special attraction for the rich'. However, the College was already exploring how to make its Old Members feel more involved: in 1980/1 a short-lived Univ. Society was created which arranged garden parties and other events. There were also occasional initiatives, such as when GEC endowed a series of Visiting Fellowships in the 1980s. It was not, however, until 1987—under, significantly, the Mastership of a former President of Yale—that the College began to raise money more systematically. A new College official called a 'Procurator' was created, a post first held by George Cawkwell, to oversee fund-raising. There was some apprehension: an Appeals Committee meeting in June 1987 observed that 'No College, to our knowledge, has endeavoured to set up a fund-raising organisation on the American pattern. The College must recognise that it may secure very little money in the early stages.'[13]

Nevertheless the Appeal began. The 1987 *University College Record* included the following warning:

One hundred and forty posts [within the university] will disappear permanently over the next five years. In addition, many more will be 'frozen', with no likelihood of any 'unfreezing' in the near future. All Oxford Colleges are being forced to look to their resources to defend their current teaching strengths and practices, not least the tutorial system.[14]

The Univ. Old Members' Trust was established in 1988 to raise money for College-related projects. It is administered by a Board of Trustees, independent of the College, almost all of whom are Old Members, with up to three Fellows. By November 1988 almost one-fifth of Old Members had responded to this first Appeal. Kingman Brewster himself led the way by persuading an old friend to endow two Fitzgerald Scholarships, equivalent in value to Rhodes Scholarships, and open to students at the US Naval Academy at Annapolis, whose holders were sent in strict annual rotation to University, Brasenose, and Christ Church.[15]

In the mid-1990s the College engaged a full-time Appeals Director. The aim was to use the College's 750th anniversary to appeal to endow nine existing Fellowships in order to secure their future continuation. The result was a great success: the 750th anniversary appeal raised almost £10,000,000, and about a quarter of the College's Old Members gave to it. Among the

---

[13] Goodman 1993: 435; Univ. Society: *UCR* Vol. VIII no. 2 (1981), 92–3; GEC Fellowships: *UCR* Vol. IX no. 2 (1986), 20.

[14] *UCR* Vol. IX no. 3 (1987), 1.

[15] Interview with Brian Loughman (who administered the scheme), 18 December 2006.

Fellowships thus created were an A. D. M. Cox Fellowship in Medieval History and a George Cawkwell Fellowship in Ancient History. At first the latter Fellowship's endowment could only support holders for a term of five years, but in 2005 it became possible to make the Fellowship permanent once again. Furthermore, after tutorial fees were imposed, a fund was created for undergraduate and graduate bursaries, and the College became among the first in Oxford to offer significant support to students in financial need.[16]

Special initiatives were created through the interests of particular donors. Several members of the Swire family, which has extensive business interests in the Far East, had attended University College, and in 1990 a set of Swire Scholarships was created, in order to give undergraduates from Hong Kong the chance to study in University College.[17]

Such benefactions were no real innovation: today's fund-raisers are the spiritual heirs of John Martyn, Thomas Walker, and Obadiah Walker. Just as early College Fellowships were named after benefactors like Henry Percy or Simon Bennet, or in memory of great men like Lord Stowell, so modern Fellowships and Scholarships are similarly named. Techniques might have changed—while Fellows of the 1660s could only use pen and ink, the first telephone appeal, or 'telethon', to Old Members was held in January 1999—but the aims were identical, and the results just as successful.[18]

Certain trends observed in the last chapter continued to develop, not least in the nature of the Fellowship. At last it became generally accepted that Fellows had a family life, and ever fewer Fellows lived in. For a while some married Fellows had lived, if not within College, then nearby in a College house, and other Fellows who did live in might have a place to which they could retreat at weekends, but this ceased to be the case. Dinner changed its function, becoming more of a special occasion, often when one brought in a guest, rather than something one did as a matter of course. A recent survey of Fellows at several colleges found that they devoted less time to college life, both because of family life, and because fewer of them could live near their colleges, thanks to the huge increase in Oxford's property prices. Some feared that not all Fellows were willing to take their turn at assuming college duties.[19]

Meanwhile, as Robin Butler himself observed, 'the paradox is that the Government's contribution to Oxford's budget in recent years has been declining and yet the degree of control has increased and is increasing'.[20] In

---

[16] 1999 Appeal: *UCR* Vol. XI no. 4 (1996), 36–7, *UCR* Vol. XII no. 1 (1997), 30–2; money raised: *UCR* Vol. XII no. 3 (1999), 32–6 and *UCR* Vol. XII no. 4 (2000), 26–7; student bursaries: *UCR* Vol. XII no. 1 (1997), 31; *UCR* Vol. XII no. 2 (1998), 37–8.

[17] *UCR* Vol. X no. 2 (1990), 9–10.

[18] The first telethon: *UCR* Vol. XII no. 3 (1999), 33; gift-giving elsewhere: Hopkins 2005: 442–3.

[19] Other colleges: Twigg 1987: 390 (Queens'), and Hopkins 2005: 439–42 (Trinity); survey: Tapper and Palfreyman 2000: 14–17.

[20] Butler 2003: 6. See too Anderson 2006: 170–5.

particular, questions have begun to be asked from on high about the quality and quantity of Fellows' published work. Since 1992, at regular intervals the government has carried out a Research Assessment Exercise (RAE) into exactly what research is being carried out in universities throughout the country. Almost inevitably research came to be more highly valued in these quarters than teaching, as academics were pressed into producing their quota of publications. Some might say that it is no bad thing to keep academics up to the mark; but a system which could write off a Freddie Wells as unproductive has perhaps gone from one extreme to the other.

With such novel pressures, to say nothing of the increasing complexity of employment legislation and financial administration, it was perhaps not surprising that another new development was the election of Fellows whose sole duties were administrative. After the Domestic Bursarship had been assumed by several Tutorial Fellows, the College once more elected a professional Domestic Bursar in 1986, who was later elected to a Fellowship. In the 1990s, the Tutorial Fellow acting as Senior Tutor found herself working about seventy hours a week on all her various duties in return for just a three-hour reduction in teaching, a situation which was unsustainable. Several Cambridge colleges had been employing professional Senior Tutors, and in 2000 University College became the first Oxford one to do the same, appointing Clare Drury, a former Senior Tutor of Newnham College. Drury proved a happy choice, and her premature death in 2004 was a great loss to the College. Likewise, when Gordon Screaton retired as mathematics Fellow and Estates Bursar in 2001, he too was succeeded by a professional. Screaton handed on a College in a more than respectable financial state: a survey of Oxford published in 2000 reckoned what had been one of the poorest colleges in Oxford, was now one of the financial 'big boys' [sic].[21]

University College was not unique in this professionalization: at Trinity College, for example, the posts of Domestic and Estates Bursar and of Senior Tutor went to full-time professionals in 1987, 1997, and 2001 respectively, and Magdalen College, having had professional Home and Senior Bursars for much longer than University College, appointed its first professional Senior Tutor not long after Trinity. Furthermore it would be unthinkable now for a college not to employ a qualified accountant or professional librarian, and many colleges even took the step of employing a professional archivist. In short, the tradition whereby Fellows were expected to try their hand at any college office collided with a world which demanded ever greater specialization, with consequences which only later generations will be able to assess.[22]

[21] Senior Tutorship: interview with Helen Cooper, 7 September 2004, and *UCR* Vol. XII no. 4 (2000), 3–4; Clare Drury: *UCR* Vol. XIV no. 1 (2005), 32–7; Estates Bursarship: *UCR* Vol. XIII no. 1 (2001), 2; Screaton as Bursar: *UCR* Vol. XIII no. 1 (2001), 12–14; the College's finances: Tapper and Palfreyman 2000: 156.
[22] This phenomenon is discussed in more detail in Hopkins 2005: 443–51.

Among the College's students, a significant change occurred in 1985, when in an attempt to give maintained-school applicants a fairer chance, undergraduates could only apply before, rather than after, A-levels, and Scholarships and Exhibitions were awarded only at the end of the first year.[23] Once they came up, the most popular subjects among undergraduates after 1979 continued to be chemistry, history, law, and PPE, with classics, English, mathematics, modern languages, and physics following. The proportion of scientists continued to grow. In 1983 not quite 40 per cent of the College's undergraduates were reading a science subject, roughly in keeping with the rest of the university; by 2006 almost half of them were. There were also new subjects. Some were merely existing subjects combined in new ways; but others, such as computing science, whether combined with mathematics or engineering, were completely new. The College responded to this development when in 1983 it became the first College in Oxford to elect a Fellow in computing science.[24]

The proportion of the College's undergraduates educated abroad remained small, but the proportion of postgraduates who had attended foreign universities grew considerably. In 1973 one-third of them came from abroad; this proportion had risen to two-fifths by 1995; and after 2000 foreign students came to make up almost half the membership of the WCR. Just as in earlier years, North America provided the most students, with Australasia as runner-up. However, the political changes of the 1990s had an impact, as postgraduates arrived from Russia, other former members of the Warsaw Pact, and even China. On the other hand, whereas between one-quarter and one-third of postgraduates of the 1980s and 1990s had done their undergraduate degrees at University College, by the early twenty-first century such students made up only about 5 per cent of the total. Students were evidently more receptive to the idea of trying somewhere new for their second degree.[25]

Postgraduates assumed a more prominent role in College life. For most of the 1980s and 1990s, they constituted between one-quarter and one-third of the student population of University College, and by 2006 that proportion had settled at one-third. This development was common throughout Oxford, as the university determined to create more postgraduate places, though this left less room for undergraduates.[26]

---

[23] Brock 1994: 754–5 and Tapper and Palfreyman 2000: 82–3.
[24] Figures taken from Tutorial lists; scientists elsewhere in Oxford: Soares 1999: 281; first Fellow in computing science: *UCR* Vol. VIII no. 4 (1983), 236.
[25] Information from Tutorial lists.
[26] Compare Davies and Garnett 1994: 142.

Certain trends were common to all students, however, including attitudes towards dining. In 1981 the College began to offer two types of dinner, a self-service cafeteria meal and a traditional Hall, and the buttery was converted into a self-service area. Students have increasingly turned away from formal dinners, to cafeteria-style meals, or cooking for themselves. It was eventually even decided to remove a room from each floor in Stavertonia to create a larger space for cooking and eating. Just as with the Fellows, Formal Hall came to be seen not so much as a meal attended as a matter of course, than as one reserved for special occasions. An occasion which had changed its nature—and, indeed the very time at which it took place—was metamorphosing once again to suit the needs of the College's current members.[27]

This continuous remoulding of College custom is seen elsewhere. Once upon a time new undergraduates simply turned up on the Thursday before term started, and were given a few short talks in the Hall before the business of meeting one's tutors and getting down to work. This did not always make for an easy transition for students who had never lived away from home before, and in 1993, for the first time, a week of timetabled activities was created for freshers. College societies and clubs continue to come and go—and return. Even the Shakespeare Society and the Martlets died in the mid-1990s, before being revived in 2001.[28] Under the auspices of Robin and Jill Butler, the 'new' Martlets took on a different role, as a society offering postgraduates in any discipline the chance to deliver a paper about their research to an interested non-specialist audience. This might seem a long way from a Victorian literary society, but the basic ethos of students reading out papers in a congenial atmosphere has survived.

The last quarter of the twentieth century did see some continuity. Bill Warren, Head Porter in 1984–2002, was as significant a figure in the lives of the students he knew as either of his predecessors, and Bill Sykes, Fellow and Chaplain in 1978–2005, showed himself the spiritual heir of Hubert Burge and Giles Alington in his pastoral duties. Sykes's role extended far beyond Chapel services. He created a system of reflection groups, open to all members of the College, irrespective of belief or lack of it, which afforded much-appreciated quiet time in busy lives.[29]

To look at the later careers of the College's recent Old Members is to encounter a world of such diversity that a neat summing-up is well nigh impossible, as can be seen in an examination of the 'News from Old Mem-

---

[27] Cafeteria meal: *UCR* Vol. VIII no. 2 (1981), 112–13. At Corpus Christi College Formal Hall was abolished in 1982, but then reintroduced later in the decade for two days a week by popular demand of the students (Harrison 1994a: 419–20, 459–60, and 479–80).

[28] *UCR* Vol. XIII no. 1 (2001), 4.

[29] Sykes's reflection groups were based on the use of anthologies on given subjects for meditation which he published between 1986 and 2002. Snow 1991: 114–19 is very perceptive on College staff in the 1990s.

bers' sections in the most recent issues of the *University College Record*. Old Members are scattered throughout the world. They are represented in all the traditional professions of the law, the church, teaching, and medicine. One, Festus Mogae (m. 1965), was President of Botswana in 1998–2008;[30] four of them were returned as MPs in the British General Election of 2005. There are academics of course, including several present or former heads of other Oxford colleges; there are journalists; there are diplomats; there are businessmen in all areas; there are novelists, poets, and playwrights; there are architects and classical and pop musicians. Some Old Members have become famous in their field; others are known just to a few.

Meanwhile the College and university which they knew is once again changing, and it is no easier for someone writing in 2007 to know what the future will bring than it would have been for someone writing in the immediate aftermath of the great Commissions of the 1850s. A century and half ago, neither the worst fears of the pessimists nor the keenest hopes of the modernists quite came to pass. The fact that one of the most interesting recent examinations of Oxford can use the word 'decline' in its title is significant, and yet its authors can also observe:

If collegiality as commensality for dons has been weakened, that process of change may at the same time have had a positive benefit in liberating dons from collegiality as a cloyingly complacent and conservative clubbability.[31]

University College in the early twenty-first century is analogous to a car which has had every part replaced. It is certainly not the College envisaged by William of Durham, so much has it changed in the last seven and a half centuries. It would indeed be hard for College members from most succeeding centuries to detect an institution which they completely recognize. Yet the College has preserved a continuous succession of Fellows, even in such turbulent times as the Civil War or the First World War. Throughout that time its members have responded similarly to the institution, ranging from dislike by way of indifference to affection. Each era has had personalities to dominate the College, and to give it a particular style. Above all the College has continued to offer scholars the opportunity and place to study and teach. One hopes that William of Durham, a scholar and teacher himself, would appreciate that this central aspect of his bequest in Rouen still remains. It is for the next generations of Fellows, students, and staff of University College to take that inheritance into the next century.

---

[30] President Mogae is the third Old Member of University College to be head of an African state, the others being Edgar Whitehead (m. 1923), Prime Minister of Southern Rhodesia, 1958–62, and Kofi Busia (m. 1939), Prime Minister of Ghana, 1969–72.
[31] Tapper and Palfreyman 2000: 70.

Appendix I
Masters of University College to 2007

The list of Masters does not become complete until the 1390s; before that date only a few people are specifically identified as Master of the College.

Hugh de Warknetheby possibly Master 1307
William de Nadale possibly Master 1332
Robert de Patrington possibly Master 1340–3
Roger de Aswardeby fl. 1353–62
William Kexby fl. 1376–9
John Middelton possibly Master early 1390s
Thomas Foston 1393–6
Thomas Duffield 1396–8
Edmund Lacy 1398–c.1401
John Appleton c.1401–08
John Castell c.1408–20
Robert Burton 1420–3/4
Richard Witton 1423/4–8
Thomas Benwell 1428–41
John Martyn 1441–73
William Gregford 1473–1487 or 1488
John Roxborough 1487 or 1488–1509
Ralph Hamsterley 1509–18
Leonard Hutchinson 1518–46
John Crayford 1546–7
Richard Salveyn 1547–51
George Ellison 1551–7
Anthony Salveyn 1557–8
James Dugdale 1558–61
Thomas Caius 1561–72
William James 1572–84
Anthony Gate 1584–97
George Abbot 1597–1610
John Bancroft 1610–32

Thomas Walker 1632–48 & 1660–5
Joshua Hoyle 1648–54
Francis Johnson 1655–60
Richard Clayton 1665–76
Obadiah Walker 1676–89
Edward Farrar 1689–91
Thomas Bennet 1691–2
Arthur Charlett 1692–1722
Thomas Cockman 1722–45
[William Denison 1722–9]
John Browne 1745–64
Nathan Wetherell 1764–1807
James Griffith 1808–21
George Rowley 1821–36
Frederic Charles Plumptre 1836–70
George Granville Bradley 1870–81
James Franck Bright 1881–1906
Reginald Walter Macan 1906–23
Sir Michael Ernest Sadler 1923–34
Arthur Blackburne Poynton 1935–7
William Henry Beveridge, Baron Beveridge of Tuggall 1937–45
John Herbert Severn Wild 1945–51
Arthur Lehmann Goodhart 1951–63
John Primatt Redcliffe Maud, Lord Redcliffe-Maud 1963–76
Arnold Abraham Goodman, Lord Goodman 1976–86
Kingman Brewster 1986–8
Wyndham John Albery 1989–97
Frederick Edward Robin Butler, Lord Butler of Brockwell 1998–

In August 2008 Lord Butler will be succeeded as Master by Sir Ivor Martin Crewe.

Appendix II
Fellows of University College to 2007

This is a list of Fellows of the College who have a place and a vote on its Governing Body. After 1945, therefore, it omits Junior Research Fellows and Special Supernumerary Fellows. Fellows are listed in order of seniority as given in successive issues of the *University College Record*, but the dates given are when they were actually admitted to the Governing Body, hence one or two anomalies below. Some Fellows, like Harold Wilson, served as Junior Research Fellows before being elected Fellows; but they appear in this list at the moment when they were admitted actual Fellows.

This list does not include the Radcliffe Travelling Fellows, both on account of their anomalous status within the College, and because they are listed to 1990 in I. Guest, *Dr. John Radcliffe and his Trust* (London, 1991), 493–6. A list of Stowell Law Fellows to 1918, however, is given at the end of this appendix.

Exact dates of Fellows' tenures cannot be determined before the early sixteenth century. Before that date, 'there' signifies the dates at which someone is known to have been a Fellow of the College. Dates of tenure are also uncertain in the late 1640s and early 1650s. (M) signifies that a Fellow became Master; (C) that a Fellow rented rooms in the College before or after his Fellowship; and (U) that a Fellow had been an undergraduate or postgraduate of the College.

Thomas de Clifford (possibly a commoner?) there in 1299
Hugh de Warknetheby there 1307–10
Roger de Bruges there 1307
Robert de Kigheley there 1307
Adam de Burleye there 1307–11
John Lokington there 1307–1311
Hugh of St Ives possibly there 1311
William de Nadale there 1332
William de Cundale there 1332–40
Robert de Patrington probably there 1332, possibly Master 1340–aft.1343
John de Poklyngton there 1340 (possibly even there 1336)
William de Polmorva there 1340
Richard de Radford there 1340, and again 1343
Robert de Scroton there July 1340
John de Suttone there July 1340
William de Peggeworth prob. there 1343; still there 1346
Adam de Pothow prob. there 1343; still there in 1346
Armand de Elstanwyke there 1346–8
John de Whixlay there 1348
Laurence Radford there 1349–61
Roger de Aswardeby there 1350–3 (M)
Robert de Elwyke there 1350–1
Peter de Curraf there 1356–63
Henry Hopton there 1356–61
William de Wilton there 1360–1
William de Trevelles possibly there 1360
William de Wymondham possibly there 1369

APPENDIX II: FELLOWS OF UNIVERSITY COLLEGE 531

William Kexby there 1374–8 (M)
Thomas Furneys before 1381
John Middelton there 1381/2–1388/9
Robert Gower there 1381–1392
John de Poklyngton there 1381–8
John Taylor there 1382–1385/6 (C)
John Alkebarow there 1383–90
Richard Gysborne there 1383–4
Richard Hethe there 1389–91
Thomas Foston there 1391/2–1393 (M) (C)
Thomas Heth there 1391–1404
Edmund Lacy there 1391–1396/7 (M) (C)
John Marshall there 1391 (C)
Thomas Nafferton probably there 1396 (C)
John Appleton there 1399–c.1401 (M) (C)
John Fayt there 1399–1401/2
Adam Redyford there 1406/7–1421
Robert Burton there 1406/7–1420 (M) (C)
John Ryvell there 1407/8–1414/5 and possibly 1420
John Hamerton there 1408/9–1419/20
John Castell there 1410–1411 (M)
John Elwyk there 1420/1–1438/9
Thomas Benwell there 1421/2–1428 (M) (C)
Thomas Butler there 1421/2–1430/1 (C)
William Prentys there 1421/2–1430
Richard Witton there 1421–1423/4 (M)
Thomas Hunter there 1422/3–1427 (C)
John Alnwyk there 1426/7–1427/8
John Martyn there 1427/8–1441 (M)
John Goldsmyth there 1430–1436/7
William Sharpe there 1433/4–1444/5
William Asplyon there 1439/40–1443
Alexander Surtays there 1439–41
William Castell there 1443/4–1445/6
Robert Hartilpole there 1444/5–1462/3
Gilbert Haydok there 1444/5–1446/7 (C)
William Dalton there 1444/5–1445/6
Thomas Pray there 1444/5–1452/3 (C)
John Davyson there 1452/3–1455

Henry Strother there 1452/3–1460
William Gregford there 1453/4–1474 (M)
John Hulle there 1453/4–1468
Richard Marshall there 1453/4–1474/5; apparently back again 1479/80–1480/1
John Mercer there 1453/4–1454/5
James Baynbridge there 1454/5–1463/4
John Watson there 1456/7–1460/1
Thomas Thurlby there 1463/4–1468/9 (C)
——Mulcaster there 1463/4–1470/1
Robert Middelham there 1465/6–1476/7
Christopher Almgyll there 1466/7–1467/8
Richard Witton there 1467/8–1478/9
John Hyton there 1468/9–1470/1
Simon Baxter there 1468/9–1476
Alan Hyndmersh there 1468/9–1474/5
William Snayth there 1474/5–1477/8
Robert More there 1475/6–1477 (C)
William Hall there 1477/8–1485
Richard Blenkynsop there 1478/9–1481/2
William Gilyot there 1478/9–1489
John Roxborough there 1478/9–1488 (M)
John Surdevall there 1481/2–1493
Richard Hyndmersh there 1484/5–1493/4
Christopher Forster there 1483/4–1491/2
William Danby there 1484/5–1496/7
Nicholas Minskype there 1484/5–1485/6
Edward Underwode there 1484/5–1491
Thomas Cramer there 1489/90–1495
Robert Benson there 1493/4–1495
John Lethom there 1493/4–1506/7
John Scott there 1493/4–1500/1
Robert Marshall there 1493/4–1502
Edward Carr there 1501/2–1504/5 (C)
——Hardying there 1504/5
John Barnaby there 1504/5–1508/9 (C)
Edward Collyer there 1504/5–1509/10
William Thomson there 1506/7
Robert Style there 1506/7–1510/11
Thomas Makerell there 1508/9–1509/10
Peter Person there 1508/9–1510/11
John Claxton there 1509/10–1516/17
Thomas Thomson there 1509/10–1514

William Bydnall 1510–12
Peter Bentlay there 1510/11–1514/15
John Garth 1510–17
John Hobson 1511–26
John Newton 1511–12
John Hartborne (alias Alborne) 1511–13
John Falowfelde 1512–33
Richard Fetherstonehaugh there 1513/14–1514/15
Robert Harryson there 1513/14–1521/2
Leonard Hutchinson there 1514/15–1518 (M)
John Hastings there 1514/15–before 1532
Robert Squire there 1515/16–possibly 1521
'Master Peter' there 1515/16
William Cocke there 1517/8
Cuthbert Gryfin/Greveson there 1518–26
John Hutchinson 1518–42
John Crayford 1519–before 1526 (M)
John Walker 1521–34
John Wright 1524–30
George Hutchinson 1526–after 1530
Richard Salveyn 1526–47 (M)
Thomas Skewing/Skowringe 1527–?
Antony Frobisher 1527–after 1537
Antony Salveyn 1531–7 (M)
Richard Kee 1531–3
William Morwayn 1531–after 1535
Anthony Carre 1531–after 1539
Robert Dayle 1533–after 1535
Hugh Hogeson 1533–after 1535
Hugh Hutchinson 1537–after 1547
John Tyffynge 1537–after 1542
Thomas Pentland 1537–c. 1540
Paul Boswell 1539–43
Laurence Trolope 1539–44
Christopher Wilson 1540–?
George Ellison 1543–51 (M)
Edmund Thomson 1543–56
Christopher Richardson 1545–?
Ralph Cockeye 1545–after 1557
Christopher Greenwell 1545–57
James Dugdale 1547–58 (M)
Henry Brachinburye 1549–after 1552

William Rawson 1550–before 1560 (C)
Thomas Wilson 1551–7
Anthony Wright 1556–between 1561 and 1563
Robert Walbancke 1556–after 1567
Henry Stapper 1558–61
John Peacock 1558–?
John Best 1558–?
Robert Grenacres 1559–before 1569 (C)
Thomas Chewe 1559–c.1575 (C)
Thomas Portyngton 1559–61
Otho Hunt 1559–after 1566
William Pulleyn 1562–after 1573/4
Thomas Wright 1562–after 1570/1
Robert Dewhurst 1563–71 (C)
Robert Boite/Booth 1569–after 1573/4
Peter Medford 1569–after 1572/3
Robert Hagthorpe there 1569/70–1573/4
Richard Slatter there 1571–6 (U) (C)
Edward Ashton 1572–81 (C)
Giles Cartwright 1572–after 1578/9 (U) (C)
Richard Jennens 1573–85 (U)
Richard Waring 1573–82
John Browne 1575–1612
Thomas Hook 1575–85 (U)
Walter Wardropper 1575–86 (U)
Robert Kizby 1579–86 (U)
Philip Waterhouse 1579–after 1586/7 (U)
John Wigglesworth 1581–2 (U) (C)
Robert Batt 1584–97
Ralph Ironside 1584–90
Anthony Crowther 1585–after 1589/90
Richard Browne 1585–after 1597 (U)
John Waldridge 1586–after 1586/7 (U) (C)
Alexander Cooke 1587–97
John Smith 1587–after 1592/3
Cuthbert Clavering 1588–90
Hugh Watmough 1590–1600 (U) (C)
Gilbert Horseman 1590–after 1594/5 (U) (C)
John Brooke 1591–1604 (U) (C)
Henry Newman 1593–1600 (C)
Arthur Coldcoll 1597–1608 (U) (C)
Charles Greenwood 1597–1614 (U) (C)

APPENDIX II: FELLOWS OF UNIVERSITY COLLEGE 533

Lancelot Gryme 1597–1603 (U) (C)
James Harrison 1598–1616 (U)
Thomas Gates 1598–? (U?)
Jonas Radcliffe 1600–26 (U) (C)
Henry Tilson 1600–14
Jonas Rookes 1603–19
John Reyner 1604–13 (U)
John Wilson 1608–after 1617 (U)
John Batty 1609–13 (U)
Robert Dickson 1612–34 (U)
Francis Allott 1613–14
Thomas Radcliffe 1613–48 & 1660 (U)
Philip Washington 1614–35 (U)
Francis Hilton 1614–after 1615/6 (U)
Michael Thomson 1614–after 1623/4 (U)
William Nutter 1616–29 (U)
Laurence Farrington 1619–after 1623/4
John Elmhirst 1621–51 (U)
Thomas Hooke 1624–33 (U)
Richard Washington 1626–40 & 1644–51 (U)
Matthew Wentworth 1626–35 (U)
Richard Clayton 1629–39 (U) (M)
Abraham Woodhead 1631–48 & 1660–78 (U)
John Dighton 1633–44 (U)
Henry Watkins 1635–48 (U)
Obadiah Walker 1635–48 & 1660–76 (U) (M)
Francis Rockley 1639–47 (U)
William Richardson 1641–51 (U)
Ezreel Tonge 1648–c.1652 (U)
William Woodward 1648–50 (U)
George Gale 1648–1655
—— Roc/Rock there 1649/50
John Wakeley 1648–50
Robert Norton 1648–65 (U)
Ezra Price 1649–58
Richard Bures 1649–after 1654 (U)
Thomas Jones 1649–58
Robert Hampson 1649–after 1653
Ambrose Bennet 1649–before 1658
John Brickenden c.1650–2 (U)
Thomas Jennings 1650–c.1655
Sampson Fyton 1650–60
Edward Terry 1650–60

Anthony Fidoe 1650–8
Thomas Thornton 1651–6
William Offley 1651–9
Edward Farrar 1651–89 (M)
Matthew Bee 1651–before 1656 (U)
Thomas Cupper 1652–60 (U)
Edward Anderson 1655–61
Richard Griffith 1655–65
William Squire 1655–61
Marmaduke Lambert 1657–60 (U)
Thomas Clent 1658–64 (U)
Thomas Harley 1658–60
Edward Burlton 1658–66 (U)
Timothy Nourse 1659–74 (U)
William Shippen 1659–68 (U)
Henry Warren 1660–4 (U)
Henry Thomas 1660–73 (U)
John Armitage 1660–75 (U)
Richard Lowther 1661–6
Samuel Jemmatt 1661–6 (U)
Abraham Crowther 1665–76 (U)
George Elcock 1665–71 (U)
Thomas Laurence 1666–75
William Pindar 1669–78 (U)
John Savile 1669–72 (U)
Joseph Lodge 1669–86 (U)
Michael Bingley 1672–84 (U)
John Ledgeard 1672–83 (U)
John Giles 1673–91 (U)
Nathaniel Boyse 1674–89 (U)
William Smith 1675–1705 (U)
Edmund Marshall 1675–84 (U)
John Wickham 1676–85 (U)
John Naylor 1676–1704 (U)
Thomas Bateman 1678–90 (U)
Hugh Todd 1678–1700
Edward Hinchliffe 1683–6 (U)
Thomas Bennet 1684–9 (U) (M)
Thomas Deane 1684–9 (U)
John Hudson 1686–1711
Francis Forster 1686–95
John Hinckley 1689–1701 (U)
Albermarle Bertie 1689–1721 (U)
John Siser 1689–98 (U)
Joseph Bingham 1689–95 (U)
John Boraston 1689–1741 (U)

Richard Farrer 1690–5 (U)
Thomas Allen 1692–1711 (U)
John Nevile 1695–1708 (U)
William Elstob 1696–1704
Robert Clavering 1697–1713
William Denison 1698–1729 (U)
Thomas Cockman 1700–13 (U) (M)
William Greenwood 1700–7 (U)
Samuel Lindsey 1704–29 (U)
Cavendish Nevile 1705–29 (U)
John Hodgson 1706–21 (U)
Benjamin Baynes 1708–22 (U)
George Ward 1708–33 (U)
John Burman 1711–16 (U)
John Browne 1711–39 (U) (M)
William Standfast 1713–22 (U)
Francis Rogers 1713–38 (U)
Thomas Cockerill 1716–29 (U)
Francis Taylor 1721–49 (U)
Robert Eden 1721–40
Thomas Heather 1722–9 (U)
James Scott 1722–34 (U)
Francis Walwyn 1729–45 (U)
John Marshall 1729–57 (U)
Thomas Kay 1729–37 (U)
Robert Swinburn 1729–49
Henry Tennant 1729–66 (U)
Thomas Collins 1733–8 (U)
John Aynsley 1735–44 (U)
Thomas Nelson 1737–60 (U)
John Shepard 1738–61 (U)
Thomas Forster 1739–60
Joseph Wood 1739–77 (U)
Henry Hobson 1740–77
Joseph Betts 1741–65 (U)
John Coulson 1744–80
Thomas Brome 1745–7 (U)
George Watson 1747–54 (U)
John Morton 1749–52 (U)
Nathan Wetherell 1750–64 (M)
John Cockerill 1752–66 (U)
John Alleyne 1754–80 (U)
Samuel Horne 1757–69 (U)
Seth Pollard 1760–7 (U)
John Rotheram 1760–7
Robert Chambers 1761–75

William Scott 1764–82
Samuel Swire 1766–88 (U)
William Jones 1766–83 (U)
George Strahan 1767–73 (U)
John Scott 1767–73 (U)
Robert Dale 1768–72
Philip Fisher 1770–88 (U)
George Croft 1772–80 (U)
Richard Lane 1773–7 (U)
Henry Utrick Reay 1774–86 (U)
Henry Ridley 1775–82 (U)
William Coates 1777–82 (U)
Robert Clarke 1777–82
William Couture 1777–90 (U)
Thomas Plumer 1780–94 (U)
Matthew Surtees 1780–94 (U)
Francis Simpson 1781–98 (U)
Robert Fenwick 1782–90 (U)
Edward Davison 1782–5
James Griffith 1782–1808 (M)
John Francis Allen 1783–1806 (U)
Jonathan Parker Fisher 1783–1806 (U)
William Ettrick 1785–1801 (U)
Hugh Moises 1786–1813 (U)
Nathan Croke Wetherell 1788–1840 (U)
Richard Heslop 1788–1809 (U)
William Hooper 1790–1805 (U)
Charles Fielding Ward 1790–9 (U)
George Shepherd 1794–1809 (U)
Robert Bates 1794–6
William Burrell 1796–9 (U)
Samuel Swire 1798–9 (U)
John Watson Askew 1799–1810 (U)
Henry Burrell 1799–1814 (U)
James Barmby 1799–1817 (U)
Charles Thorp 1801–8 (U)
Edward West 1805–23 (U)
Eardley Norton 1806–10 (U)
George Rowley 1807–21 (U) (M)
John Stapylton 1808–35 (U)
Edward Davison 1809–17
Matthew Rolleston 1809–17 (U)
William Crabtree 1809–21 (U)
Thomas Dawson Allen 1811–28 (U)
Nathaniel Clayton 1811–33 (U)
Charles John Ridley 1813–54 (U)

APPENDIX II: FELLOWS OF UNIVERSITY COLLEGE

George Francis Grey 1814–53 (U)
Frederick Charles Plumptre 1817–36 (U) (M)
Charles Carr 1817–25 (U)
John Watts 1817–29 (U)
William Glaister 1821–38 (U)
James Charnock 1821–46
James Rust 1823–30 (U)
Charles Hotham 1825–38 (U)
Edmund Hammond 1828–47 (U)
Peter Hansell 1829–36 (U)
Travers Twiss 1830–63 (U)
William Boyd 1833–6 (U)
Piers Calveley Claughton 1836–46
William Fishburn Donkin 1836–43 (U)
John William Wing 1837–44 (U)
Frederick William Faber 1837–44 (U)
Arthur Penrhyn Stanley 1838–51
Thomas Shadforth 1839–52 (U)
John Woolley 1840–3 (U)
Henry Ellison 1843–53 (U)
Joseph Cox Algar 1843–8 (U)
William Hedley 1844–63
George Granville Bradley 1844–50 (U) (M)
William Bright 1847–69 (U)
John Conington 1847–55 (U)
John Henry Slessor 1847–62 (U)
Thomas Valpy French 1848–53 (U)
Goldwin Smith 1850–68
William Basil Tickell Jones 1851–7
Peter Goldsmith Medd 1852–77 (U)
Charles Musgrave Bull 1853–66 (U)
Francis John Headlam 1854–74 (U)
Charles Stewart Parker 1854–69 (U)
Horace Davey 1856–64 (U)
Charles Joseph Faulkner 1856–92
Charles John Abbey 1862–6
Alan Becher Webb 1863–8
Albert Sidney Chavasse 1864–1902
Charles Septimus Medd 1864–74 (U)
James Lee-Warner 1866–72 (U)
Francis Allston Channing 1866–70
James Albert Owen 1868–71
Sydney William Skeffington 1869–1917
Charles Comyns Tucker 1869–80 (U)

Charles Alan Fyffe 1870–92
Bernard Bosanquet 1870–84
Ernest John Payne 1872–1904
Arthur Dendy 1873–1900
James Franck Bright 1874–81 (U) (M)
Frank Hesketh Peters 1874–1900
Samuel Henry Butcher 1876–82
Lazarus Fletcher 1877–80
Frederick Cornwallis Conybeare 1880–7 (U)
Joseph Thomas Cunningham 1882–9
William Gunnion Rutherford 1883
Lewis Amherst Selby-Bigge 1883–94
John Thomas Augustus Haines 1883–90
Reginald Walter Macan 1884–1906 (U) (M)
Hubert Murray Burge 1890–1900 (U)
Alexander James Carlyle 1893–5
Arthur Blackburne Poynton 1894–1935 (M)
Vernon Faithfull Storr 1895–9 & 1905–13
Edgar Frederic Carritt 1898–1945
Arthur Spencer Loat Farquharson 1899–1942 (U)
James Hamilton Francis Peile 1900–7
William Johnson Sollas 1901–36
Reginald John Elliott Tiddy 1902–5 (U)
Ernest William Ainley Walker 1903–38
Arthur Hugh Sidgwick 1905–12
George Hope Stevenson 1906–49
Richard Godfrey Parsons 1907–11
Kenneth King Munsie Leys 1908–42
Cuthbert Leyland Parker 1912–17
Robert Benedict Bourdillon 1913–23
Francis Paul Walters 1913–20 (U)
Cyril William Emmet 1920–3
Carleton Kemp Allen 1920–31 & 1940–62
David Lindsey Keir 1921–39
Edmund John Bowen 1922–65
Laurence William Grensted 1924–30 (U)
George Douglas Howard Cole 1925–44
Walter Ashburner 1926–9
Arthur Duncan Gardner 1927–48 (U)
John Primatt Redcliffe Maud 1929–39 (M)
Archibald Hunter Campbell 1930–5 (U)
Arthur Lehman Goodhart 1931–51 (M)

APPENDIX II: FELLOWS OF UNIVERSITY COLLEGE

John Herbert Severn Wild 1933–45 (M)
Arthur Frederick Wells 1935–66
Richard William Gilbert Holdsworth 1936–42
James Archibald Douglas 1937–50
Robert Henry Stewart Thompson 1938–47
Kenneth Clinton Wheare 1939–44
Anthony David Machell Cox 1939–80
James Harold Wilson 1944–5
Giles Alington 1944–56
George Andrew Paul 1945–62
George Hugh Nicholas Seton-Watson 1946–51
Norman Stayner Marsh 1946–60
Thomas Wilson 1946–58
Homer Hasenpflug Dubs 1947–59
Daniel John Chapman Cunningham 1947–87
John Wintour Baldwin Barns 1948–53
Peter Charles Bayley 1948–72 (U)
Peter Frederick Strawson 1948–68
George Law Cawkwell 1949–87
Lawrence Rickard Wager 1950–65
Herbert Lionel Adolphus Hart 1952–73
Thomas Maynard Parker 1952–73
Robert Berman 1955–83
Anthony Gordon Guest 1955–65
Maurice Shock 1956–77
Anthony Edward Firth 1957–76 (U)
David Hawkes 1959–71
David Ker Stout 1959–76
John Denis Egbert Campbell 1959–78
Leonard Hubert Hoffmann 1961–73
Gordon Robert Screaton 1962–2001
Alexander Chalmers MacIntyre 1962–6
Wyndham John Albery 1963–78 (M)
Martin Litchfield West 1963–74
Arthur Colin Day 1964–89
John Lister Illingworth Fennell 1964–7
John Clifton Taylor 1964–80
Kenneth Stuart Sandford 1965–7 (U)
Robert Percy Beckinsale 1965–75
Michael David Yudkin 1965–93
Jeffrey Alan Gray 1965–83
Brian Michael Barry 1965–6

Sir Peter William Gretton 1965–79
John Edward Allen 1965–96
John Mitchell Finnis (U) 1966–
John Henry McDowell 1966–86
David Ewart Albert Vincent 1967–86
John Leslie Mackie 1967–81
David William Soskice 1967–90
Anthony Derek Stokes 1967–87
Anthony Frederick Orchard 1967–2005
James Julian Bennet Jack 1968–2003
David John Burgess 1969–78
Derek Norton Stacey 1969–87
Michael Gareth Justin Evans 1969–80 (U)
Ronald Myles Dworkin 1969–98
Michael John Collins 1970–
John David Bell 1970–2000
Brian Crayford Loughman 1970–92
Leslie George Mitchell 1971–2001
Piet van der Loon 1972–87
Roy Park 1972–96
Azriel Adrian Sorin Zuckerman 1973–
Martin Hubie Matthews 1973–
Anthony Cuthbert Baines 1975–80
Christopher Brendan Reginald Pelling 1975–2003
Norman Henry March 1977–94
Nicholas Francis Robert Crafts 1977–87
Hartmut Johann Otto Pogge von Strandmann 1977–2005
Iain Sinclair McLean 1978–91
Robert Kemeys Thomas 1978–
Elizabeth Helen Cooper 1978–2004
William George David Sykes 1978–2005
David Dew-Hughes 1979–2000
Roy Butler 1980–4
Alexander Murray 1980–2001
Mark Joseph Smith 1980–
David Robert Priestley Wiggins 1981–9
John Nicholas Pepys Rawlins 1981– (U)
Robin John Nicholas 1982–
Andrew William Roscoe 1983– (U)
Patrick Edmund George Baird 1984– (U)
Kevin Andrew Charles Martin 1985–95
John Feather Wheater 1985–
John Frederick Dewey 1986–2000
Raj Bhikhu Pareck 1987–95 (U)

Michael Andrew Nicholson 1987–
Stephen John Golding 1987–
David Miller Clark 1988–2000
Timothy Williamson 1988–95
Vanessa Catherine Fry 1988–92
Kathryn Jane Wood 1989–94
Glen Dudbridge 1989–2005
Stephen James Gundle 1989–93
Keith Leonard Dorrington 1989–
Timothy William Child 1989–
Hyun Song Shin 1990–4
Christiane Sourvinou-Inwood 1990–5
Elizabeth Jane Crawford 1991–
John Hilary Smith 1991–4 (U)
Catherine Jane Pears 1992–
Ngaire Woods 1992–
Paul Leslie Burn 1992–2007
Peter James Wilson 1993–5
Philip Arthur Reay 1993–2000
Daniel James Parry Maldoom 1994–7
Mark Sheard Child 1994–2004
Rosina Pullman 1995–6
Mark Edward Newton 1996–9
Jonathan Anson Mee 1997–2007
Dorothy Edgington 1996–2001
Henrik Bindslev 1996–8
Mark Peter Taylor 1997–9
Ian Patrick Rumfitt 1998–2005
Teresa Jean Morgan 1998–2000
Stephen Collins 1998–
Lucio Sarno 1999–2000
Sujoy Mukerji 1999–
Monica del Carmen Serrano Carreto 1999–2001
John Blair Gardner 2001–
Gideon Mark Henderson 2000–
Gregor Irwin 2000–2
Andrew King 2000–1
Frances Clare Nineham Drury 2000–4
Barbara Kowalzig 2000–5
Philip Christopher England 2001–
Denis Peter Howell 2001–
Catherine Joy Holmes 2001–
Frank Nairn Marshall 2001–
Jotun John Hein 2001–
Gavin Robert Screaton 2001–4
Kathryn Jane Gleadle 2002–4
Katherine Doornik 2002–
Tania Jane Rawlinson 2002–3
Marc Stears 2003–
Peter Jezzard 2003–
Amanda Dickens 2003–4
William Robb Allan 2004–
Thomas Povey 2004–
Tarek Coury 2004–
Anne Knowland 2004–
Oliver Zimmer 2005–
Tiffany Paula Stern 2005–
Andrew Gregory 2005–
David Logan 2005–
Julie Maxton 2006–
Rahul Rao 2005–
Lisa Kallet 2007–
Benjamin Edward Jackson 2006–
Nicholas Yeung 2006– (U)
Michael Benedikt 2007–

STOWELL LAW FELLOWS

Stowell Law Fellowships were originally designed to last for seven years only, but in 1920 the ordinances were amended to made the Fellowships permanent.

George Tickell 1837–40
Stephen Charles Denison 1840–6
Goldwin Smith 1846–50 (later Fellow)
George Osborne Morgan 1850–8
Alfred Bailey 1858–65
Edgar Henry Lockhart 1865–8 (U)
Arthur Dendy 1868–73 (later Fellow)
Alfred Hopkinson 1873–80
John Davenport Rogers 1880–7
William Temple Franks 1888–95
Thomas Baty 1895–1902
William Henry Beveridge 1902–9 (M)
John Clifford Valentine Behan 1909–18

Appendix III
Members of University College in the *Oxford Dictionary of National Biography*

(M) signifies Master, (F) Fellow, (U) undergraduate, (MC) mature commoner, and (RF) Radcliffe Travelling Fellow. The descriptions alongside each name are those given in *ODNB*. Some of these entries are only available in the on-line version.

Abbot, George (1562–1633), Archbishop of Canterbury (M)
Acland, John Dyke (1747–78), army officer and politician (U)
Akers-Douglas, Aretas, first Viscount Chilston (1851–1926), politician (U)
Allen, Sir Carleton Kemp (1887–1966), jurist and Warden of Rhodes House (F)
Allen, (Herbert) Warner (1881–1968), journalist and writer (U)
Anderdon, William Henry (1816–90), Jesuit (U)
Annand, William (1633–89), Dean of Edinburgh (U)
Arbuthnot, John (1667–1735), physician and satirist (MC)
Arnold, Sir Edwin (1832–1904), poet and journalist (U)
Arnold, Thomas (1823–1900), literary scholar and teacher (U)
Arnold, William Thomas (1852–1904), journalist and author (U)
Arnold-Forster, Hugh Oakeley (1855–1909), politician and author (U)
Ashton, Thomas Gair, first Baron Ashton of Hyde (1855–1933), industrialist and politician (U)
Attlee, Clement Richard, first Earl Attlee (1883–1967), Prime Minister (U)

Bankes, Sir John Eldon (1854–1946), judge (U)
Bancroft, John (1574–1641), Bishop of Oxford (M)
Barnes, Leonard John (1895–1977), writer and campaigner against colonialism (U)
Barrett, Stephen (1719–1801), schoolmaster and Church of England clergyman (U)
Bathurst, Charles, first Viscount Bledisloe (1867–1958), agriculturist and politician (U)
Beaufort, Charles Noel Somerset, fourth Duke of (1709–56), politician (U)
Best, Henry Digby (1768–1836), Roman Catholic convert and author (U)
Beveridge, William Henry, Baron Beveridge (1879–1963), social reformer and economist (F) (M)
Beverley [Ingelberd], Philip (d. 1323×5), benefactor (gave land to College)
Bingham, Joseph (1668–1723), ecclesiastical historian (U) (F)
Blackett, Sir Basil Phillott (1882–1935), civil servant (U)

III: MEMBERS OF UNIVERSITY COLLEGE IN THE *ODNB* 539

Bosanquet, Bernard (1848–1923), philosopher and social theorist (F)
Bowen, Edmund John (1898–1980), chemist (F)
Bradley, Francis Herbert (1846–1924), philosopher (U)
Bradley, George Granville (1821–1903), Dean of Westminster and schoolmaster (U) (F) (M)
Brassey, Thomas, first Earl Brassey (1836–1918), politician (U)
Bree, Robert (1758–1839), physician (U)
Brereton, Joseph Lloyd (1822–1901), educational reformer (U)
Bright, James Franck (1832–1920), college head (U) (F) (M)
Bright, William (1824–1901), church historian (U) (F)
Brightman, Frank Edward (1856–1932), liturgical scholar (U)
Brinknell or Brynknell, Thomas *c.*1470–1539 (possible MC)
Broughton, Thomas (1712–77), Church of England clergyman (U)
Broxholme, Noel (1686–1748), physician (RF)
Budge, Sir Ernest Alfred Thompson Wallis (1857–1934), orientalist (incorporated 1898)
Bull, Hedley Norman (1932–85), university teacher (U)
Burge, Hubert Murray (1862–1925), Bishop of Oxford and headmaster (U) (F)
Burges [later Lamb], Sir James Bland, first baronet (1752–1824), politician and poet (U)
Burley, Adam (d. 1327/8), schoolman (F)
Burney, Charles (1726–1814), musician and author (took D.Mus. from University College)
Busia, Kofi Abrefa (1913–78), sociologist and politician (U)
Butcher, Samuel Henry (1850–1910), classical scholar (F)
Butler, Arthur Gray (1831–1909), headmaster (U)
Butler, John (1717–1802), Bishop of Hereford and pamphleteer (U)

Caius [Kay, Key], Thomas (*c.*1505–72), antiquary and college head (M)
Carlyle, Alexander James (1861–1943), historian and social reformer (F)
Carte, Thomas (1686–1754), historian (U)
Cartwright, Edmund (1743–1823), Church of England clergyman and inventor of a power loom (U)
Cecil, Edgar Algernon Robert Gascoyne- [known as Lord Robert Cecil], Viscount Cecil of Chelwood (1864–1958), politician and peace campaigner (U)
Cecil, Hugh Richard Heathcote Gascoyne-, Baron Quickswood (1869–1956), politician and educationist (U)
Cecil, James Edward Hubert Gascoyne-, fourth Marquess of Salisbury (1861–1947), politician and lay churchman (U)
Chambers, Humphrey (1599?–1662), Church of England clergyman (U)
Chambers, Sir Robert (1737–1803), jurist and judge (F)
Charlett, Arthur (1655–1722), college head (M)
Chedworth, John (d. 1471), Bishop of Lincoln (MC)
Christison, Sir (Alexander Frank) Philip, fourth baronet (1893–1993), army officer (U)
Christopherson, Sir Derman Guy (1915–2000), engineer and university administrator (U)
Church, Sir William Selby, first baronet (1837–1928), physician (U)
Claughton, Piers Calveley (1814–84), Bishop of Colombo (F)
Clavering, Robert (1675/6–1747), orientalist and Bishop of Peterborough (F)

Clay, Sir Henry (1883–1954), economist (U)
Clive, Sir Edward (1704–71), judge (U)
Cole, George Douglas Howard (1889–1959), university teacher and political theorist (F)
Collingwood, Robin George (1889–1943), philosopher and historian (U)
Collingwood, William Gershom (1854–1932), author, artist, and antiquary (U)
Conington, John (1825–69), classical scholar (U) (F)
Conybeare, Frederick Cornwallis (1856–1924), biblical and Armenian scholar (U) (F)
Cooke, Alexander (1564–1632), Church of England clergyman and religious controversialist (F)
Cooper, Edward Herbert (1867–1910), novelist (U)
Cooper, Thomas (1759–1839), political writer and college head (U)
Cornwallis, Sir Kinahan (1883–1959), diplomatist (U)
Courtney, William Leonard (1850–1928), philosopher and journalist (U)
Crawley, Richard (1840–93), translator and writer (U)
Croft, George (1747–1809), Church of England clergyman and religious writer (U) (F)
Croft, Sir Herbert, fifth baronet (1751–1816), writer and lexicographer (U)
Crump [Crumpe], Henry (fl. c.1376–1401), Cistercian monk and religious controversialist (MC)
Culpeper, Sir Thomas (1625/6–1697?) the younger, writer (U)
Cunliffe-Lister, Philip, first Earl of Swinton (1884–1972), politician (U)

Davey, Horace, Baron Davey (1833–1907), judge (U) (F)
Davison, Edward (1789–1863) Church of England clergyman (F)
Deane, Thomas (1651–1735), Roman Catholic convert (U) (F)
Deane [Dean], Thomas (b. 1686/7), musician (took D.Mus. from University College)
Denton, Nathan (1635–1720), clergyman and ejected minister (U)
Digges, Sir Dudley (1582/3–1639), politician and diplomat (U)
Digges, Dudley (1613–43), royalist political writer (U)
Digges, Leonard (1588–1635), poet and translator (U)
Diplock, (William John) Kenneth, Baron Diplock (1907–85) judge (U)
Dodd, Charles Harold (1884–1973), biblical scholar (U)
Dodds, Eric Robertson (1893–1979), classical scholar (U)
Donkin, William Fishburn (1814–69), astronomer and mathematician (U) (F)
Duckworth, Richard fl. 1695, campanologist (U)
Dundas, William (1762–1845), politician (U)
Dunnett, Sir (Ludovic) James [Ned] (1914–97), civil servant (U)
Durham, William of (d. 1249), theologian and university benefactor (Founder)
Dwarris, Sir Fortunatus William Lilley (1786–1860), lawyer and writer (U)

Ellerton, Edward (1771–1851), educational philanthropist (U)
Elstob, William (1674?–1715), Anglo-Saxon scholar and Church of England clergyman (F)
Evans, (Michael) Gareth Justin (1946–80), philosopher (U) (F)
Evans, Sir (Robert) Charles (1918–95), surgeon and mountaineer (U)
Eyre, Ronald (1929–92), theatre and television director (U)

Faber, Frederick William (1814–63), Church of England clergyman and Roman Catholic priest (U) (F)

Faber, George Stanley (1773–1854), Church of England clergyman and religious writer (U)
Faulkner, Charles Joseph (1833–92), university teacher and associate of William Morris (F)
Faussett, Bryan (1720–76), antiquary (U)
Fergusson, Sir James, of Kilkerran, sixth baronet (1832–1907), politician and colonial governor (U)
Ferne, Sir John (d. 1609), administrator and writer on heraldry (possibly U)
Fetherston, Richard (d. 1540), Roman Catholic ecclesiastic and martyr (F)
Fiddes, Richard (1671–1725), Church of England clergyman and writer (U)
Fisher, William Hayes, Baron Downham (1853–1920), politician (U)
Fitzhugh, Robert (c.1383–1436), Bishop of London (MC)
Flavell, John (1630–91), Presbyterian minister and religious writer (U)
Flemming [Fleming], Richard (d. 1431), Bishop of Lincoln (MC)
Flemming, Robert (1416–83), ecclesiastic and humanist (MC)
Fletcher, Sir Lazarus (1854–1921), museum director and mineralogist (F)
Francis, Sir Richard Trevor Langford (1934–92), broadcasting executive and public servant (U)
French, Thomas Valpy (1825–91), Bishop of Lahore (U) (F)
Freshfield, Douglas William (1845–1934), geographer and mountain explorer (U)
Fyffe, Charles Alan (1845–92), historian (F)

Garrod, Sir (Alfred) Guy Roland (1891–1965), air force officer (U)
Gladstone, Herbert John, Viscount Gladstone (1854–1930), politician and Governor-General of the Union of South Africa (U)
Glyn, George Grenfell, second Baron Wolverton (1824–87), politician and banker (U)
Goodhart, Arthur Lehman (1891–1978) jurist (F) (M)
Goodman, Arnold Abraham, Baron Goodman (1913–95) solicitor and public servant (M)
Gordon, John Campbell, first Marquess of Aberdeen and Temair (1847–1934), politician (U)
Gray, Robert (1809–72), Bishop of Cape Town (U)
Green, (James) Maurice Spurgeon (1906–87), journalist (U)
Grey, Sir Charles Edward (1785–1865), judge in India and colonial governor (U)
Grey, Thomas, fifteenth Baron Grey of Wilton (1575–1614), soldier and courtier (U)
Gretton, Sir Peter William (1912–92) naval officer (F)
Griffith, Richard (1635?–91), physician (F)
Gurney, Sir Henry Lovell Goldsworthy (1898–1951), colonial administrator (U)
Gwynn, (John) Peter Lucius (1916–99), administrator in India and linguist (U)

Hall, William Edward (1835–94), writer on international law (U)
Hammond, Edmund, Baron Hammond (1802–90), diplomatist (U)
Hannay, Robert Kerr (1867–1940), historian of Scotland (U)
Hare, Augustus John Cuthbert (1834–1903), author (U)
Harley, (John) Brian (1932–91), geographer and map historian (U)
Hart, Herbert Lionel Adolphus (1907–92), legal philosopher (F)
Harwood, Thomas (1767–1842), Church of England clergyman and writer (U)
Hastings, Francis Rawdon, first Marquess of Hastings and second Earl of Moira (1754–1826), army officer and politician (U)

Henriques, Sir Basil Lucas Quixano (1890–1961), founder of youth clubs and magistrate (U)
Henshaw, Thomas (1618–1700), alchemist and writer (U)
Herbert, Edward, first Baron Herbert of Cherbury and first Baron Herbert of Castle Island (1582?–1648), diplomat and philosopher (U)
Hewart, Gordon, first Viscount Hewart (1870–1943), judge (U)
Higgins, Matthew James [pseud. Jacob Omnium] (1810–68), journalist (U)
Hills, Arnold Frank (1857–1927), shipbuilder and philanthropist (U)
Hobson, Geoffrey Dudley (1882–1949), historian of bookbindings (U)
Hogg, Thomas Jefferson (1792–1862), biographer of Percy Bysshe Shelley (U)
Holderness, Sir Thomas William, first baronet (1849–1924), administrator in India (U)
Homer, Henry Sacheverell (1719–91), writer (U)
Homer, Philip Bracebridge (1765–1838), schoolmaster and poet (U)
Horne, George (1730–92), Bishop of Norwich (U)
Hopkinson, Sir Alfred (1851–1939), lawyer (F)
Hoyle, Joshua (d. 1654), college head (M)
Hudson, John (1662–1719), librarian and classical scholar (F)
Hutton, Alfred (1839–1910), swordsman (U)

Inett, John (1646/7–1718), Church of England clergyman and ecclesiastical historian (U)

Jago, Richard (1715–81), Church of England clergyman and poet (U)
James, William (1542–1617), Bishop of Durham (M)
Jenkin, (Alfred) Kenneth Hamilton (1900–80), social historian and industrial archaeologist (U)
Jenkins, Sir Lawrence Hugh (1857–1928), judge in India (U)
Jenkinson, Charles, first Earl of Liverpool (1729–1808), politician (U)
Jex-Blake, Thomas William (1832–1915), headmaster and Dean of Wells (U)
John, Nicholas Andrew (1952–96), operatic editor and dramaturge (U)
Johnson, William Percival (1854–1928), missionary and translator (U)
Jones, Thomas (d. 1682), Church of England clergyman (F)
Jones, William [known as William Jones of Nayland] (1726–1800), Church of England clergyman and religious controversialist (U)
Jones, Sir William (1746–94), orientalist and judge (U) (F)

Keir, Sir David Lindsay (1895–1973), university teacher and administrator (F)

Lacy, Edmund (c.1370–1455), Bishop of Exeter (F) (M) (MC)
Langbaine, Gerard (1656–92), dramatic cataloguer and writer (U)
Levy, Benn Wolfe (1900–73), playwright and theatre producer (U)
Lewis, Clive Staples (1898–1963), writer and scholar (U)
Lewis, Sir Wilfrid Hubert Poyer (1881–1950), judge (U)
Liddiard, William (1773–1841), travel writer and poet (U)
Lindsay, Alexander Dunlop, first Baron Lindsay of Birker (1879–1952), educationist (U)
Lister, Sir John (1587–1640), merchant and politician (U)
Llewellin, John Jestyn, Baron Llewellin (1893–1957), politician and Governor-General of the Federation of Rhodesia and Nyasaland (U)
Loftus, Dudley (1618–95), orientalist and jurist (U)
Logan, Sir Douglas William (1910–87) university administrator (U)

III: MEMBERS OF UNIVERSITY COLLEGE IN THE *ODNB* 543

Lowe, Robert, Viscount Sherbrooke (1811–92), politician (U)
Lyttelton, Charles (1714–68), Bishop of Carlisle and antiquary (U)

Macdonell, Alexander Ranaldson, of Glengarry (1773–1828), Chief of Clan Macdonell or Macdonnell of Glengarry and soldier (U)
McDonnell, Sir Schomberg Kerr (1861–1915), civil servant (U)
McFadyean, Sir Andrew (1887–1974), public servant and politician (U)
Mackay, Aeneas James George (1839–1911), legal and historical writer (U)
Mackie, John Leslie (1917–81), philosopher (F)
MacLeod, Norman, of MacLeod (1754–1801), army officer and politician (U)
Mansfield, Robert Blachford (1824–1908), author and sportsman (U)
Maples, Chauncy (1852–95), Bishop of Likoma in Nyasaland (U)
Marson, Charles Latimer (1859–1914), Church of England clergyman and folk-song collector (U)
Marten [Martin], Henry [Harry] (1601/2–80), politician and regicide (U)
Maskell, William (1814–90), Roman Catholic convert and liturgical scholar (U)
Massey, John (1650/51–1715), Dean of Christ Church, Oxford, and Roman Catholic convert (U)
Matthew, Tobie (1544?–1628), Archbishop of York (possibly U)
Maud, John Primatt Redcliffe, Baron Redcliffe-Maud (1906–82), public servant (F) (M)
Maurice, Thomas (1754–1824), oriental scholar and librarian (U)
Medd, Peter Goldsmith (1829–1908), Church of England clergyman and ecclesiastical historian (U) (F)
Mellish, Sir George (1814–77), judge (U)
Mercer, Cecil William [pseud. Dornford Yates] (1885–1960), novelist and short story writer (U)
Metcalfe, Sir Charles Herbert Theophilus, sixth baronet (1853–1928), civil engineer (U)
Middleton, John (d. 1429), physician (F) (possibly M)
Milbanke, Ralph Gordon Noel King, second Earl of Lovelace (1839–1906), mountaineer (U)
Monckton, Sir Philip (1622–79), royalist army officer (U)
Monier-Williams, Sir Monier (1819–99), orientalist (U)
Moore, John (d. 1619), Church of England clergyman and author (possibly U)
Morgan, Sir George Osborne, first baronet (1826–97), lawyer and politician (F)
Morison, Robert (1620–83), botanist (MC)
Musgrave, Samuel (1732–80), physician and classical scholar (RF)

Naipaul, Shivadhar Srinivasa [Shiva] (1945–85), writer (U)
Nelson, Thomas Arthur [Tommy] (1877–1917), member of publishing house (U)
Neville, Henry (1620–94), politician and political writer (U)
Newdigate, Sir Roger (1719–1806), politician and architect (U)
Nicholson, Francis (1650–1731), Roman Catholic convert (U)
Nourse, Timothy (c.1636–99), agricultural and religious writer (U) (F)

Oxenden, Ashton (1808–92), Bishop of Montreal (U)

Page, Sir Leo Francis (1890–1951), magistrate (U)
Palmer, Roundell Cecil, third Earl of Selborne (1887–1971), politician (U)
Palmer, William Waldegrave, second Earl of Selborne (1859–1942), politician (U)
Parker, Charles Stuart (1829–1910), politician and biographer (U) (F)

Parsons, Richard Godfrey (1882–1948), Bishop of Hereford (F)
Parsons, Robert (1646/7–1714), Church of England clergyman (U)
Paterson, Sir Alexander Henry (1884–1947), penal reformer and prison commissioner (U)
Paton, William Roger (1857–1921), epigraphist and classical scholar (U)
Payne, Edward John (1844–1904), historian (F)
Phillipps, Sir Thomas, baronet (1792–1872), collector of books and manuscripts (U)
Playfair, Sir Nigel Ross (1874–1934), actor and theatre manager (U)
Plot, Robert (1640–96), naturalist and antiquary (MC)
Plumer, Sir Thomas (1753–1824), judge and politician (U) (F)
Plumptre, Edward Hayes (1821–91), Dean of Wells (U)
Plunkett, Sir Horace Curzon (1854–1932), agricultural reformer and politician (U)
Potter, John (1673/4–1747), Archbishop of Canterbury (U)
Poulett, John, first Baron Poulett (1586–1649), local politician and royalist army officer (U)
Pryor, Alfred Reginald (1839–81), botanist (U)

Rackett, Thomas (1755–1840), Church of England clergyman and antiquary (U)
Radcliffe, Sir George (1593–1657), lawyer and politician (U)
Radcliffe, John (1650–1714), physician and philanthropist (U)
Ramsbotham, Herwald, first Viscount Soulbury (1887–1971), politician and Governor-General of Ceylon (U)
Rayne, Max, Baron Rayne (1918–2003), property developer and philanthropist (Honorary Fellow)
Reading, William (1674–1744), librarian (U)
Richardson, Sir John (1771–1841), judge (U)
Richardson, Richard (1663–1741), physician and botanist (U)
Ridley, James (1736–65), writer and Church of England clergyman (U)
Robinson, Sir Christopher (1766–1833), judge (U)
Rogers, William (1646/7–c.1730), Roman Catholic convert (U)
Rotheram, John (1725–89), theologian (F)
Rubens, Paul Alfred (1875–1917), musical comedy writer and songwriter (U)
Russel, Richard (1685–1756), journalist (U)
Russell, George William Erskine (1853–1919), politician and writer (U)

Sadler, Sir Michael Ernest (1861–1943), educationist (M)
Sargeaunt, John (1857–1922), classical scholar and teacher (U)
Savile, Sir George (c.1583–1614) (U)
Savile, Sir William, third baronet (1612–44) (U)
Say, William (1604–66?), politician and regicide (U)
Scafe, John (1776–1843), poet and writer on geology (U)
Scott, John, first Earl of Eldon (1751–1838), Lord Chancellor (U) (F)
Scott, William, Baron Stowell (1745–1836), judge and politician (F)
Selby, Prideaux John (1788–1867), naturalist (U)
Selby-Bigge, Sir Lewis Amherst, first baronet (1860–1951), civil servant and author (F)
Sélincourt, Ernest De (1870–1943), literary scholar and university teacher (U)
Seton-Watson, (George) Hugh Nicholas (1916–84), historian and political scientist (F)
Shadwell, Sir John (1671–1747), physician (U)

III: MEMBERS OF UNIVERSITY COLLEGE IN THE *ODNB*   545

Sheldon, Edward (1599–1687), translator (U)
Shelley, Percy Bysshe (1792–1822), poet (U)
Sherrey [Sherry], Richard (b. c.1505), schoolmaster and author (F)
Shirley, Walter Waddington (1828–66), ecclesiastical historian (U)
Sibthorp, John (1758–96), botanist (RF)
Sibthorp, Richard Waldo (1792–1879), Church of England clergyman and Roman Catholic convert (U)
Smith, Goldwin (1823–1910), journalist and historian (F)
Smith, William (1651?–1735), antiquary (U) (F)
Sollas, William Johnson (1849–1936), geologist and anthropologist (F)
Sonnenschein, Edward Adolf (1851–1929), classical scholar (U)
Sorley, Charles Hamilton (1895–1915), poet (accepted for matriculation)
Spencer, George Trevor (1799–1866), Bishop of Madras, India (U)
Spender, Sir Stephen Harold (1909–95) poet (U)
Squire, William (d. 1677), Church of England clergyman (F)
Stanihurst, Richard (1547–1618), literary scholar and translator (U)
Stanley, Arthur Penrhyn (1815–81), Dean of Westminster (F)
Stedman, Rowland (d. 1673), clergyman and ejected minister (U)
Stone, Francis (1738–1813), Church of England clergyman and religious controversialist (U)
Stone-Wigg, Montagu John (1861–1918), Bishop of New Guinea (U)
Stoop, Adrian Dura (1883–1957), rugby player (U)
Strode, Thomas (d. 1697), mathematician (U)
Sutton, Sir Bertine Entwisle (1886–1946), air force officer (U)
Swete [formerly Tripe], John (1752–1821), antiquary and topographer (U)
Swire, John Kidston [Jock] (1893–1983), businessman (U)

Tarleton, Sir Banastre, baronet (1754–1833), army officer and politician (U)
Thompson, Sir Edward Maunde (1840–1929), palaeographer and librarian (U)
Thorp, Charles (1783–1862), university principal (U) (F)
Thorpe, John (1682–1750), physician and antiquary (U)
Thorpe, John (1715/16–92), antiquary (U)
Thrale, Henry (1728–81), brewer and politician (U)
Thurlby, Thomas (d. 1486), mathematician and teacher (F) (MC)
Tiddy, Reginald John Elliott (1880–1916), collector of folk plays (U) (F)
Tiptoft, John, first Earl of Worcester (1427–70), administrator and humanist (C)
Todd, Hugh (c.1657–1728), Church of England clergyman and antiquary (F)
Tolley, Cyril James Hastings (1895–1978), golfer (U)
Tomson, Giles (1553–1612), Bishop of Gloucester (U)
Tonge, Israel (1621–80), informer and Church of England clergyman (U) (F)
Tozer, Henry Fanshawe (1829–1916), geographer and classical scholar (U)
Tracy, John, seventh Viscount Tracy of Rathcoole (1722–93), college head (U)
Trevelyan, Sir Walter Calverley, sixth baronet (1797–1879), naturalist (U)
Trigge, Francis (1547?–1606), Church of England clergyman and writer on social issues (U)
Turner, Sir Michael William (1905–80), banker (U)
Turton, John (1735–1806), physician (RF)

Twiss, Sir Travers (1809–97), jurist (U) (F)
Twysden, John (1607–88), physician (U)

Urswick, Christopher (1448?–1522), courtier, diplomat, and ecclesiastic (MC)
Ussher, Henry (c.1550–1613), Church of Ireland Archbishop of Armagh (MC)

Wager, Lawrence Rickard [Bill] (1904–65), geologist and explorer (F)
Walker, Obadiah (1616–99), college head and author (U) (F) (M)
Wait, Daniel Guilford (1789/90–1850), Hebrew scholar (U)
Waller, Charles Henry (1840–1910), Church of England clergyman and college head (U)
Wanley, Humfrey (1672–1726), Old English scholar and librarian (U)
Ward, Henry Leigh Douglas [Harry] (1825–1906), literary historian (U)
Warneford, Samuel Wilson (1763–1855), philanthropist (U)
Watson, George (1723–73), Church of England clergyman and classical scholar (U) (F)
Webbe, George (1581–c.1642), Church of Ireland Bishop of Limerick (U)
Wenman, Thomas Francis (1745–96), civil lawyer and botanist (U)
Wentworth, Thomas (1567/8–1628), lawyer and politician (U)
West, Sir Edward (1782–1828), judge and political economist (U) (F)
Wetherell, Sir Charles (1770–1846), politician and lawyer (U)
Wheare, Sir Kenneth Clinton (1907–79), constitutional expert (F)
Wheeler, (William) Gordon (1910–98) Roman Catholic Bishop of Leeds (U)
Whitehead, Sir Edgar Cuthbert Fremantle (1905–71), Prime Minister of Rhodesia (U)
Wightman, Sir William (1784–1863), judge (U)
Wigram, Ralph Follett (1890–1936), diplomatist (U)
Williams, (Laurence Frederic) Rushbrook (1890–1978), historian and civil servant (U)
Williams, Moses (1685–1742), Welsh scholar and translator (U)
Wilmot, John Eardley Eardley (1749–1815), politician and writer (U)
Wilson, (James) Harold, Baron Wilson of Rievaulx (1916–95), Prime Minister (F)
Windham, William (1750–1810), politician (U)
Wood, John (1728–81), architect (U)
Woodhead, Abraham (1609–78), Roman catholic controversialist (U) (F)
Woolley, John (1816–66), educationist (U)

Yerburgh, Robert Armstrong (1853–1916), politician (U)
Young, Sir William, second baronet (1749–1815), colonial governor and politician (U)

Appendix IV

(1) Social Backgrounds of Members of University College, 1550–1807 (%)

Father's Status	1551–1600	1601–42	1643–60	1660–89	1689–1722	1723–64	1764–1807
Peer, baronet, or knight	1.5	12	0.5	4	6.5	6.5	5.5
Esquire	12	18	7	12	14	28.5	58.6
Gentleman	18	16	28.5	29	29.5	28	11.4
Clergy	2	7	11	8	14	17	18.5
Other profession	—	—	0.5	4.5	0.5	2	2.6
'Plebeian'	34.5	28	36.5	38	28.5	15	1.2
Unknown	32	19	16	4.5	7	3	2.2

(2) Ages of Undergraduates on being admitted to University College, 1550–1807 (%)

Father's Status	1551–1600	1601–42	1643–60	1660–89	1689–1722	1723–64	1764–1807
13 or under	4.7	1.5	[—][a]	1	1.3	0.6	—
14	4.7	5		2	1.5	0.6	0.2
15	8.3	12.6		9.1	14.1	3.9	3.1
16	8.1	20.25		26.	15.4	13	10.7
17	9.25	22.1		25.1	30	30.3	32.2
18	9.75	10.8		17	18.9	32.4	31.2
19	6.1	4		4.4	7.6	11.8	13.6
20	4.5	2		1.6	3.7	4.1	4.1
21	2.25	0.75		0.3	—	1.5	3
22 or older	4	1		—	1.4	1.6	1.9
Unknown	38.35	20		13.2	6.1	0.2	—

[a] Of the 163 undergraduates known to have come up to the College at this time, the ages of just 11 are known.

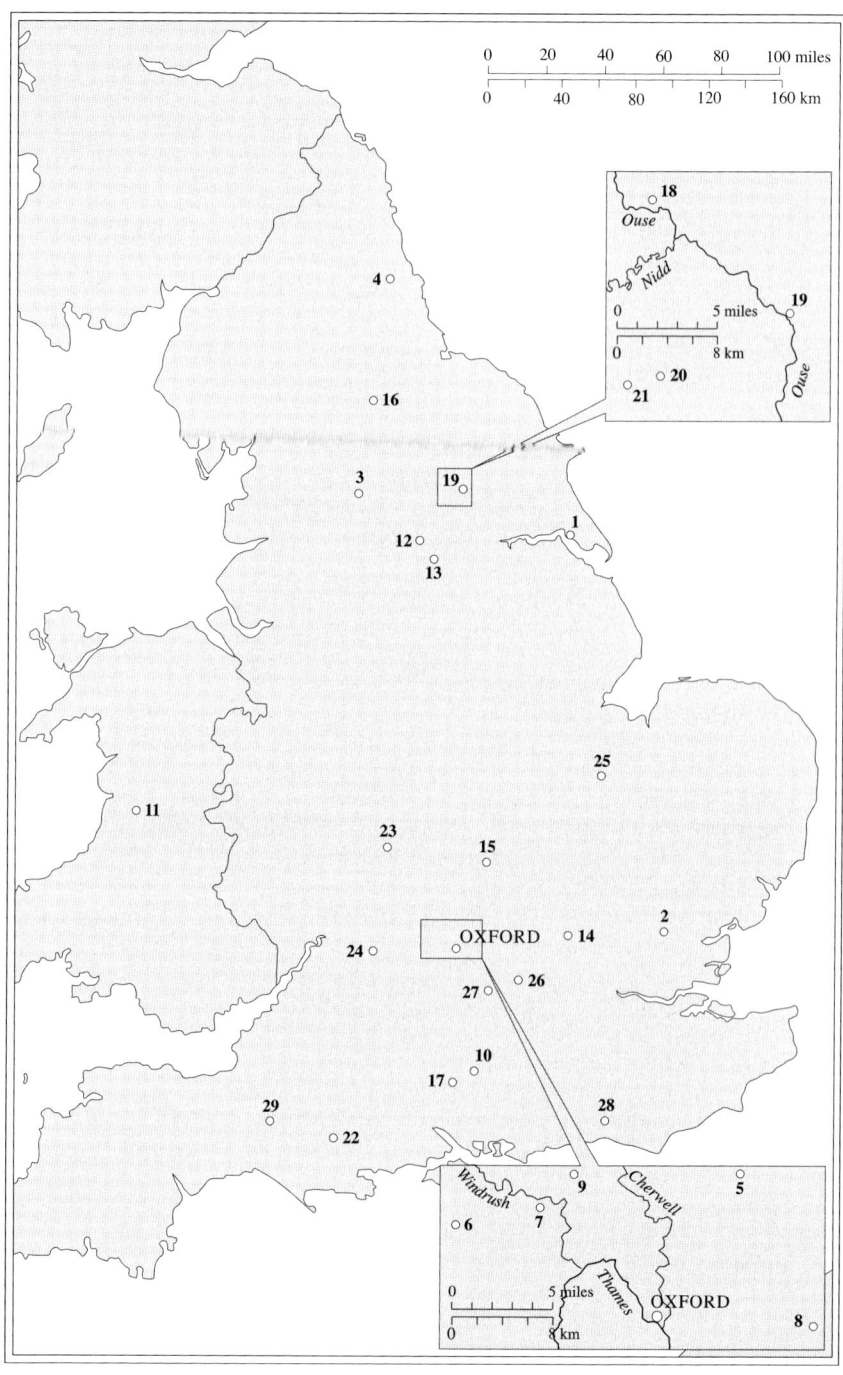

Map App. V Properties outside Oxford acquired by University College before 1850.

Appendix V

Properties outside Oxford acquired by University College Before 1850

1. Land at Paull, Yorkshire (given 1318–21).
2. The Manor of Marks Hall, Essex (given 1403).
3. The Rectory of Arncliffe, Yorkshire (given 1443).
4. Various properties in Newcastle-upon-Tyne (acquired 1447).
5. Land at Merton, Oxfordshire (acquired 1505/6)
6. Land at Hailey, Oxfordshire (acquired 1540/1).
7. Land at Hanborough, Oxfordshire (acquired 1540s; sold after 1567).
8. & 9. Land at Waterstock and at Woodstock, Oxfordshire (given 1584).
10. Rents from land in Rotherwick, Hampshire (given 1588)
11. Various farms in and near Llanidoes, Trefeglwys, and Caersws, Montgomeryshire (given 1588).
12. Land at Methley, Yorkshire (given 1590)
13. Land at Pontefract and surrounding areas, Yorkshire (given 1592).
14. The Rectory of Flamstead, Hertfordshire (given 1618).
15. Land at Handley Park, Northamphire (given 1631).
16. The advowson of Melsonby, Yorkshire (purchased 1692).
17. The advowson of Headbourne Worthy, Hampshire (given to trustees, 1714).
18. Land at Linton-on-Ouse, Yorkshire (given to trustees 1714; given to the College 1744).
19, 20, & 21. Land in the city of York, and in Healaugh and Wighill, Yorkshire (given 1737).
22. The advowson of Tarrant Gunville, Dorset (bought 1747).
23. Land at Edgiock, Worcestershire (bought 1749).
24. The advowson of North Cerney, Gloucestershire (bought 1753).
25. The advowson of Elton, Huntingdonshire (bought 1760/1).
26. Land at Marlow, Bucks. (given 1764).
27. The advowson of Checkendon, Oxfordshire (bought 1765/6).
28. The advowson of Beckley, Sussex (bought 1817).
29. The advowson of Kingsdon, Somerset (bought 1829).

References

Anon. (1723), *A vindication of the Proceedings at University College in the late Election of Mr. Cockman to be Master of that College* (1723).
Anon. (1747), *A letter to the Heads of the University of Oxford on a Late very Remarkable Affair* (London).
Anon. (1748), *A fair representation of the case between the Principal of M. Hall and Mr. E——s late Manciple thereof: with a few observations on some extraordinary pieces lately published and dispersed in Oxford; submitted to persons of sense and seriousness* (no place of publication).
Anon. (1816), *Statutes of the Realm, Volume II* (London).
Anon. (1852), *Report of Her Majesty's Commissioners Appointed to Enquire into the State, Discipline, Studies and Revenues of the Universities and Colleges of Oxford* (London).
Anon. (1874), *The Sho tover Papers* Vol. I no. 4.
Anon. (probably Michael Sadler) (1930/1), 'William Morris, Edward Burne-Jones, and C. J. Faulkner', *UCR* 1930/1: 17–21.
Anon. (probably Michael Sadler) (1934), 'The Duke of Wellington's Encaenia, 1834', *UCR* 1934: 28–32.
Anon (1950), 'The Martlets', *UCR* 1949/50: 11–16.

Abbot, G. (1605), *A briefe Description of the Whole Worlde wherein is particularly described all the Monarchies, Empires and Kingdomes of the same: newly augmented and enlarged; with their seuerall titles and situations thereunto adioyning* (2nd edn. London).
—— (1613), *An Exposition upon the Prophet Jonah: Contained in certaine Sermons, preached in S. Maries Church in Oxford* (2nd edn. London).
Abbott, E., and Campbell, L. (1897), *The Life and Letters of Benjamin Jowett* (2 vols., London).
Abrahams, H., and Bruce-Kerr, J. (1931), *Oxford versus Cambridge: A Record of Inter-university Contests from 1827–1930* (London).
Adams, P. (1996), *Somerville for Women: An Oxford College 1879–1993* (Oxford).
Addison, P. (1994), 'Oxford and the Second World War', *HUO* viii. 167–88.
Albery, J., Mitchell, L. G., Park, R, and Bell, J. D. (1992), *Shelley and Univ. 1810–11: Papers Delivered by the Master & Three Fellows of University College at a Seminar to Commemorate the Bicentenary of Shelley's Birth* (Oxford).
Alington, H. M. (1957), *C.A.A. and G.A.* (Durham).
Allen, D. (1960), *Sunlight and Shadow* (Oxford).
Allfrey, E. W. (1909), 'The Architectural History of the College', *Brasenose Quatercentenary Monographs* i (OHS lii), Monograph III.
Amherst, N. (1754), *Terræ-Filius; Or the Secret History of the University of Oxford* (3rd edn., London).
Amyot, T. (1812), *Speeches in Parliament of the Right Honourable William Windham; to which is prefixed, some Account of his Life* (3 vols., London).

REFERENCES

Anderson, R. D. (2004), *European Universities from the Enlightenment to 1914* (Oxford).
—— (2006), *British Universities Past and Present* (London).
Anstey, H. (ed.) (1868), *Munimenta academica, or Documents Illustrative of Academical Life or Studies at Oxford* (2 vols, Rolls Series l).
—— (ed.) (1898), *Epistolae Academicae Oxon.* (2 vols., OHS xxxv–xxvi).
Archer, M. (1975), 'English Painted Glass in the Seventeenth Century: The Early Work of Abraham van Linge', *Apollo* (Jan.): 26–31.
Ashworth, E. J., and Spade, P. V. (1992), 'Logic in Late Medieval Oxford', *HUO* ii. 35–64.
Aston, N. (1993), 'Horne and Heterodoxy: The Defence of Anglican Beliefs in the Late Enlightenment', *English Historical Review*, 108: 895–919.
Aston, T. H., and Faith, R. (1984), 'The Endowments of the University and Colleges to *circa* 1348', *HUO* i. 265–309.
Athill, D. (2002), *Yesterday Morning* (London).
Attlee, C. R. (1954), *As It Happened* (London).
Attwater, A. (1936), *Pembroke College Cambridge: A Short History* (Cambridge).
Austen Leigh, A. (1899), *King's College* (London).
Auvray, L. (ed.) (1907), *Les Régistres de Grégoire IX*, vol. ii (Paris).
Ayliffe, J. (1723), *The Ancient and Present State of the University of Oxford* (2nd edn. London).
Aylmer, G. E. (1986), 'The Economics and Finances of the Colleges and University *c.*1530–1640', *HUO* iii. 521–58.
Babbage, S. B. (1962), *Puritanism and Richard Bancroft* (London).
Bailey, M. (2006), *Van Gogh and Britain: Pioneer Collectors* (Edinburgh).
Baker, J. N. L. (1971), *Jesus College Oxford 1571–1971* (Oxford).
Bamford, B. (1959), *The Substance: The Story of a Rhodes Scholar at Oxford* (Cape Town).
Barber, G. (1997), 'The Taylor Institution', *HUO* vi. 631–40.
Barker-Benfield, B. C. (1991), 'Hogg-Shelley Papers of 1810–12', *Bodleian Library Record*, 14/1: 14–29.
Barton, J. (1986), 'Legal Studies', *HUO* v. 593–605.
Bayley, K. E., and others (eds.) (1916), *Miscellanea Volume II* (Surtees Society cxxvii).
Bayley, P. C. (1952) 'The Betting Book I', *UCR* 1952: 25–32.
—— (1954*a*), 'The Betting Book II', *UCR* 1953/4: 20–9.
—— (1954*b*), 'Three Old Members', *UCR* 1953/4, 29–34.
—— (1958–60), 'The Summer Room Carvings', *UCR* Vol. III no. 3: 192–201, Vol. III no. 4: 252–6, and *UCR* Vol. III no. 5: 341–6.
—— (1959*a*), 'The Grand Judges', *UCR* Vol. III no. 4: 238–40.
—— (1959*b*), 'A Gentleman Commoner at Univ.', *UCR* Vol. III no. 4: 257–66.
—— (1963), 'Master Bradley on Dean Stanley', *UCR* Vol. IV no. 3: 183–90.
—— (1964), 'A Reminiscence of Shelley', *UCR* Vol. IV no. 4: 248.
—— (1993), 'Painting Old Masters', *UCR* Vol. XI no. 1: 53–60.
—— (2000), 'Univ. Players', *UCR* Vol. XII no. 4: 92–6.
—— (2002), 'Family Matters', *UCR* Vol. XIII no. 2: 91–4.
—— (2006), 'Family Matters III: The English Rising', *UCR* Vol. XIV no. 3: 115–21.

BEDDARD, R. A. (1997*a*), 'Restoration Oxford and the Remaking of the Protestant Establishment', *HUO* iv. 803–62.
—— (1997*b*), 'Tory Oxford', *HUO* iv. 863–905.
—— (1997*c*), 'James II and the Catholic Challenge', *HUO* iv. 907–54.
BENDALL, S., BROOKE, C. N. L. and COLLINSON, P. (1999), *A History of Emmanuel College, Cambridge* (Woodbridge).
BENNETT, G. V. (1986*a*), 'Against the Tide: Oxford under William III' *HUO* v. 31–60.
—— (1986*b*), 'The Era of Party Zeal 1702–1714', *HUO* v. 61–97.
—— (1986*c*), 'University, Society and Church 1688–1714', *HUO* v. 369–400.
BERGER, É. (ed.) (1887), *Les Régistres d'Innocent IV*, vol. ii. (Paris).
BERLIN, I. (2004), *Flourishing: Letters 1928–1946*, ed. H. Hardy (London).
BERNSTORFF, A. VON, and GRUNELIUS A. C. (1912), *Des Teutchen Scholaren Glossarium in Oxford* (place of publication unknown).
BEVERIDGE, W. H. (1953), *Power and Influence* (London).
BICKERTON, F. (1953), *Fred of Oxford; being the Memoirs of Fred Bickerton, until recently Head Porter of University College, Oxford* (London).
BILL, E. G. W. (1988), *Education at Christ Church Oxford 1660–1800* (Oxford).
—— and MASON, J. F. A. (1970), *Christ Church and Reform 1850–1867* (Oxford).
BLACK, L. G. (1977), 'The College Chapel Windows', *UCR* Vol. VII no. 3: 122–36.
BLOXAM, J. R. (1853–85), *A Register of the Presidents, Fellows, Demies, Instructors in Grammar and in Music, Chaplains, Clerks, Choristers, and Other Members of Saint Mary Magdalen College in the University of Oxford* (8 vols., Oxford).
—— (1886), *Magdalen College and James II 1686–88* (OHS vi).
BOASE, C. W. (ed.) (1885), *Register of the University of Oxford Volume 1 (1449–63; 1505–71)* (OHS i).
BOLTON, G. (1962), *History of the O.U.C.C.* (London).
BOSANQUET, H. (1924), *Bernard Bosanquet: A Short Account of his Life* (London).
BOSWELL, J. (1831), *The Life of Samuel Johnson*, ed. J. W. Croker (London).
—— (1980), *Life of Johnson*, ed. R. W. Chapman (Oxford).
BOTT, A. (1964), *The Monuments in Merton College Chapel* (Oxford).
BOURGUIGNON, H. J. (1987), *Sir William Scott Lord Stowell: Judge of the High Court of Admiralty 1798–1828* (Cambridge).
BOWDEN, J. E. (1869), *The Life and Letters of Frederick William Faber, D.D., Priest of the Oratory of St. Philip Neri, 1814–63* (London).
BOWEN, E. J. (1932/3), 'Scratched Inscriptions on Window Panes in College', *UCR* 1932/3: 16–18.
BOYD, W., and SHUFFREY, W. A. (1893), *Littondale: Past and Present* (Leeds).
BOYD CARPENTER, W. (1911), *Some Pages of my Life* (London).
BRADLEY, G. G. (1873), *Two Letters to the Right Honourable the Lord Chancellor of Great Britain* (Oxford).
BREWER, J. S. (ed.) (1858), *Monumenta Franciscana* (Rolls Series iv).
—— and GAIRDNER, J. (1862–1910), *Letters and Papers, Foreign and Domestic of the Reign of Henry VIII, Preserved in the Public Record Office, the British Museum, and elsewhere in England* (21 vols. in 33; new edn. of vol. i. in 3 pts. 1930; vol. of addenda in 2 pts. 1929–32).

BRIGGS, J. (c.1791), *A Tour from Oxford to Newcastle upon Tyne in the Long Vacation of the Year 1791* (no place or date of publication given).
BRIGHTON, T. (1970), 'The Lost East Window by Gyles of York', *UCR* Vol. V no. 5: 358–60.
BRIVATI, B. (1999), *Lord Goodman* (London).
BROADLEY, A. M. (1910), *Doctor Johnson and Mrs. Thrale* (London).
BROCK, M. G. (1994), 'The University since 1970', *HUO* viii. 739–74.
—— (1997), 'The Oxford of Peel and Gladstone, 1800–1833', *HUO* vi. 7–71.
—— (2000a), 'A "Plastic Structure"', *HUO* vii. 3–66.
—— (2000b), 'The Oxford of Raymond Asquith and William Elmhirst', *HUO* vii. 781–819.
—— (2000c), 'Epilogue', *HUO* vii. 855–74.
BROCK, W. R., and COOPER, P. H. M. (1994), *Selwyn College: A History* (Durham).
BROCKLISS, L. (1996), 'Curricula', in H. de Ridder-Symoens (ed.), *A History of the University in Europe, Volume II: Universities in Early Modern Europe (1500–1800)* (Cambridge), 563–620.
—— (1997), 'The European University in the Age of Revolution, 1789–1850', *HUO* vi. 77–133.
—— (ed.) (forthcoming), *Magdalen College, Oxford: A History*.
—— HARRISS, G., and MACINTYRE, A. (1988), *Magdalen College and the Crown: Essays for the Tercentenary of the Restoration of the College 1688* (Oxford).
BROOKE, C. N. L. (1993), *A History of the University of Cambridge Volume IV 1870–1990* (Cambridge).
—— (1996), *A History of Gonville and Caius College* (Woodbridge).
BURNETT, A. (2005), 'John Evelyn (1620–1706) and Obadiah Walker (1616–1699): Their Significance for Numismatics', in C. Dekesel and T. Stäcker (eds.), *Europäische Numismatische Literatur im 17. Jahrhundert* (Weisbaden): 47–57.
BURROWS, M. (ed.) (1881), *Register of the Visitors of the University of Oxford from A.D. 1647 to A.D. 1658* (Camden Society new ser. xxix).
BURTCHAELL, G., and SADLEIR, T. (eds.) (1935), *Alumni Dublinenses* (Dublin).
BURY, P. (1952), *The College of Corpus Christi and of the Blessed Virgin Mary: A History from 1822 to 1952* (Woodbridge).
BUTCHER, A. F. (1978), 'Rent, Population and Economic Change in Late-Medieval Newcastle', *Northern History*, 14: 67–77.
BUTLER, F. E. R. (2003), 'Financing Higher Education: A Public Policy Dilemma', *UCR* Vol. XIII no. 3: 5–11.
BUXTON, J., and WILLIAMS, P. (eds.) (1979), *New College Oxford 1379–1979* (Oxford).
CAIUS, J. (1568), *De antiquitate Cantabrigiensis Academiæ libri duo. In quorum secundo de Oxoniensis quoq[ue] Gymnasij antiquitate disseritur, & Cantabrigiense longè eo antiquius esse definitur Londinensi authore; Adiunximus assertionem antiquitatis Oxoniensis Academiæ, ab Oxoniensi quodam annis iam elapsis duobus ad Reginam conscriptam, in qua docere conatur, Oxoniense Gymnasium Cantabrigiensi antiquius esse. Vt ex collatione facilè intelligas, vtra sit antiquior* (London).
—— (1574), *De Antiquitate Cantebrigensis Academiae Libri duo Aucti ab ipso Authore plurimum* (London).

CAIUS, T. (1730), *Vindiciae Antiquitatis Academiae Oxoniensis*, ed. T. Hearne (Oxford).
CAMDEN, W. (1695), *Camden's Britannia, Newly Translated into English; with large Additions and Improvements*, ed. E. Gibson (London).
CANNON, G. (ed.) (1970), *The Letters of Sir William Jones* (2 vols., Oxford).
—— (1990), *The Life and Mind of Oriental Jones: Sir William Jones, the Father of Modern Linguistics* (Cambridge).
CANT, R. G. (1970), *The University of St Andrews: A Short History* (2nd edn., Edinburgh).
CARD, T. (1994), *Eton Renewed: A History from 1860 to the Present Day* (1994).
—— (2001), *Eton Established: A History from 1440 to 1860* (London).
CARPENTER, H. (ed.) (1981), *The Letters of J. R. R. Tolkien* (London).
—— (1985), *O.U.D.S.: A Centenary History of the Oxford University Dramatic Society* (Oxford).
CARR, W. (1902), *University College* (London).
CARRITT, E. F. (1958), 'And yet what days were those', *UCR* Vol. III no. 3: 183–92.
—— (1960), *Fifty Years a Don* (Typescript).
CARTER, H. (1975), *A History of the Oxford University Press Volume I: To the Year 1780* (Oxford).
CATTO, J. I. (1984a), 'Citizens, Scholars and Masters', *HUO* i. 151–92.
—— (1984b), 'Theology and Theologians', *HUO* i. 471–517.
—— (1992a), 'Wyclif and Wycliffism at Oxford 1356–1430', *HUO* ii. 175–261.
—— (1992b), 'Theology after Wyclifism', *HUO* ii. 263–80.
—— (1992c), 'Scholars and Studies in Renaissance Oxford', *HUO* ii. 769–83.
—— (2004), 'The Triumph of the Hall in Fifteenth-Century Oxford', in R. Evans (ed.) *Lordship and Learning: Studies in Memory of Trevor Aston* (Woodbridge): 209–23.
CHANDLER, T. J. L. (1988), 'The Development of a Sporting Tradition at Oxbridge: 1800–1860', *Canadian Journal of History of Sport*, 19/2: 1–29.
CHARLETT, A. (1707), *Mercurius Oxoniensis, or the Oxford Intelligencer for the Year of our Lord 1707* (London).
—— (1708/9), 'A Letter Concerning a Colliery that Took Fire, and Was Blown up Near Newcastle, Killing 69 Persons, on August 18, 1708. Communicated by the Reverend Dr. Arthur Charlett, Master of University College in Oxford', *Philosophical Transactions* 26/318: 215–17.
CHARNWOOD, G. R. B. (ed.) (1930), *Discourses and Letters of Hubert Murray Burge* (London).
Chronicon Rhotomagense (1894), in *Receuil des historiens des Gaules et de la France* xxiii: 331–43.
CLARENDON, EDWARD, Earl of (1759), *The Life of Edward Earl of Clarendon* (Oxford).
—— (1888), *The History of the Rebellion*, ed. W. D. Macray (6 vols., Oxford).
CLARK, A. (ed.) (1887–9), *Register of the University of Oxford Volume II (1571–1622)*, parts I–IV (4 vols. OHS x–xii & xiv).
CLARK, A. G. (2007), *A Village on the Nene, Volume I: 1085–1870* (Stamford).
CLARK, G. N. (1953), *Cecil Rhodes and his College* (Oxford).

CLARK, J. C. D. (1985), *English Society 1688–1832* (Cambridge).
CLARK, W. (2006), *Academic Charisma and the Origins of the Research University* (Chicago).
CLARKE, M. L. (1986), 'Classical Studies', *HUO* v. 513–33.
CLARKE, S. (2006), 'Bishop Walter Skirlaw: Univ.'s Forgotten Medieval Patron', *UCR* Vol. XIV no. 2: 98–114.
CLAY, J. W. (1920), 'The Savile Family', *Yorkshire Archaeological Journal*, 25: 1–47.
CLIFFORD, H. (1996), 'Oxford College Cooks 1400–1800', in H. Walker (ed.), *Cooks and Other People: Proceedings of the Oxford Symposium on Food and Cookery 1995* (Totnes): 59–67.
CLINTON, W. J. (2004), *My Life* (New York).
COBBAN, A. B. (1969), *The King's Hall within the University of Cambridge in the Later Middle Ages* (Cambridge).
—— (1973), 'Origins: Robert Wodelarke and St. Catharine's' in E. E. Rich (ed.), *St Catharine's College Cambridge 1473–1973* (Cambridge): 1–32.
—— (1975), *The Medieval Universities: Their Development and Organisation* (London).
—— (1988), *The Medieval English Universities: Oxford and Cambridge to c.1500* (Aldershot).
—— (1992), 'Colleges and Halls 1380–1500', *HUO* ii. 581–634.
—— (1999), *English University Life in the Middle Ages* (London).
COCKMAN, T. (1695), *M. Tullius Cicero de officiis, recens. T. Cockman* (Oxford).
—— (1696), *M. Tullius Cicero de oratore, recens. T. Cockman* (Oxford).
—— (1699), *Tully's Three Books of Offices* (London).
—— (1732), *Salvation by Jesus Christ alone asserted and vindicated, and the objections made against it by some modern unbelievers, particularly by the author of Christianity as old as the creation full considered and answered: in two sermons preached before the University of Oxford, Jan. 2, and Jan. 6, 1731–2* (London).
—— (1733), *The duty of not conforming to this world. A sermon preach'd before the university of Oxford, at St. Mary's on Act Sunday 1733* (Oxford).
COGHILL, N. (1948), *The Masque of Hope* (Oxford).
COLE, C. (1883), *Reflections on the Zulu War and the Future of Africa* (London).
COLE, M. (1971), *The Life of G. D. H. Cole* (London).
COLLINSON, P. (1990), *The English Puritan Movement* (Oxford).
COLVIN, H. M. (1964), *A Catalogue of Architectural Drawings of the 18th and 19th Centuries in the Library of Worcester College, Oxford* (Oxford).
—— (1983), *Unbuilt Oxford* (New Haven).
—— (1986), 'Architecture', *HUO* v. 831–56.
—— (2000), 'The Townesends of Oxford: A Firm of Georgian Master-Masons and its Accounts', *Georgian Group Journal* 10: 43–60.
—— and SIMMONS, J. S. G. (1989), *All Souls: An Oxford College and its Buildings* (Oxford).
COOPER, J., and CROSSLEY, A. (1979), 'Medieval Oxford', *VCH Oxon.* iv. 3–73.
COOPER, J. P. (ed.) (1973), *Wentworth Papers 1597–1628* (Camden Fourth series xii).
COSTIN, W. C. (1958), *The History of St John's College Oxford 1598–1860* (Oxford).

COURTENAY, W. J. (1980), 'The Effect of the Black Death on English Higher Education', *Speculum* 55: 696–714.
—— (1992), 'Theology and Theologians from Ockham to Wyclif' *HUO* ii. 1–35.
COX, A. D. M. (1949), 'William of Durham and the Archbishopric of Rouen', *UCR* 1948/9: 11–20.
—— (1953), 'The French Petition', *UCR* 1952/3: 14–24.
—— (1956), 'An Inscription from the Old Library', *UCR* Vol. III no. 1: 32–4.
—— (1960), 'The College at the Restoration', *UCR* Vol. III no. 5: 324–30.
—— (1971a), 'Hanley Park', *UCR* Vol VI no. 1: 57–63.
—— (1971b) 'The College Statutes of 1736', *UCR* Vol. VI. no. 1: 63–72.
—— (1972a), 'The Earliest Known Fellow', *UCR* Vol. VI no. 2: 130–1.
—— (1972b), 'Hanley Park—A Postscript', *UCR* Vol. VI no. 2: 171–3.
—— (1973), 'The John Savile Affair', *UCR* Vol. VI no. 3: 262–70.
—— (1977), 'The Bursar and the Beer', *UCR* Vol. VII no. 3: 136–41.
—— (1981), 'Who was William of Durham?', *UCR* Vol. VIII no. 2: 115–23.
—— and DARWALL-SMITH, R. H. (eds.) (1999–2001), *Account Rolls of University College, Oxford* (2 vols, OHS new ser. xxxix, xl).
COX, G. V. (1870), *Recollections of Oxford* (2nd edn. London).
CRAVEN, J. (2000), *Mac Cooper: A Biography* (Edinburgh).
CRAWLEY, R. (1983), 'Alfred's Avatar', *UCR* Vol. VIII no. 4: 275–9.
CREE, C. E. (1974), *1871: An Oxford Diary*, ed. A. Cree (Oxford).
CROSS, C. (1986), 'Oxford and the Tudor State from the Accession of Henry VIII to the Death of Mary', *HUO* iii 117–49.
CROSSLEY, A. (ed.) (1979), *A History of the County of Oxford* (VCH) iv (London).
—— (1990), *A History of the County of Oxford* (VCH) xii (Oxford).
CUNICH, P., HOYLE, D., DUFFY E., and HYAM, R. (1994), *A History of Magdalene College, Cambridge 1428–1988* (Cambridge).
CURLEY, T. M. (1998), *Sir Robert Chambers: Law, Literature, and Empire in the Age of Johnson* (Winsconsin).
CURRIE, R. (1994), 'The Arts and Social Studies, 1914–39', *HUO* viii. 109–38.
CURTHOYS, M. C. (1997a), 'The "Unreformed" Colleges', *HUO* vi. 146–73.
—— (1997b), 'The Examination System', *HUO* vi. 339–74.
—— (1997c), 'The Careers of Oxford Men', *HUO* vi. 477–510.
—— (2000), 'The Colleges in the New Era': *HUO* vii. 115–57.
—— and DAY, C. J. (1997), 'The Oxford of Mr. Verdant Green', *HUO* vi. 268–86.
DAHRENDORF, R. (1995) *LSE: A History of the London School of Economics and Political Science 1895–1995* (Oxford).
DANIEL, H. (ed.) (1888–95), *Our Memories: Shadows of Old Oxford* (Oxford, 22 nos.).
DARLINGTON, I. (ed.) (1967), *London Consistory Court Wills 1492–1547* (London Record Society iii).
DARWALL-SMITH, R. H. (1996), 'Medieval Skullduggery: Some Forged Deeds from the Archives', *UCR*, Vol. XI no. 4: 58–69.
—— (1998), 'Obadiah Walker in his own Words', *UCR* Vol. XII no. 2: 56–68.
—— (1999), 'The Great Mastership Dispute', *UCR* Vol. XII no. 3: 58–85.
—— (2000a), 'The Shelley Memorial; or the Monument Nobody Wanted', *UCR* Vol. XII no. 4: 74–87.

—— (2000b), 'Not so Invisible: Women at Magdalen before 1979', *Magdalen College Record*, 2000: 86–96.
—— (2001), 'Charles Alan Fyffe: A Victorian Tragedy', *UCR* Vol. XIII no. 1: 72–84.
—— (2002a), 'Letters to Mother: The Undergraduate Correspondence of Sir George Radcliffe', *UCR* Vol XIII No. 2: 68–82.
—— (2002b), 'A Master's Widow writes …', *UCR* Vol. XIII no. 2: 104–5.
—— (2003), 'Univ.'s First Overseas Members', *UCR* Vol. XIII no. 3: 64–75.
—— (2005a), 'The Medieval Buildings of University College, Oxford', *Oxoniensia*, 70: 9–26.
—— (2005b), 'The Student Hoaxers: The New Shelley Letters', *UCR* Vol. XIV no. 1: 78–87.
—— (2005c), 'Univ. during the Second World War', *UCR* Vol. XIV no. 1: 100–11.
—— (2006), 'Henry Percy's Gift: Univ. and the Parish of Arncliffe', *UCR* Vol. XIV no. 2: 83–97.
DARWIN, J. G. (1994), 'A World University', *HUO* viii. 607–36.
DAVENPORT-HINES, R. (ed.) (2006), *Letters from Oxford: Hugh Trevor-Roper to Bernard Berenson* (London).
DAVIES, C. S. L., and GARNETT, J. (1994), *Wadham College* (Oxford).
DAVIES, M., and DAVIES, D. (1997), *Creating St. Catherine's College* (Oxford).
DAY, C. J. (1997), 'The University and the City', *HUO* vi. 441–76.
DENLEY, P. (1991), 'The Collegiate Movement of Italian Universities in the late Middle Ages', *History of Universities* 10: 29–91.
DENT, C. M. (1983), *Protestant Reformers in Elizabethan Oxford* (Oxford).
DOBLE, C. E. (1888–9), 'Letters of the Rev. William Ayerst, 1706–21', *The English Historical Review*, 3/12 (Oct. 1888): 751–60 and 4/14 (Apr. 1889): 338–350.
DOBSON, R. B. (1973), *Durham Priory 1400–1450* (Cambridge).
—— (1992), 'The Religious Orders 1370–1540', *HUO* ii. 539–79.
DODDS, E. R. (1977), *Missing Persons: An Autobiography* (Oxford).
DOOLITTLE, I. G. (1986), 'College Administration', *HUO* v. 227–68.
DRUMM, W. (1991), *The Old Palace: A History of the Oxford University Catholic Chaplaincy* (Oscott Series 7).
DUFFY, E. (1992), *The Stripping of the Altars: Traditional Religion in England 1400–1580* (New Haven).
DUNBABIN, J. (1984), 'Careers and Vocations', *HUO* i. 565–605.
DUNBABIN, J. P. D. (1986), 'College Estates and Wealth 1660–1815', *HUO* v. 269–307.
—— (1994), 'Finance Since 1914', *HUO* viii. 639–82.
—— (1997), 'Finance and Property', *HUO* vi. 375–440.
DUNCAN, G. D. (1980), 'The Heads of Houses and Religious Change in Tudor Oxford, 1547–1558', *Oxoniensia* 45: 226–34.
DURNING, L. (2006), *Queen Elizabeth's Book of Oxford* (Oxford).
EDEN, R. (1744), *Jurisprudentia Philologica sive Elementa Juris Civilis* (Oxford).
EDWARDS, E. (1999), *A New History of Flamstead* (Flamstead).
EDWARDS, J. (1749), *The Substance of Two Actions and the Proceedings therein in the University Court of Oxford* (London).
EDWARDS, K. (1956), 'The College of De Vaux, Salisbury', R. B. Pugh and Elizabeth Crittall (eds.), *The Victoria County History of Wiltshire*, iii (London): 369–85.

ELLIOTT, I. (1934), *The Balliol College Register, Second Edition: 1833–1933* (Oxford).
ELLIOTT, J. R. Jr. (1997), 'Drama', *HUO* iv. 641–58.
EMDEN, A. B. (1957–9), *A Biographical Register of the University of Oxford to 1500* (3 vols., Oxford).
—— (1968), *An Oxford Hall in Medieval Times* (2nd edn., Oxford).
—— (1974), *A Biographical Register of the University of Oxford A. D. 1501 to 1540* (Oxford).
ENGEL, A. J. (1983), *From Clergyman to Don: The Rise of the Academic Profession in Nineteenth-Century Oxford* (Oxford).
ESDAILE, K. A., and TOYNBEE, M. (1952–3), 'The University College Statue of James II', *UCR* 1952–3: 24–32.
EVANS, J. (1981), 'Univ. and the Oxford Group 1927–9', *UCR* Vol. VIII no. 2: 123–36.
EVANS, M. (ed.) (1887), *Letters of Richard Radcliffe and John James of Queen's College, Oxford, 1755–83* (OHS ix).
EVANS, T. A. R. (1992), 'The Number, Origins and Careers of Scholars', *HUO* ii. 485–538.
—— and FAITH, R. J. (1992), 'College Estates and University Finances 1350–1500', *HUO* ii. 635–708.
FAIRER, D. (1986), 'Anglo-Saxon Studies', *HUO* v. 807–29.
FARNELL, L. R. (1934), *An Oxonian Looks Back* (London).
FARQUHARSON, A. S. L. (1934), 'College Athletics', *UCR* 1934: 9–13.
FARRER, W., and BROWNHILL, J. (eds.) (1911), *A History of the County of Lancaster* (VCH) iv (London).
FEHRENBACH, R. J., and LEEDHAM-GREEN, E. S. (eds.) (1993), *Private Libraries in Renaissance England Volume II* (Medieval and Renaissance Texts and Studies no. 105).
—— (1994), *Private Libraries in Renaissance England Volume III* (Medieval and Renaissance Texts and Studies no. 117).
—— (1995), *Private Libraries in Renaissance England Volume IV* (Medieval and Renaissance Texts and Studies no. 148).
—— (1998), *Private Libraries in Renaissance England Volume V* (Medieval and Renaissance Texts and Studies no. 189).
FEINGOLD, M. (1997*a*), 'The Humanities', *HUO* iv. 211–357.
—— (1997*b*), 'The Mathematical Sciences and New Philosophies', *HUO* iv. 359–448.
FENDLAY, J. (1996/7), 'William Rogers and his Correspondence', *Recusant History* 23: 285–317.
FERDINAND, C. Y. (2006), 'The Mystery of Cookery and the Art of Wheedling: What Magdalen Undergraduates Read in the Eighteenth Century', *Magdalen College Record* 2006: 127–36.
FINCHAM, K. (1990), *Prelate as Pastor: The Episcopate of James I* (Oxford).
—— (ed.) (1993), *The Early Stuart Church 1603–1642* (London).
—— (1997), 'Oxford and the Early Stuart Polity', *HUO* iv. 179–210.
FIRTH, A. E. (1962), 'Obadiah Walker. I', *UCR* Vol. IV no. 2: 95–106.
—— (1964), 'Obadiah Walker. II', *UCR* Vol. IV no. 4: 261–73.
—— (1970), 'Note by an ex-Proctor', *UCR* Vol. V no. 5 (1970), 361–5.
—— (1972), 'Univ. and the Oxford Movement 1830–50', *UCR* Vol. VI no. 2: 160–7.

FLETCHER, J. M. (ed) (1976), *Registrum Annalium Collegii Mertonensis 1567–1603* (OHS n.s. xxiv).
—— (1981), 'Change and Resistance to Change: A Consideration of the Development of English and German Universities during the Sixteenth Century', *History of Universities* 1: 1–36.
—— (1984), 'The Faculty of Arts', *HUO* i. 369–99.
—— (1986), 'The Faculty of Arts', *HUO* iii. 158–99.
FORBES, M. D. (ed.) (1928), *Clare College 1326–1926* (2 vols., Cambridge).
FORRESTER, C. D. I. (1969), 'The Arms of University College', *UCR* Vol. V no. 4: 270–2.
FOSTER, J. (1887–8), *Alumni Oxonienses: the members of the University of Oxford, 1715–1886; their parentage, birthplace and year of birth, with a record of their degrees; being the Matriculation Register of the University* (4 vols., Oxford and London).
—— (1891–2), *Alumni Oxonienses: the members of the University of Oxford, 1500–1714; their parentage, birthplace, and year of birth, with a record of their degrees; being the matriculation register of the University* (4 vols., Oxford and London).
FOX, A. (2000), *Oral and Literate Culture in England 1500–1700* (Oxford).
FOX, R., and GOODAY, G. (eds.) (2005), *Physics in Oxford 1839–1939: Laboratories, Learning, and College Life* (Oxford).
FOXE, J. (1583), *Actes and Monuments* (4th edn., London).
FUGGLES, J. (1981), 'William Laud and the Library of St. John's College, Oxford', *The Book Collector* 30: 19–38.
FULLER, T. (1840), *The History of the University of Cambridge*, ed. M. Prickett and T. Wright (Cambridge).
FYFE, C. (1993), *A History of Sierra Leone* (Aldershot).
GARDINER, A. B. (2003), 'Abraham Woodhead, "The Invisible Man": His Impact on Dryden's *The Hind and the Panther*', *Recusant History*, 26/4: 570–88.
GARDNER, A. D. (1975), *Some Recollections* (Typescript).
GEE, T. P., and WILD, J. H. S. (1979), 'Social Work in London: The Univ. Connection', *UCR* Vol. VII no. 5: 251–9.
GEORGE, H. B. (1906), *New College 1856–1906* (Oxford).
GETSY, D. J. (2004), *Body Doubles: Sculpture in Britain 1877–1905* (New Haven).
GIBBON. E. (1796), *Miscellaneous Works of Edward Gibbon, Esquire, with Memoirs of his Life and Writings Composed by Himself*, ed. John, Lord Sheffield (2 vols., London).
GIBSON, S. (1931), *Statuta Antiqua Universitatis Oxoniensis* (Oxford).
—— (1935 and 1937/8), 'Stone's Hospital', *Bodleian Library Record*, Vol. VIII nos. 88: 133–5, and 96: 453–5.
GIEYSZTOR, A. (1992), 'Management and Resources', H. de Ridder-Symoens, (ed.), *A History of the University in Europe, Volume I: Universities in the Middle Ages* (Cambridge): 108–43.
GILLAM, S. G. (1952), 'Arthur Charlett's Letters and Manuscripts', *Bodleian Library Record*, 4: 105–14.
—— (1999), 'Humfrey Wanley and Arthur Charlett'. *Bodleian Library Record*, 16: 411–29.

GILLON, L. B. (1937), *La Théorie des Oppositions et la Théologie du Péché au XIIIe Siècle* (Paris).
GILMOUR, I. (2002), *The Making of the Poets: Byron and Shelley in their Time* (London).
GLORIEUX, P. (1938a), 'Les 572 Questions du manuscrit de Douai 434: description du Tome I', *Recherches de théologie ancienne et médiévale* 9: 123–52.
—— (1938b), 'Les 572 Questions du manuscrit de Douai 434: description du Tome II', *Recherches de théologie ancienne et médiévale* 9: 225–67.
GOLDIE, M. (1996), 'Joshua Basset, Popery and Revolution', in D. E. D. Beales and H. B. Nisbet (eds.), *Sidney Sussex College Cambridge: Historical Essays in Commemoration of the Quatercentenary* (Woodbridge): 111–30.
GOODMAN, A. (1993), *Tell Them I'm On My Way* (London, 1993).
GOUDGE, H. L. (1940), *Glorying in the Cross: A Memorial Volume with a Biography by Elizabeth Goudge* (London).
GRAHAM, R. (1905), 'Description of Oxford, from the Hundred Rolls of Oxfordshire, ad 1279', *Collectanea IV* (OHS xlvii): 1–98.
GRANT, E. (1992), *Memoirs of a Highland Lady*, ed. A. Tod (Edinburgh).
GRAVES, R. (1788), *Recollections of Some Particulars of the Life of the late William Shenstone Esq.* (London).
GRAY, A., and BRITTAIN, F. (1979), *A History of Jesus College, Cambridge* (revised edn., London).
GREAVES, R. (1986), 'Religion in the University 1715–1800', *HUO* v. 401–24.
GREEN, G. (1995), *Water Wings* (Lewes).
GREEN, S. J. D., and HORDEN, P. (2007), *All Souls under the Ancien Régime: Politics, Learning and the Arts, c. 1600–1850* (Oxford).
GREEN, V. H. H. (1957), *Oxford Common Room: A Study of Lincoln College and Mark Pattison* (London).
—— (1979), *The Commonwealth of Lincoln College 1427–1977* (Oxford).
—— (1986a), 'The University and Social Life', *HUO* v. 309–58.
—— (1986b), 'Religion in the Colleges 1715–1800', *HUO* v. 425–67.
—— (1986c), 'Reformers and Reform in the University', *HUO* v. 607–37.
GREENSLADE, S. L. (1986), 'The Faculty of Theology', *HUO* iii. 295–334.
GREENSTEIN, D. I. (1994), 'The Junior Members, 1900–1990: A Profile', *HUO* viii. 45–77.
GRIER, L. (1952), *Achievement in Education: The Work of Michael Ernest Sadler 1885–1935* (London).
GROOT, J. DE (2002), 'Space, Patronage, Procedure: The Court at Oxford, 1642–46', *English Historical Review*, 117: 1204–27.
GUEST, I. (1991), *Dr. John Radcliffe and his Trust* (London).
HALSEY, A. H. (1994a), 'Oxford and the British Universities', *HUO* viii. 577–606.
—— (1994b), 'The Franks Commission', *HUO* viii. 721–36.
HAMMERSTEIN, N. (1996a), 'Relations with Authority', in H. de Ridder-Symoens (ed.), *A History of the University in Europe, Volume II: Universities in Early Modern Europe (1500–1800)* (Cambridge): 113–53.

—— (1996b), 'Epilogue: The Enlightenment', in H. de Ridder-Symoens (ed.), *A History of the University in Europe, Volume II: Universities in Early Modern Europe (1500–1800)* (Cambridge): 621–40.

HANNABUSS, S. C. (2000), 'Mathematics', *HUO* vii. 443–55.

HARE, A. J. C. (1896–1900), *The Story of My Life* (6 vols., London).

HARGREAVES, J. (1991), *L. R. Wager: A Life 1904–1965* (Oxford).

HARGREAVES-MAWDSLEY, W. N. (1969), *Woodforde at Oxford 1759–1776* (OHS new ser. xxi).

HARINGTON, SIR JOHN (1804), *Nugæ antiquæ: being a miscellaneous collection of original papers, in prose and verse; written during the reigns of Henry VIII. Edward VI. Queen Mary, Elizabeth, and King James by Sir John Harington. Selected from authentic remains by the late Henry Harington, M.A. and newly arranged, with illustrative notes, by Thomas Park* (2 vols, London).

HARMSEN, T. (2000), *Antiquarianism in the Augustan Age: Thomas Hearne 1678–1735* (Oxford).

HARRIS, J. (1994), 'The Arts and Social Sciences, 1939–70', *HUO* viii. 217–49.

—— (1997), *William Beveridge: A Biography* (2nd edn., Oxford).

HARRISON, B. (ed.) (1994a), *Corpuscles: A History of Corpus Christi College, Oxford in the Twentieth Century, Written by its Members* (Oxford).

—— (1994b), 'College Life, 1918–1939', *HUO* viii. 81–108.

—— (1994c), 'Politics', *HUO* viii. 377–412.

—— (1994d), 'Government and Administration, 1914–1964', *HUO* viii. 683–719.

HARVEY, J. H. (1992), 'Architecture in Oxford 1350–1500', *HUO*, ii. 747–68.

HARVIE, C. (1997), 'Reform and Expansion, 1854–1871', *HUO* vi. 697–730.

—— (2000), 'From the Cleveland Commission to the Statutes of 1882', *HUO* vii. 67–95.

HAVENS, P. S. (1979), 'The General Strike of 1926: A Reminiscence', *UCR*, Vol. VII no. 5: 267–73.

HAWKE, R. (1994), *The Hawke Memoirs* (London).

HAYTER, A. (ed.) (1996), *A Wise Woman: A Memoir of Lavinia Mynors from her Diaries and Letters* (Banham).

HEARNE, T. (1885), *Remarks and Collections of Thomas Hearne Volume I 1705–7*, ed. C. E. Doble (OHS ii).

—— (1886), *Remarks and Collections of Thomas Hearne Volume II 1707–10*, ed. C. E. Doble (OHS vii).

—— (1888), *Remarks and Collections of Thomas Hearne Volume III 1710–12*, ed. C. E. Doble (OHS xiii)

—— (1897), *Remarks and Collections of Thomas Hearne Volume IV 1712–14*, ed. D. W. Rannie (OHS xxxiv).

—— (1901), *Remarks and Collections of Thomas Hearne Volume V 1714–16*, ed. D. W. Rannie (OHS xlii).

—— (1902), *Remarks and Collections of Thomas Hearne Volume VI 1717–19*, ed. Committee of the Oxford Historical Society (OHS xliii).

—— (1906), *Remarks and Collections of Thomas Hearne Volume VII 1719–22*, ed. Committee of the Oxford Historical Society (OHS xlviii).

HEARNE, T. (1907), *Remarks and Collections of Thomas Hearne Volume VIII 1722–5*, ed. Committee of the Oxford Historical Society (OHS l).
—— (1914), *Remarks and Collections of Thomas Hearne Volume IX 1725–8*, ed. H. E. Salter (OHS lxv).
—— (1915), *Remarks and Collections of Thomas Hearne Volume X 1728–31*, ed. H. E. Salter (OHS lxvii).
—— 1921), *Remarks and Collections of Thomas Hearne Volume XI 1731–35*, ed. H. E. Salter (OHS lxxii).
HERBERT, E. (1976), *The Life of Edward, First Lord Herbert of Cherbury, Written by Himself*, ed. J. M. Shuttleworth (Oxford).
HEWART. G. (1936), 'William, Lord Stowell', *UCR* 1936: 20–4.
HIGDEN, R. (1865–86), *Polychronicon Ranulphi Higden monachi cestrensis*, ed. C. Babington and J. R. Lumby (9 vols., Rolls Series 41).
HIGHFIELD, J. R. L. (1984), 'The Early Colleges', *HUO* i. 225–63.
—— (ed.) (2006), *Registrum Annalium Collegii Mertonensis 1603–1660* (OHS new ser. xli).
HILL, R. M. T. (ed.) (1975), *The Rolls and Register of Bishop Oliver Sutton, 1280–1299, Volume VII* (Lincoln Record Society lxix).
HINCHLIFF, P. (2000), 'Religious Issues, 1870–1914', *HUO* vii. 97–112.
HINCHLIFFE, T. (1992), *North Oxford* (New Haven).
HINDE, T. (1992), *Paths of Progress: A History of Marlborough College* (London).
HISCOCK, W. G. (1946), *A Christ Church Miscellany* (Oxford).
HMC (1883), *Ninth Report of the Royal Commission on Historical Manuscripts Part I: Report and Appendix* (London).
—— (1901), *Report of the Royal Commission on Historical Manuscripts: The Manuscripts of his Grace the Duke of Portland, Preserved at Welbeck Abbey*, Vol. VII (London).
HODGKIN, R. H. (1949), *Six Centuries of an Oxford College: A History of the Queen's College 1340–1940* (Oxford).
HOGG, T. J. (1906), *The Life of Percy Bysshe Shelley* (London).
HOLLAND, S. M. (1987), 'George Abbot: "The Wanted Archbishop"', *Church History* 56/2 (June): 172–87.
HOLMES, G. (1982), *Augustan England: Professions, State and Society 1670–1730* (London).
HONEY, J. R. DE S., and CURTHOYS, M. C. (2000), 'Oxford and Schooling', *HUO* vii. 545–69.
HONEYBALL, J. (1986), 'Seventeenth Century Rebuilding in Univ.', *UCR* Vol. IX no. 2: 65–9.
HOPKINS, C. (2005), *Trinity: 450 Years of an Oxford College Community* (Oxford).
HOPKINSON, A. W. (1958), *Pastor's Progress* (London).
How, F. S. (1904), *Six Great Schoolmasters* (London).
HOWARD, H. F. (1935), *An Account of the Finances of the College of St John the Evangelist in the University of Cambridge 1511–1926* (Cambridge).
HOWARTH, J. (2000a), '"In Oxford but...not of Oxford": The Women's Colleges', *HUO* vii. 237–307.
—— (2000b), 'The Self-Governing University, 1882–1914', *HUO* vii. 599–643.

HOWELL, P. (2000), 'Oxford Architecture 1800–1914', *HUO* vii. 729–77.
HOYLE, J. (1641), *A Reioynder to Master Malone's Reply Concerning Reall Presence* (Dublin).
—— (1645), *Jehojadahs iustice against Mattan, Baals priest: or, The Covenanters justice against idolaters, a sermon preacht upon occasion of a speech utter'd upon Tower-hill, by J.H., Minister of the Gospel* (London).
HUNT, R. W. (1950), 'The Manuscript Collection of University College, Oxford: Origins and Growth', *Bodleian Library Record* Vol III no. 29: 13–34.
HUXLEY, L. (1900), *Life and Letters of Thomas Henry Huxley* (2 vols., London).
INGPEN, R. (ed.) (1912), *The Letters of Percy Bysshe Shelley* (2 vols., London).
INGRAM, J. (1837), *Memorials of Oxford* (3 vols., Oxford).
INGRAMS, R. (2005), *My Friend Footy: A Memoir of Paul Foot by Richard Ingrams* (London).
JACKSON, R. (1959), *The Chief: The Biography of Gordon Hewart, Lord Chief Justice of England, 1922–40* (London).
JACOB, E. J. (ed.) (1947), *The Register of Henry Chichele, Archbishop of Canterbury 1414–1443, Volume IV* (Oxford).
JARRATT, G. (2004), *The Life of Walter Skirlaw: Medieval Diplomat and Prince Bishop of Durham* (Beverley).
JENKYNS, R. (2000), 'Classical Studies, 1872–1914', *HUO* vii. 327–31.
—— and MURRAY, O. (1997), 'The Beginnings of Greats, 1800–1872', *HUO* vi. 513–42.
JONES, H. S. (2000), 'University and College Sport', *HUO* vii. 517–543.
JONES, J. (2005), *Balliol College: A History* (2nd edn. revised, Oxford).
JONES, M. J. (1997), 'The Agricultural Depression, Collegiate Finances, and Provision for Education at Oxford, 1871–1913', *Economic History Review*, 50/1: 57–81.
JONES, W. (1795), *Memoirs of the Life, Studies, and Writings of the Right Reverend George Horne D.D. late Lord Bishop of Norwich* (London).
KABASERVICE, G. (2004), *The Guardians: Kingman Brewster, his Circle, and the Rise of the Liberal Establishment* (New York).
KARDAR, A. H. (1987), *Memoirs of an All-Rounder* (Lahore).
KAY, D. (1994), 'Architecture', *HUO* viii. 499–518.
KAY, D. C. (1976), 'A Univ. Poem of 1626', *UCR* Vol VII no. 2: 75–8.
KEENE, N. (2003), 'John Fell: Education, Erudition and the English Church in Late Seventeenth-Century Oxford', *History of Universities*, 18/1: 62–101.
KENNICOTT, B. (1756), *A Word to the Hutchinsonians: Or Remarks on Three extraordinary Sermons Lately preached before the University of Oxford, by The Reverend Dr. Patten, The Reverend Mr. Wetherall, and The Reverend Mr. Horne, By a Member of the University* (London).
KENNY, A. (ed.) (2001), *The History of the Rhodes Trust 1902–1999* (Oxford).
KENYON, J. (1972), *The Popish Plot* (London).
KER, N. R. (1959), 'Oxford College Libraries in the Sixteenth Century', *Bodleian Library Record*, 6/3: 459–515.
—— (1986), 'The Provision of Books', *HUO* iii. 441–77.
KEYNES, S. (1999), 'The Cult of King Alfred the Great', *Anglo-Saxon England*, 28: 225–356.

KIDD, B. J. (ed.) (1903), *Selected Letters of William Bright, D.D.*, with an introductory Memoir by P. G. Medd (London).
KIESSLING, N. K. (2001), *The Library of Anthony Wood* (Oxford Bibliographical Society 3rd ser. v).
KUHN, A. J. (1961), 'Glory or Gravity: Hutchinson vs. Newton', *Journal of the History of Ideas*, 22/3: 303–22.
LACEY, N. (2004), *A Life of H. L. A. Hart: The Nightmare and the Noble Dream* (Oxford).
LANDER, J. R. (1969), *Conflict and Stability in Fifteenth-Century England* (London).
LANGFORD, P. (1986), 'Tories and Jacobites 1714–51', *HUO* v. 99–127.
LAWRENCE, C. H. (1984), 'The University in State and Church', *HUO* i. 98–150.
LEADER, D. R. (1988), *A History of the University of Cambridge Volume I: The University to 1546* (Cambridge).
LEEDHAM-GREEN, E. (1996), *A Concise History of the University of Cambridge* (Cambridge).
LEFF, G. (1968), *Paris and Oxford Universities in the Thirteenth and Fourteenth Centuries* (New York).
—— (1992), 'The Trivium and the Three Philosophies', in H. de Ridder-Symoens (ed.), *A History of the University in Europe, Volume I: Universities in the Middle Ages* (Cambridge), 307–36.
LE NEVE, J. (1979), *Fasti Ecclesiae Anglicanae 1541–1857 Volume V: Bath & Wells Diocese*, ed. J. M. Horn and D. Sherwin Bailey (London).
—— (1986), *Fasti Ecclesiae Anglicanae 1541–1857 Volume VI: Salisbury Diocese*, ed. J. M. Horn (London).
—— (1992), *Fasti Ecclesiae Anglicanae 1541–1857 Volume VII: Ely, Norwich, Westminster and Worcester Dioceses*, ed. J. M. Horn (London).
—— (1996), *Fasti Ecclesiae Anglicanae 1541–1857 Volume VIII: Bristol, Gloucester, Oxford, and Peterborough Dioceses*, ed. J. M. Horn (London).
LENNON, C. (1981), *Richard Stanihurst the Dubliner, 1547–1618: A Biography* (Blackrock).
LEWIS, C. S. (1991), *All my Road before me: The Diary of C. S. Lewis 1922–7*, ed. W. Hooper (London).
—— (2000), *Collected Letters Volume I: Family Letters 1905–1931*, ed. W. Hooper (London).
—— (2004), *Collected Letters Volume II: Books, Broadcasts and War 1931–1949*, ed. W. Hooper (London).
LINCOLN, A. L. J., and McEWEN, R. L. (eds.) (1960), *Lord Eldon's Anecdote Book* (London).
LOACH, J. (1986), 'Reformation Controversies', *HUO* iii. 363–96.
LOGAN, D. W. (1974), 'Lubens Subscribo sub Tutamine Leys Farquharson et Walker', *UCR* Vol. VI no. 4: 367–76.
LOVATT, R. (1995/6), 'The Triumph of the Colleges in Late Medieval Oxford and Cambridge: The Case of Peterhouse', *History of Universities* 14: 95–147.
MACCARTHY, F. (1994), *William Morris: A Life for our Time* (London).
McCONICA, J. (1986a), 'The Rise of the Undergraduate College', *HUO* iii. 1–68.
—— (1986b), 'Elizabethan Oxford: The Collegiate Society', *HUO* iii. 645–732.

—— (ed.) (1996), *Unarmed Soldiery: Studies in the Early History of All Souls College Oxford* (Oxford).
MacCulloch, D. (2003), *Reformation: Europe's House Divided 1490–1700* (London).
McDowell, R. B., and Webb, D. A. (1982), *Trinity College Dublin, 1592–1952: An Academic History* (Cambridge).
McFadyean, A. (1964), *Recollected in Tranquillity* (London).
Macgregor, A. G., and Turner, A. J. (1986), 'The Ashmolean Museum', *HUO* v. 639–68.
Mackenzie, C. (1964), *My Life and Times: Octave Three 1900–1907* (London).
McLachlan, D. (1968), *Room 39: Naval Intelligence in Action 1939–45* (London).
Macphail, J. G. S. (1980), 'Trinity Term—Oxford 1919: The Buckshee Term at Univ. College', *UCR* Vol. VIII no. 1: 40–52.
Macray, W. D. (1901), *A Register of the Members of St Mary Magdalen College, Oxford, Volume III: Fellows 1576–1648* (London).
Madan, F. (1909), 'The Site of the College before the Foundation, including Brasenose and Little University Halls', *Brasenose Quatercentenary Monographs* i (OHS lii), Monograph I.
—— (1925), *Oxford outside the Guide-Books* (2nd edn., Oxford).
Magrath, J. R. (ed.) (1903), *The Flemings in Oxford Volume I* (OHS xliv).
—— (ed.) (1913), *The Flemings in Oxford Volume II* (OHS lxii).
—— (1921), *The Queen's College* (2 vols., Oxford).
—— (ed.) (1924), *The Flemings in Oxford Volume III* (OHS lxxix).
Mallet, C. E. (1924–7), *A History of the University of Oxford* (3 vols., London).
—— (1932), *Herbert Gladstone, a Memoir* (London).
Marshall, P. J. (1986), 'Oriental Studies', *HUO* v. 551–63.
Martin, G. H., and Highfield, J. R. L. (1997), *A History of Merton College* (Oxford).
Mason, J. F. A. (2000), 'Christ Church', *HUO* vii. 221–36.
Matthews, A. G. (1934), *Calamy Revised: Being a Revision of Edmund Calamy's Account of the Ministers and Others Ejected and Silenced 1660–2* (Oxford).
Maurice, T. (1819–20), *Memoirs of the Author of Indian Antiquities* (2 vols., London).
Max Müller, F. (1901), *My Autobiography* (London).
Melikan, R. A. (1999), *John Scott, Lord Eldon 1751–1838: The Duty of Loyalty* (Cambridge).
Mendl, R. W. S. (1971), *Reflections of a Music Lover* (London).
Merrick, J. (2003), 'Morellet's "Mélanges sur l'Angleterre" ', D. Medlin and J. Merrick (eds.), *André Morellet: Texts and Contexts* (Oxford): 31–64.
Miller, E. (1961), *Portrait of a College: A History of the College of St. John the Evangelist in Cambridge* (Cambridge).
Miller, J. (1978), *James II: A Study in Kingship* (Hove).
Miller, J. (2008), *We will Remember Them* (Oxford).
Milton, A. (1995), *Catholic and Reformed: The Roman and Protestant Churches in English Protestant Thought, 1600–1640* (Cambridge).
Mitchell, H. (1974), *The Spice of Life* (London).
Mitchell, L. G. (1970), 'The First Univ. Dining Club?', *UCR* Vol. V no. 5: 351–8.

MITCHELL, L. G. (1973), 'Univ., Sir William Jones, and the 1780 Election', *UCR* Vol. VI no. 3: 257–62.
—— (1986), 'Politics and Revolution 1772–1800', *HUO* v. 163–90.
—— (1989), 'Thomas Cooper: Univ.'s Revolutionary in France', *UCR* Vol. X no. 1: 86–92.
—— (1995), 'The Shooting of the Master', *UCR* Vol. XI no. 3: 66–9.
—— (1996), 'The Screwing-up of the Dean', *UCR* Vol. XI no. 4: 69–81.
—— (1998), 'Obadiah Walker: Addendum', *UCR* Vol. XII no. 2: 69–73.
—— (2002), 'The Stanhopes at Univ.', *UCR* Vol. XIII no. 2: 83–90.
—— (2004), 'The Arrival of Women in Univ.', *UCR* Vol. XIII no. 4: 69–75.
—— (2005), 'Murder, Univ., and G. D. H. Cole', *UCR* Vol. XIV no. 1: 112–18.
—— (2007), 'The Tribulations of a Bursar 1779–81', *UCR* Vol. XIV no. 3: 77–84.
MITCHELL, R. J. (1938), *John Tiptoft (1427–1470)* (London).
MITCHELL, W. T. (ed.) (1980), *Epistolae Academicae 1508–96* (OHS new ser. xxvi).
—— (ed.) (1998), *Register of Congregations 1505–1517* (2 vols., OHS new ser. xxxvii–xxxviii).
MONEY, D. (1998), *The English Horace: Anthony Alsop and the Tradition of British Latin Verse* (Oxford).
MONOD, P. K. (1989), *Jacobitism and the English People 1688–1788* (Cambridge).
MOORE, A. M. (1954), *Recollections of University College 1896–1900* (typescript).
MORRELL, J. (2005), *John Phillips and the Business of Victorian Science* (Aldershot).
MORRELL, J. B. (1994), 'The Non-Medical Sciences, 1914–39', *HUO* viii. 139–63.
MORGAN, V., with a contribution by BROOKE, C. N. L. (2004), *A History of the University of Cambridge Volume II 1546–1750* (Cambridge).
MORRIS, R. (1990), 'Reminiscences', *UCR* Vol. X no. 2: 54–61.
MORRIS, W. (1984), *Political Writings of William Morris*, ed. A. L. Morton (London).
MÜLLER, R. A. (1996), 'Student Education, Student Life', in H. de Ridder-Symoens (ed.), *A History of the University in Europe, Volume II: Universities in Early Modern Europe (1500–1800)* (Cambridge): 326–54.
MURRAY, A. (1985), *Reason and Society in the Middle Ages* (Oxford).
—— (2000), '1249', *UCR* Vol. XII no. 4: 52–73.
NAIPAUL. V. S. (1999), *Letters between a Father and Son*, ed. G. Aitken (London).
NEWMAN, J. (1986), 'The Physical Setting: New Building and Adaptation', *HUO* iii. 597–644.
—— (1997), 'The Architectural Setting', *HUO* iv. 135–77.
NEWTON, R. (1723), *The Proceedings of the Visitors of University College, with regards to the late disputed Election of a Master, vindicated* (Oxford).
NICHOLS, J. (1828), *The Progresses, Processions and Magnificent Festivities of King James the First* (4 vols., London).
NOCKLES, P. B. (1994), *The Oxford Movement in Context: Anglican High Churchmanship, 1760–1857* (Cambridge).
—— (1997), ' "Lost Causes and…Impossible Loyalties": The Oxford Movement and the University', *HUO* vi. 195–267.
NORTH, J. D. (1992), 'Astronomy and Mathematics', *HUO* ii. 103–74.
NUTTALL, B. H. (1986), *The Saviles of Thornhill: Life at Thornhill Hall in the Reign of Charles I* (Leeds).

OATES, J. (2003), 'The Rise and Fall of Jacobitism in Oxford', *Oxoniensia* 68: 89–111.
OCKWELL, A., and POLLINS, H. (2000), ' "Extension" in all its Forms', *HUO* vii. 661–88.
OLIVER, A. M. (ed.) (1924) *Early Deeds Relating to Newcastle upon Tyne* (Surtees Society cxxxvii).
ORME, N. (2006), *Medieval Schools from Roman Britain to Renaissance England* (New Haven).
OSWALD, A. (1954), 'University College', in *VCH Oxon.* iii. 61–81.
OVENELL, R. F. (1986), *The Ashmolean Museum 1683–1894* (Oxford).
OXENDEN, A. (1891), *The History of my Life* (London).
PALMER, D. J. (2000), 'English', *HUO* vii. 397–411.
PALMER, K. N. (1997), *Ceremonial Barges on the River Thames: A History of the Barges of the City of London Livery Companies and of the Crown* (London).
PANTIN, W. A. (1954), 'Oriel College', *VCH Oxon.* iii. 119–31.
—— (1964), 'The Halls and Schools of Medieval Oxford: An Attempt at Reconstruction', *Oxford Studies Presented to Daniel Callus* (OHS new ser. xvi): 31–100.
PANTIN, W. A., and MITCHELL, W. T. (eds.) (1972), *The Register of Congregation 1448–1463* (OHS new ser. xvii).
PARIS, M. (1872–83), *Matthaei Parisiensis, monachi Sancti Albani chronica majora*, ed. H. R. Luard (7 vols., Rolls Series lvii).
PARK, R. (1989), 'Our Ex-Porter's Voice', *UCR* Vol. X no. 1: 46–57.
—— (1992), 'O Statua Gentilissima, Or, Lord Eldon vs. the Science Library', *UCR* Vol. X no. 4: 55–62.
PARRY, G. (2006), *The Arts of the Anglican Counter-Reformation: Glory, Laud and Honour* (Woodbridge).
PARSONS, M. (2003), *Room to Swing a Cat* (Spennymoor).
PASMORE, S. (1982), 'Thomas Henshaw, F.R.S. (1618–1700)', *Notes and Records of the Royal Society of London*, 36/2: 177–88.
PATTERSON, D. (1986), 'Hebrew Studies', *HUO* v. 535–50.
PATTISON, M. (1988), *Memoirs*, ed. V. H. H. Green (London).
PAUL, G. A. (1954/5), 'The Chapel Organ', *UCR* 1954/5: 70–4.
PETTER, H. M. (1974), *The Oxford Almanacks* (Oxford).
PETTIS, W. (1715), *Some Memoirs of the Life of John Radcliffe M.D.* (London).
PHELPS BROWN, E. H., and HOPKINS, S. V. (1956), 'Seven Centuries of the Prices of Consumables, Compared with Builders' Wage-Rates', *Economica*, n.s. 23/92 (Nov.): 296–314.
PHILIP. I. G. (1986), 'Libraries and the University Press', *HUO* v. 725–55.
PIGGOTT, S. (1986), 'Antiquarian Studies', *HUO* v. 757–77.
PINKNEY, T. (2007), *William Morris in Oxford: The Campaigning Yean, 1879–1895* (Grosmont).
PLAYFAIR, N. (1930), *Hammersmith Hoy: A Book of Minor Revelations* (London).
PLUMMER, C. (ed.) (1887), *Elizabethan Oxford* (OHS viii).
PLUMPTRE, F. C. (1847), 'Some Account of the Parish Church at Bakewell in Derbyshire and of the Early Grave-Stones and Other Remains Discovered during the Recent Repairs', *Archaeological Journal*, 4: 37–58.
—— (1861), 'Some Account of the Remains of the Priory of St. Martin's and the Church of St. Martin-le-Grand at Dover', *Archaeologica Cantiana*, 4: 1–26.

PORTER, S. (1997), 'University and Society', *HUO* iv. 25–103.
POTTER, J. (1994), *Tennis and Oxford* (Oxford).
POWICKE, F. M. (1931), *Medieval Books of Merton College* (1931).
PREST, J. (1994), 'The Asquith Commission, 1919–1922', *HUO* viii. 27–43.
—— (2000), ' "Balliol, For Example" ', *HUO* vii. 159–69.
PREST, W. R. (1972), *The Inns of Court under Elizabeth I and the Early Stuarts 1590–1640* (London).
PROTHERO, R. E. (1895), *Letters and Verses of Arthur Penrhyn Stanley* (London).
—— and BRADLEY, G. G. (1893), *The Life and Correspondence of Arthur Penrhyn Stanley* (2 vols., London).
QUARRIE, P. (1986), 'The Christ Church Collection Books', *HUO* v. 493–511.
QUICK, A. (1990), *Charterhouse: A History of the School* (London).
RASHDALL, H. (1936), *The Universities of Europe in the Middle Ages*, new edn. by F. M. Powicke and A. B. Emden (3 vols, Oxford).
RAYNER, M. E. (1993), *The Centenary History of St. Hilda's College, Oxford* (Oxford).
REDCLIFFE-MAUD, J. (1978), 'The University College Musical Society', *UCR* Vol. VII no. 4: 188–98.
—— (1991), *Peace and War: The Memories of an Octogenarian: Book One* (Cirencester).
REDCLIFFE-MAUD, J. P. R. (1973), 'Master Sadler after Fifty Years', *UCR* Vol. VI no. 3: 250–3.
—— (1981), *Experiences of an Optimist* (London).
REDFORD, B. (ed.) (1992–4), *The Letters of Samuel Johnson* (5 vols., Oxford).
REITZEL, J. M. (1971), 'The Founding of the Earliest Secular Colleges within the Universities of Paris and Oxford' (unpublished Ph.D. thesis, Brown University).
RENTON, D. (2006), *The Spice of Life* (London).
RIDDER-SYMOENS, H. DE (1992), 'Mobility', in H. de Ridder-Symoens (ed.), *A History of the University in Europe, Volume I: Universities in the Middle Ages* (Cambridge): 280–304.
—— (1996), 'Management and Resources', in H. de Ridder-Symoens (ed.), *A History of the University in Europe, Volume II: Universities in Early Modern Europe (1500–1800)* (Cambridge): 154–209.
ROCHE, J. (1994), 'The Non-Medical Sciences, 1939–70', *HUO* viii. 251–89.
ROGERS, F. (1711), *Orationes ex poetis Latinis Excerptae* (Oxford).
ROOPER, W. H. (1893), *Reminiscences of my Life*, ed. T. G. Rooper (Bournemouth).
ROSE, K. (1975), *The Later Cecils* (London).
ROTHBLATT, S. (1997), 'An Oxonian "Idea" of a University: J. H. Newman and "Well-Being" ', *HUO* vi. 287–305.
ROY, I., and REINHART, D. (1997), 'Oxford and the Civil Wars', *HUO* iv. 687–731.
RUDD, A. (1990), *One Boy's War* (London).
RUSHWORTH, J. (1659), *Historical Collections of Private Passages of State, Weighty Matters in Law, Remarkable Proceedings in Five Parliaments. Beginning in the sixteenth year of King James anno 1618. And ending the fifth year of King Charles, anno 1629* (London).

Rushbrook Williams, L. F. (1975), 'Recollections of pre-1914 Oxford', *UCR* Vol. VII no. 1: 22–9.
Russell, E. (1977), 'The Influx of Commoners into the University of Oxford before 1581: An Optical Illusion?', *EHR* 92 (1977): 721–45.
—— (1985), 'Marian Oxford and the Counter-Reformation', in C. M. Barron and C. Harper-Bill (eds.), *The Church in Pre-Reformation Society: Essays in Honour of F. R. H. Du Boulay* (Woodbridge): 212–27.
Sadleir, M. (1949), *Michael Ernest Sadler* (London).
Sadler, M. E. (1933), 'Opie's Portrait of Dr. Johnson', *UCR* 1932/3: 10–11.
Salter, H. E. (ed.) (1912), *Records of Medieval Oxford: Coroners Inquests, the Walls of Oxford etc.*, (Oxford).
—— (ed.) (1914), *The Cartulary of the Hospital of St. John the Baptist Volume I* (OHS lxvi).
—— (ed.) (1920), *Munimenta Civitatis Oxoniae* (OHS lxxi).
—— (ed.) (1920–1), *Mediaeval Archives of the University of Oxford* (2 vols., OHS lxx and lxxiii).
—— (ed.) (1923), *Registrum Annalium Collegii Mertoniensis 1483–1521* (OHS lxxvi).
—— (ed.) (1924), *Snappe's Formulary and other Records* (OHS lxxx).
—— (ed.) (1929), *Cartulary of Osney Abbey, Volume II* (OHS lxxxix).
—— (ed.) (1932), *Registrum Cancellarii Oxoniensis 1434-1469* (2 vols., OHS xciii–xciv).
—— (1964–9), *Survey of Oxford*, ed. W. A. Pantin and W. T. Mitchell (2 vols., OHS new ser. xvi, xx).
—— and Lobel, M. R. (eds.) (1954), *A History of the County of Oxford*, vol. iii (London).
Saul, N. (1997), *Richard II* (Yale).
Sayers, J. E. (1999), *Original Papal Documents in England and Wales from the Accession of Pope Innocent III to the Death of Pope Benedict XI (1198–1304)* (Oxford).
Schlepegrell, A. (1934), 'A German Student in Oxford', *UCR* 1934: 24–8.
Schwinges, R. C. (1992), 'Student Education, Student Life', in H. de Ridder-Symoens (ed.), *A History of the University in Europe, Volume I: Universities in the Middle Ages* (Cambridge): 195–243.
Scott, D. (1971), *A. D. Lindsay: A Biography* (Oxford).
Screaton, N. (1984), 'Univ. in the First World War', *UCR* Vol. XI no. 5: 340–50.
Searby, P. (1997), *A History of the University of Cambridge Volume III 1750–1870* (Cambridge).
Selborne, Earl of (1896), *Memorials Part I: Family and Personal 1766–1865* (2 vols., London).
—— (1898), *Memorials Part II: Personal and Political 1865–1895* (2 vols., London).
Shadwell, C. L. (1898), *The Universities and College Estate Acts, 1858 to 1880: Their History and Results* (Oxford).
Shaftesbury, Ashley, Earl of (1716), *Several letters written by a noble lord to a young man at the university* (London).
Sharpe, R. (2005), 'Thomas Tanner (1674–1735), the 1697 Catalogue, and *Bibliotheca Britannica*', *The Library*, 6/4 (Dec.): 381–421.

SHAW-MILLER L. (ed.) (2001), *Clare through the Twentieth Century* (Lingfield).
SHEEHAN, M. W. (1984), 'The Religious Orders 1220–1370', *HUO* i. 193–221.
SHERRIFF, C. (2003), *The Oxford College Barges: Their History and Architecture* (London).
SHERWOOD. J., and PEVSNER, N. (1974), *Oxfordshire* (London).
SHERWOOD, W. E. (1900) *Oxford Rowing: A History of Boat-Racing at Oxford from the Earliest Times* (Oxford).
SHUFFREY, W. A. (1903), *Some Craven Worthies* (London).
SILVESTER, T. (ed.) (1750), *Select Theological Discourses Written by the Late Rev. Thomas Cockman, D.D.* (2 vols., London).
SIMONE, M. R. DI (1996), 'Admission', in H. de Ridder-Symoens (ed.), *A History of the University in Europe, Volume II: Universities in Early Modern Europe (1500–1800)* (Cambridge): 285–325.
SIMPSON, A. W. B. (1986), *A History of the Land Law* (2nd edn., Oxford).
SLADEN, D. (1915), *Twenty Years of my Life* (London).
SLUSSER, M. (1979–81), 'Abraham Woodhead (1608–78): Some Research Notes, Chiefly about his Writings', *Recusant History* 15: 406–22.
SMALLEY, B. (1952), *The Study of the Bible in the Middle Ages* (Oxford).
SMITH, G. (1864), *A Plea for the Abolition of Tests in the University of Oxford* (2nd edn., Oxford).
—— (1895), *Oxford and her Colleges: A View from the Radcliffe Library* (London).
—— (1910), *Reminiscences*, ed. A. Haultain (New York).
SMITH, M. H. (ed.) (2000), *Keyingham and its People: The Story of a Millennium* (Keyingham).
SMITH, W. (1728), *The Annals of University College* (Newcastle).
SNOW, P. (1991), *Oxford Observed* (London).
SOARES. J. A. (1999), *The Decline of Privilege: The Modernization of Oxford University* (Stanford).
SOUTHERN, R. W. (1954), 'Exeter College', *VCH Oxon* iii. 107–18.
—— (1984), 'From Schools to University', *HUO* i. 1–36.
—— (1995), *Scholastic Humanism and the Unification of Europe: Volume I - Foundations* (Oxford).
SPELMAN, J. (1678), *Ælfredi Magni Anglorum Regis Invictissimi Vita* (Oxford).
SPENDER, S. (1951), *World within World* (London).
SPRAGGON, J. (2003), *Puritan Iconoclasm during the English Civil War* (Woodbridge).
STEVENSON, W. H., and SALTER, H. E. (1939), *The Early History of St John's College Oxford* (Oxford).
STIRLING, A. M. W. (1911), *Annals of a Yorkshire House* (2 vols., London).
STOKES, A. D. (1977), 'The Admission of Women', *UCR* Vol. VII no. 3: 121–2.
STONE, L. (1975), 'The Size and Composition of the Oxford Student Body 1580–1910', in L. Stone (ed.) *The University in Society* (2 vols., Princeton), i. 3–110.
—— (1993), *Broken Lives: Separation and Divorce in England 1660–1857* (Oxford).
STURDY, D. (1988), 'The Fellows' Garden in Regency and early Victorian Times', *UCR* Vol. IX No. 4: 59–62.
—— (1990), 'The Building of the Front Quad: (i) The West Side', *UCR* Vol. X no. 2: 63–71.

—— (1991), 'The Building of the Front Quad: (ii) The North Side', *UCR* Vol. X no. 3: 80–4.
SUTHERLAND, L. S. (1986*a*), 'Political Respectability', *HUO* v. 129–61.
—— (1986*b*), 'The Laudian Statutes in the Eighteenth Century', *HUO* v. 191–203.
—— (1986*c*), 'The Administration of the University', *HUO* v. 205–25.
SWEET, R. (2004), *Antiquaries: The Discovery of the Past in Eighteenth-Century Britain* (London).
SYMONDS, J. A. (1984), *The Memoirs of John Addington Symonds*, ed. P. Grosskurth (London).
SYMONDS, R. (1986), *Oxford and Empire: The Last Lost Cause?* (New York).
TAPPER, T., and PALFREYMAN, D. (2000), *Oxford and the Decline of the Collegiate Tradition* (London).
TEIGNMOUTH, LORD (1804), *Memoirs of the Life, Writings, and Correspondence, of Sir William Jones* (London).
THOMAS, K. (1994), 'College Life, 1945–1970', *HUO* viii. 189–215.
THOMPSON, E. M. (ed.) (1875), *Letters of Humphrey Prideaux to J. Ellis 1674–1722* (Camden Soc. n.s. xv).
TODD, R. B. (2004), 'Technique in the Service of Humanism: A. B. Poynton's Legacy to E. R. Dodds', *Eikasmos* 15: 463–76.
TOMLINSON, H. (2000), 'Restoration to Reform, 1660–1832', in G. Aylmer and J. Tiller (eds.), *Hereford Cathedral: A History* (London): 109–55.
TOULMIN SMITH, L. (1896), 'Parliamentary Petitions relating to Oxford', in M. Burrows (ed.) *Collectanea III* (OHS xxxii): 77–161.
TREVELYAN, G. M. (1990), *Trinity College: An Historical Sketch*, ed. R. Robson (Cambridge).
TROWBRIDGE, A. B. (1976), *An Auld Acquaintance who'll ne'er be forgot. Memories of a Rhodes Scholar at University College, Oxford, 1920–23* (Boston).
TUCK, J. A. (1971), 'Richard II's System of Patronage', in F. R. H. du Boulay and C. M. Barron (eds.), *The Reign of Richard II: Essays in Honour of May McKisack* (London): 1–21.
TUCKWELL, W. (1900), *Reminiscences of Oxford* (London).
TUILIER, A. (1994), *Histoire de L'Université de Paris et de la Sorbonne* (2 vols., Paris).
TURNER, F. M. (1994), 'Religion', *HUO* viii. 293–316.
TURNER, W. H. (ed) (1871), *The visitations of the county of Oxford taken in the years 1566 by William Hervey Clarencieux, 1574 by Richard Lee Portcullis and in 1634 by John Philpott Somerset and William Ryley Bluemantle, together with the gatherings of Oxfordshire collected by Richard Lee in 1574* (Harleian Society v).
TWIGG, J. (1987), *A History of Queens' College, Cambridge, 1448–1986* (Woodbridge).
—— (1997), 'College Finances 1640–1660', *HUO* iv. 773–802.
TWISS, H. (1844), *The Public and Private Life of Lord Chancellor Eldon* (3 vols., London).
TYACK, G. (1998), *Oxford: An Architectural Guide* (Oxford).
—— (2005), *Modern Architecture in an Oxford College: St. John's College 1945–2005* (Oxford).
TYACKE, N. (1987), *Anti-Calvinists: The Rise of English Arminianism c.1590–1640* (Oxford).

TYACKE, N. (1997), 'Religious Controversy', *HUO* iv. 569–619.
TYERMAN, C. (2000), *A History of Harrow School 1324–1991* (Oxford).
USHER, C. (1699), *A letter to a member of the Convocation of the University of Oxford: containing the case of a late fellow elect of University-college* (London).
VARLEY, F. J. (1941), 'The Oriel College Lawsuit 1724–26', *Oxoniensia* 6: 56–69.
VERGER, J. (1992), 'Patterns', in H. de Ridder-Symoens (ed.), *A History of the University in Europe, Volume I: Universities in the Middle Ages* (Cambridge): 35–74.
VIRGIN, P. (1989), *The Church in an Age of Negligence: Ecclesiastical Structure and the Problems of Church Reform 1700–1840* (Cambridge).
VON MALAISE, N. (1985), 'Arthur Charlett as Master of University College', *UCR*, Vol. IX no. 1: 64–84.
WAINEWRIGHT, J. B. (1911–12), 'Fellows of Oxford Colleges Deprived at the Accession of Queen Elizabeth', *The Ushaw Magazine*, 21/63 (Dec.): 255–67, and 22/64 (Mar.): 51–7.
WALKER, J. (ed.) (c.1809), *Oxoniana Volume II* (London).
WALKER, J. M. (1974), 'John Webster', *UCR* Vol. VI no. 4: 364–7.
WALKER, O. (1677), *Of Education, Especially of Young Gentlemen* (3rd edn., Oxford).
—— (1685), *An Historical Narration of the Life and Death of our Lord Jesus Christ* (Oxford).
WALKER, R. B. (1974), 'The Newspaper Press in the Reign of William III', *The Historical Journal*, 17/4: 691–709.
WARD, W. R. (1958), *Georgian Oxford: University Politics in the Eighteenth Century* (Oxford).
—— (1965), *Victorian Oxford* (London).
—— (1997), 'From the Tractarians to the Executive Commission, 1845–1854', *HUO* vi. 306–36.
WATERHOUSE, E. (1986), 'Paintings and Painted Glass', *HUO* v. 858–64.
WATERS, I. (1973), *Henry Marten and the Long Parliament* (Chepstow).
WEBER, T. (2008), *Our Friend "The Enemy": Elite Education in Britain and Germany before World War I* (Stanford).
WEBSTER, C. (1986), 'The Medical Faculty and the Physic Garden', *HUO* v. 683–723.
WEDGWOOD, C. V. (1961), *Thomas Wentworth, First Earl of Strafford 1593–1641: A Revaluation* (London).
WEISS, R. (1957), *Humanism in England during the Fifteenth Century* (2nd edn., Oxford).
WELSBY, P. A. (1962), *George Abbot: the Unwanted Archbishop 1562–1633* (London).
WENDEN, D. J. (1994), 'Sport', *HUO* viii. 519–39.
WHALE, J. (1983), 'A Univ. Tractarian: Peter Goldsmith Medd', *UCR* Vol. VIII no. 4: 265–75.
WHITAKER, T. D. (ed) (1810), *The Life and Original Correspondence of Sir George Radcliffe* (London).
WHITE, A. W. A. (ed.) (1995), *The Correspondence of Sir Roger Newdigate of Arbury, Warwickshire* (Dugdale Society xxxvii).
WHITE, M., and GRIBBIN, J. (1992), *Stephen Hawking: A Life in Science* (London).

WHITEHEAD, D. (2000), 'The Architectural History of the Cathedral since the Reformation', in G. Aylmer and J. Tiller (eds.), *Hereford Cathedral: A History* (London): 241–85.
WHYTE, W. (2001), ' "Rooms for the Torture and Shame of Scholars": The New Examinations Schools and the Architecture of Reform', *Oxoniensia*, 66: 85–103.
WIGRAM, S. R. (1895–6), *The Cartulary of the Monastery of St Frideswide at Oxford* (2 vols., OHS xxviii & xxxi).
WILD, J. H. S. (1971), 'University College in Wartime, 1939–1945', *UCR* Vol. VI no. 1: 47–50.
—— (1972), 'Aid Raid Precautions in University College during the War, 1939–45', *UCR* Vol. VI no. 2: 153–60.
—— (1988), 'Reminiscences of the Very Revd. J. H. S. Wild', *UCR* Vol. IX no. 4: 41–52.
WILD, M. (1999), 'The Lodgings 1945', *UCR* Vol. XII no. 3: 92–6.
WILKINSON, L. P. (1980), *A Century of King's 1873–1972* (Cambridge).
WILLIAMS, P. (1986), 'Elizabethan Oxford: State, Church and University', *HUO* iii. 397–440.
WILSON, J. M. (1985), *Charles Hamilton Sorley: A Biography* (London).
WINTER, J. M. (1994), 'Oxford and the First World War', *HUO* viii. 3–25.
WITHERIDGE, J. (2005), *Frank Fletcher 1870–1954: A Formidable Headmaster* (Norwich).
WOLLENBERG, S. (2001), *Music at Oxford in the Eighteenth and Nineteenth Centuries* (Oxford).
WOOD, A. (1786), *The History and Antiquities of the Colleges and Halls in the University of Oxford*, ed. J. Gutch (2 vols., Oxford).
—— (1792–6), *The History and Antiquities of the University of Oxford*, ed. J. Gutch (2 vols., Oxford).
—— (1813–20), *Athenæ Oxonienses: An exact history of all the writers and bishops who have had their education in the University of Oxford. To which are added the Fasti, or Annals of the said University*, ed. P. Bliss (4 vols., London).
—— (1891), *The Life and Times of Anthony Wood*, ed. A. Clark, vol. i (OHS xix).
—— (1892), *The Life and Times of Anthony Wood*, ed. A. Clark, vol. ii (OHS xxi).
—— (1894), *The Life and Times of Anthony Wood*, ed. A. Clark, vol. iii (OHS xxvi).
—— (1899), *Survey of the Antiquities of the City of Oxford*, ed. A. Clark, vol. iii (OHS xxxvii).
WOODCOCK, M. (1998), ' "Breeding a Gentleman, or a Scholar": An Introduction to Obadiah Walker's *Of Education, especially of Young Gentlemen*', *UCR* Vol. XII no. 2: 74–83.
WOODS, M. (1941), 'Oxford in the 'Seventies', *Fortnightly*, 140: 276–82.
WORDEN, B. (1997), 'Cromwellian Oxford', *HUO* iv. 733–72.
WORDSWORTH, C. (ed.) (1904), *The Ancient Kalendar of the University of Oxford* (OHS xlv).
YORK, M. (1991), *Travelling Player: An Autobiography* (London).
YOUNG, B. W. (1998), *Religion and Enlightenment in Eighteenth-Century England: Theological Debate from Locke to Burke* (Oxford).
YOUSSOUPOFF, F. (1953), *Lost Splendour* (London).

ZOELLER, J. (2005), 'Unravelling the Story of Sampson Eyton', *UCR* Vol. XIV no. 1: 88–99.

—— (ed.) (2006), *Reminiscences: A Collection of Perspectives and Anecdotes about University College, Oxford* (privately printed).

—— (2007), 'Ambrose Bennet: College Fellow, Adventurer, and Scoundrel—I', *UCR* Vol. XIV no. 3: 95–104.

Index

The following abbreviations are used: (M) Master; (F) Fellow; (U) Undergraduate or Postgraduate; (MC) Mature commoner; (RF) Radcliffe Travelling Fellow; (S) Servant or member of staff; (T) Tenant of a College property. Places are assigned to counties as defined before 1974. Holders of peerages are usually listed under their family names, with a cross-reference from their title. Numbers in bold italics signify colour plates; numbers in italics signify a page with a black and white figure or graph.

This index does not cover Appendices I–III, and therefore people who appear there and nowhere else are not listed here.

Abbot, George (M), Archbishop of Canterbury 109, 120–6, *121*, 130, 135, 143, 177
Abbs, George (U) 319
Abendana, Rabbi Isaac 310
Acland, John 303
Acland, John Dyke (U) 294, 303
Acland, Thomas 303
Adams, Herbert Windham (U) *432*, 443
Addams, John 151
Addison, Joseph 313
Adlington, William (C?) 105
Aeschylus 313, 363
Africa, College members from 395–6, 495, 528
Ainley Walker, Ernest William (F) *15*, 447, 463, 466
Ainsworth, Michael (U) 235–6
Albertus Magnus 144, 313
Albery, Wyndham John (F) (M) 502, 505, 506, 518–19, *519*
Alcock, Edwin (U) 326
Alfred, King of Wessex, alleged founder of University College 54, 56–7, 106–7, 112, 161, 185, 200–1, 204, 215, 232, 260–1, 268, 312, 390–1, 401, 433
  alleged links with first claimed 37–40, *39*
  depictions of *frontispiece*, 69, 184–5, 200, 223, 224, 261, 261, 268, 269, 285, 421
  lawsuit concerning claims of 251–3, 254–5
  links with College disputed 201, 224, 256–7, 390
Alington, Cyril 479, 484
Alington, Giles (F) 470, 479–82, *480*, 484, 487–8, 491, 497, 498, 503, 505, 527

Alkebarow, John (F) 42–3
Allan, James Lambertini (U) 426
Allen, Sir Carleton Kemp (F) 450, 465, 466, 473, 491, *494*
Allen, Dorothy, Lady Allen 466
Allen, John Edward (F) 508
Allen, John Francis (U) (F) 319
Allen, Thomas (U) (F) 236, 260, 306, 319
Alleyne, John (U) (F) 325, 331
All Souls College, Oxford 68, 73–4, 79, 82, 86–7, 95, 101, 106, 170, 176, 232, 239, 266, 307
  buildings of 72, 162, 240
Althorp, *see* Spencer
Altschul, Frank, benefactor 486, 488–9, 491
Altschul, Helen (née Goodhart), benefactor 486, 488–9, 491
Amherst, Nicholas 229–30
Anderdon, John (U) 235
Andrews, Roger, Master of Jesus College, Cambridge 156
Andrews, Wardell (U) 305
Annand, William (U) 179
Anne, Queen of Great Britain 202, 242
  statue of 235
Anne of Bohemia, Queen of England 40
Appleton, John (F) (M) (MC) 45–6, 57, 73
Apuleius 105
Aristotle 139, 144, 145, 358, 416
Armagh, Richard of 38
Armitage, John (U) (F) 188
Arncliffe, Yorks., College living at 2, 60–4, *61*, 82, 84, 94, 105, 129, 153, 168–9, 233, 241, 327–8, 347–8, 360, 399, 548–9
Arnold, Thomas 356, 357, 362

Arran, Lord, *see* Butler
Arundel, Thomas, Archbishop of York and then Canterbury 41, 47–50
Ashburner, Walter (F) 466
Ashmole, Elias 200
Asplyon, William (F) benefactor, 66, 79
Asquith, Herbert Henry, Prime Minister 389, 446–7
Asser 201, 223
Aston Ingham, Herefordshire 134
Aswardeby, Roger de (F) (M) 33, 35
Athelham, Geoffrey (T) 55
Atterbury, Francis, Dean of Christ Church 237
Attlee, Clement Richard, Earl Attlee (U), Prime Minister 410, 411, *428*, 429, 433, 437, 462, 472, 474, 478, 484–5, 497, 510
Auckland, Co. Durham 21
Auden, Wystan Hugh 457
Australia, College members from 417, 475, 495, 526
Aycliffe, Co. Durham 74
Ayerst, William (U), Gunsley Scholar *c.*1662–91 266, 306
Ayerst, William (U), Gunsley Scholar 1698–1716 226, 266, 306
Aylesbury, Sir Thomas, resident in 1642/3 166
Ayliffe, John 10, 236

Babelak, Agnes 55
Bach, Carl Philipp Emmanuel 290
Bailey, Charles Henry (U) *428*
Ballard, Gregory 151–2
Balliol, John de 15–16
Balliol College, Oxford 15–17, 18, 24–5, 27–9, 68, 104, 111, 113, 125, 189, 251, 358, 371, 379, 389, 419, 444, 465, 470, 479, 503, 513
  buildings of 58, 72, 162
  finances of 155–6, 322, 393
  members of 15, 30, 47, 76, 93, 95, 117–18, 120, 276, 303, 353, 356–7, 373, 377, 392–3, 416, 423, 444, 446, 468
  reputation of 285, 390, 396, 406, 417, 463, 498
Bamford, Brian Reginald (U) 496
Bancroft, John (M) 109, 126–31, *127*, 144, 149, 157, 161, 177
Bancroft, Richard, Chancellor of Oxford 109, 116, 125, 126
Barker, Edward Burton (U) 316
Barker, Robert, joiner 226–7

Barling, Fiona (U) 517
Barmby, James (U) (F) 350
Barnaby, John (F) (MC), benefactor 75, 90–2, 156
Barnard, John, Fellow of Brasenose 208, 213
Barnes, Surrey 386–7
Barnes, George Stapylton (U) 402–3
Barnett, John (U) 317
Barns, John Wintour Baldwin (F) 492
Barry, Sir Charles, architect 352–3
Basset, Alan 11
Bateman, John (U) 266, 326
Bateman, Thomas (U) (F) 201
Bateson, William (S) 411, 415, 438, *476*
Bath, Somerset 304
Bathurst, Ralph, President of Trinity College, Oxford 221, 245
Batt, Robert (F) 114, 117, 147
Batt, Thomas (U) 117
Baxter, Simon (F) (T) 65
Bayley, Peter Charles (U) (F) *454*, 469, 473, 479, 493, *494*, 497, 499, 513
Bayne-Jardine, Colin Charles (U) 482, 496
Baynes, Benjamin (U) (F) 243, 308
Beaufort, Duke of, *see* Somerset
Beaufort, Henry, Cardinal, benefactor 60
Beaverbrook Foundation, benefactor 512
Beckinsale, Robert Percy (F) 503
Beckley, Sussex, College living at 347, 548–9
Bede, the Venerable 6, 5, 38, 79, 144, 203
Behan, John Clifford Valentine (F) 417, 440
Belfast, Queen's University 465
Bell, Edward Nevinson (U) *432*, 443
Bell, John David (F) 503
Bellasis, Alice 62, 84
Belsize Architects 520
Bemmerton, — (U?) 94
Bennet, Ambrose (F) (T) 177, 181, 184, 208
Bennet, John 219
Bennet, Sir Simon (U), benefactor 157–8, *158*, 177, 186, 238, *261*, 491, 509, 524
  disputes over benefaction of 161, 164, 173–5, 184
Bennet, Thomas (U) (F) (M) 207–8, 215, 216, 219–20, 249
Bentham, Jeremy 276
Bentley, Richard, Master of Trinity College, Cambridge 237
Benwell, Thomas (F) (M) (MC) (T) 54–7, 76, 94, 106
Bereblock, John 69, *70*

INDEX

Berlin, university of 362
Berlin, Sir Isaiah 481
Berman, Robert (F) 502
Bertie, Albemarle (U) (F), benefactor 220, 221, 226, 230–1, 232, 307–8
Betts, Joseph (U) (F) 275–7, 278
Beveridge (formerly Mair), Janet, Lady Beveridge 454, 456, 471, 473, 475
Beveridge, Sir William Henry, Baron Beveridge of Tuggall (F) (M) 454–6, *454*, 468, 469–74, 475, 477, 490, 510
Beverley, Philip of (also Philip Ingleberd), benefactor 25, 27, 40
Beza, Theodore 144
Bickerton, Fred (S) 407, 424, 432, 434–5, 437–8, 439, 445, 468, 472, *476*
Bingham, Joseph (U) (F) 222, 310
Birkbeck College, London 465
Birley, Sir Robert 480, 487
Bishopwearmouth, church of (now Sunderland Minster) 5–6, *6*
Black Death 26, 30
Blackett, Basil Phillott (U) *428*
Blair, Tony, Prime Minister 520
Bland, Sir John (U) 194
Boccaccio 313
Bodley, George Frederick, architect 397
Boer War 434, 439
Boethius 79, 269
Bologna, university of 1
Bolt, Thomas 145
Booth, Ledeboer, and Pinckheard, architects 489
Boraston, John (U) (F) 221, 233, 247–51, 256, 259, 260, 308, 326
Bosanquet, Bernard (F), 393
Boswell, Lady —, resident in 1643/4 166
Boswell, James 287, 334
Boteler, George (U) 169
Bouchier, Anna Maria, wife of William Denison 253
Bouchier, James, Professor of Civil Law 235, 247, 249–50, 253, 255, 257, 259
Bouchier, Thomas, Professor of Civil Law 230, 235, 247, 249–50, 253
Bourbon, Stephen de 3
Bourdillon, Robert Benedict (F) 440
Boustead, Thomas (U) 402
Bouverie, Bartholomew (U) 303
Bouverie, Jacob, 2nd Earl of Radnor (U) 280, 303, 329

Bouverie, William, 1st Earl of Radnor (U) 292–3, 303
Bouverie, William Henry (U) 303
Bowen, Edmund John (F) *15*, 416, 424, 446, 447, 452, 454, 463, 466, 479, *494*, 502
Bowra, Sir Maurice 501
Boxall, Alleyne Percival (U) *428*
Boyd, William (U) (F) 346–7, 360
Boyle, Cecil William (U) 439
Boyle, Robert 180, 283
Boyse (also Boyes), Nathaniel (U) (F) 190–2, 205–8, 209, 217
Brachinburye, Henry (F) 100, 102
Brackley, Northants., Hospital of St James at 12
Bradley, George Granville (U) (F) (M) 357–8, 360, 362, 365, 366, 386–406, *387*, *404*, 407, 425
Bradley (later Woods), Margaret 392
Brasenose College, Oxford 83, 105, 114, 170, 208, 249, 260, 346, 402, 409, 492, 502, 513, 523
  site of 12, 21, *22*, 29
Brawne, Hugh (U) 205
Bredon, Simon de, benefactor 29
Brewster, Kingman (M) 517–18, *518*, 523
Bridgeman, Sir Orlando, resident in 1644, and benefactor 166, 186
Bridport, Giles de, Bishop of Salisbury 11
Briggs, John (S) 319, *320*
Bright, Emily 413
Bright, James Franck (U) (F) (M) 394–5, 402, *404*, 405, 407–22, *408*, 424, 434, 465
  marrying off daughters 407–8, 413, 415, 434
  shooting of 413–14
Bright, Margaret (later Carr) 407, 422
Bright, William (U) (F) 362–3, 370–1, 373, 378, 386
Bringnell, — (U?) 94
Bristol 58, 331
Britten, Benjamin 501
Broadgates Hall, Oxford 125–6
Brodribb, Harold Swainson (U) 456–7
Broughton, Thomas (U) 270
Browne, John (F) 114, 117–20, 123, 126–8, 151, 156
  pupils of 117, 134, 137, 139, 141, 145, 146, 148, 152, 154
Browne, John (U) (F) (M), benefactor 248–51, 254, 258, 261, 266–74, 276, 305, 325, 337
Browne, Richard (U) (F) 151

Browne, Thomas, benefactor 117–18, 143
Bruce, David 489
Brudenell, Francis 192–3
Brudenell, Thomas (U) 192
Buchman, Frank 462
Buckeridge, Charles, architect 419
Buckhurst, Lord, *see* Sackville
Buckingham, Duke of, *see* Villiers
Buckingham, W. (S) 467
Budge, Sir Ernest Wallis, benefactor 464
Bullinger, Heinrich 101
Bulstrode, Henry (U) 169
Burdet, John (U) 137, 154
Burdet, William (U) 137, 154
Burge, Hubert Murray (U) (F) 414–15, 433, 444, 447, 487, 527
Burgess, David John (F) 500, 503, 509
Burghley, Lord, *see* Cecil
Burn, John Henry (U), benefactor 453–4
Burne-Jones, Sir Edward 372
Burne-Jones, Sir Philip (U) 372
Burney, Charles, D. Mus. from University College 289–90
Burra, Lancelot Toke (U) *432*
Burton, John (F) (M) (MC) (T?) 48–50, 52–3, 58, 73–4
Burton, John (U) 461
Bushnell, John, sculptor 215
Busia, Kofi Abrefa (U), Prime Minister of Ghana 528
Butcher, Samuel Henry (F) 394–5
Bute, Earl of, *see* Stuart
Butler, Arthur Gray (U) 358
Butler, Arthur Stanley George, architect 448, 453
Butler, Charles, Lord Arran, Chancellor of Oxford 243, 257
Butler, Frederick Edward Robin, Lord Butler of Brockwell (U) (M) *18*, 519–20, 521, 522, 524, 527
Butler, James, 2nd Duke of Ormonde, Chancellor of Oxford 242, 243
Butler, Jill, Lady Butler *18*, 519–20, 527
Butler, Theobald Richard Fitzwalter (U) 443
Bydnell, William (F) 144

Caesar 263
Caius, John, Master of Gonville and Caius College, Cambridge 106–7, 260
Caius, Thomas (M) 89, 101, 104–8, 141, 148, 149, 161, 185, 260

Calamy, Edmund 176
Calcutta, university of 448
Caldwell, Robert, possible benefactor 34
Callaghan, James, Prime Minister 511
Callimachus 280, 310, 314
Calvin, John 113, 144, 145
Cambridge, university of 4, 60, 76, 99–100, 196, 244, 309, 310, 325, 499, 502, 522
  colleges of in general 51, 68, 87, 110–11, 133, 174, 237, 446–7, 513–14, 525
  effects of English Civil War at 169–70
  examinations at 300
  hostels at 51
  incorporation of 111
  origins, genuine and mythical 2, 106–7, 201
  outside interventions in 103, 110
  postgraduate degrees at 464
  Royal and Parliamentary Commissions at 367, 369, 400–1, 446–7
  servants at 383
  sizars at 304
  study of theology at 2, 68
  see also under individual colleges
Campbell, John Denis Egbert (F) 502
Campion, Edmund 105
Canada, College members from 417, 493–5, 526
Carew, Sir Francis (U) 166
Caribbean, College members from 305, 495, 497
Carlisle, diocese of, College members from 30, 60
Carlyle, Alexander James (F) and Lecturer 410, *428*, 444, 449, 462, 466
Carr, William (U) m. 1781 319
Carr, William (U) m. 1882 258–9, 266, 407–8, 422, 516
Carritt, Edgar Frederic (F) *15*, 393, 407, 411, 415, 423, *428*, 436, 444, 449, 451, 465, 465, 466, 470, 478
Cartwright, Edmund (U) 305
Cassiodorus 79
Castell, John (F) (M) 45, 49–50, 52, 57, 73–4, 79, 106
Catcott, Alexander 271
Catherine of Aragon, Queen of England 96, 203
Cavendish-Bentinck, William Henry Cavendish, Duke of Portland, Chancellor of Oxford 300, 339

Cawkwell, George Law (F) 479, *494*, 499, 508, 510, 522, 523, 524
Cawkwell, Pat 491
Cecil, Lord Edgar Algernon Robert Gascoyne, Viscount Cecil of Chelwood (U) 396, 452
Cecil, Lord Hugh Richard Heathcote Gascoyne, Baron Quickswood (U) 396, 427, 452
Cecil, James Edward Hubert Gascoyne, Viscount Cranborne, later 4th Marquess of Salisbury (U) 396, 452, 520
Cecil, Lady Maud Gascoyne (later Palmer) 396
Cecil, Robert Arthur Talbot Gascoyne, 3rd Marquess of Salisbury, Chancellor of Oxford 396, 414
Cecil, William, Lord Burghley 110, 114
Cecil, Lord William Gascoyne (U) 396, 452
Chambers, Sir Robert (F) 273, 275, *276*, 278–80, 281, 282, 284, *286*, 287–8, 302, 309, 314–15, 317, 331, 335
  monument to in Chapel 329
  sons of 303
Champneys, Basil, architect 419–21, 520
Chantry, Sir Francis, sculptor 375
Chapman, John (U) 328
Charles I, King of Great Britain 124, 125, 161, 163, 164, 166–9, 184–5, 265, 272
Charles II, King of Great Britain 181, 183, 189, 206, 242
Charlett, Arthur (M) 211, 219–46, 247, 253, 258–9, 267, 285, 296, 305, 306, 310, 316, 326, 352, 447
  political interests of 227–8, 242–3
  relations with Fellows 229–32, 236–7, 259, 262
  scholarly patronage of 221–6, 301, 337
Charterhouse school 353, 360, 377, 425, 480
Chavasse, Albert Sidney (F) 402–5, *404*, 429
Checkendon, Oxon., College living at 269, 291, 298, 326–7, *327*, 548–9
Chedworth, John (MC) 59, 71–2, 77
Cherbery, Lord, *see* Herbert
Cheshire, College members from 136
Chichele, Henry, Archbishop of Canterbury 52
China and Hong Kong, College members from 524, 526
Cholmeley, Lewin 402

Christ Church, Oxford 74, 138, 155, 162, 199, 221–2, 297, 313, 324, 384, 389, 402, 406, 418, 514, 523
  members of 114, 117, 183, 193, 210, 211–12, 213, 237, 285, 303, 303–4, 308, 353, 377, 396, 409, 414, 417, 457
Churchill, Oxon. 172
Churchill College, Cambridge 513
Cicero 139, 145, 222, 263, 280, 312, 358
Clare College, Cambridge 99–100, 507, 513
Clarendon, *see* Hyde
'Clarendon' Schools 377, 417, 425, 461
Clarke, Francis Peter Courtenay (U) *432*
Clarke, George 239
Clarke, Mordaunt Edward Leonard Hannam (U) 440
Clarke, Robert (F) 298, 319
Claughton, Piers Calveley (F) 349, 360–1, 390–1
Clavering, Robert (F) 223, 257, 325
Clayton, John (U) 187
Clayton, Richard (U) (F) (M) 180, 185, 187–93, 195
Clayton and Bell, stained glass manufacturers 376
Clifford, Thomas de (F?) 21
Clifton College 406
Clinton, William Jefferson (U), President of the USA 483, 519, *519*
Cockerill, Thomas (U) (F) 248–50, 254, 257, 307
Cockey, Ralph (F) 100
Cockman, John (U) *10*, 241, 247, 253, 258, 302
Cockman, Thomas (U) (F) (M) *10*, 222, 234, 241, 247–66, *248*, 267, 296, 302, 305, 307, 309, 311–12, 318, 337, 422
coffee, consumption of 179, 445
Coghlan, William Humphrey (U) 440
Coke, Desmond Francis Talbot (U) 429
Cole, Christian (MC) 395–6, 434
Cole, George Douglas Howard (F) *15*, 449–51, 454, 460, 462, 464, 466–7
Cole, Margaret 450, 451, 467, 471
Colet, Isabel (T) 82, 85
colleges
  definitions of 10, 27
  in European universities 51, 87, 111
  see also Cambridge, Oxford, and Paris, universities of
Collett, Frank (S) 468
Colman, Henry (U) 177

INDEX

Comestor, Peter 29
Coney, Thomas (U) 306
Conington, John (U) (F) 363–4, 367–9
Constable, Cuthbert 214–15, 217
Contarini, Cardinal Gasparo 144
Conybeare, Frederick Cornwallis (U) (F) 395, 423, 443
Cook, Henry, artist 227
Cooke, Alexander (F) 117
Cooke, Beatrice (S) 499
Cooke, Colin Arthur (U) 464
Cooper, Anthony Ashley, 3rd Earl of Shaftesbury 235–6
Cooper, Edward Desmond Cecil (U) 458, 462
Cooper, Elizabeth Helen (F) 515, 517, 525
Cooper, Frank (T) 418
Cooper, Malcolm McGregor 'Mac' (U) 458–9, 464
Cooper, Thomas (U) 295
Copleston, Edward 341
Corneille, Pierre 313
Cornell University 370
corn rents 152–3, 163
Cornwall, College members from 30
Corpus Christi College, Cambridge 369, 377, 466
Corpus Christi College, Oxford 167, 241, 278, 363–4, 390, 406, 411, 442, 465, 476, 479, 527
Cosin, John 130
Coulson, John (F) 275–6, 278, 290–1, 296, 298, 309, 314
Courtney, William (U) 196
Couture, William (U) (F) 297–8
Coveney, Thomas, Vice-Chancellor 103–4
Coventry, War. 114
Cox, Anthony David Machell (F) 479, 481, 487, 491–2, 493, 494, 510, 524
   as authority on the history of University College 2, 5, 34, 491
Cox, George 342, 343, 350, 351, 375
Cox, Richard, Chancellor of Oxford 101
Crabbie, John Edward (U) 432
Cracknell, Gabriel (S) 139, 154
Cranmer, Thomas, Archbishop of Canterbury 102
Crawford, John (U) 385
Crawley, Richard (U) 370
Crayford, John (F) (M) 99–100, 106
Cree, Charles (U) 380, 381, 388, 389, 393
Cricklade, Wilts. 106

Croft, George (U) (F) 324, 328, 332–3
Cromwell, Oliver, Lord Protector 169, 175, 176, 178, 181, 204
Crosby, John (MC), benefactor 66, 77, 81
Croughton, Northants. 99
Crowder, —, College land agent 318
Crumpe, Henry (MC) 47–8, 49, 75
Cuffield, — (U) 210
Cumberland, College members from 194, 200
Cundale, William de (F) 29–30
Cunningham, Allan, sculptor 375
Cunningham, Daniel John Chapman (F) 502
Cupper, Thomas (U) (F) 181
Curraff, Peter de (F) 31

Dakin, Alec Naylor, Lady Wallis Budge Fellow 464
Danvers, Joan, benefactor 59
Darwin, Charles 373, 405
Davenport, Francis William (U) 382
Dawson, Stewart (U) 382
Deane, Thomas (U) (F) 206, 207–8, 213, 215, 217
Deane, Thomas, D. Mus. from University College 290
Dedham, Essex 117
Delaune, William, President of St John's College, Oxford 237, 243
Demosthenes 395
Dendy, Arthur (F) 393, 395, 401, 402
Denison, William (U) (F) (elected M) 229–31, 234, 244, 247–59, 260, 262, 308
Dervorguilla, widow of John de Balliol 16, 18, 20, 25
Devas, Jocelyn (U) 410
Devas Institute 410
Digges, Dudley (U), m. 1600 122, 155
Digges, Dudley (U), m. 1630 155
Digges, Leonard (d. 1571) 155
Digges, Leonard (U) (MC) 137–8, 143, 155
Digges, Thomas 155
Digges, Thomas (U) 155
Dix, Norman (S) 467, 467–8, 471, 478, 479, 485, 498, 499–500, 505, 515, 516–17
Dixon, Thomas, Fellow of Queen's 204
Dodds, Eric Robertson (U) 416, 424–5, 434, 439, 440, 443
Dolben, Sir William, MP for Oxford University 293–4
Dominican friars, order of 9, 42

Donkin, William Fishburn (U) (F) 354–6, 355, 357, 359, 361, 367–8, 369
Dormer, Charles (U) 210
Douglas, James Archibald (F) 470
Douglas-Home, Sir Alec Frederick, Lord Home, Prime Minister 479
Dowson, Sir Philip Manning (U), architect 476, 507–8
Dowson, William (MC) 80–1
Drury, Frances Clare Nineham (F) 525
Dryden, John (U?) 210
Dublin, Trinity College 163, 165, 170, 171, 177
Dubs, Homer Hasenpflug (F) 492
Dudley, Robert, Earl of Leicester, Chancellor of Oxford and benefactor 106, 109–10, *110*, 114–15, 116–17, 132, *261*
Duffield, Thomas (M) 45
Dugdale, James (F) (M) 103–4, 109
Duncan, John Finch (U), m. 1954 493
Duncan, John Graham (U), m. 1958 496
Dunnet, John (U) 145, 149
Duns Scotus 79, 144
Durham
  Cathedral 103, 114, 484–5
  Priory 5–7, 72
  university of 204, 468
Durham, county of, College members from 8, 16–17, 20, 46, 58, 60, 66, 72, 132–3, 136, 194, 195, 305, 308–9, 348, 351
Durham, William of, Founder of University College 2–15, 74, 528
  bequest of, and misuse of same 7–14
  coat of arms attributed to 112
  posthumous reputation of 20–1, 56–7, 71, 106, 112, 161, 185, 223, 224, 256, *261*, *261*, 390, 478, 520
  writings of 3–4, 32
Durham College, Oxford 16, 72, 91
Dworkin, Ronald Myles (F) 517
Dykes Bower, Stephen, architect 477–8

Easby, Yorks. 233, 258
Eastwick Farm, Grandpont (originally Berkshire), owned by College 93–4, 98, 105, 166, 168, 181, 322, 430, 504
Eden, Robert (F) 249–50, 260, 263, 310, 324
Edgiock, Worcs., College property at 322, 399, 445, 548–9

Edinburgh, Prince Philip, Duke of 520, *521*
Edinburgh, university of 333, 366
Edmonds, Edward Leslie (U) 452
Edward I, King of England 13
Edward VI, King of England 96, 100, 102
Edward the Confessor, King of England 40
Eldon, Lord, *see* Scott, John
Eliot, Thomas Stearns 451
Elizabeth I, Queen of England 96, 103, 106, 114, 132, 155
Elizabeth II, Queen of Great Britain 478, 520, *521*
Elliott, Rosamund (S) 468
Ellis, Clough Williams, architect 430
Ellison, George (F) (M) 98, 100–3
Ellison, Nathaniel (U) 300
Elmhirst, John (U) (F) 129–30, 133–4, 163, 164–5, 166, 171, 172
  pupils of 134, 137, 145, 146–7, 148, 149, 150, 152
Elstanwyke, Armand de (F) 26
Elstob, Elizabeth 223
Elstob, William (F) 223, 224, 229, 230, 233
Elton, Hunts., College living at 268, 326–7, 360–1, 373, 548–9
Elwyk, John (F) (T) 72
Ely Cathedral 119
Emmanuel College, Cambridge 118, 322, 446, 499
Emmet, Cyril William (F) 463
English Civil War 164–71
entry fines 152–3, 254, 259, 322, 398
Eslake, Thomas (MC) 81
Eton College 153, 346–7, 353, 377, 385, 417, 425, 439, 479, 481
Euclid 145, 311
Euripides 333
Eusebius 144
Evans, Howell Justin (U) 451, 458
Eveleigh, John, Provost of Oriel 300
Exeter College, Oxford 25, 27, 29–31, 45, 51, 58, 77, 82, 104, 154, 353, 389, 423
Eyton, Sampson (F) 175–6, 177, 181

Faber, Frederick William (U) (F) 359–61
Fairfax, Sir Thomas 169–70
Farmer, Antony 210–11
Farnell, Lewis Richard, Rector of Exeter College 423, 434
Farnham, Nicholas of, Bishop of Durham 5–6, 16

582   INDEX

Farquharson, Arthur Spencer Loat (U) (F) *15*, 413, 415–16, 427, *428*, 429, 430, 439, 440, 447–8, 449, 452, 457, 464–5, 470, 472, 473
Farquharson, James Charles Lancelot (U) *428*, 443
Farrar, Edward (F) (M) 176, 177, 178, 181, 219
Faulkner, Charles Joseph (F) 371–3, *372*, 378, 380, 389, 394, 397–400, 402, 403, 405, 409–10, 412, 414, 502
Faussett, Bryan (U) 268
Faversham, Simon de 21–3
Fayt, John (F) 74
Fell, John, Dean of Christ Church 183, 186, 188, 190, 193, 199, 203, 204, 205, 206, 210, 232
Fennell, John Lister Illingworth (F) 502
Ferguson, John Alexander (U) *428*
Ferrers, Benjamin, artist *10*, 258
Fetherstonehaugh (also Fetherston), Richard (F) 96–7
ffolliott, John (U) 358
Ffoulkes, John 350
Fidoe, Anthony (F) 179
Fiennes, William, Lord Saye and Sele 166, 167
First World War 437, 440–3, *442*
Firth, Anthony Edward (F) *494*, 503–4, 505
Fisher, Philip (U) (F) 297, 331, 360
Fitzhugh, Robert (MC) 77
Fitzjames, Richard, Bishop of London 91
Flamstead, Herts., College living at 129, 219, 233, 241, 345, 400, 445, 548–9
Flavel (also Flavell), John (U?) 178–9
Flaxman, John, sculptor 295, 329
Fleming, Anne 511
Fleming, George 220
Fleming (also Flemyng or Flemming), Richard, Bishop of Lincoln (MC) 48–9, 56, 75–7
Fleming (also Flemyng or Flemming), Robert (MC) 56, 75–7, 79–80
Fletcher, Sir Frank 424
Fletcher, Sir Lazarus (F) 373
Fletcher, Philip Cawthorne (U) *428*
Fletcher, Thomas (U) 235
Ford, Edward Onslow, sculptor 419–21
Foston, Thomas (F) (M) (MC) 45
Fox, Adam (U) *428*
Foxcroft, Anthony 180–1, 184, 185
Foxe, John 102–3, 113, 144
Fradisham, Edward (U) (MC) 136

Francis, Edmund 35–42
Francis, Idonea 35–42
Franciscan friars, order of 4, 9
Francklin, Philip (U) (MC) 137
Fraser, Thomas Cameron (U) 457
Freeston, John, benefactor 118, 126, 217–18
Freeston charities 412
French Revolution 299–300, 329, 340
Fridaythorpe, John de (MC?) 23
Frognell, Thomas, benefactor 126
Froissart 143
Fryman, John, architect 508–9
Fyffe, Charles Alan (F) 393, 397, 405, 414

Gagnier, Jean 310
Gale, George (F) 175–6
Galen 144
Galileo 313
Gardner, Arthur Duncan 'Duncs' (U) (F) *15*, 425, 427, 433, 434, 447, 455–6, 463, 466, 473
Garner, Thomas, architect 397
Garter, Knights of from University College 520
Gate, Anthony (U?) (MC) (M) 114–20, 130, 136, 140, 177, 423
Gate, Geoffrey 115
Gate, Judith, wife of Anthony 115, 120
Gate, Nathaniel (U) 115
Gate, Peter (U) 115
Gate, Thomas (U) 115, 119
Gate, Timothy (U) 115, 119
Gaunt, John of, Duke of Lancaster 47
Gem, Harvey (U) 375–6
General Strike 450–1
George I, King of Great Britain 242–3, 251–3
George II, King of Great Britain 265, 334
George III, King of Great Britain 284, 287
George IV, King of Great Britain 284
Georgian, Karen 511
Germany
    College members from 417, 433, 435, 439, 442, 463
    universities in 144, 334, 362, 422–3; *see also* Berlin and Göttingen, universities of
Gibbon, Edward 276, 278
Gibson, Edmund 226, 230–1
Giles, John (U) (F) 220
Gilliatt, John (U), benefactor 376
Gladstone, Herbert John, Viscount Gladstone (U) 396

INDEX

Gladstone, William Ewart, Prime Minister 338, 364, 368, 396
Glaister, William (U) (F) 344
Glasgow, university of 333
Gloucester Cathedral 331
Gloucester Hall, Oxford 104, 136
Godfrey, Walter, architect 478
Gold, Thomas, benefactor 105
Goldberg, Herbert Walter (U) *432*, 443
Goldsmith, Joan 35
Goldsmith, John 35
Gonville and Caius College, Cambridge 322, 377, 499
Gonwardby, John 34–5, 41, 291
Gooday, Joshua (T) 412
Good Easter, Essex 55
Goodhart, Arthur Lehman (F) (M), benefactor *15*, *454*, 454, 464, 466, 470, 479, 485–91, *486*, 492, 493, *494*, 499, 501, 508–9, 511
  see also Altschul
Goodhart, Cecily 485, *486*, 490, 504, 508–9
Goodman, Arnold Abraham, Baron Goodman (M) 492, 510–15, *512*, 517, 523
Göttingen, university of 334
Goudge, Henry (U) 411
Gourdon, Richard 235
Gower, Robert (F) 38, 43
Grant, Elizabeth 336–7, 339–40, 343
Gravesande, Willem 311, 313
Gravesend, Stephen de, benefactor 29
Green, Stanley George 'Gus' (U) 469
Greenwell, Christopher (F) 100
Greenwood, Charles (U) (MC) (F), benefactor 123–5, 133, 147, 157–8, 180–1, 184, 186, *261*, 509
Greenwood, William (U) (F) 317
Gregford, William (F) (M) 63–6
Gregory IX, Pope 4–5
Grenville, William Wyndham, Lord Grenville, Chancellor of Oxford 339, 340
Gretton, Sir Peter William (F) 500
Griffith, James (F) (M) *13*, 297, 331, 336–42, 352
  as artist and architect *11–12*, 298–9, 336, 376, 477
Griffith (née Ironside), Mary 336
Grimage, Mrs — (S), fl. 1711, bedmaker 319
Grimage, Mrs — (S), fl. 1787/8, bedmaker 319
Grimston, Sir Harbottle 204

Grosseteste, Robert 10, 12
Grunelius, Alexander Carl (U) 433, 439
Gryme, Lancelot (U) (MC) (F) 119, 148
Guest, Anthony Gordon (F) *494*
Gunsley, Robert (C?), benefactor 129
Gyles, Henry, artist 214, 375
Gylis, William (S) 138–9

Hailey, Oxon., College property at 94, 322, 399, 445, 548–9
Haileybury School 358, 437
Haines, John Thomas Augustus (F) 413
Hales, Edward (U) 208, *209*, 215, 217
Hales, Sir Edward, father of preceding 208, 217
Halifax, Earl of, see Savile
Hall, William (MC) 96, 103–4
Hambledon, Bucks. 234, 237, 326
Hamerton, John (F) (T) 49
Hamilton, Eric Knightley Chetwood (U) 436, 478
Hampden, Renn Dickson 351
Hampshire, College members from 72
Hamsterley, Ralph (M) 89–92, *92*, 156
Hanborough, Oxon. 163, 253, 258
  College property at 105, 548–9
Handel, George Frideric 265
Handley Park, Northants., College property at 157–8, 161, 163, 164, 167, 173, 181, 184, 188, 322, 345, 399, 548–9
Hanover Club 439
Hansell, Peter (U) (F) 348, 373
Harcourt, Henry (U) 236
Harcourt, Simon, father of preceding 236
Hare, Augustus John Cuthbert (U) 354, 378, 381
Harley, Thomas (F) 179
Harper, Hugh, Principal of Jesus College, Oxford 406
Harrison, James (U) (F) 119, 146, 151
Harrow School 275, 346–7, 353, 377, 417, 425, 439
Hart, Herbert Lionel Adolphus (F) 486, 492–3, *494*, 501, 504, 513
Hartburne, John (F) 109, 148
Hart Hall, Oxford 136, 251
Hartwell, Robert (U) 149
Harvard College 177
Hastings, Marquess of, see Rawdon
Havens, Paul Swain (U) 450–1

Hawke, Robert James Lee (U), Prime Minister of Australia 475, 495, 496
Hawking, Frank (U) 462
Hawking, Stephen William (U) 495, 520
Hawkins, John David (U) 492–3, *494*
Hawkins, Joseph (U) 316
Hawksmoor, Nicholas, architect 240
Hawsten, Matilda (S) (T) 77
Haydok, Gilbert (F) (MC) 72–3
Haygarth, Emma Shevvan (U) 517
Headbourne Worthy, Hants., College living at 7, 222, 238, 242, 263, 327, 373, 548–9
Headington, Oxon., College property at 105
Healaugh, Yorks., College property at 260, 548–9
Hearne, Thomas 107, 203, 220, 221, 222, 223–4, 224, 225, 227–8, 228, 231, 232–3, 234, 234–5, 243–4, 244, 245–6, 249, 250–1, 252, 253, 256, 257, 259, 260, 260–1, 304, 306, 308, 317, 318, 319, 326
Heath, Sir Edward, Prime Minister 462
Heath, George (S) 499
Heather, Thomas (U) (F) 248, 253, 255, 257, 258–9
Hedley, William (F) 375
Henry III, King of England 4, 57
Henry IV, King of England and benefactor 43, 45–6, *261*
Henry V, King of England 49, 74
Henry VII, King of England 77, 185
Henry VIII, King of England 96–8, 100
Henshaw, Thomas (U) 146–7, 169, 198
Herbert, Edward, Baron Herbert of Cherbury (U) 122, 142, *143*, 146, 149, 155
Herbert, Philip, Earl of Pembroke, Chancellor of Oxford 164, 173
Hereford Cathedral 30, 49, 292, 295, 299, 485
Herodotus 263, 358, 422
Heron, Edmund (U) 213, 216
Heron (or Hearne), William, benefactor 113
Hertford College, Oxford 336, 416, 513
Hewart, Gordon, Viscount Hewart (U) 328, 417, 432–3
Hewett, Roger (T) 98
Heywood, James 366
Hickes, George 225, 228
Higden, Ralph 38
Hill, John (U) 378, 384
Hilton, Robert John (U) 452–3

Hinchliffe, Edward (U) (F) 210
Hinckley, John (U) (F) 230–1, 308
Hobson, Henry (F) 269
Hodgson, Leonard 484
Hogg, Thomas Jefferson (U) 339–42, *341*
Holcot, William (U), benefactor 102–3, 113, 115, 153–4
Holdsworth, Richard William Gilbert (F) 468, 470–2; see also Zvegintzov
Holton, Thomas 63–4
Homer 145, 280, 395
Honeycombe, Gordon (U) 496
Hood, Paul, Rector of Lincoln 156
Hooper, Odiam (U) 318
Hooper, William (U) (F) 297
Hopkins, John, College steward 188
Hopkinson, Arthur (U) 415
Hopkinson, David (U) 462, 464, 468
Hopkinson, Martin (U) *428*
Hopkinson, Thomas (U) (MC) 137
Hopton, Henry (F) 32
Horace 280, 360
Horne, George (U), President of Magdalen 269–73, 287, 305, 306, 309, 311, 331, 351, 360
Horsfall, John (U) 378
Hoyle, Joshua (M) 171–5, 177, 184
Hubberholme, Yorks. 84, 327–8, 376
Hudson, John (F) 213, 215, 221, 222, 225, 227, 228, 229, 230, 233, 235, 243, 245, 278
Hughes, Samuel (U) 461–2
Humberston, Edward, Catholic chaplain at University College 210
Humfray, John (T) 55
Humphrey, Thomas, President of Magdalen 105
Hungerford, Robert, Lord Hungerford and Moleyns (MC) 56, 59, 73, 75–7
Hunt, Otho (MC) (F), benefactor 118–19
Huntley, Francis Osmond Joseph (U) *432*
Hutchinson, George (F) 93
Hutchinson, Hugh (F) 93
Hutchinson, John (F) 93
Hutchinson, John, theologian and philosopher 270–1
Hutchinson, Leonard (F) (M) 93–9, 106
Hutchinson, Thomas (T) 98
Huxley, Thomas 392, 405
Hyde, Edward, Earl of Clarendon 125, 169, 314
Hyndmersh, Alan (F) 65–6
Hyndmersh, Richard (F) (MC) (T) 67

India, College members linked to 284
Innocent IV, Pope 6–7
Inns of Court 147, 203, 273, 280
Ireland, College members from 136, 422, 424–5, 443
Irish Mead, Grandpont 105, 115

Jackson, Cyril, Dean of Christ Church 285, 300
Jacob, Hildebrand (U) 317
Jago, Richard (U) 315
James I, King of Great Britain 120–1
James II, King of Great Britain 189, 202, 205, 206, 208–10, 215–16, 219, 227, 253, 256, 520
　statue of 215, 313
'James III', see Stuart, James
James, John 271, 281–2
James, Katherine, wife of William 111
James, William (M) 3, 111–14, 116, 117, 120–1, 139
James, William (m. Christ Church 1593) 111
Jedwell, Joan 35
Jedwell, Philip 35
Jeffreys, Edward (U) 227
Jelley, Frederick, architect 477, 487
Jenkinson, Charles, Earl of Liverpool (U) 270, 275, 286, 287, 292–3, 296, 301, 303, 306
　sons of 303
Jennings, Thomas (F) 174
Jesus College, Cambridge 156
Jesus College, Oxford 154, 241, 346, 353, 369, 406, 455–6, 513
Jewish members of University College 485
Johnson, see York
Johnson, — (U?) 94
Johnson, Arthur, Chaplain of All Souls and Lecturer at University College 411
Johnson, Bertha 411
Johnson, Francis (M) 176, 178–81
Johnson, George 361
Johnson, Samuel 273, 282, 287–90, 289, 293–4, 295, 297, 309–10, 312, 314, 315–16, 331, 334–5
Johnson-Marshall, Stirrat, architect 489
Jolliffe, Thomas (U) 243
Jones (née Shipley), Anna Maria 317
Jones, Thomas (F), 205
Jones, Sir William (U) (F) 275–8, 276, 283–4, 287–8, 291, 293–5, 297, 301, 309, 312, 316, 317, 324, 328, 329, 333, 335
　monument to in Chapel 295, 329, 332

Jones 'of Nayland', William (U) 269–73, 275, 309
Jordon, Docea 318
Josephus 144, 205, 222
Jowett, Benjamin, Master of Balliol College 358, 361–2, 366, 371, 396, 419–20
Juvenal 144
Juxon, William 133

Kardar, Abdul Hafiz (U) 481, 495
Kay, Thomas (U) (F) 261–2
Keble, John 350
Keble College, Oxford 370
　based in University College during part of Second World War 469
Keene, Henry, architect 285–6, 286, 422
Keir, Sir David Lindsay (F), Master of Balliol 15, 457, 465
Kempis, Thomas à 144
Kent, College members from 129, 136, 155, 179, 195, 245, 305, 306
Kexby, John (MC) 49
Kexby, William (F) (M) 37, 48
Keyingham, Yorks. 25
Killingworth, Thomas 79
King, N. (S) 467
King's College, Cambridge 77, 413, 443, 446, 451, 513
Kingham, Oxon. 111
Kingsdon, Somerset, College living at 347–8, 373, 548–9
King's Hall, Cambridge 57, 63, 68, 75, 77–8
Knox, Ronald 460
Knylt (or Knytt), — (U?) 94
Kremer, Gidon 511
Kymer, Gilbert (MC) 57
Kytley, John (MC) 148

Lack, Alistair Iliffe (U) 483
Lacy, Edmund (F) (M) (MC), benefactor 45, 49, 60, 73–4, 85
Lady Margaret Hall, Oxford 514
Lambert, Marmaduke (U) (F) 181
Lang, Andrew 395
Langbaine, Gerard (U) 317
Latimer, Hugh 102
Laud, William, Chancellor of Oxford and Archbishop of Canterbury 126, 130, 157, 161, 163, 164, 170, 171, 179, 184, 187

Laurence, John (U) 230–1
Laurence, Thomas (F) 188, 204
Lawrence, John (U) 305
Lawson, Digby Richard (U) 444
Lean, Edward Tangye (U) 457–8
Ledgeard, John (U) (F) 194
Lee, Jennie 511
Leeds, university of 447, 452
Leicester, Earl of, *see* Dudley
Leigh, John (U) 198–9
Leland, John 314
Lendon, Edwin (U) 371–3, 389, 398
Levi, Rabbi Philip 310
Lewis, Cecil Day 460
Lewis, Clive Staples (U) 415, 416, 424, 441–2, *442*, 443, 445, 449, 450, 453, 460, 461, 463, 464–5, 466, 469, 479
Lewis, Richard (S) 139
Leys, Agnes 467
Leys, Kenneth King Munsie (F) *15*, 451, 466–7, 470
Leys, Margaret 467
Liddell, Henry George, Dean of Christ Church 406
Limerick 31
Lincoln Cathedral 21, 31, 49
Lincoln College, Oxford 49, 66, 77, 80, 83, 113, 118, 126, 162, 165, 179, 201, 238, 338, 377, 383–4, 396, 443, 444, 466, 492
 finances of 86, 181, 189, 324, 346, 399, 413, 446
 members of 68, 74, 95, 156, 214, 223, 249, 270, 272, 273, 304, 305, 353, 391
Lindsay, Alexander Dunlop, Baron Lindsey of Birker and Master of Balliol College (U) 423
Lindsay, Samuel (U) (F) 248–50, 257
Linge, Abraham van, designer of Chapel windows 4–5, 162–3, 165, 166, 179, 227, 376
Linge, Bernard van 162
Linton, John (U) 462
Linton on Ouse, Yorks., College property at 237–8, 241–2, 268, 299, 320, 328, 345, 399, 412, 548–9
Litchfield, Leonard, printer 211
Little Rollright, Oxon. 157
Liverpool, Earl of, *see* Jenkinson
Locke, John 198, 263
Lodge, William (U), benefactor 260

Logan, Douglas William (U) 457
Lombard, Peter 19, 32, 79, 144
London, College members from 305
London School of Economics 454–5, 468, 477
Long Compton, War. 273
Longinus 222
Lorenz, Robert Ernest (U) 439
Loughman, Brian Crayford (F) 503, 513, 514, 523
Loughton, Essex 74
Louth, Lincs. 117
Lowe, Robert, Viscount Sherbrooke (U) 338, 367–8, 390
Luther, Martin 144
Lympany, Dame Moura 511
Lyra, Nicholas de 79
Lyttelton, Charles (U) 264

Macan, Mildred 444
Macan, Reginald Walter (U) (F) (M) 396, 409, 414, 418, 422–5, *423*, 433, 440–7, 462, 472
McFadyean, Sir Andrew (U) 424, 427
Mackenzie, Compton 429
Mackie, John Leslie (F) 513, 522
Mackintosh, Christopher Charles Ernest Whistler (U) 459
Macleod, Norman (U) 329
Macmillan, Harold, Earl of Stockton 462
McNair, John Babbitt (U) 439
Macphail, James Gordon Stewart (U) 444, 456
Madan, Falconer 350, 379–80
Magdalen College, Oxford 62, 68, 78, 80, 138, 212–13, 215, 297, 418, 466, 525
 buildings of 71–2, 162, 240–1, 313, 314, 509
 finances of 86, 155, 324, 400, 413, 498, 499, 509
 members of 94–6, 101, 113, 119, 137, 138, 170, 210–11, 216, 266, 270, 276, 295, 305, 308, 325, 331, 343, 363, 417, 426, 429, 430, 449, 491, 493
Magdalene College, Cambridge 133, 241, 413
Magdalen Hall, Oxford 62, 119, 171, 257–8, 336
Magrath, John Richard, Provost of Queen's College, Oxford 369, 370
Maidstone, Kent, school at 129, 213, 266, 306, 353, 385, 417
Malmesbury, William of 201

INDEX

Manchester
  grammar school 417
  university of 448, 464
Mansfield College, Oxford 419
Marcus Aurelius 416, 472
Marks, Harold Edward Suter (U) 450, 451, 462
Marks Hall, manor of, Margaret Roding, Essex, College property at 45–6, 55, 62, 82, 84–5, 322, 399, 412, 417, 498, 548–9
Marlborough College 385, 386–7, 393, 394–5, 406, 424, 425, 513
Marlow, Bucks., College property at 273, 548–9
Marsh, Adam 12–13
Marsh, Norman Stayner (F) 498
Marshall, Richard (F) (T?) 65–6, 72–3
Marten, Henry (U) 169
Martyn, Charles (U) 305
Martyn, Christopher (U) 148–9
Martyn, John (F) (M) (T) 57–63, 65, 67, 72–3, 106, 524
Martyr, Peter 144
Mary I, Queen of England 96, 101–2
Mary II, Queen of Great Britain 227
  statue of 240, 243
Mary, Queen of Scots 116
Mason, William (U) 119
Masque of Hope 478
Massey, John (U), Dean of Christ Church 208, 210, 211, 216, 217
Maud (née Hamilton), Jean, Lady Redcliffe-Maud 460, 473, 486, 501
Maud, John Primatt Redcliffe, Lord Redcliffe-Maud (F) (M) *15*, 449, 450, 451–2, 454, 460, 462, 465, 466, 468, 473, 483–4, 486, 500–5, 508, 510, 513, 520
Maude, Michael William Vernon Hammond (U), Domestic Bursar 500
Maude, Richard, mason 160–1
Maude, Thomas (U) 338
Maurice, Archbishop of Rouen 4
Maurice, Thomas (U) 270, 279–80, 281, 283, 288, 297, 310, 331
Max Müller, Friedrich 352, 355
Medd, Charles Septimus (U) (F) 391
Medd, Peter Goldsmith (U) (F) 370–1, 373, 384–5, 386–7, 391
Melrose, Denis Graham (U) 470–1
Melsonby, Yorks., College living at 233, 241, 258, 319, 326–8, 331, 336, 548–9

Mendl, Robert William Sigismund (U) 432, 440
Menuhin, Sir Yehudi 511
Mercator 143
Mercer, Cecil William (alias Dornford Yates) (U) 429
Mercer (also Garston), Richard (T) 36
Merchant Taylors' School 377
Merton, Oxon., College property at 66, 103, 548–9
Merton, Walter de, Bishop of Rochester 16–18, 20, 28
Merton College, Oxford 16–7, 18–19, 24–5, 27–9, 52, 68, 81, 111, 113, 201, 307, 393, 402, 498
  based in University College during part of Second World War 469
  buildings of 28, 58, 71, 126–7
  finances of 25, 78, 87, 189, 413
  members of 47, 79, 89–92, 96, 241, 502
Methley, Yorks., College property at 118–19, 548–9
Metternich, Prince Klemens Wenzel von 348
Middelham, Robert (F) 74
Middleton, John (F) (M?) 43
Middleton, Edward (U) 308
Millin, Douglas Hubert (S) 468, 482–3, 492, 500, 515, 516–17, 519, *519*
Milton, John 280, 314
Misell (later Mitchell), Warren (U) 476
Mitchell, Sir Harold Paton (U), benefactor 444, 462, 508
Mitchell, Leslie George (F) 505, 506
Mixbury, Oxon. 157
Moffat, Charles Frederick Lorraine (U) 470
Mogae, Festus Gontebanye (U), President of Botswana 528
Moira, Earl of, *see* Rawdon
Moises, Hugh, Master of Newcastle Grammar School 302–3, 331, 334
Moises, Hugh (U) (F) 297, 302, 325, 331, 334, 337
Monckton, Philip (U) 169
Monday, Thomas (T) 98
Montagu, Richard 130
Montfort, Simon de 13
Montgomeryshire, College property in 116–17, 128, 152, 167, 322, 323, 398, 399, 412, 445, 548–9
Monyns, Edward (U) 141
Moore, Arthur Montagute (U) 415, 433, 435

Moore, Henry Wilkinson, architect 418, 421–2
Moorsom, Joseph (U) 363
Mordaunt, Gerald John (U) 427
Morellet, André 324, 334
Morison, Robert (MC) 199–200
Morocco, Ambassador to 202
Morris, Robert (S) 484, 496
Morris, William 372, 398, 409–10
mortmain, licences of 25
Murdoch, Rupert 520
Musgrave, Samuel (RF) 333
Musgrave, Thomas (U) 347
Mynors, Robert (U), benefactor 449

Nafferton, Thomas (F) (MC) 73
Naipaul, Shivadhar (Shiva) Srinivasa (U) 497
Naipaul, Sir Vidiadhar Surajprasad (U) 497, 520
Naylor, John (U) (F) 207
Nelson, George, sculptor 375
Nettleship, Henry 364
Nevill, Henry (U) (MC) 169
Nevile, Cavendish (U) (F) 248–51, 257
Nevile, John (U) (F) 227
Neville, H. (S) *384*, 384
Newcastle-upon-Tyne
  College property at 62, 66, 84–5, 128, 303, 548–9
  Newcastle Grammar School 302
New College, Oxford 20–1, 31, 51, 68, 74, 78, 82, 83, 95, 104, 162, 229, 295, 373, 375, 377, 389, 390, 396, 406, 492, 513
  buildings of 58, 72, 162, 240, 419
Newdigate, Sir Roger (U) 264, 267, 285–6, 293, 328, 329, 331, 332
New Inn Hall, Oxford 280, 282, 287
Newman, John Henry, later Cardinal 207, 350–1, 359–60
Newnham College, Cambridge 525
Newton, Sir Isaac 271, 311, 313, 314
Newton, Richard, Principal of Hart Hall 251–2
Newton Tony, Wilts. 117
New Zealand, College members from 417, 458, 479, 495, 526
Nicholson, Francis (U) 165, 205, 208, 217
Neibuhr, Barthold 348
Nix, Gerald (S) 496, 499–500
Nixon, William (S) 138–9
Normanton, Yorks., school at 118, 461

North, Frederick, Lord North, Prime Minister and Chancellor of Oxford 292–3, 485
Northampton
  All Saints church 74
  proposed university of 11
North Cerney, Glos., College living at 8, 268, 303, 325, 326–7, 373, 548–9
Northcote, Sir Stafford 396
Northumberland, College members from 60, 136, 194, 195, 278, 305, 308, 348
Northumberland, Earl of, *see* Percy
Norwich Cathedral 331
Nourse, Timothy (U) (F) 203, 207

Oates, Titus 204
Ockham, William of 31
Oddington, Oxon. 90–2, *92*
Offley, William (F) 175, 180
Oglethorpe, Owen, Vice-Chancellor of Oxford 101
Orchard, Anthony Frederick (F) 506, 511
Orchard, William 72
Oriel College, Oxford 20, 29, 68, 72, 83, 113, 126, 159, 254, 260, 292, 300, 303, 350, 353, 356, 358, 364, 396, 419, 514
Ormonde, Duke of, *see* Butler
Orum, John (MC) 49
Osney Abbey 54
Oughtred, William 147
Ovenstone, Gwynne (S) 481, *483*, 484, 493, 510, 515, 516–17
Ovid 139, 145, 280, 317
Oxenden, Ashton (U) 343, 352
Oxford, city of (asterisked properties have been owned at some time by University College)
  *Alfred's Head 273, 377
  see also University College, buildings: University Hall
  All Saints Church 410
  Angel Inn 179
  Ashmolean Museum 199, 224
  Bostar Hall, *see* High Street, nos. 86–7
  *Brasenose Hall 12–13, 21, 22, 44, 83, 94
  *Carfax, house on north-east corner of 34–5, 291–2
  *Cock on the Hoop, the 22, 44, 62, 240
  Covered Market 291
  *Crown Inn, Cornmarket 105, 112, 345–6
  *Deep Hall 22, 180, 283, 298

demolition of 352
see also University College, buildings: Shelley Memorial
*Drawda Hall (33 High Street) 12–13, 21, 83, 418
economic decline of 82
*Edward Hall 23, 83
*Grandpont, fields in, including Irish Mead 34–6, 38, 40, 166, 445
*Hampton Hall 22, 29, 83
*Hart Hall 22
Headington Quarry church 352, 375
*High Street, house owned by Studley Priory 22, 103, 118
   demolished 126–7
*High Street, three houses now part of Covered Market 34–5, 82, 291
*High Street, no. 9 44, 54, 94
*High Street, nos. 83–4 12, 23, 62, 364, 418
   taken into College use 453
*High Street, no. 85 418, 448
   taken into College use 477
*High Street, nos. 86–7 (also Bostar Hall) 62, 418, 448
   taken into College use 477
*High Street, no. 90 418, 460
   taken into College use 418, 441, 520
*High Street, no. 91, taken into College use 509–10, 520
Holy Trinity church 352
Irish Mead, see Grandpont, fields in
*Little Clarendon Street, properties in 34–5, 338–9
*Little University Hall in High Street 22, 44, 62
   converted into Master's Lodgings 93
*Little University Hall in Schools Street 12–13, 21–3, 22, 28, 83
*Ludlow Hall 22, 26, 58–9, 63, 83
   taken into College use 44
Magdalen Bridge 291
*Magpie Lane, nos. 2, 4 and 5, taken into College use 520
*Maiden Hall 23, 83
Martyrs' Memorial 359, 375
*Merton Street, nos. 9–12 418
*Merton Street, no. 18, taken into College use 477
*Merton Street, other college properties in, taken into College use 520
*New College Lane, house in 23, 28

*Old Parsonage Hotel 339, 507
*Olifaunt (or Olyfaunt) Hall 22, 29, 83
*Park Villas, nos. 1–9 339, 507
*Parsons' Almshouse, see University College, buildings: Helen's Court
Randolph Hotel 418
*Rose Hall 22, 26
St Ebbe's church 352
*St Giles, nos. 49–51 105, 112
*St Giles parish, fields in 34–5, 338–9
St John the Baptist church 28
St Mary Magdalen church 352, 375
St Mary the Virgin church 2, 28, 49, 93, 106, 120, 124, 203, 205, 213, 251, 255, 460
St Peter in the East church 187
   sermons preached in on SS Simon and Jude's day 113, 222
*St Peter-le-Bailey parish, garden in 34–5
*St Thomas parish, garden in 34–5
*schools in Schools Street, later garden 44, 95
*Sekyll Hall 22, 29, 83
*Sheld Hall 22, 29, 83
*Spicer Hall 22, 26, 27
   see also University College, buildings: Great University Hall
*Stanton Hall 22, 29, 83, 152, 180, 283
   demolition of 352–3
   see also University College, buildings: New Building
*Staple Hall (later St. Thomas Hall) 22, 29, 83
*Thames, islands in 34, 346
*White Hall 22, 26
Oxford, university of
   academic dress 196, 291
   academic halls at 2, 51, 76, 82–3
      change in nature of 69, 80, 83, 94–5
   accommodation of medieval students at 2, 51, 71, 76
   Act, the 265
   Almanacks, 199, 225, 261, *261*, 268, 269
   Bodleian Library 216, 222, 277, 291
   Clarendon Building 503
   colleges at 68–9, 237
      disputed elections in 251, 254, 266, 364
      finances of 86–7, 322, 413
      libraries at 313–14
      livings, necessity of owning 241–2, 373
      payments to university 400
      quadrangles at 58

Oxford, university of (*cont.*)
  regional affiliations of 73
  servants at 78, 383–4
  servitors at 304
  travelling Fellowships in 241
  undergraduates at, origins of 94–5, 134
  undergraduate teaching at, origins of 80, 112–13
  Visitors of colleges at 24, 81, 109–10, 251
  women admitted to formerly male colleges 513–15, 517
Commissions
  Executive Commission of 1854 368–9, 528
  Executive (Selborne) Commission of 1877 400
  Royal Commission of 1850 366, 367–8, 528
  Royal (Cleveland) Commission of 1872 400
  Royal (Asquith) Commission of 1919 446–7, 499
compared with universities elsewhere 1, 87, 268, 333–4, 362, 502–3
Congregation 24, 90, 101, 110–11
Convocation 24, 230, 249, 256, 351
  membership of 332
degrees awarded by 1–2
Divinity Schools 58, 102
early curriculum of 1–2
early history of, genuine 1–2
early history of, legendary 38, 106–7, 201
Examination Schools 397, 418, 503
examinations held at 299–300, 312, 337–8
Franks Commission 501–2
government funding of 478, 497–9, 522
Hebdomadal Council 110–11, 231, 249, 256, 265, 351, 367, 465
incorporation of 111
Indian Institute 419
Jacobitism at 227–8, 242–4, 259, 267–8
loan chests 10–11, 80, 93
misappropriation of bequest of William of Durham by 12–13
MPs of 267, 284, 287, 293–4, 332–3, 344–5
Newdigate Prize 267
non-jurors at 227
Norrington Table 506–7
postgraduate degrees at 464
Radcliffe Camera 237
Radcliffe Infirmary 237

Radcliffe Observatory 237
reform of 361–6
religious restrictions on entry 293, 369, 391
sport at 346–7, 380, 429, 434, 504
student unrest in 42, 242–3, 503–4
study of arts at 1–2, 80, 145
study of law at 2
study of medicine at 2
study of theology at 2, 8–9, 31, 46–50, 53, 73–4, 78–9
teaching at arranged centrally 1–2, 44, 80, 95
undergraduate scholars at 51, 132
University Museum 355–6, 386
women students at 395
see also under individual colleges and halls
Oxford Bach Choir 458
Oxford Improvement Act 291
Oxford Movement 273, 350–1, 359–61
Oxfordshire, links to University College 136
Oxford University Press 199, 201, 205, 224–5, 465

Padua, university of 147–8
Paestum 314
Painter, William 145
Pakistan, College members from 481
Palmer, Francis (U) 148
Palmer, Roundell, 1st Earl of Selborne 364, 366, 396, 400
Palmer, William Waldegrave, 2nd Earl of Selborne (U) 396, 520
Papillon, John (U) 346
Paris, university of 1–4, 362
  colleges of 9–10, 15–17, 51, 87, 111
  'pédagogies' at 51
  theology faculty of 3, 9
Paris, Matthew 4, 6–7
Park, Roy (F) 506
Parker, Charles Stuart (U) (F) 371
Parker, Cuthbert Leyland (F) 462
Parker, Matthew, Archbishop of Canterbury 106–7
Parker, Richard (MC) 117
Parker, Thomas Maynard (F) 487, 492, *494*
Parsons, Alfred Alan Lethbridge (U) 426
Parsons, John, Master of Balliol 285, 300
Patrington, Robert de (F) (M?) 29–30
Patrington, Yorks. 30
Pattison, Mark, Rector of Lincoln College 355, 356, 362, 363, 366

INDEX

Paul, George Andrew (F) 479, 513
Paull, Yorks., College estate at 25, 82, 84–5, 93–4, 548–9
Payne, Ernest John (F) 422
Peacocke, Thomas Arthur Hardy (U) 457
Pears, Peter 501
Peel, Sir Robert 344–5
Pelling, Christopher Brendan Reginald (F) 491, 506
Pembroke, Earl of, *see* Herbert
Pembroke College, Oxford 125–6, 287, 294, 371, 514
Pentland, Thomas (F) 102
Pepys, Samuel 220
Percival, John, President of Trinity 406
Percy, Henry, 2nd Earl of Northumberland, benefactor 60–2, *61*, 80, *261*, 509, 524
Percy, Henry, 4th Earl of Northumberland 63–4
Perrot, Simon, benefactor 113
Persius 363
Person, Peter (F) 90–1, 144
Peterborough Cathedral 267
Peterhouse, Cambridge 113
Peters, Hugh 180
Philip II, King of Spain 105
Philippa, Queen of England 31
Pitt, William the Younger 297, 300
Plato 139, 145, 280
Playfair, Sir Nigel Ross (U) 414, 429, 435
Pliny the Elder 144
Pliny the Younger 263
Plot, Robert (MC), benefactor, 199–200, 215, 221
Plumer, Thomas (U) (F) 283, 331
Plumptre, Edward Hayes (U) 359
Plumptre, Frederick Charles (U) (F) (M), benefactor *349*, 351–66, 367–77, 383–6, 401
  architectural interests of 352–3, 359, 373–7
Plutarch 143, 200, 222
Poklington, John de (F) 29–30
Pogge von Strandmann, Hartmut Johann Otto (F) 495
Pole, Reginald, Cardinal, Archbishop of Canterbury 102
Polmorva, William de (F) 29–31
Polybius 314
Pontefract, Yorks., College property at 118, 128, 154, 322–3, 399, 400, 412, 445, 548–9

Poore, Richard, Bishop of Durham 5
Pope, Alexander 264, 313
Porphyry 105
Portland, Duke of, *see* Cavendish-Bentinck
Pothow, Adam de (F) 33
Potter, John (U) 222, 257, 304, 305
Powell, William, Master of St John's College, Cambridge 285
Poynton, Arthur Blackburne (F) (M) *15*, 416–17, 440, 447–8, 451, 452–4, *453*, 464, 472
Pray, Thomas (F) (MC) (T) 73, 79
Pricket, John (S), College butler 190, 229–30, 235, 318
Prideaux, Humphrey 193
Primer, P. (S) *467*
Provost, Peter (MC) 75
Ptolemy 144
Pusey, Edward 360, 409

Queens' College, Cambridge 68, 73, 133, 308, 351, 377, 451, 524
Queen's College, Oxford 20–1, 28, 51, 66, 82, 83, 361, 364, 369, 371, 378, 379, 381, 418
  buildings of 72, 91–2, 162, 240, 313
  members of 30–1, 48, 73, 76–7, 95, 113, 126, 153, 200, 202, 204, 212, 223, 225–6, 276, 361, 391
Quintilian 145

Racine, Jean 313
rack rents 322, 345, 398–9
Radcliffe, Sir George (U), benefactor 124, 128, 146, 147, 149–51, 152, 154–5, 158, 166, 177, 198, 278
Radcliffe, John (U), benefactor 213–14, 217–18, 221, 222, 228, 237–42, *238*, *261*, 308, 439, 491
  statue of 240
Radcliffe, Jonas (U) (F) 123–4, 133, 146, 148, 154, 236
  monument to in Chapel 124
Radcliffe, Joshua (U) 154
Radcliffe, Savile (U) 154
Radcliffe, Thomas (U) (F) 133, 151, 154, 166, 171, 180, 181, 185
Radcliffe, Thomas (U) 154–5, 166
Radford, Richard de (F) 29–30
Radley College 417
Radnor, Earl of, *see* Bouverie

Raleigh, Walter 311
Ramsbotham, Herwald, Viscount Soulbury (U) 489
Ramus, Peter 145
Randolph, Edmund (U) 147–8
Randolph, Herbert (U) 147
Ranken, George Elliott (U) 361
Ratcliff, Richard Charles (U) 451
Rathbone, Reginald Blythe (U) 445
Rawdon Hastings, Francis, Earl of Moira and Marquess of Hastings (U) 283, 294, 520
Rayne, Max, Baron Rayne, benefactor and Honorary Fellow 512
Read, Catherine, benefactor 186
Reay, Henry Utrick (U) (F) 304
Redcliffe-Maud, *see* Maud
Reddyhoff, James William (U) 446
Redyford, Adam (F) 49
Reich, Robert Bernard (U) 483
Renton, David Lockhart-Mure, Lord Renton (U) 451, 462
Repton School 385
Responsions 338
Rhodes, Cecil 396
Rhodesia, College members from 417, 495
Rhodes House 465, 495
Rhodes Scholarships 417
Ribbentrop, Joachim von 449
Richard II, King of England 38–41, 43, 46
Richards, George (U) 304
Richardson, Sir Albert, architect 477, 487
Richardson, Thomas (U) 305
Richardson, William (U) (F) 168, 171, 172
Ridley, Charles John (U) (F) 342
Ridley, Henry (U) (F) 303
Ridley, Matthew 303
Ridley, Nicholas (U) 303
Ridley, Nicholas (refused Fellowship) 93, 102
Ridley, Richard (U) 303
Riordan, Catherine 413
Ripplingham, Robert de, benefactor 25–6
Ritchie, Henry (T) 417
Robbins Report 501
Roberts, John Varley 426
Robin, Charles Janvrin (U) *382*
Robinson, Alfred (U) 373, 383
Robinson, Sir Christopher (U) 331
Robinson, Henry 126
Robinson, William (U) 235
Rochester, Kent

Cathedral 331
school at 129, 306, 417
Rockley, Thomas (U) 149, *150*, 169
Rogers, General Bernard William (U) 482
Rogers, Francis (U) (F) 234, 247–50, 254, 257, 259, 260
Rogers, William (U), benefactor 203, 215, 216
Rolleston, Matthew (U) (F) 346
Rooper, William (U) 343, 347
Rosenberger, Oskar Jacob Wilhelm (U) 435
Rossall School 353
Rotherwick, Hants., quit rent paid to College from property on 118, 548–9
Rouen 1, 4–6
Routh, Martin, President of Magdalen College 300–1
Rowley, Francis 343
Rowley, George (U) (F) (M) 300, 337, 342–51, 381
as Vice-Chancellor 349–51
Roxborough, John (F) (M) (MC) 66–7, 73, 89, 148
Royal Holloway College, London 467
Rubens, Paul Alfred (U) 429, 435
Rugby School 353, 356, 362, 365, 377, 379, 386, 417, 425
Rushbrook Williams, Laurence (U) 415, 425, 433
Ruskin, John 409
Russell, Lord John, Prime Minister 366
Russell, Richard (U) 228
Russia, College members from 435–6, 526
Rygge, Robert, Chancellor of Oxford 38, 47
Ryneveld, Clive Berrange van (U) 495
Ryvell, John (F) 49

Sacheverell, Henry 242
Sackville, Thomas, Lord Buckhurst, Chancellor of Oxford 120
Sadler, Sir Michael Ernest (M) *15*, 227, 447–52, 458, 461, 464, 468, 472, 490, 520
St Alban Hall, Oxford 117
St Andrews, university of 87, 177
St Anne's College, Oxford 514
St Augustine 79, 143
St Basil 144, 222
St Bonaventure 3, 144
St Catharine's College, Cambridge 68, 322
St Catherine's Society (later St Catherine's College), Oxford 482, 502, 513

St Cuthbert, patron saint of University
    College 6, 5, 45, 71, 203
St Edmund Hall, Oxford 82-3, 223, 225,
    304, 354, 502
St Frideswide's priory, Oxford 11-12, 35
St Hilda's College, Oxford 467, 517
St Hugh's College, Oxford 83, 339
St Jerome 144
St John of Beverley 38, 69, 71
St John Chrysostom 143
St John's College, Cambridge 94, 124, 285,
    308, 322, 323, 325, 328, 413, 446
St John's College, Oxford 104, 126, 137,
    143, 151, 157, 160, 170, 193, 237,
    241, 243, 245, 279, 339, 369, 418,
    476, 507, 509
St Jude 71
St Mary Hall, Oxford 233
St Neot 38
St Paul's Cathedral, London 67, 130
St Paul's School 377
St Peter's Hall (later St Peter's College),
    Oxford 443
St Thomas à Becket 97
St Thomas Aquinas 3-4, 79, 143, 313
Salisbury
    Cathedral 104, 187
    proposed university of 11
Salisbury, Marquess of, *see* Cecil
Sallust 306
Salvesen, Harold Keith (U), benefactor 499
Salveyn, Anthony (F) (M) 103
Salveyn, Richard (F) (M) 100-1, 103
Sandbach, Samuel Henry (U) 402-3
Sanderson, Robert 145
Sandford, Kenneth Stuart (U) (F) 503
Saône, Guillaume de 10
Savege, — (U?) 94
Savile, George (U) 154, *155*
Savile, Sir George (U) 122, 124-5, 154-5, *155*
Savile, George, Earl of Halifax 177, 188,
    189, 195
Savile, John (U) (F) 189
Savile, Sir William (U) 141, 154-5, 169, 177
Say, William (U) 169
Saye and Sele, Lord, *see* Fiennes
Scarisbrick, Robert (U) 210
Scarron, Paul 313
Schlepegrell, Adolf Friedrich Karl (U) 463
Scotland
    College members from 179, 506

universities of 144, 333-4, 362; *see also*
    Edinburgh, Glasgow, and
    St Andrews, universities of
Scott, Sir Gilbert George, architect 374,
    375-6, 448, 453
Scott, James (U) (F) 248, 253, 255
Scott, James Yuill (U) 428, 443
Scott, John, Earl of Eldon (U) (F) 278, *279*, 281,
    282-3, 284, 285, *286*, 287, 295, 297,
    301, 302-3, 309, 312, 316, 317, 328-9,
    331, 334-5, 339, 349-50, 373
sons of at University College 303, 305
statue of 373-5, *374*, 453-4, 521-2
Scott, John Oldrid, architect 378
Scott, William, Baron Stowell (F) 278-82,
    279, 284, *286*, 287-8, *289*, 290, 292-5,
    297, 301, 302-3, 305, 309, 310, 314,
    324, 328, 329, 331, 332-3, 334-5, 354,
    389, 524
son of at University College 303
statue of 373-5, *374*, 453-4, 521-2
Screaton, Gordon Robert (F) 502, 511-12,
    521, 525
Scroton, Robert de (F) 29-30
Second World War 469-74
Selborne, Lord, *see* Palmer
Seldeneck, Rolf Wilhelm von (U) 442
Sélincourt, Ernest de (U) and Lecturer 411,
    419-20, *428*, 460
Selwyn College, Cambridge 489
Seneca the Younger 145
Shadforth, Thomas (U) (F) 378
Shadwell, John (U) 210, 213
Shadwell, Thomas 210, 213
Shaftesbury, Earl of, *see* Cooper
Shakespeare, William 138, 145, 314, 429
Sheldon, Gilbert, Archbishop of Canterbury
    and Chancellor of Oxford 193
Shelley, Jane, Lady Shelley,
    benefactor 419-20
Shelley, Percy Bysshe (U) 339-42, *341*,
    419, *420*
see also University College, buildings:
    Shelley Memorial
Shelley, Timothy (U) 339-40
Shenstone, William 315
Shepherd, Frederick Hawkesworth Sinclair,
    artist *15*, 452, 501
Shepherd, George (U) (F) 306
Sherborne Priory 12
Sherborne School 406

Shippen, Robert, Vice-Chancellor and
    Principal of Brasenose 244, 247,
    249–51, 255, 257, 259
Shippen, William (U) (F) 202, 204, 247
Shipton-under-Wychwood, Oxon. 63, 253
Shock, Sir Maurice (F) 488–9, 501, 509
Shrewsbury School 353, 377
Sidgwick, Arthur Hugh (F) 443
Sidmouth, Marianne, Viscountess,
    benefactor 354
Sidney Sussex College, Cambridge 211
Silvester, Thomas (U) 170–1
Simonburn, Northumberland 74
Simpson, Francis (U) (F) 331
Skeffington, Sydney (F) 392, 394
Skirlaugh, Yorks. 40
Skirlaw, Walter, Bishop of Durham,
    benefactor (MC or F?) *1*, 40, 45–6,
    54, 71, 80, *261*, 509
Slater, Richard (U) *426, 432*
Slatter, Richard (MC) (F) 144, 149
Sleidan, Johannes 146
Smith, Goldwin (F), benefactor 364–6, *365*,
    367–70, 375, 376, 385, 390, 391, 392,
    396, 405
Smith, Dame Maggie 495–6
Smith, Oliver (T) 166, 169
Smith, R. (S) 467
Smith, Thomas (T) 166
Smith, William (U) (F) 217, *225*, 230, 233, 235,
    240, 258, 317, 323–4, 516
    as authority on the history of University
        College 2, 21, 56–7, 224, 249
    as eyewitness 185, 186, 200, 206–8, 211,
        214–15, 216, 220, 226, 229, 231,
        232, 236, 306
    opinions on legend of King Alfred 39,
        224
    publication of *The Annals of University
        College* 256–7
    transcripts of 94, 137, 214–15, 256
Sollas, William Johnson (F) 411, 466
Somerset, Lord Charles Noel, later 4th Duke
    of Beaufort (U) 254, 260, 268
Somerset, Henry, 3rd Duke of Beaufort (U)
    244, 247, 250–1, 257, 260, 312,
    315
Somerset, Henry, 5th Duke of Beaufort 292
Somerton, Oxon. 163
Somerville College, Oxford 83, 467, 499,
    507, 517

Sophocles 280, 310, 389
Sorbon, Robert de 10, 15
Sorley, Charles Hamilton (accepted for
    matriculation) 440
Soulbury, *see* Ramsbotham
South Africa, College members from 417,
    495, 496
Southern, Sir Richard 501
Southey, Robert 276
South Scarle, Notts. 30
Southwell, Thomas (MC) 75, 76–7
Spelman, Sir John 200–1, 204, 232
Spencer, George John, Viscount Althorp, later
    Earl Spencer 276–7, 312
Spender, Sir Stephen Harold (U) 451, 457–8,
    460, 461–2
Stael, Peter (MC) 199–200
Standfast, William (U) (F) 228, 324–5
Stanford, Lincs., proposed university of 11
Stanford Rivers, Essex 123, 128
Stanhope, Walter (U) 278–81, 283, 289, 290,
    309, 310–11, 314, 316
Stanley, Arthur Penrhyn (F) 353, *355*,
    356–66, 367–9, 386, 390–1, 405–6
Stanyhurst (or Stanihurst), Richard (U) 105–6
Stapper, Henry (F) 103–4
Statius 313
Staunton, Henry of, Chancellor of Oxford 1, 13
Stell, Leslie Vernon (U) 481
Stevens, the widow (S) 235, 319
Stevenson, George Hope (F) *15*, 465, 466,
    470, 477, 498
Stokes, Anthony Derek (F) 514
Stoop, Adrian Dura (U) *428*
Storr, Vernon (F) 373, 408
Stowell, Lord, *see* Scott, William
Strafford, Earl of, *see* Wentworth
Strahan, George (U) (F) 288, 312, 314,
    315–16, 331
Strahan, William 288
Stratford, William 244, 247, 249, 250, 251,
    256–7, 257, 259
Strawbridge, David James (U) 438, 469
Strawson, Sir Peter (F) 468, 479, 485, 488, *494*,
    501, 513
Strete, Edmund (MC) 42, 71, 75, 77
Strother, Henry (F) (T) 74
Stuart, Charles Edward, also 'Charles III' or
    'the Young Pretender' 267–8
Stuart, James Francis Edward, also 'James III'
    or 'The Old Pretender' 216, 227, 242

INDEX

Stuart, John, Earl of Bute 287
Suetonius 263, 313
Sunderland, *see* Bishopwearmouth
Surtees, Matthew (U) (F) 303
Sutherland, Graham, painter 511, *512*
Suttone, John de (F) 29–30
Swire, Samuel (U) (F) 296, 319, 331
Sykes, William George David (F) 505, 517, 527
Symonds, John Addington 364
Syon monastery, Middx. 66, 79

Tacitus 263
Tanner, Thomas 225, 230–1, 232, 256, 257
Tarleton, Sir Banastre, Bt. (U) 294, 329
Tarrant Gunville, Dorset, College living at 268, 326–7, 348, 386, 548–9
Taylor, Francis (U) (F) 249–51, 254, 257, 259, 261–2, 266
Taylor, John (F) 42–3
Tennant, Henry (U) (F) 261–2, 275, 327–8
Tennant, Miles (U) 327–8
Tennant, Richard (U) 167
Terence 139, 145, 280
Terry, Edward (F) 175, 181
Terry, Harold Frank (U) *432*
Terry, James, benefactor 448
Thatcher, Margaret 520, 522
Theocritus 263
Theyer, Charles (U) 203
Theyer, John 203
Thinne, Thomas, MP for Oxford University 193
Thomson, Edmund (F) 100, 102
Thomson, Michael (U) (F) 151
Thomson, Thomas (F) 91, 144
Thomson, William (F) 144, 148
Thornhill, Yorks. 124–5, 154–5, *155*, 177, 189
Thornton, Joshua (U) 184
Thornton, Thomas (F) 175–6, 184
Thrale, Henry (U) 290
Thrale, Hester 290, 294, 318, 490
Thucydides 222
Thurlby, Thomas (F) (MC) 79
Tickell, George (F) 354, 361
Tiddy, Reginald John Elliott (U) (F) *428*, 443
Tildesley, Edward (U) 141
Tildesley, Richard (U) 141
Tinne, Christopher Edward (U) 426, 430, 443
Tinne, Michael Capellen (U) 430, 443
Tiptoft, John, Earl of Worcester (MC) 56, 75–7, 79–80, 95, 520

Titzabetsi, Caspar (MC) 178
Todd, Hugh (F) 200, 212, 220, 225, 226, 231, 326
Toke, John (U) 302
Toke, Nicholas (U), m. 1721 245, 254, 258, 302, 310–12, 318
Toke, Nicholas (U), m. 1756 302
Toke, Nicholas (U), m. 1782 302
Tolkien, John Ronald Reuel 460
Toller, Charles Richard Alfred (U) 439
Tolley, Cyril James Hastings (U) 459
Tonge, Ezreel (also Israel) (U) (F) 170, 172–4, 175–6, 204–5
Torre, Henry (U) 317
Tottenham, George Leonard (U) *432*
Townesend, William, architect 238–40
Townshend, Charles, Lord Townshend 242
Tractarianism, *see* Oxford Movement
Transylvania, College residents from 178
Tredington, Worcs. 104
Treitel, Sir Guenter, Lecturer 485, 491
Trevor-Roper, Hugh Redwald, Lord Dacre 481
Trinity College, Cambridge 57, 193, 237, 402
Trinity College, Oxford 16, 104, 170, 211, 220–1, 338, 369, 381, 389, 392, 396, 406, 433, 443, 444, 447, 451, 470, 476, 502, 506, 517, 524, 525
  buildings of 240, 313
Trinity Hall, Cambridge 68
Trithen, Francis (MC) 338
Trowbridge, Alexander Buel (U) 444, 445, 456, 458, *459*, 462–3
Trudeau, Garry 518
Tucker, Ken (S) 497, 499–500
Turin, Lucia (S) 468
Twiss, Sir Travers (U) (F) 348–9, *349*, 354, 356, 357, 358, 360, 361, 367–70, 391
Twyne, Brian 35, 107, 185, 187
Tydeman, William Marcus (U) 496

Underwode, Edward (F) 67
United States of America, College members from and links with 177, 294, 305, 417, 444, 450, 482–3, 485, 493–5, 517, 526
University Challenge 507
University College, buildings
  Alington Room 190, 487–8, *488*
  barges 378, *379*, 429–30, *431*, 504–5
  bathrooms installed in 418, 477

University College, buildings (*cont.*)
 boathouses 504–5, 520
 Bostar Hall, *see* Oxford, city of: High Street, nos. 86–7
 buttery 196, 375
 Catholic Chapel in 209–10, 211–12, 215–16, 219
 Cecily's Court 508–9
 Chapel, lack of 28
 Chapel, medieval 35, 44–5, 69–71
  attendance at 66, 112, 179
  burials in 124, 138, 152, 175
  dedication of 66
  destruction of 187
  disputations held in 80
  effects of Reformation in 97, 97, 100, 102
  furnishings of 163
  memorials in 71, 91, 124
  missal used in *1*, 80, 97, *97*
  services held in 64, 71, 80
  stained glass windows in 69
 Chapel, modern 210, 251, 255
  as built 161–2, 186–7
  as rebuilt in 19th century 299, *374*, 375–6
  as restored in 20th century 448, 477, 520
  attendance at 226, 388, 391, 425, 425–6, 462
  burials in 220, 245, 266, 300, 342
  choir and singing in 376–7, 424, 426, 517
  consecration of 187, 219
  marriages celebrated in 497, 517
  memorials in 124, 295, 329, *332*, 347
  organ in 376, 477
  paintings in 227, 336, 376
  screen at west end 226–7
  seating arrangements in 315
  sermons preached in 359, 406, 408–9, 424
  services held in 315, 337, 371, 444, 517
  stained and painted glass windows in *4–5*, 162–3, 165, 166, 179, 186, 213–14, 227, 375–6, 448, 469, 520
  war memorials in 439, 442, 444, 471, 478
  see also University College, general: religion in
 cricket pavilion 430, 515
 Durham Buildings 421, 489, 498
 electricity installed in 417–18
 first home of 21–23, *22*
  see also Oxford, city of: Little University Hall in Schools Street
 Front Quadrangle, *see* Main Quadrangle

gardens 196, 235, 316, 352–3, 375, 416
Goodhart Building and Seminar Room 488–90, *490*, 507
Great University Hall 22, 26, *27*, 28, 44, 58–9
 see also Oxford, city of: Spicer Hall
Hall, medieval 59, 69, 163, 180, 190
 disputations held in 112
 seating arrangements in 141
Hall, modern 356, 475
 as built 161–2, 179–80
 as rebuilt in 1766 285–6, *286*
 as rebuilt in 1904 421–2
 lectures and disputations given in 245, 395, 409
 portraits in 329, 511
 seating arrangements in 196, 226, 285, 315
 see also University College, general: meals
Helen's Court (formerly Parsons' Almshouses) 488, 489
High Street, houses in converted to College use 418, 453, 477
 see also Oxford, city of: High Street, nos. 83–4, no. 85, nos. 86–7, no. 90, and no. 91, and Merton Street, no. 18
kitchen 162, 190
Kybald House (also Tutor's House) 418, 488, 499
lavatories 432, 477
Law Library 498
Library, medieval 19, 69, 71, 142–4, 167
 books given to 29, 46, 66, 79, 113, 118, 125, 143–4, 187
Library, 17th century *191*, 313–15, 352, 487
 as built 162, 190
 books bought for 314
 books borrowed from 314–15
 books given to 203, 204
 chains in 313–14
 gutting of 375
Library, 19th century
 as built 373–5, *374*
 as rebuilt in 1930s and 1990s 453–4, 521–2
 books borrowed from 373
 statues in 373–5, *374*, 453–4, 521–2
Library, undergraduate 313–14
Logic Lane, bridge over 421
Magpie Lane, *see* Oxford, city of: Magpie Lane, nos. 2, 4, and 5

Main Quadrangle 316
  as originally built 126–8, 158–63, *159*, *160*, 166, 186–7, 190–3, *192*
    costs of 161, 163, 190, 193
    designs for 158–60
    fund-raising for 135, 154, 158, 179–80, 186–7, 190–3
  as rebuilt in early 19th century *12*, 299
  as rebuilt in 1950s 477–8
  requisitioning of 441
  statues erected on 215, 235
Master's Lodgings, as first recorded 59
Master's Lodgings, in Little University Hall in High Street 93, 104, 136, 141, 180, 209, 216
  printing press in 211, 216
  demolition of 240
Master's Lodgings, in Radcliffe Quadrangle 238–40, *239*, 251, 253, 256, 336–7
  conversion into undergraduate accommodation 397–8
  donation of Browne Library to 273
  possible depiction of room in *10*, 258
Master's Lodgings, modern 397, 413
medieval quadrangle of 58–9, 69–72, *70*
  demolition of in 1660s and 1670s 190
  residential space in 71–2, 139–42
  stained glass windows in 69
Merton Street, houses in, *see* Oxford, city of: Merton Street, no. 1college properties in
Mitchell Building *16*, 508
modernization of after 1945 477–8, 520–1
New Building 352–3
  requisitioning of 441
  see also Oxford, city of: Stanton Hall
Payne Library 422, 477
Porter's Lodge 520
Radcliffe Quadrangle *9*, 268, *269*, 285, 421, 432, 477, 520
  building of 238–41, *239*
  requisitioning of 441, 471
  statues erected on 240, 243
  see also Master's Lodgings, in Radcliffe Quadrangle
Senior Common Room 201, 210, 226, 288, 290, 316, 352–3, 421–2, 451, 452, 477
Shelley Memorial 419–21, *420*, 448, 478, 520–1
  see also Oxford, city of: Deep Hall

squash court 448
Stavertonia *17*, 507–9, 513, 527
Treasury 254, 313
Tutor's House, *see* Kybald House
unbuilt designs for *11*, 158–60, *159*, *160*, *162*, *239*, 239–40, 298–9, 397, 419, 448, 478, 487
University Hall 377, 421
  carvings from transferred to Summer Common Room 421
  see also Durham Buildings and Oxford, city of: Alfred's Head
University College: general
  accents at 154, 371, 417, 422
  accounts and finances of 19–20, 37, 42, 44, 52–3, 60–2, 64–5, 81–7, 86, 98, 99, 104–5, 112, 128–9, 152–3, 163, 167–8, *168*, 173–5, 180–1, 188–9, 254, 259–60, 320–5, *321*, 345–6, *345*, 398–400, 411–14, 443, 445–6, 498–9, 509–10, 511–12, 522–4
  accounting systems of 85, 400
  effects of agricultural depression of 1880s 411–13
  effects of inflation 98, 509
  estates, lawsuits concerning 34–43, 54, 116–17, 118, 161, 164, 173–5, 184
  estates, management of 55, 82–5, 98, 128, 152–3, 167–8, 254, 259, 318, 321–3, 338–9, 345–6, 398–400, 412, 416, 443, 445, 498
  government grants to 487, 497–9, 522
  income from internal sources 44–5, 62–3, 96, 399, 443
  stocks, investment in 291–2, 322, 354, 398, 445–6, 498
  anniversary celebrations of 356, 390–1, 478, 520, *521*, 523
  balls held at 401
  benefactions to and fund-raising at 58–60, 77, 135, 179–80, 190–3, *191*, 223, 224, 227, 260, 285, 375, 491, 499, 508, 512, 523–4; *see also under individual benefactors*
  prayers to benefactors 19, 24, 64, 185
  bible clerks at 52
  Bump Suppers 380, 456–7
  Bursars 15, 19, 23, 103, 398, 416
  Catechist, office of 112, 146, 222, 260, 265, 278, 296, 310

University College: general (cont.)
  Chaplain Fellow 462
  clubs and societies
    Cecil Club 460
    Churchwardens 429, 437, 460
    Durham Society 429, 460
    Eldon Society 460, 495
    Inklings 460
    Martlets 427, 428, 437, 440, 444, 451, 458, 460, 478, 527
    Robert Boyle Society 460, 495
    Shakespeare Club (or Society) 401–2, 427, 527
    Shakespeare Reading Club 401
    University College Boat Club 14, 346–7, 357, 378–80, 379, 429–30, 431, 437, 439, 458–9, 495, 504–5, 516–17, 519
      see also servants and members of staff: servants' sports clubs; University College, buildings: barges and boathouses
    University College Debating Society 381
    University College Essay Society 401
    University College Musical Society 460, 478, 501, 511
    Univ. Players 469, 478, 495–6
    Utopers 458–9
    see also recreations at
  coat of arms of 112
  collections 389, 463, 498
  commoners (mature) at 20, 73, 75–7, 137–8, 199–200, 302
    numbers of 62–3, 75, 137
    origins of 20, 73
    participating in life of College 45, 75, 77, 80–1
  contraceptive machine 505
  costs of living in College 76, 315–16
  customs at 370–1, 496
  Dean, office of 112, 265, 480–1
  Domestic Bursarship 416, 479, 500, 525
  Estates Bursarship 398, 414, 416, 525
  excommunication of Fellows at 49–50
  family networks at 154–5, 177, 189, 208, 302–3, 396
  feasts
    St Cuthbert's Day Feast 44, 244, 254, 288
    SS Simon and Jude's Day Feast 157–8, 174, 201, 254, 260

Fellows
  academic qualifications of 31, 52–3, 73–4, 309, 464, 487, 492
  administrative demands made on 525–6
  admission procedures for 15, 114, 255, 277, 307–8, 356
  appointments of made by outsiders 100, 171–2, 175–7, 189, 204, 213
  as College Officers 112, 291, 296, 347, 525–6
  as Common University Fund (CUF) lecturers 499, 522
  betting books of 297, 299, 337, 343, 347
  books owned by 130, 144
  books written or published by 32, 79, 186, 197–8, 200–1, 205, 221–2, 234, 265, 277–8, 333, 355, 356, 363–4, 393, 395, 416, 422, 450, 464–6, 472, 479, 491, 506, 525
  careers of 31, 72–4, 163, 194, 283–4, 325–8, 465
  disputed elections of 229–32, 266, 363
  educational backgrounds of 176–7, 194, 307, 309, 373
  Emeritus Fellows 447
  Fellows of undergraduate status 277, 282, 309
  freezing of posts 184, 210, 412, 522
  Honorary Fellowships 369
  killed in action 443, 471–2
  laicization of 371–3, 393, 401
  lengths of tenure 24, 31, 72–3, 133, 194, 308, 334
    limits imposed on 391–2, 401
  geographical origins of 20, 72, 132–3, 177, 194, 308–9, 417
    changes to geographical restrictions on 348–9, 368–9
  holy orders taken by 24, 64, 188, 232, 368, 414–15
  marriage of 317, 368, 391–2, 395, 401, 418, 466
  misbehaviour by 66–7, 151–2, 156, 179, 229, 244, 255, 443, 457
    financial 129–30, 151–2, 235, 261–2, 297–8
    sexual 55, 179, 234–5, 282, 317, 348, 414
  pension schemes for 393–4, 401
  pluralism of 58, 64–6, 133–4, 292
  political sympathies of 227–8, 242–3, 259, 267, 285, 293–5, 329, 344–5, 371,

386, 393, 395, 409–10, 422–3, 443, 450–1, 466
'prize' Fellows 392, 401, 447
Professorial Fellows 411, 447, 466, 492–3
proportion of scientists among 502
residence in College 73, 81, 133, 137, 139–42, 148, 179, 277, 291, 296, 328, 392, 440, 491, 505, 524
residence in College after resigning Fellowship 73
size of Fellowship 42, 53, 62–3, 502
social life among 80–1, 201, 253–4, 255, 294, 297, 355, 368, 393, 395, 423, 451, 466, 491–3, 524
social status of 72, 132–3, 403
Special Supernumerary Fellows 447
specialization of in particular subjects 392
Stipendiary and non-Stipendiary Fellows 447
stipends of 19, 23–4, 64, 133–4, 152–3, 163, 254, 323–5, 346, 399, 412–13
subjects of study 15, 23, 78–80, 142, 177, 188, 265
see also subjects studied by members of
suicides among 220, 414
vacancies, lack of 308
Fellowships created at 15, 25, 512, 523–4
Bennet Fellowships 157–8, 164, 173–5, 184, 188, 194, 207–8, 220, 249–50, 258–9, 265, 308, 365
Lady Wallis Budge Fellowships 464
Mynors Fellowships 449, 464
Percy Fellowships 60, *61*, 265, 282, 349
Radcliffe Travelling Fellowships 237, 241, 320, 333, 447
Salvesen Fellowships 499
Skirlaw (or Henry IV) Fellowships 45–6, 265, 349
Stowell Law Fellowships 354, 361, 364, 446
Weir Fellowships 499
William of Durham Fellowships 265, 282, 349, 356, 363
forging of documents at 41, 54, 57, 254
General Purposes Committee 492, 513
government scrutiny of 49–50, 522, 524–5
graces said at Hall 113, 371, 450, 496
humanism 79–80
'illuminations' at 205, 216, 290
incorporation of 111–12

Jacobitism at 227–8, 242–4, 267–8, 272, 288
Junior Common Room 427, 440, 444, 462, 495, 496, 517, 519
Junior Research Fellows 447, 449, 456
lecturers at 410–11
livings owned by 60, 84, 129, 233, 238, 241–2, 268–9, 326–8, 347–8, 373, 412, 548–9
Masters
domestic lives of 295–6, 336–7, 407–8
elections to Masterships 65, 90, 100–1, 104, 109–10, 114, 119–20, 157, 171, 175–6, 187, 193, 219–21, 247–59, 252, 265, 266–7, 275, 336, 342–3, 351, 386–7, 405, 407, 422, 447–8, 452, 454–5, 473–4, 485, 500–1, 510
lay Masters 114–15, 423–4, 462
limits to tenure and powers of 393–4
married Masters 111, 115
origins of 19, 33
relations with Fellows 66–7, 90–1, 119–20, 123, 180, 200–1, 213–15, 230–3, 236, 253, 255–6, 259, 260–2, 282, 294–5, 367–8, 393–4, 406, 407, 424, 451, 473–4, 484, 490, 501, 511
relations with undergraduates 122, 128, 226, 262–3, 278, 337, 388, 405–6, 407, 424–5, 451–2, 455, 485, 501, 510–11
stipends of 152–3, 323–4, 399, 412
meals and timings of meals 163, 244, 315, 340, 343–4, 380, 390, 427, *432*, 441, 445, 455, 457, 496–7, 505, 524, 527
effects of rationing 471, 478
food, standards of 357, 383
see also University College, buildings: Hall
Middle Common Room (also Weir Common Room) *16*, 495, 508, 513
murders committed or attempted in 42, 413, 470–1
name of 21, 23–5, 27–8, 111–12, 379
'non-dons' 503
numbers of people at 53, 62, 101, 134–5, *135*, 141, 161, 165–6, 168, 194, *195*, 212–13, 228, 254, 263, *264*, 268, 283, 299, 343, *344*, 353, 396–7, 405, 411, 440, *441*, 444, 476, 503
Old Members
concept of 77, 153–6
keeping names on books 331–3
patronage among 331
portraits of 329

University College: general (*cont.*)
    relations with College 180, 190–3, 283, 285–7, 328-333, *330*, 433, 437, 438, 527–8
    University College Record 433, 437, 445, 448, 491, 527–8
    see also University College Club
  origins of, genuine, *see* William of Durham
  origins of, mythical, *see* Alfred, King of Wessex
  outsiders' opinions of 107, 125, 132, 280–1, 288, 390, 394, 396, *404*, 405–6, 414, 433, 481, 507
    'The Pub on the High' 456
  plague, reactions to 152
  'poor scholars' at 138, 161
  'portionists' at 52, 76, 94, 138
  postgraduates at 464, 492, 493–5, 526
  Praelector, office of 112, 146, 266, 347, 377
  racism at 434, 445
  recreations at 148–51, 264, 316, 346–7, 378–81, 427–36, 456–60
    athletics 380, 430, 459
    archery 128, 149
    boating 264, 316
    bowls 264
    chess 495
    cricket 264, 316, 346–7, 415, 416, 427, 430, 458–9, 495
      see also clubs and societies: Utopers
    dancing 149, *150*, 198, 264
    drama 201–2, 381, *382*, 429, 348, 478, 495–6, 519
      College revue 505, 517
    fencing 149, *150*
    football 380, 427, 430
    golf 380, 415, 445, 459
    hockey 458, 517
    journalism 429, 497
    music 149, 198, 201, 264, 289, 355, 427, 429, 432, 435, 458, 460, 478, 501, 511, 517, 520
    riding and hunting 149, 264, 316, 343, 352, 378, 393, 411
    rowing; *see* clubs and societies: University College Boat Club
    rugby 380, 429, 430, 439, 458–9, *459*
    skating 316
    skiing 459
    squash 448

    tennis 149, 202, 427, 430
    see also clubs and societies
  religion in 408, 415, 462–3, 527
    Arminianism at 130–1, 162, 177
    Hutchinsonianism at 270–3, 285, 309
    laicization of 369, 390–1, 395, 401
    Oxford Group at 462–3
    Oxford Movement at 359–61, 370–1
    Puritanism at 115–16, 117, 171, 177, 178–9
    Reformation, effects of at 96–104, 97
    Roman Catholicism at after 1558 103–4, 185–6, 202–18, 360–1
    see also University College, buildings: Chapel
  Restoration, effects of at 181–4
  Rhodes Scholars at 417, 430, 435, 461, 463, 479, 484–5, 495, 496
  roll calls 391, 425–6, 455
  St Lucy's Dinner 497
  scholarships endowed at 96, 119, 266, 273, 305–7, 354
    Bennet Scholars 157–8, 164, 173–5, 184, 306, 326, 365
    Browne Scholars 118, 119, 273
    Dr Browne Scholars 273, 307
    Fitzgerald Scholars 523
    Freeston Scholars 118, 119, 214, 263, 273, 304, 306, 369, 461–2
    Gunsley Scholars 129, 208, 213, 266, 270, 273, 305, 306, 326, 353, 369, 385, 461
    Heron Scholars 113
    Hunt Scholars 118–19, 214, 273
    Leicester Scholars 116–17, 273, 306, 339
    lengths of tenure 266
    Lodge Scholars 260, 304, 338
    Swire Scholars 524
  sconcing 457, 496
  Senior Research Fellows 447
  Senior Tutorship 480–1, 482, 491, 493, 525
  servants and members of staff 19, 64, 77–8, 138–9, 196, 255, 299, 318–19, *320*, 370, 381–4, *384*, 437–8, 455, 456, 467–8, 476, 482–4, 499–500
    books owned by 139
    changes in membership 499–500
    daily routine 438, 499–500
    honours bestowed on 484
    nomenclature 468, 499
    opinions on Fellows and undergraduates 407, 415, 424, 438, 482, 515

payment of 264, 381–3, 427, 438
professionalization of 525–6
relations with Fellows and undergraduates 319, 383–4, 438, 468, 482–4, 504, 519, *519*, 527
reorganization of in 1938 455
servants' sports clubs 437, 467, *467*, 500
silver 125, 154
  loss of during Civil War 166, 167
sport, attitudes towards 346–7, 378–80, 415, 429–34, 458–9, 504–5
sports field for 430, 435
statutes 249
  of 1280/1 7–8, 13–15, *14*
  of 1292 7–8, 18–21, 66, 265
  of 1311 23–5, 109, 111, 250
  of 1475 and 1478 64–6, 80, 90, 249–50
  of 1561 103–4
  of 1736 259, 265–6, 282
  of 1857 and later 368–9, 391–2, 393–4, 400–1, 447
student representation in College administration 504
subjects studied by members of 280, 310–13, 377, 463–4, 502–3, 526
  agriculture 464
  anatomy 311, 314
  Anglo-Saxon 200–1, 223, 228
  antiquarianism 200, 223–4, 264, 314
  archaeology 223, 352, 366
  arithmetic 79, 146
  astronomy 79, 197, 281, 313, 355–6
  biology 392
  botany and plant sciences 199, 326, 503, 512
  chemistry 199, 200, 281, 340, 430, 446, 463, 476, 493, 502, 526
  Chinese 492
  classics 79–80, 112, 144–6, 222, 263–4, 269, 275, 277, 280–1, 288, 306, 310–12, 313, 333, 337–8, 354, 358–9, 363–4, 370, 389, 395, 413, 416–17, 427, 445, 449, 463, 465, 491, 497, 502, 526
  computing science 526
  Egyptology 464, 492
  engineering 463, 502, 526
  English 411, 449, 463, 479, 497, 512, 515, 526
  geography 122, 146, 200, 222, 311, 503
  geology 411, 466, 489, 503
  geometry 146, 270, 275, 311
  Hebrew 223, 272, 309, 310
  history, ancient 222, 280, 281–2, 348, 358, 409, 422–3, 465, 479, 522, 524
  history, modern 146, 311, 313, 314, 393, 394–5, 411, 422, 463, 502, 524, 526
  jurisprudence 265, 277, 280, 282–3, 313, 377, 417, 463, 465, 466, 486, 492, 502, 512, 526
  law, canon 23
  law, civil 177, 197, 263, 270, 281, 311, 348, 354, 369–70, 389, 417
  logic 32, 112, 145–6, 199, 245, 264, 280, 311
  mathematics 146–7, 197, 281, 311, 347, 348, 354, 359, 371, 377, 502, 526
  medicine and physiology 114, 146, 147–8, 177, 197, 214, 241, 265, 333, 425, 447, 463, 476, 493, 502, 512
  modern languages 197, 338, 463, 502, 526
    French 146, 280, 311, 312, 313, 389
    German 348, 362, 439
    Italian 146, 311, 313
    Russian 502, 514
    Spanish 146
  numismatics 199, 223
  oriental studies 276–7, 284
  philosophy 64, 112, 146, 269, 280, 311, 338, 393, 465, 479, 522
  physics 281, 311, 313, 354, 359, 377, 463, 502, 512, 526
  political economy 348
  politics, philosophy, and economics 449, 456, 463, 502, 526
  rhetoric 146, 264, 269
  science (or 'natural philosophy'), general 197, 199, 270, 281, 311, 355, 377, 425, 502, 526
  theology 7–8, 23, 31–2, 47–50, 64, 78–9, 112, 122–3, 142, 144, 145–6, 177, 222, 265, 310–11, 313, 314, 338, 358, 359, 370, 377, 389, 409, 462–3, 492
teaching at 95, 112, 309–12, 410–11
  costs of 324
  endowment of lectureships 105, 112, 389
  lectures 278, 280, 309–10, 315, 347, 357–8
  opening up of to members of other Colleges 358, 389
  private tutors 309, 338

INDEX

University College: general (cont.)
    standards of 123–4, 146–7, 236, 244–5, 263, 269–70, 275–6, 278–82, 309–11, 333–4, 338, 340, 343, 352, 357–8, 370, 377–8, 389–90, 395, 410, 424, 450, 470, 479, 481, 491, 505–7
    timetable of lectures at 197, 198, 280, 315, 359
    tutors at 146, 197–8, 222, 228, 263, 278, 282, 309, 346, 360
  tutorials at 389, *465*
  undergraduates
    academic standing of 358–9, 389–90, 414, 425, 463–4, 498, 505–7
    accommodation in College *17*, 139–42, 148, 160–1, 279, 483, 344, 426–7, *426*, 436, 477, 507–9, 514–15
      discomfort of 427, 436, 475
      electric heating installed in 455
    accommodation outside College 436, 476, 496, 507–9
    activism among 281, 381–3, 503–4
    admissions initiatives 493, 497–8, 506
    admissions procedures 354, 377, 425, 463, 493, 510, 526
    admissions register, creation of 194
    aesthetes versus athletes 416, 434, 457–8
    ages of 115, 136–7, 195, 303–4, 444, 476, 493, 547
    batellers 196
    becoming Fellows 133, 176–7, 194, 307–8, 373
    books borrowed by 314–15
    books owned by 145–6, 263–4, 280, 310, 313, 427
    bullying among 385, 434–5, 457–8
    careers of 135, 147–8, 178, 196, 283, 310, 325–8, 329–31, 437, 527–8
    charitable work carried out by 410, 427, 437
    clothing 148–9, *150*, 427, 496, 504
    daily life of 148–51, 196–7, 315–18, 343–4, 346–7, 378–81, 425–37, 445, 456–69, 495–7, 503–5
    degrees taken by 147–8, 178, 196, 325, 359, 444, 506–7
    disciplining of 202, 226, 262, 340–2, *341*, 388, 401–5, 404
    early undergraduate scholars at 51–2, 75–6, 94–6
    examinations sat by 300, 312, 337–8, 359, 389–90, 414, 425
    finances of 134, 145–6, 148–51, 315–17, 427, 430, 461, 522–3
    financial aid for 461–2, 478, 497–8, 510–11, 522, 524
    Freshers' Week 527
    gentlemen commoners and noblemen at 147–8, 196, 244–5, 280, 312, 316, 338
    geographical origins of 135–6, 154, 195, 304–5, 417; *see also under individual counties and countries*
    killed in action 169, 439, 442–3, 471–2
    migrations to other colleges 137, 178, 196, 305
    misbehaviour of 148–51, 202, 234–6, 243, 244–5, 316, 340–2, 384–5, 388, 401–6, 429–35, 444–5, 456–8
      financial 148–9, 316–17
      sending down of in 1880 402–5, *404*, 411, 414
      sexual 235, 317–18
    nomenclature of 51, 504
    Officer Training Corps 415, 439
    political sympathies of 243, 329, 340–1, 410, 437, 450–1, 462, 503–4
    possessions of 148, 426–7
    practical jokes played by 290, 340–1, 343, 384–5, 401–5, 421, 430–2
    proportion of scientists among 502, 526
    see also subjects studied by members of
    relations with Fellows 281, 357–8, 371, 381–5, 403–6, *404*, 414–15, 429, 480–1, 487–8, 504, 505
    schools attended by 302, 353, 377, 417, 425, 461, 497–8, 506
    service cadets at 471, 476
    servitors 196, 260, 288, 304, 315, 338
    slang of 371, 379–80, 407, 424
    social divisions among 136, 141–2, 147–9, 196, 226, 236, 245, 315, 385, 426, 433–5, 462
    social status of 136, 177, 195, 228, 304, 343, 353, 377, 396, 417, 425, 461–2, 547
    study, attitudes towards 234, 236, 244–5, 262–3, 272, 278–81, 310–12, 343, 357, 396, 433–4, 463, 505–7
Univ. Old Members Trust 523
Vice-Master 266, 472–3, 510

Visitations of and interference in by outside bodies 47–50, 100, 104, 170–1, 173–6, 181, 189, 204, 209–10, 213
Visitors of
  the Crown 251–3, 254–5, 256–7, 266, 363, 390, 393–4, 397
  University of Oxford 19–20, 24, 46, 64, 66–7, 81, 90–1, 101, 109–10, 114, 176, 180, 187–8, 217, 221, 230–1, 232, 249–53, *252*, 254–5, 256
visits made to by the famous 132, 202, 215–16, 287–90, 349–50, 478, *519*, *519*, *520*, *521*
war, effects of on 63, 85, 164–71, 299–300, 322, 345–6, 439, 440–3, 444–5, 469–74, 475–6, 478, 491, 493
Weir Common Room, *see* Middle Common Room
women at
  admitted to lectures in College 409
  as evacuees 471
  as servants and members of staff 77–8, 139, 235, 319, 383, 468, 484
  as students and Fellows 513–15, 516–17
    proportion of 517
  as visitors or guests 497, 504
  as wives of Fellows 395, 466–7, 491
  as wives or daughters of Masters 111, 115, 120, 141, 157, 318, 336–7, 407–8, 424, 456, 485
  dining in Hall 290, 318, 490, 504
University College Club 329, *330*
Urban IV, Pope 7
Ursinus, Zacharias 145
Urswick, Christopher (MC) 77
Usher, Charles (U) 229–32

Valence, Simon de 12
Velleius Paterculus 222
Vertue, George, engraver 223
Vickers, Henry Reginald (U) *432*
Villiers, George, 2nd Duke of Buckingham 172
Virgil 106, 139, 145, 280, 313, 363–4, 370

Wadham College, Oxford 126, 140, 159, 170, 193, 271, 402, 413, 414, 476, 500, 513, 517
Wager, Laurence Rickard (F) 489, 492–3
Wake, William, Archbishop of Canterbury 243

Wakefield, Yorks., school at 118, 214, 417
Wakeman, Joseph, Catholic chaplain at University College 210, 217
Waldrige, John (MC) (F) 112
Wales, College members from 136, 139
  College property in, *see* Montgomeryshire
Walker, J. W. and Sons, organ manufacturers 376, 477
Walker, Obadiah (U) (F) (M) 135, 137, 146–7, 165, 167, 170–1, 172, 173, 181, 183–218, 219, 220, 226, 247, 452, 524
  Roman Catholicism of 202–18, *212*
  scholarly activities of 197–201, 217
Walker, Thomas (M), 52, 157–71, 172, 174, 177, 181–2, 183–7, 193, 197, 204, 223, 524
Walsingham, Sir Francis 116, 119–20
Walwyn, Francis (U) (F) 263, 306, 310
Waneman, — (U?) 94
Wanley, Humfrey (U) 223–4, 230–1, 232
Ward, George 'Jolly' (U) (F) 234–5, 244–5, 247–51, 253, 254, 255, 257, 259, 260, 263, 317, 324
Warham, William, Archbishop of Canterbury 90–1
Warren, Bill (S) 527
Wars of the Roses 63, 76, 85
Warwickshire, College members from 305
Wase, Christopher 200
Washington, Richard (U) (F) 163, 165, 167, 170–1, 172, 174
Waterhouse, Stephen (MC) 114
Waterstock, Oxon., College property at 113, 548–9
Watkins, Henry (U) (F) 170–1
Watson, George (U) (F) 271–3, 309, 311–12
Watson, Musgrave Lewthwaite, sculptor 375
Watts, John (U) (F) 344, 348, 386
Waynflete, William, Bishop of Winchester and founder of Magdalen College 62
Wearmouth, *see* Bishopwearmouth
Webster, John (U) 460, 477, 478
Weir, James, benefactor 495, 499
Weir, James Colin (U) 499
Wellesley, Arthur, Duke of Wellington, Chancellor of Oxford 349–50, 367
Wellington College 417
Wells, Arthur Frederick 'Freddie' (F) *454*, 470, 479, 491–2, *494*, 501, 505, 507, 513, 525
Wentworth, George (U) 124, 154

Wentworth, Matthew (U) (F) 124, 133, 151–2, 154, 202
Wentworth, Philip (U) 124, 137, 154
Wentworth, Thomas, Earl of Strafford 124–5, 133, 137, 149, 151, 154–5, 158, 169
Weskew, John (T) 82
Wesley, John 270
West, John 42
Westminster Abbey 292, 405
Westminster School 244, 377
Wetherell, Sir Charles (U) 295–6
Wetherell, Henry (MC) 295–6
Wetherell, James 295
Wetherell, Nathan (F) (M) 272–3, 275–301, 305, 308–9, 318, 321–2, 325, 329, 331, 333, 339, 381, 401, 485
  monument in Chapel 329
  political machinations of 284–5, 287, 291–5, 300
  Vice-Chancellorship of 291–2
Wetherell, Nathan Croke (U) (F) 295–6, 346
Wetherell, Richard (U) 295
Wetherell, Robert 295
Wheare, Sir Kenneth Clinton (F) 470, 473, 485
White, John, elected Fellow 175
Whitehead, Sir Edgar Cuthbert Fremantle (U), Prime Minister of Rhodesia 528
Whithall, Giles (U) 243
Whittington, John (T) 152
Whixlay, John de (F) 26
Wighill, Yorks., College property at 260, 548–9
Wild, John Herbert Severn (F) (M) *15*, 447, 450, 451–2, 455, 470–1, 472, 473, 474, 475–85, *476*, 501
Wild, Margaret 475, 485
Wilkinson, Henry (U) 243
Wilkinson, William, architect 418
William I, King of England 56–7, 106
William III, King of Great Britain 202, 216, 227, 232
Williams, Edgar 'Bill' 495
Williams, Ralph Augustine (U) 432
Wilson, Francis Heathcote (U) *382*
Wilson, James Harold, Baron Wilson of Rievaulx (F), Prime Minister 455–6, 462, 470, 473, 479, 481, 510, 520
Wilson, Mary, Lady Wilson 456, 481
Wilson, Samuel (U) 151

Wilson, Steuart 460
Winchester College 153, 353, 377, 415, 417, 425
Windham, William (U) 278, 280, 283, 287–8, 300, 314, 328
Windsor, St George's Chapel 31, 49
Winwick, Lancs. 219
Witton Richard (F) (M) (T) 53–4
Wolveridge, John (U), benefactor 134–5, 186
Wood, Anthony 57, 60, 91, 102–5, 128, 165, 171, 172, 177, 178–9, 181, 183, 186, 187, 199, 201, 202, 204, 206, 209, 210, 214, 219, 220, 314
  on the buildings of University College 59, 69–71, 70, 179, 190
Wood, Derek Alexander (U) 485
Wood, John the Elder 304
Wood, John the Younger (U) 304
Wood, Richard (U) 230
Woodforde, James 316
Woodhead, Abraham (U) (F) 146–7, 161, 165, 166, 171, 172, 181, 185–6, 190, 193, 198, 203, 206, 217
  works of 186, 205, 209, 211, *212*, 217
Woods, Henry, President of Trinity 392
Woodstock, Oxon., College property at 113, 168, 445, 548–9
Woodward, William (U) (F) 170, 172
Woolley, John (U) (F) 353
Worcester, Earl of *see* Tiptoft
Worcester College, Oxford 239, 389, 429
Worcestershire, College members from 194, 305
Wright, Samuel (S), cook 318–19
Wyatt, James 299
Wyclif, John 47–50
Wynford, William 72

Xenophon 145

Yale, university of 517–18
Yanofsky, Daniel Abraham (U) 495
Yarburgh, Charles (U) 263–4, 310–11, 313, 316, 319, 324
Yarnold, Frederick Herbert (U) 451–2, 465
Yates, Dornford, *see* Mercer, Cecil
Yeldham, John Lermitte (U) 458
York
  College property at 260, 399, 548–9
  York Minster 26, 30, 37, 74
York (formerly Johnson), Michael (U) 496

Yorkshire, links to University College 30, 46, 60, 72, 114, 118–19, 132–3, 135–6, 154–5, 177, 189, 194, 195, 273, 304–5, 306, 308–9, 349, 356, 363
Young, Sir William (U) 283

Yudkin, Michael David (F) 510
Yusupov, Prince Felix (U) 435–6, *436*, 478

Zvegintzov (later Holdsworth), Mary (S) 468
Zwingli, Huldrych 144

University College, Oxford, in 2007

⑨ Numbers in white circles indicate staircases or entrances to rooms

The Radcliffe Quadrangle is built on the sites of Little University Hall and the Cock on the Hoop; the Shelley Memorial is built on the site of Deep Hall; and the New Buildings are built on the site of Stanton Hall